THE TWO HORIZONS OLD TI

MW01200494

J. GORDON McCONVILLE and CRAIG BARTHOLOMEW, *General Editors*

Two features distinguish THE TWO HORIZONS OLD TESTAMENT COMMENTARY series: theological exegesis and theological reflection.

Exegesis since the Reformation era and especially in the past two hundred years emphasized careful attention to philology, grammar, syntax, and concerns of a historical nature. More recently, commentary has expanded to include social-scientific, political, or canonical questions and more.

Without slighting the significance of those sorts of questions, scholars in THE TWO HORIZONS OLD TESTAMENT COMMENTARY locate their primary interests on theological readings of texts, past and present. The result is a paragraph-by-paragraph engagement with the text that is deliberately theological in focus.

Theological reflection in THE TWO HORIZONS OLD TESTAMENT COMMENTARY takes many forms, including locating each Old Testament book in relation to the whole of Scripture — asking what the biblical book contributes to biblical theology — and in conversation with constructive theology of today. How commentators engage in the work of theological reflection will differ from book to book, depending on their particular theological tradition and how they perceive the work of biblical theology and theological hermeneutics. This heterogeneity derives as well from the relative infancy of the project of theological interpretation of Scripture in modern times and from the challenge of grappling with a book's message in Greco-Roman antiquity, in the canon of Scripture and history of interpretation, and for life in the admittedly diverse Western world at the beginning of the twenty-first century.

THE TWO HORIZONS OLD TESTAMENT COMMENTARY is written primarily for students, pastors, and other Christian leaders seeking to engage in theological interpretation of Scripture.

Job

Lindsay Wilson

WILLIAM B. EERDMANS PUBLISHING COMPANY
GRAND RAPIDS, MICHIGAN / CAMBRIDGE, U.K.

Published 2015 by
Wm. B. Eerdmans Publishing Co.
2140 Oak Industrial Drive N.E., Grand Rapids, Michigan 49505 /
P.O. Box 163, Cambridge CB3 9PU U.K.

Printed in the United States of America

21 20 19 18 17 16 15   7 6 5 4 3 2 1

Library of Congress Cataloging-in-Publication Data

Wilson, Lindsay, 1955-
    Job / Lindsay Wilson.
        pages   cm.   — (The two horizons Old Testament commentary)
    Includes bibliographical references and index.
    ISBN 978-0-8028-2708-1 (pbk.: alk. paper)
    1. Bible. Job — Commentaries.   2. Bible. Job — Theology.   I. Title.

    BS1415.53.W55   2015
    223'.107 — dc2

                                                    2014044654

www.eerdmans.com

Contents

Contents

Acknowledgments

The book of Job has never been an easy book to read or write about, but it is certainly an engaging one. It cries out for the kind of treatment possible in the Two Horizons Old Testament Commentary series, which deals not only with the meaning of the text but also with the theological ideas that emerge, understood as part of Scripture as a whole. My initial excitement at undertaking such a project has been steadily supplanted by an awareness of my own limitations in many of the areas needing to be explored and explained. It has been both humbling and stimulating to explore the implications of the book for all areas of theology — biblical, systematic, moral, and practical. The result has been that it has taken much longer than I originally envisaged, and I would like to thank the series editors for their patience.

My original academic involvement with Job came in a course on Wisdom literature taught by Barry Webb, followed by a research thesis on Job's protests supervised by John Woodhouse. Since then I have returned to Job often, sometimes in writing and regularly in my teaching. I would like to thank my students (including a research student, Andy Prideaux) for stimulating my thinking on this book, as well as colleagues at conferences and especially the Tyndale Old Testament study group. Ridley College, Melbourne, has been a fruitful place for ministry for the last twenty-three years, and I would like to thank its principals (Maurice Betteridge, Graham Cole, Peter Adam, and Brian Rosner), my Old Testament colleagues (Robin Payne, Paul Barker, Andrew Sloane, Andrew Reid, and Andrew Abernethy), and other members of the faculty for their support and encouragement. I particularly want to thank the librarian, Ruth Millard, and the office staff for all their work behind the scenes, which makes possible the production of a book like this. I also thank the board of Ridley for granting several periods of study leave during which much of this commentary was written.

Finally, I would like to record my deep appreciation and thanks to my family. I have learned much over the years from my (now adult) children, Melanie, David, and Samara, about some of the issues and struggles in daily life which emerge in the book of Job. Of course, my debt to my wife, Clarissa, is beyond words. Job's wife does not get good press in the book of Job, but my wife is an ongoing source of support, encouragement, and godly challenge.

Above all I wish to express my gratitude to the true and living God whose words are found in the surprisingly contemporary book of Job. I am thankful for its rich picture of God's active kingly rule, and its call for raw honesty in our relationship with him.

LINDSAY WILSON
January 2014

Abbreviations

AB	Anchor Bible
AnBib	Analecta biblica
AThR	*Anglican Theological Review*
BCOTWP	Baker Commentary on the Old Testament Wisdom and Psalms
BDB	F. Brown, S. R. Driver, and C. A. Briggs, *A Hebrew and English Lexicon of the Old Testament* (Oxford: Clarendon, 1906)
BETL	Bibliotheca ephemeridum theologicarum lovaniensium
Bib	*Biblica*
BIS	Biblical Interpretation Series
BJRL	*Bulletin of the John Rylands Library*
BSac	*Bibliotheca sacra*
BST	The Bible Speaks Today
BTB	*Biblical Theology Bulletin*
BZAW	Beihefte zur Zeitschrift für die alttestamentliche Wissenschaft
CBQ	*Catholic Biblical Quarterly*
CBQMS	Catholic Biblical Quarterly Monograph Series
CNTUOT	*Commentary on the New Testament Use of the Old Testament* (ed. G. K. Beale and D. A. Carson; Grand Rapids: Baker, 2007)
ConBOT	Coniectanea biblica: Old Testament Series
CurTM	*Currents in Theology and Mission*
DCH	*Dictionary of Classical Hebrew* (ed. D. J. A. Clines; 8 vols.; Sheffield: Sheffield Phoenix, 1993-2011)
DOTWPW	*Dictionary of the Old Testament Wisdom, Poetry and Writings* (ed. T. Longman and P. Enns; Downers Grove, IL: InterVarsity Press, 2008)
DTIB	*Dictionary for Theological Interpretation of the Bible* (ed. K. J. Vanhoozer; Grand Rapids: Baker Academic, 2005)

ESV	English Standard Version
ET	English translation
ExpTim	*Expository Times*
FOTL	Forms of the Old Testament Literature
GKC	*Gesenius' Hebrew Grammar* (ed. E. Kautzsch; trans. A. E. Cowley; 2nd ed.; Oxford: Clarendon, 1910)
GNB	Good News Bible
HALOT	*Hebrew and Aramaic Lexicon of the Old Testament* (ed. L. Koehler et al.; trans. and ed. M. E. J. Richardson; repr. 2 vols.; Leiden: Brill, 2001)
HAR	*Hebrew Annual Review*
HBT	*Horizons in Biblical Theology*
HTR	*Harvard Theological Review*
HUCA	*Hebrew Union College Annual*
ICC	International Critical Commentary
Int	*Interpretation*
ITQ	*Irish Theological Quarterly*
JB	Jerusalem Bible
JBL	*Journal of Biblical Literature*
JETS	*Journal of the Evangelical Theological Society*
JSOT	*Journal for the Study of the Old Testament*
JSOTSup	Journal for the Study of the Old Testament Supplement Series
KAT	Kommentar zum Alten Testament
KJV	King James Version
LXX	Septuagint
MT	Masoretic Text
NAC	New American Commentary
NASB	New American Standard Bible
NCBC	New Century Bible Commentary
NEB	New English Bible
NIBC	New International Biblical Commentary
NICOT	New International Commentary on the Old Testament
NIDOTTE	*New International Dictionary of Old Testament Theology and Exegesis* (ed. W. VanGemeren; 5 vols.; Grand Rapids: Zondervan, 1997)
NIGTC	New International Greek Testament Commentary
NIV	New International Version
NIVAC	NIV Application Commentary
NJPS	New Jewish Publication Society Version
NRSV	New Revised Standard Version

NRT	*Nouvelle revue théologique*
NSBT	New Studies in Biblical Theology
NT	New Testament
OT	Old Testament
OTL	Old Testament Library
OTSWA	*Ou-Testamentiese Werkgemeenskap van Suid-Afrika*
RB	*Revue biblique*
RevExp	*Review and Expositor*
RSV	Revised Standard Version
RTR	*Reformed Theological Review*
RV	Revised Version
SBT	Studies in Biblical Theology
SJT	*Scottish Journal of Theology*
SR	*Studies in Religion/Sciences religieuses*
StBL	Studies in Biblical Literature
SwJT	*Southwestern Journal of Theology*
TBT	*The Bible Today*
TD	*Theology Digest*
TDOT	*Theological Dictionary of the Old Testament* (ed. G. J. Botterweck et al.; trans. J. T. Willis et al.; 15 vols.; Grand Rapids: Eerdmans, 1974-2006)
TOTC	Tyndale Old Testament Commentary Series
UBS	United Bible Societies
VT	*Vetus Testamentum*
VTSup	Vetus Testamentum Supplements
WBC	Word Biblical Commentary
WTJ	*Westminster Theological Journal*
ZAW	*Zeitschrift für die alttestamentliche Wissenschaft*

Introduction

This introduction is a response to questions commonly asked by readers of Job when they approach the book for the first time. It will cover the following issues:

Who wrote the book, and when was it written?
Are these real historical events and the actual words spoken?
How should we read the book?
Why was the book written?
How have others understood it?
How do the different parts of the book fit together?
What is the structure of the book?
Is the text of Job reliable?
Why is the book so long and repetitive?

Some of the other commonly asked questions will be dealt with in the remainder of this commentary as we look at the text, the theological themes, and the connection of the book with biblical, systematic, moral, and practical theology. Coverage will be given there to the following issues (among others):

Why do good people suffer?
Why is Satan in the heavenly council?
Does Job have a firm hope in a redeemer?
How does the book of Job fit with the rest of the OT?
How should we read Job as Christians?
Why is Job restored?
Why does God allow what happens to Job?

Many other questions will emerge as we explore this captivating but uncomfortable book.

Who Wrote the Book, and When Was It Written?

This is a sensible question to ask when reading any book, but the short answer is that we do not know who wrote Job, and it does not seem to matter much. There are some biblical books whose authorship has not been disclosed in the text itself (e.g., Joshua or Ruth in the OT; Hebrews in the NT). Such is the case with the book of Job, which makes no claim for any particular human author. It is a book *about* Job, not necessarily *by* Job. Some have suggested Moses (on the assumption of it being dated very early); some have proposed Solomon (since it is wisdom literature); others propose Job (since he is the main character) or Elihu (probably because they do not know what else to do with him). However, we simply do not know who wrote the book because the book itself does not tell us, and there is not enough external evidence to come to a conclusion.

This means that the question of authorship must not be particularly important for interpreting the book, and we would need to be cautious of any scholar who builds too much on the basis of any one theory of its authorship. It also means that the question of authorship is not a litmus test of orthodoxy.

Different theories about authorship have led to specific views about the book's time of writing (e.g., if it was written in the era of Moses or of Solomon). However, if the authorship cannot be determined, then the time of writing is a matter for further exploration based on the text itself.

It is helpful to distinguish between the setting of the story and the writing of the book. The *story* of Job seems based in patriarchal times, but the *book* of Job was written at a much later date. A number of indicators connect the tale to the time of the patriarchs. As was common in Israel before the establishment of a priestly family, Job is the head of the family who would offer sacrifices (1:5). In the time of the patriarchs, wealth was measured in the number of animals (reflected in 1:3), and the main figures lived extraordinarily long lives (for Job see 42:16-17). The unit of currency referred to in 42:11 is known elsewhere only by its mention in Gen 33:19 and Josh 24:32. A connection between an individual named Eliphaz, a son of Esau, and Teman is made in Gen 36:4, 11, 15. The patriarchs were largely nomadic, although they occasionally lived near cities (e.g., Shechem in Gen 34). Job's family seems at least seminomadic in 1:1-5, although chapter 29 describes his prominent role in city affairs (e.g., 29:7-10, 21-25).

For reasons like these, many have quite sensibly suggested that the story of Job was *set* in patriarchal times and written down soon afterward. This would make good sense if the book was understood as a verbatim account of events and conversations, but would be less persuasive if it was seen as the later wisdom adaptation of an earlier tale. Clearly, Job was a famed historical figure — he is mentioned as a person of great righteousness in Ezek 14:14, 20 (see also Jas 5:11, where he is a model of perseverance).

However, there are good reasons for dating the *writing* of the book of Job at a later time. First, the book presupposes the individual retribution theology of the book of Proverbs.[1] The book of Proverbs claims to be substantially Solomonic (Prov 1:1), with other parts added in the time of Hezekiah (25:1). I will argue that the book of Job is responding to a fossilized misunderstanding of Proverbs, which would have meant that significant time will have passed after Hezekiah. This argument proposes that the book must be written at a later time, and more will be said about this as we explore the ideological setting of the book. It is also important that in our collections of biblical books Job is gathered among the poetical books, not the historical ones. This suggests that the extensive speeches in the book were not uttered in patriarchal times.[2]

The second argument that permits (but does not demand) a later date to the book is that there are good literary and theological reasons for the "patriarchal" features of the book. An author can give a setting to a story that is earlier than her or his own time, so the time setting of the story does not determine the time of writing. Here, even though there is a patriarchal flavor to the story, there is no mention of any historically datable events, nor is any information used that would not have been available to a later writer.

There are good reasons why the story is given such an early setting, and the most significant of these is that it would then predate the Mosaic law. If a wisdom writer wanted to explore and nuance the idea of retribution found in Proverbs, dating a narrative prior to Moses would preclude characters trying to resolve it by appealing to the law, including the book of Deuteronomy.

A further way to keep this as an intrawisdom debate was to make the main character a non-Israelite, so that emphasis could be given to Job's struggle as a human being to persevere in faith. There can be no easy appeals to Israelite traditions or solutions. This seems to be why the book is set in the land of Uz.

---

1. The book of Deuteronomy also has a strong emphasis on the theology of retribution, but it is more at the national rather than individual level. Both Job and Proverbs belong to Israelite wisdom literature, and the debates about retribution were an intrawisdom discussion dealt with in both books in wisdom ways.

2. Estes, *Handbook*, 12, also points out that the epilogue, with the comment that Job lived for 140 years (42:16), would demand a date for the final form of the book long after the actual dialogue between Job and his friends. On the book's language and the implications for dating, see most recently Seow, *Job 1–21*, 17-26.

Some contend that trying to find it on a map is futile, with Dermot Cox assert-ing, "One might just as well search for the Land of Oz."[3] Most identify Uz with Edom, the land to the southeast of Israel, on the basis of the parallelism of Lam 4:21. As a personal name Uz is found in lists of Edomite kings (Gen 36:28; 1 Chr 1:42). In Jer 25:19-26 the land of Uz (v. 20) is included in a list of nations outside Israel, although Edom is separately mentioned (v. 21). Edom was known for its wisdom (Jer 49:7), and would later become the home of the Nabatean traders. David Clines helpfully comments, "The importance of the name Uz lies not in where such a place is, but in where it is not. Israelites themselves may not have known its precise location, but they will have known, as we do, that it is not in Israel."[4] In other words, locating the story in Uz has more to do with it taking place outside Israel rather than identifying it on a map.

However, the setting of the book outside Israel and involving charac-ters not identified as Israelite does not mean that there is no connection with Israelite faith. Indeed, this is an Israelite book, written for Israelites, and its teachings are both consistent with and part of Israelite theology. In the same way that many of the sentence sayings of Proverbs are not explicitly connected to the Israelite historical, prophetic, or legal traditions but are part of Israel's Scripture, so too is the book of Job. There is a backgrounded Israelite perspec-tive throughout.[5] This is echoed by the use of the Israelite name of "Yahweh" in the prologue and epilogue, but almost never on the lips of the characters in the dialogue (only in 12:9).

It is intended to be read by Israelites, but the discussion takes place by bracketing out certain distinctives of Israel's covenant faith. As is common in the Israelite wisdom literature, it makes connections and seeks solutions based on our general humanity rather than on what is specifically Israelite. In so doing, it adds other levels of richness to OT theology that would be largely missing without wisdom literature (see the section on "Job and Theology: Job and Biblical Theology").

Various answers about the dating of the book have been given, but the debate has not been conclusive. If it was written significantly after Hezekiah, this brings it at least to the late preexilic period since Hezekiah's reign ended about a hundred years before the exile. Many would seek to date it in the exile, but two main objections have been made to an exilic dating. First, the issue of suffering in the exile is that of national suffering caused by Israel's sin (e.g.,

3. Cox, *Man's Anger and God's Silence*, 21.

4. Clines, *Job 1–20*, 10.

5. See Walton, "Job 1: Book of," 344-45. Walton mentions the insistence on the justice of God, the denial of bowing to the sun and the moon (31:26-28), the futility of trying to appease God by ritual, and the absence of syncretism.

Lamentations), but in Job the issue is undeserved suffering of a righteous person. Second, Edom was instrumental in the destruction of the temple, so it is unlikely that an Edomite would be pictured as utterly righteous in an exilic setting. However, as the exile progressed many examples of individual righteous people would also have emerged, even if the reason for the exile itself was Israel's unfaithfulness. In relation to the second objection, it is interesting that Job is not specifically identified as an Edomite, but rather as a human being. The exile was certainly a time of rethinking and intellectual activity that would make a good background for the writing of the book of Job, and it may well have been written late in the exilic period, or perhaps in early postexilic times.

Others seek to date it on the basis of alleged Aramaic expressions in the book (usually giving a late date) or on the basis of literary dependence (e.g., Job 3:3-10 and Jer 20:14-18 or Gen 1; comparisons with Isa 40–55 and Job 38–41). It cannot be later than 200 B.C. because of the clear reference to the book of Job in Ben Sira (Sir 44:9) and also the discovery of the Targum of Job at Qumran.

In the end, it does not really matter. The setting is important (set before the Mosaic law, in a non-Israelite culture) but the dating is not, for its message is not dependent on any historical circumstances or its place in the history of Israel. It is a timeless, universal book. What is important about its date is that it must be set significantly after the book of Proverbs, and read against some of the misunderstandings of this foundational wisdom book. The actual date of writing is less important than its place in the sequence.

Are These Real Historical Events and the Actual Words Spoken?

Behind the question of the genre of the book of Job is the issue of whether the book is a record of actual events and speeches. Some believe that, since the book of Job is Scripture, then it must be historically reliable and therefore must be seen as a chronological record of exactly "what happened." While this is a reductionist view of history (since history is always a selection of events, rather than an exhaustive account), the more significant problem is that a story should only be read as history if it was intended to be an historical record. Of course, the OT contains many other kinds of literature (e.g., hymns, laws, visions, oracles), and so it is always worth asking about the genre of any biblical book or passage. Even if the book is fundamentally a story, this does not necessarily mean that it is an historical retelling of actual events that were recorded at that time. The prophet Nathan tells a story of a rich man who took a poor man's lamb (2 Sam 12:1-4), and Jesus tells the parable of the good Samaritan (Luke 10:25-37). These stories ring true to life (and make their point) even if there was no historical good Samaritan, or no special lamb that drank from its owner's cup. These stories are parables, in which the story form is used to convey important truths.

Some read the book of Job as an historical story, recounting actual events in the ancient Near East in patriarchal times, and recording speeches given and heard at that time. Most of the OT stories are of this kind, and Job is probably regarded in Ezek 14:14, 20, as an historical figure like Noah. One difficulty of this view is that it leads to the historicity of the heavenly events of the prologue. This involves God agreeing to test Job without cause by killing all his children, puts the accuser possibly in the heavenly court, and allows all Job's suffering to occur just to prove a point.[6] If, however, the tale is regarded as a hypothetical story or parable, then these details are simply examples of the author using literary license in order to make the impact much greater.

A further difficulty of the "historical story" view is that Job is a wisdom book, and one of the features of wisdom literature is its lack of focus on history. Though wisdom ideas can be present in historical narrative (e.g., the Joseph story, Gen 37–50), it is unlikely that a wisdom book is only historical narrative. It is much more likely (and leads to a less problematic reading) that a wisdom author has started with the historical legend of Job and reworked it to serve his wisdom purposes. He is using a well-known story to explore a contemporary issue that had arisen because of how some were reading the book of Proverbs. The truth in the words of Job and his friends lies not in whether they were actually spoken at a particular time, but whether they ring true to life and to the issues in this intrawisdom debate.

It may be that the book of Job is an historical account of what was said and what happened in Uz some thousands of years ago. Although this is not my view, readers with that view will still benefit from the observations and analysis made in this commentary. However, even if the book of Job is to be read in this way, the more important perspective is to read the book as part of a debate within the wisdom movement.

Scholars have proposed a number of other genres for the book of Job. Indeed, many different subgenres are contained in the book. As F. I. Andersen notes, "The book of Job is an astonishing mixture of almost every kind of literature to be found in the Old Testament."[7] Some scholars wish to make one or other of these subgenres into the genre of the book as a whole. Claus Westermann, for example, regards it as a lament, although he has to excise the Elihu

---

6. Walton, *Job*, 27, comments, "The book reveals how things work in the world, not how things work in heaven."

7. Andersen, *Job*, 33. He notes that it includes proverbs, riddles, hymns, laments, curses, nature poems, lawsuits. See also Hartley, *Book of Job*, 40-41.

speeches to make it fit his pattern.[8] Others have proposed "lawsuit drama" as its genre, but it is better to see the litigation idea and legal imagery woven through the book rather than determining its genre.[9] Katharine Dell has proposed that the book be read as "sceptical literature" in its content, setting, and structure, and a parody as its genre.[10]

Some who date it quite late view it as a Greek drama. A more promising background is found in the parallels with ancient Near Eastern wisdom books from Egypt and Mesopotamia. The three most likely works here are the Sumerian "A Man and His God," the Akkadian *Ludlul bel Nemeqi* ("I Will Praise the Lord of Wisdom"), and the so-called Babylonian Theodicy.[11] There is some value in these parallels, as Job fits into the kind of "protest wisdom" found in the international wisdom movement. However, the parallels are not close enough (e.g., there are none with prose narratives; none focuses on a righteous sufferer) to determine Job's genre, and what they have most in common is the setting of suffering. Perhaps part of the fascination of the book of Job is that there is no other book like it, even in the ancient world.

How Should We Read the Book?

A suggested reading strategy for the book of Job in the light of biblical theology will be developed later, but a brief introduction is in order. As with all biblical books, any individual verse or chapter needs to be read as part of the entire book, in the wider context of the Bible as a whole. This is particularly vital for Job.

The first principle for reading Job, then, is that any section of the book needs to be understood in the light of the whole book. We need to be wary about taking individual verses out of context and claiming that their teaching is part of the message of the book. For example, both Eliphaz and Elihu tell Job that suffering can have an educative purpose (5:17; 33:19). This is true, but it is not the truth that Job needed to hear, nor is it the message of the book as a whole. It is a truth that is proposed but dismissed if these sections are read as part of the book as a whole.[12]

A second reading principle for the book of Job is the need to pay attention

---

8. Westermann, *Structure of the Book,* 1-13.

9. See "Theological Themes" below. On the legal metaphor see Habel, *Book of Job,* 54-57.

10. Dell, *Sceptical Literature.*

11. See, e.g., Newsom, "Book of Job," 328-34; Walton, *Job,* 31-38.

12. See the section below "How Do the Different Parts of the Book Fit Together?" This should be read before reading any individual chapter or unit.

to its wisdom context. Its ideological setting as part of the wisdom corpus is more crucial than its historical setting. While many of the other OT books deal with the history of the covenant, the covenant people Israel, and God's entry into history in redeeming his people, the wisdom books have a broader, more universal concern with all of creation. Thus there is often a greater focus on everyday life issues than on what God has done in order to save us. The book of Job stands in counterpoint to Proverbs' insistence that order exists in the universe, due in part to the presence of Wisdom at creation (Prov 8:22-31; 3:19-20). While Proverbs allows for temporary setbacks (24:15-16), it does proclaim that the righteous will be rewarded and the wicked punished (3:9-10; 10:27-32). This idea is commonly known as the doctrine of retribution.

The book of Job protests not against Proverbs but against a fossilized misunderstanding of retribution that had misrepresented the mainstream wisdom tradition of Proverbs.[13] This narrowing or calcifying of the teaching of Proverbs is represented in the book by Job's friends, and they are his conversation partners. They are examples of those who have ignored the flexibility of Proverbs (as seen in Prov 26:4-5), and simply read off a person's spiritual state from their circumstances. The prologue to Job (chs. 1–2) reveals that Job's suffering is not a consequence of his sin, and God's failure to rebuke Job in chapters 38–41 clearly shows that his honest protests throughout the dialogue are legitimate. The book of Job is not rejecting the doctrine of retribution, but simply insisting that retributive justice is not the only principle on which God runs his world.

Why Was the Book Written?

A work as profound as the book of Job is likely to have multiple purposes. However, many readers approach the book hoping to find answers that it never intends to give. For example, the book does not intend to make pronouncements about the problem of suffering (though suffering is a problem), or about whether a righteous person can suffer (obviously one can). If you are looking to the book of Job to give fresh or conclusive answers to these questions, then you will be sorely disappointed. The book of Job will be a valuable resource for those who are suffering and those caring for them, but only after the purposes of the book are clarified.

As part of the Bible as a whole, the first purpose of the book is to correct a misunderstanding of the book of Proverbs. Indeed, if we want to understand Job, then we probably need to start by reading Proverbs. The book of Proverbs

---

13. See Holmgren, "Barking Dogs Never Bite."

helps us to be aware of the nature of life. It outlines the kind of attitudes, actions, people, and situations to avoid, and the ones to embrace in order to live well. The truths found in this book differ from those truths characteristically found in the Bible. Fred Holmgren suggests that "proverbs are not infallible statements that are valid for every person or situation. Rather they tell us what generally, usually, or often is the case."[14] Proverbs are true — but not exhaustively or exclusively true — from a certain perspective in a specific situation. Most proverbs need to be balanced by other equally true proverbs, and sometimes they appear to conflict. Examples in English proverbs include "out of sight, out of mind," yet "absence makes the heart grow fonder"; "many hands make light work," yet "too many cooks spoil the broth"; "look before you leap," yet "he who hesitates is lost." Each of these proverbs is true, but they are not the whole truth. This understanding of proverbial truth is also seen in Prov 26:4-5, which exhorts the reader not to answer a fool according to his folly in v. 4, but the very next verse urges them to answer a fool according to his folly. Thus proverbs, including biblical proverbs, describe what usually or frequently happens, but the wise person is one who recognizes when it is better to listen to one rather than the other.

In Job the issue in dispute is the doctrine of retribution — whether God always rewards the righteous and punishes the wicked. A number of proverbs highlight that those who are righteous will receive blessings. For example, Prov 16:7 (NRSV) says, "When the ways of people please the LORD, he causes even their enemies to be at peace with them." Proverbs 3:1-10 indicates that if you trust in God you will get long life, prosperity, and the favor of God and others (see also 9:10-12). These are never meant to be universal promises — they are partial perspectives that accurately reflect part of the truth. Yet some people seemingly wanted the proverbs to say more than that godliness often leads to a healthy, successful life. They pushed this line as if it alone was true, so that misfortune in a person's life witnessed to their evil character, while good fortune disclosed a person's righteousness. Such a view is represented in the book of Job by the friends. Holmgren notes that "Job's Friends are person who have cast flexible proverbial sayings into rigid laws. . . . They made words say more than they were meant to say."[15] While what they say is often true, it is usually not true in Job's case, and is certainly not the whole truth.

A key purpose of the book, then, is to reexamine the relationship between individual righteousness and rewards, and to rediscover the nuanced teaching of the book of Proverbs. The book of Job is a form of protest wisdom, but it is a protest against those who had hijacked and distorted the teaching of Proverbs.

---

14. Ibid., 341-42.
15. Ibid., 347, 353.

This leads to the second purpose of the book, which is to explore the proper relationship between God and humanity or, to put it another way, the nature of true faith or righteousness. Gregory Parsons argues that "the relationship between God and man is the basic problem of the book," which involves the refutation of a dogmatic theology of retribution that binds God. We shall see that this is not a book about suffering, but the losses inflicted on Job shed light on the book's purpose. Parsons suggests that "Job's suffering as an innocent party was not the main focus but was introduced only as a means of isolating and intensifying the question of the proper basis of man's relationship with God."[16] The challenge of the prologue is whether Job fears God for no reason (1:9), and the book explores this issue of whether it is possible to have a faith in God free from ulterior motives. The accuser questions whether such a faith is possible, and the book as a whole responds with a resounding yes.

Allied to this purpose is the desire to explore what kind of responses to God may be regarded as legitimate expressions of faith. This is a distinctive contribution of the dialogue. In this book Job makes many laments and complaints to God. He accuses God (e.g., 6:4; 13:21; 16:11-14) and calls for litigation against a God who seems to be absent. The book as a whole endorses Job's complaints and questioning as a legitimate expression of the faith of a righteous person. They are God-directed and reveal that Job believes, despite God's apparent absence, that God alone can resolve his dilemma. Job can be described by God in 42:9 as "speaking of him what is right," not only in the prologue but also throughout the dialogue. A stance of meek submissiveness is not the only permissible response to God. Protest and questioning — with an underlying desire to draw near to God — can in some circumstances be appropriate.

A final purpose of the book is to focus on the character of God. This is an underlying issue right through the dialogue as the friends pontificate about how God *must* act. Yet Job insists that the way he had previously thought about God cannot account for his present experience of God's apparent displeasure. God is silent toward, and seemingly absent from, him in the face of his great suffering. The theophany and Yahweh speeches (chs. 38–41) insist that God cannot be constrained by narrow human categories. As the sovereign creator and maintainer of order, God reaffirms his freedom to run the world as he chooses and insists that he must be treated as God. The book presents a majestic picture of God's power and greatness as a foundational truth. Only when God is treated as God can humans become the people they were meant to be. We cannot exhaustively know God's design or purposes, so we need to be content with letting God be God.

16. Parsons, "Structure and Purpose," 143.

How Have Others Understood It?

Some understanding of the way Job has been interpreted over the years will help us to see the range of possibilities for interpreting the book.[17] There has probably been more written on Job than on any other OT book except the Psalms.

Two trends in early Christian interpretation can be seen in John Chrysostom (ca. 347-407) and Jerome (ca. 347-419), both of whom were responding to the allegorizing of Origen.[18] Chrysostom found in Job a model of self-denial and a contrast with Adam. Central were his struggle with the devil and his perseverance under trial, both of which were to be imitated. Chrysostom's focus was largely on the Job of chapters 1–2, not the protesting Job of the dialogue. Jerome, instead of emphasizing the prologue, used texts that he thought could be read christologically (e.g., 19:23-27) to establish the hope of bodily resurrection as a key to reading the book. Thus Job's trust in his redeemer is the book's clear and distinctive contribution.

Gregory the Great (ca. 540-604) argued for allegorical and moral readings in *Moralia in Iob*. On the moral level, he sought to explain away Job's bold words to God, and to portray him as the patient saint of the prologue.[19] His preferred reading was an allegorical one; for example, the ostrich in 39:13-14 is the synagogue, her eggs are the apostles "born of the flesh of the synagogue," and Job's seven sons refer to the twelve apostles (7 = 3 + 4; 3 × 4 = 12).[20] The book thus outlined the great doctrines of the Christian message with Job himself being a type of Christ and of the persecuted church. He held that Job's suffering was "medicinal, purgative and pedagogical."[21] There is a greater focus in his book on sin than suffering, as it gives warning to the sinner and the hope of salvation to the believer.

Two important medieval views are those of Maimonides (1135-1204) and Thomas Aquinas (1225-1274), who moved away from Gregory's allegorical hermeneutic.[22] Both saw that Job centered on the issue of God's providence, but Maimonides in *The Guide of the Perplexed* understood the story as a parable about a nonhistorical person who, though righteous, lacked some wisdom. He suggested that Job had wrong beliefs instigated by Satan (the sole cause of Job's suffering), and it was Elihu's role to introduce the concept of the angel of cor-

17. An earlier form of this material is found in L. Wilson, "Job, Book of," 384-85.

18. Glatzer, *Dimensions of Job*, 24-27.

19. See Dell, *Sceptical Literature*, 25.

20. For other examples see Glatzer, *Dimensions*, 28-31. On Gregory see also Schreiner, *Where Shall Wisdom Be Found?* 22-54.

21. Schreiner, *Where Shall Wisdom Be Found?* 158.

22. On both these scholars see ibid., 55-90.

rection and intercession, a kind of counterpart to Satan (the "evil inclination"), who enables the "knowledgeless" Job to hear "the prophetic revelation" of the Yahweh speeches.[23] In *The Literal Exposition of Job,* however, Aquinas viewed Job as a real historical figure who despite his advanced wisdom was still sinful in his protests. He argued against "spiritual" readings of the story (allegorical, moral, anagogical), and opted for the "literal" or historical sense. Aquinas perceived that the book of Job properly explained God's sovereign ordering of the universe.

The Reformers strongly affirmed the literal sense rather than the allegorical. In his preface to the German translation of Job, Martin Luther (1483-1546) contended that the book's theme is whether the righteous can suffer misfortune. He thought that Job, in his human weakness, erred by speaking wrongly against God, but was still more righteous than the friends. He did not explore how to read the book christologically.[24] John Calvin (1509-1564) wrote 159 sermons on the book, but no commentary, and opted for the "clear," "simple," or "natural" sense of the text.[25] Even Behemoth and Leviathan were not to be read symbolically as describing the devil (so Gregory) but in their natural sense referring to an elephant and a whale, respectively.[26] He found in Job a resource for enduring suffering, although he often contrasted the more "humble" or submissive approach of the David of the psalms to Job's angry and impatient outbursts, which cross the line of genuine piety.[27] He found much truth in the words of the friends, but especially in Elihu's view of God's providence and the place of suffering.[28] Despite his pride, Job came to see that God could be trusted to run his world justly. For Calvin, the reality of the resurrection was something grasped by Job but not by his friends, and this enabled Job to rise above their arguments without denying the justice of God. Life beyond death meant that justice may not be fully apparent in this life.

In more recent times (nineteenth–mid-twentieth century; even earlier in Germany), the historical-critical approach has dominated Joban studies, generally focusing on innocent suffering as the central theme of Job, and thus foregrounding the prologue and epilogue. This approach has led to some clarification of matters of language, date, authorship, and literary parallels in the

---

23. Glatzer, *Dimensions,* 20-22; Schreiner, *Where Shall Wisdom Be Found?* 64-67.

24. Glatzer, *Dimensions,* 32.

25. Detailed studies of Calvin's sermons on Job have been undertaken by Schreiner, *Where Shall Wisdom Be Found?* 91-155 (focusing on suffering and justice, nature and history); and Thomas, *Calvin's Teaching on Job,* who argues that the incomprehensibility of God is the interpretive key for Calvin. He also explores the pastoral and christological dimensions of Calvin's reading of Job.

26. Schreiner, *Where Shall Wisdom Be Found?* 143-44.

27. Ibid., 100-105.

28. On Calvin's high regard for Elihu, see ibid., 131-35.

ancient Near East, but has been accompanied by doubts about the authenticity of many segments of the book (e.g., the poem on wisdom, ch. 28; the Elihu section, chs. 32–37; the Yahweh speeches, chs. 38–41; the epilogue, ch. 42). The aim in such studies was generally to get back to the original or authentic parts of the book of Job and to identify any later additions that may have attempted to skew the author's intention. Behind this is an assumption that the present form of the text often disguises the "real" meaning of the book.

Dell has pointed out that, in the mid-twentieth century, the focus shifted to the dialogue and its discussion of the doctrine of retribution, often seen to be in tension with the prologue and epilogue. This focus also raised the issue of theodicy, or how God's moral governance of the universe can be justified. A third movement in modern times has been to concentrate on Yahweh's speeches and Job's reply, which present the nature of God as the key issue and focus on how humans can respond to God. The final movement discerned by Dell is to propose that all the various parts are integral to the book's literary unity and then to argue that the message of the book is protesting and unorthodox, calling into question such ideas as retribution or traditional understandings of God.[29]

The onset of the new literary and canonical approaches and the resurgence of evangelical scholarship have led to English-speaking scholars tending toward reading the book as a literary and theological whole (e.g., Andersen, Habel, Hartley, J. Janzen, Newsom, G. Wilson, Walton, Estes). Such final-form approaches have sought to give full weight to each section of the book, and have regained a sensitivity to lament as a legitimate stance before God. Other contemporary interpretations include the liberationist approach of Gustavo Gutiérrez, deconstructionist readings by David Clines, an historicized reading by David Wolfers (Job is the nation of Israel), and a variety of feminist, psychoanalytical, and philosophical perspectives.

A number of important issues have emerged from this survey. First, an emphasis on different parts of the book will yield vastly different interpretations. While all commentators are products of their age, our goal in reading the book of Job is to arrive at an interpretation that accounts for all of the book, giving appropriate weight to the function and importance of each part. The prologue, dialogue, and epilogue must all play a part, and the human and divine verdicts given by Elihu and by God himself (his words together with his appearance) will need to shape our reading. The change of direction by Job in chapter 42, and God's endorsement of Job rather than the friends, will also need to be accounted for. It will also be necessary to read this book as part of the wisdom books, part of the OT, and as part of the Bible as a whole.

---

29. Dell, *Sceptical Literature*, 29-56.

How Do the Different Parts of the Book Fit Together?

In any complex book (and Job certainly is that!) an overview of the component parts and the flow of thought is a very useful tool.[30]

The prologue (chs. 1–2) gives the setting. Job is blameless and not suffering because of any sin. But neither Job nor his friends are told that. Job's faith is then tested by the losses of his possessions and children, as well as his health, in the rest of the prologue. Within the prologue, suffering clarifies and isolates the central issue of whether Job is only a "fair-weather" believer (1:9). Job responds to his suffering first with the traditional piety in chapters 1 and 2, and then with lament, complaint, and other protests from chapter 3 on.

The greater part of the book consists of interaction between Job and his friends. Job's initial self-lament and self-curse in chapter 3 trigger various responses from the three friends who have arrived to comfort and console him. During nearly three complete cycles, the friends speak in turn, with Job responding after each. This continues as far as chapter 27, by which time the friends have become silent. However, chapters 3–27 have been difficult to classify. To call them a "discussion" or "debate" implies too intellectual an exercise and downplays Job's ever-present turmoil. "Dialogue" implies that each is seeking to answer the issues raised by the previous speaker, an aspect often frustratingly absent from Job.[31] Andersen suggests that this is a form of "contest" literature, a type of debate in which each person tries to make the best speech, though not necessarily refuting his opponents.[32] Despite the apparent problems of classifying these chapters as "dialogue," I shall use this label as the most apt, familiar, and convenient.

Clearly, if the book is to be read as a whole, this section must be given proper weight. Job's God-directed cries and complaints throughout the dialogue are best viewed as calls on the seemingly absent God to become present. Though he strongly accuses God (6:4; 13:21; 16:11-14), he longs to speak to God in person (13:15), in a relationship in which God would call and Job would answer (14:15). Job explores imaginative possibilities, including a figure variously described as an arbiter, witness, and redeemer (9:32-35; 16:18-22; 19:23-27). A legal metaphor is woven through the book, as Job desperately pleads for justice from God.[33] Job

---

30. An earlier form of this is found in L. Wilson, "Job, Book of," 385-87.

31. However, Course, *Speech and Response,* passim, argues that the repetition of words and themes in the introductions to each speech suggests that each speech in chs. 4–24 is a genuine response to the preceding speech; while Pyeon, *You Have Not Spoken,* 38, concludes more generally that "recent scholarly debate suggests that the speeches of Job actually do interact with one another."

32. Andersen, *Job,* 96-97.

33. See the section "Theological Themes: The Litigation Motif."

persistently believes that only God can resolve his crisis (7:20-21; 10:1-2; 13:3, 15-19, 22-24; 19:25-27; 23:10-16).

The dialogue breaks down in the third cycle, thus witnessing to the inability of the exponents of traditional wisdom to resolve Job's dilemma. The three cycles of speeches are followed by a wisdom poem (see below) and then Job's summing up of his case. In this summary, he outlines his previous righteous life and his current treatment as one of the wicked. These are followed by an oath of clearance in chapter 31, which climaxes in a cry that God might answer him (31:35).

A number of false trails suggest some unsatisfactory answers to Job's dilemma. The first is the advice of the friends. The final verdict of the book is that Eliphaz, Bildad, and Zophar have not spoken about God what is right, but that Job has (42:7-8). This has puzzled many readers since Job is the one who is challenging, accusing, and complaining to God, while the friends attempt to defend God's justice and explain Job's suffering. On their trite formulas, Job is a sinner suffering for his sins (4:17; 5:7, 17-27; 8:3-7; 11:6, 13-16). Their analysis and advice has missed the mark in the case of Job.

Another false trail is the suggestion that the wisdom poem of chapter 28 provides the answer, implying that Job needed to learn to fear God (28:28). However, the prologue has already stated that Job feared God (1:1, 8; 2:3). Furthermore, Job 28 is placed before Job's summing up in chapters 29–31, where Job repeats his complaints and calls for the presence of God. Chapter 28 has not provided the solution, and Job is still calling for a resolution. It is best understood not as the anticipated conclusion, but rather as an anticlimax. Its answer, in traditional but overly rigid wisdom terms, is qualified by what follows in chapters 38–42. When God finally does appear, he does not mention fearing him as the way forward.

The final false trail is found in the Elihu speeches (Job 32–37). While some misunderstand Elihu to be a fourth friend, his function is rather that of an adjudicator. The Elihu speeches give the human verdict on Job's case, but one that is to be overruled by the following chapters. His speeches provide a summary of the preceding dialogue and concede that the friends have not bettered Job. Elihu narrows in on Job's words in the debate (34:3, 5-6, 9, 35-37; 35:16) rather than on Job's conduct before the dialogue. His conclusion is that Job has not "spoken of God what is right," a verdict that is thus intentionally set up as a rival to the later words of God. Elihu thus anticipates, and provides a theological foil for, God's long-awaited appearance.[34]

When God finally appears and utters two speeches, the book begins to clarify. There is debate over whether these should be called the Yahweh

34. L. Wilson, "Role of the Elihu Speeches," 90; McCabe, "Elihu's Contribution," 76-77.

speeches, drawing attention to what God said, or rather labeled a theophany, which highlights God's appearance. The fact of God's presence entirely satisfies Job's deepest longings, while the reminder that God is not bound to human views of justice effectively answers Job's pursuit of litigation. Thus they provide a compelling resolution for Job. God's speeches bring about a paradigm shift in the book, and God even needs to speak twice before Job finally understands. His survey of the natural world decisively shifts the issue from Job's question, "Why am I not dealt with justly?" to the broader one of how God orders his creation. The dialogue is thus shown to have been telescopic rather than panoramic. When God reveals that the way he orders the world is wider than our understanding of justice, Job reacts appropriately to this new information.

A delicate balance has to be maintained in these chapters, as Yahweh seeks to redirect Job's energies without crushing him. If Yahweh is too harsh, he would appear to endorse the views of the friends; if Yahweh is too soft, then Job will not hear what is needed. The playful irony of the Yahweh speeches achieves a right balance. Thus both God's words and his appearance provide a platform from which we can view the work as a whole.

In chapter 42 Job does not need to, and does not, repent of any sin, even his words uttered in the debate. Instead he changes his course of action now that Yahweh has appeared. In particular, Job ceases to pursue his protests now that he has understood them to be misdirected. This change of perspective is exactly what is found in Job's response (42:2-6). He concedes that he spoke of "things too wonderful for me, which I did not know" (v. 3, referring to the Yahweh speeches). Furthermore, before God's appearance, he had only heard of God "by the hearing of the ear, but now my eye sees you" (v. 5, referring to the theophany). His new direction is recorded in v. 6, which many have misunderstood as Job repenting of his sin. This is most unlikely in view of God's endorsement of Job's words (42:7-8, including the honorific title "servant") and Job's intercession for the friends, leading to their restoration (42:9-10). In this commentary I argue that Job is now rejecting and turning away from his previous laments ("dust and ashes"). Now that Job's horizons have been expanded and his thinking reconfigured, Job needs to change his perspective in life, which is precisely what he proceeds to do as he rejoins society (42:10-17).

The epilogue (42:10-17) has often been regarded as sounding a jarring note, seemingly restating the discarded theory of retribution. Yet Job's restoration is pictured as an act of grace, and the book as a whole points out that God's relationship to people is wider than simply retribution, so that the doctrine of retribution is qualified, not overturned. The picture at the end of the book is of Job as a righteous person of faith, surrounded by even more abundant evidence of his active trust in God.

What Is the Structure of the Book?

The discussion in the previous section gives the following structure to the book:

The Prologue (chs. 1–2)

The Dialogue (chs. 3–31)
Job's Self-Lament (ch. 3)

Round 1 (chs. 4–14)	Round 2 (chs. 15–21)	Round 3 (chs. 22–27)
Eliphaz (chs. 4–5)	Eliphaz (ch. 15)	Eliphaz (ch. 22)
Job (chs. 6–7)	Job (chs. 16–17)	Job (chs. 23–24)
Bildad (ch. 8)	Bildad (ch. 18)	Bildad (ch. 25)
Job (chs. 9–10)	Job (ch. 19)	Job (chs. 26–27)
Zophar (ch. 11)	Zophar (ch. 20)	
Job (chs. 12–14)	Job (ch. 21)	

Interlude — A Poem on Wisdom (ch. 28)
Job's Summing Up (chs. 29–31)

The Verdicts (32:1–42:6)
Elihu's Verdict (chs. 32–37)
God's Appearance (Yahweh Speeches) and Job's Responses (38:1–42:6)
God's First Speech (38:1–40:2)
Job's First Reply (40:3-5)
God's Second Speech (40:6–41:34)
Job's Second Reply (42:1-6)

The Epilogue (42:7-17)

While this overall structure is the most crucial pattern to grasp, more detail is given in the following outline of the contents of the book:

1:1–2:13: The Prologue

1:1-5	Job Is Utterly Righteous
1:6-12	The First Heavenly Court Scene
1:13-19	The First Test — Loss of Possessions and Family
1:20-22	Job's First Reaction to His Loss and the Narrator's Verdict
2:1-6	The Second Heavenly Court Scene
2:7-10	The Second Test — Ghastly Sores
2:11-13	The Arrival and Mission of the Friends

3:1–31:40: The Dialogue

3:1-26: Job's Self-Curse and Self-Lament

4:1–14:22: Round One

4:1–5:27: Eliphaz

6:1–7:21: Job

  6:1-30: Job to Friends

  7:1-21: Job to God

8:1-22: Bildad

9:1–10:22: Job

Is the Text of Job Reliable?

Two issues are related here. First, do we have what was originally written, in the order in which it was written? Another way of expressing this is to ask, Is all of the book genuine and meant to be there? This question is frequent, and a number of scholars have suggested rearrangements of the book. The second main issue is whether the Hebrew text (the MT) is the best textual witness. This is sometimes raised because of the difficulty of translating some verses,[35] and is reflected in two different English versions giving vastly different translations of a verse (e.g., the NRSV and NIV translations of 13:15).

---

35. An example of this is Good, *In Turns of Tempest*, 100-101, when he leaves 19:25b-26 untranslated because he does not think that he can make meaningful sentences out of them with any confidence. A clear recent summary of the textual witnesses is found in Seow, *Job 1–21*, 2-17.

Many scholars doubt the authenticity of parts of the book. Some see only the prologue and epilogue as original; others view the dialogue as the original writing that was later given a narrative setting. Many see the incomplete third cycle of speeches as evidence of textual corruption; some see chapter 28 as a misplaced poem. A lot of scholars would remove the Elihu speeches, though some now want to insert them before chapter 28. Some suggest that either the second Yahweh speech or both speeches are later additions, while many object to the epilogue as contradicting the rest of the book. If this were to be a commentary on only those parts of the book that scholars agreed to be authentic, it would be a very short book!

Two examples will suffice. In the third cycle of speeches, a number of difficulties have been proposed: Bildad's speech is much shorter than his previous speeches (25:1-6), lacks both introduction and conclusion, and would be suitably finished by 26:5-14; a third speech from Zophar is missing; there are not enough poetic lines to make a full cycle; Job's last response is very long (chs. 26–31); Job's words in 24:18-24 seem to counter his complaint in 24:1-17; and 27:13-23 seems out of place in Job's mouth. While it is quite possible that there is textual corruption here, few can agree about how the text is to be re-allocated. A number of scholars add 26:5-14 to Bildad's otherwise short speech (e.g., Rowley, Gordis, Pope, Terrien, Habel); but Clines adds all of chapter 26; John Hartley instead adds 27:13-23; while Peter Zerafa ascribes 24:18–25:6 to Bildad. Many have assigned 27:13-23 to Zophar, but others add 24:18-24 and sometimes 27:7-10 (or 27:7-12). We might conclude with E. J. Kissane that "the text has suffered much more at the hands of some modern critics than it had suffered throughout the ages of its history."[36] The end result is that the atttempts to "restore the original text" have failed to come to any compelling conclusion. I will argue that the third cycle purposefully ends in disarray, and grinds to a halt as a way of showing the bankruptcy of the friends' arguments.[37]

The Elihu speeches are commonly regarded as a later insertion into a previously existing book of Job, and several lines of argument have been adduced in support of this view.[38] First, Elihu is not mentioned in the book outside chapters 32–37 (even though a bystander is quite naturally not mentioned until

---

36. Kissane, *Book of Job*, xli; quoted in Smick, "Job," 965. For a fuller survey of earlier and foreign writers see Zerafa, *Wisdom of God*, 19-29. Pope, *Job*, xlvi, notes that the Qumran Targum substantiates the order of chs. 24–27 in the MT. Hartley, *Book of Job*, 25, observes, "The wide variety of the multiple reconstructions cautions further against major reapportioning of the verses in chs. 24–31 in order to achieve a full third cycle."

37. Loader, "Answer or Enigma?" 25-26; Tsevat, "Meaning of the Book of Job," 2; Gutiérrez, *On Job*, 28. Most recently see Long, "On the Coherence," 113-22.

38. On this see Johns, "Literary and Theological Function," 1-8.

he intervenes). His absence from the epilogue and his failure to be rebuked by Yahweh are due to the fact that his role is not that of a friend but an arbiter. Second, his diction is claimed to differ from the rest of dialogue, in particular containing more Aramaisms; but Robert Gordis uses this information to conclude that the speeches were written by the same poet in his later years, inserting the new insights gained from his further experience in life. Third, he differs from Job's friends in that he quotes and then refutes Job's words, and also in that he addresses Job by name. Yet it has been plausibly suggested that Elihu's method of verbatim quotation is unique because his task in the book is unique, while the use of a person's name was an appropriate court procedure. Fourth, many say that Elihu adds nothing to the debate but merely rehashes the traditional theology of the three friends, but this overlooks that Elihu has a literary function even if his views contribute little beyond the arguments of the friends. Fifth, others claim that the content of Elihu's speeches is inconsistent with the rest of the book, but this is a matter to be decided by careful exegesis. Lastly, if chapters 32–37 were removed, no one would suggest that there was a lacuna. However, even if this were true, it is simply to say that there could have been a different story about Job.

The external evidence for including Elihu is strong — three out of the four manuscript fragments of Job from Qumran include portions of Elihu's speeches.[39] Significantly, a growing body of modern writers has found it fruitful to explore their literary and theological functions in their present context.[40] Thus, while it is possible to read Job without the Elihu speeches, there is no compelling reason to do so unless the content of the Elihu speeches demands it. Their literary and theological functions will be pointed out in the study of chapters 32–37.

My approach in this commentary is to use the heuristic principle that the book of Job is to be interpreted in its present form in order to see if it makes sense. Often the motivation for rearrangement of the text is that the commentators believe that the text does not make sense as it stands. J. H. Eaton observes, "Attempts at reconstruction of an original Job, though in principle quite justifiable, do not seem to have repaid the effort which has gone into them, and the very number of them, by a law of diminishing returns, has tended to reduce the credibility of each new one."[41] My growing conviction from studying Job is

---

39. Parsons, "Structure and Purpose," 153. Some details are set out in Seow, *Job 1–21*, 5.

40. McKay, "Elihu — A Proto-Charismatic?" 167; Hemraj, "Elihu's 'Missionary' Role," 52-60; Tate, "Speeches of Elihu"; Johns, "Literary and Theological Function"; McCabe, "Elihu's Contribution"; Wolfers, "Elihu"; L. Wilson, "Role of the Elihu Speeches"; and the commentaries by Andersen, Habel, Simundson, Hartley, Smick, J. Janzen, G. Wilson, Walton.

41. Eaton, *Job*, 33. He concludes that "effort may be better spent in trying to read the present text as positively as possible."

that, when the book is read in its present form, many of the supposed inconsistencies and contradictions can be resolved, and the book can be read as a coherent whole. In the exegetical sections of this commentary I will explain how each section can be seen as a legitimate part of the whole, and how some of the "difficulties" have important literary and theological functions. The reader will need to assess this after working through Job, by asking whether this holistic reading accounts for what is in the book better than any other theory.

In terms of the preserved text, Marvin Pope comments, "The Book of Job is textually the most vexed in the Old Testament, rivaled only by Hosea which has the advantage of being much shorter."[42] While a detailed study of the textual issues is outside the scope of this commentary series, there are good grounds for seeing the MT as the foundational and most important source. The earliest form of the Greek Septuagint is about four hundred lines shorter and is at times just a paraphrase of the MT.[43] The other Greek versions have been preserved only in fragments, and the oldest Syriac version, the Peshitta, is generally a literal translation from the Hebrew. The Qumran Targum on Job (11QtgJob) is not complete, but appears to be based on a Hebrew text very close to the MT.[44]

However, many of our problems with the text of Job arise out of our limited knowledge of the Hebrew language. It is not so much that the text is corrupt; it is simply difficult. The book has a greater number of hapax legomena (words used only once in the OT) and rare words than any other book in the OT.[45] Frederick Greenspahn notes that the prose sections and Zophar speeches have fewer hapax legomena, but that the Eliphaz, Bildad, and Elihu speeches have a large but not overwhelming number. Yet there is an even higher proportion in both Job's speeches and in Yahweh's speeches.[46] The large number of uncommon words calls for humility as we seek to understand the precise thrust of parts of the book of Job.

Why Is the Book So Long and Repetitive?

Admittedly, the dialogues in the book of Job are long, and seem at times to trawl over the same ground. Roland Murphy comments, "The traditional phrase, 'the

---

42. Pope, *Job*, xliii. He still regards the MT as the primary source for the book of Job (xlvii).

43. See, e.g., R. Smith, "Introduction to Job," 6-7; Pope, *Job*, xliii-xlvii.

44. Sarna, "Book of Job," x. Nothing remains of chs. 1–16, but there are substantial later sections. See Pope, *Job*, xlv-xlvii, who sees its origins in the second century B.C.; Hartley, *Book of Job*, 4-5.

45. Greenfield, "Language of the Book," xiv.

46. Greenspahn, "Number and Distribution," 15-16.

patience of Job,' might better be bowdlerized as 'the patience of the reader of Job.' The back and forth of the discourses is repetitious and stubborn, on both sides."[47] This does make the book of Job difficult to read at one sitting (the ideal way to read the book); even a few verses or a chapter at a time can be trying. Many a Bible reader who has waded through the cultic laws of Leviticus, crossed over the allocation of the land in Joshua, and got bogged down in the genealogies of 1 Chronicles might experience a similar sense of boring repetition as they confront the talkfest of Job.

It is a long book, but it needs to be long. The issues dealt with in the book are those that people grapple with at length. A "Reader's Digest" version of Job — attractive though that might seem — could give the book a different message. Part of the reason for the length of the dialogue is a legal system in which a party loses by running out of relevant arguments to add. The slow grinding to a halt of the dialogue is the writer's way of demonstrating the futility of the friends' views in this case. Similarly, God uses a flurry of examples (and indeed two speeches), when he simply could have told Job what he wanted him to know. There are two good reasons why he did not. First, if all that God does is to correct Job, then it looks like the friends are right after all. Second, the many different examples in God's first speech change the tone of the speech into a leisurely stroll around the creation, while still giving Job enough information to rethink his stance.

The length of the book of Job is not the result of having a bad editor, but often serves a literary and thematic purpose. It seems long to us because we live in a media-driven culture that is looking for sound bites and short text messages.

It is also a long book because it invites the reader into the process of reflection, and this takes time. Christopher Ash suggests that the issue of suffering and the questions that it raises about God cannot be answered by a postcard, but only by a journey that takes time. Trying to take shortcuts defeats the purpose of a deliberately long book like Job.[48] The book does not simply arrive at propositional answers, but explores the process of loss and grief, the reworking of faith, and the transformation of Job.

The size of the book of Job suggests that it may take a lengthy series of sermons to cover its riches. While it is tempting to do Job in a nutshell by looking at the prologue, Yahweh speeches, and the epilogue, time spent grappling with the book as a whole will reveal many other riches.

---

47. Murphy, "Last Truth about God," 585.
48. Ash, *Out of the Storm*, 14.

Commentary

1:1–2:13: The Prologue

These two chapters provide the setting or background against which the central dialogue is to be read. They invite the reader to explore the following questions:

> How does Job react to his great loss, and what is the basis for his reaction?
> How does this response affect our understanding of the dialogue that follows?
> How is Job's character viewed by God, by the narrator, and by Job himself?
> What does the prologue tell us about the nature of Job's relationship with God?
> What is at stake here?

Questions like these indicate the issues that are opened up as the book begins.

The prologue seems to be structured around seven scenes, often alternating between heaven and earth (1:1-5, 6-12, 13-19, 20-22; 2:1-6, 7-10, 11-13).[1] The scenes are juxtaposed side by side, some with no connective other than "One day" (NRSV, NIV), resulting in a staccato effect.[2] These scenes introduce the character of Job and then raise some of the issues that will be later developed.

1:1-5: Job Is Utterly Righteous

At the outset, the writer hints at the issue of what it means to be human before God. In an atypical Hebrew word order (commonly used for emphasis), the word "man" is at the beginning of the first

---

1. However, some scholars make a break between 2:7a and 2:7b, or combine some of the units.

2. So Ash, *Out of the Storm*, 19.

verse (lit. "A man there was in the land of Uz"). This suggests that the book will teach us not only about God but also about humanity. His location (Uz) and his name are given.

The setting in the land of Uz is significant. While its exact location is hard to determine, its main significance is that it is outside Israel.[3] This is the implied setting of the story and, as will become clearer in v. 5, it is set prior to the giving of the OT law. The stage is put in place for a universal rather than an exclusively Israelite answer to the issues that will be raised.

The name Job (אִיּוֹב/*ʾiyōb*) sounds like the Hebrew word for "enemy" (אֹיֵב/ *ʾōyēb*); but even if this link is established, its significance is not clear. Though Job sometimes feels under attack by God (e.g., 6:4; 13:24), God does not regard him as an enemy (42:7-8). It is best not to read too much into his name, and nothing is made of his name anywhere in the book.

What is emphasized about this man is his righteous character. A fourfold description is given, which is unparalleled in the rest of the OT. Job is "blameless and upright, one who feared God and turned away from evil" (NRSV). While each term has a distinct meaning, it is probably the cumulative effect of all four terms that is significant. In terms of the first pair, Meir Weiss suggests that "blameless" refers to character, and "upright" to his actions, but this is probably too neat a distinction.[4] "Blameless" (תָּם/*tām*) refers to a person's moral character and is elsewhere used in the sense of integrity (e.g., Gen 20:5, 6; 1 Kgs 9:4; Pss 7:8; 25:21; 26:1, 11; 41:12; 78:72).[5] Bildad later disputes Job's "blamelessness" (8:20), but Job insists that he is blameless (9:20-22). The description of Job as "upright" (יָשָׁר/*yāšār*, "straight, whole, just") is similar in meaning, and the two words are parallel in Ps 37:37. Calling Job blameless and upright is not an assertion that he was sinless (for he is human), but simply that he was a person of genuine and thorough integrity.

The remainder of v. 1 adds further testimony to the righteousness of this man. The most crucial description is that he feared God, which is often mandated in wisdom texts.[6] Interestingly, this characteristic of Job fearing God is picked up by "the satan" in v. 9 ("Does Job fear God for nothing?") as a representative description of Job's supposed righteousness. "Fearing" God is not cringing in his presence, but fundamentally an attitude of respecting God as

---

3. See "Introduction: Who Wrote the Book, and When Was It Written?"

4. Weiss, *Story of Job's Beginning*, 25.

5. A related word, תָּמִים/*tāmîm*, is also often translated as "blameless," and is used of Job in 12:4. The two words are parallel in Ps 101:2.

6. The expression "fearing God/Yahweh" is used in Prov 1:7, 29; 2:5; 3:7; 8:13; 9:10; 10:27; 14:2, 26, 27; 15:16, 33; 16:6; 19:23; 22:4; 23:17; 24:21; 31:30; Eccl 5:7; 7:18; 8:12; 12:13; Pss 15:4; 19:9; 34:9, 11; 111:10.

God and treating him accordingly. "Turning away from evil" means to reject godlessness as a path of life.

In v. 2 the focus is clearly on Job. There could be an implication that the items in vv. 2-3 follow on from his piety in v. 1 (the conjunction "and" can be used in this way). At the very least, the juxtaposition of his righteousness and his wealth hints at the fittingness of the blessing. As the patriarch, the children were born *to him,* not to his wife. The numbers are stylized, ideal, symbolic figures (again suggesting completeness), seven and three with their total ten, like the round figures that will describe his possessions in v. 3. Perhaps his wife is not mentioned in the introduction because of her role in the testing of Job, but it is more likely that her absence is for a literary reason. She will be introduced in 2:9, when her previous absence will heighten the dramatic impact of her words. It is common in Hebrew narrative for a character to be introduced just before they become the focus of attention.

In v. 3 the narrator outlines Job's substantial animal holdings. The numbers are again round and complete figures: ten thousand sheep and camels; one thousand oxen and donkeys. This catalogue in v. 3 then leads to the conclusion that "this man was the greatest of all the people of the east." The way in which Job was greater is not specified. Some (e.g., Weiss) interpret this as "greater in wisdom," for the east was most renowned for its wisdom (Jer 49:7; Obad 8; 1 Kgs 5:10). The immediate context, however, more probably suggests that it is in his wealth or possessions that Job is greater than all others. "East" (קֶדֶם/*qedem*) can also mean "antiquity," so that "sons of antiquity" might mean the patriarchs.

Robert Fyall proposes that it is significant that his character is mentioned in v. 1 before his wealth in v. 3.[7] However, it is better to regard all of vv. 1-5 as being all about character. The aim of describing Job's possessions is not just to show how rich he was. Rather they have a literary function of providing evidence of his great righteousness. This is how the traditional wisdom circles understood wealth — as the blessings of a just God. The positive aspect of the doctrine of retribution — that God rewards righteousness — seems to underlie this opening picture of Job and will be explored and expanded during the course of the debate.

This understanding of vv. 2-3 reveals the unity of the first five verses. It is Job's righteousness that is highlighted in v. 1; the evidence of it is given by the description of his blessings in vv. 2-3; and vv. 4-5 show the great care Job took to ensure he and his family were right with God.

The details in vv. 4-5 thus establish how scrupulous Job was. He would offer sacrifices for the possible sins of his sons, rising early to make offerings for each one. The imperfect tense at the end of v. 5, combined with the phrase

7. Fyall, *How Does God Treat His Friends,* 21.

"all the days" (ESV, NASB "continually"), implies this was his habitual practice. Some see in v. 4 a record of life in the fast lane, but this is unlikely to be a weekly cycle (contra Dhorme, Fohrer, Rowley). The text reads "each [on] his day," and in 3:1 "his day" means the day of Job's birth. So this most likely describes an annual cycle. The invitation to the sisters to join these feasts implies unity and harmony within the family. Verse 4 not only introduces the children, who will be crucial in the subsequent events, but also explains how they will happen to be in the one place (v. 13).

Verse 5 gives further evidence of Job's character, showing that he is concerned with the spiritual well-being of his children. Andersen suggests that "rise early in the morning" is a common Hebrew idiom for conscientious activity, not primarily a focus on the time of the sacrifice, though it is clearly in the morning.[8] Some incorrectly suggest that Job is here pictured as obsessive in his piety, overscrupulous as a sign of inward insecurity and lack of trust in God. That is not the most natural reading of the text and would undermine the carefully constructed picture of Job as fittingly righteous. This verse also introduces the motif of cursing God as the litmus test of unrighteousness, which is picked up later in the prologue (1:11; 2:5, 9). The verb בֵּרַךְ/*bārak*, "bless," is used euphemistically to mean "cursed" here, as in 1 Kgs 21:10, 13.

The resulting picture is one of Job in patriarchal times, where the head of the family, rather than a cultic official, is the priest. As suggested in relation to v. 1, the patriarchal timing of the story and the location in Uz give a setting outside Israel and before the giving of the law. The later picture of Job (e.g., 29:7) as a city dweller means that he was not entirely nomadic, but is initially presented as such to give the flavor of the patriarchal period.

These opening verses establish Job as a person of unblemished righteousness. This is the narrator's initial verdict on Job before his faith is tested. Any understanding of Job must start from this point where the book starts — that Job is, before he is tested, a model righteous person. Neither Job nor the friends are told any of this, but it is included to shape the reader's understanding of Job's circumstances.

1:6-12: The First Heavenly Court Scene The focus here moves to the gathering in heaven, where the hidden drama is disclosed. The two heavenly court scenes help the reader to understand what is going on, but for Job (and his friends) they are unseen right to the very end. When Job interacts with the friends, with Elihu, and finally with Yahweh, he is not privy to what has gone on in heaven.

---

8. Andersen, *Job*, 81. GKC §113k suggests that the Hiphil infinitive הַשְׁכֵּים/*hiškîm*, "get up early," used as an adverb, often has the connotation of "earnestly."

The first scene closed with what Job used to do "all the days"; this scene starts with "one day" and focuses attention on a crucial meeting and dialogue. The effect of this heavenly gathering is to narrow our focus down to the one figure of Job. This has implications for the character of Job but also for God's integrity. If God is treating Job as righteous when he is not, then God is not acting fairly. Much is at stake.

The figure of "the satan" or "the accuser" makes his appearance in this scene, and there has been some debate about his identity. A number of scholars (e.g., Gibson, Newsom, Weiss, Clines, Seow) regard "the satan" as an expression of the dark side of God himself. However, none of these scholars demonstrates from the text of the prologue that "the satan" should be so understood. Yet "the satan" may be different from the devil, or representing one whose actions later became "satanic" in a deeper sense. The word שָׂטָן/*śāṭān* is the common Hebrew word for an "accuser," and can refer to either an earthly or a heavenly "accuser." When it is preceded by the definite article (as here), it refers to a role — *the* accuser or adversary — not a person's name. Most English versions translate *haśśāṭān* as "Satan," but this is reading later ideas of Satan or the devil back into this text. In the OT *śāṭān* is first used as a proper noun in the very late text 1 Chr 21:1.[9]

Is he God's accuser or Job's? Most regard him as the accuser of (sinful) human beings in general or Job in particular. Others suggest that he is a court official, and that the setting is like a Persian court, where there were informers, or perhaps even *agents provocateurs,* whose role was to identify those who were disloyal. More likely, we see here the role of one who was later to become Satan as we know him.

A common question is, What was such a figure doing in the heavenly court? The Hebrew permits, but does not demand, us to see the accuser as properly belonging to the "sons of God," which is perhaps a reference to the assembly of angelic beings (as in 1 Kgs 22:19-22; Dan 7:9-14).[10] Some (e.g., Driver and Gray) take the phrase "among them" (v. 6) to imply that he belonged in the heavenly court. Yet Andersen suggests that it is because he does not belong that he alone is asked his business.[11] The Hebrew is not decisive, and it is likely that he is singled out here for a narrative purpose. It is common in Hebrew narrative to name the one who is about to speak or take on a major role.

His insidious nature, however, may be discerned by listening to the tone

---

9. See further comments below on the identity of "the satan" in "Job and Theology: Job and Satan."

10. So Clines, *Job 1-20,* 18.

11. Andersen, *Job,* 82.

of his comments. His language is abrupt and peremptory, using imperatives to address God, and failing to use the deferential language associated with court etiquette (addressing a superior as "my Lord," not "you"; himself as "your servant," not "I"). Perhaps these are indications of insulting speech, hinting that he does not belong to the circle of God's respectful servants. Clines, however, suggests that it reflects the naivete of the prologue and its economical use of words (e.g., there is no description of the heavenly court).[12] This is more difficult to determine, for at times the description is wordy, not brief (e.g., the repetition of "the accuser said to Yahweh," or "Yahweh said to the accuser," rather than "he said" or "the accuser said"). The careful selection and use of words in the prologue suggest that the accuser's tone is a significant detail.

God's question in v. 7 does not imply that God lacks information (see his questions in Gen 3:6; Exod 4:2) but serves a narrative function. It establishes Yahweh as the initiator of the conversation and of the action that follows. The accuser's answer appears at least evasive, but it may just be formulaic court language.

The narrator's verdict on Job (v. 1) is repeated by Yahweh in almost identical terms (v. 8). Indeed, Yahweh seems almost to boast about Job's righteousness. Any understanding of Job, then, must start from the point where the book starts — that Job, before he is tested, is the model righteous man. Moshe Greenberg rightly indicates that one implication of this is that "our judgment on what Job and his Friends will say about his character must be determined by this information."[13] The additional comment in v. 8 that "there is none like him on the earth" is a way of emphasizing that, if it is possible for a human being to act righteously for motives other than self-interest, then Job is presented by God as the one likely to do so.

Verse 9 gives the key question that will hang over the whole book: "Does Job fear God for no reason?" (ESV). Is Job a genuine believer? It will seem so from his initial responses in 1:22 and 2:10, but the matter will only finally be solved when God gives his verdict at the end (42:7-8). Some (e.g., Clines, Gordis) have suggested that the ambiguous Hebrew form (either a perfect tense or a participle) ought to be translated as a perfect tense because of word order, and is only conceding that Job had feared God up to that time, leaving open the question of whether Job will continue to do so. This is possible, but a stative verb can refer to a present attitude as a result of a past decision or action, and so can have an ongoing sense anyway.

The phrase "for no reason" or "for nothing" (v. 9, translating חִנָּם/*ḥinnām*)

---

12. Clines, *Job 1–20*, 23, 30.
13. Greenberg, "Job," 286.

has a range of meanings.[14] It can mean "without cause, undeservedly" (e.g., Ps 35:19; 1 Sam 19:5); "without payment/reward/recompense" (e.g., Gen 29:15; 2 Sam 24:24); or possibly "without success, in vain" (Prov 1:17; Mal 1:10; Ezek 6:10; perhaps in Job 2:3). Here it means "without payment or reward," implying that Job trusts God only because God makes his herds prosper and his circumstances comfortable.

The language of putting a hedge or fence (v. 10) around Job is an agricultural metaphor, best understood as a hedge rather than a fence.[15] In this part of the ancient Near East, people had thorn hedges around vineyards or animal pens to keep out wild animals and robbers. The image is one of making something safe.

The motif of cursing God — so important to the prologue — starts to be developed in v. 11. Job has shown an earlier fear that his children might curse God (v. 5); here the accuser argues that Job will curse God (v. 11; 2:5); later Job's wife urges him to curse God (2:9). Whether a person curses God seems to be a clear indicator of whether one is righteous.

This is a questioning not just of Job's motives but also of God's rule. The accuser is saying to God that Job does not deserve all his blessings, and thus God is not ruling the world with justice. He also charges Job with having an ulterior motive of either becoming or remaining prosperous. His function is twofold — to raise this issue of whether "Job's piety is merely a pretense for his selfishness,"[16] and to put into effect the divine permission to test Job by removing the hedge around all that Job has, but not yet striking Job physically.

Why does God allow — indeed, initiate — this? Is it not immoral to have a heavenly wager (better, a challenge to a test) in which Job is put through so much suffering? That is more our question than one that arises in the book, and is problematic only on the view that this is an historical narrative rather than a literary use of an historical figure. Yet, for the purpose of the story, this test is needed. We must be in no doubt that Job is innocent and not suffering because he deserves it. How can God test whether Job is in it for the money and other blessings unless they are taken away?

Is it that God himself does not know what the outcome will be (so Clines)? Is it that God himself is satisfied but is prepared to allow "the satan" to satisfy himself (so Rowley); or, more positively, is it that God accepts the challenge in order to vindicate his servant (so Peake) or to refine Job's faith (Clines says this is most improbable of all, but it strikes me as the most likely)? However,

---

14. See Clines, "Does the Book of Job," 104; BDB 336b; *HALOT* 1:334; *DCH* 3:271-72.
15. A similar idea, though using a different Hebrew root, is found in Job 3:23.
16. Estes, *Handbook*, 30.

the picture is clearly one of God still in control. The accuser is powerless to act without God's permission. He cannot just do whatever he likes. The prologue does not give us any encouragement to draw the fine line between God permitting and God causing these disasters to happen. While God delegates the task to the accuser, Job's complaints in the dialogue will always be against God, never against the accuser.

The first heavenly scene centers on Yahweh's assertion of Job's righteousness and asks, "Is it for nothing?" Does Job only serve God as long as life is comfortable or trouble free? The focus is not on the identity or role of the accuser, but rather on the issues he raises — what is true righteousness, and is Job righteous after all?

1:13-19: The First Test — Loss of Possessions and Family From Job's point of view, he is simply called on to respond to a series of disasters, of different kinds, that pile up on top of one another. The hand of the accuser and the purposes of God remain concealed. The repetitious, formulaic expressions of vv. 13-19 have the cumulative effect of picturing a personal world shattered by disaster. The recurrence of the phrase, "While he was still speaking, there came another and said . . ." (vv. 16, 17, 18), highlights that there was no time between reports to adjust to each new loss. The very objects that symbolized Job's righteousness (his "possessions" listed in vv. 2-3) are taken away.

There is symmetry in the pattern of disasters. The losses alternate between those caused by human agents (Sabeans, Chaldeans) and those given natural or supernatural explanations (lightning, whirlwind). The disasters strike from all four points of the compass.[17] There appears to be an increase in intensity. There are a thousand oxen and donkeys; seven thousand sheep; three thousand camels (larger and more valuable than the other animals); and the children, most valuable of all, come last. The round numbers and hyperbolic nature of the descriptions (e.g., lightning to consume seven thousand sheep) are common features of stories passed down many generations. Noticeably absent is any mention of God or the accuser (the reference to "the fire of God" in v. 16 refers to lightning).

The first and last reports (vv. 14-15, 18-19) include descriptions of a peaceful scene before the destruction. There is also great narrative artistry in v. 18, when the pace of the story is slowed down and much seemingly unnecessary detail is given. Each announcement is followed by the formulaic phrase, "I alone have escaped to tell you." It is as if the life of the messenger is spared only so that Job can be told and his suffering made worse. The house of the eldest brother is presumably not a tent — they are settled agriculturalists, not nomads. There is

17. Hartley, *Book of Job*, 77.

no condemnation on the brothers and sisters for drinking wine, for that would cut across what the narrator is intending to do here. We are waiting for and fearing the worst. That new reality ("they are dead") is only given at the end and very tersely. The final messenger does not even call them "the children," but uses נְעָרִים/*nĕʿārîm*, the same word used in vv. 15-17 for servants or young people. Yet it clearly refers to Job's children.

The test has begun.

1:20-22: Job's First Reaction to His Loss and the Narrator's Verdict Job's first response to his loss is outlined in vv. 20-21 and presents Job as a model of piety. The tearing of garments is a common rite of mourning (Gen 37:29; Josh 7:6), as was shaving the head (Isa 15:2; 22:12; Jer 7:29; 16:6; 41:5; 47:5; 48:37; Ezek 7:18; Amos 8:10; Mic 1:16). These were accepted practices at times of great sorrow. However, since they are outward in nature, their exact significance can be a little ambiguous (e.g., is it just for show?). All is clarified by his subsequent falling to the ground and worshiping (v. 20). He understands that behind the human enemies and natural forces, God is at work and is ultimately responsible. God — not just the Sabeans, Chaldeans, or some forces of nature — has taken away (v. 21). This is, for the first-time reader, an apparent resolution of the problem — a godly person suffers greatly yet retains his faith.

The words Job uses in v. 21 reflect the affirmation of God ordering his world seen in the mainstream wisdom tradition as reflected in the book of Proverbs (Prov 16:9; 20:24; see also Eccl 5:15; Sir 40:1). Since Job, a non-Israelite, uses the name Yahweh, this is a reminder that the book is designed to be read by the people of God.

In v. 22 the narrator endorses the righteous nature of Job's initial response. This will be reinforced by having Yahweh repeat and magnify his assessment of Job (2:3). Of course, this is not to say that Job's first response *exhausts* the response of a righteous man. However, it is clear that his response, as far as it goes, is acceptable to God. The double denial of wrongdoing is a clear endorsement of Job's righteousness — "in all this Job did not sin or charge God with wrong" (v. 22 ESV). The uncommon word תִּפְלָה/*tiplâ*, "wrong" (also used in 24:12), is related to a word meaning "insipid, without taste," and so has a mild sense. If Job has not done even this, then clearly he has not cursed God.

2:1-6: The Second Heavenly Court Scene The second heavenly scene is modeled very closely on the first, and there is much repetition. Verses 1-2 repeat 1:6-7 with two exceptions (a different word for "where"; the addition of "to present himself before Yahweh"), which do not appear to be of any major significance.

It concerns the same issue of whether Job is righteous. Again God does not directly address this issue as he asks the accuser where he has come from, though this is probably to accentuate the parallels between the two heavenly scenes. The question ("From where have you come?") has a different narrative function here. In chapter 1 Yahweh's question was simply to initiate the conversation and perhaps to indicate that the accuser had thoroughly explored the earth. Now Yahweh invites an admission of failure from the accuser. The accuser again seems evasive and vague in his response ("going to and fro . . . walking up and down"), though this might simply be to reflect the first heavenly court scene. Yahweh's further response in v. 3 also has a fuller significance. The Job about whom he now boasts is one who succeeded in the face of testing. Yahweh repeats his claim about Job's righteousness. He is inviting the accuser to concede the apparent success of the "experiment."

Yahweh also adds further words, "He still holds fast his integrity, although you incited me against him to destroy him without reason" (v. 3b). The phrase "he persists in/holds fast to his integrity" may mean that the issue has been settled, or simply that they have not *yet* been been able to cause Job to abandon his integrity. Yahweh seems to mean the former, but the accuser is suggesting that it is the latter. The trial has not been severe enough, and needs to be extended to include his mental and physical health.[18]

The verb "you incited/provoked/moved me" probably is being used delocutively (so Clines), signifying an attempt to persuade, rather than a successful persuasion.[19] "Without reason" (v. 3) is the same Hebrew word used in 1:9, and could mean "without cause" or "without success," or perhaps imply both.

The accuser simply responds that the testing did not go far enough. A further test is needed to clarify the same issue as in the first heavenly scene. Some (e.g., G. Wilson) understand the phrase "Skin for skin" to mean that the exchange must be equal — therefore involving all he has, even his health, to make it a fair test. Others (e.g., Gordis) see it as the skin of others (animals and family) to save his own skin. Still others (e.g., Rowley) refer to the idea in Arabic literature of an outer and an inner skin — so this means one skin beyond another, that is, dig deeper. Edwin Good, followed by Carol Newsom, translates it as "skin up to skin," that a person would be willing to trade anything up to the value of a skin for a skin. Here it would mean all that a man gives *up to* his life. However, Clines rightly argues that the meaning is clear from the rest of vv. 4-5. It does not refer to any past events (loss of children, animals, etc.) but to the future.[20] If

---

18. Alden, *Job,* 42, speaks of a test of wealth in ch. 1 and a test of health in ch. 2.

19. Clines, *Job 1-20,* 5.

20. See the useful discussion in ibid., 43-45.

Yahweh were to touch Job's skin (= life), then Job would attack him (i.e., his life, by cursing him).

As in 1:11-12, the accuser is the appointed agent of Yahweh to carry out the test. He can touch (i.e., harm or strike) Job's bone and flesh, but his life must be preserved. "Flesh and bone," in distinction to "life," must therefore refer to his physical aspect or body. It is possible that "his bone and his flesh," in view of Gen 2:21-23, might suggest his wife, but that does not fit the subsequent unfolding of the story. In any event, from this point onward God will not speak again until chapter 38.

2:7-10: The Second Test — Ghastly Sores In the second wave of the satan's attack, Job himself is afflicted by ghastly sores. Just as he lost all his possessions, so now he is afflicted from the sole of his foot to the crown of his head — a comprehensive rather than partial affliction. There must not be any suggestion that the disease was not extensive enough. Attempts to identify the disease are not in principle wrong, but in practice are not very fruitful or conclusive in the light of the general language used here and the poetic descriptions that we find during the dialogue. Although the active role of the accuser is more explicit than in chapter 1, it is equally clear in the context of 2:1-6 that the hand of God is at work.

His physical setting ("in the ashes," v. 8) would be a burning dump outside the town, where "he sat, amid rubbish, rotting carcasses, playing urchins, homeless beggars, village idiots, and howling dogs."[21] This would be a place of isolation, physical hardship, and social rejection. The scraping with broken pottery would be a vain attempt to relieve his symptoms — much like scratching an itch — but would only worsen the problem.

That the description of his affliction is immediately followed by his wife's foolish advice (v. 9) implies that Job has now also lost her emotional support. When the accuser strikes "his bone and his flesh," the one who is "bone of his bones and flesh of his flesh" (Gen 2:23) does not aid Job by her words. The very one who should support him in such a time of crisis rebukes him for insisting on his integrity and tempts him to "curse God and die." Her reference to his "integrity" reminds us that God used this same description of Job in 2:3. She appears to believe that Job's suffering will continue until he acknowledges his sin, so that insisting on his integrity equals refusing to repent. If so, she is expressing a traditional understanding of the doctrine of retribution.

What does she mean by "Curse God and die"? It could mean, "Curse the God who has so afflicted you, before you die" (i.e., to suggest to Job a final act of defiance). Alternatively, it could be understood as, "Curse God, who will

21. Terrien, "Job," 920.

then strike you dead" (putting into train a process that will put him out of his misery by doing the one forbidden thing that will ensure his immediate destruction and end his endless agony; Terrien calls this a "theological method of committing suicide"). She seems to be rightly motivated by a care for Job, to end his misery (and perhaps hers) by ending his life. However, in its narrative context she serves to tempt Job to do what the accuser has said Job would do (2:5). If Job does curse God, Job would have failed, and Yahweh would have been shown to be wrong.

Interpreters through history have often portrayed her very negatively. Augustine called her the "devil's assistant"; Calvin called her "Satan's tool"; Aquinas suggested that the accuser only spared her from the disasters of chapter 1 in order to use her in chapter 2. More recently, feminist critics (e.g., Clines, van Wolde, Brenner, Penchansky) have sought to read her as a wronged victim. Through no fault of her own, simply due to the social structures of the time, her well-being is dependent on Job. Now *she,* Job's unnamed wife, has lost everything — family, possessions, status — although her pain is neither acknowledged nor described. Job is to blame since this has all happened because of his piety. Yet Job has uttered no regret, but insists on "maintaining his integrity." The only honorable thing to do would be for Job to call down on himself the wrath of God. Thus Job continues to wrong her by his submissiveness to God. By accepting it he brands her and her children as wrongdoers (on the theory of retribution). The LXX here inserts a long speech in the mouth of Job's wife, designed to portray her more sympathetically.[22]

The Hebrew text takes us down neither of these paths. A worthwhile story could have been written about Mrs. Job, but that is not this story.[23] This book is about a particular godly person in the land of Uz, and his struggle to persevere in faith. Job's wife has literary roles in *his* story.

First, her narrative function is to elicit a verbal response from Job. In the first test, Job responded not only with actions but also with a speech, which revealed his state of mind (1:20-21). After this second test, Job's response was only with actions (v. 8), until his wife prods him to speak in reaction to her words.[24]

Second, her words articulate a possible response (most likely, some form of suicide) that Job could make to his circumstances. She raises the issue of whether it is better "to be or not to be." This option Job decisively rejects in v. 10a. Here Job sees God as the sovereign bringer of both prosperity ("good"

---

22. See Gordis, *Book of God and Man,* 223.

23. In the Aramaic Targum Job's wife is called Dinah, an allusion to Gen 34. In the pseudepigraphal *Testament of Job,* she is called Sitis, a corruption of the LXX translation of Uz (see Alden, *Job,* 66). Van Wolde, *Mr and Mrs Job,* passim, simply calls her Mrs Job.

24. See J. Janzen, *Job,* 48-49.

bears this sense here) and adversity. "Evil" does not refer to moral evil but is used in the nonmoral sense of "disaster" or "pain" (see also the "painful" or "loathsome" sores in 2:7, and the "troubles" in 2:11).

Some regard the narrator's verdict on Job's subsequent response as more ambiguous than his earlier summary (1:22), endorsed by Yahweh (2:3). Here there is no verdict from Yahweh, and the narrator simply concludes, "In all this Job did not sin *with his lips*" (v. 10b). Some suggest that the change from chapter 1 implies that Job did not sin in his speech but did in his heart (e.g., the Talmud).[25] Yet Proverbs does not commend the practice of thinking one thing but saying another (e.g., Prov 12:19, 22; 14:5; 20:14; 26:24-25, 28).[26] The narrator's verdict is best read as a wholehearted endorsement of Job's approach. Yair Hoffman proposes that the phrase "with his lips" (v. 10) may still be important.[27] It focuses our attention on the words of Job, which will be heard at some length in the dialogue. We are meant to study the future *words* of Job rather than his actions, for his words will disclose whether Job perseveres in his faith. This book centers on how to speak rightly to and about God.

2:11-13: The Arrival and Mission of the Friends Three new characters are introduced in v. 11, serving as a bridge between the prologue and the dialogue. The places of origin of these friends are not entirely clear, but they are, like Uz, obviously outside Israel. They first heard the news of Job, next met together, and then came to be with Job, a few weeks or months later.

The introduction of Job's friends is especially significant for its mention of their purpose in coming. His friends are not there to rebuke him for his "sin," but "to show him sympathy and comfort him" (v. 11b). They come for the laudable purpose of supporting him in his (presumably temporary) setback. Their inability to recognize him (v. 12a) is a reminder of the extent of his changed circumstances. They mourn and identify with him by tearing their clothes (like Job in 1:20), sprinkling dust on themselves, and sitting with Job, thus identifying with his plight. It has been suggested that their action of sprinkling dust on their heads is a magical act of self-defense, to *prevent* their being afflicted like Job, but this is not a natural way to read the story.[28] At this stage, there seems to be no rebuke implied for the friends.

25. Weiss, *Story of Job's Beginning*, 72.
26. See also Hartley, *Book of Job*, 84; Andersen, *Job*, 94.
27. Hoffmann, "Relation between the Prologue," 166.
28. See Weiss, *Story of Job's Beginning*, 75-76; cf. a helpful survey in Clines, *Job 1-20*, 62-63. As a sign of mourning ashes/dust were put on the head, as in 2 Sam 13:19; see also Isa 61:3; Josh 7:6; 1 Sam 4:12; 2 Sam 15:32; Ezek 27:30; Lam 2:10; though the verb "sprinkle" is not used in this connection.

Verse 13 paints a picture of much lamenting, as was common in an ancient Near Eastern setting. Seven days is the period that Joseph mourned for his father Jacob (Gen 50:10), and also the time that the people of Jabesh-gilead mourned for Saul (1 Sam 31:13). Clines sees this period of silence as less positive, carrying a customary external convention to absurd lengths, implying that the sufferer was to be identified with the dead.[29] He assumes that they would have had mixed feelings about Job — that of their head and their heart. However, there seems to be no evidence of this in the text, and their silence could easily be explained by viewing Job's circumstances as a temporary setback to a righteous person. Indeed, their not speaking a word to Job (v. 13) does not mean they were silent for all this time — simply that they did not speak a word *to him*. This again serves to focus the reader's interest on the issue of words or speech. One's speech is a good indicator of one's righteousness.

Two matters have become clear in these opening two chapters. First, the issue at stake in the prologue is the nature of Job's response. Is his faith disinterested, or does he only serve God for what he gets out of it? Second, the picture that emerges from the prologue is a portrayal of Job as a man of unblemished righteousness. This must govern the way we read the dialogue. Yet attention has been drawn to his future spoken words. We are enticed to read on in order to find out how the trial of Job's faith will turn out.

3:1–31:40: The Dialogue

3:1-26: Job's Self-Curse and Self-Lament

This chapter includes a self-imprecation or self-curse in vv. 1-10, and a self-lament in vv. 11-26. Others make the division between the curse and lament after v. 13.[30] It would appear, however, that there is a change of focus after v. 10, so that vv. 11-13, like vv. 14-26, center on Job's situation rather than the cosmos, and are largely in question form, not curse.

3:1-10: Job's Self-Curse Chapters 1 and 2 have set the background of the book. We would expect Job's opening words in the dialogue to be crucial in setting out the issues and the problems of the book. It is surely significant that chapter 3 leads quickly into a lament.

Job's first action is to open his mouth, thus continuing the focus on

29. Clines, *Job 1–20*, 63-64.
30. Fishbane, "Jeremiah IV 23-26," 165; Hartley, *Book of Job*, 88-89, 101-2.

speech. The mention of "his lips" in 2:10 drew our attention to Job's future speaking, and now Job opens his mouth to speak. The mention of Job cursing (קָלַל/*qālal*) in v. 1 casts our minds back to the use of בָּרַךְ/*bārak*, "bless," as a euphemism for "curse" in the prologue. Will Job now curse God as asserted by the accuser (1:11; 2:5) and as encouraged by his wife (2:9)? Indeed the different verb used arouses our interest. Is what Job is about to do the same as cursing God? At the very least, the transition from submissiveness to uttering a curse signals a major change in Job.

Yet when he does curse there is again ambiguity. He does not curse God, but instead curses the day of his birth. As Norman Habel notes, "his curse falls on a past event which would appear to be irreversible."[31] The very fact that Job is asking for something impossible would suggest that here is a bold and dramatic way of addressing the apparent lack of proper order in Job's experience of the world. This may explain why the curse is not addressed to God, or why God is not invoked. It is primarily a cry from the heart, a call of extreme frustration, rather than intended to be an efficacious curse. It is an upsurge of emotion that needs to be vented rather than implemented. Andersen rightly insists that showing one's emotions is not the issue, because "the Lord's testing is not to find out if Job can sit unmoved like a piece of wood."[32]

Some argue that this curse against part of creation also implies a curse against his Creator, perhaps even seeking an undoing of creation itself and all human existence.[33] The focus of vv. 3 and 10 is, however, only on Job rather than on the wider creation. It is not the day or night that are damned, but the birth events that happened during them. Common to all cursing is the use of hyperbole, so Job's real complaint is about the current disorder in his life.

The curse itself expresses no explicit animosity to God, and in v. 4 Job calls on God to be his ally in the curse. Indeed, he does not curse anyone else, not even his father or mother. In v. 7 he simply asks that that *night* be barren. This is the first of a number of impossible scenarios that Job will explore in the course of the book (9:33-35; 14:13-17; 16:18-22; 19:23-27).[34] On the face of it, then, this curse is asking for the impossible, a way of saying, "I can't cope! I want a way out!" Daniel Simundson colorfully suggests that "Job's cry is a bitter irony, a perverse upside-down version of 'Happy Birthday to Me.'"[35] However, for Job, cursing God is still not an option.

31. Habel, *Book of Job*, 107.

32. Andersen, *Job*, 100-101.

33. For example, Cox, *Desire*, 38, 48; Robertson, "Book of Job," 449-51; Fishbane, "Jeremiah IV 23-26"; Hartley, *Book of Job*, 102.

34. See J. G. Janzen, *Job*, 70-71.

35. Simundson, *Message of Job*, 47.

Verses 3-10 are a carefully structured curse. D. N. Freedman notes that v. 3 and v. 10 form a neatly balanced opening and closing pair of lines.[36] The "day" and "night" are introduced in v. 3, and each is in turn picked up: "that day" in vv. 4-5 and "that night" in vv. 6-9. The "day/night" as a single entity seems then to be the subject of the verbs in v. 10. Verses 4-9 are best seen as an explanatory parenthesis, so that the כִּי/*kî,* "because," clause in v. 10 gives the reason for the curse in v. 3 — it did not prevent Job from being born, nor hide trouble from his eyes. The word "trouble" (עָמָל/*'āmāl*) also has the sense of "toil," and it is interesting that "rest," the opposite of toil, is a key theme of vv. 11-26 (vv. 13, 17, 18, and especially v. 26).

Job is reflecting what he himself was experiencing. In his darkness, he asks for the day to be one of darkness (vv. 4a, 5) and deep gloom (a deathly or deep shadow, lit. "the shadow of death," v. 5). For the night, he asks for "thick darkness" (v. 6), using yet another word for darkness, so that the images overwhelm. He calls for a lack of light (vv. 4, 9) and an absence of joy (v. 7). The mirroring of his own circumstances in what he now asks for again suggests that Job is responding at an emotional level as a way of expressing his own pain.

Much has been made of the mythological background of the curse, especially in the reference to Leviathan (v. 8). However, a decision about whether the curse has a mythological background is not the key to understanding its function. Verses 4-9 are simply expansions or an unpacking of the curse of v. 3. Leviathan is mentioned as an aside in v. 8b, and probably refers to the mythological sea monster that was a symbol of chaos in the ancient world, and even in the OT.[37] Verse 8 also refers to "those who curse the day," but it is probably best not to make an identification of them. It likely refers to a hypothetical rather than an actual group of people.

The place of the curse in the flow of the book is significant. It provokes a response from the friends in the following chapters, just as Job's oath of clearance/innocence (31:35-37) will later require an answer. Job's questionings and complaints do not simply arise in response to the barbed comments of his friends, for this curse and the following lament both precede and engender the response from the friends. Job complains even before he is lectured by his friends.

The following observations can be made:

- Nothing in this self-curse is inconsistent with true faith. It is not the cursing of God that the satan promised and his wife suggested.

36. Freedman, "Structure," 503.
37. Pss 74:13-14; 104:25-26; Isa 27:1; see also Habel, *Book of Job,* 108-9.

- Because it is incapable of literal fulfillment, it is best understood as a great cry of pain rather than an incantation designed to destroy the creation.
- It is thus a cry of protest that springs out of an existential dilemma — it is part of Job's struggle to preserve his faith in the midst of his experience of disorientation.

3:11-26: Job's Self-Lament The rest of the chapter is a single lament, though with two parts. A number of scholars suggest that there are two separate sections here (vv. 11-19 and 20-26, with minor breaks before vv. 16 and 23), each of which commences with לָמָה/*lāmmâ*, "why."[38] In vv. 11-19 Job focuses on his own death, while in vv. 20-26 he considers the suffering of humanity in general. However, Job often appears to explore the general case of humanity but actually has his own situation in mind (see, e.g., 7:1, 3; 14:1-12, 13-17).

Habel has rightly observed the unity of the lament by noting its parallels to the curse of vv. 3-10. There is a similar framing device in which the opening statement announces the subject of the outcry (vv. 3, 11), while the reason for the outcry is given at the end of the unit in a כִּי/*kî*, "because, for" clause (vv. 10, 24-26).[39] In addition, there are parallels in subject matter in vv. 3 and 11, while both units end with the related ideas of trouble (v. 10) and turmoil (v. 26). The unity of this section can also be seen in the recurring motifs of light (vv. 16, 20), turmoil (vv. 17, 26), and rest (vv. 13, 17, 26), while the idea of death pervades the lament (vv. 11, 13, 16, 21, 22).

Verses 11-26 are a self-lament *(Ichklage),* which, unlike the lament psalms, is not uttered to God but about him (e.g., v. 23). Habel suggests that it may be an alternative way of expressing the curses of vv. 3-10, hence the parallel shape.[40] That is, although it may not be formally a curse, it functions in the same way. However, a better way of viewing this self-lament is that it reflects the same undergirding theology as vv. 3-10. Thus the conclusions reached about Job's curse should affect our reading of this section as well.

Job does not refer to enemies in the lament, nor does he rebuke the friends (who have yet to speak).[41] This might provide clues about what Job's motives were. If his first lament includes neither a complaint addressed to God nor a condemnation of any enemies, then Job appears to be using the lament form to come to terms with his own circumstances. He is trying to hold together his

---

38. For example, van der Lugt, "Stanza-Structure," 5; Clines, *Job 1–20*, 75-76; Freedman, "Structure," 504-6. Verse 12 begins with a different word, sometimes translated as "why" in English versions.

39. Habel, *Book of Job,* 102-3.

40. Ibid., 110.

41. Westermann, *Structure,* 9.

understanding of the God he has known with the treatment he is now experiencing. Job is pouring out his frustration and confusion. Timothy Gorringe describes this chapter as "a spine-chilling howl of despair."[42]

Verses 11-15 are governed by the question, "Why did I not die at birth?" (v. 11a). The twin images of death in v. 11 (dying and expiring/perishing) are contrasted with two symbols of life in v. 12 (knees to receive me, and breasts to nurse). The verb "receive" (קָדַם/*qādam*) literally means "meet." This meeting can be with hostility, but it can also mean meeting as a friend or receiving, which is the sense suggested here by the parallelism. Being on the knees could mean being cared for by a male relative (as in Gen 48:10-12), but the parallelism of nursing suggests that it is being accepted on the mother's knees (as in Isa 66:12) in order to nurse. Verses 11-12 give a life-and-death contrast, with Job asking why he was allowed to live rather than die.

The intensity of the longing for rest is indicated in v. 13 by the use of four different terms: to lie down, to be quiet, to sleep, and to be at rest. This is what Job desperately wanted, but his reality was exactly the opposite (v. 26). Job's aim is not for extinction or an active ending of his life; he primarily longs for relief from his distress. This is perfectly natural, even for a person of strong faith. The kind of rest he longs for is filled out in vv. 14-15 — that of the leaders of the community and those who prospered. The images speak of a death that implies that a person has been favored by God.

Verse 16 raises a related question: Why was I not a buried stillborn, dying even before birth? The motivation is again made clear by the explanation given in the following verses (vv. 17-19). It is not that Job prefers death to the gift of life, but simply that he longs for an end to his misery. The examples given in vv. 17-19 are no longer confined to those for whom life was easy, but include the wicked, the weary, prisoners, and slaves (vv. 17-18), who experienced great hardships in life. In death there would be a ceasing of rage or turmoil (v. 17a, the same word used in v. 26), rest (v. 17b, used in 12:5 of things being comfortable), being at ease (v. 18a), and freedom from forced toil (vv. 18b, 19b). What is driving Job's longing is a desire to be liberated from his current distress. Thus death is not seen as more welcoming than God; rather, it is a graphic, stereotypical way of announcing the depth of his distress.

Job then appears to be talking about humanity in general in vv. 20-22, but vv. 23-26 are syntactically dependent on the "why is light given" in v. 20 (the ESV inserts these words in v. 23 to make this clear). While v. 23 also appears to be talking in general terms, it becomes clear in vv. 24-26 that Job has his own situation in view all the time. This gives us a further window into Job's self-

---

42. Gorringe, "Job and the Pharisees," 19.

understanding. He is "in misery" and "bitter in soul" (v. 20); he vainly longs for death (v. 21a); he digs or searches for death like hidden treasures (v. 21b; the root is used in 11:18 in the sense of "look around thoroughly"); and he would rejoice exceedingly if his misery could come to an end (v. 22).

Verse 23 gives perhaps the clearest image of Job's experience. His way is hidden, and God has hedged him in. The accuser used a similar verb in the opposite sense in 1:10 — God preventing evil from reaching Job. Now Job's situation seems as if God is preventing any good in life from reaching him. Yet Job has just as big a view of God here as in the prologue, and his theology has not changed. In both, he believes that God is in total control, and that what comes to him only happens because God permits it. Indeed, here God has actively hedged him in. Even in the midst of hardship, Job does not seek to reduce God to a more manageable size. He refuses the way out of limiting God's power or adopting a dualistic understanding of the world.

He describes his present situation in v. 24 as "sighing" and "groaning" at the level of life's necessities (bread and water). This is filled out in the final verse of the chapter. Andersen sees v. 26 as having "four sharp clauses, each of which stabs like a knife," and he vividly translates it as: "I cannot relax! And I cannot settle! And I cannot rest! And agitation keeps coming back!"[43] In between these two descriptive clusters, Job describes his situation as what he utterly dreaded (the Hebrew expression is intensive) and feared (v. 25). This is not a denial that he feared the Lord, nor is it refuting the idea that he is a person of faith. He is simply saying that his worst-case scenario has now arrived, which is exactly what the accuser planned.

4:1–14:22: Round One

4:1–5:27: Eliphaz

In chapters 4 and 5 Eliphaz begins the friends' response to Job. The major divide in chapter 4 is between vv. 1-11 and 12-21, with Eliphaz's vision in the night beginning in v. 12. Verses 1-11 divide into two sections, vv. 1-6 (an introduction) and vv. 7-11 (a summary outline of retribution).

4:1-6: Introduction Verses 1-6 fit together well. After the narrator's introduction (v. 1), Eliphaz states his intention to address a matter with Job (v. 2). In vv.

---

43. Andersen, *Job*, 110. Hartley, *Book of Job*, 100, also argues that the use of the perfect forms in v. 26 suggests that the quality of the action indicated by the verbs is completely absent from Job's present experience.

3-4 he outlines Job's past wisdom and his practice of using it to care for others in difficult times. This is the background to the observation he makes in v. 5, and the question or proposal for a way forward in v. 6.[44]

In the prose introduction of Eliphaz he is described as a Temanite (2:11). Teman is linked to Edom and wisdom in several OT prophetic texts (Ezek 25:13; Jer 49:7; Obad 8-9; Amos 1:11-12). Clearly he is not an Israelite, and he may be giving an answer that reflects ancient Near Eastern wisdom more broadly. Hence, when he first uses a title for God (4:9, 17), he uses the generic title "Eloah." Eliphaz "answered" or perhaps "responded" to Job (v. 1), which in the light of v. 5 suggests that Eliphaz is responding to Job's outburst in chapter 3, rather than the circumstances of his suffering.

He starts off in a respectful, almost deferential way in v. 2a (ESV: "If one ventures a word with you, will you be impatient?"; NRSV "offended"). The root תלא/*tl'* means "be weary in vain endeavor" or "be impatient," and the same word is usually translated as "impatient" in v. 5.

Similarly, in vv. 3-4 he praises and honors Job's former ministry of instruction ("you have instructed many").[45] He also mentions his support for the struggling: "you have strengthened the weak hands" (v. 3b, lit. "sinking hands," and used of people losing heart or energy); "your words have upheld those who were stumbling," and "you have made firm the feeble knees" (v. 4). The images are of those burdened by their circumstances. The use of the same term for "words" (v. 4) as in v. 2 shows that Eliphaz sees himself as mirroring to Job exactly what Job had done to others.

However, in both cases such respect for Job leads him to say "Yet/but" or "But now" (vv. 2b, 5), so that the initial (genuinely) positive comment is a prelude to what Eliphaz really wants to say. In v. 2b he is explaining or justifying why he must now speak.[46] In v. 5 there is a mild rebuke addressed to Job, implying that he should apply to himself the advice he has given to others. The assumed subject in v. 5 is trouble or suffering (the verbs are third person feminine singular), while the verb "touches" (the same word used by the accuser in 1:11 and 2:5) clarifies what Eliphaz is referring to.

Instead of Job responding with impatience and dismay (v. 5), Eliphaz suggests that he should be demonstrating confidence and hope (v. 6). Already Eliphaz's way of thinking can be seen as he explains to Job what should be the

---

44. See also Course, *Speech and Response,* 21.

45. The verb translated "instructed" perhaps means "discipled" here. It is related to the noun מוּסָר/*mûsār,* a prominent wisdom word for discipline in a positive, shaping sense. In 5:17 *mûsār* describes the positive "instruction, shaping, or discipline" done by God.

46. Literally it reads "who is able to restrain (themselves) with respect to words/speech."

grounds of his stance. In v. 6 these are outlined as his "fear"[47] and "the integrity of your ways." For the reader, this is a clear echo of Job in 1:1 as one who "feared" God (the verbal form of the noun) and was "blameless," the word translated here as "integrity" (ESV, NRSV, NJPS). Eliphaz assumes that Job is basically godly and so suggests that this will be the way to gain consolation. He is urging Job to rely on his wise character, for that will soon be rewarded by restoration. While the word כִּסְלָה/*kislâ* (v. 6a) is related to a word for stupidity or folly and seems to have that sense in its only other occurrence (Ps 85:8 [MT 9]), the parallelism with "hope" in v. 6b suggests something positive like "confidence." Interestingly, Eliphaz is the only one of the three friends to talk to Job in the language of the "fear of God," and he will do so in his remaining two speeches (Job 15:4; 22:4). This is the traditional language of wisdom teachers, seen prominently in Proverbs (e.g., Prov 1:7; 9:10). Thus Eliphaz begins with a conventional expression of the wisdom theology of retribution. Furthermore, in Job 4:8-11 and 5:2-7 he will outline further aphoristic wisdom reminiscent of Proverbs.

4:7-11: A Summary Outline of Retribution These verses follow on quite logically from Eliphaz's introduction and amplify his retributive understanding of how God organizes this world. It begins in v. 7 with an appeal to "remember" (= "think now," NRSV) the theological concept of retribution. Job will later call on God to remember, but largely for God to remember him as a person (14:13; 7:7; we should probably understand 10:9 in this way too, for it is God's remembering of Job that is at issue), not simply to call to mind an idea or concept. Verse 7 asks two rhetorical questions (with the implied answers "no" and "nowhere") reinforcing that aspect of retribution that Job is questioning — do the innocent or upright (the description of Job in 1:1) perish or become cut off? Eliphaz's fundamental position is that the innocent are never "cut off" (v. 7), which is a simplistic application of the principle of retribution. For him, the good man *must* always be delivered and rewarded by God.

Verse 8 is a simple affirmation of the seemingly relevant aspect of retribution (the wicked will reap what they sow), and this is based on Eliphaz's experience ("as I have seen").[48] While v. 7 asserts that the righteous will not be cut off or perish, vv. 8-11 describe with more force the destruction that will happen to the wicked. Thus the emphasis of his doctrine of retribution (while it

---

47. The words "of God" are not present but implied and so added by ESV and NRSV. It is roughly equivalent to "piety" (so NIV) or "godliness."

48. However, Hoffman, "Equivocal Words," 116, notes that "wickedness" (אָוֶן/*'āwen*) and "trouble" or "mischief" (עָמָל/*'āmāl*) are equivocal terms. The noun *'āwen* can mean iniquity, but may simply mean "sorrow"; *'āmāl* can mean "transgression or evil," but can simply mean "toil" or "trouble/misery." The saying works at both levels.

includes both the righteous and the wicked) is weighted much more on the side of the punishment of the wicked rather than the vindication of the righteous.

The wicked are described in v. 8 as those who plow iniquity and sow trouble, an agricultural metaphor continued in the rest of the verse, where they reap the trouble they have sown. What happens to them (v. 9) is a natural consequence of their character. The involvement of God in this retribution is made clearer in v. 9, which states that God will actively punish the wicked, rather than simply that the wicked will be punished. Thus, while this can be viewed as a natural process, it is also seen to be God's work through this process.

The meaning of the analogy with lions (vv. 10-11) is not immediately obvious. A major clue is that "the lion is a standard metaphor for the wicked in the biblical traditions."[49] All three nouns for lion in v. 10, as different ways of describing the wicked, are subjects of the verb that is left to the end of the sentence. This abnormal placement of the verb gives plenty of chance to nuance the description of the wicked.[50] The force of it is something like: "The wicked — whether they think of themselves as lions roaring, or fierce lions rejoicing over a kill, or younger lions ripping into their prey — they will all come to nothing."

This is further clarified by the lion imagery of v. 11. If there is no prey, then the lion that depends on prey will starve, and the young lion cubs will not able to be fed and will therefore scatter or disperse in search of food. This last verb is a picture of helplessness. Eliphaz has seemingly begun to shift his position and now implies, but does not openly state, that Job is wicked, since his circumstances fit the expected outcome of the wicked.

4:12-21: Eliphaz's Vision and Its Implications In vv. 12-16 Eliphaz receives a vision or spiritual experience, the content of which is told from v. 17 onward. His spiritual experience is vivid, though the mention that the word was brought to him stealthily suggests that it has a shroud of mystery around it. Indeed, he has heard only a whisper or perhaps a small piece of it.[51] He receives disquieting or excited thoughts (see 20:2) in the context of a dream at night (v. 13). Verse 14 indicates that this was not an "easy" or uplifting spiritual experience, since it involved trembling and shaking. Verse 15 may be describing a further physical action ("the hair of my flesh stood up," ESV), though this may be a metaphor. It is not clear whether it has come from a wind[52] or spirit moving past, as the word

---

49. Pyeon, *You Have Not Spoken*, 103, citing Pss 17:12; 22:13, 21; Prov 28:15.

50. The verb "broken" (נִתָּעוּ/*nittāʿû*, v. 10) occurs only here, and may be an Aramaic form or possibly a textual error for a similar root (נתע/*ntʿ* in place of נתץ/*nts*, "pull down, break down").

51. So Newsom, "Book of Job," 377-78; Clines, *Job 1–20*, 111. The word is only found here and in 26:14, with a related word in Exod 32:25.

52. So Clines, *Job 1–20*, 111.

רוּחַ/*rûaḥ* could mean either. Verse 16 puts more emphasis on shape or form, implying that it was more than wind. Finally, there is a voice, though it is not explicitly said that the spirit speaks, simply that with the appearance of the spirit a voice is heard (not a "hushed voice" as in the NIV, but one that gives clarity).

It is not clear whether Eliphaz's emphasis is on the spiritual experience or on the message itself in v. 17. It may well be both, but the primacy is likely to be on the content of the message. In v. 12a it is introduced as "a word"; in v. 12b the focus is on what was heard ("my ear received"), not what was seen. That the message aspect of the experience is developed in 5:6-7 also implies that the idea that humans are not righteous is more important to Eliphaz than the fact of the mystical experience.

Thus v. 17 is crucial. It could be translated as "more righteous than God" or "more pure than his maker" (cf. NIV), but this makes no sense theologically. The traditional rendering ("righteous before God") is preferable.[53] Eliphaz is suggesting that, given the absolute purity and righteousness of God, no human being (including Job) could ever measure up. Since perfect innocence is not possible, even a comparatively righteous person — as Job claimed to be — can expect to suffer for a little while on occasion, but can never be destroyed.

The content of this vision is, at best, a word of illumination or a spiritual word. What finally prevents it from being a revelation from God is that it is not consistent with the message of the book as a whole. A general truth is the subject of the vision, but it does not provide the answer in this book. The content of Eliphaz's dream has nothing to do with the reason the prologue gives for Job's suffering.

However, where do the words of this vision finish? The ESV, NIV, and NRSV all opt for the end of v. 21, implying that all of vv. 17-21 was the content of what was spoken, not simply v. 17. It is better to view only v. 17 as the content of the vision,[54] with Eliphaz drawing out the implications of this in vv. 18-21. This would make vv. 18-21 a series of reflections on the human condition, directed implicitly toward Job and his situation. Verse 18 explains that the servants and angels God is most likely to regard as righteous or pure — presumably due to their proximity to him — are fallible, not trustworthy. If even these heavenly beings ("his servants" are probably those in the heavenly court) are not trusted and are charged with error, then v. 19 says, how much more humans? A fairly pessimistic view of humanity is then developed, especially in vv. 19-21, and later resurfacing in 5:6-7. The phrase "those who dwell in houses of clay" refers to

---

53. So Habel, *Book of Job*, 129. Walton, *Job*, 158-59, argues for "righteous in God's perspective," an idea similar to "righteous before God," but closer to "in the light of God's character."

54. So Clines, *Job 1–20*, 133-34.

their bodies, not their dwelling places. It is clarified by "whose foundation is in the dust," recalling the creation account in Genesis 2. "Crushed like the moth" is a symbol of the precarious nature of human life, filled out in vv. 20 and 21a with a variety of verbs: beaten to pieces, perish forever, plucked up. These vivid descriptions are all crystallized in the simple question in v. 21, "do they not die?" (ESV). The clinching phrase is that they will die "without wisdom" (v. 21b). This gives a clear hint that for Eliphaz the issue is, What is wisdom? However, the issue for Job in chapter 3 was rather, Can I still have faith?

5:1-7: The Experience of the Fool There are three sections in chapter 5 — vv. 1-7, 8-16, and 17-26, with v. 27 simply finishing the speech. Having outlined his vision and its implications, Eliphaz turns to Job's request to be answered (v. 1), raising the possibility of a response even from a heavenly being ("the holy ones"). Eliphaz is speaking directly to Job at this point. Yet there is also a focus on the fool by the double mention in vv. 2-3, perhaps implying that Eliphaz regards Job a fool. So, while Eliphaz is speaking in traditional and generic terms in vv. 2-5, the focus on Job in v. 1 suggests that Job needs to learn something from these words. Vexation, and having one's dwelling cursed, fit Job's situation, but the significance of jealousy (v. 2b) is less clear. Perhaps it is simply part of the proverbial couplet, or it may be that Eliphaz is implying that Job may be jealous of those who are not suffering. This may, however, simply be a general homily on the fate of the wicked, perhaps spoken as a warning to Job not to go down that path. It is at least a statement of the negative side of classical retribution theology.

The outcomes in vv. 4-5 are precisely the kind of outcomes one would expect for someone who would be the opposite of the wise person (a "fool"). The consequences are all echoes of the losses that Job suffered in 1:13-19, a fact surely not lost on Job. The mention of children being crushed (v. 4) seems particularly insensitive in the light of 1:19. While there are some textual and translational difficulties in v. 5, it seems to envisage people other than the fool enjoying the fool's possessions.

Verses 6-7 round off this section by generalizing from the experience of the fool. The implication is that the human lot is one of trouble.[55] That is just the way things are, and there is no need for troubles to be coming out of nowhere (dust, ground, v. 6). There are a number of allusions to the Genesis creation

---

55. In v. 6 Habel, *Book of Job*, 114, 117, followed by Perdue, *Wisdom in Revolt*, 120, repoints לֹא/*lō'*, "not," as לֻא/*lû'*, "surely," both times, giving the sense, "for surely evil/disaster comes forth from the dust." While the double mention of "not" in v. 6 makes this less likely, the force of vv. 6-7 would not be substantially changed. It would then mean: "trouble comes out of nowhere, but is the lot for humanity."

account (dust, sprout from the ground, humanity), highlighting the importance of a theology of creation for the wisdom books.

5:8-16: Commit Your Cause to God, Who Is Active Verse 8 begins with a strong adversative ("But I"/"As for me"), indicating a new section and change of topic. The solution that Eliphaz commends is for Job to "put his matter," or "commit his cause" (NRSV, ESV), to God. His mention of Job appealing to God as the way forward (v. 8) ironically introduces the litigation motif that Job will later pursue in a different direction. As a further note of irony, Job is the only one who does talk *to* God in the book, for the friends and also Elihu restrict themselves to pontificating *about* God.

All of vv. 9-13 are grammatically or syntactically dependent on the mention of God in v. 8. Verse 9 starts with a participle meaning "the one doing/who does." Then two more participles in v. 10 (giving and sending), a governing infinitive construct (to set; this would take on the value of the participles) in v. 11; and then governing participles in vv. 12 and 13 (frustrates and catches/captures). This enables us to see what Eliphaz is doing here, and it is rhetorically quite clever. He first of all urges Job to entrust his cause to God (presumably rather than continue in his outburst), and seeks to transform the situation by filling out the activity and character of this God. As the onlookers would hear this, they would nod in agreement and say, yes, God is like this. Rhetorically, it is an astute way to get his hearers on his side.[56]

In terms of content, God is depicted as a powerful creator and sustainer in vv. 9-10. There is no mention of retribution at this point. God is just a worker of great and indescribable wonders, and the supplier of life-giving rain and water on the earth and the (lit.) "outsides" (presumably the fields or countryside). Then vv. 11-13, while still talking about God, begin to outline how God rewards and punishes humans. First, v. 11 claims that God sets the lowly on high and lifts the mourners to safety — in other words vindicates the (presumably godly) suffering ones. Job might have thought at this point that Eliphaz might have then moved on to identify Job as one brought low, one mourning.

But Eliphaz's speech has a sting in its tail, and he spends vv. 12-14 on a subgroup of the wicked described as "the crafty" and "the wily." These descriptions may not have been heard negatively by their original audience, since the first two descriptions of this group are the "crafty" and the "wise in their craftiness." The word for "crafty" (the plural of עָרוּם/ʿārûm) is itself a neutral word, used to describe the serpent in Genesis 3, but can also mean "shrewd" or "prudent," a

---

56. The syntax changes in vv. 14-16 with a series of finite verbs, all imperfect tenses (waw consecutives in vv. 15-16a) until the final perfect tense in v. 16b — injustice has shut her mouth.

desirable characteristic for the wise in Prov 1:4. Again, this is rhetorically clever, and is suggestive for Job. Has his "shrewdness" and "wisdom" passed over into "craftiness" or even "folly"? The word "devices" (v. 12) can be either positive or negative. It is used of God's thoughts in Isa 55:8-9 and Jer 29:11, but can also describe wicked thoughts (e.g., Isa 59:7; 65:2; Jer 18:12). In the book of Proverbs it can refer to the thoughts of the righteous (12:5) or those of the wicked (6:18). Thus, when combined with "crafty/shrewd," it is not determinative of either a positive or negative meaning. The description "wily" (v. 13; lit. "having been twisted," even physically twisted as in wrestling, Gen 30:8) may suggest that something good has been altered out of its usual shape, but it would take its meaning from the parallel expression, "the craftiness of the wise." The word for "schemes" (plural of עֵצָה/ 'ēṣâ) is used in Job 38 for his plan for how he runs the world.[57]

The frustration and despair of v. 14, which echoes Job's experience (e.g., 7:13-14), might be, according to Eliphaz, due to God's righteous and just activity of catching out and frustrating the schemes and plans of the crafty. Eliphaz has thus moved in this part of the speech from the great activity and character of God through a brief mention of his lifting up the lowly to a stronger focus on his punishment of the "craftiness of the wise." Does Eliphaz, therefore, believe that Job is one of the wicked, at least temporarily? It appears to be a real possibility for Eliphaz, but he seems to qualify it in vv. 15-16. Here there is a focus on the "needy" being rescued and the poor having hope. Verse 15 could speak of deliverance from military foes (from the edges of their swords), or more likely from the sharp tongue of ordinary enemies (from a sword in their mouth). The needy are saved not from sharp swords but from sharp words (see v. 21). The last part of v. 16 reinforces the emphasis on retributive justice with a declaration that injustice has shut its mouth. This is a win-win conclusion for Eliphaz. If Job is suffering for his (temporary or other) craftiness, then he deserves it; if he is among the poor and needy, he has hope and will be rescued; but on either scenario justice (understood in terms of the doctrine of retribution) will win out. It is hard to work out exactly what Eliphaz thinks of Job, and in light of the other double entendres in his speech, this is probably an intentional ambiguity here. There is at least some hope implied in this section because God is depicted as the one who transforms situations or brings about reversals.[58]

5:17-27: God Will Reward the Righteous Verses 17-26 are the final substantial section of Eliphaz's speech, followed by a commendation and exhortation in

---

57. Incidentally, v. 13 is the only verse from Job that is quoted in the NT (1 Cor 3:19).

58. So Nam, *Talking about God,* 39. However, Perdue *Wisdom in Revolt,* 117, believes that Eliphaz has twisted God's universal reign so that it has become "a cold system of retributive justice."

v. 27. Again the tone changes to an emphasis on blessing, deliverance, protection, and peace. In v. 17 Eliphaz shares with Job the conviction that what has happened to Job is the work of God (also v. 18 — he wounds, he shatters). While he and Job draw different conclusions from this, they both see God acting in what Eliphaz calls "reproving" and "disciplining."

Eliphaz's conclusion, however, is wrong in Job's case. Despite his vision in 4:17, his opinion in 5:17 is faulty. Verse 17 shows a disciplinary view of suffering that Elihu will develop in more detail. God does sometimes discipline his people, but the prologue has shown that this is not the reason for Job's suffering. So irony arises as Eliphaz concludes his analysis with such certainty, but with the reader knowing that he is certainly wrong. The idea in itself has merit; it simply does not apply to Job in this particular instance.

What does Eliphaz assert about the fate of the righteous? Though they will be wounded or shattered at times, God will bind up and heal. Difficulties and setbacks are not all that there is in life, and they will certainly have a time limit for the righteous. The righteous will suffer to some extent in life, but never finally. The possibility of falling but ultimately triumphing (delivered from six or seven troubles, v. 19) is an echo of Prov 24:16. In Job 5:20 they will experience famine and war; in v. 21, physical and verbal attacks from their enemies.

These troubles are, however, soon left behind as Eliphaz waxes eloquent about the rewards of the righteous. Verses 22-23 highlight some potential dangers (destruction, famine, wild beasts), but the righteous will be in league with the stones of the field, presumably the opposite of destruction and famine, and implying that the fields will bear fruitful crops. The beasts will not pose a threat but will be at peace. The tent of the righteous will be at peace (an image of the household being a place of harmony and prosperity), and they will lose no animals from their flocks (v. 24). They will have many descendants of their own (v. 25). It is hard to say how Job would have responded to this, but it must have struck him as insensitive. He too knew the theory, but this was not his experience. All this would have been of little comfort to Job, who had already experienced many of these losses, so the final reassurance of a ripe old age (v. 26) would have brought little comfort.

In this speech Eliphaz has emphasized that the wicked will be punished, but he also expresses this positive aspect of the doctrine of retribution — the righteous will be rewarded. The significance of Eliphaz finishing his speech on this fairly positive note is that, despite his warnings to Job, Eliphaz still seems to believe (or perhaps hope) that Job is among the righteous and that therefore his suffering will be over soon.

In the final verse he also makes an appeal to the authority of the collective mind of the wise, which is close to an appeal to tradition. The "we" of v. 27 is at least the three friends, but probably also the "wise" whom they represent. Yet it is clear that even Job's great losses will not cause Eliphaz to reexamine his ideas, and he urges Job to know all this for his own good (lit. "know it for yourself"). Job's only task, according to v. 27, was to apply the traditional teachings to himself, not to persist in his protest. This is the climax to Eliphaz's first speech.

6:1-30: Job to Friends

Job now responds to Eliphaz's misdirected words. Chapter 6 is essentially Job's response to Eliphaz, and he will turn in chapter 7 to addressing God himself. This pattern of first speaking to the friends and then turning to God is typical of Job in the dialogue. After the introductory v. 1, vv. 2-7 make up the first section, which is a sketch or outline of his complaint. Verses 8-13 are his request, followed by a rebuke of the friends' failure to care for him in vv. 14-23. Verses 24-30 finish the chapter with a challenge addressed to the friends. The purpose of chapter 6 is "to point out that the friend's explanation of Job's current plight in the light of tradition is insensitive and amounts to deception."[59]

6:1-7: Job's Complaint Outlined In v. 1 Job "answered" in the sense of "responded," not necessarily answering every matter raised by Eliphaz. Verse 2 starts with a request that his angst and suffering be taken seriously. It could be understood as Job asking that his vexation be weighed against his calamities ("if only my vexation and calamity were properly weighed; let them be balanced together against each other"), but more likely means that he wants his vexations to be properly weighed (an intensive expression), and his calamity as well, against what is just or right, so that they would be shown to be excessive. This would fit even better with the call for vindication in v. 29. Thus his vexations and calamity are different things — the subjective response and objective happenings or his mental anguish and physical sufferings.[60]

This combination of mental and physical sufferings provides the subject for v. 3. The comparison with the sand of the sea (usually a metaphor for what is uncountable) refers to an enormous and therefore heavy body of sand. In response to these overwhelming sufferings, Job's words have been "(justifiably) extreme" or "unrestrained," rather than "rash" (ESV, NRSV) or "impetuous" (NIV). He hints at the extent of his pain in v. 4 with a strong accusation that

---

59. Pyeon, *You Have Not Spoken*, 123-24.

60. Hartley, *Book of Job*, 131-32, suggests that the vexation is the anguish that the trial provoked, and the misfortune refers to Job's actual losses.

God has fired poisoned arrows at him and has marshaled terrors against him. Theologically, this is a very significant verse, for it draws attention to the fact that Job believes that God is the one in total control, and so it is he who has been aiming at him. It implies a big view of God, even as it accuses him.

A series of proverbial sayings follows in vv. 5-6. A donkey legitimately brays in order to be fed, but once it has been given grass to eat, it does not continue to bray (v. 5). A similar scenario applies for the ox. This suggests that Job, by still crying out to God, believes that God has not yet answered him. Verse 6 has two parallel proverbs, which are then applied in v. 7. First, tasteless food cannot be eaten without salt, for food is meant to delight the tastebuds. Second, the food is tasteless, like the juice of the mallow.[61] But what is the "them" of v. 7a, which is described as loathsome to Job in v. 7b? It is unlikely to be his sufferings of v. 2, or the arrows of God of v. 4, for these would have been unpleasant, not bland. In the light of v. 5, it could refer to his continual cries to God, saying that they are as uninteresting to him as tasteless food. However, most likely Job has in view Eliphaz's words, which were bland, tasteless, and missed the point of Job's anguish.

6:8-13: Job's Request Job announces to the friends in v. 8 that he has a way forward, a longing expressed to the God whom he still believes is in absolute control of his circumstances. He discloses his petition in v. 9 — that God would finish his life (crush him, cut him off). The language of crushing and God loosing his hand to cut Job off clearly relates to death, but this is probably not an actual request to be killed. The prospect of death as comfort is a striking way of expressing the intensity of his pain. His suffering is so severe that he cannot cope with it and longs for it to stop. Is his request of v. 9 then a failure of faith? It is interesting that both in his accusation (v. 4) and now his longing for death (vv. 8-9) he reveals a big view of God. God is the one in control and is thus the cause of what happens to him. He does not reduce the size of God, or admit the possibility that God might not be able to restrain other powerful forces at work. This is part of true faith.

In vv. 10-13 he justifies why he asks for this, first, in v. 10 by saying it would bring him comfort, but also insisting that he has kept true to God and his words. Immediately after his request to die (v. 9), he insists that he has not denied God's words (v. 10). Verse 10 is difficult to translate with precision as the verb (וַאֲסַלְּדָה/ *wa'ăsallĕdâ*) is a hapax legomenon.[62] It is traditionally translated as "I exult,"

---

61. If that is what is meant. BDB 321, 938, suggests "in slime of purslane"! KJV and NIV opted for the white of an egg, on the basis of the rabbis. If it is a vegetable we do not know what it is.

62. Andersen, *Job*, 129 observes, "The text is difficult, and no solution is in sight."

giving the sense: "even though I am in endless pain, I exult, for I have not denied the words of the Holy One." Clines, following Gordis, argues for the translation "I recoiled," in which case the sense would be, "I recoil from/in the midst of my endless pain, because I have not denied the words of the Holy One."[63] On either reading, Job is making a claim that he has not denied his God. These factors suggest that it is not a failure of faith at all, and that his request is more a voicing of how desperate his circumstances are rather than a measured petition.

Indeed, the rhetorical questions of vv. 11-13 seem to be expressing his human weakness, so that he is simply overwhelmed by his circumstances. The imagery of the questions in vv. 11-12 is fairly clear. In v. 11a Job is implying that he has no strength or power that would enable him to wait with any confidence that he would be able to see his way through the crisis. Job then reveals that he does not have a clear end or outcome that would make it easier for him to be patient (v. 11b). Verse 12 seems to unpack v. 11a and make the same point about his lack of strength. In other words, he is saying to the friends that he is feeling weak and feeble, unable to see any real prospect of a good outcome, despite the pious and optimistic words of Eliphaz in 5:17-26.

Verse 13 is another rhetorical question with the implied answer no. He concludes that he does not have any help in himself (or perhaps "with him"), and that there is no prospect of a change for the better. Job is telling his friends to stop putting a nice veneer on his troubles.

6:14-23: The Friends' Failure to Care The opening verse is difficult to translate but quite crucial for the passage as a whole. Some understand Job to be the subject and translate it: "the despairing [need] the loyalty of a friend, when they forsake the fear of the Almighty *(Shaddai)*."[64] However, many emend למס/*lms*, on the basis of Hebrew manuscript support, to למאס/*lm's*, "to reject," which would give the translation: "the one who rejects/withholds loyalty from a friend has abandoned/forsaken the fear of the Almighty." This makes Eliphaz the subject and suits the flow of thought of the passage better. Job is not here conceding that *he* has forsaken the fear of God, for he has just insisted the opposite in v. 10. It is rather an allusion back to Eliphaz's words in 4:6, where Eliphaz challenges Job to let his fear of God be his ground of confidence. Job is turning that around now and saying that the way Eliphaz has spoken is to have abandoned the fear of God.

Verses 15-17 are a series of interconnected nature images that speak of the friends' failure to stick to the role they set out to do — to comfort and console

---

63. Clines, *Job 1–20,* 159.
64. For example, Habel, *Book of Job,* 138, 140, 148.

Job (2:11-13). He says to them that they should be giving him support but are not (vv. 14-15). The image of a dry water source is a familiar one to those in the Middle East. In the desert areas of contemporary Israel and Jordan are many wadis, which can have flash floods (the "torrential streams" of v. 15), but for much of the year are dried-up riverbeds. The friends came with floods of promises and good intentions, but that has passed by and nothing helpful is left. Verses 16-17 refer to the storehouses of ice and snow, seemingly immovable and inexhaustible, but they melt away and dry up in the heat. What seemed much is now nothing. Such is, according to Job, the help offered by the friends.

Verses 18-20 are the next subsection. The caravans could be understood in a number of ways.[65] It could simply be a parallel image of travelers forming caravans to ensure the success of their specific journey, but it ends in failure. This could be a parallel to the purposeful visit of these three friends, who came to comfort Job but failed. It could also be that the caravans, the caravans of Tema, and the travelers of Sheba describe Job's three friends. Though the friends are not from Tema or Sheba (both in Arabia), the caravans might have been, or it could simply be a stereotypical way of describing those who have journeyed from afar. Whether it is a comparison or an actual description, the same point is being made. The friends have been purposeful in coming but have failed in their mission, according to Job.

This leads nicely on to v. 21, where Job focuses in on the three friends ("you" is plural, implying that Job regards Eliphaz as speaking on behalf of the other two), although the first part of v. 21 is difficult.[66] Job says that they have seen his circumstances and are afraid. Perhaps they are afraid that this might happen to them, but it is more likely that the friends are frightened that their core belief in retribution is at risk, and in need of defense.

This section is rounded off by a number of rhetorical questions, just like the previous section. Verse 21 is the punchline (so Andersen), but Job now forces his point home with a number of questions aimed at the friends. The implication is that Job has not asked the friends for a gift or bribe from their wealth, nor has he asked them to rescue or ransom him. In the light of vv. 22-23, the friends could have been afraid (v. 21b) that the cost of helping Job might put them in financial or personal jeopardy. Many commentators who see v. 22 beginning a new part of the speech do not see the connection between the

---

65. The noun אָרְחוֹת/ʾŏrḥôt in v. 18 literally means "ways" or "paths" but is used as a metonymy for a traveler or wayfarer, as in 31:32 and in 6:19, in parallel to "travelers."

66. The Ketib is, "for now you have not become [or become nothing]," but the Qere reads, "for now you have become to him." Presumably the word "such" is implied, i.e., "for such you have now become." The LXX and Syriac here are helpful: "for [such] you have now become *to me*," which rendering is more natural than "to him," and is followed by Dhorme, Fohrer, Pope, RSV, NRSV.

"being afraid" of v. 21 and the questions of vv. 22-23, and therefore consider they follow on a little oddly.

6:24-30: A Challenge to the Friends The new section starts in v. 24 with a call to his friends (the verb "teach" is plural) to teach or correct him, if they can. He is asking for explanation and not simply condemnation. If it is demonstrated that he deserves to suffer, he will be silent. Verses 25-26 are further reflections on how the friends (in the person of Eliphaz) have used words. He concedes that they are using upright or respectable words, but asks what good they have achieved, presumably because the focus on Job's words misses the fact that Job is speaking out of his desperation.[67] Job describes his speech (the speech of a despairing or desperate person) as wind, but it is not clear whether this is his own verdict or that of the friends. Andersen reads this verse as saying that the friends have treated Job's words as something of little value, to be blown away (lit. "for the wind"). Verse 27 reveals the extent of Job's pain. There is no real evidence that the friends would cast lots over the fatherless (divide the spoils?), but he feels that they are prepared to rewrite his life rather than question whether he is being dealt with justly. Their words show no care for Job as a person.

The closing words addressed to the friends are in vv. 28-30. In vv. 28-29 Job is still claiming to be a person of integrity, and he is asking them to reconsider. He asks them twice to turn (שׁוּב/*šûb*, "repent, change direction"). He is urging the possibility of change, for much is at stake. He does not want injustice/ unrighteousness to continue, and he knows his vindication as a righteous person is at stake. Whereas Eliphaz has talked about wisdom (4:21), Job sees that the issue at stake is his "integrity" or "righteousness" (צִדְקִי/*ṣidqî*, v. 29). This is the issue that the accuser raised in 1:9. Does Job fear God for nothing, or is his faith based on self-interest? Verse 30 rounds this off with two rhetorical questions with the implied answer no.

7:1-21: Job to God

There seems to be a change of audience in chapter 7. Job now addresses God, not Eliphaz. This is made explicit in vv. 7-8, and the "you" of vv. 12, 14, and 16-21 is clearly Yahweh.[68] Chapter 7 is a balanced poem comprising three major

---

67. In v. 25a Clines, *Job 1-20*, 156, 161, translates נִמְרְצוּ/*nimrĕṣû* as "distressing" (cf. ESV "forceful") to describe these "upright words."

68. Contrast, e.g., 6:25, 26, 28, where the "you" is Eliphaz (and his friends) involved in the dialogue with Job.

units (vv. 1-8, 9-16, 17-21). Each unit is framed by an opening axiom about the human condition and a closing cry to God (vv. 1-2/7-8; 9-10/15-16; 17-18/21).[69] This structure suggests that the focus of the chapter is on the axioms that begin each section, leading to a pointed cry to God.

7:1-8: The Hardship of Human Life The opening axiom is possibly a quotation or formula from traditional wisdom sources.[70] The images are of the misery and hardship of human existence, apparently for all people but specifically in Job's case. The question form, with the implied answer yes, presents this hardship as a self-evident truth. Dianne Bergant argues that this emphasis on the misery of human life pervades all of vv. 1-6 (in contrast to ch. 14, where the focus is on its brevity), although there is mention of life's brevity in v. 6.[71] In saying that a person's life is like that of a hired hand, Job is asserting that humans are being treated in a way that does not suit their dignity, that they are being treated like something that is at odds with the Hebrew creation traditions of Genesis 1 and 2 or Psalm 8.

In vv. 3-6 Job extrapolates from the axiom to his own life. The lingering wretchedness spoken of in v. 3 ("months of emptiness" and "nights of misery") is elaborated on in both vv. 4 and 5. In v. 5 we see that extreme physical torment accompanies Job's mental anguish, although the poetic nature of the language and the lack of specific details preclude any medical diagnosis. However, it is important to notice that his physical sufferings do not lead to a petition for their removal, implying that the restoration of his physical health is not the key issue for Job. The section ends with mention of the brevity of life and lack of hope in v. 6.

The imperative "Remember" in v. 7 not only signals that Job is addressing God directly but also, in the context of the OT, is a call for God to act toward him in accordance with God's prior commitments (as in Gen 8:1; Exod 2:24). Indeed, a central theme in the laments is to move God to "remember" the one afflicted.[72] However, Job is not here summoning God to remember his covenant promises (as is common in Hebrew laments), but is calling on God to remember the commitment that a creator has to his creature. He is asking God to act on the basis of his creaturely weakness.

---

69. Habel, *Book of Job,* 153-54. This structure is also argued for by van der Lugt, "Stanza-Structure," 12.

70. So Habel, *Book of Job,* 157.

71. Bergant, "Anthropological Traditions," 150.

72. For example, in Ps 25:6-7, when God remembers someone in his mercy, he no longer holds their sins against them, while the writer in Lam 5:1 calls on God to remember Israel by activating his saving power in a new way. Hartley, *Book of Job,* 147, concludes that "the summons to remember in a prayer of distress, then, is a fundamental petition for deliverance."

The surveillance metaphor in v. 8, where God is depicted as the "seeing eye," is crucial for our understanding of v. 7. In 7:20 God is described as a "watcher of humanity" (NRSV), while in 10:14 God is also pictured as one who is the celestial watcher. This should be understood not as a mocking reminder but as a genuine plea.[73] The individual lament was a cry of faith in times of disorientation and distress. For this reason, it is best to see here a genuine, heartfelt cry that has arisen because of the seeming absence of God. Thus vv. 7 and 8 display, in the midst of Job's despair and anguish, a genuine calling on God to remember and act before it is too late.

7:9-16: The Short-Lived Nature of Human Life Job's second axiom (vv. 9-10) highlights the ephemeral nature of human beings. As Habel expresses it, "Mortality means life in transit; to be human is to be displaced."[74] In v. 11 Job again turns to his own oppressive circumstances, responding not in silent submission but with unrestrained lamenting of his distress. The terms he uses (the "anguish of my spirit"; the "bitterness of my soul") reveal his present emotional and spiritual state. The use of cohortatives ("let me/I will"), however, underscores Job's determination and resolve.

Verse 12 is unique in this section in that it contains a question, thus sharing a characteristic of the third section (vv. 17-21). There has been much debate over the mythological background to "sea" and "sea monster," and whether Job is "guarded" or "muzzled." The thrust of v. 12, however, is that God should not keep strict surveillance on humans, for they are insignificant. Only if they had the dimensions of mythological troublemakers would divine attention be warranted.[75] The tone seems to be one of disorientation rather than sarcasm.

In vv. 13-14 he recounts his emotional and physical agony. The dreams or visions of v. 14 are not sources of a message from God (see Gen 28:10-17; 46:2-4) nor even disciplinary warnings (Job 33:14-17); they are experienced as destructive and overwhelming nightmares. Even in the place where Job could expect to find "rest," there is terror.

Job then weighs up death and life in vv. 15-16. He is using the traditional lament hyperbole to express the extent of his despair (see 3:11-26). This is not an embracing of death as something positive, but only the dismissal of the hypothetical possibility of living forever. In v. 16 Job concludes with a plea to God to leave him alone or, more literally, to "cease from me." This is not a lack

73. Contra Habel, *Book of Job*, 155. There is nothing in the text by this stage that would alert us to read this in a mocking, almost sarcastic tone. Indeed, Habel draws his argument from parallels in later parts of the book.

74. Habel, *Book of Job*, 161.

75. Diewert, "Job 7:12," 211, 214-15.

of faith, but rather Job struggling to persevere in his faith. The irony of this is that "in the very act of begging God to desert him he approaches him."[76]

7:17-21: Why? How Long? This section is a barrage of questions. Verses 17-18 together ask "why," as do vv. 20-21a, while v. 19 asks, "how long?" These are the two characteristic questions of the laments, implying that they should be interpreted in the light of the biblical laments.[77]

Verses 17-18 call to mind, and perhaps parody, Ps 8:4-5, which reflect on the status God has given to humans and how he examines and tests them. While in other contexts this may speak of the value of humanity, here it serves only to deepen Job's despair. God's presence in testing, coupled with his absence in comfort, becomes a burdensome oppression.[78] In v. 17 the root גדל/*gdl*, "make so much of" (ESV), which normally implies an amount of care, here refers to punitive attention. Also in v. 18 the root פקד/*pqd*, which can mean "visit" in the sense of either "with care" or "with punishment," here takes on a negative thrust.

After the general axioms of vv. 17-18, Job turns again to his own situation in v. 19. This suggests that the asking to be left alone in v. 19 is more an expression of anguish and despair than a rational request. To simply analyze the questions in v. 19 is to ignore what is involved in "the rhetoric of outrage."[79] Laments use stereotyped expressions as well as strongly emotive language that can be misunderstood if it is dissected too analytically. One clue in interpreting this verse is to notice that Job keeps on initiating conversations with God, at the same time as asking to be "left alone."

Verses 20-21 are an interesting passage on the connection between sin and suffering. Job is not denying that he sins,[80] and it is clear from vv. 20-21 that the fact of his sin is undisputed. What Job cannot understand is why he has not been forgiven, for he has shown penitence and made the necessary sacrifices (e.g., 1:13). He is unaware of any further sin, let alone a sin of such a magnitude to warrant the suffering he now faces. He is accusing God, directly and pointedly, of being excessively harsh. The ending of this speech is not primarily a confession of sin, but rather an expression of bewilderment about how his current circumstances are connected to his admittedly imperfect, but still

---

76. Clines, *Job 1–20*, 196.

77. Westermann, *Structure*, 51.

78. Cox, *Triumph of Impotence*, 56.

79. A helpful phrase I first heard used by D. A. Carson. See Carson, *How Long*, 87-88.

80. The word "if" at the beginning of v. 20 is not in the Hebrew text; this verse can be understood as a conditional sentence leading to the rendering "if I have sinned." See GKC §159b, h; Hartley, *Book of Job*, 150; Gordis, *Book of Job*, 82; Dhorme, *Job*, 110. On Job's admission of sin, see also 13:26.

righteous, former life.[81] The image of God as a "watcher of humanity" in v. 20 is an ironic contrast with the supposed protective hedge of 1:10 and the twist this was given in 3:23.

Verse 21 closes with Job's desperate reminder to God that, unless he intervenes to deliver him soon, it will be too late, as Job will have died. This chapter is designed to move God to come to his aid, not to desert him or leave him alone. At the end of chapter 7, there is a tension between Job wanting God's presence and his absence. On the one hand, we see Job's accusations against God; and, on the other, he directs accusations toward the God whom he still sees in absolute control.

8:1-22: Bildad

Bildad's speech is shorter than Eliphaz's, lasting only twenty-two verses but having several distinct parts. Verses 2-7 give the core of his argument, insisting that God will not pervert justice. Verses 8-10 outline the authority for this argument. One side of his doctrine of retributive justice (the punishment of the wicked) is then the subject of a more discursive set of comments in vv. 11-19, while vv. 20-22 finish on a more optimistic note, perhaps even implying (at least leaving it as a real possibility) that since Job is righteous he will be vindicated.

8:1-7: The Essence of Bildad's Argument Verse 1 simply announces that Bildad is the second of the friends to speak. Bildad clearly believes that Job's words are inappropriate, and describes them as a strong or mighty wind (רוּחַ/*rûaḥ*). The word for "mighty" (כַּבִּיר/*kabbîr*, v. 2) is used only in Job and Isaiah, and generally denotes some aspect of strength; but if the wind is destructive (as in Job 1), then a mighty wind is even more destructive. He may be picking up Job's self-description in 6:26 of his speech as "despairing wind." In the context, it is clearly a rebuke of Job, and so the reference back to Job's previous address to the friends would make sense.[82]

The heart of Bildad's theology is found in his core sentence in v. 3. Unlike Eliphaz's vision (4:12-17), we do not yet know the source of his views, but they are unambiguous in their content. He will not shift from his base principle that Almighty God will not pervert justice (מְשָׁפָּט/*mišpāṭ*) or righteousness (צֶדֶק/

---

81. A parallel might be the book of Daniel, where there is no description of any sin committed by Daniel, for the focus in the book is on Daniel as a model of righteousness. However, he confesses sin in Dan 9:4-11.

82. So Course, *Speech and Response*, 49.

ṣedeq, "rightness, what is right"). This pairing of "justice" and "righteousness" is a classic one, and highlights the importance for Bildad (and the doctrine of retribution generally) of these key ideas. Whereas Eliphaz starts from God's utter holiness, Bildad clearly focuses more on God's justice and righteousness. The verb "pervert" (v. 3, עות/ʿwt, "to be bent, crooked") occurs twice, and the Piel has a factitive sense of "making crooked, falsifying, perverting." God does not twist justice or righteousness into something else, regardless of what Job may claim.

The syntax of this section is interesting. There is an interrogative marker (indicating a question) at the beginning of v. 3, followed by the hypothetical particle (אם/ʾim) beginning the second part of v. 3 as well as the start of vv. 4, 5, and 6. It appears in v. 3 to be used to indicate that the question of v. 3a continues with a similar question in v. 3b. The pattern in vv. 4-6 suggests that it must have the same force and so require a similar translation in each case. This would be the hypothetical or conditional sense of "if" rather than "since," most clearly in vv. 5-6. Thus Bildad may simply be considering the possibility in v. 4 that Job's children have sinned toward God and brought this calamity on themselves (lit. "he sent them away into the hand/power of their transgression"). However, while Bildad expresses this conditionally, he builds on it as if it is an established fact, as it probably was in his mind.

His suggestion that the death of Job's children was their own fault is coldly logical (given his presuppositions) but pastorally insensitive. He starts with the belief that suffering is punishment, and so the death of Job's children is proof they have sinned. Bildad argues from the contrast between the fate of Job and of Job's children in order to offer a warning; Bildad urges Job to search his heart before God in order to ensure that he is not guilty of crimes such as those for which his children have died (vv. 5-6), so that God can restore him (v. 7).

In v. 5 Bildad urges Job to seek God and to amplify that seeking by asking God to show him favor or grace. The point here is that Job must cease his call for "justice" — since God is just — and throw himself on God's grace. This is the choice that Job must make. In v. 6 Bildad suggests that, if Job is upright, then he will be restored to נְוַת צִדְקֶךָ/nĕwat ṣidqekā, which can mean "place of your righteousness" or "place that is rightly yours" ("your rightful habitation," ESV) or both.[83] Verse 6, however, shows that Bildad understands "grace" as deserved rather than undeserved favor. The success or otherwise of the choice urged in v. 5 is dependent, according to Bildad, on Job being pure and upright (v. 6). At this point, Bildad is aware of the importance of upright living, but he

---

83. Habel, *Book of Job*, 175.

has misunderstood grace. This section closes off in vv. 6-7 with a rich picture of God as the restorer, the one who will rouse himself,[84] restore a person's proper place, and honor that person with even greater success.

8:8-10: The Basis of Bildad's View Bildad now outlines the source of his authority — tradition. Verse 8 is urging Job to consider the long-held traditions; the parenthetical v. 9 justifies this on the basis of the short-lived nature of individual human life; and v. 10 exhorts Job to listen to the tradition and learn.

In v. 8 he appeals to those from the former generations (since they are to be inquired of, probably the people from former times) or what was searched out by their fathers. The point of v. 9 is not that the current generation did not live as long, but rather that the short span of an individual human life cannot measure up to the collective number of years of all the sages of the past. The teaching is handed down from generation to generation, tested, modified when needed, but confirmed and proven again and again. Hence the focus in v. 10 is on their teachings or words, which come from their minds/understanding (lit. "hearts"). Of course, what has been handed down by the previous generations is a theology of retribution such as that seen in the book of Proverbs. It is this that Bildad proceeds to outline. Many commentators raise the possibility that Bildad is not just talking about previous generations, but the first or prime generation — those really from antiquity. On either reading, it is an appeal to teaching that has appeared to have stood the test of time.

8:11-19: Discursive Comments The most revealing aspect of Bildad's outline of this traditional doctrine of retribution is that vv. 11-19 focus almost entirely on the punishment of the wicked, not the reward of the righteous. Job would have agreed with Bildad that God would certainly punish the wicked. What may have been in dispute was whether Job belonged among the wicked. Interestingly, both Job and Bildad would have agreed that God rewarded the righteous, but they drew different conclusions from it. Job asked why he as a righteous person was not being rewarded; Bildad is suggesting to Job that if he were righteous he would have been rewarded.

The amount of detail here is excessive and overwhelming. Why is it included when it is more than is needed to establish a point that Job agrees with anyway? The answer is most likely that Bildad believes that Job has not understood the implications of these truths for his situation. In other words, as long as Job does not see that his suffering is caused by sin, Bildad feels that he needs to keep on talking so that Job will get the hint. It does not mean that Bildad

---

84. Or perhaps "enrich Job" — so Andersen, *Job*, 140.

thinks Job is utterly unrighteous, but at least sufficiently wicked to deserve the punishment he is getting.

Verses 11-12 contain an extended image about papyrus reeds. Verse 11 seems to say there is no effect without a cause — unless you have marshy water, you will not get papyrus reeds. This idea probably comes from Egyptian wisdom,[85] so it is likely that Bildad is appropriating some of the international wisdom current in his day. Yet the point of v. 12 is that they can die suddenly. They appeared to be thriving, but the effect (withering) would come because of their nature. He is effectively saying to Job, "You have prospered for a while, but if you are not utterly righteous, this will ultimately be made clear." That would lead nicely into his conclusion in v. 13 that such destruction will happen to the profane, who "forget God." Forgetting God in the OT is not simply a lapse of memory but a morally accountable choice (e.g., Deut 8 and many other places). He is wrongly implying that this description fits Job.

Verses 14-15 are trying to fill out the picture of what such a person is like. His confidence is broken and his ability to trust (or perhaps the object of his trust) is the web (lit. "house") of a spider. This image may mean "insubstantial, not strong enough to hold him," or "entrapping, beguiling." Verse 15 inclines me toward the image of insubstantial, for it will not stand up when one leans against it, nor will it be able to be firmly held.

Verses 16-19 then emphasize the ephemeral nature of the unrighteous flourishing, like a plant that begins to grow but withers. While these verses do not explicitly state that they are referring to an unrighteous person, Bildad's theology would not permit the final destruction (v. 18) of a righteous person. Thus the mention of destruction rather than correction means that he is referring not to an incompletely righteous person, but to one who is utterly unrighteous. Verse 19 is problematic, since it is difficult to see how his destruction and replacement by others is "the joy [or exultation] of his way." This most likely means that the righteous will rejoice that the way of the wicked leads to destruction. What is clear is that the wicked will cease to be, and will be replaced by another.

8:20-22: An Optimistic Finish Given what Bildad has said in vv. 11-19, it is surprising that he concludes in vv. 20-22 on a fairly positive note (echoing Pss 126:2; 132:18). It may, however, be only a theoretically optimistic note. Bildad is clear that God can accept a righteous man, but he may not be hopeful (in the light of Job's words) that Job will be acceptable. Thus the optimistic tone

---

85. Habel, *Book of Job,* 176, thinks that "papyrus" and "reed" are Egyptian loanwords; but Clines, *Job 1–20,* 207-8, notes that papyrus still grows in the Huleh valley in Israel and along the coastal plain.

of vv. 20-22 is conditional on Job's repentance, on his turning away from his accusations that God is perverting justice. There is very little material on the rewarding of the righteous when compared to the extensive teaching on the punishment of the wicked, which indicates Bildad's understanding of the tradition handed down from the fathers. For the reader, however, there is irony in v. 20, since the description of Job as blameless was established in 1:1, 8; 2:3. Job was and presumably still is blameless, yet he experiences God's apparent rejection. This serves to undercut the force of what Bildad has said, and also makes his cheery words in vv. 21-22 seem flawed and therefore hollow. Yet the comparatively cheerful note on which Bildad ends at least leaves open the possibility of Job's innocence.

Bildad may have meant well, but he did not speak in a way that cared for the suffering Job. He failed to perceive where Job was at, or to engage him. Job believed that God rewards the righteous and punishes the wicked, but his beliefs did not meet with his experience. He wanted to know why this God did not come to him and care for him. Bildad had not really listened before he spoke.

9:1-35: Job

This is Job's second speech in the first cycle, and he responds to Bildad's topic of righteous justice. The issues of righteousness and justice have already been raised by the time the reader reaches chapter 9. In his first speech, Eliphaz asked whether humans are righteous (יִצְדָּק/*yiṣdāq*) before God (4:17). Job clearly insists that it is his righteousness (צִדְקִי/*ṣidqî*) that is at stake (6:29). Bildad also has asked whether God perverts justice (מִשְׁפָּט/*mišpāṭ*) or righteousness (צֶדֶק/ *ṣedeq*, 8:3). Thus, when Job asks how can a person be righteous (יִצְדַּק/*yiṣdaq*) before God (v. 2), he is replying to this string of references begun by Eliphaz's question in 4:17.

Some scholars see the major break in the speech after 9:24,[86] but the traditional chapter divisions divide the speech well into a section that considers litigation against God, and a section in which Job actually speaks to God (though in the form of what he *would* say to God; see below). Habel sees these chapters as an extended speech on the futility of litigation, but this issue is largely confined to chapter 9 and only dribbles into the first two verses of chapter 10.[87]

---

86. For example, Clines, *Job 1–20*, 223-24. One of his criteria is that God is spoken about in 9:2-24, but addressed in the second person in 9:25–10:22. However, he concedes that God is spoken about in 9:32-35.

87. Habel, *Book of Job*, 186-87.

9:1-4: Being Righteous before God The exact translation of Job's question in v. 2b is disputed. While most translations opt for something like "How can a person be in the right/justified before God?" Gerald Wilson suggests that it should be translated in a declarative sense: "How can a mortal be declared righteous [or publicly vindicated] before God?"[88] In other words, Job is asking how his righteousness can be recognized by God. This would make good sense of the context, but the Qal stem of this root is not otherwise used in this sense in the book.[89] Indeed, later in this chapter (vv. 15, 20) it means to "be in the right" rather than "declared to be right." A better way is to translate it as "be in the right," but to note that the strong litigation motif in the chapter implies some legal vindication of this. This would explain the connection with vv. 3-4.

While it is not surprising to see the issues of righteousness surfacing, an unexpected turn of events is that Job uses the question of his righteousness to contemplate the cut-and-thrust of litigation with God. In v. 3 the terms "contend with" and "answer" are legal expressions, and a courtroom setting seems envisaged. At the outset, then, litigation is contemplated not to usurp God but to establish the truth of Job's righteousness before God — a truth to which God has already testified (1:8; 2:3). In v. 4 Job finds the prospect of litigation against God daunting — who has hardened himself (probably in the sense of taken a firm stand) against him and succeeded? Job's consideration of litigation is, however, assuming a high view of God, evident in his clear description of God as wise in heart (mind) and mighty in strength (v. 4).

9:5-13: God's Power and Force Here Job focuses on the power and force of God. The God-sized view of God seen in v. 4 continues in this section and owes much to the doctrine of creation. This unit does not greatly advance Job's argument, but it does reveal his understanding of God as active in his creation. Having contemplated litigating against God (v. 3), he now reflects on God's grandeur as Creator. Verses 5 and 13 bracket the section with comments about God's anger, implying that Job feels that he is currently experiencing the anger of God.

Connected with this is the notion that God is a mover and shaker. He removes and overturns mountains (v. 5, possibly a reference to the eruption of a volcano) as well as causing earthquakes (v. 6). He is the one who can stop the rising of the sun (or prevent it from being seen, whether by heavy clouds or some other way) and the shining of the stars by his speech (v. 7). Job clearly

88. G. Wilson, *Job*, 83.
89. BDB 842 notes that the Qal stem can mean (1) "have a just cause, be in the right" (Job 9:15, 20; 13:18; 34:5; 33:12); (2) "be justified" (11:2; 9:2; 25:4; 40:8); (3) "be just" (of God); (4) "be just, righteous, in conduct and character" (used in 4:17; 10:15; 15:14; 22:3; 35:7). The Hiphil stem is, however, used to mean "declare righteous, justify," in 27:5.

understands that God is actively and powerfully intervening in his world. Job is putting the disasters that have happened to him into this broader creational context of God's activity.

In vv. 8-10 he focuses on God as the Maker or Creator. The stretching out of the heavens (v. 8a) is in parallel with the trampling on the waves (lit. "high places," some [e.g., Clines, Hartley] emend to "back") of the sea. This appears to be a reference to God creating the heavens and the seas, reminiscent of Genesis 1. The references in v. 9 apparently refer to stars or constellations, although the precise meaning of "the chambers of the south" is difficult to grasp.[90] The series of participles that bind together vv. 5-10 suggest that v. 10 is a resting place in Job's thought. It outlines in summary form that God is the doer of great and marvelous acts (of creation) that cannot be fully fathomed or found by human beings (by searching or counting).

Verses 11-12, which both begin with the particle הֵן/*hēn*, "Behold," speak of God's activity in terms of movement — he passes by near to Job, but Job is not able to see him or what he is doing (v. 11 — the two halves of the verse are parallel). In v. 12 God is described as seizing or snatching (the verb occurs only here in the OT), but no object is expressed. It is almost as if whatever God takes, he cannot be stopped or turned back. The second part of v. 12, in parallel with the first, is not saying that it is illegitimate to question God, but rather that one cannot efficaciously stop God from acting by asking him to justify his actions. The conclusion in v. 13 is that God will not turn back his anger, no matter how mighty the foe. Rahab refers to a sea creature subdued by God (see Job 26:12; Isa 51:9).

9:14-20: The Difficulties of Litigation against God Job's mind drifts back to litigation in v. 14, but this is not entirely unrelated to the description of God as Creator. The power of this active Creator makes it seem a daunting prospect to constrain him within the boundaries of legal procedure, but vv. 14-20 are riddled with legal language. This section begins with Job considering the practical problems of defending oneself against God (vv. 14-15). In vv. 14-15 there is a kind of desperation in Job's words. "Answer" in vv. 14a and 15a has a legal context (it refers to legal argument), as do "I am in the right/innocent" (v. 15a, צָדַקְתִּי/*ṣādaqtî*) and "for my case" (v. 15b, לִמְשֹׁפְטִי/*limšōpĕṭî*). Literally v. 15 reads, "Though I am in the right, I cannot answer him. For my case, I must appeal for mercy." His complaint is essentially that being legally right is not enough to gain a legal victory against God.

Job then anticipates what would happen if God responded to his legal

---

90. Andersen, *Job*, 146, says its meaning still eludes us.

claim (vv. 16-18), joining the image of God as Creator to the litigation theme. Behind v. 16 is the idea that the awesome God of vv. 5-13 is too big to be concerned with Job. The Creator image is more explicit in v. 17 with the mention of God being able to use a tempest to attack Job, while in v. 18 God is the one who has power over human breath. This big view of God as a powerful creator is important to observe, for otherwise Job's accusations might seem as if he has little regard for God. Thus, when he accuses God of multiplying his wounds without good cause (v. 17, a point God conceded in 2:3), or that God fills (lit. "satisfies") him with bitter things (v. 18), the real thrust is to point out how God as Creator determines all that happens to Job.

The end result is a twin focus on the threads of justice and righteousness in vv. 19-20. As Creator, God is "mighty" (v. 19a, same word as in v. 4), so he cannot be overcome. In relation to a legal case, no one can ensure that God can be made to appear (v. 19b). Job therefore anticipates that he would lose the court case (or perhaps "justice," v. 19), but that this would be unjust (v. 20). The climax is found in v. 20, where he expresses frustration that, despite his being righteous (אֶצְדָּק/'*eṣdāq*, NRSV "I am innocent"; ESV "I am in the right"), he would condemn himself; and though blameless (תָּם/*tām*), God would declare him crooked or perverse. Against a human opponent, Job could win, but how can he be vindicated against his mighty Creator? That is Job's dilemma.

9:21-24: How Does God Rule the World? In these verses Job is trying to sum up or clarify to himself how God rules the world. Some suggest that Job here is no longer acting righteously.[91] However, unlike his complaints to God, Job is not here talking *to* God directly. He is instead speaking *about* God to the friends and any others who are assembled. Indeed, he is still contemplating his next step, rather than accusing, and the tone is one of despair.[92]

Two significant observations emerge from vv. 22-24. First, the actions of God are so hard to comprehend because Job sticks so carefully to the doctrine of retribution. Job cannot understand why the blameless (תָּם/*tām*) and the wicked are not treated differently (v. 22). Second, Job still seems to hold to the view that God is in sovereign control of the world (v. 24). Andersen accurately observes that "Job has no doubt that it is God, and God alone, who orders the world in this way."[93] Since v. 24 ends with a question, it suggests that Job is still only exploring possibilities. Job wants to understand more, but cannot.

91. O'Connor, "Reverence and Irreverence in Job," 89, sees Job's accusation in 9:23b that God would give an unjust verdict against the innocent as being "surely the low point of his irreverence."
92. Clines, *Job 1-20*, 225.
93. Andersen, *Job*, 149.

9:25-35: Exploring Other Options This unit commences with a cry of futility (vv. 25-26), based on the brevity of life. While Job elsewhere talks of how his days linger (e.g., 7:1-4), they can also be regarded as passing swiftly in the sense being gone without achieving anything (here and in 7:6). The images of a runner (used of one bringing news of victory in battle in 2 Sam 18:19-33), "skiffs of reed," or a swooping eagle are those of fast-moving objects.

He then explores a number of options. The first two (vv. 27, 30) start with the word "if," a hint that they will not be pursued. The first option (vv. 27-29) is to forget about his complaint and snap out of it, yet that would lead to his condemnation, not vindication (vv. 28b-29a). The next option (vv. 30-31) is to clean himself up (v. 30), but he believes that God will throw him back into the muck (v. 31).

The third option explored by Job (vv. 32-35) — and the real focus of the section — is his call for an umpire. Here Job returns to the concept of litigation, but is still overwhelmed by the thought of confronting God in court (v. 32). The force of v. 32 is that it is not a level playing field, since God has a divine advantage over humans. So Job searches for someone who will mediate between him and God (v. 33), vindicating him on the basis of his integrity.[94]

His desire for a mediator or arbiter or umpire (מוֹכִיחַ/*môkîaḥ*) is confined to v. 33. Little detail is given of what kind of figure Job had in mind, as if that should not be our focus. That the umpire is to go between Job and God suggests that the umpire is not God, but possibly an unidentified third party, perhaps a helper in a lawsuit to get justice done. However, it is also useful to ask whether Job is looking for an actual or simply a hypothetical figure. Three factors suggest the latter. First, Job is at this stage still only exploring possibilities, not actualities. Verse 33 is probably a hypothetical sentence, assuming that the MT לֹא/*lōʾ*, "not," is repointed to the wish particle לֻא/*luʾ* or לוּ/*lû*. If it were a hypothetical figure, this would account well for the little detail given of his identity.[95] Second, the image of vv. 34b-35a is one of the dread of God terrifying Job. It would be unusual to ask one who terrifies you to act as an arbiter. Third, v. 35b is best understood as Job saying that he cannot find this hypothetical figure. Habel translates this as, "But this is not so for me," and

---

94. Parsons, "Structure and Purpose," 148, argues strongly that his appeal for an impartial "umpire" in 9:33 is for someone who would come up with a "settlement proposal" to be weighed up by the parties. See also Habel, "Only the Jackal," 232; L. Wilson, "Realistic Hope," 244-45.

95. The repointing is implied by the LXX and Syriac versions. Smick, "Job," 915, suggests that the MT pointing probably arose for theological reasons. Clines, *Job 1–20*, 220, 243, agrees that in 9:33 the negative particle should be read as the wish particle. Some who resist this alteration do so because v. 32 has already ruled this possibility out, but Clines notes that לוּ/*lû* can express a wish contrary to fact, so this can be taken as a (hopeless) wish.

notes, "In spite of his bold idea Job knows of no such mediator."[96] This follows the pattern that we will also see when Job further explores the possibility of an arbiter in 16:18-22 and 19:23-27.[97] It also explains why Job pursues this line of thinking no further in this speech.

10:1-22: Job

After finding no hope of getting a legal settlement in chapter 9, Job turns to lamenting in chapter 10. Habel sees this and the preceding chapter as having a common theme of the futility of litigation. He thus reads chapter 10 in a forensic context and sees only vv. 18-22 as a complaint. The rest of chapter 10 instead becomes the rehearsing of a possible case against his legal adversary. However, Habel's keenness for the "legal metaphor" has made him extend it too far in this speech. Roland Murphy is right when he notes that, despite echoes of the judicial process (especially in vv. 1-2), the chapter is primarily a complaint and ends in vv. 18-22 on a clear complaint note.[98]

While chapter 10 is formally a description of a lament rather than Job actually lamenting, the existential nature of the language indicates that Job is complaining rather than theorizing. Clines sums it up well: "Chap. 10 contains the words he would use (no, the words he *does* use) in the confrontation he here steels himself for."[99] Even though it is presented as what Job would say to God (v. 2), it is primarily a complaint and is addressed to God in the second person.

10:1-2: Transition to a Lament The first indicator of the complaint is in v. 1, which is similar to the transitional v. 11 in the complaint in chapter 7. This suggests that the accusations of this chapter are to be understood as a lament form and not as part of a closely reasoned legal argument. The agony churning inside him compels him to speak his thoughts boldly and freely.

Behind v. 2 is the idea that a plaintiff is obliged to make known to a defendant the charges he has against him, although even here it is God's silence that tests him far more than the emotional and physical pain. Yet the reversion to direct address of God in v. 3, and for the rest of the chapter, suggests rather that v. 2 is the last whimper of the litigation, as it gives way to complaint to God. This section is thus transitional.

96. Habel, "Only the Jackal," 232.
97. L. Wilson, "Realistic Hope," 244.
98. Habel, *Book of Job*, 54-55, 186-88; Murphy, *Wisdom Literature*, 28.
99. Clines, *Job 1–20*, 242.

10:3-7: Three Sharp Questions In vv. 3-5 Job probes to discover God's motive for afflicting him by asking three sharp rhetorical questions. The first question is, what advantage does God gain (lit. "what is the good to you?") from oppressing Job? The phrase "to despise/reject the product of your hands" (v. 3) contributes to the emphasis in this complaint on God as Creator, and therefore on God's obligations to humans as his creatures.

The second and third questions (vv. 4, 5) are absurd questions in the style of a disputation. Job asks why God uses methods that humans have to use because of their limited knowledge. In v. 4 Job asks whether God has the limited human vision that Job has. In v. 5 he asks whether God is subject to the same time limitations that bind Job. The key issue for Job (vv. 4-5) is this human struggle of being in a relationship with God, but not understanding God's motives and goals.

Verse 6 seems to pick up the thread of v. 3a and seeks to amplify Job's understanding of how God is oppressing him. He describes God's presence in suffering yet absence in care in the parallel expressions (chiastic in Hebrew) of "seeking/searching out" his "iniquity/guilt" or "sin." At this stage Job is firmly convinced of his innocence, and also perplexed because he believes that God too knows he is not guilty (v. 7a). Job is thus still acting out of faith, since "the conviction that God knows his true situation is a conviction born of faith."[100] Whereas Job had earlier looked for an umpire to settle his case (9:32-34), he now looks for, or at least longs for, a deliverer or rescuer (v. 7b).

10:8-12: Remember How You Made Me Westermann suggests that the next two sections are an unpacking of the two thoughts of v. 8: "Verse 8 takes up the accusation of v. 3, with vv. 9-12 expanding upon v. 8a and vv. 13-17 expanding upon v. 8b."[101] Verse 8a speaks in very tender and anthropomorphic terms of God's hands shaping and making him. Yet Job finds it anomalous that the one who showed commitment to his creature has now destroyed him or swallowed him up (v. 8b). The juxtaposition of God's creational care and his present activity (at least from Job's perspective) is what Job cannot fathom.

As v. 8a is unpacked, there is, in vv. 9-12, an appeal to a theology of creation, based on the assumption that God's purposes in creating humanity were good. The call on God to "remember" (זְכָר־/*zĕkār*) in v. 9 is significant. Not only is this word frequent in lament psalms, but its function in 7:7 has already been seen. It is asking God to intervene and rescue him on the basis of past commitments. Job seems to imply that in the very act of creating him, God has

---

100. Gutiérrez, *On Job*, 60.
101. Westermann, *Structure*, 52.

committed himself to care for his creation, and so Job is asking God to act on that basis. It would be out of character now for God to destroy his handiwork. Since Job believes that he has been faithful, he now calls on God to be true to the commitment he entered into by creating Job, and so guard Job from premature death. In 14:13, in the beginning of the pivotal hope (14:13-17), we again see Job asking for God to set a time and then remember him. It seems significant that the call on God to remember Job occurs in chapters 7, 10, and 14. Thus, in the midst of the darkest laments in Job and in each speech in the first cycle, Job is still concerned to have his relationship with God restored by having God remember him.

In v. 9 the images of "clay" and "dust" are echoes of the Genesis creation account and highlight Job's earthy fragility as a human being. The process of actually making Job is spoken of metaphorically in v. 10, but the images imply gentle care, as if making a prize-winning cheese.[102] This is reinforced by images of clothing and knitting in v. 11, thus completing the process of making Job. Verse 12 leaves the metaphors behind and thus clarifies their meaning. Here he mentions the gift of life (which he feels is now endangered), steadfast love (חֶסֶד/*ḥesed*), and preserving (or "watching") care.[103] This outlines what Job wants from God his Creator.

10:13-17: Now You Have Destroyed Me These verses unpack the second half of v. 8, "now you have destroyed me altogether" (ESV). Job's claim is that he has been unduly afflicted by God and expresses the darkness of not experiencing God's providence as caring, as if life has been turned upside down. This is evident in how the word שָׁמַר/*šāmar*, "watch," is used with different implications in v. 12b and v. 14a. In v. 12 Job speaks of God's providential, caring "watching" over him, but in v. 14 he describes God spying on him to detect even small mistakes in order to correct him.[104] This captures the tension between the way Job would like God to act toward him and the way he feels God is now treating him.

The language that Job uses here is quite accusatory. As an indication of the depth of his pain, he protests that God had a hidden purpose in view (v. 13); that God is hunting him like a lion hunts its prey and even performs "wonders" (echoing God's wonders in creation) against him (v. 16); and that the witnesses God uses and the trouble/vexation he adds are as if God is sending wave after wave of armed troops against him (v. 17). Against the backdrop of this perceived

---

102. G. Wilson, *Job*, 109, thinks "milk" is a reference to semen, and the cheese possibly an embryo, but they are better understood metaphorically.

103. For a useful study of חֶסֶד/*ḥesed*, see Andersen, "Yahweh, the Kind and Sensitive God."

104. See Hartley, *Book of Job*, 189.

divine activity, Job feels disgraced and afflicted (v. 15c), not only when he sins/ is guilty (vv. 14a, 15a), but even when he is "in the right" (v. 15a ESV, צִדְקִתִּי/ *ṣādaqtî*).

10:18-22: Closing Words of Despair Job's second speech closes in a way reminiscent of his opening outcry (3:11-26) and his brief plea in chapter 7 (7:19). The theme of transitoriness is seen in vv. 18-22, whereby vv. 20-22 take up the theme of chapter 7, while vv. 18-19 point back to chapter 3. Two significant changes are made from that opening salvo in 3:11, 16. First, the onus for his tragic birth is now laid squarely on God, not some mysterious force of destiny. Thus the tone is more accusatory here, as God is addressed directly. Second, the self-lament of chapter 3, "Why have I been born?" has now become, "Why did you bring me out of the womb?" (v. 18a). This wish that he had never been born could not, of course, have been granted, but it does help us to see what is going on in Job's mind. Job is again indulging in wild imaginings. The depth of his despair is driving him to explore any avenue, no matter how impossible. He spoke similarly in wanting to undo his day of birth in chapter 3, and will do so in his request to be hidden in Sheol in 14:13. These courses of action are not seriously proposed, but rather they testify to the pain behind them that has driven Job to such desperation. They are, in the words of J. Gerald Janzen, "imaginative outreaches."[105]

In this section, Job is preoccupied with death. Since this is a complaint or lament, we should not interpret these verses literalistically to suggest that he sees death as desirable. Indeed, the description in vv. 21-22 would preclude us from doing so, with the accumulation of terms for death — "darkness and deep shadow," "gloom like thick darkness," and then a repeat of both "deep shadow" and "thick darkness" (as reflected in ESV). Even his call to be left alone (v. 20), like that of 7:16, is in the context of speech in which he asks God to remember him (v. 9), and he keeps on talking to the seemingly absent God. Given the impossibility of the wish here, Job goes on in v. 20 to ask for some relief in the remaining few days of his life. He still petitions the God he feels is not present.

Another feature of the laments is also seen here. The mention of the grave (v. 19, and implied in "before I go," v. 21) is intended to remind God that no praise or love for God can be declared in the grave, so that God will be moved to answer his petition (see also Ps 88:10-12). This course of action is thus motivated by a desire to stir God into coming to his rescue, which is his ultimate aim.

Thus, in chapter 10, Job is in despair, but he is not giving up. He is still acting out of faith, but his circumstances drive him to accuse God and to ex-

---

105. J. Janzen, *Job*, 125.

plore imaginative possibilities. His aim at this point is not primarily getting relief from his suffering, but rather having his relationship with God restored.

11:1-20: *Zophar*

After the introductory v. 1, Zophar states his fundamental position in vv. 2-6. Verses 7-12 are a discrete unit arguing that the depths of God are beyond human knowing. In the final section, vv. 13-20, Zophar proposes to Job a way forward. This has a strong focus on the reward that will come to the (repentant) righteous, but comes with a closing sting in the tail in v. 20 that outlines the destruction of the wicked. Andersen describes Zophar's platitudes as "flat beer compared to Job's seismic sincerity."[106]

11:1-6: Zophar's Fundamental Position Zophar is a Naamathite (v. 1), whose geographical location is unknown; but, like the other two friends, he is clearly a non-Israelite.

His initial description of Job (v. 2) gives a clear impression of his attitude. He implies that Job is a "man full of talk" (lit. "a man of lips"; Clines suggests "glib talker") who has spoken many words, and his implication is that such a person should not be unanswered (= left uncorrected) or (regarded as being) in the right (יִצְדָּק/*yiṣdāq*). This is filled out in v. 3 when his talk is described as babble or idle talk, or mocking (לְעַג/*lāʿag*, already used by Job in 9:23), so that Job deserves silencing and being shamed. Zophar wrongly thinks that any protest directed to God is to be regarded as mocking God.

Verse 4 sets out Zophar's understanding of Job's pivotal claim — that his teaching or instruction is pure and that he too is clean in God's sight. Both his words and his character are acceptable ("pure," "clean") to God. This verse is not a quotation from Job's words earlier in the dialogue, but Zophar's attempt to sum up the essence of what he hears Job saying.

In vv. 5-6 he moves on to what God might say in response. Zophar has a high view of God's wisdom and understanding (lit. "double in sound wisdom," v. 6b), but suggests that this is a secret kept from Job (v. 6a). However, the interesting assumption Zophar makes is that he is privy to this wisdom, so that he pronounces a verdict on God's behalf against Job. It is clear from the book as a whole (especially 42:7-8) that Zophar is wrongly claiming to speak for God. Zophar tries to have it both ways — to state that God's wisdom is secret, but then to pronounce words on God's behalf without any revelation from him. His

---

106. Andersen, *Job*, 156.

tone is patronizing; he speaks as if he has insider knowledge. There is a great danger in giving spiritual counsel that we presumptuously claim is a message from God when our opinion (however sound) is simply our own view. Since Zophar has attacked both Job's words and his character, a gap emerges between God's verdict (1:8; 2:3) and Zophar's.

If Zophar is measured against the benchmark of his purpose in coming (to comfort and console Job, 2:11), then he fails miserably.[107] This is particularly the case in v. 6c, when Zophar proclaims that Job has been let off with a discount, that God has forgotten some of (partitive *min*) his sin. In other words, the full punishment of his guilt would have to be more than the death of all ten children, all his possessions (which were also symbols of his righteousness), the loss of his wife's support, and the physical agony of the sores to all parts of his body. This, Zophar suggests, is to be let off lightly. The irony of Zophar's observation is that it undercuts his strong view of the doctrine of retribution, which will be filled out in vv. 13-20. In claiming that God has allowed part of Job's guilt to be forgotten (v. 6c), Zophar is surrendering the idea that God justly rewards righteousness and punishes wickedness. He does not explore the concept of mercy, but he fails to explain how this "discount" is compatible with the doctrine of retribution.

11:7-12: The Depths of God Are beyond Human Knowing The governing questions of v. 7 are crucial. Zophar asks Job whether he can think deeply or completely about God. In other words, he is challenging Job about whether he has an exhaustive knowledge of God (and his purposes). Humans can never answer such questions affirmatively.

In vv. 8-9 God's doings are given a fourfold description: higher than the sky/heaven, deeper than the depths of Sheol, longer than the earth/land, broader than the sea. The cumulative effect of these creation terms is to give a picture of God's being and actions that one cannot fathom entirely. The application to Job is that he is undertaking a futile exercise in trying to understand why God is acting as he does. Zophar comments in v. 8, "what can you do? . . . what can you know?" In v. 10 Zophar is responding to some of Job's legal language, asking, if God pierces and imprisons a person, or calls him to a (legal) assembly, who can cause God to turn back?[108] The implication is that Job should refrain from his pursuit of litigation before the consequences become even worse.

Zophar then applies the ideas of vv. 8-10 to the issue of the punitive side

---

107. Campbell, "Book of Job," 23, observes that Zophar "goes straight for the jugular."

108. The verb חָלַף/*ḥālap* can mean "vanish/pass away," as in Job 9:26, or "pierce/pass through," as in 20:24.

of the doctrine of retribution. Like Eliphaz and Bildad before him, Zophar first focuses on the greatness of the God of creation in order to say something to Job about the punishment of the wicked. In v. 11 God's all-embracing wisdom enables him to identify people of worthlessness and iniquity. God will not be fooled. Verse 12 contrasts God's wisdom with that of a hollow-minded or stupid person, who is as unlikely to get a mind or understanding as the colt of a donkey can be born a human being. The reason that Zophar is outlining this to Job is that he believes that Job fits into the categories of a worthless or hollow-minded person.

11:13-20: A Way Forward The flow of thought here is seen in the move from the conditions of vv. 13-14 (If. . . . If . . .) to the positive consequences or results in vv. 15-19, followed by a final warning about the fate of the wicked in v. 20. Many of the words Zophar says are true, but the prologue has already demonstrated that they do not explain Job's circumstances, and are therefore not what Job needs to hear.

This section is not about the righteous being rewarded but rather about the repentant. The conditions of vv. 13-14 are an outline of the repentance that Job must do, according to Zophar. His suggestions reveal his assessment of Job. In v. 13a he urges him to "prepare your heart" (ESV), but the word for "heart," לֵב/*lēb,* is related to the verb used in v. 12, and should probably have the same sense of "understanding."[109] The precise significance of "stretch out your hands toward him [God]" in v. 13b is not clear, but it is at least an exhortation to Job to call on God in prayer. The nature of the prayer is not specified, but the surrounding tone is one of repentance.

Verse 14 is conditional in its form, but the impression already given is that Zophar believes Job is already wicked. The word for Job's hypothetical "iniquity" (אָוֶן/*'āwen*) in v. 14 is the same word Zophar used to describe Job's actual guilt or iniquity in v. 6. The image of v. 14b is one of injustice characterizing his way of life and the community ("tents") over which he had exercised control. Thus Zophar views Job as one who needs to fix up his understanding and repent by putting away his wickedness and changing the injustice of his lifestyle. He urges Job to repent, setting out four steps to repentance in vv. 13-14 (fix up your understanding; stretch out your hands to him in prayer; put away the sin in your hand; and allow no injustice to dwell in your tent). Only if Job does all this will the glowing pictures of vv. 15-19 come to fruition.

---

109. The word לֵבָב/*lēbāb* will be used by Job in the sense of "understanding" in 12:3. The Hiphil of כּוּן/*kûn* can have the sense of "fix," "make firm," or "prepare," and Zophar's exhortation most likely means "fix up your understanding."

Having stated his view strongly, Zophar proceeds to clothe it in apparent niceties as he ponders the restoration of a repentant sufferer. The images of v. 15 are about security and self-respect in the community. The fear mentioned here is most likely the fear of other human beings, not of God. Verse 16 adds that the dark times of the past will then soon be forgotten. This contrast between Job's present and his future circumstances is so glaring that it is like juxtaposing darkness and the midday sun (v. 17). Even the darker times of Job's future will be so much brighter than the present. The key words of v. 18 are "security/trust" and "hope." It is an idyllic picture of a reversal of Job's circumstances of fear and despair. It is reinforced in v. 19 by the vision of "stretching out" (parallel to "sleeping/resting" in v. 18) without fear (again of other humans), and many people seeking his presence.

So, while vv. 15-19 may give the initial impression that Zophar views Job positively, all of this restoration is dependent on Job's "necessary" turning from his wickedness in vv. 13-14. One final indication of Zophar's real attitude is evident in v. 20, when he reverts to some traditional statements about the destruction of the wicked. Zophar appears to believe that Job is currently one of the wicked. Zophar is half right, for God does give blessings of hope, security, and peace to his people, but God also allows unpredictable and seemingly unfair suffering. He is also wrong in thinking that the way forward for Job is to repent.

Zophar seems the least sympathetic and compassionate of the three friends. Eliphaz at least wondered if this might be a temporary setback. Bildad tried to distinguish between the greater guilt of Job's children and his lesser guilt. With Zophar all of these subtleties are lost, as he insists that Job is even getting off lightly. Since Job is suffering, he must be a sinner indulging in folly and wickedness.[110]

12:1-25: Job

In this closing speech of the first round, Job begins by addressing the friends. This is explicit in vv. 2-3, and they still appear to be his audience in 13:2, 4-12. God is spoken about in the third person (e.g., 12:4). The first section, 12:2-6, deals with the issues raised by the prospering of the wicked and the affliction of righteous Job. There is a focus on the created world in vv. 7-11/12, but the key issue is signaled in v. 9b — that the hand of the Lord has done all this. Verses 12 and 13 only loosely belong to their subsections, but have a lot in common

---

110. Clines, *Job 1–20*, xl.

and are perhaps hinge verses. Verses 13/14-25 examine God's active control of and involvement in the world.

12:1-6: The Wicked Prosper but I Am Suffering Job starts somewhat sarcastically in v. 2, but the following verses disclose that this has come from his deep pain and genuine questioning. Job is in effect saying that they do not have exclusive domain on knowledge of how God works in his world. This flows naturally into v. 3a, where Job claims that he has "understanding" (lit. "heart," but related words mean "understanding" in 11:12-13). In the rest of 12:3 Job implies that what the friends have spoken is fairly commonplace rather than particularly insightful. Job does not need to be persuaded about the doctrine of retribution — which is why he still cannot understand what God is doing.

Thus Job repeats the core of his complaint in v. 4. Rather than being held in the honor that befits a righteous person, Job has become an object of derisive laughter. This dilemma is exacerbated whenever Job recalls his previous relationship with God. What Job longs for is the time when he would call out to God and God would answer. In other words, his core request is for a restored relationship. This loss of a right relationship with God is exacerbated by the intellectual enigma of how God is allowing one who is just and blameless to be mocked. It is as if the rules governing the universe have changed.

If v. 4 sets out Job's existential puzzle and intellectual enigma, then vv. 5-6 push past Job's personal situation to show that the issue is much wider. Job points to some realities that are hard to square with the doctrine of retribution as espoused by his friends. In v. 5 those who are comfortable are seemingly unrighteous in that they have only contempt for those who slip into disaster or misfortune, assuming that it is a consequence of their sin. Verse 6 is even clearer, for here robbers and those who provoke God enjoy lives characterized by peace and security. The exact meaning of "who bring their god in their hand" is not clear, but it is a way of describing the group of people who provoke God. It could refer to idolatry, or to something carried in or wielded by the hand (e.g., a weapon) in which these God-provokers trust. It might also be that "hand" is simply an image of power (common in Hebrew), and so could refer to those who control their own destiny as if they were gods. Of course, vv. 5-6 indicate that Job sees the problem as not simply that he is suffering unfairly. There is a broader issue that some who are wicked are prospering. Thus even if Job's suffering is taken away, Job is insisting that the problem is still present, if less acutely so.

12:7-12: God's Hand in Creation Verses 7-11 are an excursus on nature, and they seem to make a common point. In vv. 7-8 the animals, the birds, the earth (or, on the basis of a slight emendation, the bushes of the earth), and the fish all will teach and declare the key truth of v. 9b, "that the hand of Yahweh [the LORD] has done this." This verse is (inadvertently?) highlighted by being the only occurrence of the name Yahweh in the dialogue. Perhaps the author's real theological convictions break through at this point.

What, however, is the "this" that God has done (v. 9b)? There is no new action or event introduced in vv. 7-9, so presumably it is what Job has been talking about previously. In vv. 4-6 Job has been pointing to his own reversal and to the prospering of the wicked. In other words, Job is focusing on the way the world is run, with all its apparent anomalies. All the activity that happens in the world is done by the hand of God.

This leads nicely on to another nature picture (v. 10) of God as the creator and sustainer. In this way the hand of God is active in giving life and breath. Now that the theological principle has been established, it is applied in vv. 11-12. Just as the palate is designed to discriminate among foods and to reveal what is tasty or bland, so the ear is designed by God to test words (v. 11). The words that need to be tested are introduced in v. 12. Habel rightly understands the force of these words by translating them as a question — "Does wisdom come with age, as you say, and understanding with longevity?"[111] Job is challenging the friends, who are appealing to age-old traditions, that God always rewards the righteous and punishes the wicked. Job is urging them to test those beliefs in the light of his situation (v. 4) and the prospering of the wicked (vv. 5-6), all of which have come from Yahweh himself (v. 9). In arguing like this, Job is suggesting that they need to look behind their past dogmas to the God who is both the source of all wisdom as well as the one in charge of all activity.

12:13-25: God's Active Control of the World If v. 12 is to be understood as a question, then v. 13 is the foundation of the answer. It literally reads "with him is wisdom and might; he has counsel and understanding." The "him" is not specified, but v. 9b governs all of the previous section, outlining the activity of God. Thus most translations rightly translate v. 13 as "with God is wisdom and might, etc." Once it is seen that this is a response to the question of v. 12, it emerges that Job is urging the friends to go behind their traditions back to the God who gives wisdom and understanding. Such a desire may well ground Job's words in 13:3, where he longs to speak directly to God. This truth is so fundamental that it is repeated in slightly different words in v. 16.

---

111. Habel, *Book of Job*, 212. So also NJPS, NRSV; cf. ESV. The NIV translates it as a question implying the answer yes. If it is to be translated as a statement, it seems to be citing the friends' view, perhaps even being a virtual quotation, with the goal of assessing it.

The remainder of vv. 14-25 deal with the sovereign activity of God in all areas and situations of life. Indeed, the whole chapter now can be seen as unpacking the notion that God is sovereignly controlling his creation. It is a much bigger view of God than the friends will allow. So in vv. 4-6 Job is insisting that the friends' narrow formulation of the idea of retribution needs to be rethought in the light of a reality test. Verses 7-12 insist on the same rethink (v. 12) without diminishing the role of God (v. 9). Now in vv. 13-25 God is pictured as both the source of wisdom (v. 13) and the one who is actively involved in ruling all aspects of his world (vv. 14-25).

God's rule is first seen in his ability to intervene in the human world. He can tear down something built by people (v. 14a) and he can restrict a person's freedom or circumstances (v. 14b), which may be a reference to how Job feels that God has treated him (a different verb, but perhaps the same idea as in 3:23). The images of v. 15 refer to the drastic realities of drought caused by lack of rain (v. 15a) and the destruction caused by floodwaters (v. 15b). If v. 14 focused on God intervening in history and society, then v. 15 explores the impact on humanity of God intervening as Creator.

Verse 16 repeats the assertion of v. 13 that God is both powerful and wise. He knows what to do and is able to bring it about. The second part of v. 16 focuses on two groups of people, the deceived and the deceivers, but does not bother to identify who is in each group. This injects a note of ambiguity as vv. 17-21 describe groups such as counselors, judges, kings, priests, elders, and princes without clarifying whether they are best understood as deceivers or deceived.

Verses 17-21 clearly focus on God's activity in the human world, and the theme is one of reversal caused by God's intervention. This is seen in v. 17 with judges, who were sources of wisdom, being made fools, and the (well-regarded) advisers being humiliated by being stripped. Verse 20 echoes this with the elders losing their discernment (like the judges), and the "trusted" (advisers) being deprived of their tool of trade (their speech). The kings of v. 18 have the tight restrictions they imposed on others loosened, but then have a waistcloth (perhaps a symbol of serving, but at least one of effort) bound on them. In v. 19 priests who are both dressed finely and would lead processions are now stripped and themselves led away. The mighty are overcome by God's power. The kings and the mighty are both reflected in v. 21, where both princes and the strong suffer reversal, with the princes treated with contempt and the strong[112] so vulnerable

---

112. אֲפִיקִים/'ăpîqîm should be read as "the strong" (cf. KJV) rather than "channels" or "streams," which it means in Ps 18:15 (MT 16); Joel 1:20. *HALOT* 1:78 lists homographs to cover both meanings.

before their opponent's power that their belt can be undone, making them no longer ready for battle.

The great opposites of darkness and light form an envelope around the remaining verses (vv. 22, 25), with the theme of active reversal in nature being especially prominent in v. 22. God determines the destiny and circumstances of the nations in history (v. 23), both in making them great and influential, as well as destroying them and leading them off the world scene. What happens at this national level is then reflected in vv. 24-25 when the leading individuals of the nations (or perhaps "the land") have their understanding or wisdom taken from them, and they wander away aimlessly and stagger like a drunkard.[113] Throughout this section, the theme is not that God is capricious, but simply that he cannot be confined to the categories that Job's friends are espousing.

13:1-28: Job

Verses 1-12 make up the first section, with vv. 1-3 being a statement of Job's stance and vv. 4-12 his rebuke of the friends. It is harder to know where the section that begins in v. 13 ends, and where the subsequent breaks have to be made.[114] In vv. 15-16 he is speaking about God in the third person; in v. 20 he is speaking to God in the second person. Yet it is not entirely clear where this transition happens. Most likely vv. 18-19 are also addressed to the friends, which would divide the second half of the chapter into vv. 13-19 (addressing the friends) and vv. 20-28 (addressing God).

13:1-3: Job's Stance Verse 1 appears to sum up what Job has said in chapter 12. Job asserts that this was his genuine experience as he has seen and heard all the happenings mentioned there. In v. 2 Job addresses the friends (see also vv. 4-5). He considers their limited ideas, which preclude what Job has just seen and heard, and insists that he has mastered those ideas as well. Job proposes a direction different from that of his friends because of this wider reality that he has been confronted with. He announces his plan to argue his case (v. 3), which has a primary reference to settling a legal dispute.[115] This is a clear and unambiguous statement of his intention.

---

113. Many note that both vv. 21a and 24b are present in Ps 107:40.

114. See the suggestions in Habel, *Book of Job*, 226; Hartley, *Book of Job*, 222; and Clines, *Job 1–20*, 285-87.

115. Andersen, *Job*, 164, notes, however, that the use of the same root in Isa 1:18 includes the desire not to win the suit, but to reconcile the offending party by sorting out the misunderstanding.

13:4-12: Job's Rebuke of His Friends A clear contrast is drawn between the stances of Job (v. 3, "But I") and his friends (v. 4, "But you"). This change reflects the content of vv. 4-12, where Job now outlines and critiques the approach of the friends.

A physician comes to help and to heal, but since Job's friends whitewash rather than address the problem, they are worthless, and they have used lies (v. 4). The depth of Job's emotional pain is evident in v. 5, when he asks for silence from the friends, a call that he will repeat in v. 13. We might have expected Job at this point to say that each word they utter adds to his pain, but he observes rather that whatever they say results in them being less and less wise (see Prov 17:28). From Job's perspective, and ultimately from God's (Job 42:7-8), their lack of wisdom is seen in their refusal to take into account Job's argument and pleadings. These very things are what Job has outlined in chapter 12 and referred to here in 13:1. So in v. 6 he asks the friends to listen to his pleas.

While v. 7 is in question form, it is really an accusation of what Antony Campbell calls "the ultimate sin that any theologian must fear"[116] — speaking falsely and deceitfully for God. This is the exact charge that God will finally bring against them (42:7-8). Verse 8 speaks of showing partiality or favor (lit. "lifting up his face") to God, even arguing his case for him. They are more concerned with defending God rather than finding out what is true. Verse 9 then addresses how the friends might go when God calls them to account. Job's question in v. 9a has the clear answer of no from Job's corner, and he somewhat cheekily suggests in v. 9b that their only chance would be to try to deceive God, as they have tried in the debate to deceive humans. This leads in vv. 10-11 to the certainty of God's overwhelming rebuke of the friends. Verse 12 rounds off this section with two parallel statements that describe the worthlessness and emptiness of their seemingly wise words. They have the form of wisdom (proverbs, maxims) but no substance. Like anything built out of ashes or clay, their "wisdom" will not last.

13:13-19: Addressing the Friends As in v. 5, Job calls for silence from the friends (v. 13) and wants to boldly pursue truth as he comes before God. He is fearful of the consequences, realizing that his course of action may place his life at stake (v. 14b; the image of v. 14a seems also to be an image of self-destruction). Yet he is willing to accept the consequences of his approach (v. 13b). The power of God looms large in Job's thinking and makes the prospect of litigation very daunting.

Verses 15 and 16 seem pivotal for understanding Job's current mind-set. Verse 15a has been variously translated, for example, NIV "Though he slay me, yet will I hope in him"; NRSV "See, he will kill me; I have no hope." The

116. Campbell, "Book of Job," 24.

difference is based on the Hebrew text, where the Ketib is לֹא/*lō'*, "not/no," but the Qere is לוֹ/*lô*, "in him."[117] The different readings result either in Job hoping in him or having no hope, while the first part of the verse becomes either a hypothetical statement or a statement of fact, respectively. Clines concludes that "only one's sense of the context can determine an answer."[118] The context suggests the more positive reading ("I will hope *in him*"), yet one that retains a tension between Job's hope and despair. Verses 4-12 are an extended rebuke to the friends for their view that God would not vindicate him. In such a setting, Job is unlikely to concede that he has no hope before God. Yet, while Job expresses his fear of approaching God (vv. 13b-14; later v. 21), that fear does not deter Job, and he presses for litigation in the remainder of the chapter. He has an awareness of the risk and yet a hope for vindication. This leads on to chapter 14, which contains elements of both outreaching hope and deep hopelessness. This note of at least guarded hope is echoed in the possibility of deliverance in v. 16. Although he is not sure that he will be delivered, he knows his deliverance, if it comes, must come from God. This would lead to the following translation of v. 15: "Though he may slay me, I will hope in him; even so [i.e., even though he may slay me], I will present my case to his face."

Having prepared his case (מִשְׁפָּט/*mišpāṭ* — v. 18), his goal is to be vindicated or shown to be righteous. However, v. 18b is best translated as "I know that I am in the right." Being in the right will not necessarily lead to vindication, but this is another affirmation of his innocence before his friends, and it is a necessary precondition of being vindicated. In v. 19, still talking to the friends, he calls for litigation by way of legal charges being brought against him (רִיב/ *rîb*, "contend," has this legal sense). The end result is that if the charges are established, Job will be silent. The connection between silence and death is a temporal one — he will no longer dispute with God until the time of his death. Job has already suggested (v. 5) that the way of wisdom for the friends is to remain silent. Thus it seems that the outcome of the litigation, in conformity with Israel's legal practice, will be determined by who is silenced at the end.[119]

13:20-28: Addressing God At v. 20 Job turns to address God, and this further reveals Job's perception that only God can give or withhold a solution to his di-

---

117. The Qere is followed by the Vulgate and Syriac. Gordis, *Book of Job*, 144, notes that both the Ketib and the Qere are attested in the Mishnah. My translation follows the Qere reading, on the basis that it is more difficult (and therefore more likely to be original) to read a note of hope in the context of despair. Smick, "Job," 922-23, prefers to translate "If he slays me, I will not wait" (but defend his ways, being sure God would vindicate him). Similarly, Habel, *Book of Job*, 224-25.

118. Clines, *Job 1–20*, 312.

119. Köhler, *Hebrew Man*, 159-60.

lemma. Verses 20-27, often classified form-critically as a lament, are a transitional unit to the complaint to God in chapter 14. Job is still thinking in courtroom terms in 13:20-21, asking for God to ensure a fair trial by not overwhelming him with his power (lit. "hand") or terrifying/intimidating him. The litigation setting is still apparent in vv. 22-23, with v. 22 outlining the court process of speech and reply, and v. 23 outlining what Job wants God to prove in court. Job is not denying that he is a sinner in v. 23 (he admits sin in v. 26), but is challenging God to prove that the number of his sins warrants the punishment he has received.

The lament tone emerges more clearly from v. 24 onward, when Job moves on from the legal solution to his existential anguish. His desire here is more to restore a relationship than to win a case. Beginning with the typical lament question "why," he reveals what is hardest about his plight. It is not the physical suffering or the financial losses, but rather the absence of God's care (hiding his face), and God counting him as an enemy. In other words, he longs for a restoration of his friendship with God (v. 24). The images of a driven leaf and dry chaff (v. 25) are of something insignificant or insubstantial, blown about by a powerful wind. In more specific language in v. 26, he charges God with prescribing ("write" has this sense in Isa 10:1) bitter things against him, and giving to him the consequences of the sins of his youth. His present oppressive situation is then outlined in images of imprisonment and restriction of movement (v. 27). This imagery, together with v. 24a, will be taken up by Elihu in 33:10-11. The final, more reflective image in v. 28 is of a person without human dignity, like something rotting away or destroyed by moths.

14:1-22: Job

Habel discerns two major units in this chapter (vv. 1-6 and 7-22) with each one centering on key questions (vv. 3-4, 13-17).[120] Verses 1-6 focus on the brevity of human life, while vv. 7-22 explore the issue of hope. There are three sections in vv. 7-22 — vv. 7-12, 13-17, and 18-22. The first and third of these point to the lack of hope for humanity, but in the center of these two sections is Job's imaginative exploration of hope, which is the real focus of the chapter. This chapter is also complicated by a juxtaposition of bold nature analogies and traditional axioms about mortals, thus importing a tension or dialectic between a pessimistic, orthodox tradition and his bold new theme of hope. This tension integrates well with his complaint to God, which blossoms when faith in one's traditions conflicts with the reality of one's experience.

120. Habel, *Book of Job*, 236.

Chapters 12–14 show the same progression of thought that has been evident in Job's two previous speeches. Both those speeches moved from the pursuit of litigation to the pressing of a lament or complaint to God. So here there is a progression from the pursuit of litigation in chapter 13 to the complaint of chapter 14.

14:1-6: The Brevity of Human Life As in chapter 7, Job here laments his pain against the backdrop of human sorrow in general, made more acute by the finality of death. This section opens with the generic subject אָדָם/*'ādām*, "man/humanity," which might suggest his links with the "ground" (אֲדָמָה/*'ădāmâ*) and thus his limited and weak nature. The three subsequent phrases ("born of a woman," "few of days," and "full of trouble") underscore human limitations. The phrase "few of days" seems to be an intentional reversal of the standard description of a happy life as "full of days" (Gen 25:8; 1 Chr 29:28). The analogies of a flower and a shadow (v. 2) also illustrate the brevity of human life, as both do not last long.

In v. 3 Job turns to direct address of God in bold questions. Here the surveillance motif (7:8, 17-20; 10:6, 14; 13:27) resurfaces, seemingly describing God watching over human beings in general. Yet Job's real focus is on his situation, not that of a "typical human." This can be seen clearly when, after talking about how God treats humans in general, Job asks, "Do you bring *me* into judgment with you?" A number of versions and translations have emended "me" to "him,"[121] but the tone of the rest of this poem seems to support the view that Job, despite speaking generically, has his situation in mind all along. On either reading, the issue in v. 3 is the existential tension between his theoretical understanding of God and humanity, and his present bitter experience. This is Job's pivotal question at the center of vv. 1-6.

This suggests a way of interpreting the next verse. Verse 4 seems to say that not even God can make a person pure, for humans are impure by nature. However, the complaint context of v. 3 suggests that this is an emotive outburst, rather than the rational conclusion to a closely reasoned argument.[122] In vv. 5-6 Job's apparent focus is on humanity in general, and he petitions God to turn his

---

121. The LXX, Vulgate, and Syriac have emended "me" to "him" (as does the NIV), which makes for a neater parallelism, although the MT ("me," followed by ESV and NRSV), as the harder reading, probably ought to be preferred — if it yields good sense. Gordis, *Book of Job*, 147, suggests that the MT could be maintained because Job "frequently oscillates between his own tragic lot and that of all men," as in 3:22-26.

122. Against Hartley, *Book of Job*, 232, who seems to suggest that Job is asking a theoretical question of God as to why he expects man to be flawless and why he holds him responsible for every wrong he has done. On this verse see Zink, "Uncleanness and Sin."

gaze away. Again, the emotive tone of the petition, as well as the lament setting, suggests that he is trying to reconcile his faith with his own experience, being firmly committed to give full weight to both. Thus v. 6 is not just a request that God leave him alone, for he affirms in v. 5 that this same God is sovereign and the only one who can help. Instead, Job is protesting that God is treating him as a "hired man," that is, in a way unsuited to his limitations, or perhaps even his true nature or righteousness.

14:7-12: The Lack of Hope for Humans This section unpacks human limitations by contrasting the hope of new life of a tree with the lack of such hope for humans. The word תִּקְוָה/*tiqwâ,* "hope," occurs in v. 7 and in eleven other places in Job, more than in any other book. It will reappear later in this chapter — here in v. 7 a tree has hope; but God destroys human hope in v. 19. Hope is crucial to Job's struggle to persevere in faith. Given our fragile ecological context, we do not normally think of a tree having "hope," but here it refers to the prospect of regeneration, of being able to come to life again. In vv. 8-9 a tree may appear to be lifeless, but when it is touched by water it can spring to life and put forth new growth.

In v. 10 the word for "man" is גֶּבֶר/*geber,* which often emphasizes his strength and virility in contrast to the earthiness and limitedness of אָדָם/*'ādām* in v. 1. If so, the word is used ironically, for even in their strength, humans are depicted as not having the opportunities that are open to a resilient tree. While humans cannot rise, a tree can sprout forth new life. A person's anguish must therefore be resolved while she or he is still alive; it cannot be deferred. Job is working with the common wisdom assumption that this life is where it all happens, and so the idea of survival after death is not appealed to as a way of resolving the crisis. This focus on the time between birth and death has implications for reading vv. 13-17. The tension in Job is crying out for an urgent resolution.

The image of v. 11 is not one of seasonal waters failing, but a final failure when a stream changes course or when an earthquake cuts off a feeder spring. It is a picture of irreversible vanishing, a drying up for good. This leads into the image in v. 12 of death as sleep, but a permanent sleep from which one cannot wake — "till the heavens are no more."

14:13-17: Job's Imaginative Exploration of Hope The place of vv. 13-17 within the chapter is important. Some see the possibility of a revitalization after death explored in vv. 13-17, and then rejected as not possible in vv. 18-22.[123] Habel's

---

123. Bergant, "Anthropological Traditions," 155, suggests that the waw adversative at the beginning of v. 18 means that the last section of the chapter "expresses despair of any hope, even

structural analysis, however, shows that this is the pivotal hope of the poem in vv. 7-22, so that it is bracketed and highlighted (rather than overruled) by the surrounding sections.[124]

Job here expresses his wishful longing to the God he knows is in charge, but whose ways he does not fully understand. The standard request to God is to be protected from Sheol (the place of the dead), but Job subverts that by asking to go to Sheol for protection (v. 13). He longs so much for relief from his present situation (God's "wrath") that he is exploring the most unlikely of possibilities.[125] He is not asking to die, but rather to be hidden for a period of time and then set free from Sheol, which he has already said is not possible (7:9-10; 10:21).

However, Job's core longing still has not changed, for he wants God to "remember" him (v. 13). As in 7:7 and 10:9, this call to remember, that is, to care for him on the basis of his past commitment as his Creator, is what Job desperately wants. It is also the typical cry of the lament psalms, where it is rightly understood as a cry of faith. A further indication that Job is still clinging to faith here is that God is the one who is addressed (second person singular verb forms), as the only one who can solve the problem. It is an appeal *to* God *against* divine wrath. Job clings to the thought of God's loving care, even if that involves grabbing at straws, doing so because he believes that God will, in time, vindicate him.[126]

At the beginning of v. 14 even Job concedes that his approach is anomalous, as he asks whether a person can live again once one dies. Some see in his answer the hope of a personal resurrection as he speaks of waiting for חֲלִיפָתִי/ *ḥălîpātî* to come. This term has been variously translated as "my renewal" (NIV, ESV), "my replacement" (NJPS, Habel), or "my release" (NRSV, Gordis, Dhorme). It commonly has the idea of being released from hard service, and is used to speak of replacement troops relieving battle-weary ones. In translating it as "renewal," some understand it as the release from the hard service of this life for a new vital life in a restored body.[127]

---

that suggested in the previous section." On this view, even if the thought of resurrection was present in v. 14, there is in vv. 18-22 no hope expressed in resurrection.

124. Habel, *Book of Job*, 236. Andersen, *Job*, 170, suggests that here we find the author's real convictions, flanked before and after by contrasting opinions, which he rejects. He thus sees these verses as the high point of the speech, and reaffirming the faith previously expressed.

125. Zimmerli, *Man and His Hope*, 23, describes it as "an impossible desire."

126. Hartley, *Book of Job*, 236, comments, "the deep-flowing current of Job's genuine trust in God surfaces again. He appeals to God's mercy as the way of escape from God's wrath."

127. For example, Andersen, *Job*, 169, who argues that the continuation of personal life with God after death was part of Israel's distinctive faith from the beginning. See also Alexander, "Old Testament View."

However, while the concept of personal resurrection might solve Job's struggle (and does so in the context of the whole Bible), it is better to see that Job has no realistic hope of resurrection here. This is just Job's dream of a provocative alternative, as Job indulges in lateral thinking, "imaginative outreach," rather than a realistic hope.[128] It is tempting for Christians, for whom the resurrection from the dead is a central cause of hope, to read back into Job's use of the word "renewal" more than Job had in mind.

In v. 15 Job himself indicates what he means by "renewal" — it refers to a restoration of his relationship with God. What Job longs for here is a reestablishment of reciprocal communication between God and him, which is another way of asking God to remember him. It reveals what Job is missing most, rather than what he realistically expects will happen. Job's faith is evident in that his hope is to have his relationship with God restored, rather than regaining his possessions or status or health.

The opening phrase of v. 16, "For then" (NRSV, ESV), would imply a continuation of Job's wishful thinking, as he dreams of experiencing God's attention as blessing.[129] Job longs for God to pay such caring attention to him ("number my steps," v. 16a) that he would no longer be punished for any sin, transgression, or iniquity (vv. 16b-17). God's treatment of him would be relational and supportive, rather than condemnatory and punitive.

14:18-22: The Lack of Hope — Again The theme of apparent hopelessness reappears in vv. 18-22. However, what we have here is a reminder of Job's present anguish and of his struggle to keep his hope alive in that setting. Verse 18 begins with a disjunctive conjunction ("But"). However, this does not necessarily deny the hope of the previous section. The despair of this section is to be read alongside the projections of hope of vv. 13-17. Lament is not about logical sequence, but rather flows with a raw and often desperate honesty.

Verses 18 and 19 contain four analogies from nature that describe human hopelessness. The mountain steadily erodes, and rocks are dug out and taken away. As the years go on, less mountain and fewer rocks are found. Verse 19 speaks of water wearing down rocks and eroding soil, while the end of the verse draws out the point: "so you destroy the hope of mortals" (NRSV).

Job's dilemma is expressed in the form of a complaint (v. 20). He complains that God prevails "forever" — presumably in a way that cannot be re-

---

128. Habel, *Book of Job*, 242, describes it as "a provocative alternative"; Clines, *Job 1-20*, 338, calls it "an impossible dream"; Hartley, *Book of Job*, 238, uses the language of "utopian fantasies."

129. For a different view see Hartley, *Book of Job*, 236, 237, who opts for the translation "But now," meaning that Job is coming back to reality.

versed. The reference to God changing his countenance is not clear (it might refer to rigor mortis, or to a change of face due to a change within).[130] In vv. 21-22 those who are afflicted by God, in anticipation of their imminent death, become so self-focused (v. 22 — only feeling their own pain, and mourning their own loss) that they do not care ("know," v. 21) whether their own children prosper or suffer. They are consumed by their hopelessness and isolation as they linger in the face of death. It is this conflict of ideas, experiences, and hopes that causes Job's anguish. Yet he does not choose letting go of God as the way out.

15:1–21:34: Round Two

15:1-35: Eliphaz

This chapter is made up of three sections. Eliphaz first introduces his rebuke of Job (vv. 1-6). Verses 7-16 outline the essence of his dispute with Job, with vv. 7-10 dealing with the source of authority for Job's ideas, while vv. 11-16 discuss how God views and treats human beings. The final section (vv. 17-35) concerns the fate of the wicked.

15:1-6: A Rebuke of Job Eliphaz begins by rebuking Job for the choices he has made and the effect his words will have (vv. 1-6). The tone is one of mild correction since it begins with a series of questions (vv. 2-3) rather than direct accusations. He raises the inappropriateness of a wise person (Job has claimed to be wise in 12:3) expressing knowledge that is little more than hot air. Ironically, Elihu will later pick up and apply to himself a very similar expression (32:18-19). It is an image of emptiness, of lacking substance.[131] He suggests that Job's words are unprofitable and can do no good (v. 3), a view that God will overrule (42:7-8).

Eliphaz argues that the effect (even if not the intention) of Job's words is to do away with the fear of God and to slight (so Clines) or hinder meditation before God (v. 4).[132] He is the only one of the three friends to refer to the fear of God (the words "of God" are not in the Hebrew text, but are inserted properly

---

130. See Hartley, *Book of Job*, 239 n. 5.

131. Contra Clines, *Job 1–20*, 340, 347, who translates רוּחַ דַעַת/*da'at rûah* as "violent notions," assuming a violent wind is being spoken of in 8:2. He is suggesting that Job's words are not sober or restrained enough for Eliphaz.

132. The root שִׂיחַ/*śyh* can mean "complain," as in Job 7:11, 13, but that does not fit the sense here.

to give the sense), and his concern here is that Job's attitude is undermining the proper attitude of respecting God as God, both for himself and others.

Eliphaz concludes that Job's words show his error (vv. 5-6). This is made clearest in v. 6, which parallels his mouth declaring Job wicked (or "condemning him," the Hiphil of עשׁר/*rš'*) and his lips giving evidence against him. The clarity of this verse can then help us to understand v. 5. It could be rendered "your mouth teaches [in the sense of "makes clear"] your iniquity" (cf. NRSV, ESV) or "your iniquity teaches [in the sense of "instructs"] your mouth" (cf. NIV, Clines, Gordis), but on either translation it is Job's words (as in v. 6) that are linked with folly. Verse 5b on its own could be neutral ("crafty, shrewd" can be negative as in Gen 3:1 or positive as in Prov 1:4), but in the context it appears to have a negative thrust. Eliphaz believes that Job has spoken wrongly, and in a way that will cause great harm.

15:7-16: How God Views and Treats Humans Here Eliphaz challenges Job's authority to speak as he does. He explores a number of possible justifications that Job might offer, and rejects each in turn. In v. 7 he asks whether Job has some primacy in creation, echoing Prov 8:22-31 (especially vv. 22, 25). If Job were present at creation (an impossible scenario), then and only then would he able to pontificate with such certainty about how the world is run.

The second possible justification is that he may have access to God's mind and purposes if he were present in the heavenly council (v. 8a). This too is impossible for a human being.

The third possibility — and seemingly the real issue for Eliphaz — is that Job might think that he has information that others do not have. He asks this in two ways: Do you limit wisdom to yourself? (v. 8b); What do you know that we do not know? (v. 9). The first of these implies that Job denies there is (full?) wisdom in anyone other than himself; the second asks the crucial question of how Job claims to know things that the friends do not. While there is an apparent defensiveness in Eliphaz's words, it is a very natural question. Eliphaz responds to this issue in v. 10, appealing to the body of the sages (also in v. 18), in some ways reminiscent of Bildad's appeal to tradition in 8:8-10.

His analysis of Job's response is evident in vv. 11-13. He believes that Job should be satisfied with what he already has, rather than searching for some further answers. What he already has includes the comforts or consolations of God or the words of his friends, optimistically described as dealing gently with Job. In other words, in the midst of a crisis like Job's, sufferers need to accept the general care of God (v. 11a) and the specific attempts by their friends to support them (v. 11b). It is not right to look for some special intervention by God. Job's desire to grab at something more is evidence of his hubris, which is filled out by

Eliphaz as the core of Job's being (his heart) taking him away; his eyes flashing (with anger or rage?) and his turning his spirit toward (in the sense of "against") God (vv. 12-13a). The evidence for all of this pride is the words that Job allows to emerge from his mouth (v. 13b). Disputing with God is unacceptable to Eliphaz.

Eliphaz buttresses his argument by some general reflections on the human condition (vv. 14-16) followed by his reflections on the fate of the wicked (vv. 17-35). The phrase "one born of woman" (v. 14) is simply another description of a human being, rather than implying anything unclean about women. Thus he asserts (by a question) that no human being can be pure or clean (זכה/*zkh* has overtones of being justified before God, as in Ps 51:7 [MT 8]; Job 25:4) or righteous. He then develops an *a minore ad majus* argument (from the lesser to the greater) in vv. 15-16. Since God does not trust (in the sense of regarding as entirely blameless) his holy ones (the parallelism suggests angelic beings), and the heavenly beings have polluted the heavens (the sphere in which these beings operate), then how much less will God regard any human being as pure and uncorrupted (v. 16). Eliphaz is not saying in v. 16 that Job in particular is abominable or unjust, but is rather asserting that this is the condition of each human being, so that no human can come before God with a clean slate. Job cannot take the stance before God that he is attempting since his human actions disqualify him from being entirely innocent.

15:17-35: The Fate of the Wicked This lengthy section explores the fate of the wicked. Clines comments on the second cycle of speeches, "the description of the wicked serves a different function in the mouth of each of the three friends: for Eliphaz, it is a picture of what Job is not; for Bildad (chap. 18) it is a picture of what Job may become; for Zophar (chap. 20) it is a picture of what Job must avoid."[133] A closer reading of vv. 17-35 suggests that Clines is trying to make too sharp a distinction here, for Eliphaz implies that the description may apply to Job. Rhetorically, it seems to be placed here as a warning to Job, presumably to go no further down this track. Eliphaz addresses Job specifically ("you," v. 17, a singular suffix) and urges him to hear, as if he needs to learn from this description; Eliphaz backs up his claims again with an appeal to the tradition of the sages (vv. 18-19).[134] If this was known to the wise, then Job too would have known it. Therefore, Job is not hearing new teaching but rather teaching that he already knows but needs to act upon.

---

133. Clines, *Job 1–20*, 344.

134. The exact reason for including the detail of v. 19 is not clear. Bartholomew, "Wisdom Books," 122, notes that this suggests that the OT wisdom writers are aware of God's acts in the history of his covenant people.

In any event, Eliphaz vividly describes the negative aspect of the doctrine of retribution (i.e., that God will punish those who do evil) in an elaborate treatment of the fate of the wicked. He extensively describes their fate in vv. 20-24, and again in vv. 27-35. In between these sections is the fundamental reason why Job will fail — because he has taken a stance against God (vv. 25-26). This appears to be the thrust of Eliphaz's address, urging Job to change his approach to God. Eliphaz describes the way of the wicked as stretching out their hand toward (as in v. 13, in the sense of "against") God and defying him (v. 25).[135] This is illustrated by the feeble picture of running to ram God with "a thickly bossed shield" (v. 26, ESV, NRSV; one which has been thickened by additions to strengthen it). Eliphaz's analysis of why the wicked will fall (v. 25) is thus very similar to his understanding of why Job needs to change (vv. 11-13). This makes it likely that Eliphaz is describing the fate of the wicked as a warning to Job.

Verse 20 begins with an emphatic "all" ("all the days of the wicked"), signaling that what is being described is universally true. A wicked person writhes (commonly, as here, "in pain") during all his days, in parallel with the number of his years in which his sufferings are stored up (v. 20). There is some realism in Eliphaz's words, for he acknowledges that there will be, for the wicked, times of prosperity (v. 21) and wealth (v. 29); but where there is mention of ease, the point being made is that it will not last (vv. 21, 29). In v. 21 the "sound of terror" being in his ears implies that he is living in dread of this destruction coming. As in wisdom literature generally, the focus is not on God bringing about the judgment on his wickedness, but rather on the certainty of punishment, however it will come.

The wicked person is on an irreversible descent to a premature death whether by sword (v. 22) or by hunger (v. 23a). There is a foreboding sense that destruction is just around the corner (vv. 21a, 23b). His physical distress and emotional anguish terrify him and undercut his morale, like troops defeated even before they go into battle (v. 24). His previously sumptuous lifestyle (the "fat" of v. 27) and housing (the cities of v. 28 that will become desolate and ruined) will be a thing of the past as his wealth will not last and his possessions will not increase (v. 29). Verse 30 concludes that he will not be able to turn aside from "darkness," a symbol of the coming disasters; his "shoots" (his promise of ongoing life or prosperity) will be burned up; and he will depart by the breath or spirit of his mouth (v. 30).[136]

---

135. The Hitpael of the verb גָּבַר/*gābar*, "to be strong, mighty," is used here and in Job 36:9 to describe a false claim to be great, but in Isa 42:13 of God showing himself to be mighty.

136. The NRSV emends this to read, "their blossom will be swept away by the wind," but the MT should be retained. This appears to be an allusion back to "spirit" and "mouth" in v. 13,

Verses 31-35 reinforce the picture already painted of the fate of the wicked. Verse 31 describes their way as "emptiness," with the principle of retribution evident in that those who trust in emptiness will end up with emptiness. Verses 32-33 portray a similar fate with a succession of agricultural images — his branch will not be green (v. 32b, no life, so no yield of fruit); his grapes will be shaken off the vine before they ripen (v. 33a); and his blossom will be prematurely cast off like that of the olive tree (v. 33b).[137] Verse 32a could be translated, "it [his empty way of life] will be repaid in full before his time" (ESV) or perhaps "his day will not be filled." On either translation it confirms the principle of retribution. The negative application of this principle is restated in v. 34, with the gathering of the godless being barren, not fruitful, and fire consuming what was unjustly gained by bribery. A final verdict is rendered in v. 35 through the imagery of birth — the wickedness and deceit they conceive will grow up in kind to be evil. This concludes the extensive description of the outcome of wickedness. Eliphaz is pointedly firing this shot across Job's bow.

16:1-22: Job

There are three main sections in this chapter, which begins Job's first speech of the second round. In vv. 2-5 Job reflects on the friends as "miserable comforters"; in vv. 6-17 he laments his lot and explores how God is treating him; and in vv. 18-22 he considers the possibility of a heavenly witness.

16:1-5: You Are Miserable Comforters Job reflects not only on Eliphaz's past speech (ch. 15), but on the words of all the friends ("miserable comforters are you all," v. 2). He complains to the friends that have given him nothing new: he has heard many things like these (v. 2a); he also was able to speak as they did (v. 4a). He describes their words as "windy" (lit. "words of spirit/wind"), a concept used by Eliphaz in 15:2 (accusing Job of speaking with "windy knowledge" and filling himself with the east wind). He asks them what has provoked (lit. "sickened") them to answer (v. 3b).[138] Verse 4 gives a scathing description of their "comfort"

---

and thus a further warning to Job. The NIV renders, "the breath of God's mouth will carry him away," but this misses the allusion back to v. 13.

137. G. Wilson, *Job*, 171-73, and Clines, *Job 1-20*, 363, think it refers to the blossom falling off before it is pollinated and so having nothing left to form into fruit. Habel, *Book of Job*, 260, notes that most of the blossom of the olive tree falls before reaching maturity.

138. Although the singular verb תַּעֲנֶה/*taʿănâ,* "you answer," is used in v. 3b, it is likely that Eliphaz is simply representative of the friends, so that all are in view. There may also be a play on

as stringing words together and shaking their heads against Job. This latter image is here not one of nodding in sympathy (as it was in 2:11) but shaking the head in derision (as in the actions of the enemies in Pss 22:7; 109:25). Verse 5 should probably be read as Job speaking tongue in cheek, ironically implying that their words (symbolized by mouth and lips) did not strengthen him or assuage his pain. Alternatively Job could be saying that, if he were in their shoes, he would have used the opportunity to do something useful.[139] However, this does not appear to fit the flow of thought as well, since vv. 2-4 describe their unkind words, and there is no indication of a change of direction here.

16:6-17: Lamenting His Lot Though some commentators (e.g., Clines, Hartley) link v. 6 with the previous section, it seems better to view it as describing his present sufferings and thus linked with what follows. His pain is not eased by speaking (certainly to the friends, perhaps also to God) and is not diminished if he refrains from speaking about it.

The agency of God pervades the whole section and is introduced in v. 7: God has exhausted me (the subject "God" is implied in v. 7, but explicitly mentioned in v. 11); you have driven off (lit. "ravaged" or "devastated") my former friends ("all my company"). This whole section outlines what Job believes God has done to him, and there is a strong accusatory tone. However, it is based on the premise that God is responsible since he is in charge of his world. In vv. 7b-8a this reality of God breaks through when Job leaves off talking to the friends and addresses God directly (a change to second person singular forms; many Bible translations, e.g., ESV, NRSV, try to tidy up the text here). Job complains that God has shriveled him up.[140] Job says that his being shriveled up is evidence or "witness," but he does not say what it is evidence of. Most commentators and Bible translations add the words "against me," perhaps inferred from later in the verse. It could have a broader sense as well that it is evidence of how God has treated Job. Job will pick up the same word "witness" (עֵד/'ēd) in v. 19. Certainly Job's leanness or gauntness testifies against him on the basis of the principle of retribution (v. 8). There is also very strong language in v. 9, where Job claims that God's anger has torn him apart and that God, his adversary/enemy, has hated him. God gnashes his teeth at Job and sharpens the focus of his eyes on him. This is bold language, for in this one verse Job has called God his enemy and claims that God hates him.

The wicked enemies, common in biblical laments, are described as staring

---

words here, for four Hebrew terms have the same root consonants, one of which means "answer" and another "afflict." Job may well be implying both.

139. As Clines, *Job 1–20*, 367, suggests (also RV, NIV).

140. Many commentators, e.g., Gordis, Habel, Clines, and Hartley, translate this verb, which has a core meaning of "seize" as in 22:16, by "shriveled" since it also means "wrinkle."

insolently at Job, physically striking him, and ganging up against him (v. 10). However, they are only a temporary aside and do not distract Job from his complaint that God has given him over to such people (v. 11). The God who should have protected him is the very one who has surrendered him so easily to the ungodly.

God's treatment of Job is filled out further in vv. 12-14. His starting point was one of being "at ease" or untroubled (v. 12a), but the subsequent imagery arises from the language of battle and siege. He is seized and broken into pieces (v. 12); he is God's target and surrounded by archers (vv. 12-13); he has suffered damage to his vital organs (v. 13); he is like a city that has had its walls breached and is overrun (v. 14). The combined effect is that God is actively and relentlessly pursuing Job as a target, inflicting severe punishment on him and utterly overwhelming him.

In vv. 15-17 Job summarizes his present circumstances as a result of all that God has inflicted. The image of sewing sackcloth (used for mourning) on his scaly or scabby skin (the word used for skin implies a scaly surface) is a vivid way of saying that his lamenting has lasted so long that it looks likely to be his enduring condition, and so sackcloth can be sewn on as his permanent clothing (v. 15a). The precise translation of v. 15b is difficult, but it likely refers to Job's present humiliation.[141] Verse 16 reflects the consequences of much weeping and lamenting with the image of dark or death shadows perhaps being the black rings under the eyes. Then v. 17 notes that all this suffering has been despite him having committed no violence, and even though his prayer (perhaps for deliverance?) is clean or pure. In saying this, Job is claiming again that his present level of suffering is undeserved.

16:18-22: The Possibility of a Heavenly Witness In this final section of the chapter, Job is calling for a change in his situation. This is made clear in v. 18 when he calls on the earth (meaning anyone or anything) not to cover up the suffering evidenced by his spilled blood. He also calls on his cry for help and for justice to find no (resting) place where it might stop and be silent. He does not want his situation and his anguish to be forgotten.

At this point Job cries out for a heavenly figure to come to his aid. Whether his call to the witness in heaven is presented as renouncing the fear of God may depend on the identity of the heavenly figure, and at this point commentators are divided.[142] Some see the heavenly figure as God. This is based

---

141. The root עלל/*'ll* has been rendered "insert," "thrust," "bury," "laid"; and his "horn" could be a container or more likely a symbol of his strength, glory, or even body.

142. See the later section "Job and Theology: Job and Resurrection."

on the very reasonable assumption that no other figure could be in authority over God, but it does not fit well with this figure arguing Job's case with God (v. 21). Others therefore conclude that it must be some identifiable figure other than God, although there is little agreement over who this could be. A better way forward is to view this figure as neither God nor someone other than God, but rather a hypothetical figure. As in 9:33, 19:25, and 31:35, this legal figure is an imaginative outreach, a wishful longing explored by Job simply because of the depth of his pain.

The role of this figure (what Job longs for) is to argue the legal case of Job with his God (v. 21). This is why he describes his tears in v. 20b as being God-directed ("my eyes leak/drip to God"), probably in the face of scorn from his friends.[143] The tone of sadness and the prospect of death characterize the closing verse of the chapter, leading appropriately into the rest of Job's speech in chapter 17.

17:1-16: Job

The structure of chapter 17 is much less clear, with vv. 1-2 being a continuation of 16:18-22. Verses 3-4 are addressed to God, while v. 5 is a proverbial saying that could be linked either with what precedes or follows. Verses 6-10 talk about God (v. 6) and then address the friends (v. 10) in a complaint. The speech ends in vv. 11-16 with a description of his present despair.

17:1-2: A Lack of Hope The anguish of the previous verses is filled out in the first two verses of this chapter, both in his expectation of death (v. 1; cf. 16:22) and by the presence of mockers (v. 2; cf. 16:20). He complains in v. 1 that his spirit is broken or destroyed, which leads him to say that he expects an imminent death.[144] As in the lament psalms, the afflicted one is surrounded by mockers who rebel against God, or perhaps conspire against Job.[145]

---

143. There are various renderings of v. 20a, which are well set out by Curtis, "On Job's Witness," 552-53. Since Curtis's article, Hartley, *Book of Job*, 263, has proposed, "Behold, my interpreter is my friend"; while Clines, *Job 1–20*, 371, argues for, "It is my cry that is my spokesman."

144. Literally "my days are extinguished; graves [are] for me." Hartley, *Book of Job*, 265, notes that the plural on "graves" makes it likely to mean "graveyard."

145. The Hiphil participle of מָרָה/*mārâ*, translated "provocation" (ESV, NRSV) or "hostility" (NIV), always connotes rebellion against God except in Deut 21:18, 20 (rebellion against parents), and here — so Eugene Carpenter and Michael A. Grisanti, "מרה," *NIDOTTE* 2:1101. Since it often implies Israel agreeing to rebel, it may have a derived sense here of conspiring against Job.

17:3-5: Speaking to God Job turns here to address God directly, made patent by the use of "you" in v. 4. The thought of v. 3 appears to be a continuation of his imaginary exploration of 16:19, 21, and the exact nature of the pledge or security (indeed, the transaction involved) is not clear. The concept in v. 4a is that God has closed the friends' minds to understanding Job's plight. Since God cannot let the friends triumph over him (v. 4b, probably because that would be unjust), then God himself must find a way to support Job (v. 3).[146] Verse 5 is a wisdom proverb that describes, in a retribution setting, the importance of being a supportive friend. Following on from v. 4, it is likely to be a further reflection on the friends' treatment of Job.

17:6-10: Complaining to the Friends In this section Job is speaking about God ("he," v. 6), and speaking either to the onlookers or more probably the friends ("among you," v. 10; also, in a few manuscripts, "all of you" earlier in the verse). He complains that God, as the one who runs the world, is responsible for his present plight of being belittled and spat at (the phrase could mean "spit in the face" or "spit in front of/in the presence of") by others (v. 6). There have been real physical effects as well, with weakened eyesight (it could be temporary from continual weeping) and loss of body mass (v. 7). He outlines for them in vv. 8-9 how the righteous should respond to such a calamity, implying that the friends have not acted like this. Then he focuses on the friends in v. 10, charging them with lacking wisdom.

17:11-16: Job's Present Despair Job sinks back to despair at the end of the speech. It is as if his life were over ("my days are past") and the things he longed for in the future (his "plans" and "desires") are destined not to be (v. 11). The stark differences between night and day are bleached out as the two become indistinguishable (v. 12). Job explores another imaginative scenario in vv. 13-14, "going over to the dark side," seeking to make his home ("house," "bed," v. 13) in the darkness of Sheol, pretending that he belongs there and is related to the pit and the worm (v. 14). Of course, none is this is realistic, but it is a vivid way (perhaps like 16:19) of expressing his desperation for the hope of a way out (v. 15). Job is searching for a genuine way forward in the midst of his present darkness. He ends on a note of apparent defeat (v. 16), conceding that this would not be feasible.

---

146. For a different way of understanding this verse, see Clines, *Job 1-20*, 393-94, who argues that it is Job's pledge.

18:1-21: Bildad

Bildad's second speech is almost entirely devoted to the fate of the wicked (vv. 5-21), but how it relates to Job is not made explicit. Both Eliphaz and Bildad focus in their first speeches on the nature of God, but in their second speeches they explore the theme of the fate of the wicked. This suggests that their initially tentative convictions that Job is among the wicked are firming up as the debate progresses.

18:1-4: Get Some Perspective! He begins by asking whether Job intends to go on talking forever (v. 2a) and urges him to "be sensible" or "consider" (v. 2b).[147] He pours scorn on Job for considering the friends to be stupid like cattle (v. 3; see 17:10). Bildad's intention is to urge Job to have a bit of perspective, since the earth/land or even a rocky wall or cliff should not be made to revolve around Job or be adjusted for his pleasure (v. 4, probably a reference back to Job's words in 14:18). Of course, the usefulness of this advice depends heavily on whether Job or the friends are speaking the truth.

18:5-21: The Fate of the Wicked In vv. 5-21 Bildad gives an extended description of the insecurity, terror, and hopelessness of the wicked. It is likely that he is implying that Job is at least well on the way to becoming one of them, so that this section is meant rhetorically to be heard by Job as a strong warning.

Bildad uses a variety of images in his rather colorful if dark description. The key metaphor in vv. 5-6 is one of light ("lamp," "flame") being extinguished, which seems to be an image of life coming to an end (as in Prov 13:9). The fourfold repetition of this image, each time subtly different, is a way of insisting that this outcome is certain. No further information is given at this stage about how it will come to pass.

Verses 7-10 focus on the twin themes of feet and traps. The focus is initially on the feet, with the strong steps of the wicked being restricted (v. 7a). This might be thought of as due to weakness (as in the previous image of weakness leading to death), but the picture of being restricted or cramped fits nicely with the theme of being caught up in a trap or impediment in vv. 7b-10. So it is his own plans (the plural of עֵצָה/ʿēṣâ, v. 7b) that set him back (lit. "throw him down"). This is filled out in vv. 8-10, when he walks on a mesh net (v. 8), which

---

147. The plural "you" and "your" arouses the interest of the commentators. Pope, *Job*, 133, suggests that Bildad is classing Job as belonging to the "impious" and addressing the wicked; Habel, *Book of Job*, 280, says it is more likely that he is just using language of the traditional exordium style, echoing the plural language of Job in 12:2; 19:2. However, Job is speaking there to a group of friends, whereas Bildad is speaking only to Job.

is a trap because of a hidden rope (v. 10), so that he is caught and securely held in the trap by his foot (v. 9). Thus the first general image of the light of his life being snuffed out is followed by a more precise picture of his way of life (walking with his feet) ensnaring or trapping him.

The different metaphor of being pursued begins in v. 11 and continues as far as v. 13. There is some mythological background to much of the language of this chapter, with images like the "firstborn of death" (v. 13) and the "king of terrors" (v. 14) being allusions to the Canaanite god of the underworld, Mot.[148] Bildad compares the fate of the wicked to being surrounded or encircled by terrors (either mythological beings or terrors more generally, as in 30:15), and chased closely as if his pursuers are right at his feet (v. 11). His inner resources ("his strength") are sapped of their power (v. 12a), with calamity or disaster waiting for him to stumble (v. 12b). The image of v. 13 fills out what Bildad says will happen when his pursuer catches the wicked: it will eat his limbs covered with skin (lit. "the limbs of his skin"), with the eater being identified as the firstborn death or firstborn of death. Clearly vv. 11-13 outline a relentless pursuit of the wicked resulting in death, destroying his body.

The next section (vv. 14-16) continues the mythological references (most prominently, the "king of terrors," v. 14) but moves away from the pursuit motif to the image of being uprooted from their home and destroyed. In ancient Near Eastern thought, one's home, even as humble a home as a tent (vv. 14-15), is depicted as a place of security and safety. The wicked is ripped away from his tent (in parallel with "from [the object of] his trust," v. 14a) and is made to march[149] to the king of terrors (v. 14b), an image of death or judgment/punishment. Verse 15 is not entirely clear about what is in the tent of the wicked.[150] On any reading, it continues the picture of his home no longer being under his control or benefiting him in any way. His home will be either destroyed (the image of v. 15b) or under the control of someone else.

---

148. See Sarna, "Mythological Background," 315-18; and, more recently, Fyall, *Now My Eyes,* 121-23.

149. The verb appears feminine, so it is some unspecified feminine noun that causes him to march. Clines, *Job 1-20,* 406, covers the possibilities well, but arrives at no convincing conclusion. The most likely suggestion is that it is a rare masculine form, and thus a reference back to the firstborn of death in v. 13.

150. Fyall, *Now My Eyes,* 123, notes that renderings such as "things of what are not his" (ESV is similar) are virtually meaningless and emends to "fire," following Dahood, "Northwest Semitic," 312-14. This would give good sense (the only thing left in the destroyed tent is the burning fire consuming it) and would be a good balance with the sulphur or brimstone scattered over the location in v. 15b. If the text is to stand, it could mean that once the wicked person has been taken from their tent, all their possessions are taken too. Alternatively, it could mean "terror [implied from earlier] dwells in his tent so that it is no more his."

Verse 16 rounds off vv. 14-16 with a vivid image of the idea of being up-rooted from one's home, resulting in death. There may be an allusion here back to Job's use of the tree being compared with a human life (14:7-12). Certainly the result of being plucked out of one's dwelling place will lead to an outcome symbolized by roots drying up and branches withering.[151]

Verses 17-19 deal with a fate worse than death in some cultures — that of being forgotten, as if one had never lived. This is certainly the case in Hebrew society. The motif of remembrance is very strong in a book like Deuteronomy (e.g., Deut 8:2, 11, 14, 18, 19; 25:19; also Eccl 12:1), and in contemporary Jewish thought memory is a key way of overcoming the horror of the Holocaust.[152] Thus this section climaxes the fate of the wicked by pointing out that their memory will perish from the earth and they will have no name (v. 17). The horror of this is pictured in v. 18 as being thrust out into darkness and driven out of the world. There is a return to more realistic language in v. 19 with the wicked having no descendant and no survivor in the place where they used to dwell. Not only are the wicked destroyed, but so is any memory of them.

The last two verses close off Bildad's speech. The use of a merism (east, west) in v. 20 means that all the people on the earth are appalled and horror-struck, presumably at the extent of the judgment on the wicked. The lesson is drawn out in the final verse. Their dwelling places (plural of emphasis) or the consequences of their wicked behavior (including, ironically, no longer living in their dwelling place) will be as Bildad has vividly described in vv. 5-19. This is what is assigned to the one who does not know God. This strong conclusion implies that Bildad is giving Job a forceful warning to refrain from going down the path of the wicked, and seems to betray his view that Job has already gone too far.[153]

19:1-29: Job

This chapter is largely a lament, but with some additional elements. In vv. 2-6 Job is rebuking the friends for their treatment of him. Verses 7-20 are the lament proper, with vv. 7-12 describing his treatment by God and vv. 13-20 describing

---

151. If it introduces the following section, it may be an image of being removed from its place so that there is no more memory of it. Clines, *Job 1–20,* 420, regards it as referring not to the wicked man but to his family and possessions, anticipating v. 19.

152. This is why the Holocaust Museum in Jerusalem is called Yad Vashem, "a remembrance and a name," and why stones are left on Jewish graves.

153. Fyall, *Now My Eyes,* 123, suggests that in this verse Bildad has thrown off all pretense and is calling Job an evil person; Clines, *Job 1–20,* 408, suggests that the tone of the speech as a whole is "to *encourage* Job to amend his life."

the way in which others have abandoned or rejected him. Verses 21-22, balancing vv. 2-6, are a concluding plea to the friends to stop. In the well-known passage of vv. 23-27, Job explores the possibility of a redeemer, while vv. 28-29 bring the focus back to the friends.

19:1-6: Rebuking the Friends The second person plural forms ("you") in vv. 2-6 indicate that Job is not simply answering Bildad, but rebuking all of the friends. He condemns them in vv. 2-3 for tormenting him (lit. "causing him grief"), crushing him with words (דכא/*dk'* is used to mean "crush" in 4:19; 5:4; 6:9; 22:9; 34:25, which is better than ESV and NRSV "break in pieces"), humiliating him (lit. "caused him to be shamed," hence "cast reproach on") and shamefully wronging him (a hapax legomenon whose meaning is not certain). In Job's eyes it is a litany of mistreatment toward him.

There is debate over whether v. 4 is to be read as a confession of sin or whether it is hypothetical. On either view, he disputes their right to correct him by arguing that even if he has gone astray, then his error is his concern ("remains with me"), not theirs.[154] The logic here is not entirely clear, since one person's wrong actions often affect others, and so this is likely to be an emotional expression of pain rather than a rational argument.

Differences in applying the doctrine of retribution are evident in vv. 5-6. Job charges his friends with using the idea that God rewards the righteous and punishes the wicked to establish their superiority to Job (magnifying themselves against him) and to use his humiliation or disgrace as evidence that he must be a sinner (v. 5).[155] Job, however, responds in v. 6 by complaining that God is treating him as if he is in the wrong category. He seems to assume that the doctrine of retribution has been misapplied in his case. Both Job and his friends agree that God is treating Job as an enemy, but the friends think that he is right in doing so, while Job knows it cannot be.[156] Job's ongoing presupposition is that everything that happens to him has come from the God who is in charge of the world. Thus God has wronged him or put him in the wrong (the verb is used by Bildad in 8:3), and is the one who has "closed his net about me" (v. 6).[157]

154. Hartley, *Book of Job,* 283, points out that this root refers to an inadvertent mistake, but see Clines, *Job 1-20,* 440-41. Newsom, "Book of Job," 475, translates it as "my inadvertent sin would lodge with me," i.e., its consequences would.

155. Andersen, *Job,* 191, calls this "the theological calculus of the friends."

156. Habel, *Book of Job,* 299, says that they "rationalize rather than sympathize."

157. Gordis, Habel, and Clines make a small emendation and translate this as throwing up his siegeworks around/against him. However, the "net" imagery seems more likely in view of Bildad's use of the same idea in 18:8-10, although different words are used. In any event, the theological thrust is the same.

19:7-12: God's Treatment of Him Quite logically, vv. 7-12 turn to God's treatment of Job. Verse 7 makes a summary complaint before the details are subsequently given. The essential point is that God is not responding to his legal claim for help. A cry of "violence" or a call for help should be met, Job thinks, by God's intervention to right the injustice.[158] Legal language ("answer," "justice") is found here, suggesting that this is a complaint not against the friends but against God, upon whom he has been calling to meet him in the court (e.g., 16:19, 21).

He particularizes his claim in vv. 8-12. Verse 8 describes how God has stopped his life progress, in that he has built an unpassable wall in front of him (see Lam 3:9; Hos 2:6), as well as depriving him of light to see his path. He claims that God has taken away his dignity and reputation (his glory and crown, v. 9) and that God is dismantling all parts of his life (probably by destroying his possessions) so that his life is diminishing ("I am departing," often translated as "I am gone," v. 10a), and his hope for a secure future has been uprooted (v. 10b). In v. 11 Job considers God's attitude toward him, concluding that God regards him as an enemy and God's wrath burns against him. The image of v. 12 is one of sending troops to surround and lay siege to Job, a mismatch (Habel calls it "divine overkill") accentuated by the siegeworks surrounding not a walled city but Job's tent.

It is very clear in this section that Job has a big view of God actively behind all that has happened to him, which leads him to speak in such bold and accusatory words. There is no doubt that God has done it; Job simply cannot understand why.

19:13-20: Others Have Abandoned Him In this next section Job complains that his family and others have deserted him, but this too is caused by God — *he* has put my brothers far from me (v. 13a). There follows a catalogue of those who have abandoned Job: his brothers (v. 13a), all who knew him (vv. 13b, 14b), those near him (v. 14a, perhaps his relatives), houseguests and maidservants (v. 15), his male servant (v. 16), his wife and children (v. 17), other children (v. 18), his closest friends (v. 19). The cumulative picture is of his being totally and utterly abandoned by the entire community, a theme that Job will pick up in his summing up in chapter 30.

Much of this language is typical of biblical laments. However, unlike a lament or God-directed complaint, he is speaking (at least initially) to the friends about God rather than directly to God. One possible example of the

---

158. "Violence" could be a summons to God to deliver from disaster as in Hab 1:2, or that God has inflicted violence on him, which is probably to be preferred in light of the description in Job 16:9-14.

stereotypical language of the lament is when he complains he is loathsome to his own children (v. 17), even though they are now dead.[159]

It is not entirely clear whether v. 20, which appears to describe his physical situation, should be treated together with vv. 13-19 or as part of the summary of vv. 21-22. It does seem different in nature to the challenge questions of vv. 21-22, so it may best be understood as a description of his emaciated condition (he is skin and bones),[160] which was a result of his exclusion from the community, as described in vv. 13-19. There is a hint of this connection in v. 17a. Verse 20b is the source of the expression "to escape by the skin of my teeth," but many think that a narrow escape does not fit the context here. However, while it is not entirely clear what is intended by the "skin of my teeth," it is a vivid image for "almost nothing at all," and the language of "skin" will be picked up in v. 26. It seems best to understand Job as saying that, up to this point, he has escaped death by the narrowest of margins.[161] Such is the extent of his physical wasting away as a result of his rejection by the entire community.

19:21-22: Plea to the Friends to Stop As a result, Job calls to his friends for "mercy" or "grace," since he has been "struck" (NIV, NJPS; better than simply ESV and NRSV "touched," as also in 1:11) by God's powerful hand (v. 21). He can instinctively see that running his situation through the grid of retribution theology is not working. He needs care and support, not rebuke and correction (contra Habel and Clines, who suggest that Job's call for "pity" is ironic). In v. 22 he asks why they are "persecuting" (so KJV, NASB; רָדַף/*rādap* can mean simply "pursue," but often means "persecute" in the context of enemies, e.g., Pss 69:26; 109:16) him as God has been doing. Again Job is insisting that God is treating him as an enemy. The phrase "not satisfied with my flesh" seems to be elliptical for "not satisfied that my flesh has wasted away," the very thing pointed out in v. 20a.

159. So Hartley, *Book of Job*, 289. Literally the phrase לִבְנֵי בִטְנִי/*libnê biṭnî* means "sons of my womb/belly," which Rowley, *Job*, 136; Clines, *Job 1–20*, 449; and others take to be elliptical for "the sons born from the same womb as me." Thus some English versions (NIV, RSV, NASB) translate it as "brothers." The parallels cited by Clines and others (Gen 43:29; Judg 8:19) do not refer to this phrase but explicitly to "sons of my mother." Better support for rendering it as "brothers" is given by the parallel in Job 3:10, where *biṭnî* clearly means "the womb from which I came." However, the absence of this phrase elsewhere to mean "brothers" possibly implies that Job simply has on his lips stereotyped lament language and uses it without adjustment to his particular circumstances. Wolfers, *Deep Things*, 135-36, gives a different explanation: it means "my sons." Gordis, *Book of Job*, 202, suggests that the author/editor is just careless about harmonizing details.

160. However, see Clines, *Job 1–20*, 430, 450-52, who argues that that he is deprived of vigor and has collapsed in a heap.

161. See the list of suggested emendations in Rowley, *Job*, 136-37; Clines, *Job 1–20*, 431-32.

19:23-27: The Possibility of a Redeemer For many, the high point of Job's faith and hope is seen in 19:25-27. However, we need to be careful, lest we read into the book what we expect to find. A more detailed study of this difficult passage is in order.

The point of 19:23-24 is the recording of Job's legal case on durable materials. Job wishes that the testimony to his innocence could be written in some enduring, permanent form. Habel suggests that the "words" of v. 23 are not the words that follow in vv. 25-27, but rather those of his legal case. In juridicial contexts (and very frequently in Job), "words" (מִלִּין/*millîn*) normally mean the words or argument of a case.[162] The need for such evidence implies that Job envisages that he will die before his vindication, for otherwise there would be little need for a permanent record.

Some see in v. 25a the high point of Job's faith, as he believes with confidence in a living redeemer. Although, they say, he has previously spoken in an accusatory and angry way toward God, finally in this purple passage Job's real faith bursts through. I have suggested, however, that Job's previous angry complaints and protests are a legitimate part of faith, so that there is no need to read this passage as a high point of faith in order to make Job acceptable to God. It might still be a model of clarity in Job's faith, but it does not *need* to be.

A closer reading of the passage confirms that vv. 25-27 speak more of the intensity of Job's longing rather than of any settled conviction. Clines proposes, "In vv 23-27 we have a wish, a conviction, and a desire."[163] His wish (impossible to fulfill) is that his testimony be engraved on the mountain (vv. 23-24). His conviction is that his case will be won, even if after his death (vv. 25-26a); his desire is that, at a later time, he will see God. He is expressing his desire rather than his conviction.[164]

The verb "I know" governs all of vv. 25-27, so it is likely that Job's "conviction" about his redeemer in v. 25 or his vindication might also be a longing or desire. It is not clear that Job has a conviction that his case will be won on the basis that his redeemer lives. Indeed, Clines's view starts to dissolve when he concedes that Job's conviction "is much more a conviction that he is innocent

---

162. Clines, *Job 1-20*, 456, suggests that they are his legal depositions referred to in 13:3, 6, 13, 17, 18, and are stated more or less directly in 13:23-24.

163. Clines, *Job 1-20*, 437.

164. Clines, *Job 1-20*, 461, notes that the verb "I will see" is either a modal imperfect (GKC §107m-n, "I might see") or a cohortative (GKC §48b-e, "let me see"), expressing a will or desire rather than a simple prediction. Clines's view is that vv. 25-26a and 26b-27 refer to different times. In vv. 25-26a he is affirming his conviction that a redeemer will vindicate him after his death. The conjunction beginning v. 26b should be translated "but," not "then," and the rest of this verse and v. 27 outline what is his underlying desire, leaving aside for the moment the possibility of a redeemer.

than a conviction that he will really be vindicated."[165] His belief ("I know") is that he ought to be or must be vindicated — not that he will be. Thus it cannot be used to establish that he really believes that he has a "redeemer" who lives. Indeed, he no more believes that he will be vindicated than he believes that he will see God. Yet he desperately longs for both realities.

This is made clearer by examining the identity of his "redeemer." A "redeemer" (גֹּאֵל/*gōʾēl*) is a hypothetical legal figure, like that of the "umpire/arbiter" of 9:33 and the "witness" of 16:19. These are not several different figures being called on by Job, but the one "hope" who is variously described. There is a recurring pattern in each passage of call for an arbiter being preceded by angry protest and succeeded by despair (9:35b; 16:22; 19:27c) following the floating of unfulfilled hope.[166] In other words, this "redeemer" is none other than the "witness" of 16:19 and the "umpire" of 9:33. As in 16:19, where Job appears to express a longing in the language of conviction ("my witness is in heaven"), so here the strength of the language is an indication of the intensity of his longing rather than the certainty of his belief. Underlying the entire passage is a strong desire for help that leads to several imaginative possibilities rather than definite scenarios — his words permanently preserved; his redeemer standing on earth; seeing God from his flesh.

Job is not just making a demand for justice or vindication, but looks forward to seeing God. While one nuance of "redeemer" is vindication, that concept is not explored in this passage. Verses 26 and 27 focus instead on seeing God, as if that would meet his existential dilemma. So underlying this picture of wanting a redeemer is Job's deeper desire for a restored relationship with God.

To some extent, this conclusion undercuts an issue that has been the subject of much academic debate: when will this vindication be — before or after death? Dhorme, for example, contends that Job expects a fair hearing before his death; others (e.g., Andersen, J. G. Janzen), that Job will be vindicated by an inquiry after his death. The agenda behind this debate is whether an incipient doctrine of bodily resurrection can be found here. Does the phrase "in/apart from my flesh I shall see God" imply that Job will be in an embodied or disembodied existence after his death?

Even if this is more than just Job's "desire," there is no solid ground here for a doctrine of bodily resurrection. The preposition מִן/*min* in the phrase "in my flesh" has a core meaning of "from" and could either be translated as "in" ("from the location of," implying an embodied state) or "out of/apart from"

---

165. Clines, *Job 1–20*, 461.

166. Michel, "Confidence and Despair," 176, notes that a literal translation of v. 27c is "my kidneys are spent in my loins" and suggests that it means that he has been wetting himself so many times that he is now completely dry and no longer able to wet himself. Cf. NIV "How my heart yearns within me!"; NRSV and ESV "My heart faints within me."

("away from," a privative use, implying a disembodied state). The Hebrew preposition does not favor one or the other. Some have argued, however, that the use of "skin," "flesh," and "eyes" in vv. 26-27 suggest an embodied form in any event.[167] However, a better view is that the limits of language have been reached here, and the details should not be pressed too far.

Westermann, then, is close to the flavor of the passage when he asserts, "The whole discussion about whether or not Job here expresses hope in resurrection bypasses the sense of the text."[168] Indeed the dialogue contains many other hypothetical scenarios — for example, cursing the day of his birth in chapter 3; "although he will slay me" in 13:15; being hidden in Sheol in 14:13; considering taking God to court in 9:14-20. None of these is a realistic possibility, but Job explores them all. Perhaps anyone would if they were covered in Job's scabs.

That Job so quickly slides back into despair (19:27c) again suggests that no identifiable figure is in view. Thus what may initially strike us as a great expression of trust is rendered ambiguous as it is more closely examined. It is likely that here Job is exploring resurrection only as an imagined possibility to which he is driven by his anguish, rather than a confident affirmation that he will be raised. Yet even this is rightly motivated, for he pushes in a new direction in the hope that God can and might do something to vindicate him.

19:28-29: Back to the Friends The chapter is rounded off by a warning addressed to all the friends ("you say," v. 28a, is plural). In v. 28 Job is assuming that they will continue to press him (from his point of view, pursuing or persecuting), based on their conclusion that the source of problem ("the root of the matter") is found in Job. In other words, since Job has sinned, his suffering is the consequence of his sin. In response to this restatement of the doctrine of retribution, Job strongly warns them to be afraid of the judgment that will come upon them, seemingly for their wrongful treatment of him.

20:1-29: Zophar

This is Zophar's second and final speech. After his initial response (vv. 2-3), his comments about the fate of the wicked can be divided into three sections.

---

167. Andersen, *Job*, 193; J. G. Janzen, *Job*, 144.

168. Westermann, *Structure*, 103-4. He adds, "It is a complete misunderstanding so to generalize the expressions here that they become a 'presentiment' of resurrection or of life after death. The emphasis does not lie upon how it will be possible for Job to receive justice from God despite his having to die; the point is only that it will happen." Or, even better, that he simply wishes it might happen.

Verses 4-11 develop the idea of the brevity of the wicked due to premature death. The middle section (vv. 12-22, united by its distinctive food imagery) focuses on the self-destructive nature of sin. The final section deals with God's active wrath against the wicked (vv. 23-29). There is some difference of opinion about the break between these last two sections. The ESV, NRSV, and NIV make a division between vv. 19 and 20, while others suggest a break after either v. 22 or v. 23.[169] The virtual absence of any emphasis on God's agency in vv. 12-22 (mentioned only in v. 15), and its predominance in vv. 23-29 make vv. 12-22 and 23-29 the most natural sections.[170]

20:1-3: Zophar's Initial Response Zophar talks with increasing impatience (ESV "my haste within me," v. 2).[171] The image of his thoughts answering him (v. 2a) is not transparent. Hartley notes that the word "thoughts" occurs only here and in 4:13 (worrying thoughts in night visions), and this usage suggests the sense of "troubled thoughts."[172] Zophar's problem is that these thoughts keep on cropping up as he listens to Job.

Zophar is responding to being censured by Job (v. 3a), probably a reference back to Job's rebuke in 19:28-29. His final claim is that "a spirit from/out of his understanding answers me" (v. 3b), but the meaning is again not entirely clear. Is it a claim to an inner voice from God? Or is it simply a reference to the inner voice of a seasoned sage? Zophar may not see a difference, but it is apparent from v. 4 that the source of his words is the tradition of the sages.

20:4-11: The Premature Death of the Wicked Zophar thus begins with an appeal to tradition, just as Bildad did in the first cycle and Eliphaz in chapter 15. This tradition stretches right back to the creation of humanity, a hyperbolic way of describing his certainty about what he is about to say.[173] His key sentence is in v. 5 — "the exulting of the wicked is short, and the joy of the godless but for a moment." His observation of life is that, at any given point of time, some who

---

169. For the former see Habel, *Book of Job*, 310-11, 317-18; for the latter see G. Wilson, *Job*, 216-19. Clines, *Job 1–20*, 480, notes that vv. 12-23 are united by the image of food, which is absent from the previous strophe (vv. 4-11) and only alluded to in the following strophe (vv. 24-29) in v. 26b-c.

170. The emphasis on God's agency is seen in vv. 23 and 27, with "heavens" as a euphemism for God, 28, 29 (twice). Although vv. 23 and 28 read "he" or "his," God is clearly the intended person.

171. Cf. Gordis, *Book of Job*, 210, who translates "the feelings within me"; similarly Clines, *Job 1–20*, 471. However, "haste" fits the context well and reflects the tone of the speech.

172. Hartley, *Book of Job*, 300.

173. The word "not" is rightly added in the translation in v. 4. See Gordis, *Book of Job*, 214.

are wicked will be prospering, but insists that any delight in such prosperity will only be for a short time. It is as if the punishment of the wicked is a creational principle, part of the world order.

Two themes are emphasized in this section — the shortness of time for the godless to prevail, and their certain (early) death. The concept of brevity is prominent. In v. 5 this exulting is "short" and "for a moment"; in v. 7 they will perish "forever" (not a statement about the eternal punishment of the wicked, but the utter or complete nature of their perishing); in v. 8 it will be short-lived like a dream or night vision; in v. 10 their wealth will have vanished so that their children will need to beg; and in v. 11 they will lie down in the dust.

These words have an important role in their context. In vv. 5-6 Zophar concedes that the godless may temporarily prosper and, indeed, prosper greatly (e.g., "his height mount up to the heavens," v. 6 ESV). Here he probably has Job in view, for Job has been arguing that his abundant blessings were outward signs of his righteousness. Zophar is responding to this by saying that even when the wicked attain great riches or status (as Job did), this will be soon forgotten.

There is also a strong emphasis on death. The wicked person will perish (v. 7), chased away and not found (v. 8), no longer seen (v. 9); and his body will lie down in the dust, a metaphor of death. Images of the transience of the wicked are piled up in vv. 7-9, with some more concrete pictures of their fate in vv. 10-11. The focus is not only on premature death (vv. 7a, 11b) but also on the loss of possessions in this life (v. 10). The image of v. 11 is a suitable climax — though youthful vigor fills his bones (hence a premature death), that will be of little value once he dies.

20:12-22: Sin Will Destroy Having considered the fate of the wicked in vv. 4-11, Zophar now has a narrower focus on the effect that the wickedness has on the godless people themselves. The food imagery, which is woven throughout this section, appears to be a metaphor for their wicked actions. This is made explicit in v. 15a, when the food of v. 14 becomes the riches (presumably ill-gotten) of v. 15. The central idea is thus that wickedness will consume them even as they devour it. Specific examples of their wickedness include crushing and abandoning the poor, seizing a house they did not build (v. 19), and their greed (leaving nothing after eating, v. 21a; also v. 20a). These particular descriptions then flavor the way we read "riches" (v. 15a), "the fruit of his toil/gain" (v. 18a), and "the profit of his trading" (v. 18b), so that these should be understood as wrongfully gained wealth and profits. Zophar's implication that Job is like this will be answered by the oath of clearance in chapter 31.

The traditional understanding of retribution is seen in Zophar's concentration on the fact that wickedness will reap its destructive consequences (e.g.,

vv. 14, 16, 18-19, 21) rather than on God's overt involvement in the process. Of course, Zophar recognizes that God is behind this process (stated explicitly in v. 15b), but the emphasis is on the self-destructive nature of human evil. It is even stated that other people will exercise this retribution, so that "the hand of a sufferer will come upon him" (v. 22b).

20:23-29: How God Deals with the Wicked Verses 23-29 describe God's more active wrath against such a person.[174] Verse 23 operates as a hinge verse, continuing the food imagery ("fill his belly"), but taking a step further to talk of God's active intervention in judgment (lit. "he," but clearly a reference to God, as in v. 28). Thus God will send his "burning anger" against him, and cause it to shower on him into the core of his body (lit. "his bowels"). In Job's situation, it would point to the disasters that have come upon him, as well as the physical affliction.[175]

Verses 24-25 explore a wider scenario than Job's situation, seemingly referring to suffering inflicted in battle,[176] but the point is very clear. The wicked will not avoid their just outcome, for even if they flee from one weapon or attack, they will be struck in another way (בָּרָק/*bārāq* in v. 25b is probably a vivid image of the flash of a spear or arrowhead; it sometimes means "lightning").

This idea of retribution is drawn out in more general terms in vv. 26-28, before the principle is clearly enunciated in v. 29. Verse 26 explains that complete darkness (lit. "all darkness") is hidden in wait for the wicked person's ill-gotten treasures; that even an unfanned fire will devour them, and that there will be either nothing or very little left in their tent (v. 26c).[177] Such will be the extent of his devastation.

A cosmic picture is given in v. 27 with "the heavens and the earth" being either a merism (meaning everything in between as well) or that God (euphemistically called "the heavens") will lay bare his iniquity while the people of the earth will rise up against him. Either reading implies an overwhelming force

---

174. Clines, *Job 1–20*, 494, sees the principal theme here as "the inescapability of the end of the wicked."

175. Hartley, *Book of Job*, 309, comments: "While speaking in principle, Zophar definitely has Job in mind." See also Holbert, "Skies."

176. As Habel, *Book of Job*, 319, suggests, however, it may be a reference back to Job's earlier accusation that God is shooting arrows at him (6:4; 16:12-13).

177. Verse 26c could be translated, "let him feed on [only] what is left in his tent" (giving the jussive form of the verb its normal sense) or "the survivor/one who is left will graze in his tent" (keeping up the pattern of the earlier parts of the verse). The Hebrew can mean either "what is left over" or "the one who is left alive." Andersen, *Job*, 197, has suggested that "tent" has the sense of "all a person's property" rather than his home. Habel, *Book of Job*, 319, sees a reference to the property (v. 26a), the person (v. 26b), and the household (v. 26c) of the wicked.

unable to be resisted by the wicked person. This is continued by the image of their possessions carried away and dragged off in the day of God's (lit. "his") wrath (v. 28).

Zophar's conclusion is stated clearly in v. 29 — this is what is allotted to the wicked person by God, and it is what God says is their inheritance. There is no room in Zophar's thinking for mercy, let alone for the wicked to turn from their wickedness and live. The suffering Job would understand Zophar's point all too clearly, for he is one whose possessions have been taken away, and all of his society has risen up to reject him.

21:1-34: Job

As the second cycle of speeches draws to an end, Job utters this lengthy discourse in which he explores how the wicked are not always dealt with as the friends have insisted. There are apparent anomalies in how the world is run, and Job is suspicious of any attempt to trim the picture down to make it fit into a tidy theological system. Job confronts the friends and complains that their neat and ordered world simply does not match reality.

The chapter can usefully be divided into four sections (vv. 1-6, 7-16, 17-26, and 27-34), although many scholars divide the third section in two (after either v. 21 or v. 22). The second section begins with the question "Why" (v. 7), the third with "How often" (v. 17), and the final one with "Behold/Oh" (v. 27). Each of these subsequent sections focuses either on what the wicked say (vv. 14-15), or what the friends have said about the wicked ("you say," vv. 19, 28). This speech is unusual, in part because it is the only speech in which Job "confines his remarks to his friends."[178]

21:1-6: Change Your Attitude to Me After the author's formulaic reintroduction of the speaker (v. 1), Job calls on the friends to listen to him, but then expects that they will mock him and his words (vv. 2-3). They are asked to listen carefully (the imperative plus infinitive absolute is an emphatic construction), and so bring him real comfort.[179] Job is saying in v. 2 that if they had listened carefully to his words, they would have brought him comfort and so have fulfilled their purpose in coming. It is clear from v. 3, however, that Job does not expect this desired outcome to happen, for he expects them to keep on mocking

---

178. Andersen, *Job*, 197.

179. The word תַּנְחֻמֹת/*tanḥûmōt*, "comfort," at the end of v. 2 is related to the verb נחם/ *nḥm*, which was used in 2:11 to describe the friends' purpose in coming.

him after he has finished speaking. The singular verb "mock" may indicate that Job has only Zophar in mind, but more likely implies that he is a representative of the three as a group.

Job continues to call for a different response from the friends in vv. 4-6. He asks why, since his complaint is not against, or addressed to, a human being (implying that it is addressed to God), should he not be impatient (v. 4)? While this might refer to being impatient with God for not acting quickly enough, in the context it more likely refers to Job's impatience with the friends for interfering when his complaint is with God. This is why they should realize the enormity of their folly or presumption and be silent ("laying a hand over the mouth," v. 5; see 29:9; 40:4). In v. 6 Job remembers what a dangerous task it is to lay a complaint before an all-powerful God, and hence his response is dismay and trembling. Having rebuked the friends for stepping in so blithely (v. 5), he now considers how precarious his own position is (v. 6).

21:7-16: The Prospering of the Wicked Job is asking why and how the wicked prosper, and what their attitude is toward God. The general problem is stated in v. 7 — why the wicked not only exist but "live a long life" (or "advance to old age") and grow mighty in power or wealth.[180] They not only escape punishment but also have a seemingly successful life.

Job then particularizes the issue by referring to their offspring (v. 8), their security (in their house, and more generally, v. 9), the fertility of their animals (v. 10), their enjoyment of life and family (vv. 11-13a), and their peaceful rather than premature death (v. 13b; Sheol is "the place of the dead"). Verses 14-15 highlight the stance of the wicked before God, and the effect is one of dissonance. People who say such things should, according to the doctrine of retribution, receive punishment, not prosperity. At first glance, Job has said something close to the words of the wicked. He has earlier told God to depart from him (v. 14a; see 7:19), and he has asked whether he has gained any profit from praying to God (v. 15b; see 19:7-8). But this is only a superficial comparison, for Job has strongly wanted to know God's ways (v. 14b) and has refused to give up serving him (v. 15a). Verse 16a seems to be a summarizing statement, setting out that prosperity is the present experience of the wicked. Verse 16b is difficult but is best understood in its context (following Gordis) as a kind of prayer: "May the path of the wicked be far from me," or perhaps, as Habel suggests, a personal disclaimer ("The counsel of the wicked is beyond me!").[181]

---

180. The word חַיִל/*ḥāyil* can mean either power or wealth; in 20:15 and 18 it refers to wealth.
181. Gordis, *Book of Job*, 230; Habel, *Book of Job*, 321, 328.

21:17-26: Why Are the Wicked Not Punished? This section is bracketed by the reality of death, which is raised in vv. 17-18 ("putting out the lamp of the wicked") and returned to in vv. 23, 25-26. Job is asking, "How often do the wicked die prematurely?" All the images of vv. 17-18 are pictures of death (lamp being put out, calamity, God distributing pain, carried away by the wind like straw or chaff), but what hangs over each of them is, How often does this happen to the wicked? This is a series of rhetorical questions with the implied answer, "Hardly ever." Since the wicked do not die prematurely, v. 19a introduces the rationalization: "God stores up the punishment [or iniquity] for their children" (introduced in many versions by a supplied "You say" or "It is said" to give the sense).

Job calls for change, asking that the punishment due to the wicked (in the context, presumably early death) be paid out to them (v. 19b), filled out in v. 20 as "seeing their own destruction" and "drinking the wrath of the Almighty." A further reason for this is given in v. 19b as "that they may know it" (lit. "and they will know"), with the sense being that the wicked will experience (know) that their wickedness has real and deadly consequences. A reason is given in v. 21 for Job's request — for the wicked will not care what happens after they die, and thus presumably will not change their ways. Verse 22, marked as a question, seems to be an aside by Job as he reflects on God, rather than a continuation of the argument.

Verses 23-25 provide a contrast between two men ("One," v. 23; "Another," v. 25) who die. The second one dies in a bitter spirit and has not tasted prosperity (v. 25). Even the details of his life are less full than those of the first man described in vv. 23-24. The first man experienced complete prosperity (there is a play on words with "bones" in v. 24 here), and during his life was entirely (lit. "all of him") secure and at ease (v. 23). His full life is further emphasized in v. 24, although the details are less clear. The first part of the verse is rendered in the NIV as "his body well nourished" and more literally by the NRSV and ESV as "his pails full of milk" (i.e., prosperous). Hebrew עֲטִינָיו/'ăṭîn, often translated "pails," is found only here, and Hartley's translation, "his testes full of milk," provides a good parallel with the second half of the verse (the marrow of his bones moist).[182] Both images would then speak of physical bodily vigor right up to the time of death.

The exact force of v. 26 is not clear, though it is plainly asserting that both these men die and return to dust (Eccl 3:20). It could be implying that, even though they have different experiences in this life, they have a common destiny, but this does not seem to fit the flow of thought in the chapter. More likely, then,

182. Hartley, *Book of Job*, 317-18.

v. 26 is simply recording the fact that both men die, but the emphasis in vv. 23-26 is on the contrast between one man who had a full and rich life while the other experienced bitterness and deprivation. What seems to be implied is that there is an arbitrariness here, for no connection is made (as Job thinks should be) between a person's righteousness and the fullness of one's life. Thus Job is again protesting that divine retribution is not reflected in the world.

21:27-34: The Failure of the Friends "Behold" was used in v. 16 to round off an earlier section, but it seems to be used here to begin a new topic. Job starts by saying that he knows the friends' thoughts and wrong schemes (v. 27).[183] Job perceives them as adversaries, not friends. The issue at stake is introduced by "For you say" in v. 28. Job hears the friends to be challenging him to show any evidence that wicked people are living in fine houses. Since the word "tent" appears to be resumptive of the "house of the prince" (v. 28a), the question v. 28b asks is, "Where is a wicked person living like a prince?"

Job immediately responds in vv. 29-33 that anyone who keeps their eyes and ears open will know this, implying that the friends are blind and deaf to reality because they are blinkered by their rigid theological systems. In v. 29 he urges them to ask the travelers who would have knowledge of what happens in different lands (ironically, the friends have traveled long distances to see Job, 2:11). The testimony of the travelers is that the evil person is held back from disaster and sustained in a day of destruction (v. 30). Furthermore, such wicked people are not confronted to their face or rebuked for their wrongdoing (v. 31), and even in their death they are given special honor (v. 32, their wrongly gained wealth enables their tomb to be watched and preserved). Verse 33 begins with an image of agricultural prosperity for the wicked, followed by a statement that they can influence the community, and that many gather before or around them.[184]

Finally Job closes off this speech, and the second cycle of speeches, by concluding that the comfort offered by the friends is insubstantial, lightweight, mere hot air.[185] In terms of what is left standing of their answers, Job suggests

---

183. There are two verbs חָמַס/*ḥāmas*, with the common one having undertones of violence; the rare one occurs only here. Andersen, *Job*, 201, notes that 11QtgJob confirms that the emphasis is on scheming rather than physical violence.

184. Alternatively, v. 33c could be understood as Job insisting this is not an isolated case, since there is a long line of wicked people who have prospered, as suggested by the translation "goes before him." The Hebrew clause is verbless and could be translated "many are before him" in a physical sense of gathering in front of him. Hebrew לְפְנֵי/*lipnê*, "before," can refer to either time or place.

185. The word is הֶבֶל/*hebel*, a key word in Ecclesiastes, and having a base meaning of "vapor" or "breath."

that there is nothing but faithlessness or treachery (v. 34). The tone on which this speech ends does not augur well for an imminent resolution of this dispute.

22:1–27:23: *Round Three*

As it stands, the third cycle of speeches is incomplete, with no speech from Zophar and only a short address by Bildad (25:1-6). Many commentators either explain this as a result of textual corruption or reallocate the existing text.[186] The approach taken here is to see this breakdown in the third cycle as a symptom of the disintegration of the arguments of the friends.

22:1-30: *Eliphaz*

When the text is read in its present form, the change in Eliphaz's attitude becomes a significant catalyst. In his third speech, Eliphaz has a nastier tone and shifts his position strikingly, pushing even further the position previously outlined by Bildad and Zophar. He abandons his former belief in the genuineness of Job's piety and outdoes his two friends in making specific allegations branding Job as a sinner. Eliphaz confronts Job with a list of his offenses (vv. 2-11), reflects on God's knowledge and power (vv. 12-20), and finally urges Job to repent (vv. 21-30).

22:1-11: Job's Offenses Eliphaz starts his speech with a gentle tone, which he will soon abandon. In vv. 2-3 he considers the theoretical issue of whether human righteousness benefits God in any way. The rhetorical questions, with the implied negative answer, assume the self-sufficiency of God and that he therefore will get no gain (v. 3b), benefit (v. 2a), or pleasure (v. 3a), even from right and blameless human actions. His lesson for Job (stated in v. 2b) is that a person's insight will be of use only to himself, not to God. He seems to imply that Job's hubris is making him think too highly of his own importance in God's scheme.

Verse 4 is a clever hinge verse, in which Eliphaz appears to imply at first that it is not because of Job's (undoubted) piety that God has acted against him, but presumably for some other reason. However, in the light of Eliphaz's rebuke of Job in v. 5 as greatly wicked (filled out in vv. 6-11), what he means here is that Job's attitude to God (his "piety" or lit. "fear of him," v. 4) is defective, perhaps being an attempt to bribe God into overlooking his real life of wickedness.

186. See the section in the introduction, "Is the Text of Job Reliable?"

His summary is stated in v. 5 and then illustrated in vv. 6-11. It is not clear why Eliphaz makes the accusations that follow in this section, since they seem entirely out of character with the pious Job before his afflictions. They are specifically denied by Job in his oath of clearance in chapter 31. All of these charges concern the neglect of some social duty, what he failed to do, and so may simply be a hyperbolic way of saying that not every member of his community was touched by his social concern. They may be a recital of a preexistent wisdom text, thus explaining the change in Eliphaz's position and the lack of fit with Job's life. Perhaps Eliphaz is so steeped in retribution theology that he believes that only great guilt can explain great suffering, and so he now thinks that Job's refusal to heed the warnings of his three friends must mean that Job has been guilty of great wickedness and that there is no end to his iniquities (v. 5).

In any event, he accuses Job of specific sins and the heartless oppression of the needy. He has been unjust to his brothers (v. 6a), requiring a pledge when their word should be enough (hence חִנָּם/*ḥinnām*, "for nothing," here means "without cause or justification"). He has taken away the few garments of those barely clothed (v. 6b; see 24:7, 10), perhaps as a pledge to secure a loan. He has been uncaring to the hungry and thirsty (22:7), withholding from them water and bread. He is charged with creating or tolerating institutional injustice in v. 8, for the man with power has the land, and it is occupied by the one who is favored or preferred.[187] The implication is that power and influence determine one's enjoyment of the land, rather than need. Two categories of the marginalized are referred to in v. 9 — the widows who are sent away empty and the orphans whose arms (as a symbol of strength) are crushed.

Thus Eliphaz concludes in vv. 10-11 that Job's present torment has come upon him because of his unrighteousness, rather than despite his righteousness as Job has claimed. Four images here depict a state of helplessness: surrounded by snares (v. 10a), overwhelmed by sudden terror (v. 10b), unable to see in the darkness (v. 11a), and covered by floodwaters (v. 11b). None of these describes Job's situation precisely, but the cumulative effect of the images is to portray Job's helplessness and to argue that it is fully deserved.

22:12-20: God's Knowledge and Power Eliphaz then describes God's majesty, picturing him as high in the heavens and even higher than the stars (v. 12). The thrust of the verse is that we can see how lofty the stars are, and how much more the one who is higher still. This exalted picture of God is meant to be in contrast with Eliphaz's perception of Job's attitude in v. 13. Eliphaz accuses Job

---

187. The expression "the favored man" is literally "whose face is lifted up," but it is used to refer to favor shown to someone.

of saying (either by his stance or his words) that God has limited knowledge and is unable to see through the deep darkness and therefore to judge. There is no evidence in the dialogue that Job said anything like this. The deep darkness is explained in v. 14, as the sight of the God who is in the heavens is obscured by the clouds that cover part of what happens on earth. In other words, Eliphaz is now imagining that Job is claiming that he is innocent in the hope that God will not have seen, and therefore does not know about, his wicked actions.

In vv. 15-20 Eliphaz contends that Job is guilty by association, as he describes the wicked man and implies that Job is like that. He accuses Job of following the well-worn path that the wicked have previously trodden, with the implication that he should cease to do so (v. 15). The argument of vv. 16-20 is a little tortuous since the events are not in chronological order. Verse 17 is the beginning of the actions of the wicked, with the defiant words to God dismissing him, and the boastful words addressed to others, "What can the Almighty do to us?"[188] Initially, they enjoy the good things of this life (v. 18a). At this point, Eliphaz interjects to say that the "plan [מֵצָה/ʿēṣâ is used in the sense of plan in 38:2] of the wicked is far from me."[189] God's decisive response has been brought forward to the beginning of the poem for emphasis and is described in v. 16 — snatching them away in premature death and washing away their foundation. The response of the righteous to the destruction of the wicked is then outlined in vv. 19-20. They delight in the right action of God and pour scorn on the folly of those who opposed him (v. 19). After concluding that their opponents are cut off, they note that anything the wicked left over has been destroyed by fire (v. 20; cf. 1:16). Eliphaz is making very clear that the defiance of the wicked will be met forcefully with the definite and decisive response of God.

22:21-30: Urging Job to Repent Eliphaz finally outlines, in fairly formulaic terms, the way forward for Job to return to God. While this conclusion contains many fine words (e.g., vv. 21-22), it does not seem to be grounded in Job's actual situation (e.g., in v. 23b the mention of injustice in Job's tents, and in v. 24 the need to renounce gold, both of which Job no longer has).

Eliphaz begins with a call to "agree with God [or, more literally, "show harmony with him"; perhaps even "come over to his side"] and be at peace" (v. 21a). The expected consequence of this is that good or well-being will come to him (v. 21b). Eliphaz urges Job to do more than this initial returning to God, for in v. 22 he then calls on Job to receive instruction from God and place God's

---

188. MT has לְמוֹ/lāmô, "to them," but LXX and Syriac support לָנוּ/lānû, "to us."

189. The LXX, followed by Dhorme, *Job,* 334-35, has "him," not "me," which makes it a reference to God.

words in his heart (a metaphor for allowing what God says to control the core of his being). The irony is that this is exactly what Eliphaz will need to do in 42:7-9. If Eliphaz's diagnosis of Job was right, then his advice would be good. This is the only occurrence of the word תּוֹרָה/*tôrâ* in Job; it often means "law" in the OT, but fairly commonly has a more general sense of instruction (as here).

His misdirected advice continues in vv. 23-28. He calls on Job to return to God to be built up, but the truth is that Job has doggedly refused to let go of God. The mention of removing unrighteousness from his "tents" overlooks the fact that Job has been driven out of his community. Job will later present a sustained defense of his social righteousness (ch. 31). The thought of vv. 24-25 is that if Job puts away his gold, then God will be his special treasure. However, this too overlooks Job's loss of all his possessions. While it could have been argued in the prologue (as the accuser did) that Job trusted in his wealth, such an allegation can no longer be leveled against him. Eliphaz's goal for Job is that he will then be able to delight in God and lift up his face to him — a picture of a positive relationship (v. 26). The next stage of this reconciliation is that Job will pray to God, God will hear him, and then Job will pay his vows (v. 27, probably by a sacrifice). Verse 28 gives a picture of godly, prosperous living. Job's decisions will be established because they will come from his right desires, and God will honor him with the good things in life. All this analysis and advice is neat and tidy, but is based on a misdiagnosis of Job's situation. Eliphaz is trotting out formulas that he would have used many times, but he is simply wrong about how Job needs to move forward. As Andersen puts it, "The only thing wrong with Eliphaz's exhortation is that it is completely irrelevant to Job's case."[190]

Verses 29-30 are more difficult to interpret, in large part due to the change to the plural ("when *they* are humbled," v. 29). Such an unexplained change is often accounted for by a quotation or use of a formulaic expression that has not been adapted to the particular circumstances. Since Eliphaz has used formulaic expressions earlier in the speech (e.g., vv. 23-24), this is the most likely explanation. It would also fit well with the fact that Eliphaz is running out of arguments as the dialogue is grinding to a halt. Verse 29 is a commendation of humility, for the lowly are saved but the proud are humbled. What is added by v. 30 is that, once a person is delivered, that person can intercede for others. While there are proposals to emend the text, if the text is to stand it means that God would deliver those who are not innocent through Job being an acceptable intercessor because of the cleanness of his hands (purity of life). This is, for the reader, an ironic anticipation of what will happen in 42:8-9.

Eliphaz's speech would have been suitable if Job's stance before God were

---

190. Andersen, *Job*, 205.

different. His words, however, are misdirected and therefore serve to make Job's anguish even more miserable. Misapplied truth about God can be deeply wounding in the practice of pastoral care. True words can be right but not appropriate.

23:1-17: Job

In chapters 23 and 24, Job responds in a way that is different from his previous speeches. Especially in the first cycle, Job starts with the friends and the comments they make together with any charges they level against him. Then he characteristically moves on to talk to God, usually in the second person, but occasionally (e.g., 10:2) in the third person. In chapters 23–24 Job begins by speaking to God (23:1-17), but in an indirect way. God is spoken about (third person), not directly addressed (second person), but it is clear that God is in view. Job wants these words to be heard by God, even if they are overheard by the friends.[191] Perhaps the use of the third person is due to Job's growing despair that God might not answer him. Then in chapter 24 Job responds to Eliphaz and the issue he raised about Job's involvement in the mistreatment of the needy and marginalized.

In chapter 23 the language of litigation is very prominent in vv. 2-7 as Job continues toying with the idea of a legal case against God.[192] However, in the second part of the chapter more relational terms are evident (e.g., vv. 10-12), and the section is bracketed by the absence and presence of God (vv. 8-9, 15-17).

23:1-7: Pondering Litigation against God Since in these verses Job uses much litigation language, his complaint (v. 2) is likely to refer to his desire to pursue God in the courts as a way of seeking justice.[193] Job acknowledges that his pursuit of litigation is "rebellious."[194] He freely acknowledges in v. 3b that the path he has chosen is a painful one. His use of power is difficult ("heavy") on account of his distress. Even behind this desire to pursue his legal case, Job's deepest longing appears to be for the presence of God. Thus in v. 3 he expresses a wish that he might find God, that he might come to his dwelling place. For

---

191. Along similar lines Andersen, *Job,* 206, describes it as a soliloquy.

192. The legal terms include "complaint," v. 2; "case," "arguments," v. 4; "answer," "say," v. 5; "contend," v. 6; "argue," "acquitted," "judge," v. 7.

193. "Complaint" has a legal sense in 9:27, but a lament sense is possible in 7:13; 10:1.

194. Many English translations, e.g., NIV, NRSV, ESV, adopt the reading of the Syriac and Vulgate and emend MT מְרִי/*měrî* to מַר/*mar,* "bitter." This fits the parallelism, but the MT is acceptable, and preferred as the harder reading.

Job the fiction of a legal case is to bring God near and accessible, not to drive him away.

He speaks more explicitly of his legal action in vv. 4-7. This is another imaginary scenario, since Job runs through not only his own case against God (v. 4) but also God's response (v. 5). He has previously thought of the danger of coming before an all-powerful God in litigation (e.g., ch. 9), but now he imagines that God would not enter into contention with him, but would give heed to Job (23:6).[195] Verse 7 is very revealing, for it discloses Job's self-understanding (that he is "an upright person," one of the descriptions given of Job by God in 1:1, 8; 2:3) as well as his ultimate goal ("I would be acquitted forever by my judge"). His desire is not for the kudos that might come from victory over God, but only for his vindication on the just grounds of his uprightness. His pursuit of litigation is driven not by insolence but by an unshakable belief in the justice of God and a firm conviction that he has not deserved what has been meted out to him. His understanding of how God rules the world is thus confined to retributive justice, but he wishes to honor rather than dethrone his God.

23:8-17: Searching for a Terrifying God In the rest of this chapter, Job both longs for and yet is terrified of the presence of God. He is desperately seeking God, looking in all directions (forward and back, v. 8; right and left, v. 9),[196] wanting to see God and thus know his presence. Job uses three different verbs of seeing and a particle of nonexistence ("he is not there," "perceive," v. 8; "behold," "see," v. 9). He still has a conviction that God will justly vindicate him on the grounds of his righteousness.

This conviction is based on God's knowledge of his way of life (v. 10a) and God's "testing" him to show his authentic faith (v. 10b; בָּחַן/*bāḥan* used of testing the purity of gold in Zech 13:9). Job claims to be righteous not only in what he did ("held fast," "kept," v. 11) and what he shunned ("turned aside," v. 11b; "departed from," v. 12a), but also in his underlying attitude ("treasured," v. 12b).[197] What Job was committed to living out is variously described as God's "steps," "way," "commandment," and "words." He is claiming a comprehensive righteousness and will provide more details in chapter 31.

Verses 13-14 espouse a big view of God, but this is tied in with the sur-

---

195. Most see here an ellipsis, with the verb "set" (שִׂים/*śîm*) implying "set his mind on" or "give heed to" (שִׂים לֵב/*śîm lēb*). The use of "no" and "surely" clearly implies Job will be victorious.

196. This is not greatly affected by whether Job (Syriac, Vulgate) or God (MT) turns to the right (v. 9b).

197. מֵחֻקִּי/*mēḥuqqî*, "from/more than my statute," is often translated "more than my portion (daily bread)" (e.g., ESV, NJPS), as in Gen 47:22; Prov 30:8; 31:15. See Clines, *Job 21–37*, 579, for other options.

rounding material. Job is not thinking here about God's immutability,[198] but rather his determination to carry out his purposes. This is clear in the rest of vv. 13-14. First, there is the rhetorical question, "who can turn him back/dissuade him?" (v. 13b) with the implied answer, "No one." Next, v. 13 states that what God desires (to do), he performs. Finally, v. 14 asserts that God will complete what he had decreed for Job (lit. "my decree") and according to the things in his mind (lit. "these many things with him"). In other words, Job is focusing on God's ability and determination to bring about what he intends for Job.

However, in the light of his prolonged affliction, Job testifies that God's presence, which is what he longs for (vv. 15-16), actually terrifies him. He believes that God should be on his side (vv. 10-12), but the prolonged absence of God and his pervasive afflictions make him fear what is God's purpose for him. Bracketed by statements that he is terrified/God has terrified him (vv. 15a, 16b, using the same verb), he also confesses that he is in dread of God (v. 15b) and that God has made his inner being weak (v. 16a). This fourfold description indicates the extent of his terror. However, in v. 17 we see Job's determination to press on, even though he describes his situation as "darkness/deep darkness." Despite his oppressive circumstances, Job boldly perseveres. As he does so, he both longs for, and fears, the presence of God.

24:1-25: Job

Eliphaz had raised the issue of the oppression of the poor (22:6-20), which Job now addresses. He agrees that oppression exists, but asks why God does not act in judgment against the oppresssors. As Job outlines his argument, we see the kind of actions and attitudes that Job regards as morally reprehensible, anticipating his more extensive list in chapter 31.

24:1-12: Reflecting on Oppression Verse 1 sets the tone of the chapter, with Job asking why the "times" and God's "days" have not been stored up by God or seen by those who know him. Some versions (e.g., ESV, NIV) translate "times" as "times of/for judgment," but the context of the passage suggests a positive element as well. They are the "times" when the wicked will be called to account, but also marked by the righteous being vindicated and the victims

---

198. Contra RSV, ESV: "he is unchangeable," v. 13a. הוּא בְאֶחָד/*hû' bĕ'eḥād,* lit. "he [is] with one" = single-minded. The NRSV and NIV opt for a different sense of *'ēḥād,* "alone," and translate, "he stands alone."

protected. Instead, Job sees ample evidence that the wicked are prospering, and would locate himself among the oppressed. His big question is, "Why does God allow it?"

The subject of the verbs in vv. 2-4a is not specified, but it is clear from the content (and the rest of the chapter) that some wealthy, wicked people are in view. The actions of v. 2 involve manipulating the means of wealth. Moving a landmark (on terms favorable to oneself) is a way of claiming possession of the land of others (Prov 23:10). Seizing and pasturing the flocks of others is also depriving them of their ability to earn a living. Verses 3-4a outline three examples of discriminating against the marginalized — the fatherless, the widow, and the poor. The donkey is the means of transport, while the ox is the animal that works the field. Taking an ox as security for a pledge is probably excessive, and possible only because of the power of the lender and the desperation of the widow. Thrusting the poor from the road (v. 4a) describes personal and physical humiliation of the marginalized, on top of the earlier economic oppression.

The subject of the verbs changes in vv. 4b-12, with the focus now on the poor. The oppressions that afflict them are viewed from their perspective. For them, suffering is not primarily a theoretical issue but rather an existential and personal one. The poor of the land are made to hide themselves (v. 4b). They are described as wild desert donkeys, going further away from "civilization" in their work of seeking "prey," which will be food for their children (v. 5). They work as laborers in the fields of the wealthy, gathering food for him (the pronoun is singular), but all that they can do is glean what is left behind in the vineyard (v. 6). Verse 7 (also v. 10a) picks up the detail of Eliphaz's earlier speech (22:6b), and refers to their garment having been taken in pledge for a loan. As a result they are cold, wet, and exposed during the night (vv. 7-8). Verse 9 appears to be a parenthetical aside (reverting to the wicked as the subject), highlighting the defenselessness of the victimized widow and explaining how the poor were deprived of their clothing. The power imbalance is clear. Verses 10-11 return to the poor, describing them as naked, hungry, and thirsty, but nonetheless forced to work, carrying sheaves and making olive oil and wine. Verse 12 is a summary verse that rounds off the section. Away from the city, men (מְתִים/*mĕtîm*, often revocalized to מֵתִים/*mētîm*, "dying," but having a more general sense in 11:3) groan under their oppression ("groan" is related to the groaning land in Exod 6:5), and the spirit of the wounded cry out for help. The last phrase could be rendered, "but God does not charge/attribute anyone with wrongdoing," or "but God does not give heed to their prayer" (following the Syriac).[199] On ei-

---

199. The first is preferable since שִׂים/*śîm* has been used to mean "charge/attribute" in 4:18, and תִּפְלָה/*tiplâ* is used in the sense of "wrongdoing" in 1:22.

ther reading, the scandal for Job is that God has not intervened to remedy the wrongs done to the oppressed.

24:13-17: Serious Wrongdoing Further categories of even more serious wrong-doing are then outlined in vv. 13-17, with the wicked again being the subjects. The three wrongs of murder (v. 14), adultery (v. 15), and stealing (v. 16, digging through the wall in order to steal) occur in the same order as they appear in the Ten Commandments, which may suggest literary dependence. However, there is a need to be cautious here, for the key image in this section is of darkness (vv. 15, 16, 17) and light (vv. 13, 14, 16), which does not appear to have been derived from the Decalogue. A key implication is that Job observes much serious wrongdoing in the world, and his complaint is that those who choose the paths of darkness are not caught or held to account. Darkness covers their evil actions, whereas God's light should expose them.

24:18-20: The Fate of the Wicked These verses describe how suddenly (vv. 18-19a) and completely (v. 20) the wicked are swallowed by Sheol or death (v. 19b). This suddenness is emphasized by (something unspecified) moving quickly over the surface of the waters, or of a portion of land so immediately cursed that one does not even look to the vineyards, since there will be no fruit (v. 18). The ice-cold "snow waters" from the mountains come to nothing due to the drought and heat (v. 19a). The images of v. 20 speak of the wicked being utterly forgotten, as if they never existed.

These verses sit awkwardly as words of Job. Is this a misplaced speech of one of the friends?[200] How can they be understood as part of Job's words, in light of what he says earlier in the chapter about the chronic problem of the wealthy oppressors seeming to succeed? Several explanations are possible. This may be designed to balance what Job has said earlier, admitting that sometimes the wicked do come to a speedy end. But there is no picture here of the oppressed being released or wrongs righted. A second possibility is that this sudden, complete end comes to the same wicked oppressors mentioned in the first part of the chapter. This view may not account for the material that follows in vv. 21-24, and would seem to undercut the force of Job's earlier protest about the extent of oppression by the wicked. A third possibility is that these verses are best explained as expressions of Job's wishes, not his actual observations. A fourth option, and the one most likely if these are regarded as the words of Job, is that these verses

200. Some see it as part of Bildad's final speech, but more take it as belonging to Zophar's missing speech. See a useful summary by Clines, *Job 21–37*, 589-90; and an assessment by Lo, *Job 28*, 104-18.

(and some of the ones that follow) are a kind of virtual quotation, holding up the friends' views alongside the reality that Job has described in vv. 2-17. This would fit with the flow of the chapter so far, with the challenging question of v. 1 and the thrust of the summary v. 12. If this were so, then the tone of Job's words in vv. 18-20 would be deeply sarcastic, spoken in order to show how far short of the mark they fall. Habel objects to this view, since it would seem to require a more detailed response or comment than simply v. 25.[201] However, vv. 21-23 may provide an appropriate critique. Either of the last two options is a possible way in which these verses can be read as a useful part of Job's speech.

24:21-24: The Prospering of the Wicked Verses 21-23 focus again on the prospering of the wicked, and seem consistent with the earlier parts of the chapter. Verse 21 describes how they wrong (lit. "feed/graze on") the childless, barren woman and cause the widow not to prosper. What Job cannot understand is that God (lit. "he," but God is in view) preserves and prolongs the lives of such wicked (v. 22), and indeed gives them security and protection. Job cannot understand why the wicked are left to prosper.

Verse 24 is difficult, but the best explanation is that Job is conceding that ultimately the wicked will die (the images of "gone/they are not," "gathered up," and "cut off/wither"), and that is part of the picture that he does not wish to deny. However, his essential point is that they have been left to flourish for so long — and what is worse, God has seemed to give them security and protection (v. 23).

24:25: A Final Challenge to the Friends This last verse is usually agreed to be from the mouth of Job, and comes as a final challenge to the friends, to play the ball and not the man. For the friends to answer Job's argument, they will need to establish that there are no examples of the wicked prospering, and that wickedness will always be quickly and completely overcome. They will effectively have to argue for the truth of vv. 18-20, words so effectively undercut by Job's juxtaposition of them with the realities he has described in vv. 2-17.

25:1-6: Bildad: Humans Are Worthless before God

Bildad's short third speech, with its lame echo of Eliphaz's, confirms that the dialogue is breaking down.[202] The legal scenario behind this is that adversaries

---

201. Habel, *Book of Job*, 357.
202. Gordis, Habel, Rowley, Terrien, and Pope all complete this speech with 26:5-14 (as does

would continue to talk until they ran out of new or compelling arguments.[203] In the third cycle, Eliphaz has resorted to sounding like the other two, Bildad gives us the shortest chapter in the book, and Zophar has nothing more to say. If an author wanted to show that the friends could not match Job in the dialogue, this is a most appropriate way of doing so.

He begins by speaking of the majestic nature of God (vv. 2-3) and concludes that no human can be righteous before God (vv. 4-6). Bildad pronounces that dominion or rule and the ability to create terror are with God,[204] and that he imposes peace in his heaven (v. 2b). This imposing of peace most likely refers to his present ordering of creation.[205] His greatness is then emphasized by two rhetorical questions in v. 3: Can the number of his armies be counted? Is there anyone on whom his light (and therefore control) does not shine? Both expect the answer no.

Bildad then turns his attention to humanity, but his underlying intention is still to exalt God by establishing a contrast. The discrepancy between God and humans is such that no person could be right(eous) or pure when compared to God. However, this speech adds little that is new, since Bildad just mechanically repeats what Eliphaz had said in his first two speeches (4:17; 15:14; in effect, conceded by Job in 9:2; 14:4): no one is righteous before God, and Job should therefore accept that he is a sinner. There are no specific allegations against Job, nor even any reference to him, since Bildad only considers humanity in general (vv. 4, 6). Bildad has nothing more to say about Job's case, so he is reduced to recycling platitudes, merely repeating what has already been said.

Verse 5 is a hyperbolic assertion that even heavenly objects are not bright or clean in God's eyes. This is another way of saying that God is dazzling in his light and absolutely pure, and that nothing compares to him. Clearly this is true, but it does not advance the dialogue.[206] Bildad's speech ends not with a bang but with a whimper. If the bright heavenly objects cannot match God,

---

Clines, but he also inserts 26:2-4 after 25:1), but concede there is still something missing. Hartley completes it with 27:13-23, but with similar reservations. For a useful table see Lo, *Job 28*, 127.

203. Köhler, *Hebrew Man*, 159-60, notes that this was the customary legal process: "Before the legal assembly the speech and counterspeech continue back and forth until the one party has nothing more to say. For this reason the third friend finally speaks no more." See also Kidner, *Wisdom*, 79; Clines, *Job 1–20*, 460.

204. The noun פַּחַד/*paḥad* can mean "fear," but more commonly "terror," and thus the ability to cause terror here, v. 2a. Gordis, *Book of Job*, 276, reads it as a hendiadys meaning his "awe-inspiring rule" or "dominion of fear." Clines, *Job 21–37*, 631, notes in passing that "Bildad's language is as lapidary and indeterminate as a haiku."

205. However, Clines, *Job 21–37*, 632, understands it to describe God's past act of creation.

206. Rowley, *Job*, 170, comments, "It is hard to see how Bildad could suppose that any of this was an answer to Job."

how much less a human being, who is nothing more than a maggot or a worm, insignificant creatures of little value and attractiveness. Indeed, they are symbols of uncleanness, decay, and death as they consume animal and vegetable matter. Of course, Bildad is arguing much more than was needed since all he had to do was establish a case against Job, not denigrate all of humanity. The irony of his argument is that logically it establishes that his own views are those of a maggot or a worm.

26:1-14: Job

Chapter 26 can be neatly divided into two sections: vv. 1-4 are Job's rejection of Bildad's arguments, while vv. 5-14 are Job's praise for God's majestic power. The disputed passages throughout this speech may be accounted for on the basis of the use of irony, which would make the echoes of Bildad and Zophar entirely appropriate. John Holbert, in a careful study of irony in Job, maintains that it is never enough simply to identify the literary form of materials, without regard to how they are actually being used. Thus it may well be that a hymn of praise such as in 26:5-14 is being used ironically.[207]

26:1-4: A Strong Rebuke of the Friends Job here rebukes his friends with heavy irony, perhaps even sarcasm.[208] Job challenges Bildad to show how he has helped the one who has no power, or saved the arm that has no strength (v. 2). The implication is that Bildad cannot show this because he has not done it. In v. 3 Job narrows his focus to wisdom, and sarcastically challenges Bildad in an almost identical way. He asks how Bildad has advised the one who has no wisdom, and how he has caused anyone to know or experience in abundance wisdom or success (תּוּשִׁיָּה/*tûšîyâ* means "success" in 5:12 and 6:13, and "wisdom" in 11:6). The implied answer, made more persuasive since there is no actual response from Bildad, is "Not at all." Job has previously made clear that wisdom, power, and strength belong to God (12:13-16), but he has found none of these in Bildad's words.

207. Holbert, "Function and Significance," 281, concludes that the reader needs to have an eye for irony in Job because "formal materials have been consciously twisted to function in ways different from those which their *Sitzen im Leben* would indicate." Both Skehan, "Strophic Patterns," 141, and Wolfers, "Third Cycle — Part 1," 218, see irony here.

208. Lo, *Job 28*, 128-29, notes that vv. 2-4 are sometimes rejected as Job's because the pronouns are masculine singular, whereas Job usually uses the plural to address all the friends together (except 12:7ff; 16:3; 21:3). She quite reasonably suggests that the singular pronouns imply that Job is singling out Bildad at that point.

Verse 4 is an allusion back to the words of Eliphaz's inspiration in 4:15, which were echoed in Bildad's last speech (25:4). The question of the origin of Bildad's words again implies that they are not from God, nor from any other reliable source. At this point Job ceases to answer Bildad, and turns his attention to the character of God.

26:5-14: Praise for God's Majestic Power Verses 5-14 are words of praise for God's majestic power, which many commentators suggest are more appropriate to the friends than to Job. Many scholars see parallels between Bildad's discourse in 25:2-6 and the words of 26:5-14, as if these verses are the completion of that earlier speech. While this praise of God may be appropriate for Bildad, there is no good reason to deny it to Job. Perhaps this section is not Job finishing off Bildad's speech for him, but rather Job saying that he believes this too, yet it does not solve his dilemma. Job retains a big view of God running his world. All that he laments is that he cannot see how the treatment he has received can be part of God's just plan. This leaves the friends nowhere to stand, and hence they have become silent.

Verses 5-6 are a preamble to the picture of God's majesty, emphasizing that even the dead are not hidden from God. The use of three different terms for the dead (the "shades/ghosts" in v. 5a, used of the dead in Prov 2:18; 9:18; Ps 88:10; Sheol, the place of the dead in v. 6a; and Abaddon, the place of destruction in v. 6b) is a way of emphasizing how comprehensive the assertion is that the dead are open to God's view.

The rest of the chapter unpacks God's ongoing activity in creation (with a predominance of participles in vv. 7-9), acknowledging God's lordship over the entire universe. He keeps on stretching out the sky (v. 7a; the "north" is sometimes an image of the dwelling place of the gods, as in Isa 14:13) and putting the earth in its place (v. 7b). The waters of the heavens he is storing in the clouds (v. 8). The notion that God rules in heaven is behind v. 9, and Job observes that the clouds cover the heavens.[209]

He has set boundaries to the seas and light (v. 10). The "pillars of heaven" are so under God's control that they are pictured as trembling and dumbfounded at his rebuke (v. 11).[210] His control over sea and sky is seen in his ability to disturb the sea (an image of a storm, v. 12a) and to make the skies

---

209. Verse 9a literally reads "he is covering the face of [his] throne," i.e., the heavens. NIV, NRSV, and ESV all make a slight emendation, reading כֶּסֶה/*keseh*, "full moon," for MT כִּסֵּה/*kissēh* (variant of כִּסֵּא/*kissē'*). This would make good sense of the context, but is not strictly necessary.

210. The pillars of heaven are the firm foundation on which the heavens stand, given Job's understanding of the universe. Many see it as a reference to the distant mountains that appear to support the expanse of the sky.

clear (after the storm, v. 13a). However, both of the actions are the means God uses to control the mythological forces of chaos often associated with the sea in Hebrew thought. Thus Rahab is struck (v. 12b; see 9:13), and God pierces the fleeing serpent (v. 13b). This is an anticipation of the second Yahweh speech (chs. 40–41), and shows the possibility of Behemoth and Leviathan being creatures of mythology at that point. What is asserted both here and there is that God has control over all forces that might cast fear into human hearts.

Verse 14 rounds off this section by claiming that even this majestic view of God that he has espoused is still only touching the edges of God's mighty and powerful ways. They are just the "outskirts" or a "whisper," with Job conceding that the full thunder of God's power is beyond comprehension. These words are truer than Job appears to understand at this point, for he thinks that the friends have forgotten all this as they pronounce on God's treatment of him in such glib ways. At the end of the book, Job will realize that he too has spoken of things beyond his understanding (42:3), and in particular that God's running of his creation is determined only by a narrow principle of human retributive justice.

27:1-23: Job

There are three clear sections in this chapter.[211] In vv. 1-6 Job restates his insistence on his integrity, which he has maintained all along. In vv. 7-12 he identifies the friends as belonging to the wicked before picking up on what will be the lot of the wicked in vv. 13-23. While many reassign these verses to Zophar (or some to Bildad), it is possible to read them as Job lecturing to the friends with heavy irony about the fate of the wicked.

27:1-6: Insisting on His Integrity There are two main strands of the litigation motif in the book. One seems to center on the figure described in different legal terms in 9:33, 16:19, and 19:25. In these cases, Job seems to push beyond a litigation framework in seeking a restored relationship with God. The other, most prominent in chapter 13, focuses on taking God to court since he is bound to deliver justice. At first one might think that Job has moved on from the latter approach, but this does not account for 27:1-6. Here Job resumes his case (מָשָׁל/ *māšāl*, v. 1) and complains that God has denied him justice (מִשְׁפָּט/*mišpāṭ*, v. 2).[212]

211. A chart of suggested reallocation of parts of this chapter to Zophar and/or Bildad is set out in Lo, *Job 28*, 127, with more extended discussion at 178-87. More recently, Clines, *Job 21–37*, 643-44, regards only vv. 1-6 and 11-12 as belonging to Job, and uses the rest of the verses together with 24:18-24 to reconstruct a third speech for Zophar.

212. Frye, "Use of *māšāl*," 63-64, has argued persuasively that מָשָׁל/*māšāl* is to be understood

Job acknowledges the emotional impact of all this when he insists that the Almighty has made his life (נֶפֶשׁ/*nepeš*) bitter (v. 2b). Yet, despite all this, Job expresses a determination to persist in his struggle and not seek an easy way out. In vv. 3-4 he states that as long as there is breath in him (the translation "spirit of God" in v. 3b is possible, but it seems to be in parallel with "breath" in v. 3a, and so should probably be translated "God-given breath"), he will not speak what is false or deceitful (v. 4). In the context, this does not mean "lies" in general, but rather that Job will not falsely confess to wrongdoing simply to have his situation restored. He chooses a position of integrity even in the midst of suffering and anguish. Verses 2-4 are the first time Job has used an oath formula, and this section is his first "oath of clearance/innocence," a legal form that will reappear at greater length in chapter 31.[213] Even though he believes that God has not been acting rightly toward him, he still appeals to God by swearing an oath in his name.

The implications of this stance are then worked out in vv. 5-6. Job asserts that he will not concede that God is in the right (v. 5a), nor will he deny his integrity (v. 5b) or righteousness (v. 6a).[214] Job claims a clear conscience, not reproached by his "heart" or the core of his being. Clearly, at the end of the dialogue, Job still seeks to take God to court to vindicate his integrity and righteousness. On the basis of how he understands the world is run, Job has taken a principled stand.

27:7-12: Offering to Instruct the Wicked

Job's central wish here is stated at the outset: "Let my enemy be as the wicked" (v. 7a). The identity of his enemy is clarified in v. 7b as the one who rises up/takes a stand against him. Each of the friends would fit into this category, and so Job addresses the friends in vv. 8-12.

Job asks a series of rhetorical questions in vv. 8-10. Verse 8 implies that the wicked will be cut off by God — that is, their life will be taken away. Even in this life, God will not hear the wicked's cry for help (v. 9). Furthermore, the wicked will make matters worse by not delighting in God or calling on him constantly (v. 10).

Job then turns away from the rhetorical questions and offers to act as a teacher to the friends (v. 11). The first part of the verse could be translated, "I will teach you by means of the hand/power of God," but the parallelism suggests

---

as a litigation term here and in 29:1, where it is a departure from the stereotyped formula that begins all Job's other speeches to the friends.

213. Lo, *Job 28*, 168, 188.

214. Even if Job is speaking to the friends at this point, not God, the force of his words would be the same, for they are saying that Job is wrong to persist in his claim of innocence since it is evident that he is suffering.

"I will teach you in [the matter, i.e., "about"] the hand of God." The flip side of this is that he will not conceal "that which is with God," a way of talking about God's intentions or plans.

As the dialogue grinds to a halt, Job is offering to instruct the friends. Indeed, Job regards his argument as self-evident ("all of you have seen it," v. 12) if they were to look honestly at the world. It is with a strong note of pathos, then, that Job asks the friends why they have become so utterly "vain" or "lightweight" (v. 12b; see Eccl 1:2 and many other uses in that book).[215]

27:13-23: The Fate of the Wicked There are a number of explanations for why vv. 13-23 deal with the punishment of wicked. As mentioned above, some allocate these verses to Zophar or Bildad.[216] Others see that they plausibly continue the words of Job. Andersen, for example, argues that the chapter is designed to be read as "an imprecation, not a statement of fact."[217] If it is so understood, this chapter involves Job calling on God to judge the wicked, which might include the friends. Job could also be undercutting the friends' arguments, stealing their thunder by outlining what the fate of the wicked should be. J. G. Janzen opts for the view that, in chapter 27, Job is quoting snatches of the friends' words in an ironic or sarcastic way.[218] This argument from the use of irony is a difficult one to assess.[219]

A better way to read these verses, however, is to view them as an amplification of v. 7a. In a sense, vv. 8-12 have been an aside in the argument. Having said in v. 7a, "Let my enemy be as the wicked," Job now picks what is the appointed lot or portion that the wicked will receive. Thus he is explaining the meaning of the phrase "as the wicked." Job is suggesting to the friends that they have backed themselves into a corner and will now be treated by God as the wicked. This makes the section descriptive of what happens to the wicked and by analogy what will happen to the friends, an interesting anticipation of what God himself will say in 42:7-8.

The overall impact of the passage is more important than understanding all the details. As an outline of the lot of the wicked (v. 13), Job claims that even when they appear to prosper, this will be reversed (vv. 14-19), for terrors will

---

215. An emphatic expression from the root הבל/*hbl,* having a core meaning of "vapor" or "breath."

216. For more detail see the survey in Lo, *Job 28,* 178-87.

217. Andersen, *Job,* 221.

218. J. G. Janzen, *Job,* 172-74.

219. Smick, "Semeiological Interpretation," 137, rightly observes that "this irony approach which reverses the meaning has merit but must be contextually controlled." That some have suggested the presence of irony in the immediate context makes it more cogent here.

overwhelm the unrighteous (vv. 20-23). It is clear from v. 13 that Job still has a big view of God as the one who determines what happens to a person — the wicked are allotted a portion and receive their due from God.

The multiplying of children is an apparent blessing, but they will face an early death by the sword or die during a famine (v. 14). Even if they survive these dangers, the wicked's descendants will die from disease or pestilence, unmourned by their spouse (v. 15). Verses 16-19 outline the futile attempts that the wicked will make to preserve their life. Though they may hoard silver or clothes (vv. 16-17), these will be enjoyed not by them but by the righteous or innocent. The pictures of v. 18 are those of temporary structures (a moth's house, a watchman's booth), but the folly of the wicked is that they imagine that these buildings will endure. The lesson drawn out in v. 19 is that the wealth of the wicked will vanish overnight, or in the blink of an eye.

Verses 20-23 then explain that the wicked will not only lose their wealth, health, descendants, and life, but will also experience terror and hostility. Terrors will overwhelm them and carry them off with the irresistible force of a flood or a whirlwind (v. 20). The image of a whirlwind taking them away is then developed in v. 21. They are now picked up by the east wind and swept out of their place, again without being able to resist. The powerful God throws something (not specified) at the wicked without letting up (lit. "without pity") so that the wicked flee in haste (an emphatic structure in Hebrew, an infinitive absolute and imperfect). God drives them away from their "place" with slapping of hands (used of striking people down in Job 34:6) and hissing (a symbol of derision, as in Jer 49:17; 50:13; Lam 2:15).

Looking back to v. 7, Job is wishing that his enemy (the friends) be like the wicked as outlined in vv. 13-23 — in other words, that they might receive the portion that has been given to him. This is the irony in this section, for Job is utterly orthodox when he outlines the fate of the wicked. The friends cannot, and do not, take issue with him, but Job is turning all this around to imply that this is the fate that the friends deserve.

Looking Back over Round Three

In this manner the third round of speeches finishes. An interesting by-product of this anticlimactic end is that the breakdown of the cycle has prevented the debate reaching a conclusion.[220] In a "shame" or "face-saving" culture like the

---

220. Matheney, "Major Purposes," 18, proposes that the breakdown "may be a poetic device intentionally used by the author to bring the debate to a close," but not to a conclusion.

ancient Near East, it would be virtually impossible for the friends to concede they were wrong. The other way it could have concluded was if God or someone else interrupted the proceedings and brought the conflict to a satisfactory close. However, if this were done, there might still be the suggestion that eventually the debate may have reached a resolution without such an intervention. Because there is no conclusion at this point, the reader has to make order out of the debate. The leisurely tone of chapter 28 will give the reader space to do so. This also leads to a further possible function of the third cycle. Hartley observes, "while this cycle seems trite and dull, it moves the plot along by creating in the listener the demand that the plot take a new direction."[221]

28:1-28: *Interlude — A Poem on Wisdom*

A major difficulty in understanding this chapter is deciding who spoke or wrote it. A number of scholars (e.g., J. G. Janzen, Childs, Good, Whybray, Greenberg, Lo, G. Wilson) see the chapter as a continuation of Job's words in chapter 27.[222] The peaceful tone of this poem and the absence of accusation have led few to regard it as the missing speech of Zophar, although he did cover some similar territory in 11:7-12.[223] A couple of scholars have contended that it was spoken by Elihu.[224] Some (Tur-Sinai, Settlemire) think it belongs after 42:6; others simply remove it as inauthentic (Driver and Gray, Dhorme, Geller, Pope). Quite commonly (e.g., Westermann, Andersen, Sawyer, Newsom, Hartley, Habel, Walton, Estes) it is seen as an interlude or authorial comment.

Several factors suggest that Job is not the speaker. First, the following chapter commences with "Job again took up his discourse" (29:1). While this need not imply a change of speaker, the mention of Job as the speaker in 26:1, 27:1, and 29:1, but not in 28:1, suggests that Job may not be speaking here. Second, the complete change in literary genre and the irenic tone of the poem (in

---

221. Hartley, *Book of Job,* 323.

222. Greenberg, "Job," 295, notes that ch. 28 is still formally part of the speech of Job, and suggests that the mention of silver in the first line links it to 27:16-17. More substantially, there is a possible connection between this chapter and 27:11, where Job undertakes to teach his friends, "What is with the Almighty?"

223. Gordis, *Book of God and Man,* 102.

224. Greenstein, "Poem on Wisdom," 263-72, and Clines, "Putting Elihu in His Place," argue that the chapter is the closing part of Elihu's final speech, noting that Elihu is especially interested in the topic of wisdom. Clines relocates the Elihu speeches prior to ch. 28. This is unlikely, as it would not make sense of God's rebuke of Eliphaz and Job's *two* friends in 42:7-9, and it would not fit the pattern of the cycle of speeches of the three friends.

the light of how Job speaks out in ch. 29) signal that it was unlikely to have been spoken in the debate. Though there can be widespread mood swings in grief and suffering, this chapter is clearly and inexplicably different in tone from the debate.[225] This is not to deny the appropriateness of the chapter in its present location, merely to assert that it is not part of the debate. Here, then, are sufficient signals to indicate to the reader that this chapter was not uttered by Job in the course of the debate. They provide good grounds for reading the poem — whatever its prehistory — as an appropriate reflection by the author or editor at the crucial time when the dialogue has broken down.

The chapter falls easily into three sections, separated by two refrains (vv. 12, 20), and completed by the final verse (v. 28). While some scholars see the refrains as introducing the following section, there is a nicer symmetry in viewing the first two sections building to the refrain (so vv. 1-12, 13-20) and the third section being capped off by the fear of God saying (v. 28).[226] The refrains in the chapter ask the question, "Where shall wisdom be found?" and the closing verse apparently gives the answer, "the fear of the Lord, that is wisdom."

28:1-12: The Achievements of Humanity This chapter is a collage of images about human beings and their natural environment. Initially, there are settings of remote mining activities, but the real focus is on what humans achieve in these places. Humans display great ingenuity and skill in bringing things to light. While this can be overemphasized,[227] there is a strong affirmation of human abilities to shape and extract value from the creation. This lays the groundwork for a parallel between searching for gems, bringing forth what is hidden (vv. 3, 11), and searching for wisdom, which is also concealed (vv. 13, 21).

Verses 1-4 describe the finding, mining, and processing of precious metals (silver, gold, iron, copper). Silver is mined (v. 1a),[228] and gold is purified (v. 1b).[229] Similarly, iron is taken out of the earth or dust, and copper cast from its ore (lit. "stone," v. 2). Thus four different valuable metals have been located and converted into a usable form through human cleverness. Verses 3-4 then show a series of cameos about how people do the mining activities in vv. 1-2. There is

225. Alter, *Art of Biblical Poetry,* 92.

226. Zerafa, *Wisdom of God,* 130-33, argues that the refrain consists not only of one line but covers three full lines beginning the following section: vv. 12-14 and vv. 20-22. Clark, "In Search of Wisdom," 401-2, has observed the parallel structure of vv. 12-19 and vv. 20-27.

227. For example, Geller, "Where Is Wisdom?" 159, speaks of "terms which echo godhood."

228. However, van Leeuwen, "Technical Metallurgical Usage," 113, understands v. 1a to refer to the molten silver that comes out of the smelter ready to be shaped.

229. Van Wolde, "Wisdom, Who Can Find It?" 4, notes that the root זקק/*zqq* occurs only seven times in the OT, four times in relation to purifying precious metals.

no subject identified in v. 3a, but "man" is assumed and the personal pronoun "he" appears in v. 3b. The picture of v. 3 is of pushing the exploration process to its very limits, finishing with a focus on the stone/ore in darkness. Verse 4 describes opening up or making a shaft or tunnel in a remote location.[230] The remoteness of such activity is mentioned twice ("away from where anyone lives," "forgotten by travelers"). In v. 4b "the forgotten ones" hang down low,[231] swinging to and fro in the mine shafts. It is depicted as a lonely and difficult task.

In vv. 5-6 the focus changes from the activity of mining to the earth itself. In modern terms, v. 5 is something like a split-screen TV. One screen shows the surface of the earth producing its bounty in grain that will become bread. However, a second camera goes underground, where there are powerful and destructive forces, which are turning or transforming it by fire.[232] Distinct parts of the earth tell a different story. The earth certainly contains riches of sapphires and gold (v. 6), but it is not a safe environment.

The perspective changes in vv. 7-8 as we zoom in from high above the earth, from where even the birds of prey and falcons, with their keen distance eyesight, cannot discern the path to the earth's hidden treasures. The animals in v. 8a are not clearly identified, but since שַׁחַץ/*šaḥaṣ* means "pride/conceit," it is generally seen as a generic description of proud or wild animals. This also makes a nice parallel with "lion" in v. 8b. The picture in v. 8 is of the most majestic beasts not being able to find the way to the treasures found by humans. In the light of the mention of wisdom in v. 12, the difficult search for wisdom is for humans alone, not for birds with keen eyesight, nor for animals with legendary strength.

Having set out this broader context, the poet now returns to what humans can do in vv. 9-11. In v. 9 they work on the flinty rock and overturn (used in v. 5 of the earth being turned up by fire) mountains. In v. 10a they cut through (or "carve out"; the Piel indicates that this is a forceful action) watercourses of some sort. Verse 10b picks up the contrast with the keen-eyed birds of v. 7, and asserts that humans see every precious thing, unlike the beasts and birds of vv. 7-8. Humans not only find the way to these precious items, but also shape the created world (damming streams), so that what is hidden and presumably precious is brought out to light (v. 11). While vv. 1-11 do not explicitly mention

---

230. The verb פָּרַץ/*pāraṣ* means "to break through," and נַחַל/*naḥal* is usually a wadi, but the idea is of underground channels, caves, or tunnels.

231. The root דלל/*dll* usually means "to be poor, lowly," but is used in Prov 26:7 of the leg of a cripple dangling.

232. Van Wolde, "Wisdom, Who Can Find It?" 8, notes that the verb הָפַךְ/*hāpak* is used of destruction in the flood story, at Sodom and Gomorrah, and in the threat to Nineveh outlined in Jonah 4.

wisdom, the context of the poem as a whole and the explicit question of v. 12 make clear that wisdom is in view. This poem starts as a reflection on the human search for jewels and precious metals, but is transformed into a challenge: Can human ingenuity find the way to wisdom and understanding? They have shown great enterprise, but this is beyond them (v. 12). Thus v. 12 reverses the praise of human skill in vv. 1-11 with the implied answer, "They do not know." This key question, which humans cannot answer, will be repeated in the refrain in v. 20: Where can wisdom and understanding be found?

28:13-20: Humans Cannot Buy Wisdom and Do Not Value It The next stanza builds on this limited ability of humans to master wisdom. They cannot comprehend the value of wisdom and understanding either (v. 13), nor can they offer anything to gain them (vv. 15-19). Human mining skills are of no help in finding these twin jewels of wisdom and understanding.

This section is made up of two parts; the theme of each is set out in v. 13. Verse 13a states that humans do not know wisdom's worth, which is filled out with a description of its incomparable value in vv. 15-19. Verse 13b speaks of the human inability to find the location of wisdom, as if that would enable mastery of it. It proclaims that wisdom is not found in the land of the living, while v. 14 adds that it is not found in the most remote parts of the world — the sea (יָם/*yām*) or the deep (תְּהוֹם/*tĕhôm*). There are images of places that are not under human control, which means that vv. 13b-14 together are saying that wisdom is not located in a place under human control or in any other place. In other words, humans can neither exhaustively understand wisdom nor control access to it.

Verses 15-19 make the further point, introduced in v. 13a, that humans cannot fully appreciate the value of wisdom, pointing out in particular that all the things regarded as precious by humans cannot match the worth of wisdom.[233] The whole stanza of vv. 13-20 asserts that wisdom is neither fully attainable nor properly valued.

The material in vv. 15-19 is more important for its rhetorical effect than for a careful study of the detail. A collection of precious stones, jewels, and other items are held up as possible contenders for the most valuable item. The verbs and verb equivalents used are all one of evaluation and comparison — "bought for" (lit. "be given for it"), "weighed" (שָׁקַל/*šāqal*), "valued" (Pual of סלה/*slh*, vv. 16, 19), "equal" (vv. 17, 19; lit. "arrange it"; the parallelism in both

---

233. Hartley, *Book of Job*, 378, fails to see that v. 13 ties together and introduces the two parts of vv. 13-20, and opts to translate v. 13a as "Man does not know its abode," tying it in more with vv. 13b-14. This is unnecessary.

verses indicates that it is being arranged to match or equal the gold and precious glass), "exchanged for" (strictly a noun meaning "exchange," not a verb but often translated with a verbal sense because of the sequence of verbs in these verses), "be remembered" ("mention made," ESV), "[price] is above" (lit. "bag/pouch ... more than").[234] The comprehensive nature of this list — itself a wisdom technique — is a rhetorical way of asserting that wisdom is more precious than all that humans value highly.

Wisdom is the subject throughout. This is implied by the fact that it follows on from v. 12, it is explicit in v. 18b, and it is picked up in the refrain of v. 20. The refrain in v. 20 is virtually the same as in v. 12, with the verb "come from" replacing the verb "be found." This change is of little significance but may reflect the change from the search for wisdom in vv. 1-11 to the location and value of wisdom in vv. 13-19.

28:21-27: God Knows the Way to Wisdom Verses 21-22 echo vv. 13b-14 in their focus on the inability of humans to locate and therefore control wisdom. The key assertion of v. 21 is that wisdom (the implied subject from v. 20) is hidden or concealed, generally from all living creatures (v. 21a) and especially from the birds (v. 21b), most likely an allusion back to the birds of sharp distance eyesight in v. 7. The Niphal or passive form of the verb may well imply or at least hint that God has (purposefully) hidden the location of wisdom. Verse 22, with its mention of Abaddon (the place of destruction) and Death, parallels the focus in v. 14 on the sea and the deep. All four descriptions are focusing on liminal areas of life, as if the search for wisdom has had to extend to the very edges of reality. Verse 22 asserts that even after going as far as the edges, there is no solid data about the location of wisdom.

There is a significant turn in vv. 23-27, as the poet explores the connection between God and wisdom. First, God understands דַּרְכָּהּ/*darkāh,* "its path/way" (v. 23), which could mean "its nature" but more probably (in the light of the parallelism in the verse and the concerns of the chapter) "the way to it." God alone is seen to be the one who "understands" the way to "wisdom" and its "dwelling place" (the same word used in vv. 1 and 6, and in the refrains of vv. 12 and 20). The verbs used of God ("understands" and "knows") are ones strongly associated with wisdom. God, however, looks to the ends of the earth (v. 24, echoing the extremities of vv. 14 and 22) and sees everything. Since God at least

---

234. The image appears to be a bag of money and hence "price." Others relate it to the root מָשַׁךְ I/ *mšk* I, "to draw/drag," as in drawing up oysters for pearls. *DCH* 5:525 offers three suggestions: "trail; acquisition," hence "acquisition of wisdom"; or "a bag(ful) of wisdom"; or simply "the price of wisdom."

knows wisdom's place, even if humans can never have divine wisdom, they still receive the benefits of the good and just cosmic order, as it reflects God's hidden wisdom. This can be seen in vv. 25-26 in the provision and control of wind, sea, and rain.[235] This information about God's active control of the creation serves to ground what is said about God and wisdom in v. 27.

Verse 27 is crucial. The first statement is that God "saw" wisdom, in contrast to all others (including human beings). The last statement is that he "searched" it (חָקַר/*ḥāqar*), which probably has the sense of searching it thoroughly or exploring it in detail.[236] The meaning of the middle two statements is less certain. The Piel of the root ספר/*spr* in v. 27 can be rendered as "counted," "related," or "appraised," but often has the sense of "declared" (i.e., "recounted," not just "counted").[237] The force of this is that the poet is claiming that God not only knows the location and nature of wisdom, but that he has also declared it and made it known to others. The other verb that is used of wisdom in v. 27 is that he "established it" (the Hiphil of כּוּן/*kûn*). Here the thought is that he has caused it to remain as part of the fabric of creation. He has caused it to stand firm as a genuine part of the real world. In so doing, he has caused it to be at least partially able to be discerned by others.

28:28: The Fear of God and Wisdom The same words used in the refrains ("wisdom" and "understanding," vv. 12, 20) recur in this final verse. Some have suggested that "wisdom" has a different sense here — that vv. 1-27 concern "speculative" wisdom, which is not obtainable, while v. 28 speaks of the availability only of practical wisdom. However, there are no hints that any distinction is being made between two different kinds of "wisdom," and so "wisdom" should be understood in the same way as in the rest of the chapter.[238] If vv. 12 and 20 are asking the question about where wisdom and understanding can be

---

235. Geller, "Where Is Wisdom?" 167.

236. The verb חָקַר/*ḥāqar* was used earlier in the passage (28:3), and its use here implies that what humans were unable to search out, God has done. Aitken "Lexical Semantics," 122, sees a portrayal of the work of an engineer; van Hecke, "Searching for," 154, 159, notes that the verb "always designates the searching of or the exploring of an object in order to gain understanding of it." On wisdom in Job 28, see Habel, "Of Things beyond Me," 144-45.

237. *HALOT* 1:766 lists as its meanings: "count out, count over again"; "count up"; "make known, announce"; "report, tell," though curiously it lists Job 28:27 under the group "count out, count over again." The more common meaning of ספר/*spr* in the Piel is "to make known" (Exod 9:16; 10:2), though it may have many shades of meaning, ranging from proclaiming (Ps 22:22 [MT 23]) to recounting (Job 38:37). See Zerafa, *Wisdom of God,* 153-54; Tur-Sinai, *Book of Job,* 408-9.

238. Gordis, *Book of Job,* 539, suggests that the dropping of the article from חָכְמָה/*ḥokmâ,* "wisdom," in v. 28 gives some support to this view.

found, then v. 28 is ostensibly giving the answer that it is acquired by fearing God and turning away from evil.

The expression יִרְאַת אֲדֹנָי/*yir'at 'ădōnāy* ("fear of the Lord") occurs only here in the OT, but it is equivalent to the mainstream wisdom phrase, יִרְאַת יהוה/*yir'at yhwh,* "fear of Yahweh/the LORD."[239] However, the first part of v. 28 is asserting something different from the typical wisdom maxim, "the fear of Yahweh is the *beginning of* wisdom" (Prov 1:7; 9:10; Ps 111:10). Here the assertion is "the fear of the Lord — that is wisdom (הִיא חָכְמָה/*hî' ḥokmâ*)." The change is significant. No longer is the fear of God just the beginning point or even first principle for living the life of wisdom; it is now all that there is of wisdom. It exhausts wisdom; it covers the whole field. In the book of Proverbs, the fear of Yahweh was seen as an indispensable foundation, but one that could be built upon or supplemented by other sources of wisdom such as learning from the created world, or seeing patterns in daily life. The expression found in Job has taken this vibrant understanding of Proverbs, and squeezed the life and flexibility out of it, resulting in a calcified or fossilized understanding of the fear of God. The parallel term, "to turn away from evil," is also expressed in this absolute form — it is "understanding."

The use of both expressions, fearing God and turning away from evil, recalls the similar (and expanded) description of Job in 1:1, and twice repeated by God (1:8; 2:3). This is not what Job needed to learn. This is where Job started. Yet his genuine fear of God and turning away from evil have not been enough to give him the answers or comfort that he has longed for in the midst of his sufferings and the seeming absence of God. This is a strong hint that v. 28 is not being presented as the solution to the book.

Reading Chapter 28 as Part of the Book as a Whole Moshe Greenberg has proposed that this chapter is the anticipated conclusion, giving the answer that Job needed to return to fearing God.[240] Even if v. 28 is only asserting that the fear of God is the essence of wisdom (rather than exhausting the meaning of wisdom, as I read it), it still does not provide the answer for Job. If it is to be read as the answer or solution, then its implication is that Job needs to renounce his angry protests and return to a submissive attitude of fearing God. Yet God rebukes the three friends for proposing just this, and endorses what Job has said about him (42:7-8).

The location of Job 28 within the structure of the whole book also suggests that it is not an anticipation of the conclusion and theme of the book. Wester-

---

239. See L. Wilson, "Fear of God"; and Clines, "Fear of the Lord."
240. Greenberg, "Job," 299.

mann observes that it cannot "represent the high point of the book, as some interpreters assume; this is rendered impossible already by its location before the great concluding lament."[241] The answer given by this interlude is followed and qualified by chapters 29–31, and later God's different verdict. This chapter serves the important literary function of preparing for what is to follow. The possible conclusion of v. 28, then, is reframed by chapters 29–31, in which Job insists that the issues are not resolved. The observations in chapter 28 do not resolve Job's struggle. This prevents it from being read as the answer or anticipated conclusion.

It may even operate as a reflection on the preceding dialogue. Robert Laurin sees is as a summary of the views of the friends,[242] while others read it as a dismissal of the previous discussion.[243] The chapter is, at least, a dramatic way to close off the self-perpetuating dialogue and, at the same time, to reflect on the dead-end approach taken by the friends. Furthermore, the placing of chapter 28 after the dislocation and confusion of chapters 24–27 creates uncertainty about who is speaking.

Job's big question is, "Where is God?"; and his longing is for a restored relationship. This chapter does not meet or answer his deepest need.

29:1–31:40: *Job's Summing Up*

In general terms, chapter 29 describes Job's former prosperity, chapter 30 focuses on his present suffering, and chapter 31 outlines his final defense. This makes chapters 29–31 a distinct unit that operates as a final or comprehensive review. Chapters 29–31 are framed by a longing for a restored relationship (29:2) and the issuing of a legal challenge to God (31:35-37).

29:1-25: *Job's Former Prosperity*

After the introductory first verse, vv. 2-6 describe Job's former experience of his relationship with God as well as his family situation and personal circumstances. The remainder of the chapter is concerned with Job's public roles and actions. Verse 7 draws attention to his place in the community, outlining the honor accorded him (vv. 7-10) and his active care of the community in working

---

241. Westermann, *Structure*, 136. Habel, *Book of Job*, 393, views it as a foil for Job's climactic summing up in chs. 29–31.

242. Laurin, "Theological Structure," 88.

243. Dhorme, *Job*, li; Newsom, "Dialogue and Allegorical," 300.

for justice (vv. 11-17). Verses 18-20 are a discrete section introducing the new thought of Job's expectation (at that time) of ongoing peace. Verses 21-25 close off the chapter by pointing to his prominence and community respect. In other words, Job goes back to the days when he was respected as a wise leader who feared God and turned away from evil. That did not prevent his present distress or give him an awareness of God's presence in his struggle of faith.

29:1-6: Job's Former Blessings Verses 2-6 are very revealing. In describing his former circumstances (the "months of old," v. 2), his first and most prominent thought is of his relationship with God, not of his prosperity. This period is labeled "the days when God watched over me." The verb speaks of God keeping and preserving Job, treating him with care and kind attention. This positive tone continues in v. 3 with the image of God's lamp or light, which sheds light on him and enables him to walk safely through darkness. Security and direction have come as a result of God's presence in relationship.[244]

Verse 4 reads literally, "as I was in my winter days," but it is probably a description of his former days (NRSV and ESV "my prime"), when he was younger and at the height of his powers.[245] Again, what was significant to Job at this time was not the opportunities or capabilities of youth, but rather that the friendship of God was upon his tent. The "friendship of God" is a good translation of סוֹד אֱלוֹהַּ/*sôd 'ĕlôah* (hence most ETs; see also Ps 25:14), though it literally has the sense of "counsel/council of God." It speaks of those in the intimate inner circle ("the circle of trust") who hear the private or secret conversations.

This friendship is filled out in two ways in v. 5 — as God being "with" him, and the image of wholeness in the family, with Job surrounded by his children as an outward sign of God's blessing. Even when the children are mentioned here, they are seen as the outworking of the friendship of God, which was for Job the more substantial loss. This friendship led to other things such as a full family in v. 5b and material plenty in v. 6, but what he laments is fundamentally the loss of God's watching over him, God's friendship, which led to these other goods. It was not that Job loved the gifts, not the giver; it was Job's friendship with God, his belonging to his inner circle, that he desperately misses. Verse 6a is a picture of exuberance and abundance (so much butter to spare that it could be used to wash steps), while v. 6b seems to picture a stone olive oil press (or the rock could be the whole hill, including the press), which yielded abundant amounts of oil.

244. Verse 3b is literally "to his light I used to walk [through] darkness." The force of the image may be that the presence of God is a kind of home base to which he could always return in times of darkness.

245. Clines, *Job 21–37*, 934, argues that contextually it must mean "prime" or "peak of one's power."

This passage also jogs our memory about the accuser's earlier challenge (1:9). Did Job fear God out of self-interest or out of genuine integrity? Would Job renounce fearing God once his possessions were taken? The answer given is that Job looks back to his former relationships and appears to give little consideration to his material losses.[246]

29:7-10: Job's Former Honor The picture of Job 1 and 2 is often understood to depict Job and his family as nomadic, perhaps due to the large number of animals in the flocks and herds, which would make them at least seminomadic. However, even there each of his sons had houses (1:4), and the ashes where Job ended up (2:8) were probably the rubbish heap outside a town or city. This picture of Job living for at least part of the time in the city is amplified in chapter 29. Verses 7-10 outline Job's former significant role in the public affairs of the city. The gate of a city (which we today would consider a small walled town) was not just an entrance but also a place for discussing public affairs and deciding legal disputes (Ruth 4). There was room to sit and talk, with most gates opening out into a public square as one entered the city. Here we can finally understand the reason for Job's familiarity with the litigation process, as he takes his seat in the gate.[247] The picture of v. 7 is thus one of Job assuming a high and respected public profile. In v. 8 the youth defer to him, and the aged — often viewed as the repository of wisdom — acknowledge Job's wisdom. In vv. 9-10 this picture of his great influence in the public and legal affairs of the city is furthered by even the "princes" and "nobles" refraining from speaking once Job had spoken. The identification of these people as princes and nobles may imply to modern readers that the "city" was bigger than it actually was, but it clearly refers to those who were rulers and leaders in the community.

29:11-17: Job's Former Role in Administering Justice Job's self-description in this passage is interesting. Habel has argued, from a structural point of view, that v. 14 is the central verse of the central section of this chapter.[248] Here Job describes his life in terms already frequently seen in the book, as characterized by justice and righteousness, which were his clothing that he wore every day. This is both what Job held to be valuable about his former state and what will be the basis for his oath of clearance in chapter 31. By these criteria, Job claimed that he was entitled to be cleared.

---

246. Gros Louis, "Book of Job," 256: "Job, in his own life review, barely mentions his possessions. What seems more important to him is the quality of life."

247. In relation to the connection between the city gate and justice, see the appendix "Justice in the Gate" in Köhler, *Hebrew Man*, 149-75. Job's role there is unpacked in 29:11-17.

248. Habel, *Book of Job*, 406-8.

As part of Job's review of his former circumstances, this section focuses on his just actions within the community. He delivered the righteous poor person who cried out for legal redress, as well as the marginalized such as the fatherless (v. 12b), the widow (v. 13b), the blind and lame (v. 15), and the general category of the needy (v. 16a). He intervened to rescue those about to perish, so that they blessed him once their lives had been preserved (v. 13a). He was proactive in that he searched out the legal cases of those he did not know, rather than confining himself to his immediate circle (v. 16b).

Verse 17 seems to provide a summary statement of how he took on those who were oppressing the poor and needy. These oppressors (ESV "the unrighteous"; NRSV "the wicked") are vividly pictured as sinking their teeth into their prey, but Job secures release for the oppressed. It is in this active lifestyle sense that he was clothed with justice and righteousness (v. 14). He worked through the legal system to secure what was right for the marginalized rather than what suited the rich and powerful. In so doing he resembles the wise ruler of Proverbs (Prov 28:4-6, 15-16; 31:4-5).

29:18-20: Job's Expectation of Ongoing Peace These three verses reveal what kind of future Job expected during his former prosperity. He describes the one, core thought of a peaceful, fulfilling life through a number of images. The idea of dying in the nest (v. 18a) is not one of never venturing beyond his home, but rather of having a secure home base, undisturbed by the uncertainties of life that he had experienced more recently. A long life is in view in the multiplying of days like the grains of sand that cannot be counted (v. 18b).

In a dry climate or area, having roots that extend to sources of water (v. 19a) means the ability to survive times of drought or adversity. This access to moisture is supplemented by abundant dew on the branches (v. 19b), another key source of water in a climate where rain is scarce. Together the images of v. 19 give a picture of ongoing and stable access to the source of life.

Verse 20 is more difficult. Two things are renewed or refreshed. The first is his כָּבוֹד/*kābôd*. This could be translated as "glory" (so most translations, e.g., ESV, NRSV, NIV), but the focus in the chapter on his reputation (e.g., vv. 7-10, 21-25) suggests that his "honor" before others is in view.[249] The significance of the bow in his hand is less clear. Some understand it as a metaphor for his body, full of vigor and springing back to shape. It is better to see it as a literal bow,

---

249. Contra Hartley, *Book of Job*, 393, who translates כָּבוֹד/*kābôd* as "liver" (a by-form of כָּבֵד/*kābēd*), and says the image of a new liver is of a refreshed inner being. He is building on Ceresko, *Job 29–31*, 27.

which in the context could be used to prevent injustice (vv. 11-17) or to hunt for food, with the provision of food balancing the abundant water of v. 19.[250] The significance of the bow being new, not old or brittle, is that the bow is able to shoot powerfully and accurately. חָלַף/*ḥālap*, "renewed" (KJV, NASB; most other ETs "ever new"), is used in Isa 40:31 of those waiting on the Lord to renew their strength, or in Job 14:7 of a tree sprouting forth again.

29:21-25: Job's Prominence in the Community This section picks up many of the concepts outlined in vv. 7-10, but also rounds off Job's summary of his former life by picturing Job as a respected elder in the community.

The initial focus is on Job's wise spoken advice in vv. 21-23. In v. 21 they waited for and listened quietly to his advice. On its own this verse could simply show that they listened politely, but the scenario is described extravagantly in vv. 22-23. Verse 22 shows that Job's words had the outcome of ending discussion. His advice was so patently wise that nothing more could be said or needed to be said. Verse 23 speaks of Job's advice being anticipated or looked forward to like the life-giving rain being swallowed by a thirsty earth. Thus Job's words were final and life-giving.

However, this section is not just about words but also about actions. Verses 24-25 speak of his involvement in the lives of others. The imagery of "smiling" and the "light of his face" (v. 24) is that of encouragement during difficult times. Verse 25 speaks of his exercising a leadership role (he lived as a chief or head; he dwelt like a king), but it also speaks of his identification with the people. This is seen in his choosing their path or way of life (v. 25a), living among his troops as a good king does (v. 25b), and bringing comfort to those mourning (v. 25c). The combined picture is one of great status and respect, matched with wise advice and genuine care for the people.

30:1-31: Job's Present Suffering

The juxtaposition of chapters 29 and 30 — the before and after — show that virtually all of Job's relationships have been turned upside down. The contrast with chapter 29 is stark: from enjoying "the respect of the most respectable" (29:21-25), he now suffers "the contempt of the most contemptible" (30:1, 9-12).[251]

---

250. However, Clines, *Job 21–37*, 992, suggests that bows are only used for inflicting death and injury on other people (though he adds "and animals"). He ignores the use of a bow to prevent injustice, or the most likely use of hunting for food.

251. Andersen, *Job*, 234-35.

30:1: But Now . . . In v. 1 some rough younger men are no longer silent, but are actively mocking and laughing at Job. The contrast between this present reality and his formerly being treated with honor is indicated by "But now" in v. 1.

30:2-8: How Job Would Have Viewed His Mockers Verses 2-8 are best understood as a virtual quotation referring not to Job's present views but rather representing what was said about the outcasts when Job was a respected citizen.[252] These verses, then, are an extended description of the (group of) people who are now laughing at Job (v. 1).

All the details are looking at the same group with a variety of images. They are not physically strong, for their energy has been spent (v. 2).[253] They are desperately hungry (vv. 3-4), resorting to scavenging for food among the soil, leaves, and roots. While there is debate over identifying some of the references, the overall picture is quite clear. They are driven away or banished from their human communities (v. 5), treated like wild animals in being forced to live in desolate, deserted places (vv. 6-7). They are even described as if they were animals, braying like donkeys in v. 7. Verse 8 rounds off this section by describing them as senseless and nameless, even whipped or driven out of the land.

This is a comprehensive picture of those outcasts who were beyond the fringes of human community. There may well be elements of hyperbole here, as Job is about to make the point (see vv. 9-15) that even those with no community respect at all are currently mocking and belittling him.

30:9-15: The Attacks of His Enemies The recurrence of וְעַתָּה/*wĕʿattâ*, "And now" (v. 9, the same expression translated as "But now" in v. 1) is resumptive of Job's earlier train of thought, as he proceeds to focus on their present mocking (v. 1). Verses 9-15 speak of Job's treatment by his "enemies," a common feature of biblical laments. God is still spoken of in the third person (v. 11), so Job is not yet turning directly to address God.

Verses 9-11 variously describe how these outcasts mock Job. He is the subject of their taunting songs (v. 9a.).[254] He is also to them a "byword," which is

---

252. Both Gordis, *Book of Job*, 330, and Habel, *Book of Job*, 414, regard vv. 2-8 as a virtual quotation representing what Job had formerly thought about them. However, Job may simply be identifying a group of outcasts and outlining how they were rejected by the community as a whole, rather than by him personally. Skehan, "Job's Final Plea," 53, suggests that Job is referring to the past condition of his revilers' parents.

253. See Ceresko, *Job 29–31*, 46. כָּלַח/*kālaḥ*, "vigor," used only in v. 2b and in Job 5:26, here parallels "strength."

254. Ceresko, *Job 29–31*, 58, notes that use of the root שׂחק/*śḥq*, "laugh at" (ESV), in v. 1 and

literally "a word" (מִלָּה/*millâ*), but the context suggests an insulting word. Verse 9 is made plainer by their actions in v. 10 — they abhor him; paradoxically they reject him by both keeping distant from him and yet not hesitating to come close enough to him to spit in his presence (ESV, NRSV) or face (so NIV, NJPS, NASB, KJV). Verse 11b offers the summary description that they have cast off any restraint as they show contempt for Job.

How does Job see God at work in all this? Job still clings to the belief that God is the one who determines what happens to him (v. 11a).[255] Job thus retains a big view of God despite his adversity, and does not retreat to a dualism in which God can only determine part of what happens, while evil forces account for the rest. יֶתֶר/*yeter*, "cord" (KJV, ESV), has been used in 4:21 as a symbol of life. There is a similar concept, but different word for "cord," in Eccl 12:6. The word עָנָה/*'ānâ*, "humbled," here could also be translated "afflicted" (so NIV, KJV, NASB).

Verses 12-15 fill out the attacks of his enemies with a montage of images. The descriptions of v. 12 seem to imply a physical assault on Job, but this may simply be metaphorical language describing a more verbal attack. The twin images of v. 13a-b speak of making life hard for Job, putting obstacles in his path, and increasing the difficulty of his circumstances. Verse 14 refers to a full frontal assault, bursting through the breach in a walled city now left defenseless, overwhelming Job by the relentlessness of their attack. They are portrayed in v. 15 as "terrors" turning upon him, attacking both his reputation (honor) and his circumstances (prosperity/well-being). The force of vv. 9-15 as a whole is that this attack by his enemies is overwhelming in its severity and persistence.

30:16-19: God Is Causing His Present Sufferings In vv. 16-19 Job focuses on his present sufferings, and accuses God (still spoken *about* in v. 19) of determining his circumstances. This section is again introduced in v. 16 by the structural marker וְעַתָּה/*wĕʿattâ*, "And now" (see vv. 1, 9). The key theological conclusion of v. 19 is preceded by traditional lament language in vv. 16-17 and a more enigmatic v. 18. Verse 16a could be translated "concerning me [i.e., in my situation], my soul is poured out," or as is commonly translated, "my soul is poured out within me." On either reading there is great personal anguish and despair, echoed in vv. 16b-17. This is reminiscent of the oppressive days and nights in 7:1-4, 13-15. Not only are the days of affliction unending, but the comparative ease that one might expect at night does not come. Instead, there is bone-racking

---

the word for "their song" (נְגִינָתָם/*nĕgînātām*) here in v. 9 are brought together in a lament context in Lam 3. In Lam 3:14 the ESV translates *nĕgînātām* as "the object of their taunts."

255. "God" is not in the Hebrew text, but its insertion enables the reader to understand the sense. The change to singular verbs in v. 11a makes clear that his taunting enemies are no longer in view (also in v. 19), and he addresses God directly in v. 20.

pain that gnaws away at Job, so that there is for him no rest (v. 17). Verse 18 may speak of Job's altered appearance or his maltreatment, but it seemingly continues the thrust of vv. 16-17.[256]

Job's despairing conviction in v. 19 is that God (as in v. 11, rightly implied) has thrown him down into the muddy clay (i.e., humiliated him) and that he has become like dust and ashes. Dust and ashes are symbols for lamenting in chapter 2, here, and in 42:6. Job is claiming that God has forced him into a situation where all he can do is lament both his circumstances and his sense of abandonment.

30:20-23: Accusing God At v. 20, however, Job turns to address God directly as he has done previously in his complaints to God. In vv. 20-23 Job makes his strongest accusations against God — God not answering, God turning on him and attacking him, snatching him up and tossing him about, and finally bringing him down to death.[257] As before, Job's words issue from a desire for the presence of God in the midst of his distress. What hurts Job most is that when he cries out to God, God does not answer or respond (v. 20).[258] Job desires a living relationship with God, yet he feels that God watches him (v. 20b) but does not watch over him (29:2). The attention given to him by God simply makes life harder (v. 21). He accuses God of being cruel to him, an idea filled out by his belief that God is using his power to persecute Job (16:9).

Verse 22a could be understood in one of two ways. Job could be describing his current circumstances as God unsettling him by the wind and tossing him about. It could also be read more positively as a description of his former circumstances — God lifting him up in the sense of prospering him.[259] The former is more likely in view of Job's description of his previous circumstances being confined to chapter 29, while chapter 30 simply limits itself elsewhere to his present distress (except possibly v. 25). In any event, it is clear that v. 22b describes Job's perception that God is currently tossing him about in a fierce storm. Job expects that he will receive an early or imminent death (v. 23).

256. Reyburn, *Book of Job,* 550, proposes that "garment" might be a metaphor for his skin, but it could also refer to his difficult circumstances. G. Wilson, *Job,* 330, explains the NIV as comparing God to an ill-fitting garment that binds and chafes him. Clines, *Job 21–37,* 953-55, outlines the various possibilities.

257. Habel, *Book of Job,* 417, sees three sections in the lament (vv. 20-31), based around "cry out": torment instead of justice (vv. 20-23), evil instead of reward (vv. 24-27), and lament instead of litigation (vv. 28-31).

258. There might be a play on words here as עָנָה/*'nh* I, "answer," in v. 20 is a homograph of the root used to describe days of affliction in v. 16 (noun based on *'nh* II) and in v. 11 of God "humbling" Job (*'nh* II). See *HALOT* 1:851-54.

259. For the former see, e.g., Clines, *Job 21–37,* 1007-8; G. Wilson, *Job,* 331. For the latter see, e.g., Habel, *Book of Job,* 421; Newsom, "Book of Job," 546.

30:24-31: Withdrawing into Despair As he focuses on the reversal of his circumstances and the stark contrast with his former life, in vv. 24-31 this leads Job to withdraw into despair. The Hebrew of v. 24 is difficult, and many commentators suggest emendations. If the Hebrew text is not changed, the most likely sense is, "Surely does not one in a [situation of] ruin stretch out a hand [to call for help?]; and if a disaster [happens] to them, [utter] a cry for help" (similarly ESV). In the light of v. 25, it means that a person struck by disaster would put out a hand for help, an action that most people would respond to. Verse 25 describes Job's practice, in the time of his former prosperity, of caring deeply (weeping, grieving) for the needy suffering hardship.

In v. 26 Job returns to his current experience, in which he hopes for restoration ("good" = prosperity) but faces only disaster ("evil"). Light and darkness describe these same situations. He feels that no one, not even God, has shown him any mercy and care. Indeed, this focus on Job's present hardship is amplified in the rest of vv. 27-31, and the whole section vv. 26-31 is best understood as a contrast and counterpoint to the ideal description of 29:2-6. Verse 27a shows that he has internal (health) issues that hamper his quality of life, while v. 27b summarizes his present situation as days of affliction (as in v. 16). The image of being "darkened" (v. 28a) may talk about his outlook in general (the most likely) or could be anticipating the blackening of his skin in v. 30a. Verse 28b appears to refer back to vv. 24-25 and indicates that he makes (presumably unsuccessful) appeals for help to the gathered community. He expects them to be his brothers or friends, but v. 29 shows that the only brother or friend he has are the wild animals (jackals, ostriches) who, like him, live on the outskirts of the community. His physical suffering is quickly described in v. 30, with an apparent focus on a skin disease and some internal illness. The point is clear even without a full medical diagnosis. Finally, v. 31 describes in hyperbolic terms how his musical instruments (the lyre and pipe, which he would not still have) are turned to songs of mourning and weeping, for they would no longer be needed for any song of joy.

This is a bleak and comprehensive picture of Job's world turned upside down, and of his former prosperity being so eaten up by his times of hardship that they are now only a distant, wistful memory.

31:1-40: Job's Final Defense

The legal procedure behind chapter 31 must be understood in order to make sense of the passage. The "oath of clearance" is a form of self-curse, forcing a verdict by calling down upon oneself the wrath of the god if what one is swearing is false.[260] Other OT examples reveal that this need not be an act of disrespect for the monarch whose legal system has not secured justice.[261] Undergirding this procedure is the assumption of a theology of retribution in which God will reward the good and punish the wicked. This is first seen in its negative form (the wicked will be punished) in v. 3. In v. 6 Job wants God to weigh him on the scales of justice and vindicate him because of his integrity. Other examples of retribution thinking can be seen in vv. 9-10 and vv. 21-22. The assumption is that there is a necessary correlation between action and consequence. The friends have used this equation to condemn Job; Job uses it to complain of the miscarriage of justice.

This chapter has been regarded as a fruitful source of the OT picture of the personal ethics of a righteous person. Chris Wright suggests that the negatives (what Job claims he has not been guilty of) can be processed into positive prints to build up a picture of a person fulfilling their obligations, doing what is good.[262] This chapter can be used in this way to make an "identikit" picture of the thoughts, goals, and actions of a righteous person, echoing the portrayal given of Job in chapters 1 and 29. It is not primarily one of cultic righteousness, for only the worship of the sun and moon (vv. 26-28) seems concerned with this.[263] Job's integrity extends from his outward actions to his thoughts and attitudes.[264]

There is no strong structure in this oath of clearance, since it is a succession of possible breaches, often begun by "if," and extending through vv. 1-34, 38-40. Wedged in among the last few examples is the summons for a "hearer" to listen to Job's legal complaint and vindicate him (vv. 35-37). The individual sections seem to be divided either by Job giving a reason for his rejection of such behavior (e.g., vv. 2-4, 11-12, 14-15, 23, 28) or by his calling for certain consequences for a breach (e.g., vv. 8, 10, 22, 40). On this basis, the chapter divides into vv. 1-4, 5-8, 9-12, 13-15, 16-23, 24-28, 29-34, 35-37, 38-40. The section in vv. 29-34 is incomplete because it is interrupted by Job's call for a hearer, but the standard pattern is resumed in vv. 38-40.

31:1-4: His Rejection of Lust The most striking characteristic of how the oath of clearance begins is that Job starts with an attitude, not action, denying that

---

260. Köhler, *Hebrew Man*, 160-61; Kline, "Trial by Ordeal," 82-83.

261. O'Connor, "Reverence and Irreverence in Job," 101, points out that "a citizen aggrieved by a royal official could bring his complaint before the King's tribunal without thereby being guilty of disrespect towards the monarch." Köhler, *Hebrew Man*, 164, cites the examples of 2 Sam 12:1ff.; 14:1ff.; and 15:1-6.

262. C. Wright, *Old Testament Ethics*, 372.

263. Maston, "Ethical Content of Job," 52.

264. Fohrer, "Righteous Man," 13-14.

he has looked "lustfully" (NIV) at a young (unmarried) girl or virgin.[265] The language of making a covenant with his eyes is that of a deliberate, firm resolve (a covenant, with God or with himself) to tackle the prior issue of lust and not simply refrain from overt sexual sin. His integrity is shown by his willingness to address the root cause of the problem and not simply the symptom.

An insight into Job's character or motivation is provided by the three reasons he gives in vv. 2-4. The first reason is that Job believes that "God above"/"the Almighty on high" will allot to each person the portion or heritage (language used by Zophar in 20:29) that they deserve (v. 2). Second, he understands that God will bring punishment (calamity, disaster) for the wicked (unrighteous, workers of iniquity, v. 3). Finally, he sees that nothing will escape the all-seeing God, who will hold Job to account (v. 4). Thus he has a big view of God as all-seeing and transcendent, and he believes that God will operate on the basis of the principle of retribution. The wisdom poem (28:24) has already proclaimed that God sees everything to the ends of the earth. Job here concedes that this includes his whole way of life.

31:5-8: His Denial of Falsehood and Deceit Verses 5-6 deal with falsehood and deceit.[266] The language of "walking" and "my foot hurrying to/after" are ways of describing the characteristic pattern of life in a person. The "falsehood" and "deceit" could refer to shady business practices, to idolatry, to false and deceitful associates, or to lies in general as a way of life. The word "falsehood" (שָׁוְא/*šāwĕ*) refers to what is false, vain, or empty.[267] מִרְמָה/*mirmâ*, "deceit," is used of Jacob's deception of Esau (Gen 27:35). It often refers to deceit by words (e.g., Pss 17:1; 35:20; 52:6; 109:2). However, there is a striking use of the words in relation to deceitful business practices in using scales and weights (e.g., Amos 8:5; Hos 12:8; Mic 6:11; also in wisdom texts, e.g., Prov 11:1; 20:23). The idea of being weighed in balancing scales (v. 6) may support this sense of deceit in business.[268]

Verse 7 contains three images: "turning aside from the way," "my heart

265. The word "lustfully" is not explicit in the Hebrew text. The intensive (Hitpolel) form of the verb בִּין/*bîn* (which in the Qal means "to understand, perceive") means to look intently in some unspecified way. Here it means to look at/for a girl in some improper way.

266. Hartley, *Book of Job*, 408, suggests that vv. 5-6 deal with falsehood and vv. 7-8 with covetousness.

267. It can refer to the use the name of the Lord in vain, as in Exod 20:7; Deut 5:11. It is used six times in Job, referring to idols in Job 15:31a, but meaning "empty" in 35:13. However, neither of these is spoken by Job.

268. Gordis, *Book of Job*, 345, and Wright, *Old Testament Ethics*, 372, believe that vv. 5-6 are about cheating or dishonesty in the areas of trade or business. Andersen, *Job*, 241, also suggests that the consequence of failure of his crops (v. 8) supports the view that v. 5 is referring to shady business practices.

following my eyes," and "any spot or blemish sticking to my hands." These are various ways of describing moral purity. Verse 1 has already raised the possibility of the eyes leading a person astray, but the image of a spot sticking to the hands is a clearer image of impurity.

Job's underlying theology of retribution is seen in v. 8, when he gathers up vv. 5 and 7 and asks that if he has wrongly gained from others by any false or impure actions, may what he has gained be taken away or given to another.

31:9-12: His Avoidance of Adultery These verses deal with Job's denial of any adultery, and, as with vv. 1-4, the main focus is again on the rationale and consequences. The details of this section are similar to the wisdom teaching of Proverbs 5–7.[269] An apparent exception is v. 10, but even this is a straightforward statement of retribution theology that saturates the book of Proverbs.

Verse 9 focuses on both thoughts or inner attitudes (the heart enticed) and actions (lurking/laying in wait), rather than simply on outward acts that could be prohibited by the law. Lying in wait at his neighbor's door seems, in the light of Prov 5:8, to refer to lingering near the house in order to create opportunities for sexual conquests. Verse 10 is difficult to read in a contemporary Western culture, but must be understood against the background of a society in which a wife was deemed to be the property of her husband. It is thus a cry by Job that if he has wrongfully taken the property of another man, then his property should be taken. This is a classic retribution principle, but embedded in the vastly different cultural values of times long ago. The images of his wife grinding for another, and others bowing down on her, are references to sexual intercourse.[270]

The rationale for this oath is set out in vv. 11-12 and is twofold. First, such sexual sin would be a serious offense and a wickedness deserving of punishment (v. 11). Second, it would be as foolish as playing with fire, ultimately being very destructive of his whole life (v. 12).

31:13-15: His Care for His Servants These verses are quite staggering when understood against their cultural backdrop. The "cause" (מִשְׁפַּט/*mišpaṭ*) of the servant is the legal case, and the legal obligations of masters to their servants were generally ignored and unenforced, since slaves were regarded as property. That Job considers this to be a moral issue shows the extent of his integrity.

---

269. For example, the parallels between v. 9a and Prov 6:25; v. 9b and Prov 5:8b; vv. 11-12 and Prov 5:21-23 (especially in the light of Job 31:28, where in the sight of the judges is parallel to being false to God); v. 12 and Prov 6:27-28.

270. However, Hartley, *Book of Job*, 413, understands this as doing the menial work of a slave.

The rationale for this is even more telling. He believes not only that he is accountable for how he treats his servants, but also that he is answerable to God (v. 14). This too is typical of wisdom literature (Prov 5:21; Eccl 11:9; and the wisdom-influenced Gen 39:9).[271] Even more radical is Job's assertion in v. 15 that the underlying reason for dealing fairly with servants is that they all share a common humanity based on them all being created by God.[272] The doctrine of creation is important to the book, and grounds the care for others in the book of Proverbs as well (Prov 14:31; 22:2). This is an apparent belief in the genuine worth of all human beings, despite Job's wealth and righteous reputation having made him the greatest man in all the east (Job 1:3). Job was not spoiled by prosperity and power.

31:16-23: His Righteousness in Dealing with the Poor and Marginalized Verses 16-23 are an extended description of his righteousness in dealing with the poor and marginalized, refuting Eliphaz's charges (22:5-9). The need to care for those on the outer edge of society was enshrined in OT law (see especially Deuteronomy), but it was also a common element in OT wisdom literature. The kind of actions undertaken by Job included providing what the poor and widows needed (v. 16),[273] sharing his food with starving orphans (v. 17), giving guidance and direction for the fatherless and widows (v. 18), and providing covering and bedding for the needy (vv. 19-20).

Job has not described the consequences for any failure in these obligations, but they are all gathered up in the more complete oath formula in vv. 21-22. In v. 21 Job denies the offense of raising his hand to threaten or strike the orphan. The second part of v. 21 implies a legal setting (the gate as the place of justice), with Job denying that he used the legal processes (and his prestige in that setting, 29:7-10) to oppress the orphan.[274] Verse 22 shows another clear example of Job's retributive thinking: If he used his arm to act unjustly toward the needy, let that arm become useless.

Verse 23 comes back to the motif seen earlier of Job believing that he is accountable to God for his treatment of others (vv. 2-4, 6, 14-15). His under-

---

271. For wisdom influence in this part of the Joseph story, see L. Wilson, *Joseph, Wise and Otherwise*, 102-5.

272. See further Neville, "Job's Ethic."

273. Hartley, *Book of Job*, 416, views "eyes failing" as causing the widow's eye to grow weary, in the sense of giving up hope in despair. This phrase is used in that sense in Ps 69:3 (MT 4) and perhaps by Zophar in Job 11:20.

274. The image of seeing his "help" (here probably referring to a person) in the gate (v. 21b) is an image of having one who could sway the legal decision in his favor, rather than allow a case to be judged on its merits.

standing is that a failure to care positively for the marginalized is worthy of punishment and judgment from God.

31:24-28: His Refusal to Worship Money or Other Gods This section combines offenses of trusting in riches (vv. 24-25) and adopting pagan worship practices (vv. 26-27), rounded off by a theological rationale (v. 28).[275]

The focus on riches is again a problem of attitude (trusting, rejoicing) rather than outward action. It is described from four different angles, a technique that gives examples of wrong attitudes rather than an exhaustive definition of the offense. The synonymous parallelism of v. 24 (different words are used for "gold/fine gold" and for "trust/confidence") is saying a similar thing in each half of the verse. It draws attention to the same failing of trying to gain meaning, security, and purpose in life from something that is a tempting but poor substitute for God (a point made by Prov 3:14; 8:19; 11:28a; and by Eliphaz in 22:24-25). In v. 25 the verb "I rejoiced" covers both halves of the verse, so the verse explores the nature of Job's longing or delight. Having either great wealth or a proven track record of growing wealth as one's most prized achievement would be as culpable as trusting in wealth for meaning and security. The place of our ultimate trust is a matter of deep concern to God.

Verses 26-27 are less transparent for the modern reader, but the imagery relates to the worship of the sun (אוֹר/'ôr, lit. "light") and moon. Job denies both any wrong attitude ("enticed," and this "in secret" and so not able to be noticed by other people) and any false action (lit. "my hand has kissed to my mouth," seemingly some action of homage). Tying together vv. 24-27, Job concludes that any or all of these actions and attitudes would constitute a wickedness deserving of punishment (a similar phrase to that used in v. 11b) since it was being false to God (v. 28b; the sense is betraying or being deceitful/unfaithful to God).

31:29-34: Not Guilty of a Variety of Wrongs This section is technically incomplete in that it ends abruptly with the interjection of v. 35. However, the placement of these verses in the chapter as a whole makes clear that Job is denying all these things as well. It is simply the urgency of Job's desire for vindication that make him bring his oath to an abrupt climax in vv. 35-37.

Again it begins with the mention of an underlying attitude. The twin description of v. 29 refers to delighting or rejoicing when those who have op-

---

275. C. Wright, *Old Testament Ethics*, 372, describes all these examples as avoiding idolatry, whether in the form of materialism or of astrology. Interestingly, the same connection of trusting in wealth and worshiping other gods is made in Deut 8:11-20, and in the NT by the connection of coveting and idolatry as in Col 3:5.

posed Job meet with disaster. In an aside in v. 30, Job adds that he has not even sought revenge by cursing such a person (lit. "his soul" or life) with his speech.

Verses 31-32 describe Job's active care for the homeless or traveler, providing them with food (v. 31) and a place to sleep (v. 32). "Flesh" or "meat" indicates that Job did not simply feed them scraps, for meat was a valuable food. These verses seem like a clear denial of the charges leveled by Eliphaz in 22:7-9. Job has shown care for those in need around him.

Verses 33-34 do not address the issue of whether Job has sinned. Although he is "blameless and upright, fearing God and turning away from evil" (1:1, 8; 2:3), there is no thought within the book that Job is sinless. Rather, Job is righteous, more righteous than other human beings. The point in v. 33 is whether he has attempted to conceal or hide his sin. Verse 33a could be translated, "if I have concealed my transgressions like Adam," but אָדָם/'ādām is probably used here (as commonly in Hebrew) to refer to humanity in general, and thus translated "as people do." The idea of hiding sin in v. 33 is filled out in v. 34 by describing some of the possible motivations for people to disguise their sin. Thus he denies that he concealed sin out of fear of the crowd, or to avoid being looked down upon by certain (presumably important) family groups. At the end of the verse Job returns to the idea that he is not a person who has simply sinned behind closed doors. He has earlier referred to the sins of his youth (13:26).

31:35-37: The Call for God to Answer Verse 35 begins with an appeal that would compel the plaintiff to present his evidence.[276] Job's call is for a שֹׁמֵעַ/šōmēaʿ, literally a "hearer," a legal figure.[277] This means that Job has not given up his earlier wish for an arbiter, witness, or redeemer, as he strives for God's intervention. It is another way of describing the figure mentioned in chapters 9, 16, and 19.

The other major issue that arises out of these verses is whether Job is being presented as overstepping the boundaries of true piety. Harold Knight sees here a need for Job to be released from his self-centeredness; Habel argues that "Job appears to overstep the bounds of humble faith and assume a posture of Promethean arrogance."[278] More likely is the view that he is simply taking a stand as a righteous human being seeking vindication.[279]

We may be unsure at this stage about how to take Job's words. Throughout the book our sympathy for Job has been built up, but it is hard to be sure

276. Dick, "Legal Metaphor," 38, notes that v. 35 is "a defendant's official appeal . . . at which the judge would compel the plaintiff to formalize his accusations and to present any supporting evidence."

277. O'Connor, "Reverence and Irreverence in Job," 92, citing 2 Sam 15:1-6.

278. Knight, "Job," 70; Habel, *Book of Job*, 64.

279. R. Smith, "Introduction to Job," 115. See also Gros Louis, "Book of Job," 256.

whether Job has gone too far this time. This leads us to eagerly await a reply or response from God. It is clear that Job has put his life on the line by his oath of clearance before God, and in this sense it "is an act of trust in the righteousness of God."[280]

31:38-40: His Right Treatment of the Land This final section signals a return to the oath of clearance. While some suggest it must be an afterthought or misplaced, Andersen helpfully comments, "The placement of the central idea away from the end (verses 35-37) so that the last lines (38-40) are not the climax, but an echo of a point made earlier in the poem, is a common device."[281] As readers, we regain the force of his previous words.

These verses are a straightforward example of such an oath, outlining the possible offenses in vv. 38-39, and the proposed punishment for breach in v. 40. Job is here denying any wrongdoing in relation to the land and its owners. Verse 38 is a more general and colorful description, personifying the land so that it can cry out (often used of calling out in response to injustice) and weep. A more specific example is given in v. 39 of not paying for any crops he has consumed, seemingly by ending the life of the owner of the land (actually or through despair or starvation). A clear retribution theology is found in v. 40, where Job proposes that if he has wrongly taken crops like wheat and barley from the land may his land produce thorns and weeds.

The chapter ends with a note that the words of Job are ended. While Job will make two further contributions in response to God's speeches (40:3-5; 42:1-6), Job's dispute with God ends at this point. What remains is the resolution. We await God's response.

32:1–42:6: The Verdicts

32:1–37:24: Elihu's Verdict

The Elihu speeches are a lengthy bridge between the dialogue (chs. 3–31) and the appearance and speeches of Yahweh (chs. 38–41). In 32:1-5 a prose introduction describes Elihu and explains the circumstances that cause him to begin speaking in 32:6. The remaining chapters seem to be formally divided into four speeches, each commencing with a similar formula (32:6; 34:1; 35:1; 36:1). However, 32:6-22 serves as Elihu's apologia or justification for stepping forward

---

280. O'Connor, "Reverence and Irreverence in Job," 94.
281. Andersen, *Job*, 240.

to speak. Then he addresses Job, with 33:1-7 a transitionary piece that both continues Elihu's apologia and introduces his substantive arguments, which commence at 33:8.[282]

In chapters 33–35 Elihu summarizes and evaluates the preceding dialogue. The section 33:8–35:16 comprises three speeches, commencing at 33:8, 34:1, and 35:1.[283] Each of these three speeches centers on a citation of Job's charges followed by a disputation of them.[284] Job's charges are cited in 33:8-11, 34:5-9, and 35:2-3, then disputed in 33:12-30, 34:10-33, and 35:4-13.

It is generally agreed that there is a clear break between chapters 33–35, on the one hand, and chapters 36–37, on the other.[285] In chapters 36 and 37, Elihu no longer refutes Job's charges, but simply states his conclusions or verdict.[286] Thus 36:1-21 contains a summons to Job, Elihu's verdict, the substantiation, and its application to Job. In 36:22–37:24 Elihu utters a hymn of praise to God as creator (36:22–37:13), then concludes with an address to Job (37:14-24).[287]

The Elihu speeches serve a twofold purpose.[288] First, they reflect on the preceding dialogue, summarizing and evaluating the arguments. Elihu rebukes the friends for their failure to prove Job in the wrong (32:12) and, in particular, their inability to answer Job's arguments (32:12, 15, 16). When he addresses the friends/wise about Job, Elihu narrows in on Job's words in the debate (33:8-11; 34:5-6, 9, 35-37; 35:16), rather than Job's prior conduct. For Elihu, then, the issue is not whether Job's sin caused his suffering, but rather whether he has spoken wrongly in the course of the debate. His evaluation is that the speech of Job is sacrilegious, and Job is therefore reckoned as a transgressor (34:7-8). However, Elihu has admitted that the friends' narrow view of retributive justice, inflexibly

282. Andersen, *Job,* 246. Habel, *Book of Job,* 445, helpfully sees 32:6-22 broken up into the right to answer (vv. 6-10), the need to answer (vv. 11-16), and the compulsion to answer (vv. 17-22).

283. Habel, *Book of Job,* 72; McCabe, "Significance of the Elihu Speeches," v-vi. However, see Johns, "Literary and Theological Function," 11. Andersen, *Job,* 246, and Hartley, *Book of Job,* 437, who see the first speech starting at 33:1, do not materially differ, because they both regard 33:1-7 as an opening part still in the vein of Elihu's apology in ch. 32.

284. McCabe, "Significance of the Elihu Speeches," 83, 131, 160; Habel, *Book of Job,* 455-57, 479-80, 490.

285. So, e.g., Hemraj, "Elihu's 'Missionary' Role," 63; Andersen, *Job,* 246; Habel, *Book of Job,* 72; McCabe, "Significance of the Elihu Speeches," v-vi. However, see Johns, "Literary and Theological Function," 11, who argues that 35:1–36:21 constitute a unit.

286. Habel, *Book of Job,* 72 suggests that, in 33:8–35:16, Elihu considers and analyzes Job's claims before the assembly; and in chs. 36–37 he gives a verdict, pronouncing in favor of God. Hemraj, "Elihu's 'Missionary' Role," 63, argues that chs. 33–35 constitute the negative part or refutation of Job's self-defense, followed the positive part of persuasion on God's behalf in chs. 36 and 37.

287. McCabe, "Significance of the Elihu Speeches," 200.

288. McCabe, "Elihu's Contribution," 72-80; L. Wilson, "Role of the Elihu Speeches."

applied to Job's present condition, has failed (32:3-5, 12). Elihu will at least cause the arguments of the friends to be discarded.

His own conclusion is that Job has not "spoken of God what is right" (32:2; 33:12), a verdict to be weighed and finally rejected in the light of the chapters to follow. His evaluation is thus a rival explanation to the later words of Yahweh, causing the reader to question Elihu's seemingly orthodox answer in the light of God's wider viewpoint. Elihu is thus a theological foil for Yahweh.

Their second purpose is to prepare for the final resolution of Job's dilemma in the Yahweh speeches. In addition to asserting the human verdict (which Yahweh will override), Elihu prepares for the theophany in a number of ways. First, six chapters of Elihu set the reader free from observing the dilemma solely through Job's eyes.[289] Second, the long delay caused by Elihu's lengthy speeches leads us to wonder whether God will finally appear. Third, he provides space between Job's summons and God's appearance, so that God is not seen as at Job's beck and call. Fourth, Elihu begins to set the mood of wonder and praise that will characterize the Yahweh speeches, especially in 36:22–37:24. Lastly, the nature discussion in 36:22–37:24, with its correlation of God's power and justice (37:23), anticipates the Yahweh speeches by proposing that God's power and purposes (37:23) are evident in his ordering of the world.

32:1-5: Prose Introduction of Elihu Verse 1 tells us what we already know from the breakdown of the dialogue — that the three friends have ceased to answer Job. The silencing of the friends has several functions. We expect the resolution of the book to come quickly now, since the dialogue has ground to a halt. The way in which a litigant won a case in the ancient Near East was for the other side to stop presenting arguments to dispute or rebut his claims. The legal metaphor has been strong in the book of Job; thus there is a strong hint here that, by the friends being reduced to silence, Job has been vindicated, so that he is righteous not only in his own eyes (the friends' description, v. 1) but also in the eyes of the narrator.

Another person comes forward (v. 2), the only character in the book who is called by a full name (i.e., patronymic included). Elihu's name means "he is my God," which might suggest that the author intended to present him as the one with a right appreciation of God.[290] Others see significance in the fact that the unpointed spelling of one form of Elihu (e.g., 32:4) is identical with one version of the name Elijah (e.g., 1 Kgs 17:1).[291] While this fits well with the pic-

---

289. Humphreys, *Tragic Vision*, 110-11.

290. McKay, "Elihu — A Proto-Charismatic?" 167.

291. Habel, *Book of Job*, 448. Tate, "Speeches of Elihu," 489, notes that the name Elihu is also

ture of Elihu as a forerunner of the coming of the Lord, the evidence is slender. There is no compelling argument, then, that the name of Elihu is of any great significance. Others have seen significance in his being described as a Buzite. Uz and Buz were brothers (Gen 22:21), which might suggest he came from Edom.[292]

More important is the description of Elihu as angry. This is repeated four times in vv. 2-5 (vv. 2 [twice], 4, 5). It is not likely that Elihu is speaking with the anger of God, for the prologue insists that God was not, at least at that stage, angry with Job. Elihu is angry with both Job and the three friends, but for different reasons. He is angry with Job because he justified himself (declared himself in the right, the Piel of צדק/*ṣdq*, v. 2) more than, or rather than, God.

Elihu is angry with the three friends because they had not found an "answer" (a legal term) to Job in the dialogue, but declared him to be in the wrong or condemned (v. 3).[293] The friends failed in what Elihu considered to be a straightforward task of defending God and thus establishing Job's guilt. At this point of the book, it is clear that Job has had the best of the dialogue (if he were running for office today, we would say he has won the preelection TV debate).

Verse 4 provides an explanation for Elihu's late entry into the fray, for he waited for his elders to speak before him. However, the failure of these three older men to provide a convincing legal response to Job meant that Elihu burned with anger (v. 5). It is left unclear whether Elihu's anger in v. 5 is mainly toward the three friends or at Job, but this fourth mention of Elihu's anger (without any other description of him) implies that here is someone who is too angry, one in whom anger has too prominent a place.

32:6-22: Elihu's Apology The second aid to understanding Elihu is his apologia for speaking in the rest of chapter 32, as he now addresses the friends.[294] Verses 6-7 fill out what was already stated in v. 4. He gives two rationales for not speaking in the presence of his elders. In v. 6 his timidity and fear restrained him from speaking, but in v. 7 he also thought that wisdom is learned over time, and it is

---

used of others including an ancestor of Elkanah and a brother of a David (1 Sam 1:1; 1 Chr 12:20; 26:7; 27:18), but these seem to be of no significance here.

292. On the basis of Jer 25:23-24, which mentions Dedan and Tema, Hartley, *Book of Job*, 428, and Clines, *Job 21-37*, 713, locate Buz in Edom (see Jer 49:7-8) — not northwest Arabia, as Newsom, "Book of Job," 562, asserts.

293. The Hiphil of רשע/*rš* could mean "make oneself guilty," as in Job 34:12 (but this does not fit the sense, for Job is the object); "cause to be condemned," as in Prov 17:15; Ps 37:33; or most commonly in Job "to pronounce or declare guilty," as in Job 9:20; 10:2; 15:6; 34:17, 29; 40:8.

294. Elihu uses the second person plural to speak of the friends in vv. 6, 10-12, speaking of Job in the third person in v. 14. However, in vv. 15-16 speaks of the friends in the third person. He explicitly turns to Job in 33:1. So Webster, "Strophic Patterns," 102.

therefore worth listening to his elders. He has, however, now come to a different view, which is explained in vv. 8-10. Verse 9 outlines what is denied — that simply being old makes one wise — while v. 8 proposes that it is the breath of the Almighty (i.e., a God-given gift) that is the source of wisdom. Presumably believing himself to have that gift, he proceeds in v. 10 to declare that he will announce his opinion.

Elihu feels externally compelled to speak because of the failure of the friends (vv. 12, 15, 16), and internally because the divine word has been given to him (v. 18). Elihu explains to the friends in v. 11 that he has listened for the wisdom that he expected to come from them. However, his conclusion in v. 12 is that all the friends (the "you" and "your" are plural in vv. 11-14) failed in their attempts to refute Job or to provide a convincing response to him. The Hebrew word for "one to refute" (v. 12) is מוֹכִיחַ/*môkîaḥ,* the word used by Job in 9:33 in his call for an arbiter. Presumably Elihu sees himself taking on this role.[295] The friends had failed in their attempts, and their words are to be discarded.

In v. 13 Elihu seeks to undercut the probable response from the friends — we are the possessors of wisdom, God will vanquish him (or perhaps "let God vanquish him"). The thrust here is that the friends are claiming to have responded with wise words, but that now the matter will be resolved by God's actions to drive Job away.[296] In v. 14 Elihu signals that he wants to take a different tack in responding to Job and that he will not use the arguments of the friends, presumably because they are defective.

Verse 15 starts a new subsection; the three friends are spoken about in the third person, as Elihu presumably widens his attention to the gathered assembly. To this wider audience he points out the objective facts of the friends' failure to answer Job; he mentions four times their failure to speak, answer, or utter words (vv. 15-16). Verse 16 must be understood as a question (Shall I wait . . . ?) even in the absence of an interrogative marker, and he supplies the answer to his question in v. 17 by stating his intention to give his answer and opinion.

Once Elihu starts to speak, an ironic gap appears between what Elihu intends and the meaning his words have for the reader.[297] Elihu appropriates to himself terminology used in a derogatory way by previous speakers (vv. 18-19; "full of wind" is used negatively by Eliphaz in 15:2). Thus he states he is full of

---

295. So McCabe "Elihu's Contribution," 50-51.

296. Gordis, *Book of Job,* 368, suggests that the verb נָדַף/*nādap,* "to drive away," is being used in an abstract sense to mean "rebut, refute."

297. Habel, *Book of Job,* 444, sees an ironic gap between the prose portrayal of Elihu as an angry youth and his self-perception in his apology.

words and that the spirit (or lit. "wind") within him is being held back (v. 18).[298] He probably intended this to mean that this "spirit/wind" has come from God, as in v. 8, but that is not the way he comes across here. In effect, he has a need to "break wind," in the same way that unvented wine in a new wineskin is about to burst through its container (v. 19). Here is a picture of someone who *needs* to speak rather than one who *ought* to speak. He is not in control, but his "windy words" are in the driving seat. In v. 20 Elihu indicates that he must or will speak in order to find relief. The final part of his apologia is his denial of using partiality (lit. "lift up the face of a person," which means giving them preferential treatment) or flattery, rightly believing that he is accountable before God his maker not to do so (vv. 21-22).

Thus, even as Elihu utters his apologia, his credibility is undermined by this comic self-portrayal and his admission that he is speaking out of his own needs. Elihu's arguments and conclusions are thus significantly undermined from the beginning and are unlikely to be the final verdict. As Elihu continues in the following chapters, his views will become less and less persuasive to the attentive readers. In the following chapters, he will make arrogant assertions (33:5-7, 31-33; 34:2-4, 31-33; 36:2-4; 37:19-20) and describe both himself and God as "masterminds" (36:4 and 37:16). Even his view that suffering can be educative is shown by the prologue not to be the reason for Job's suffering.[299] J. G. Janzen concludes that "Elihu is being presented as someone who does not understand himself or his role," thus giving rise to dramatic irony.[300]

First Speech

Verses 1-7 may be a continuation of his apology or a preamble to his first speech (vv. 8-33). In terms of the structure of the rest of the chapter, vv. 8-11 are a citation of Job's claim, followed by a rejection of his argument (vv. 12-13). The numerical saying in v. 14 rounds off the preceding verses by raising the view that God speaks in a variety of ways. This is then filled out by an argument that shows how God speaks through dreams (vv. 15-18), through suffering (vv. 19-22), and through an angelic go-between (vv. 23-28). Verses 29-30 are a summary conclusion before a final demand that Job listens to him (vv. 31-33).[301]

298. Pope, *Job,* 213, colorfully describes it as "Elihu is flatulent with words."

299. Habel, "Role of Elihu," 92, concludes that Elihu is the brash but intelligent fool — having intelligence but lacking wisdom. J. Janzen, *Job,* 219-21, gives some additional examples.

300. J. G. Janzen, *Job,* 220.

301. For similar structural analyses see Newsom, "Book of Job," 567-68; McCabe, "Significance of the Elihu Speeches," 83; Habel, *Book of Job,* 455-57.

33:1-7: A Transition from Apology to Argument In v. 1 Elihu addresses Job by name, which the three friends did not do. This is consistent with his having a role different from that of the friends.[302] A focus on speech and words continues through vv. 1-3, and the impression given is that Elihu is wordy or verbose. Verse 2 in particular is redundant.[303] He claims in v. 3 that he speaks from "uprightness of heart" and "pure or sincere lips." While this is a little too self-serving, it does imply that Elihu is seeking to be sincere in taking on his role.

Some see v. 4 as claiming that, as a fellow human being, he is now addressing Job as an equal.[304] However, the focus on words both before and after this verse (vv. 1-3 and 5) makes it likely that Elihu envisages that his words will lead to greater understanding. He seems to believe that the God who made him will make special use of him to speak wisdom (see Prov 8:6-8). Verse 4b repeats the phrase "the breath of the Almighty" from 32:8, but the focus here is not on God as the source of wisdom, but rather as the creator of life.

Verses 5-7 round off the preamble by a challenge (v. 5) followed by a series of reassurances (vv. 6-7). However, there is a large hint of arrogance in Elihu's words, beginning in v. 5 with the challenge to answer *if you can*. These are strong words when addressed to one who is older and who has been described as the "greatest of all the people of the east" (1:3). This is made clearer by vv. 6-7. Elihu claims a similar standing before God as Job, since they are both created by their Maker (v. 6b; see Isa 45:9). He then displays in v. 7 an exalted view of his own importance, urging Job not to be overwhelmed by fearing him and stating that his pressure on Job will not be too heavy.[305] Elihu seems to claim too much status, much too quickly.[306]

33:8-11: Citation of Job's Charges Elihu's claim is that he is citing or summarizing words that he has heard Job utter in the course of the debate (v. 8), most

---

302. Habel, "Role of Elihu," 94, comments that the use of a person's name was an appropriate court procedure, so that witnesses or defendants are regularly summoned by name (e.g., Mic 6:1-5).

303. Andersen, *Job*, 248, writes that vv. 1-7 are "overloaded with Elihu's continued prolixity." The irony of pointing out Elihu's verbosity is not lost on Clines, *Job 21-37*, 725, who concedes, "it is not for a commentator who writes a million words about the thousand verses of the book to take Elihu to task for prolixity."

304. Newsom, "Book of Job," 567. Tate, "Speeches of Elihu," views vv. 4 and 6 as a claim to share a common humanity. However, Elihu's tone appears to be more arrogant than Tate suggests.

305. אַכְפִּי/'akpî, "my pressure," could alternatively read "my hand" if it is regarded as a variant form of כַּף/kap, as in the NIV, based on its parallel use in 13:21 and in the LXX.

306. G. Wilson, *Job*, 369, colorfully describes the pompous Elihu by suggesting that if Hollywood were to cast the role of Elihu, the only choice would be John Cleese in his Basil Fawlty incarnation!

clearly in 13:23, 24, 27.[307] Verse 9 is a general summary of Job's argument rather than an exact quotation of his words, and it focuses on his claim to innocence.[308] It may be that Elihu has understood Job to be claiming to be sinless (v. 9 could be read this way), but if so he has misunderstood the nature of Job's assertion that he is righteous. Verses 10-11 incorporate some almost verbatim quotes from Job's earlier speeches, developing the question of justice under the theme that God is treating him as an enemy. Verse 10a has some echoes of 10:6-7 and 13:23, while v. 10b is essentially a quotation of 13:24b. Verse 11 is again largely a repetition of the first two sections of 13:27. The claims disputed in the rest of Elihu's speech are essentially that Job is innocent and yet has been denied justice. In basing his rebuke of Job on his words uttered in the debate, Elihu reveals his view that the dispute between Job and the friends concerns how to speak rightly about God. He is not interested in Job's prior actions, but only with his words in the dialogue. He is ostensibly delivering a verdict on the debate.

33:12-14: Job Is in the Wrong Elihu asserts in v. 12 that Job is not in the right, a conclusion that will be overturned by the words of God in 42:7-8.[309] Elihu's concern is with deciding the case in favor of God, and he focuses on the arguments and testimony of the case (the legal process) rather than Job's afflictions or anguish. His approach is a judicial rather than a therapeutic one. The reason given by Elihu is that God is greater than (the Hebrew can also mean "too great for") human beings. He therefore addresses Job's legal approach of "contending" with God in v. 13a and rightly understands that a key thread of Job's pursuit of litigation was to get God to answer Job's questions. Verse 13b does not include the word "saying" in the Hebrew text (Hebrew does not need to do so), but it is probably implied that Job has said this. It could alternatively be translated as if this is a conclusion Elihu has reached — that God will not answer human words — but the context does not support this, for Elihu then explains how God does

307. McCabe, "Elihu Speeches," 83, 131, 160, notes that each of Elihu's first three speeches centers on a citation of Job's charges followed by a disputation of them. Job's charges are cited in 33:8-11, 34:5-9, and 35:2-3, then disputed in 33:12-30, 34:10-33, and 35:4-13.

308. McCabe, "Elihu's Contribution," 51-52, has pointed out that different terminology has been used by Job in places like 9:20-21 (blameless); 27:5-6 (integrity, righteousness); 13:23 ([without] transgressions, [free from] iniquity); but v. 9 is a fair summary of what Job has been saying, most recently in the oath of clearance in ch. 31. See also Zophar's words in 11:4.

309. Ross, "Job 33:14-30," 44, suggests that Elihu represents the standard tradition of Hebrew cultic psalmody. Habel, *Book of Job,* 462, more plausibly suggests that he is trying to move Job to acknowledge the error of his position. Of course, the two views are not mutually exclusive, for Elihu may be pointing out the error of Job's claim (33:8-11) by showing that God speaks through an angelic mediator (33:13-14, 23). However, Job's complaints do not have the cultic setting that Ross appears to presuppose.

answer. It is not a specific quotation from Job, but it does reflect what he has said in many places.[310] Elihu will respond to this further in 34:23, but concludes this section by claiming that God does speak in the sense of responding to Job's cries, but that humans often do not perceive it (v. 14).

33:15-18: God Speaks through Dreams The first of Elihu's three examples is an explanation of how God speaks through dreams. However, Elihu envisages something different from what Job had in mind. God uses dreams, according to Elihu, not to answer human charges but to provide them with warnings (vv. 15-16; see 7:14, where Job admits he has received these). The purpose of the warnings is that people will change the way they are acting (turn aside from their deeds, v. 17) and turn from their pride (perhaps suggested by 31:36-37). Elihu asserts that God's goal in this is good, for it will prevent people coming to an early or violent death (v. 18). Clearly violent death is in view in v. 18b; in v. 18a "keeping back his life from the Pit" is a common Hebrew phrase that probably refers here to premature death.

33:19-22: God Speaks through Suffering Verses 19-22 begin the development of Elihu's second argument, that God speaks through suffering. The argument is close to a famous quotation from C. S. Lewis: "God whispers to us in our pleasures, speaks in our conscience, but shouts in our pains: it is His megaphone to rouse a deaf world."[311] This line of reasoning would also have been of little comfort to Job. This section is largely a progressive description of suffering from pain when lying down (v. 19a) and aching in his bones (v. 19b), which result in a loss of appetite, even for desirable food (v. 20), wasting away of flesh (v. 21a), loss of weight (v. 21b), and the prospect of death (v. 22). The most striking comment occurs at the beginning of v. 19, when Elihu argues that a person is rebuked or reproved by this suffering. This educative or disciplinary view is often regarded as Elihu's distinctive contribution to the theme of suffering in the book. The verb used here (יכח/*ykḥ*) has already been used by Eliphaz to make the same point (albeit briefer) in 5:17-18 (he also uses it in 22:4). However, while suffering can have a disciplinary or correcting role (a wake-up call), this is not the reason for Job's suffering as set out in the prologue.

33:23-30: An Angelic Mediator An interesting twist in Elihu's argument comes in vv. 23-28, as he develops the idea of an angelic mediator. Exactly what Elihu

---

310. McCabe, "Elihu's Contribution," 54, identifies 9:2, 14-19, 32-35; 13:22; 19:7; 23:2-7; and 30:20.

311. Lewis, *Problem of Pain*, 81.

had envisaged by this figure is not entirely clear, but it certainly echoes the imprecision of Job's hope for a mediator seen in chapters 9, 16, 19, and 31. Most commentators see this mediator as a heavenly figure (מַלְאָךְ/*mal'āk*, often translated "angel," can mean either an earthly or a heavenly messenger), which is more likely than those who suggest that it is actually Elihu referring to himself.[312] Seeing that Elihu's practice has been to refer to Job's explicit statements and proposals, Elihu is probably referring back to the same figure raised by Job in the earlier chapters. His argument here is that if there was such a figure (the "if" in v. 23 also implies it is a hypothetical figure), then Job should rely on his mediation and not continue his attack on God. This mediator appears to be part of a larger group ("one of a thousand," hence presumably not Elihu), and his task is to declare to a person "his uprightness." "His uprightness" could mean either "the fact that he is upright" (see NRSV, NJPS) or "what is the right/upright thing for him to do" (see ESV, NIV). The context of his sin (v. 27) and the need for grace and a ransom suggests that "what is right for him to do" is the best sense here.

The mediator is pictured in vv. 24-25 as graciously interceding for an individual, asking for deliverance from death (v. 24b) and restored health to his body (v. 25). It is not entirely clear what is the "ransom" (כֹּפֶר/*kōper*) found by the mediator, but the passage is not interested in exploring this. Rather, vv. 26-28 develop the appropriate human response of repentance and thanksgiving. The subject of the one praying to God in v. 26 ("he") is not specified. It could be an ongoing reference to the mediator, but is more likely resumptive of the individual discussed in vv. 19-22, and who continues to confess his sins and give thanks in vv. 27-28. In other words, it is the sufferer, not the angelic mediator, who prays to God and whose prayer is accepted by God. God accepts this prayer, leading to a joyful relationship and the person's righteousness restored (v. 26). The one who was delivered then proclaims through song (like a song of thanksgiving in the Psalms) his or her confessed sin and thanksgiving for forgiveness (vv. 27-28).

Verses 29-30 round off this first speech with a general reminder that God is the one who repeatedly rescues his people from death.

33:31-33: Appealing for a Response In vv. 31-33 Elihu again summons Job by name (as in 33:1) and calls for a response. In v. 32 he asks for an answer (yet preceded by the hypothetical "if there are words") and for Job to speak, but the tone of this ending suggests that he does not expect Job to reply. He calls on Job to "pay attention" (v. 31); and in both vv. 31 and 33 he calls on Job to listen

312. See, e.g., Beeby, "Elihu — Job's Mediator?" 45; Wolfers, "Elihu," 92.

to him and be silent. In v. 31 he adds, "I will speak," and in v. 33 the content of his speech is made clear: "I will teach you wisdom." Elihu is seeking to give the impression of wanting Job to respond, but he really intends to instruct Job and change his thinking.[313]

34:1-37: Second Speech

This chapter contains the second speech of Elihu. It follows the previous pattern in citing words spoken by Job during the dialogue and then disputing them. However, the twist in this speech is that Elihu not only corrects Job but also calls to the gathered sages (vv. 2, 10, 34) to confirm his view. The main issue at stake in this speech is God's justice.

After a summons to the wise (vv. 2-4), there is a citation and summary of Job's expressed views (vv. 5-9). The bulk of the speech is then a correction of Job's view (vv. 10-33). First of all he addresses the sages (vv. 10-15), clarifying what he is rejecting and the counterargument he wishes to put (vv. 10-12), followed by an initial supporting argument (vv. 13-15). Then he addresses Job directly (vv. 16-33) with a further supporting argument (vv. 16-20) and an explanatory section (vv. 21-30), before making an appeal to Job to change (vv. 31-33). In the last part (vv. 34-37) the sages come back into view and are invited to join with Elihu in his condemnation of Job.[314]

34:1-4: Call to the Wise Men to Listen This speech is introduced in v. 1, and in vv. 2-4 he addresses the sages who are present. This may simply mean the three friends, but probably refers to the wider group of sages who have gathered. He urges them to listen to him (v. 2), and for them to listen with discernment as they seek to find out ("choose" and "know") what is "good" (טוֹב/*ṭôb*)[315] and "right" (מְשְׁפָּט/*mišpāṭ*) (v. 4). The word *mišpāṭ*, while commonly meaning "justice," can also be used of a legal "judgment," and may have that sense here as Elihu is calling on the sages to join with him in pronouncing a legal judgment on Job. Verse 3 is a quotation from Job's earlier words in 12:11. This shows that he has listened well, and is now using Job's own words back on him in an example of skillful rhetoric.

---

313. Rowley, *Job*, 216, comments that "LXX, perhaps tired of the verbosity of Elihu, omitted verses 31b-33."

314. This structure is proposed by McCabe, "Significance of the Elihu Speeches," 131; and similar divisions are made by G. Wilson, *Job*, 381-95.

315. However, Habel, *Book of Job*, 481, argues for a legal sense of "defensible."

34:5-9: Citation of Job's Charges Elihu then twice cites Job's words and charges (vv. 5-6 and 9), separated by some comments on Job's attitude (vv. 7-8). The first citation (vv. 5-6) is a mixture of quotation and distillation. Verse 5b is a quotation from 27:2a (see also 14:3; 19:7), while v. 5a picks up the gist of Job's many protestations of innocence (e.g., 9:21; 13:18; 27:2-6) in a manner similar to 33:9. Job is pictured as claiming that he has been wrongly denied justice by God (v. 5). The claim "I am in the right" could mean "I am innocent," and in light of the prominent legal metaphor in the book, it is probably referring to a legal more than a moral rightness. He also claims that he has wrongly been treated as a liar (v. 6a),[316] even though he is without sin in this matter (v. 6b). In echoing Job's claim that his wound (lit. "arrow")[317] is incurable (v. 6), Elihu shows that he has heard the depth of Job's pain, which makes him even more culpable in that he does not express any comfort or care of Job in the rest of his speech.[318]

In vv. 7-8 Elihu inserts an interim judgment that Job has thrown in his lot with the wicked, described in terms that contrast with the picture of the righteous man of Ps 1:1. He has adopted the ways of the scoffers (drinking up their scoffing like water, v. 7, echoing the words of Eliphaz in 15:16) and journeyed with the wicked and evildoers (v. 8). In other words, he has adopted the practices of the wicked and preferred their company. It is unusual for Elihu to focus on Job's deeds, for he elsewhere concentrates on Job's words during the debate, not on his conduct.[319] It is possible, then, to understand "traveling" and "walking" as ways of describing Job's settled stance of angry words addressed to God.

The second summary charge (v. 9) is a synthesis of Job's comments in such places as 9:22-24 and 21:5-13. Taking this statement at face value, Elihu has interpreted Job to say that it is a waste of time to delight in God, though a fairer reading of Job would suggest that he is rightly troubled by the prospering of the wicked and the suffering of the righteous.

34:10-12: God Will Not Do Wrong In any event, vv. 10-33 outline a comprehensive refutation of Job's charges, marked by a strong insistence that God acts justly. The essence of Elihu's argument is stated in vv. 10-12. In v. 10, as in v. 2, Elihu is addressing the gathered sages rather than Job, and Andersen may

---

316. Habel, *Book of Job*, 474-75, and McCabe, "Elihu's Contribution," 56, view the verb as delocutive.

317. It is used here to describe the wound caused by God's arrows (hence NJPS "arrow-wound"; see also NIV), which are mentioned in 6:4. McCabe, "Elihu's Contribution," 56, regards it as a metonym.

318. Simundson, *Message of Job*, 137, notes that his views would be "more appropriate when speaking to a seminar on the interpretation of suffering rather than to a suffering human being."

319. So Westermann, *Structure*, 146, who notes that "only the words of Job interest Elihu."

be right in suggesting that in this speech Elihu is no longer addressing Job to help him, but is rather attacking him in order to score a point.[320] Elihu begins negatively by denying that God would do what was wrong or wicked (v. 10). The principle of retribution is then stated very clearly in v. 11 — that God will treat (pay back, recompense) a person according to their work, and he will cause them to receive what corresponds to their ways. The gist of v. 10 is taken one step further in v. 12. God neither acts wickedly nor perverts justice (מִשְׁפָּט/ *mišpāṭ*, the same word used in vv. 4, 5, 6). God is fundamentally just and committed to justice.

34:13-15: God Is in Charge of the Earth In vv. 13-15 Elihu expands on what God could do. God has always been in charge of his creation, and so the rhetorical question of v. 13 has the implied answer, "No one." Verses 14-15 consider the implications of this for humanity and assert that God could simply destroy all humans if he chose to do so. The image of humans returning to dust is an allusion to the creation account (Gen 2:7). Since this section is unpacking the previous one, it implies that God as Creator has the right to actively rule over his creation, and so could never be charged with acting unjustly.

34:16-20: God's Justice In v. 16 Job is again addressed (the verbs are second person singular). This unit explores God's fair governance of society as the outworking of his justice (v. 17a), although the term חָבַשׁ/*ḥābaš* means "govern" only here, as demanded by the context; elsewhere it means "bind." The sense is that the ruler needs to bind or restrain evil in order to secure justice. Verses 17b-19 are an extended rhetorical question implying that God is righteous and mighty and hence shows no partiality to royalty, nobles, or the rich. Job has, of course, tried to hold together the power of God and his commitment to justice, even though he cannot see how both are true in his circumstances. Elihu, however, believes that Job is condemning God rather than bringing his questions and complaints to him. In v. 19 Elihu makes clear that his theological undergirding is the belief that all humans are the work of God's hands (v. 19c). The implication in v. 20 is that God's sovereign power extends to life and death.

34:21-30: God's Knowledge Grounds His Judgment Another general principle is set out in v. 21 — God knows all the ways of each individual — and this grounds the rightness of his judgment in vv. 22-30. Since God knows all a person's ways, there simply are no hiding places available for wrongdoers (v. 22). The Hebrew of v. 23 is quite difficult; the ESV tries to retain the MT but loses

320. Andersen, *Job*, 251.

some comprehensibility.[321] With two small emendations, it can be rendered, "For it is not for a human to set a time to come before God in judgment."[322] Since God knows all the actions of a person (v. 21), then any appearance before God is unnecessary because it cannot disclose any further information. Thus Elihu is ruling out any possibility of Job benefiting from his pursuit of litigation and his insistence that God grant him a hearing in court. This is why Elihu has put himself forward as a surrogate who will judge in God's absence. His reply to Job's call for litigation is that he must settle for a human arbiter. What Elihu does not allow for is that God is still able to choose, for reasons other than gaining more knowledge, to allow humans to appear before him, as he will do in chapters 38–42. In many ways, Elihu could plausibly be seen as the answer to Job's demand for a legal figure. As such, he concludes that the transcendent Yahweh does not appear to mortals (vv. 23-24), and urges Job to redirect his vision and look for God's answers in other ways.[323]

God has no need of further information before he can act justly. Thus he can replace the powerful "without investigation" (v. 24) since he knows their deeds (v. 25). Verses 26-30 then repeat Elihu's earlier insistence that God does justly condemn those who act wickedly (v. 26), who have turned aside from following his ways (v. 27), who oppress the poor and afflicted (v. 28), and who exercise the power to rule in ungodly ways (v. 30). Verse 29 is an aside, seemingly aimed primarily at Job, asserting that since God so actively enforces justice, no one can complain when God appears to be quieter or absent.

34:31-33: Appealing for a Response Verses 31-33 are less transparent. Habel understands them to be an appeal to Job to confess his error and respond appropriately.[324] However, he probably has reverted to addressing the sages or friends, which he did in vv. 10-15 and whom he will mention again in v. 34. If so, then Elihu might be ruling out another reason why God would not appear to Job in a courtroom. In court offenders could promise to amend their ways (not offend, v. 31; do it no more, v. 32), but this is not how Job has responded, for he has instead insisted on his innocence.

---

321. It has to insert God as the subject of the first part of the verse, and the relationship between the two halves falters. The NIV is similar.

322. So Hartley, *Book of Job*, 455, based on changing the verb "to set, appoint," from an imperfect to an infinitive (following Gordis), and proposing that haplography has caused the dropping of the initial letter from מוֹעֵד/*mô'ēd,* "a time" (following Reiske). See also Clines, *Job 21–37,* 753.

323. Habel, *Book of Job,* 490, notes, "God's will is to be discerned through life and nature, not through direct confrontation with a transcendent silent God."

324. So also Hartley, *Book of Job,* 460. This would account for the use of second person singular verbs in vv. 32-33. Clines, *Job 21–37,* 782, points out that this question is irrelevant to Job's situation.

The precise thrust of v. 33 is rather opaque, but it is clear that Elihu is now addressing Job. He appears to be saying that Job needs to "choose" to repent in order for his situation to be settled, and so he calls on him to express his repentance ("declare what you know").

34:34-37: Urging the Wise to Agree with Him There is a final appeal to the wise men in vv. 34-37, urging them to adopt Elihu's analysis of Job. In v. 35 Elihu finds that Job's spoken words in the debate have been without "knowledge" or "insight" — two key wisdom words. Elihu then urges (lit. "I entreat you") that Job be tried (= condemned) to the end because he has spoken like the wicked (v. 36). Three examples are then given in v. 37: he has not only done wrong but has "rebelled" or crossed over the boundary; he claps his hands;[325] and he multiplies or increases his words to God. This last cameo is often translated, "he multiplies his words against God," but Elihu may simply be rebuking him for continuing to speak to God without changing his attitude. Elihu has not yet finished, but his conclusions and the direction of his argument are extremely clear.

In relation to Job, Elihu's evaluation is that Job's words are sacrilegious, and he is therefore reckoned as a transgressor (vv. 35-37). His conclusion is that Job has not "spoken of God what is right," a verdict to be weighed and finally rejected (42:7-8). His evaluation of Job is thus intentionally set up as a rival to the later words of Yahweh, causing the reader to question Elihu's seemingly orthodox answer in the light of God's wider viewpoint. Elihu is thus a theological foil for Yahweh. As Andersen puts it, "Elihu gives the human estimate; Yahweh gives the divine appraisal."[326]

35:1-16: Third Speech

Elihu's third speech follows the basic pattern of the first two. He begins by citing the substance of Job's words (vv. 2-3), and then disputes his claim by insisting that the transcendent God is not dependent on human beings (vv. 4-8). He then explains why the Creator does not answer cries for help (vv. 9-13), before applying this by concluding that Job's summons for God to appear in court is an empty cry (vv. 14-16).[327]

---

325. The precise import of clapping is unclear, but the context brands it as negative, probably a reference to clapping as a way of summoning God. Clines, *Job 21–37*, 763, follows others and emends יִסְפּוֹק/*yispôq* to יַסְפִּיק/*yaspîq*, "cast doubt upon."

326. Andersen, *Job*, 51.

327. See McCabe, "Significance of the Elihu Speeches," 160. Habel, *Book of Job*, 490, sees

35:1-3: Citation of Job's Charges Elihu challenges Job about whether the object of his pursuit is really justice, hinting that Job is more self-serving that he claims to be (v. 2a). The translation of v. 2b is uncertain; it could be translated "it is my right before God" or "I am more righteous than God."[328] Of course, this ambiguity might be purposeful, with Elihu being able to imply that Job is claiming to be more righteous than God, but when pressed could claim that all he was asserting was that Job was insisting that he had a legal action against God.

Elihu introduces v. 3 as the words of Job. Although they are not strictly a quotation, they echo the sentiments of passages like 7:19-20, 9:22-31, and 21:7-13. The issue at stake is whether Job has gained any advantage or blessing from choosing righteousness rather than sin, and Elihu hears Job saying that there is no such advantage. Elihu has interpreted Job to be asking an academic question, but Job's earlier expression of this thought arises out of his despair and desperation. Like the friends, Elihu is seeking to correct Job's ideas rather than deal with the pastoral or real life issue.

Together vv. 2-3 imply that Job is complaining (if Elihu understands him properly) that neither his words (his legal claim, v. 2) nor his actions (his sin or otherwise, v. 3) seem to draw any response from God.

35:4-8: The Effect of Wickedness and Righteousness on God Elihu turns to instruct both Job and the friends (v. 4); hence this speech is meant as a correction to at least Job and his three dialogue partners.[329] He reminds them in vv. 5-8 that neither human righteousness nor human wickedness will affect or benefit God.[330] Elihu's speech is based on a big view of God as the transcendent Creator in the heights of heaven (v. 5; see 22:12; cf. 9:8-10; 11:8). Whereas Job complained of divine silence, Elihu reframes this as sovereign transcendence.

Yet he quickly moves from this to Job's wickedness and righteousness. The two parts of v. 6 are really parallel expressions. Elihu is asserting that Job's transgressions do not have any effect on God, for he is detached from them.

---

two arguments from Elihu — one from cosmic order (vv. 5-8) and one from divine silence (vv. 9-12), with v. 13 as a conclusion — but his division is essentially the same.

328. Hartley, *Book of Job*, 463, opts for "I am more righteous than God"; McCabe, "Elihu's Contribution," 58, argues for "My righteousness is greater than God's." The two key issues are the role of the preposition מִן/*min* and the meaning of צִדְקִי/*ṣidqî*.

329. Instead of being a reference to Eliphaz, Bildad, and Zophar, it could have in view those evildoers and wicked mentioned as Job's fellow travelers in 34:8. Yet, since these are not actual companions, they could not be in view here.

330. Newsom, "Book of Job," 581, points out that Elihu is not really answering the question that Job has implied. Elihu cites him as asking, "What advantage do *I* have?"; but Elihu will answer by saying, "*God* gains no advantage."

In the next verse, he argues his case higher still by stating that even righteous acts do not give anything to God or confer a benefit on him (v. 7). God is not dependent on Job's actions, good or bad, for God cannot be manipulated by human actions. Although the meaning is less precise in v. 8, the thrust is that a person's righteousness or wickedness only affects that person (and presumably not God). Eliphaz has uttered something similar in 22:2-3.

This statement of God's transcendence is a statement of Elihu's fundamental position. Since this is what God is like, God's refusal to meet Job in court is not an indifferent silence, but simply an appropriate expression of his superiority.

35:9-13: Why God May Not Answer Cries for Help Verses 9-13 provide more information about why God may not answer cries for help. The first observation is that a person may be crying for help because of their difficult circumstances (v. 9) but not be seeking God (v. 10a). Underlying this is the assumption that people have obligations to God since he is their Maker. He is referring to people who may want help from God, but not God himself. This was most inappropriate to say to Job, who has consistently sought the presence of God.

God is described as the one "who gives songs in the night" (ESV, NIV). While songs (of praise) are often linked with joy, the night is a symbol of darkness and perhaps sorrow. This would suggest that the songs are either laments or songs of trust that proclaim the value of faith in God even in the midst of difficult times (e.g., Ps 23:4).[331] Elihu also says that God teaches wisdom as one observes the animals and birds (v. 11).[332] God's will is to be discerned through life and nature, not through direct contact. This is the mainstream wisdom understanding, yet one that Yahweh's appearance will soon challenge. In addition, Elihu is wrong in implying that wisdom is the issue in Job's case.

Elihu draws some of these threads together in v. 12 by reminding them that God does not answer their cry, but now adds a hint about the reason. An answer is not given because those who are asking are evildoers motivated by pride (v. 12b). This is filled out in the more general conclusion in v. 13, where a cry for help based on pride is seen as empty (v. 13). It would seem that wanting the gift but not the giver is but one example of a self-sufficient and hollow cry for help. Yet even this more general principle misses the mark in the case of Job.

---

331. Since the word זְמִרוֹת/*zĕmirôt*, "songs," is unexpected here, a number of commentators seek to emend it. While it is better to retain MT, the best suggestion for emendation is מַרְאֹות/*mar'ôt*, "visions," perhaps a reference to visions of the night that give insight like that recorded in 4:13-17.

332. Dhorme, *Job*, 534, followed by Gordis and Hartley, suggests that, while it could mean that humans are given more wisdom than these creatures (comparative use of the preposition), it is better translated as God instructing by means of the animals and birds (instrumental use).

35:14-16: Job's Pursuit of Litigation Is Empty Elihu, however, applies this to Job, pointing to his complaint about the absence of God and his insistence of calling God to court (v. 14). How much less will God answer Job's cries, says Elihu. Having talked to Job in v. 14, he then talks about him in vv. 15-16. The point in the difficult text of v. 15 seems to be that since God in his anger has not punished Job, and since he takes less notice of transgression than we think (see v. 6), then Job has not stopped. He has continued to spout forth his empty words (here הֶבֶל/*hebel,* meaning "futile" talk, the same core concept as in v. 13), and multiplies words without knowledge (v. 16), an echo of the last verse of the previous speech (34:37). The irony here in v. 16 is that it is Elihu who has multiplied words without knowledge in his long-winded speeches. Job will ultimately concede that he spoke out of limited knowledge (42:3), and God confronts Job with that (38:2), but in a different sense than that intended by Elihu. Indeed, God twice commends him for speaking what is right about him (42:7-8), but will broaden Job's understanding of how God runs his world. Elihu has spoken some words that are true in some situations, but he has misapplied them to Job.

36:1–37:24: Fourth Speech

These two chapters together constitute Elihu's fourth speech, starting with a similar formula to the previous three (34:1; 35:1; 36:1; see also 32:6, introducing his apology). The previous three began with a citation of Job's words, followed by a reasoned rejection of his views. Elihu adopts a different approach in his final speech. He no longer cites the charges that Job has made and refutes them. Now he merely presents his own views and conclusions.[333]

This speech has two component parts. In 36:1-21 Elihu recapitulates the preceding speeches by strongly arguing that God is just. In 36:22–37:24 he prepares (unknowingly) for the Yahweh speeches by describing God's powerful activity in nature.[334] The first part (36:1-21) contains a summons to Job (vv. 2-4), Elihu's verdict (vv. 5-7), the substantiation (vv. 8-15), and its application to Job (vv. 16-21).[335]

---

333. Habel, *Book of Job,* 72; McCabe, "Elihu's Contribution," 60. Hemraj, "Elihu's 'Missionary' Role," 63, argues that chs. 33–35 constitute the negative part or refutation of Job's self-defense, followed by the positive part of persuasion on God's behalf in chs. 36 and 37. See also Fingarette, "Meaning of Law," 267.

334. McCabe, "Elihu's Contribution," 60.

335. McCabe, "Significance of the Elihu Speeches," 178. Habel, *Book of Job,* 494-95, gives a similar structure, although he joins the first two sections.

36:1-4: A Summons to Job Elihu's arrogance is clear in the opening to this speech (vv. 2-4). The condescending tone of v. 2a is even more apparent when Elihu claims to be speaking on God's behalf (v. 2b), a presumption overturned by the rest of the book. Elihu claims that Job is in the wrong; God commends him for speaking of him what is right (42:7-8); Elihu says that God will not appear, but at the end of his speeches, God does so (38:1). Thus his extravagant claims to get knowledge from far off (presumably from God) and to ascribe righteousness to God his maker (v. 3) are undercut by his pompous introduction.[336] Even more damaging for Elihu's credibility is his self-description as one who is complete or perfect in knowledge (v. 4). While this seems arrogant in itself, he will later in this same speech use an almost identical description of God as the one who is "perfect in knowledge" (37:16).[337] Thus, while Elihu will articulate many lofty truths about God in this speech, they are undermined by the way he introduces himself.

36:5-7: Elihu's Verdict Elihu's essential argument is set out in vv. 5-7. His fundamental conviction in v. 5 is that God is mighty in his purpose (v. 5b, lit. "in strength of heart," with the heart representing one's mind), and his mightiness means that he does not despise or reject anyone (v. 5a).[338] This insistence on God's strong ability to carry out his purpose is then filled out with reference to the wicked and the righteous in vv. 6-7. The wicked are dealt with first (v. 6). In saying that God does not keep them alive, Elihu implies that they receive as punishment the due consequences of their wickedness. The second part of the verse is often translated, "he gives the afflicted their right" (e.g., ESV, NRSV), but a more literal translation is, "justice [placed emphatically] he gives the afflicted" (cf. NASB, NJPS). In other words, it most likely refers not to the righteous afflicted being given their reward, but rather that God will act justly toward those who deserve to be afflicted. This is not good news for the wicked. The second half of the verse therefore parallels the first half, with both talking about punishment for the wicked. Alternatively, it may simply refer to all who are afflicted (righteous and wicked), and insists that they will all get justice in the sense of deserved reward or punishment. Verse 7 explicitly deals with the

---

336. Wharton, *Job*, 151, sees him presented here as "a ludicrous caricature of all religious or intellectual arrogance." Robertson, "Comedy of Job," 48, describes him as "a youthful, high-spirited, pompous, cock-sure reincarnation of the friends."

337. Newsom, "Book of Job," 585, makes the point that תָּמִים/*tāmîm* may simply mean "sound" or "wholesome," but Elihu's use of it in relation to God suggests that he means more than this.

338. No object is present in the Hebrew text, but "anyone" is implied. Habel, *Book of Job*, 497, suggests that מאס/*m's* may mean "waver," perhaps in a wordplay on the root מסס/*mss*, "to melt."

righteous, who are exalted and placed securely with those in positions of power. Elihu, as an armchair observer, thus insists on the idea of retribution as the determiner of human destiny.

36:8-15: The Substantiation of the Verdict People who suffer are described in v. 8 as "bound [or chained] up" or "caught in cords of affliction," which v. 9 explains as a result of their transgressions and specifically (perhaps with Job in mind) their arrogance. The test of whether a person is righteous or wicked, according to Elihu, is how they respond to instruction (מוּסָר/*mûsār*)[339] and to God's call for them to turn away from their iniquity (v. 10). The two responses are set out in vv. 11 and 12: "if they hear [obey] and serve him . . . if they do not hear [obey]." These different responses lead to suitably different outcomes. Verses 11 and 15 indicate the outcome for the afflicted righteous who turn back to God. The rest of their days will be filled with good (i.e., prosperity) and what is delightful or pleasant (v. 11). They will be delivered by God's power because adversity has opened their ear to hear (obey) God (v. 15). In Elihu's disciplinary view of suffering, he sees that their affliction will ultimately have beneficial consequences.

The other outcome is for the wicked or godless,[340] who show their true nature by not listening to or obeying God. They will perish and die, prematurely (by the sword, v. 12; in youth, v. 14), unfulfilled (without knowledge, v. 12), and wasting their lives (among the [cult] prostitutes, v. 14). Instead of crying out to God for help, they harbor their anger (v. 13).

36:16-21: Application to Job The preceding material sounds like a thinly veiled warning and word of advice aimed at Job. Now Elihu turns in vv. 16-21 to address Job explicitly ("you" and "your" in v. 16 are singular pronominal suffixes). Elihu claims that Job has been offered a way out of his distress. The distress is pictured metaphorically as the endless cramps of hunger pains, but the enticing offer given to Job is a feast in an open space, with a table full of fatness (v. 16).[341] However, Elihu concludes that instead of being "full of fatness," Job has chosen to be "full of the judgment on the wicked" (v. 17a),[342] in which he receives (is

---

339. Clines, *Job 21–37*, 859, notes that "instruction" in wisdom literature can be either physical punishment or words of correction, but that the mention of ears here clearly implies spoken words.

340. Since their basic stance in life is opposed to God, they are described in v. 13 as the "godless of heart."

341. "Fatness" was not at that time a symbol of obesity or high cholesterol, but of plenty and the absence of want.

342. Clines, *Job 21–37*, 863, notes that to be "full of the judgment of the wicked" means "to suffer judgment that rightly falls on the wicked."

grasped by) just punishment (judgment and justice, v. 17b). Elihu fears that Job might respond with scoffing (v. 18a). Verse 18b is less transparent in its meaning, for it is not clear what the ransom is, and why the greatness of the ransom would turn Job aside (i.e., away from God). While it may be an allusion back to the ransom of 33:24, Elihu appears to be telling Job not to let the greatness of the cost deter him from turning back to God.

In v. 19 Elihu urges Job to discontinue his cry for help, which is presumably different from the cry that the wicked refuse to make in v. 13. The parallelism of the verse suggests that Elihu has in mind Job's cry for vindication, trusting in his own strength to take on the might of God. He also warns not to turn away from the light and long for the darkness of night (v. 20).[343] In v. 21 Elihu gives Job another warning to avoid wickedness. The verse could be translated: "Take heed; stop turning to iniquity, for this is what you have chosen from your affliction." Thus the point might be not that Job has chosen iniquity rather than affliction (as in most translations), but rather that Job has chosen the path of iniquity during his affliction, and Elihu urges him to do so no longer.[344]

36:22-25: God's Powerful Works Deserve Praise In the second part of his final speech, Elihu voices a hymn of praise to God as Creator (36:22–37:13), then finishes off with an address to Job (37:14-24).[345] Within this major division, the first section can be divided into 36:22-25, 26-29, 30-33; 37:1-5, and 6-13. The second section is made up of words to Job (37:14-20) and a more general final summary (37:21-24).

The focus on creation in the hymn quite naturally introduces Yahweh's speeches. Gerald Wilson expresses it well: "While Elihu's theology denies the possibility of God coming in response to Job's pleas, his words actually prepare for that very divine appearance."[346] Elihu begins to set the tone of praise of the Creator and wonder at the creation that will characterize the Yahweh speeches.

---

343. The "night" is perhaps referring to Job's musings about the gloomy place of the dead in 10:20-22. Alternatively, G. Wilson, *Job*, 406, suggests it might also refer to the night as a symbol of the time when darkness can cover up evil deeds.

344. Alternatively, McCabe, "Elihu's Contribution," 61, has suggested that Elihu is targeting Job's preference to complain against God rather than learn the lessons from his affliction. Habel, *Book of Job*, 499, repoints בָּחַרְתָּ/*bāḥartā*, "you chose," as a Pual or passive, בֹּחַרְתָּ/*bōḥartā*, giving the sense of "for to this end you have been tried with affliction."

345. McCabe, "Significance of the Elihu Speeches," 200-222, views the two sections as a hymn of praise describing God's magnificent control of the weather (36:22–37:13), and his concluding address to Job, marked by a change in tone (37:14-24). Bias and Waters, *Job*, 260-76, however, divide the speech into three parts: explanation of suffering (36:1-18), exhortation to Job (36:19–37:16), and his conclusions (37:17-24).

346. G. Wilson, *Job*, 400.

In particular, 36:22–37:24 draws us into a God-centered focus, "to restore God to the centre of our thinking as preparation for entry to his presence," while the rhetorical questions (37:15-20) and nature imagery set the scene for, and lead naturally into, the Yahweh speeches that follow.[347] In particular, he does not confine himself to the concept of retributive justice, but also explores how God orders and governs the universe. What is presupposed in these nature passages is a theological principle that will be crucial for understanding the Yahweh speeches: that observations from the natural world can lead to conclusions about God's moral order. As in the natural world, God's governing of the moral world is broadened far beyond a narrow understanding of retributive justice.

In this section, appropriately signaled by a "Behold" (as in vv. 26, 30), Elihu has largely moved beyond Job and will only specifically address him again in 37:14. In vv. 22-25 there is a new focus on God's power (v. 22) and his work (v. 24), each as evidence that God deserves to be lifted high or praised in song. His "work" refers to his power evident in the created world. The point of v. 25 is that all people have seen God's work in all of creation. Woven into this picture of God's majestic power is the central point developed in vv. 22b-23. God is not simply a mighty creator but a teacher without rival who has no need to be told what to do.[348] In particular, Elihu insists that no one can require God to act in certain ways (v. 23a) or say to him, "You have done wrong" (v. 23b).

36:26-29: God's Control of Rain and Storms

Verses 26-29 focus on God's control of rain and storms. In v. 27 the image is of gathering the water, then using rain to "purify" the mist (this uncommon verb, זָקַק/*zāqaq*, described refining gold in 28:1). The description of the rain is filled out in v. 28, with particular emphasis on it falling abundantly on humans. This will serve as a foil to God's wider description in 38:26, where rain will fall even where there are no human beings. Verse 29 begins with the question about whether anyone could indeed understand how God orders the pattern of rainfall. It is almost an exclamation, but is at least a question with the implied answer no. The main application of this verse — indeed this section — is that no one is able to fully understand God's active management of the weather. A similar point is made in v. 26, which begins with the statement that God is great in the sense of exalted on high. It then asserts that we do not know him (presumably exhaustively, rather than

---

347. McKay, "Elihu — A Proto-Charismatic?" 169-70.

348. Clines, *Job 21–37*, 865, makes the useful observation that the mention in v. 22 of God's power and that he is a teacher without compare implies that every aspect of his power and his ways in creation should be understood as instruction. The way God actively rules in his creation reflects what God values.

at all),[349] and cannot even search out the number of his years. In other words, God's greatness seen in his control of the rain and weather highlights our limitations of knowledge of him and his ways. Elihu is surely implying that we should not criticize what we cannot understand. Of course, the irony that emerges for the reader is that Elihu is setting himself up as one who is perfect in knowledge (36:4) and has been pontificating at length about how God runs his world.

36:30-33: God's Use of Lightning A similar process is at work in vv. 30-33, this time with the illustration of the destructive force of lightning. After outlining its forceful nature (v. 30), he adds that God executes judgment on peoples by these (v. 31a). The verb יָדִין/*yādîn* (ESV "judges") could be translated "governs,"[350] which might ground his comment that the rain from these storms provides much food (v. 31b). However, the bounty of abundant food is introduced because that is what is struck by the lightning in v. 32. The dominant image of vv. 30-33 is thus not one of beneficence, but rather one of targeted destruction. Elihu's underlying theology as seen elsewhere is that the mighty Creator will use his power to reward human righteousness and punish human wickedness. This subsection is about retribution, with God using lightning to attack his mark (v. 32b). While a reference to thunder is introduced in v. 33a, the exact meaning of v. 33b is not entirely clear.[351] However, the verse asserts that God's verdict will be unmistakable and plain for all to see.

37:1-5: God's Purposes through Thunder and Lightning The lightning and thunder that were the focus at the end of chapter 36 remain at center stage in 37:1-5. Verses 1-4 deal relatively unproblematically with God's thunder and lightning (symbols of God's active presence in 36:33a) going forth into all the world (v. 3). The expected response of this overwhelming reality (v. 1) is that we should listen intently (v. 2),[352] and the result is that God's voice is heard (v. 4). The point of this extensive description is crystallized in v. 5 by drawing out the principle already seen. God displays his awesome power in creation (v. 5a), doing great things (a different word from 36:26) that we cannot or do not know.

---

349. The word "him" (v. 26a) may be implied in the Hebrew text. Alternatively, it might mean that we do not know his greatness.

350. So, e.g., NRSV, NIV. Hartley, *Book of Job,* 476, emends the verb to יָזוּן/*yāzûn,* "he feeds/ nourishes"; see also NIV margin.

351. ESV translates it as "the cattle also declare that he rises"; NRSV, "he is jealous with anger against iniquity." They reflect choices between similar words in Hebrew (מִקְנֶה/*miqneh,* "cattle"; and מַקְנִיא/*maqnî',* "jealous"; עוֹלֶה/*ʿôleh,* "rising"; and עַוְלָה/*ʿawlâ,* "iniquity").

352. An emphatic expression in Hebrew, thus meaning not just "listen" but "listen carefully/ attentively" ("Keep listening," ESV). It is in the plural here to emphasize its application to all.

God's greatness in nature is again coupled with our limited understanding of him and his ways.

37:6-13: God's Activity in the Rest of the Natural World The narrow focus on thunder and lightning is then broadened out in vv. 6-13 to other aspects of the natural world. There is mention of snow falling and strong showers of rain (v. 6). The image of sealing up human hands (v. 7) is one that is foreign to contemporary people. Perhaps the closest analogy is sealing off a crime scene so that it cannot be disturbed or so that there can be no unauthorized access. The picture is of stopping human work so that all whom God has made may know him or his work.[353] The same point, but without the purpose clause, is made in v. 8 with the animals ceasing from their activity of roaming and either hibernating or being confined to their dwelling places (perhaps by the storm). Verses 9-11 explain the frozen weather, which keeps the animals confined to their winter homes, with mention of storms, the cold winds, ice, frozen water, thick clouds, and lightning. In v. 12 another principle emerges that God is using and guiding these forces of nature to accomplish his purpose (lit. "what he commands") over the surface of the entire earth.[354] Finally, Elihu insists that God causes all this to happen (v. 13b). The reasons given in v. 13 for God's activity in the storms are startling — it is for correction or chastisement (lit. "for a staff/rod," a symbol of punishment), for his land, or for his committed love (חֶסֶד/*hesed*). While the reason for including the middle term ("land") is not clear,[355] the other two reasons reflect punishment and reward, the essence of the doctrine of retribution.

37:14-20: Challenge to Understand God's Great Works Elihu concludes his argument by calling on Job to hear, and urges him to understand the great works of God (v. 14). The first part of this summons is a series of rhetorical questions (vv. 15-20), with an aside or challenge to Job in v. 19. The questions

353. The object of "know" in v. 7 is "his work" (KJV, NASB). ESV and NRSV rework the difficult MT; see Clines, *Job 21–37*, 839-40. For the NIV reworking see G. Wilson, *Job*, 413, 415. Clines, *Job 21–37*, 876, notes the parallel with God sealing up the stars so that they will not do their work of shining (9:7).

354. It could mean over the productive parts of the earth (hence ESV, NRSV "the habitable world"), which would again be restricting Elihu's focus to the world of humans, not the earth as a whole.

355. Hartley, *Book of Job*, 479 n. 38, follows Tur-Sinai and Gordis in redividing MT לארצו/ *l'rṣw* to רצו לא/*l' rṣw*, i.e., רָצוּ לֹא/*lō' rāṣû*, "if they [humans] are not willing," which seems to be the most likely emendation to date. See Clines, *Job 21–37*, 843, for other suggestions. If "land" is to be retained, Elihu may be saying that God can use a storm to bring punishment (correction) or benefit (love), but perhaps also simply to provide water for the land, independent of human goodness or wickedness.

are similar to those that God will ask in the chapters that follow, but Elihu's goal is different. Indeed, what Elihu says is problematic. Although he is right in claiming that God is perfect in knowledge (v. 16), he has previously described himself in these terms (36:4). Elihu can rightly see that only God controls and coordinates the weather (vv. 15-18). While the exact symbolism of v. 17 is not clear, the contrast is between God, who can change the weather forces, and Job, who can only endure the scorching heat. Elihu then concludes that Job should stop speaking or be swallowed up by God (v. 20). Elihu continues to speak as if he knows God's mind exhaustively, and insists that we (and specifically Job) cannot proceed with a legal case against God because of darkness or lack of knowledge (v. 19).

37:21-24: Fear the Coming of God Verses 21-22 introduce the coming of God — either in Elihu's imagination or in reality as God is about to speak from the whirlwind (38:1) — in the image of the light following the storm. God's appearance is appropriately described by the coming of gold from the north, with God seen in his fearsome splendor (v. 22). When Elihu says that we cannot find God, he means that we cannot find out all that there is to know about God. Then, in language reminiscent of 36:22, 24, God is described as great in power. This power is seemingly harnessed to Elihu's key concern — that God will not mishandle justice and righteousness (v. 23). The correlation of God's power and justice (v. 23) anticipates the Yahweh speeches by proposing that God's justice and righteousness are evident in his ordering of the world, although in ways that neither Job nor Elihu has yet understood.

Elihu still believes that Job's approach has undermined justice and righteousness, and so he urges people (in particular, Job) to fear God (v. 24). Elihu's flipside is that God does not show preference to those who claim to be "wise of heart" (v. 24b). Elihu is not here saying that God does not reward those who are genuinely wise and godly in their whole being, but is referring to this as a way Job might describe himself.[356] Elihu's ultimate word to Job is that he needs to fear God, whereas the book as a whole insists that Job has already done so (e.g., 1:1, 8; 2:3), but he is still left with a need to do business with God.[357] Elihu is asserting the same point as the wisdom poem of chapter 28.[358]

356. Others see this as a negative rhetorical question with an implied positive answer, e.g., McCabe, "Elihu's Contribution," 63 (also Hartley and Gordis), which is reflected in the NIV, "does he not have regard for all the wise in heart?" This also makes good sense, and would mean that Elihu is affirming the doctrine of retribution again, as in v. 23b, and perhaps making an invitation to Job.

357. See L. Wilson, "Fear of God," 67-75.

358. Andersen, *Job*, 268: "We have come full circle to Job 28:28."

38:1–42:6: *God's Appearance (Yahweh Speeches) and Job's Responses*

When Yahweh intervenes in the proceedings, the reader expects the resolution of Job's dilemma to be fast approaching. Yahweh's appearance means that Elihu's "final" verdict must now be qualified. His long-awaited presence signals that this is the climax of the book, and so it would appear to be a most fruitful place for discovering its overall message.[359] Yet there is widespread disagreement about what answers the speeches give, and many conclude that they fail to address the key issues raised in the dialogue.[360]

Scholars divide over whether the significance of chapters 38–41 is based on what God says (the Yahweh speeches) or rather on the fact that he appears (the theophany).[361] In other words, is it the *content* of his speeches or is it the *context* within which he speaks that leads to a resolution of the issues raised in the book? Some of Job's problems are resolved simply by the appearance of Yahweh. Job's God-directed cries and complaints throughout the dialogue are a call on the seemingly absent God to become present. He has longed to speak to God in person (13:15), in a relationship in which God would call and Job would answer (14:15). This focus would account for the failure of the speeches to address the issue of suffering.[362] Once Job sees God again, he is able to accept that he does not need to know exhaustively God's purposes.

Furthermore, the intention of the Yahweh speeches is not to establish Job's guilt or sin. William Dumbrell expresses this well when he concludes, "There is no hint in these speeches that Job is being treated as a sinner; rather, he is being treated as one whose horizons need to be expanded."[363] Job has not shown a lack of respect for God, but simply that he has limited knowledge of how God orders his world. The playful tone of the Yahweh speeches confirms this.[364] The very proliferation of examples and detail in chapters 38 and 39 — much more than is needed to win an argument —

---

359. Simundson, *Faith under Fire*, 83.

360. Jamieson-Drake, "Literary Structure," 217. Bernard Shaw, quoted in Baker, "Book of Job," 17, is reported to have said, "If I complain that I am suffering unjustly, it is no answer to say, 'Can you make a hippopotamus?'"

361. This is filled out in L. Wilson, "Job 38–39," 122-25.

362. McKeating, "Central Issue," 245-46, observes that they "*never once mention the problem of suffering. . . . They do offer an answer to the problem of faith.*" See also Rowold, "Theology of Creation," 20.

363. Dumbrell, *Faith of Israel*, 258. Similarly, Habel, *Book of Job*, 528.

364. Andersen, *Job*, 271: "there is a kindly playfulness in the Lord's speeches which is quite relaxing. Their aim is not to crush Job with an awareness of his minuteness contrasted with the limitless power of God."

transforms the speech into a stroll through creation. A delicate balance has to be maintained, as Yahweh seeks to redirect Job's energies powerfully yet playfully. If Yahweh is too harsh, he would appear to endorse the views of the friends; if Yahweh is too weak, then Job will not hear what needs to be said. The playful irony of the Yahweh speeches preserves a right balance. Job's longings are met, enabling him then to proceed in a new direction. God also broadens Job's understanding so that he will continue to persevere in faith.

However, Georg Fohrer has observed that "in the Old Testament . . . it is the words spoken by God that make a theophany significant."[365] The intellectual energy expended in chapters 3–31 would seem odd if the solution was to be found solely on a nonintellectual level.[366] The need for Yahweh to address Job *twice* would be otiose if his appearance alone was sufficient to satisfy Job. Presumably Yahweh keeps on talking because something else needs to be said, something not yet understood by Job.

The speeches, by their question form, are not presented as answers to Job's questions, but themselves constitute a series of impossible challenges addressed to Job. Their very impossibility implies that they are not intended to be answered, but rather to reorient Job to take a different stance before Yahweh.[367] They are in the form of a "challenge to rival" speech also evident in Isaiah 40–55. This form of challenge question seeks to elicit the response, "You God alone," and to expose the inefficacy and deficiency of all rival deities. The additional element not found in Isaiah is the purpose or result clause, which indicates that what God desires is the restoring of a proper relationship, rather than the belittling of Job.[368] These factors suggest that the goal of the speeches is a reorientation of Job so that his relationship with Yahweh can be restored.

So it is both God's appearance and his words that are significant in chapters 38–41.

God's words here split into two speeches, commencing with almost identical phrases and having a similar structure:[369]

---

365. Fohrer, *Introduction to the Old Testament*, 327. Gutiérrez, *On Job*, 69, agrees that "the words of God give the presence of God its full meaning."

366. Tsevat, "Meaning," 10-11. Interestingly, the constellations in Job 9:9 recur in Job 38:31-32.

367. Habel, *Book of Job*, 51; Rowold, "Theology of Creation," 51-52, 60.

368. Rowold, "Theology of Creation," 61, 64-65. On 52-53 he notes that the purposes or results involve the other aspects of creation being brought to their intended richness as well: the shaking out of the wicked (38:13-15), the greening of desolate lands (38:26-27), making dust into arable clods of soil (38:38), bringing goats to life and maturity (39:3-4).

369. The structure outlined is a modification of that set out by Habel, *Book of Job*, 526-27.

A   Introductory formula (38:1)   A1 Introductory formula (40:6)
B   Thematic challenge (38:2-3)   B1 Thematic challenge (40:7-14)
   i. Theme A (key verse — v. 2)   i. Summons (v. 7)
   ii. Summons (v. 3)   ii. Theme B (key verse — v. 8)
                                              iii. Challenge expanded (vv. 9-14)
C   Particularization of theme   C1 Particularization of theme
   i. In the physical world (38:4-38)   i. With Behemoth (40:15-24)
   ii. In the animal and bird   ii. With Leviathan (41:1-34)
      kingdoms (38:39–39:30)
D   Brief Challenge to Answer (40:1-2)

The significance of this largely parallel structure is that each speech has a different thematic verse.[370] In the first speech 38:2 draws our attention to God's design and control of the world (in contrast to Job's lack of knowledge), while in the second speech 40:8 raises the issue of God's justice in contrast to Job seeking to justify himself.

38:1–40:2: God's First Speech: The Physical World and the Animal World

38:1-3: Theme Verse and Summons Verse 1 reintroduces the name Yahweh (ETs: the LORD), and mentions him speaking out of the whirlwind (a different word than in 37:9), a comment that will be repeated in 40:6. A whirlwind or storm has no particular theological significance, but it is an appropriate setting given Yahweh's power and his activity in running his world and preserving his creation.

Verse 2 is, on the surface, asking the question "who?" but its thrust is "why?" God is not asking Job to identify himself, but rather explain why he has taken the stance he has. The word "counsel" (עֵצָה/'ēṣâ) is commonly used to describe a plan or design, rather than mere advice or counsel. God's question to Job is why has he obscured God's plan or design (for his creation) with "words without knowledge." God is not claiming that this was Job's intention, but it was the effect of his words. Before seeing this as a strong rebuke to Job, we must remember that God will twice describe Job as the one who has spoken of him what is right (42:7-8). Job's basic stance before God must be right, but at least some of his words are based on too limited an understanding of God's pur-

---

370. Rowold, "Theology of Creation," 113-15. Within ch. 38, Jamieson-Drake, "Literary Structure," 220-24, further argues that the use of refrain lines (as well as content analysis) shows that ch. 38 has the twin theme of God's sovereignty over the earth (vv. 2-21) and God's sovereignty over heaven (vv. 22-38), merging in the summary (v. 33), which points to God's sovereignty over both.

poses. Job will concede as much in 42:3. The problem is not that Job had wrong knowledge of God, but that his view was telescopic (limited only to the issue of justice) rather than panoramic (concerned with how God orders his world).

Verse 3 is an invitation for Job to prepare for a contest (lit. "gird up your loins" or tuck in that clothing that will prevent you running). The contest is set out simply in v. 3b: "I will ask [question] you, and you will cause me to know [the answer]."

38:4-7: The Physical Earth God starts the body of his first speech with a consideration of the physical earth. There is a series of questions of different kinds — where were you (v. 4), on what (v. 7), but primarily who (vv. 5 [twice], 6). He is asking whether Job was around at the time of creation (v. 4), presumably to see if Job can understand how creation holds together, and whether he knows why it has the shape and size it has (v. 5). The "who" questions of vv. 5-6 are not really asking for the identity of the one who shaped the earth (that is clearly God),[371] but are really pointing out to Job that if it was not him, so he cannot claim to understand the earth. The key issue here is what does Job know. The verb "to know" is used twice in vv. 4-5, as well as the noun "understanding" (v. 4b is lit. "if you know understanding"). Job's limited knowledge is being demonstrated.

Verse 7, however, adds an interesting twist with the addition of superfluous, almost playful information. There is no need to add that the "sons of God" (probably a reference to the heavenly court) responded with joy (v. 7b). The idea of the morning stars singing (for joy) is a lighthearted, even comic picture that seems out of place if this is intended as a strong rebuke to Job. The use of humor here softens God's questioning of Job, and this sets the tone for the speech. The apparent harshness of 38:2 is thus not left to stand. What is made clear at the outset is that God is basing his moral ordering of his world on the fact that he is its Creator.

38:8-11: The Sea The playful note established in vv. 4-7 continues in vv. 8-11. In v. 8 there is the dual picture of the sea bursting forth from the womb, and also the image of shutting in the escaped waters with doors. The word "doors" has been used by Job in 3:10 to describe the "doors" of his mother's womb. God ultimately makes the crucial point that he determines the sea's boundaries and confines it (vv. 10-11), but not before continuing the image of the sea as baby. Thus v. 9 pictures the sea putting on clouds as its clothing, and being wrapped around with thick darkness as a swaddling band. The point is that God has

---

371. Habel, *Book of Job*, 537, notes that God is being pictured as the architect (v. 5a), the surveyor (v. 5b), and the engineer (v. 6).

determined the boundaries of the mighty sea, but it has been established gently and with humor. Yahweh's skillful use of rhetoric has secured his argument without demeaning Job. The initial harshness of 38:2 has been softened by the use of humor in these first two sections.

38:12-15: The Morning The next aspect of the physical world is the dawn or morning personified. There is a serious, but impossible, question being asked in vv. 13-14 — Are you, Job, able to control the morning or dawn so that the wicked can be shaken out of the earth? Of course Job cannot, but his inability is again softened by the slightly comic image of picking up the corners of the earth like a piece of clothing and shaking it as if removing dust.[372]

Verses 14-15 depart from the usual question pattern. The subject of v. 14 is not entirely clear, but it is most likely the physical earth of v. 13. The most natural reading is that God shapes or reshapes the world like a seal leaves its enduring mark on clay.[373] This leads nicely into light (meaning life) being taken from the wicked and their violent purposes (the "uplifted arm") frustrated (v. 15). Verses 14-15 are thus a little cameo of how God intervenes in his world to restrain the wicked, which reinforces the challenge for Job as to whether he is able to do this. God's design clearly entails the restraining and exposing of the wicked.

38:16-18: The Outer Limits of the Earth In this section there are three challenge questions, followed by a call to Job to publicly declare it if he knows all that is being asked. God starts in v. 16 by asking Job whether he has been to certain places, but the emerging issue is the state of Job's understanding (note the verbs in vv. 17-18: "revealed, . . . seen, . . . comprehended, . . . know"). Thus the thrust even of v. 16 is whether Job knows about these places through having been there. The parallelism of v. 16 suggests references to those parts of the earth hidden from humans, deep below the surface. Verse 17 moves to what we would more commonly call the "underworld" or place of the dead.[374] Together these two verses cover the parts of the world that cannot be seen by humans because of their location and because they could be experienced only beyond death.

372. The word כָּנָף/*kānap* in v. 13a most commonly means "wing," such as the wings of a bird, but can mean the extremities of clothing, or the edges or four corners of the physical world.

373. The NIV and ESV translate v. 14b as "its features stand out." NRSV has "it is dyed like a garment," but based on an emendation of the MT. Habel, *Book of Job,* 522, suggests that the implied subject might be the wicked, who stand out like the emerging shape of a garment as light shines on it.

374. This is patent in the phrase "gates of death" (v. 17a), while the "gates of the dark shadows" (v. 17b) appears to be saying the same thing. צַלְמָוֶת/*ṣalmāwet,* usually translated "deep darkness" in v. 17b, refers to the dark state of the dead in 10:21.

The phrase "expanse of the earth" (v. 18a) is more difficult to account for here. It could refer to the earth stretched out, or the sky (as in Gen 1), or the underworld.[375] The word רחֲב/*rāḥāb*, found here in the plural, means a broad place or expanse. It is a different word from the expanse of the sky in Genesis 1 (e.g., v. 14), and probably refers here to the broad expanses of the earth as a whole. Thus Job is again being asked whether his comprehension of the earth extends to its outer limits.

38:19-21: Light and Darkness These three verses address, in an ironic way (see v. 21), Job's limited knowledge of light and darkness. Job does not even know the path to where light or darkness rests (v. 19), so he could not lead it to where it belongs (v. 20). The implication is that Job would have no knowledge of where light and darkness fit into God's design and purposes. Job's short lifespan (v. 21) means that there is so much that he cannot know or comprehend.

38:22-30: The Waters — Snow, Hail, Rain, Frost, Ice God first asks Job about whether he has entered or seen (and hence knows all about) the storehouses for snow and hail (v. 22). The word for "storehouses" is used elsewhere for rain (Deut 28:12) and wind (Jer 10:13; 51:16; Ps 135:7), and has a broader sense of where special treasures are kept. There is a twist in v. 23 when these supplies of creation have been held back so that they can be used by God in human history. The examples God gives are times of disaster or distress (v. 23a, perhaps caused by the falling of snow and hail, similar to the natural forces causing havoc in Job 1:16, 19), and God's intervention in changing the course of battles (v. 23b). In other words Job, who does not know where snow and hail are kept, cannot know why they are being used to alter personal and national circumstances. Verse 24 broadens out the vista to include light and the wind, as if the same argument could be used for other weather features as well.

God widens the discussion even further in vv. 25-27 when he indicates that his concerns are wider than human beings alone. In v. 23 God referred to his intervention as Lord of creation into human history. Now his active kingly rule over all of creation is seen in his provision for the earth even where that has no apparent impact on humanity. The mention of torrents of rain and thunder (v. 25) lead to the beneficial bringing of rain on a land or a desert where there are no human beings (v. 26). The absence of humans is emphasized by its repetition

375. Andersen, *Job*, 276 n. 3, says "certainly the underworld," but gives no reasons. Hartley, *Book of Job*, 498-99, claims that Andersen "shows" that אֶרֶץ/*'ereṣ* here means the "underworld." Hartley cites several references (Pss 9:13; 107:18; Isa 38:10), but these relate to the "gates of death/ Sheol," not the use of "earth."

in v. 26 ("no man," using שִׁיא/*'îš*, then אָדָם/*'ādām*). The intention appears to be care for the ground and to make it flourish, even apart from its usefulness for humanity (v. 27). God's care is for all of creation, and his ordering of it is not simply to benefit human beings.[376]

The way that God runs his world cannot be reduced only to rewarding human righteousness and punishing human wickedness, for God's actions in sending rain on uninhabited land are related to neither. God's purposes here are not determined by a narrow view of human retributive justice, but reflect his wider concern for and control of all of creation. This section on the weather forces bears a strong message that Job's focus on justice as the rationale for the running of the world is too blinkered a perspective. God's active ruling of his creation is broader than justice alone.

The remaining verses of this section (vv. 28-30) reintroduce a comic element that again serves to soften God's words. This is seen in the idea of fathering rain (v. 28a), giving birth to dew or frost (vv. 28b, 29b), and ice emerging from a womb (v. 29a; see v. 8). In v. 30 the waters become frozen hard, implying that their impenetrability is an apt parallel to Job's inability to understand the weather forces in the world.

38:31-33: The Heavenly Bodies The recurring image here is that of authority and rule, seen in binding and loosing (v. 31), leading out and guiding (v. 32), knowing the regulations of heaven and the rule of these heavenly bodies over the earth (v. 33). The precise identification of each of the suggested constellations is not necessary in order to understand the main point of this section. Those constellations usually designated as Pleiades, Orion, and the Bear have already been mentioned by Job in the course of the dialogue (9:9).[377] In the context of the argument, God is inviting Job, in light of his inability to determine what happens on earth, to consider how he might cope with trying to rule the heavens as well. This is stated clearly in v. 33a, where Job's knowledge of how the heavens are organized is the issue, followed by a question (v. 33b) about whether he can implement or establish that ongoing pattern.

38:34-38: Storms The final subsection concerned with the physical world covers heavy rains and lightning typical of a thunderstorm. The storms are described in vv. 34-35 and 37-38, with a focus on wisdom and understanding in

---

376. Terrien, *Elusive Presence,* 371.

377. מַזָּרוֹת/*mazzārôt* (v. 32a) might be a general word for constellations (so BDB 561). Habel, *Book of Job,* 523, notes that it could be a variant on מַזָּלוֹת/*mazzālôt* (used in 2 Kgs 23:5), which means "constellations." But its precise meaning is not sure. Hartley, *Book of Job,* 502, therefore translates it generally as "the planets."

the centrally located v. 36. This structural observation suggests that the ability to control a storm is evidence of wisdom and understanding, and it is this that Job does not have. Words like חָכְמָה/*ḥokmâ*, "wisdom," and בִּינָה/*bînâ*, "understanding," are not simply intellectual terms, but are used of skilled craftsmen and those who pilot and sail ships (e.g., Exod 31:3-5; 35:10, 25-26, 30-35; Ezek 27:8-9). It is this practical ability to control and use what one has to achieve one's goal that is evident in God's mastery of a storm.

The key verbs in the four challenge questions of vv. 34-35 and 37-38 seem to be verbs of powerful action — "lift up, send forth, tilt." The one apparent exception is the verb סָפַר/*sāpar*, translated "number" in v. 37, but in the Piel it normally means "recount" or "declare."[378] It could mean here "determine where the clouds go, declare to them what to do," which would fit better with the parallelism of "tilt" in the rest of the verse. Thus all the challenge questions may deal with whether Job can control the elements of storms.

An ominous feature of the examples used is that they appear to cause harm and damage. There is mention of rain causing a flood (v. 34), heavy rain causing a quagmire (vv. 37b-38), and destructive lightning striking the earth (v. 35). These are all features of God's ruling of his creation, but they do not present as beneficial. The existence of order in creation thus does not preclude a certain amount of ambiguity in how God arranges his world. There are still paradoxes in the natural order.[379]

38:39-41: God Provides for the Lions and Ravens Yahweh turns to the animal kingdom for the rest of his first speech, and a striking aspect here is the remoteness of the creatures catalogued. The creatures mentioned in 38:39–39:30 are united by a common thread that they are not under human control or tamed by humans.[380] The only possible exception is the horse (39:19-25), but even here it is a picture of the mighty warhorse whose spirit is not broken by humans.

The previous verses (38:34-38) outlined aspects of the physical world that were hard to square with God's benevolent rule over creation. This survey of the animals begins on the very same note with consideration of animals feeding on other animals — with God actively hunting on their behalf. Thus God provides prey for the ravens (v. 41) and hunts the prey for the lion (vv. 39-40),

---

378. It is used once in Ps 22:17 (MT 18) with the sense of count. BDB 707-8 translates it as "count" but on the basis of repointing it to a Qal. It may also have the sense of "muster," and related words involve grouping or gathering things to count them, e.g., in a census.

379. Holmgren, "Barking Dogs Never Bite," 349-50, describes them as "certain happenings in nature that are difficult to harmonize with his absolute and benevolent rule."

380. Gordis, *Poets, Prophets, and Sages*, 293. Clines, *Job 1–20*, li, points out that this selection shows "that the world does not exist solely for the benefit of humankind."

on both occasions so that they can feed their young. The reality is that other animals die in order that the young lions and ravens are kept alive by God. In relation to the young ravens, even a cry to God for help (which is what Job has done) will, if answered, cause death and suffering elsewhere. This is another example where God's ordering of his creation seems arbitrary or incongruous, or at the very least, where it is not being rigidly governed by justice. Job is being asked whether he can order a creation that is as complicated as the one being described.

As with the beginning of the first part of the speech, there are a number of comic elements here. The image of the mighty God hunting on behalf of the lions or being at the beck and call of young ravens is a playful picture despite its deadly ramifications for other animals. This lightens or softens this second part of the speech as it gets underway, and will be carried further when the careless ostrich is described (39:13-17).

39:1-4: The Mountain Goats These verses concern the wild mountain goat or ibex (described as the "goats of the cliff/crag") and the female deer or hind at the time of giving birth (v. 1). The questions being asked of Job are whether he knows the time of such events and whether he can guard or protect[381] the animals as they bear their young (v. 1). Again the issue is Job's lack of knowledge and control. This lack of knowledge is filled out in v. 2 with further questions about the length of their pregnancy (or perhaps their lives; it is lit. "months they fill") and the actual time of birth. The birth process is then described in v. 3, followed in v. 4 by a picture of their quick growth and independence. Of course, none of the detail of vv. 3-4 is necessary to the question, and the inclusion of such otiose information changes the tone from rebuke to instruction. The animals in view appear in v. 4 to be wild animals, not those domesticated by humans.

39:5-8: The Wild Donkey The focus of this section is on the wild donkey, described by פֶּרֶא/*pere'*, a common word (used in 6:5), as well as by עָרוֹד/*ārôd*, a word found only here in the OT. This time Job is not directly asked about his knowledge or ability to control, but simply quizzed about who has set the wild donkey free to roam. The emphasis in v. 5 is on loosening the bonds or setting free, and the picture of vv. 6-8 is of such donkeys being distant from human contact, living in arid lands (v. 6), away from the cities and their people (v. 7), and at home in the remote mountains (v. 8). While Job is not asked directly, the implied question is whether his understanding of the way the world is run

---

381. The verb שָׁמַר/*šāmar* (v. 1b) is often translated with the sense of "observe," but something more active seems in view.

allows for creatures like the wild donkey that are so peripheral to humans. The wild donkey is part of creation, but what does it have to do with retributive justice?

39:9-12: The Wild Ox The powerfully strong wild ox is considered to see if Job can control such a creature and thus make it serve him (v. 9). The implied challenge is that, even if Job were able to capture such a creature, could he domesticate it? Such a creature could be of great benefit to a farmer. It could be used to till the soil in the fields (v. 10), do the heavy work because of its strength (v. 11), and bring the grain back to the threshing floor (v. 12). However, it would be of value only if Job could trust it to do what was asked ("have faith," v. 12; "depend/ trust," v. 11; "willing to serve," v. 9). This ultimately depended on whether Job could control it, and that is the question that God asks.

39:13-18: The Ostrich The comic element is reintroduced with the cameo about the ostrich, another animal outside human control.[382] It is purposefully described as a creature without understanding, which has "forgotten" wisdom (v. 17), and this is evident in it leaving eggs on the ground for it and others to tread on (vv. 14-15). Coupled with this is a dark side evident in the ostrich being cruel to its young (v. 16). Thus death and pain are part of creation. It seems that God has designed his creation to include an animal like this, though it lacks wisdom and causes pain to others.[383] The implied question is whether Job's understanding of the world can account for such a creature. Indeed, there is a surprise twist at the end, where a fleeing ostrich can outrun a horse and rider (v. 18). It may look and act foolishly, but it is magnificent when it does what it is designed to do.

There is no question to Job in this cameo, as if the challenge has been transformed into a nature walk. God is no longer asking Job about the order in creation; he is simply showing it to him. He is almost making suggestions about discoveries Job will make as he tries to find his own answers. The questions are not meant to test or examine Job, but to lead him out into the world and reorient his perspective.

39:19-25: The Warhorse A different kind of creature — one commonly used by humans — appears in vv. 19-25. Here at last is a creature that appears to be an

---

382. Verse 13 is opaque, but the point of the rest of the section is clear.

383. In relation to the ostrich, Rowold, "Theology of Creation," 104, comments, "the mystery and marvel of Yahweh's עצה is that it has room also for this wisdom-less and understanding-less ostrich. Is there, then, place for the knowledge-less Job too?"

exception to the remote creatures of the rest of the chapter. However, a careful look reveals that this horse is not a domesticated farm animal but rather a wild bundle of energy that storms into battle, and whose spirit is not broken by humans. The battle imagery is prevalent: leaping over obstacles and terrifying snorting (v. 20, designed to put others in their place), though the enemies dig themselves in.[384] He delights in his strength and goes into battle showing no fear (vv. 21-22). In v. 23 the weapons mentioned may be aimed at the horse or else carried by it into battle. However, the horse is not deterred but covers the ground quickly and can hardly wait for the trumpet to sound and the battle to begin (vv. 23-24). This is a masterly and evocative description of the mighty warhorse. Henry Rowold suggests that it "represents the epitome of the vibrant, positive joy of life, which characterizes the עצה of Yahweh."[385]

What is Job asked about such a creature? God wants to know whether Job has trained or motivated such a spirited animal. Has Job given the horse his might that is so vividly portrayed (v. 19a)? Has he given him the ability to leap so powerfully in the face of danger (v. 20)? Job is being asked about whether he has made and could control such an animal, but the challenge is distracted by the striking detail given about such a magnificent creature.

39:26-30: The Hawk and the Eagle The final examples of the animal world are the hawk and the eagle, which make a leisurely end after the intensity of the warhorse. A number of motifs recur here. First, these two birds are remote and distant from humans. The hawk soars above (v. 26); the eagle has its nest on high (v. 27), on inaccessible rocky crags (v. 28), a long way away from its prey (v. 29). Second, the existence of these predators means death to others (most clearly in v. 30), but they are nonetheless part of creation. Lastly, the questions that God asks Job are whether he can determine how these birds act. Does Job understand how to manage the air currents and decide which way to head, let alone impart that to the hawk (v. 26)? Does Job give commands to the eagle about where he should make his home and vantage point (vv. 27-29)? He is being challenged again by God about his limited knowledge and inability to control such a complex universe.

40:1-2: Brief Challenge to Answer As Yahweh concludes his first speech, he uses legal terms ("contend . . . argue . . . answer," v. 2). The language of the liti-

---

384. Most translations, e.g., ESV, NIV, NRSV, based on the Greek, Syriac, and Latin versions, have "he paws [digs]," but the verb in the MT is plural. It makes sense if read as the enemy establishing defensive positions, but the horse will not be put off.

385. Rowold, "Theology of Creation," 105.

gation motif is strikingly less frequent in the Yahweh speeches, especially in this first speech.[386] This suggests that God is not presenting evidence for the defense, but rather showing Job why the process itself is flawed. Job's desire to see God in court assumes that the world is ordered only on the basis of retributive justice, but this is shown to be too narrow.

Yahweh is not simply judge; he is also the king who is actively exercising his sovereign rule.[387] Thus, in his first speech, Yahweh has spoken of the creation of the world (38:4-11), his control of the wicked (38:12-15), his knowledge of the world's structure (38:16-23), his command over natural forces and the heavens (38:24-38), his ability as provider (38:39-41), and his control of the wild animals (39:1-30). That these are all part of God's complex governing of the world leads him to urge Job to see the futility of his stance before God. Yahweh's summation in v. 2 shows the awesome task Job has set for himself in pursuing his court case, and the implied way forward is for Job to acknowledge the pointless nature of his approach.[388]

40:3-5: Job's First Reply — An Insufficient Response

Job's reply after Yahweh's first speech is ambiguous at best. He "answers" (v. 3) by asking, "what shall I answer?" (v. 4), and then declares that he will "not answer" (v. 5). While he concedes that he is of small account, he makes no admission of wrongdoing.[389] There is no retraction of the words uttered during the dialogue, nor any withdrawal of litigation, nor any renunciation of his previous claim of innocence.[390] Some view the placing of the hand over the mouth (v. 4b) to be an expression of submission to God,[391] but the context suggests that he is simply announcing that he will now be silent.

The numerical saying in v. 5 draws attention to the second part of the

386. Tsevat, "Meaning," 29. In all of the Yahweh speeches, Parsons, "Structure and Purpose," 149, finds it only in 40:2, 8, and perhaps 38:3 = 40:7.

387. See Scholnick, "Poetry in the Courtroom," 201.

388. The unexpected feminine suffix on "answer" (v. 2) is best understood as referring in a general sense to the verbal idea of the previous sentence (in this case, it refers to the entire speech): GKC §135p. Gordis, *Book of Job*, 465, reads it as, "can he answer all this, i.e. that has been set forth?"

389. Habel, *Book of Job*, 549. He notes that "the mood is one of complaint not of confession."

390. This leads to a variety of views. Hartley, *Book of Job*, 518, understands Job as "saying that he continues to stand behind his avowal of innocence." Gordis, *Book of Job*, 466-67, notes that "Job is not submitting to God or conceding any part of His position" and calls his response "more evasive than submissive." However, Patrick, "Job's Address of God," 280, argues that Job acknowledges that he can no longer accuse God.

391. So Smick, "Job," 1045, who notes that Job has used it twice before (21:5; 29:9).

verse, but it can be variously interpreted. The verb used in v. 5b can mean either "to continue to do something" or "to do something again." It probably implies only that Job will not continue his protests or add any additional arguments.[392] This first speech by Job thus brings no clear resolution of the issues at stake. Yahweh will not be content to be merely "unanswered," and will repeat his demand for an answer in v. 7. The central thrust of Yahweh's second speech will be that his purposes are wider than a merely forensic justice and include his governing of the universe. That Yahweh needs to say this again indicates that Job has not yet understood it, and thus that his response in vv. 3-5 is insufficient.[393]

40:6–41:34: God's Second Speech

Yahweh's second speech is fairly clearly structured. Unlike the myriad of examples in chapters 38–39, there is a focus here on the two figures of Behemoth and Leviathan. The speech begins with a challenge (40:6-14) announcing the theme, which is then amplified in relation to Behemoth (40:15-24) and Leviathan (41:1-34).[394]

An initial hurdle is determining the nature and identity of Behemoth and Leviathan. Are they intended to be understood as literal creatures or as symbolic (sometimes called "mythological") images?[395] If they are to be read as natural creatures, then they are probably being described hyperbolically. This is clearest in 41:18-21, where Leviathan is depicted as breathing out fire and smoke. Various suggestions have been made for their identification as natural creatures. בְּהֵמוֹת/*běhēmôt* (Behemoth) is the normal word for a large beast such as a cow.[396] He eats grass (40:15), goes into the mountains for food (40:20), is at home in

392. BDB 415, 2a; Habel, *Book of Job*, 549; Gordis, *Book of Job*, 467; Andersen, *Job*, 285; Greenberg, "Job," 298. It is used in this sense in 41:8 (MT 40:32).

393. Rowold, "Theology of Creation," 112, suggests that "the spirit of Job's first reply is at best only provisional, and perhaps even reluctant." Gibson, "On Evil," 399, views it as "ungracious, even . . . ironic." Andersen, *Job*, 285, asserts that it is "somewhat evasive, and not at all a satisfactory end to the matter."

394. The Leviathan section is 41:1-34 in English versions, but the Hebrew versification differs: it is 40:25–41:26. The English verse numbers are used here.

395. Andersen, *Job*, 288-91, and Gordis, *Book of Job*, 569-72, set out the case for a natural or literal interpretation; Pope, *Job*, 320-34, outlines the mythological view. Smick, "Job," 1048-49, concedes that Behemoth and Leviathan are used frequently in the OT without any symbolic meaning, citing Pss 8:8; 50:10; 73:22; 104:26; Joel 1:20; 2:22; Hab 2:17. Leviathan is used symbolically in Ps 74:12-14 and Isa 27:1 (see also Rev 12–13).

396. The plural form of Behemoth is usually understood as an intensive plural, thus describing a great beast.

the river (40:21, 23 — the Jordan River), and is difficult to capture. It has been suggested that he is a hippopotamus, elephant, or water buffalo. By itself the description of Behemoth does not seem sufficient to determine whether it is a literal or symbolic/mythological creature.

Leviathan is sometimes understood to be a crocodile, a dragon, or even a whale. It is no doubt related to Lotan/Litan, the name of a seven-headed dragon in Canaanite mythology. It has thick, perhaps armored skin (41:13), scales on his back or hide (41:15-17), sharp parts underneath (41:30), and is at home in the sea (41:31-32). Other significant elements of the description include his fire breathing (41:18-21), the dread of the gods before him (41:25), his unequaled stature on earth (41:33-34), and his juxtaposition over against Yahweh (41:8-11). All these suggest that Leviathan (and hence also Behemoth) are either hyperbolic descriptions of natural creatures or, perhaps more likely, mythological creatures. It is difficult to think of any natural creature that fits the description given in Job, especially that of Leviathan. In Isa 27:1 Leviathan symbolizes moral chaos in the world.

If they are to be understood symbolically or mythologically, some have proposed that they are specifically figures of Satan (the accuser of chs. 1–2) or Satan and Death.[397] This would mean that the accuser of the prologue is more active in the book than commonly thought. However, they are more likely to be symbolic in a more general sense of the forces of chaos or of possible threats to God. Seeing them as symbolic creatures also makes sense of the flow of the book. Just as there is progression in subject matter from Yahweh's first speech to his second, so there is progression in the creatures described. We move from the natural creatures detailed in the first speech to even greater and more fearsome symbolic creatures in the second.

However, whether mythological or natural, their function is that they are difficult to be controlled or ordered. They are powerful adversaries (40:16-18; 41:7-10, 12-34) that defy human attempts to capture them (40:24; 41:5-9). In developing these examples at length, God admits there is "evil" or at least paradox in the world, but asserts that he contains it — as he has contained Leviathan and Behemoth — within certain boundaries. Yahweh has chosen not to eradicate Behemoth and Leviathan, but to place them under his sovereign governance.[398]

---

397. Gibson, "On Evil," 402-9, 417-18, sees the two figures as paralleling "the satan" of the first two chapters. This is picked up by his former student Fyall, *Now My Eyes*, 126-37, 157-72, who identifies Behemoth as Death personified and Leviathan as Satan, the one who has power over death. See also Ash, *Out of the Storm*, 94-98; Smick, "Semeiological Interpretation," 147. Another theory is that of Gammie, "Behemoth and Leviathan," who suggests that Behemoth and Leviathan are symbols of Job himself.

398. Clines, *Job 1–20*, xlvi.

40:6-8: Theme Verse and Summons The introductory formula and summons (vv. 6-7) are a virtual repetition of at the beginning of Yahweh's first speech (38:1, 3). This suggests that the two speeches are intended to be complementary, focusing on the same issue of how God runs his world, but from a different angle.[399]

In 40:8 Yahweh asks an explicit question about justice, using the word מִשְׁפָּט/*mišpāṭ*, "justice, judgment," and also the root צדק/*ṣdq*, "to be righteous." This is the theme verse of the second speech, and the thrust of it is, "Will you even [try to] make my judgment/justice ineffectual? Will you make me wicked in order that you might be righteous?" God can discern Job's assumption that he can be declared righteous only if God's treatment of him is shown to be wrong (on the basis of the theory of retribution). The key to unraveling this paradox is realizing that God's concerns are wider than simply administering justice. God is concerned with the wider brief of actively governing the universe. As in the first speech, he is trying to demonstrate that his plan/design (38:2) is not limited to rewarding human righteousness and punishing human wickedness. It even includes keeping in check the forces of evil and chaos, symbolized by Behemoth and Leviathan. Gustavo Gutiérrez expresses it well: "Job realizes that he has been speaking of God in a way that implied that God was a prisoner of a particular way of understanding justice. . . . What is it that Job has understood? . . . that justice alone does not have the final say about how we are to speak of God."[400]

This is not to say that God is unjust, nor is it to assert that justice has nothing to do with the way God runs his world. The divine speeches simply illustrate that our understanding of justice is not the sole criterion for how God acts. The doctrine of retribution is thus not rejected but rather marginalized or qualified.[401] The view that Yahweh is bound to act *only* according to the principles of retributive justice is shown to be an unsuccessful attempt to restrict his sovereign freedom.

40:9-14: The Challenge Expanded After this theme verse comes a challenge to Job about whether he can match the might and dignity of Yahweh. Verse 9 asks the rhetorical question (with the implied answer no) of whether Job has strength (an arm) like God, and whether he can bring things into being and control them ("thunder with a voice like his"). Verses 10-13 are an invitation to

---

399. Rowold, "Theology of Creation," 113-14, notes that the repetition in 40:6-7 of 38:1, 3 is a literary device that serves to "bind the two speeches into one larger whole" so that they should be read together.

400. Gutiérrez, *On Job*, 87. See also Parsons, "Structure and Purpose," 149-50; Habel, *Book of Job*, 66.

401. See the perceptive comments of Clines, *Job 1-20*, xlv-xlvi.

take on the divine roles, assuming God's majestic splendor (v. 10), then judging the wicked and proud (vv. 11-13). Only if Job were able to do this, and show himself to be God's equal, would Yahweh cede to him (v. 14). Behind this challenge, of course, is the issue of how the world is run. Is it simply a matter of executing retributive justice or not?

40:15-24: The Challenge of Controlling Behemoth The section begins "Behold, Behemoth," in v. 15a, then describes him and his habitat in vv. 15b-23, then asks a solitary question in v. 24 — can you control or subjugate him?[402] There is no longer the barrage of challenges that marked God's first speech, and the main point emerges at the end (v. 24).

The first observation about Behemoth concerns his creatureliness. He is made by God; just like Job he is God's creature; and he eats grass in common with many other animals (v. 15). His strength is the focus of vv. 16-18. Rowold sees an emphasis on his procreative strength in vv. 16-17 and mention of his physical strength in v. 18.[403] Certainly, some of the detail of vv. 16-17 is able to be understood as a picture of his virility. Verse 16 describes strength and power in his loins and belly (בֶּטֶן/*beṭen*, "belly," can describe the womb in a female), and the language may be euphemistic. What might drive this view is the common translation of v. 17a: "he makes his tail stiff like a cedar" (ESV, NRSV). There is a need for some caution, since זָנָב/*zānāb*, "tail," is used elsewhere for the tails of other animals (e.g., Exod 4:4; Judg 15:4) without any sexual overtones.[404] However, since the other option of a tail bending or swaying gives no impression of strength, it is likely that a sexual connotation is intended. Certainly there is a focus on physical strength in v. 18, as Behemoth's bones and limbs are likened to strong metals.

Behemoth is described as the first of the works of God (v. 19a), a status that humans think they have.[405] This assertion about the distinctiveness of Behemoth would certainly be hyperbolic language for any natural creature, since there is no basis on which a hippopotamus or elephant could fit this description.

---

402. Fyall, *Now My Eyes,* 131, suggests that there are four sections: the challenge (v. 15), the creature's appearance (vv. 16-19), his habitat (vv. 20-22), and his invincibility (vv. 23-24).

403. Rowold, "Theology of Creation," 134-36.

404. Furthermore, the translation "make stiff" is uncertain; the root חפץ/*ḥpṣ* II is a hapax legomenon whose main meaning given in BDB 343 is "to bend down," but may be related to the root חפץ/*ḥpṣ* I, which means "desire," and is used in Song of Songs to mean "sexual desire." See Hess, "חפץ." Gordis, *Book of Job,* 476-77, also notes that in later Hebrew זָנָב/*zānāb* colloquially has the meaning of male genitals, and that there is versional support for rendering פַּחַד/*paḥad* (only here "thighs") as "testicles."

405. A similar description is given of Wisdom in Prov 8:22.

The force of v. 19b is not entirely clear, but seems to mean that God (the one who made him) is called on to bring his (presumably God's) sword near to him, either to defend him (as a special creature) or to control him.[406]

Verse 20 then provides evidence (introduced by "For") supporting his exalted status as described in v. 19. It is not simply saying that he finds food in the mountains, but that the mountains are lifting up or offering food to him (perhaps as a tribute). As further evidence of his special place, all the living creatures of the field gather to frolic and play there. "There" appears to refer to the mountains, but v. 21 continues to explore his habitat and describes it as reeds and marsh. Possibly he lives in a river valley (later described as the Jordan in v. 23) surrounded by mountains. Indeed, the focus of most of vv. 21-23 is on a river environment (reeds, marsh, brook, river, Jordan). The scene of vv. 20-22 has Edenic or paradise elements, but there is a move in a different direction in v. 23. Here the focus is on the fearlessness of Behemoth, which is demonstrated in the face of a turbulent river. The name Jordan is used because it symbolized a river for later Israelites.[407]

The climax of the description of Behemoth comes in v. 24. Among other possibilities, v. 24a could mean, "Can one take him in his springs?" (a location), or "Can one take him while he is looking?" (a state of alertness);[408] but the rendering "while he is looking" fits the context best. The implied answer to the question in any event is no. A human being could not capture him. The second part of the verse probably describes using a trap to pierce his nose, and so lead him away captive. Alternatively, it could mean making it vulnerable to capture by piercing its nose.[409] The verse as a whole is asking whether Job can capture and therefore control a creature like Behemoth.

41:1-7: The Challenge to Contend with Leviathan The Leviathan section covers the entire chapter, and there are two major sections — vv. 1-11, largely a challenge to Job; and vv. 12-34, an extended description of Leviathan's attributes and features.[410] In vv. 1-7 Job is challenged to contend with Leviathan through

---

406. Along these lines it could be translated "its maker will approach with his sword." Fyall, *Now My Eyes*, 129, translates, "even his Maker has to bring his sword against him."

407. Gordis, *Book of Job*, 479, suggests that "Jordan" is just being used as a synonym for "river," in the same way that Carmel is used for a fertile field in Isa 32:15.

408. The latter is the meaning given in the LXX, "in his eyesight," reading "eyes" as a symbol of sight. Cf. NRSV "Can one take it with hooks?"; ESV "Can one take him by his eyes?"

409. Ruprecht, cited in Hartley, *Book of Job*, 526, notes that hunters of a hippopotamus would pierce its nose so that it would have to breathe through the mouth, since an open mouth made it vulnerable to a mortal wound.

410. However, Habel, *Book of Job*, 559-60, structures it slightly differently: vv. 1-8, the chal-

a series of challenge questions. These generally begin with interrogative markers, except vv. 1 and 6, but even there challenge questions are implied. Verses 8-11 sound like conclusions — first, in relation to Leviathan, the challenge is described as futile (vv. 8-10a); and second, in relation to Yahweh, the implication is drawn out in v. 10b ("who then is he who can stand before me?"), and followed by a concluding assertion (v. 11). Once these points have been made, there is an extensive and overpowering description of Leviathan in vv. 12-34. Verse 12 is an introductory verse, followed by a description of his armor (vv. 13-17), his fire breathing (vv. 18-21), his strength (vv. 22-25), the inability of weapons to defeat him (vv. 26-29), the turmoil he creates (vv. 30-32), and a general conclusion (vv. 33-34).

Verses 1-2 are connected in that v. 1a and v. 2b envisage capturing Leviathan with a hook, forming a neat *inclusio*. This image of catching, and therefore determining what happens to, Leviathan also seems echoed in v. 2a with the picture of placing a rope in (perhaps through) his nose. This most likely refers to being able to lead Leviathan behind as a captive or tamed creature. More difficult is the image of v. 1b of weighing down his tongue with a cord. The parallelism of these verses (fishhook/hook; cord/rope on body part) suggests a parallel sense. Perhaps the situation is one of controlling the creature by weighing down his tongue, maybe preventing him from eating or making sounds.[411]

In vv. 3-4 human characteristics are attributed to Leviathan, such as the ability to speak and to enter into agreements. If Leviathan were able to express his intentions in such ways, would he be utterly submissive and deferential? Verse 5 develops this into the area of being a domesticated animal, asking whether he would be sufficiently harmless for young girls to play with safely.

Verses 6-7 raise the issue of whether you could make some profit from selling the creature for meat. The image in v. 6 is not of selling him whole (though v. 6a would allow that sense), for v. 6b describes dividing him into pieces for different individuals.[412] Thus v. 7 anticipates the later descriptions of Leviathan, speaking here of the process of trying to kill him in order to distribute the meat.

---

lenge; vv. 9-12, the divine claim; vv. 13-32, the description of Leviathan; and vv. 33-34, a final summary.

411. "Weighing down" literally means "causing to sink." Rowley, *Job*, 259, notes that it is used in the Samaritan Pentateuch of Lev 8:13 in the sense of "bind." Keel, *Dieu répond à Job*, 109-10, 121, presents pictures in which hunters have cords attached to the nose and mouth of the hippopotamus and crocodile, as well as hooks. That may well be the basis of the imagery in 40:24 and 41:1-2.

412. So Rowley, *Job*, 259; contra Habel, *Book of Job*, 554, who suggests it might mean to divide up the proceeds of the sale. The language of v. 7 suggests killing, not just taming for sale.

41:8-11: Some Conclusions The series of challenge questions about subduing Leviathan have now ended, and there are now two mild imperatives ("lay your hands on him," "remember the battle," v. 8), followed by a conclusion, "you will not try it a second time." This theme of taking on a losing cause is reinforced in vv. 9-10a, with there being no prospect of doing a "Crocodile Dundee" and taming Leviathan. It is a hopeless ambition for a human being.

The real point of the Leviathan section is made clearer in vv. 10b-11. At this point there is an echo of God's challenge to Job (40:9). Verses 8-10a (or perhaps vv. 1-10a) are like an extended protasis — if you cannot stand up against Leviathan — then the apodosis in v. 10b is, "how can you stand up in my presence?"[413] This is quite logically followed by a concluding claim of Yahweh's ownership and sovereignty over all creation (v. 11). Though Leviathan might inspire fear in others, before Yahweh it is only a creature. Yahweh clearly asserts that as owner or ruler of the universe, he can never be *compelled* by anything, even the principle of retribution (v. 11).[414] If there is more to Yahweh's purposes than retributive justice, he cannot be *bound* simply by justice, as if it is an objective principle that can be used to shackle God or restrict his freedom.

41:12-17: Leviathan's Armor The second, descriptive section gives details about Leviathan's body or the effect he has on others. This begins in v. 12 with a general statement about his strength (his limbs and frame), but focuses in vv. 13-17 on his impenetrable armor. This armor prevents access to his limbs and to the rest of his body as mentioned in v. 12.[415]

Verse 13 is difficult to translate. The first part is a challenge as to who could uncover or strip off "the skin [or surface] of his garment," probably a reference to the outside surface of his body viewed as a garment. The second half of the verse is often translated as "coming near to him with a bridle" (so ESV, NIV), but this does not fit the sense of his skin's impenetrability, which flows through the rest of vv. 13-17. It could alternatively be translated, "Who can penetrate its double coat of mail?" (so NRSV, NJPS), which makes reasonable sense of the text and suits the context.[416] Verse 14 focuses on Leviathan's face, with the

---

413. The NRSV and many commentators emend the text of v. 10b and v. 11 to read "it" ("who can stand before *it?*" "who can confront *it?*") — but the Hebrew suffix is "me," i.e., God. God's point is that, if you think it (Leviathan) is scary, wait till you confront me.

414. Whybray, *Two Jewish Theologies*, 8; Greenberg, "Job," 299; Gutiérrez, *On Job*, 72.

415. However, Gibson, "New Look," 132-39, and Fyall, *Now My Eyes*, 161, suggest that v. 12 instead concludes the previous section. Both also note that בַּדָּיו/*baddāyw*, "his limbs," can be translated "his boasting."

416. The LXX provides support for this reading. It assumes that there has been a scribal transposition of consonants or metathesis in the underlying Hebrew text from סרן/*srn* ("coat of

"doors of his face" being a reference either to his mouth or his jaws. The implication is probably that even if you were able to pry open his mouth, you would be deterred by his terrifying teeth and thus still unable to penetrate his defenses.

Verses 15-17 give an extended description of the protection that covers his back. It is a picture of an impenetrable row of shields that are close together (v. 15), without even any room for air (v. 16). Indeed, they are joined together (lit. "a man to his brother") in some way so that they cannot be separated. His outer defenses are impenetrable (vv. 13-17).

41:18-21: His Breathing of Fire This section has a sustained picture of Leviathan as a fire-breathing creature, an aspect that is the strongest argument for seeing it as a symbolic figure rather than an identifiable animal. Something like a fire-breathing dragon is in view (v. 18), and those who wish to see a natural creature here must understand these verses to be speaking hyperbolically of an animal like the crocodile. The sneezings that flash forth light would thus be the light from the fire. Even the simile of his eyes being like the eyelids of the dawn is best understood in this way. The red shades of the dawn is a fitting image for fire, and it means either that his eyes are red and fiery or perhaps that the fire he breathes is reflected in his eyes so that they appear red.

This is made explicit in v. 19 with flaming torches emerging from his mouth, with the parallel section describing them as "sparks of fire." Smoke comes out of his nostrils (v. 20), like steam coming off a boiling pot or smoke coming from the (burning) rushes. Verse 21 contains yet another explicit mention of fire breathing with a flame coming out of his mouth, and the fire of his breath kindling coals.[417] The image of Leviathan as a fire-breathing creature serves to picture him as a fearsome opponent who cannot be easily conquered.

41:22-25: His Strength The two key themes of this subsection are the strength of Leviathan and his ability to evoke terror, both of which are introduced in v. 22. The neck is a potentially weak part of the human body, but strength is found in Leviathan's neck (v. 22a). This motif of strength is filled out in vv. 23-24, with reference to two other possible areas of weakness. The drooping or hanging parts ("the folds," ESV, NRSV, NIV) of his flesh (v. 23) and his heart (v. 24) might be thought soft enough to be vulnerable. However, the "folds" are not loose flaps, but stick together, are firm like cast metal, and will not totter or

---

mail") to רסן/*rsn* ("halter, bridle"). Reading "coat of mail" would enable a more natural reading of "double" and "enter/penetrate" in v. 13b.

417. Contra those who interpret this section as describing the steamy breath of the crocodile, and the reflection of light sparkling in the water. At best this could only be a hyperbolic description of a crocodile.

shake (v. 23). His heart is cast hard as well (the same root used in v. 23 is used twice in v. 24), and is compared to the immovable lower millstone. This creature has no soft underbelly.

The idea of causing terror is introduced in v. 22b and developed in v. 25. Terror is vividly pictured in v. 22 as dancing before him, thus possibly surrounding and certainly preceding him. Verse 25 develops two situations that epitomize his ability to instill fear — when he ominously raises himself up, and when he crashes down and presumably makes much noise and disturbance. The extent of the terror is seen in the fact that the אֵלִים/*'ēlîm*, "gods" (NRSV; "the mighty," ESV, NIV), are rattled. While this highlights the probable symbolic understanding of Leviathan, it also shows how far-reaching the terror is, with no one being immune.

Together both these key ideas buttress the notion that Leviathan is an awesome beast that cannot be controlled easily if at all by humans. He is an overwhelming adversary.

41:26-29: Weapons Cannot Defeat Him These verses logically develop this theme by exploring whether humans might be able to overcome Leviathan through the use of weapons, since his strength cannot otherwise be matched. A catalogue of weapons is mentioned, but none can prevail against him. This conclusion is reached in v. 26, but amplified in the verses that follow.

The weapons can reach or strike him (v. 26), but neither the sword nor the spear, the dart nor the javelin can inflict a decisive wound on him.[418] Their ineffectual nature is made clear by the comparisons of v. 27, where he treats iron as if it were straw and bronze as if it were as soft as rotten wood. In vv. 28-29 both sling stones and clubs are as weak as stubble, while arrows do not deter him and javelins only make him laugh. Human technology in developing weapons of warfare bring people no closer to being able to overcome Leviathan.

41:30-32: He Creates Turmoil This unit deals with the turmoil that Leviathan creates in the (mythological) setting of the deep and the sea (v. 31). The first picture is of him using the sharp, pottery-like protrusion of his underside to churn up the mud or mire (v. 30), an image connected to the sea in Isa 57:20. More explicitly grandiose is the image in v. 31 of making the deep (a symbol of

---

418. The dart may seem out of place here and is uncommon. It may refer to a small projectile that was able to penetrate where bigger objects could not. Dhorme, *Job,* 640, and Gordis, *Book of Job,* 488, propose "dart, missile, arrow." Hartley, *Book of Job,* 529, also notes that it could refer to a stone as it refers to uncut stone from a quarry in 1 Kgs 6:7. However, a different word is used for a sling stone here in v. 28.

chaos like Leviathan himself) boil like a cooking pot, and the vast sea (which in Hebrew thought was the realm of chaos) become like a pot of ointment. Over such symbols of chaos, Leviathan leaves a wake as he traverses the water (v. 32). The image of the deep having white hair is not fully transparent, but it is a picture of old age. The deep (= chaos) has the weakness rather than the wisdom of old age when compared to Leviathan. Thus the scene serves to build up an impression of the indomitable power of Leviathan.

41:33-34: Conclusion A general conclusion emerges in vv. 33-34, exalting Leviathan as one without peers. He cannot be compared to anything on earth (v. 33a), and in particular he is a creature who is without fear of anyone else (v. 33b). Job would have been thinking by this stage, "How can I control such a creature?" The answer is that he would not be able to. This creature — whether natural or symbolic of the forces of evil and chaos — would need to be controlled for the creation to continue. Can such a creature fit in Job's ordering of the world? The implication is that Job's understanding of how God orders his world, and what needs to be done, is limited and inadequate. Here is a creature Job cannot manage, one who sees everything that is high and who is king over all the proud (v. 34).[419] God's ordering of the world is more complex than Job had imagined, and is certainly more nuanced than simply rewarding human righteousness and punishing human wickedness.

42:1-6: Job's Second Reply

Chapter 42 is made up of two parts. In the first (vv. 1-6), Job's reply to Yahweh ends in an apparently puzzling way in v. 6: "Therefore I despise myself and repent in dust and ashes" (NIV, NRSV, ESV). We may well wonder whether the friends have been right after all.

Verses 2-6 are structured as follows:

A   Job's starting point — God is powerful (v. 2)
   B   Quotation from the Yahweh speeches (v. 3a)
      C   Job's response — he spoke with limited knowledge (v. 3b-c)
   B¹   Quotation from the Yahweh speeches (v. 4)
      C¹   Job's response — the situation has changed (v. 5)
A¹   Job's new direction (v. 6)

---

419. There has been mention of pride in relation to both Behemoth (40:12) and Leviathan (41:34).

Yet, in the prose epilogue (vv. 7-17), God delivers his verdict that Job, not the friends, has spoken of him what is right (vv. 7-9), and Job's losses are reversed (vv. 10-17). Job is vindicated and restored.

42:1-5: Job's Sufficient Response After the introductory verse, the unit starts in v. 2a ("I know that you can do all things/everything"),[420] where Job readily admits God's power to achieve his purposes. This is simply Job's starting point, not something he has learned during the dialogue. He has always believed that God has had the power to help him (e.g., 7:17-21; 10:2-22; 14:5, 13-17). It is why he has kept calling out to God, believing that his God-sized problem calls for a God-sized solution. As a way of nuancing this he says (v. 2b), "no purpose of yours can be thwarted."[421] He understands that God is actively ruling the world, even when he does not understand what on earth God is doing.

In v. 3 Job refers back to the opening of Yahweh's first speech (38:2) and his challenge: "Is your knowledge like mine?" There are some minor differences between 38:2 and 42:3a, but the parallels are very clear. Habel has pointed out that 38:2 is the theme verse of the first speech, and that it revolves around God's "counsel" or "plan" (עֵצָה/'ēṣâ),[422] which is best understood as how God sovereignly and freely orders his creation.

In response to this, Job concedes his limitations, thereby showing that he has at last understood the point of Yahweh's two speeches. Job has come to realize through the Yahweh speeches that God's plan for the universe is more complex than Job's blinkered knowledge of it. In wanting to know the whole plan of God, Job had forgotten that even righteous humans cannot exhaustively know God's purposes and his ordering of the world. There is a hiddenness in God's order. Perhaps a misreading of Proverbs in some wisdom circles led to the view that God's order or plans can be definitively read off from the world. The narrator of Job exposes this as a form of fossilized wisdom that tried to bind God. It emerges in the speeches of Job's friends, and was shared to some extent by Job himself. Job now concedes that his partial view of God's workings is insufficient to constrain God. So Job says, "I have uttered what I did

---

420. In v. 2 the Ketib is the second person masculine singular ("you know"), while the Qere is the first person common singular ("I know"). It is best read as the first person, Job speaking of his knowledge about God's unstoppable plans and purposes, rather than as a reference to God's self-knowledge.

421. Van Wolde, "Job 42:1-6," 239, proposes that "plan/purpose" (מְזִמָּה/mĕzimmâ) is parallel to "everything" (in the affirmative in the first line and in the negative in the second), and the parallelism implies that this word refers to any plan, good or bad.

422. Habel, *Book of Job*, 526-28.

not understand." This is the closest Job comes to confession in this chapter, an admission that his knowledge of God's doings was too limited.[423]

The structural outline shows that v. 4, like v. 3, refers back to God's words, picking up the repeated challenge from both of Yahweh's speeches (38:3; 40:7). In picking up these challenges (rather than the substance of the speeches), Job could be either referring to the key part as symbolic of the whole speeches, or perhaps more generally focusing on God's appearance itself more than the content of the speeches.

Job responds in v. 5 by acknowledging that God's appearance to him made his goal of vindication irrelevant. When God broadens Job's tunnel vision, Job realizes even more clearly that his problem was not so much to clear his name, but to see God. Each part of this verse has its complications. Verse 5a could mean either "I heard you" or "I heard about you," but most scholars rightly opt for the second translation ("I heard/had heard about you"). Since the "seeing" of v. 5b refers to the Yahweh speeches (see below), what Job had heard was prior to this time — either before he was tested or during the debate. Some interpret it to imply that Job's faith in the prologue was simply a secondhand faith.[424] However, "the hearing of you by the hearing of the ear" is more likely to refer to what he had heard about God from the friends during the debate, for his faith was genuine in the prologue (1:1, 8; 2:3). Thus v. 5a is best understood as a reference to Job having heard many things about God from the friends as they sought to bludgeon him into submissive repentance.

What, then, is conveyed in v. 5b when Job says, "but now my eyes see/have seen you"? Antony Campbell sees this as problematic, for he argues that Job has not seen God: "There have been words in plenty to hear; there has been no report of vision."[425] Robert Fyall proposes rather that, on analogy with Moses in Exodus 34 and Isaiah in Isaiah 6, to "see God" is bound up with hearing God's words. He concludes, "Truly to hear God is to see God. It is because Job has listened to God that he now sees God."[426] This needs to be nuanced a little

---

423. The phrase "things too wonderful for me" could perhaps be translated "more wonderful than me," but that is not the point being made here. The word נִפְלָאוֹת/*niplā'ôt*, "things wonderful," refers to the intricate complexity of the world.

424. Morrow, "Consolation," 212, notes that 42:5 can be translated: "Through (mere) report I had heard of you but now my eye has seen you." Raurell, "Job's Ethic," 136, also comments, "Job's prior knowledge of God — by 'hearing' — was school knowledge, second-hand. Now 'seeing' God, he has a new (first-hand) perception of God's reality."

425. Campbell, "Book of Job," 20-21. Van Wolde, "Job 42:1-6," 248, suggests that it has the sense of Job having seen Yahweh's point of view, rather than Yahweh himself, that he has a transformed understanding of Yahweh. That much at least is true, but can more be said?

426. Fyall, *Now My Eyes*, 179. Adam, *Hearing God's Words*, 59, cites Fyall with approval and

by examining how the idea of seeing God is developed in the book. Job hints at wanting to see God in 7:7-8. While he calls for God to leave him alone (e.g., 7:19, 13:21; 14:6) he also longs for a restored relationship (e.g., 10:9-12). In 13:1 he refers back to what the friends have said, and says, "my ear has heard and understood it," but in 13:3 says he still wishes to speak to the Almighty; and similarly in 13:22, 24; 14:14-17. He condemns Bildad for tormenting him with words about God in 19:2, but he longs to see God in 19:25-27. Even in 23:3-7 he longs to come into God's presence, but he feels that God is absent or even hiding in 23:8-9. In his review of his former life in chapter 29, his first thought is of God being with him in 29:2-5. It is also interesting that in 34:29 Elihu contrasts God hiding his face with the concept of seeing God. In the light of all this, "seeing God" is best seen as a metaphor for God's presence, for God is no longer hiding his face. Thus it is a reference to what has happened in chapters 38–41 — not merely hearing God's words, but hearing God's words from God who is present, from meeting God and listening to him. Having already focused on the content on God's words (the Yahweh speeches) in v. 3b, Job now refers to the appearance of this (speaking) God (the theophany). So its primary referent here is to experiencing the once-hidden God as present.

How, then, should vv. 2-5 be understood? Job begins by outlining his starting point — that God can do all things. He then cites the theme verse about God's design from Yahweh's first speech, and he shows that he gets the point of the speeches and concedes that he spoke with limited knowledge about how God runs the world. The content of God's words has expanded his horizon. Then he refers to the key challenge verse of Yahweh's speeches, and announces that his fundamental call for the presence of God has been met by God's appearance to speak to him in chapters 38–41. This satisfies him in a way that what the friends said about God did not. Both God's appearance and God's words have met Job's needs, and now enable him to move on.

42:6: Job's New Direction The key that unlocks Job's reply is v. 6, which raises the issue of whether Job's "repentance" implies that he retracts all that he has previously uttered. Up to this point Job's protests are presented as expressions of authentic, if at times misdirected, faith. Thus, when we come to chapter 42, we do not assume that Job will repent. Both parts of this verse have traditionally been given quite interpretive translations that have skewed our reading of the book as a whole.

In v. 6a Job uses the verb מָאַס/*mā'as*, commonly rendered in English

---

comments, "Job has not seen a vision, nor has he heard a description of a vision of God. . . . He has 'seen,' by receiving the words of the Lord."

versions as "despise" (NRSV, NIV, ESV).[427] Its core meaning is "reject" or "retract," and it normally takes an object. Its meaning here depends on the object supplied, and it could be that Job "rejects" himself, God, the words he uttered in the debate, the dust and ashes mentioned in this verse, or even the theology of his friends (this may be "I heard of you by the hearing of the ear" in v. 5). One suggestion that pays attention to the context is to look back to Job's previous words (ch. 31) and see that Job used this verb there meaning to reject or dismiss a legal case or suit (31:13). The meaning here could then be Job dismissing or withdrawing his litigation against God.[428] However, the number of intervening chapters (during which the verb is used by Elihu in 34:33; 36:5) suggests that we should look for another solution. Job also uses the verb here in a different sense than in chapter 31, where it referred not to him retracting litigation against God, but rather to whether he had rejected the legitimate legal causes of his female servants.

Mā'as is used quite often in Job and does not appear to have a technical meaning.[429] Thus it is best to go back to its base meaning of "reject," and to see that it has the same object as the next verb, נחמ/*nḥm,* "dust and ashes" or lamenting.[430]

Verse 6b is often translated as "I repent in dust and ashes." The verb *nḥm* is, however, most commonly used in the OT of God "repenting."[431] While *nḥm* can refer to human repentance for wrongdoing (Jer 8:6; 31:19), it can also refer to a change of attitude out of compassion (Judg 21:6, 15) or even moving from a right course of action to a wrong one (Exod 13:17). God can even speak of "repenting" of the good he intended to do (Jer 18:10).

Despite this, the standard view is to see that Job recants and shows re-

---

427. Other versions and commentators have adopted other translations: "melt away" (NEB), "recant" (NJPS, Pope), "retract" (JB, NASB), "ashamed of" (GNB), "withdraw my case" (Habel), "loathe" (J. G. Janzen), "sink down" (Dhorme), "abase myself" (Gordis, Hartley), "repudiate" (Gutiérrez).

428. Scholnick, "Meaning of *mišpaṭ*," 528; Habel, *Book of Job,* 576.

429. In 5:17 (reject the discipline of the Almighty); 7:16 (I reject — no object; life implied?); 8:20 (God does not despise/reject the blameless); 9:21 (I am sick of life); 10:3 (to despise/reject the work of your hands); 30:1 (those whose fathers I would have disdained/rejected to put among my dogs); 34:33 (Job rejects — no object); and 36:5 (God does not despise/reject — no object, but "anyone" implied).

430. So Good, *In Turns of Tempest,* 170, 376; Patrick, "Job XLII 6," 370. For an example of a single object for two verbs, see Amos 9:3.

431. It is used of such actions as God making man (Gen 6:6-7), of being about to inflict evil (Exod 32:12, 14; 2 Sam 24:16; 1 Chr 21:15; Jer 18:18; 26:3, 13, 19; 42:10; Amos 7:3, 6; Jonah 3:9, 10; 4:2), or of choosing Saul (1 Sam 15:11, 29, 35). It is not the common word שׁוּב/*šûb* so often used of humans repenting of their sins (as in 1 Kgs 8:47; Ezek 14:6; 18:30).

morse for what he said prior to the theophany. God's interrogation is thought to have overwhelmed him and perhaps even convinced him that he has spoken in pride. However, the context neither demands nor suggests that Job is pictured as repenting of sin.[432] Instead, vv. 7-8 endorse Job as God's servant and as the one who has spoken of God what is right. Furthermore, Job acts as an intercessor for the friends, who urged him to repent in order to receive God's forgiveness (vv. 8-9). If Job had repented, there is a curious avoidance of any declaration of forgiveness from God that would normally follow such repentance.

Indeed, the view that Job repents seems not to have grasped that Job's complaint to God are cries of faith, not unbelief, and therefore do not require repentance. The majority of uses of *nḥm* in the Niphal mean "change one's mind" or "reverse a decision," and since God is the subject of most of these, there is no suggestion that anyone made a mistake in the first place.[433] The idea that best fits the OT examples is to "react appropriately to the (changed) circumstances," which would mean that Job is saying, "I have changed my declared course of action by no longer mourning [dust and ashes]." So the phrase here could be translated, "repent of [or turn away from] dust and ashes," that is, get on with life.[434] The change in circumstances is likely to be that Job has experienced the presence of God. Job is not denying the validity of his earlier complaints and protests. Rather, what he is saying is that now that God has come he wants to turn aside from what is no longer appropriate.

This interpretation is supported by the use of the idiom נחם על/*nḥm 'l*.[435] When *nḥm* is followed by the preposition *'al*, "about/concerning," the phrase means to change one's mind about something one had planned to do (as in Exod 32:12, 14; Jer 18:8, 10). Here it would mean to turn away from dust and ashes, since the situation has changed.[436] Thus, since usage determines meaning, then general usage is against the translation "repent in dust and ashes" and in favor of "repent concerning. . . ." In other words, Job is now ready to resume

---

432. So Estes, *Job*, 256: "This cannot be repentance of sin, or else the friends would be right in their assessment of him."

433. Patrick, "Job XLII 6," 370.

434. Ibid. Van Wolde, "Job 42:1-6," 246, 249, suggests it means "to turn a new page in the book of one's life."

435. There is a textual issue with נחם על/*nḥm 'l* in v. 6. The Masoretes placed an *athnach* (a major disjunctive accent) under נחם/*nḥm*, implying perhaps that the two words should be separated. However, van Wolde, "Job 42:1-6," 249, argues that the *athnach* is used to indicate that the phrase "concerning dust and ashes" is the direct object of both the preceding verbs and not simply connected to *nḥm*.

436. See Patrick, "Job XLII 6," 370. J. G. Janzen, *Job*, 255, notes, "In every other instance where the niphal (middle or reflexive) form of *nḥm*, 'change the mind,' is followed by the preposition *'al*, translators uniformly render the expression 'to repent *of, concerning*' (e.g., Jer. 18:8, 10)."

normal relationships in society, the very thing that he proceeds to do in the following verses. "Dust and ashes" thus seems to represent the status and role of Job as an isolated sufferer and protesting mourner. It is used by Job in 30:19 to describe his present condition as he sums up his case before God. Thus v. 6 is best rendered, "therefore I reject and turn away from lamenting."

42:7-17: The Epilogue

42:7-9: Job Has Spoken Rightly about God If there was any residual ambiguity over how to understand Job's words in 42:6, it is instantly clarified by vv. 7-9. The immediacy of God's endorsement of Job (v. 7) leads us away from a focus on Job's change of direction and toward God's approval of Job's stance throughout the dialogue. This approval is implied in Job's appointment as the mediator for his friends (v. 8b), by the costly nature of the sacrifice (v. 8a), and by his successful intercession (v. 9). Job is also called God's "servant" on four occasions (once in v. 7 and three times in v. 8), which in the OT is a title of honor, and is used by Yahweh in 1:8 and 2:3.[437] The use of this title shows he has the same high status that he had prior to his trial. Furthermore, if v. 6 were a confession, there would need to be either an absolution or acceptance of that confession, but it is glaringly absent.

Job's genuine faith is finally made explicit when God twice says that Job has spoken of him "what is right" or in accordance with the truth (vv. 7-8).[438] While this does not endorse all that Job has said, his general approach is approved of. This reinforces the view that Job was not "repenting" in v. 6, and confirms that the Yahweh speeches were not intended to establish Job's guilt or sin.

The events of vv. 7-9 are essential to the theology of the book, for otherwise Job's friends would have come out victorious, and Job alone would have been humbled. It is also impressive that Job is able to resolve his relationship with God and be chosen by God as a mediator for others, even before his family and possessions are restored. Job did indeed fear God for nothing (1:9).[439] There are also other strong echoes of the prologue in these verses,[440] which leads nicely into the description of Job's restoration in the remainder of the epilogue.

---

437. Hartley, *Book of Job*, 539; MacKenzie, "Transformation of Job," 57.

438. The term "truth" (נְכוֹנָה/*nĕkônâ*) refers to what is correct and consistent with the facts (Deut 17:14; 1 Sam 23:23). Job's answers correspond with reality. Nam, *Talking about God*, 13, makes the interesting translation, "you have not spoken about me *constructively* as my servant Job has."

439. Kline, "Trial by Ordeal," 92.

440. For example, terms like "my servant" (42:7-8 and 1:8; 2:3), and themes such as Job as intercessor (42:8 and 1:5), and the offering of sacrifices for others (42:8 and 1:5).

Verses 1-9 thus vindicate Job, rebuke the friends, and free Job up to move in a new direction now that God has both appeared and enlarged Job's horizons. Job is indeed one who fears God for nothing, thus answering the fundamental question of the book.

42:10-17: Job Is Doubly Restored The reversal of Job's circumstances is connected in v. 10a to his act of intercession for his friends, not to his change of direction in v. 6. His restoration thus is an act of grace, not a reward for a changed approach to God. God was not bound to restore Job, but in his goodness and his freedom it is fitting that he does so.

The significance of Job receiving twice what he had before (v. 10b) is uncertain. Some are concerned that this double restoration of Job's possessions overturns the book's message that there is no necessary connection between righteousness and rewards. Whybray, for example, thinks that the epilogue teaches that "God turns out to be Father Christmas after all."[441] Yet the author needed to choose between restoring Job in this life or leaving him unrestored. Neither alternative is without its problems. To restore Job may reinstate the idea of retribution. However, the doctrine of retribution is not so much overturned as qualified in the book of Job. Retribution does not exhaust the truth about how God relates to people, though it is part of that truth. Indeed, to leave Job unrestored seems unjust and unnecessary once his faith has been tested and the verdict given. The sufferings appropriately cease because they were the form of the trial.

Some see here compensation being paid by God for wrongfully depriving Job of his possessions for a while, on analogy with the laws of restitution (e.g., Exod 22:4). This is less likely than the view that the doubling of his possessions is an indicator of the generosity of a gracious God. It is also possible that the doubling of Job's possessions signals an increase in Job's righteousness. Job's possessions in the prologue were not simply an indication of his wealth but rather outward evidence of his righteousness (see on 1:1-5). The removal of these outward signs raised the question of whether Job was righteous after all. Now that God has tested and proved Job's integrity, he restores these outward signs and doubles them perhaps to indicate that Job's tested righteousness is even greater than it was before.

Verse 11 outlines the social restoration of Job. Since the respect of the community was Job's pretest situation (see ch. 29) and since it is an appropriate accompaniment to his righteousness, *all* (mentioned three times) show respect for him by coming to eat with him at his house. Sharing a meal was significant

441. Whybray, *Two Jewish Theologies*, 5-6.

in that culture and is thus a good initial indicator of his reestablished reputation. Unlike the earlier meal in his oldest son's house (1:13-19), this meal is the setting for restored community relationships in the community, not disaster. As Andersen puts it, "Job ends his days in full enjoyment of all the relationships in which a person is fully human."[442]

The changed attitude of those gathered is revealed further in the rest of the verse. They turned from rejecting him to consoling and comforting him (the same words used in 2:11) for the disasters (רָעָה/*rāʿâ*, translated as "evil" in ESV and NRSV, but used widely in the OT to describe nonmoral evils like natural disasters) that God has caused to come upon him. The reason for the gift of a piece of money (a קְשִׂיטָה/*qĕśîṭâ*, an unspecified amount)[443] and a gold ring is not entirely clear, and may be either a way of confessing their previous wrong treatment of him, or simply being an outward sign that they regard him as worthy. Given the restoration of his abundant possessions, it was not needed to help him out of his poverty.

In v. 10 the narrator records that the Lord "restored" Job; now in v. 12 he adds that the Lord "blessed" Job. While these may be different ways of describing the same action, it does highlight that Job's restoration is brought about by God's abundant blessing. The mention of doubling in v. 10b is filled out in v. 12 by an exact doubling of the number of animals he possessed in 1:3. However, v. 13 indicates that this doubling did not extend to his children, but simply that he has restored to him a family of ideal proportions and balance.[444] Perhaps twenty more children would not have seemed to be a blessing! The narrative simply does not address the contemporary issue of how ten new children could replace the loss of the previous ten. Job's wife is not mentioned (nor is the accuser), though her presence is necessary for the bearing of ten more children. However, the focus of this last section is on the restoration of what was lost, and Job's wife did not need to be restored, and therefore receives no specific mention here. She may also not have been mentioned because of her earlier involvement in the testing of Job.

The focus on Job's three daughters in vv. 14-15 is unusual in Hebrew narrative. There is not even a need to mention the restored sons; instead our attention is drawn to the women who might easily have missed out in that culture. Job's delight in his daughters is reflected in their names, which represent beauty

442. Andersen, *Job*, 293.

443. Hartley, *Book of Job*, 541, notes that it is a unit which apparently belonged to patriarchal times, referred to only in Gen 33:19 and Josh 24:32. He notes that since Jacob bought a large piece of land for a hundred *qĕśîṭâ*s, then it is probably a moderate but certainly not token amount.

444. There is an unusual form of "seven" in v. 13, which some suggest should be read as a dual, i.e., fourteen. However, that would still leave only three daughters.

and beautification.[445] In case the implication of his daughters being named is missed, v. 15 mentions their unrivaled beauty, and that they received an inheritance along with their brothers. This seems to hint at their special worth, as well as their being more than enough to share around.

The final two verses of the book describe Job's long life that befits his righteousness (e.g., Prov 3:1-2), living for either 140 years more or 140 in total. More important than this detail is the observation that he saw his sons and his sons' descendants (one or two more generations would be needed to make four, depending on whether the four includes Job's own life). The book ends with Job dying not tragically or prematurely, but after a rich life, "full of days."[446] While there is no explicit mention of Job's health being restored, his long life and the other blessings seem to imply that it was.

At the very least, the story of the restoration hints that suffering is not God's final word. Don Carson suggests that "the epilogue is the Old Testament equivalent to the New Testament anticipation of a new heaven and a new earth. God is just, and will be seen to be just."[447]

445. Habel, *Book of Job*, 585. Jemimah ("turtle dove"), a picture of gracefulness; Keziah ("cassia"), a variety of the highly valued cinnamon; and Keren-happuch ("horn/container of antimony" or "black eye makeup").

446. Hartley, *Book of Job*, 544, notes that the final verse is the epitaph of the noblest of God's servants such as Abraham (Gen 25:8), Isaac (Gen 35:29), David (1 Chr 29:28), and Jehoiada the priest (2 Chr 24:15), again highlighting Job's status.

447. Carson, *How Long*, 155.

Theological Themes

Suffering

What Kinds of Suffering Are Found?

The prologue introduces us to the suffering of Job. In chapter 1 he experiences not only the loss of his vast possessions (1:14-17), but also, in the eyes of his society, the righteousness that they symbolized. This financial and social loss is exacerbated by the emotional loss and grief of losing all of his ten children (1:18-20). His emotional loss is worsened when he apparently also loses the support of his wife (2:9-10). The second test results in extreme physical suffering for Job, affecting every part of his body from the bottom of his foot to the top of his head (2:7), leading him to seek some temporary relief by scraping at his sores with broken pottery (2:8). The end of the prologue, however, gives some promise of social support as Job's three friends travel a long way to show him sympathy and comfort him (2:11). This anticipated support is seen to be illusory as Job will soon describe his friends as "miserable comforters" (16:2). One aspect of Job's suffering that is not made explicit in the prologue is the spiritual suffering of God being silent or apparently absent.

Four types of suffering — physical, social, emotional, and spiritual[1] — can be seen throughout the book and are gathered together in a useful summary review of his present situation in chapter 30. There Job expresses such physical symptoms as burning pain in his bones that prevents him for resting by day or sleeping at night (30:16-17, 30), while his skin has turned black and is peeling away (30:28, 30). Other parts of the dialogue also mention his festering skin

1. Zuck, "Theology," 227. Waters, "Suffering," 114-15, adopts the same categories.

(7:5), physical emaciation (16:8; 19:20), problems with his eyesight (16:16? 17:7), and troubled sleep (7:4, 13-14).

His social rejection is evident in the mocking laughter and songs of the young men (30:1, 9) who despise and humiliate Job without restraint (30:10-14). The prosperity and honor he once enjoyed in that society has vanished (30:15), and he is more accepted among the animals than by people (30:29). The broader book reinforces this picture of his being abandoned and mocked by his former friends, fellow citizens, and family (12:4; 16:10; 17:2, 6; 19:13-19), in stark contrast to his former high social standing (29:7-25). On top of this, he is attacked and maligned by his three "comforters" (6:14-21, 27; 13:4-5; 16:2; 19:2-3; 21:34).

His emotional state is characterized by mourning, not joy (30:31). He is churned up internally (30:16, 27), in need of help (30:24-25) since his life is characterized by darkness (30:26) and terror (30:15). In the dialogue, there are further indications of his emptiness, misery, and darkness (7:3; 19:8), of his internal anguish, bitterness, and self-loathing (7:11; 10:1), and of his despair (19:10, 27c).

Job's spiritual suffering is probably his deepest pain as his cries to God are seemingly unanswered (30:20). He feels not only brought down by God (30:11), but also persecuted and tossed about by a God he now experiences as cruel (30:21-22; cf. 29:2-5). Elsewhere in the book, Job speaks of being targeted and hunted by God (6:4; 10:16-17), being worn out and attacked by him (16:7-9) and treated as an enemy (19:6-12). In the midst of all this he still insists on his innocence (6:10, 29-30; 16:17; 23:5-7, 11-12; 27:6; and especially his oath of clearance in ch. 31). Job's resultant state is that he is terrified and in dread of God (23:15-16), even while he longs for a restored relationship (14:14-17).

While some of this suffering is inflicted by other people (Sabeans, Chaldeans, friends, neighbors, and family), the spiritual and physical suffering are seen by Job to be from God (e.g., 30:11, 19; 6:4; 9:24; 10:3; 14:17-20), while the emotional and social pain is exacerbated by God's apparent failure to vindicate Job during the time of the dialogue.

What Is the Problem of Suffering?

How, then, is this suffering a problem for Job, and how does the book address this issue? David Clines suggests that three common issues arise concerning suffering, each of which is touched on in the book of Job:[2]

    1. Why is there suffering? In other words, what is the origin or cause of

---

2. This is helpfully set out by Clines in a number of places. See, e.g., *Job 1–20*, xxxviii-xxxix.

suffering? Or more personally, why has this suffering happened to me? It is clear that the focus is not on the philosophical question of why there is evil and suffering in a world where God is both loving and all-powerful. Those who seek answers to this legitimate question search in vain in the book of Job, and will especially find the Yahweh speeches to be a deep disappointment.

Indeed, the book is only concerned with the issue of undeserved or innocent suffering or, more precisely, situations where there is no absolute correlation between human actions and reward or punishment. It does not seek to answer the question of why each person might suffer, or why people in general suffer — the book is about the suffering of a unique individual, and the reader can see that the reason for his suffering (to demonstrate that it is possible to genuinely fear God, 1:9) is unlike anyone else's situation. The Yahweh speeches do not mention suffering, and Job's problem is resolved (42:2-6) before his suffering is removed and fortune restored (42:10). Finally, Job is never told — even in the epilogue — of the events of the prologue and why he was suffering. The reason why people suffer is not the focus of the book.

2. Is there such a thing as innocent suffering? The prologue establishes that this is a reality in the case of Job, but this truth is developed no further in the rest of the book. Job describes himself as innocent (6:30; 9:15), and more importantly this is confirmed both by the narrator (1:1) and by God himself (1:8; 2:3; 42:7-8). The book of Job, however, is not primarily concerned with this issue, and it figures nowhere in the resolution.

3. In what way am I supposed to suffer? or, What am I to do when suffering? The book touches on the issue of suffering, but not to give a philosophical answer to the problem of evil. As Samuel Terrien puts it, "the enigma of suffering is not the central concern of the poet: it is merely the instrument of his argument."[3] Thus the concern is, How can I have faith in the midst of suffering? Another way of expressing this is that suffering is not the issue, but it is a setting like no other that can disclose whether a person has genuine faith in God. "Job's suffering . . . was introduced only as a means of isolating and intensifying the question of the proper basis of man's relationship with God."[4] Suffering is a means to the end of exploring this question, not the end in itself. Job's suffering causes him to ask the fundamental dilemma of life. Thus, since Job cannot understand why he is suffering relentlessly, he questions whether he has misunderstood God's nature or purposes, and even the way the world is run.

Clines points out, "To Job the issue is how to reconcile his experience of suffering with his knowledge of his innocence; to the readers the issue is rather

---

3. Terrien, "Job," 914.
4. Parsons, "Structure and Purpose," 143.

how a righteous person is to behave when afflicted by undeserved suffering."[5] If suffering, in and of itself, is not the main issue of the book (contrary to popular perception), then what does it teach us about how to respond to innocent suffering? Clines proposes that the book gives two answers. Let the patient Job be your model for as long as you can. When you can do so no longer, use the protesting Job as a model — calling on God alone to act, believing that only in him can the tension of suffering be resolved. This appears to be more systematic than the book of Job itself, but it clearly does endorse a variety of responses to suffering that are still legitimate expressions of faith. This aspect will be explored below.

Perhaps more significant is the issue of where we turn when suffering strikes. There are ultimately only two choices: we either turn toward God or away from him. Job is one who models turning to God, first in submission, and then in lament and complaint. Yet he never turns away from God, for he knows that, despite God's apparent absence and silence, God is the one who can meet the sufferer's deepest longings.

Another issue that often arises in Christian reflections on suffering is whether suffering is ever the end of the story, or will it always be followed by restoration? In other words, will grace always triumph over suffering? Clearly in Job's case suffering is followed by restoration, but there is no basis for generalizing from his experience. For example, Job was a perfectly righteous human being, and many who suffer are not. Furthermore, God is not bound to restore Job, but rather is free to sovereignly rule his world in the way he sees fit. Job's restoration does, however, remind us that suffering can be followed by healing and restoration, so that one needs to look at the entire period of a person's life to evaluate their suffering. Our own experience of this life teaches that suffering will sometimes last until the end of a person's earthly days, and it is not the intention of the book of Job to refute this.

What Answers Are Proposed?

The friends do seek to answer the intellectual question of why suffering comes to people in general and Job in particular, and they give some answers (suffering can be a punishment, a warning, or a discipline). They do their best with their presuppositions, but get it wrong. The reader, who from the prologue is privy to certain information that is given to neither the friends nor Job, can see that their views are wrong in Job's case.

5. Clines, *Job 1–20*, 8.

The distinctive perspectives of each friend can be discerned from their initial speeches.[6] The first friend, Eliphaz, begins with the presupposition that the innocent will not suffer to the point of destruction (4:7). For him Job is essentially one of the innocent (4:6), so his suffering is bound to be soon over. The content of his vision is that no one is perfectly righteous (4:16-17), with the implication that even the comparatively righteous should expect to suffer from time to time. The retribution principle espoused by Eliphaz (4:8) stands unshaken by Job's experience. Since the suffering of a fairly righteous person is therefore likely to be minor and time-limited, Eliphaz urges Job to commit his cause to God (5:8), learn from the experience (5:17), and wait for God's healing (5:18-26). Later Eliphaz moves to a more condemnatory stance (22:5-11), and seems to agree with Zophar that Job may be a secret sinner (22:13-14). Yet even in this final speech he expresses hope that God will restore him if Job turns away from his sin.

The second friend, Bildad, is if anything more convinced of the power of sin to explain suffering, and he uses that connection to account for the death of Job's children (8:4). The very fact that Job still lives is proof that he is no gross sinner like his children. However serious his suffering, it is not as bad as it might be; therefore his sin is not as serious as he may fear. He tells Job that if he is pure and upright, he will be restored (8:6-7). Bildad, heavily reliant on tradition (8:8-10), centers his understanding of suffering on the principle that God will always act justly (8:3). While he is less definite than Eliphaz about Job's innocence, he still seems to anticipate Job's restoration (8:6-7, 20-22). In the midst of suffering, he urges Job to seek God and plead with him for mercy (8:5).

Whereas Eliphaz has set Job's suffering in the context of his whole life (his suffering is just a temporary pinprick), and Bildad has set it against the backdrop of the fate of his family (the children are dead, Job is not), Zophar, the third friend, does not wish to consider any such context for Job's pain. For Zophar suffering is inevitably the product of sin, and since Job is suffering, he must be a sinner. Since Job refuses to concede his sin (11:4), he must be a hidden or secret sinner (11:5-6). If truth be known, God is exacting less from Job than his sin deserves (11:6c). Zophar has declared that the principle of retribution is not at all a rigorous quid pro quo, for a percentage of the punishment that should be inflicted upon Job has already been deducted for mercy's sake. His solution is for Job to repent and turn from his wickedness (11:13-14). The hope of restoration that he holds out to Job (11:15-19) implies that an end to his suffering is still a possibility.

6. See Clines, "Arguments," 206-8.

The Friends as a Group

Clines sees a different goal in each friend: "Eliphaz argues from the piety of Job in order to offer consolation; Bildad argues from the contrast between the fates of Job and Job's children in order to offer warning; Zophar argues from the suffering of Job in order to denounce Job."[7] Thus, in their approach, Eliphaz assumes Job's piety and argues from it; Bildad sets up a condition — if Job were innocent, God would restore him; while Zophar simply believes that God knows Job's sin and is certainly punishing him for it.

Clines also suggests that their intentions are different: "Eliphaz's intention is to encourage Job to patience and hope (5:8; 4:6); Bildad's intention is to urge Job to search his heart before God in order to ensure that he is not guilty of crimes such as those for which his children have died (8:5-6); Zophar's intention is to summon Job to repentance for sins that he clearly has already committed (11:6c)."[8] However, all three friends have in common that Job needs to turn back to God (5:8; 8:5; 11:13-14) rather than continue in his complaints.

More importantly, what is true of all Job's friends is that they fail to comfort Job. A. S. Peake comments that "they failed him miserably, and, when he hungered for sympathy, offered him a flinty theology."[9] Daniel Simundson suggests that the friends "are so involved in their own answers and in defense of their positions that they lose their sympathy with Job and are not able to bring him any comfort at all."[10] Christopher Ash notes that there are two ways to explore hard questions in life like suffering — through asking "armchair questions" or "wheelchair questions."[11] The friends pontificate on suffering from their "armchairs"; Job asks the "wheelchair questions."

Elihu

It is important to recognize that, while these views about suffering are given in the course of the dialogue, they must not be identified with the message of the book about suffering. Elihu concludes that none of the friends has proved Job wrong or properly answered his challenges (32:12). More defini-

---

7. Ibid., 210.

8. Ibid. Vermeylen, *Job, ses amis et son dieu*, 36, suggests that these distinctions are overdrawn and are somewhat tenuous. In fact, he suggests, the three defend essentially the same point of view and the same theology, so that they are representatives of the same "party."

9. Peake, "Job," 100.

10. Simundson, *Faith under Fire*, 93.

11. Ash, *Out of the Storm*, 12-13.

tively, the words of the three friends about God and how he runs his world (and therefore about suffering) are twice rejected by God (42:7-8) as the book is resolved. Indeed, at several stages in the book it is suggested that suffering is simply the inevitable consequence of being born as a human being (Eliphaz in 5:7; Job in 7:1-2; 14:1).[12]

Some see a way forward in Elihu's observations on suffering. Larry Waters, who proposes that "Elihu presented a totally different perspective on suffering from that of the three,"[13] regards Elihu as saying that Job's suffering is not due to his past sin, but rather that it serves as a warning to draw him closer to God and to change the way he views God's rule of the world.[14] This educative view of suffering is certainly present in 33:19-20 and 36:15, but has already been hinted at by Eliphaz (5:17-18).[15] Furthermore, while suffering can have this effect, the prologue tells us that this is not the reason for Job's suffering, and the Yahweh speeches do not mention this emphasis. Thus, although Elihu's view does vary from that of the friends, it is not intended to be the solution of the book. Elihu also suggests that the proper response to suffering as a warning is confession (33:27), which is not Job's pressing need.

Furthermore, suffering is only a small part of Elihu's teaching. While much attention has been given to his view on suffering, Elihu says comparatively little directly on this subject, and his great concern is with the nature and action of God.[16] This focus on his view of suffering may have arisen from a desire of commentators to find the distinctive voices of each character, perhaps blinding them to how much the characters have in common. J. W. McKay, viewing Elihu's understanding of suffering as not the only or even the dominant theme in his addresses, is prompted to comment that Elihu's function is more important than the content of his speeches.[17] Thus, while Elihu may have a different strand of teaching on the function of suffering, this is not of great significance in the overall message of the book.

---

12. Whybray, "Freedom of God," 237.

13. Waters, "Reflections," 445. He fills this out in more detail in "Suffering in the Book of Job," 117-22.

14. Clines, "Arguments," 210, describes Elihu's view of suffering in this way: "it may not be the penalty for sin already committed, but a warning, given in advance, to keep a person back from sin (33:19-28)."

15. Gordis, *Book of Job,* 551, points out that it is also a genuinely wisdom theme, found in Prov 3:11-12. Whedbee, "Comedy of Job," 20, observes that, although the disciplinary view of suffering is mentioned by Eliphaz in 5:17, Elihu modifies it by combining it with a mediatorial figure in 33:23-26.

16. So Tate, "Speeches of Elihu," 492.

17. McKay, "Elihu — A Proto-Charismatic?" 167.

What Possible Answers Are Not Explored?

Finally, it is worth commenting on a number of biblical perspectives on suffering that are not present in the book of Job. There is, for example, no reliance on any doctrine of original or inherited sin,[18] even though this could justify why everyone deserves to suffer. Neither is mention made of vicarious suffering, a theme so richly developed in parts of the Old and New Testaments.

It is a debated point in Joban scholarship whether Job's situation is eased by the prospect of a postmortem life with God. Some see a full-blown doctrine of resurrection in such passages as 13:15, 14:13-17, and 19:25-27, while others view these Scriptures as only giving hints of ideas to be developed elsewhere. In this commentary I have argued that there is no realistic hope of resurrection in these places, but in the Bible as a whole and the NT in particular the doctrine of resurrection does ease some (but not all) of the tensions that Job and his friends were grappling with. The book of Job discloses why the biblical doctrine of resurrection makes sense of life and brings so much comfort in the midst of suffering. However, the book of Job itself (consistent with the lack of interest in eschatology in wisdom literature) does not largely explore any eschatological resolution of the problem of suffering.

Surprisingly, little is made in the book of any connection between Satan and suffering. Despite the presence of the accuser in the prologue, and his being the one who implements God's decisions, the prologue views what happens to Job to be determined by God. The dialogue does not explore the possibility of Job's suffering coming from any hand other than God's. Job himself, though he imaginatively explores many hypothetical scenarios, does not consider Satan to be the cause of his sufferings. The ending of the book ignores the accuser entirely, presumably because he was only the one who instigated the test and is no longer useful to the story.

Some Observations

Several important observations can, however, be made from the book of Job.[19] First, one of the features of severe pain is that it can be all-consuming. Carol Newsom notes that "one of the characteristics of acute suffering is its tendency to obliterate all other experience."[20] It can easily become the only reality, and

---

18. So Andersen, *Job,* 66. Contra Berkhof, *Systematic Theology,* 215, 224, who cites Job 31:33 in support of the doctrine.

19. Bias and Waters, *Job,* 317-24, make some interesting but overstated suggestions.

20. Newsom, "Book of Job," 520.

so even one's faith in God can be pushed to the side. Job holds on to two pressing realities without denying either: the extent of his suffering and his former relationship with his God.

One reason why suffering is such a difficult issue in Job is that a big view of God is present. David Atkinson observes that suffering "is only a *problem* to the person with faith in a good God."[21] There is no room for dualism, for rival deities, or for a God who is powerless or unloving. Job is committed to wrestling with a God-sized God rather than to shrink his view of God in order to explain his suffering. Job blames God and deals with God (9:24; 10:3). As Don Carson notes, "The Book of Job frankly insists that suffering falls within the sweep of God's sovereignty,"[22] and this is both the source of the problem and the path to the resolution of Job's dilemma.

It is also clear from the book that not all suffering is linked with sin. Job claims to be innocent (6:24, 30; 9:15), and the narrator and God agree (1:1, 8; 2:3; 42:7-8). The friends handcuff all suffering to sin without exception, but are shown to be wrong.

Finally, the book of Job proclaims that any individual sufferer does not need to know why the suffering has occurred in order to work out how to live with it. Job never knows, and even at the end of the book is not made aware of the events of the heavenly scenes of the prologue. In chapter 42 Job is able to move on even before his suffering is stopped and his life restored. The presence of God reorients Job and enables him to live with loss.

Retribution and Justice

What Is the Idea of Retribution?

Connected with the theme of suffering is the idea of retribution. The concept of retribution is one of several theories of justice that have prevailed in ancient and modern times. It is distinct from other theories such as the rehabilitation, restoration, and deterrent views. These are all theories about how to treat those who have committed wrongs — legal or moral; individual or social; against other people, the environment, or God.

The retribution view is sometimes called the "deserts" theory of punishment. According to this theory, punishment should be administered *only* when it is deserved, and then only to the extent that it is deserved. It has a

21. Atkinson, *Message of Job*, 26.
22. Carson, *How Long*, 139.

different goal from one motivated by revenge or retaliation. Punishment is not *in order to* reach some goal but *because of* some offense. The basic principle is: Whatever a person deserves, that should be their punishment, no more or no less. A retributive understanding of punishment sees a penalty imposed on the wrongdoer as a result of, and in proportion to, their offense. A breach of what is "right" incurs the retribution of punishment: this retribution is deserved by the wrongdoer, since the action or omission was a conscious choice to act against the rights and interests of others.

The idea of retribution in the moral ordering of the world is one way of accounting for human suffering. Many writers see the book of Job raising the issue of whether there is any moral order in the world. In other words, do we live in a world in which goodness is rewarded and wickedness is punished?

What Is the Background to the Idea of Retribution?

In the OT the concept of retributive justice is a common one, and seen even before the creation of Israel as a nation (e.g., Gen 9:5). The best-known formulation of it is found in Lev 24:17-20 ("an eye for an eye"), but it receives its classical formulation in the laws and teaching of Deuteronomy. The climax of the idea in Deuteronomy is in chapter 28, which specifies a long list of curses and blessings. The curses are a result of disobedience to the terms of the covenant, while the blessings are a reward for covenant obedience. The concept of retribution found in Deuteronomy is predominantly national or social rather than individual, and is based on a response of obedience or otherwise to the covenants laws. The link is between certain actions or omissions and some specified consequences. This understanding of retribution found in Deuteronomy shapes the historical books from Joshua through 2 Kings, which illustrate that when Israel is obedient to the covenant they prosper, but covenant disobedience leads to punishment, supremely in exile (Deut 28:63-65).

The doctrine of retribution is also found in the foundational wisdom book of Proverbs, but here it has a different flavor. Proverbs is more concerned with the individual, not the nation, and their obligations to God and others is not specifically based on Israel's covenant law. Furthermore, the link in Proverbs is not just between outward actions and consequences, but between character and consequences.[23] The teaching of Proverbs is also based largely on a theology of creation, rather than the covenant undergirding of Deuteronomy. In its Deuteronomic formulation, God actively and overtly intervenes in history to

---

23. See Boström, *God of the Sages,* 138.

reward and punish the community of Israel (in accordance with the covenant blessings and curses), but the foundational wisdom book of Proverbs simply insists that there is a correlation between character/actions and consequences without necessarily outlining the means used to reward or punish.[24]

Since the book of Job, as wisdom literature, is responding to the formulation found in the book of Proverbs, not that of Deuteronomy, a brief outline of the version found in Proverbs is needed. Proverbs clearly teaches both that the righteous will be rewarded and that the wicked will be punished. Two examples will suffice, but there are many others. In Prov 3:9-10 honoring God with one's wealth and produce will lead to overflowing barns and bursting wine vats. In a cluster of proverbs at the end of chapter 10 (10:27-32), there is a sustained contrast between a positive outcome for those of righteous character (life, joy, strength, security, wisdom, truth), with the opposite for the wicked.

It is easy to see why some could see an absolute correlation between one's righteousness and how God will reward one (as in some proponents of the "prosperity gospel"). Yet there are at least two qualifications on this idea in the book of Proverbs itself. The first is the nature of a proverb. Proverbs show regular, not universal, connections (was Prov 3:9-10 true of Jesus?), and they cannot be read as guarantees or promises. A proverb is not true in every situation, so there can be conflicting proverbs (e.g., 26:4, 5). This means that proverbs that teach that God rewards the righteous and punishes the wicked cannot be used to prove that every person who is suffering must have sinned proportionately.

Second, the book itself nuances the connection between righteousness and rewards, and between suffering and wickedness. Thus, in the sentence sayings of Proverbs, it is possible for wealth to come from either wickedness (10:2; 16:8, 19; 22:17-18) or from diligence (10:4; 12:27). Thus one's wealth at any given instant cannot be a reliable measure of one's righteousness or wisdom. There is even the explicit mention of the righteous falling seven times (24:16). If one is part of a city or nation or community, the wickedness of others can bring disaster (11:11), even for a righteous person. Justice can be perverted by false witness (12:17), greed, dishonesty, or bribes (15:27; 16:28; 17:8; 20:10, 14, 17, 23), while lies and slander (which characterize a fool, 10:18) can bring personal and social calamity. Innocent people can meet a violent end (1:11; 6:17) or be cheated of their rights (17:23, 26; 18:5) or livelihood (13:23).[25] A (righteous) man may be shamed by his foolish wife (12:4), his son (19:13), a prostitute (22:14; 23:27),

---

24. Walton, "Retribution," 650-51, makes a similar distinction between a corporate-level retribution theology as a covenant theme, and a retribution principle at an individual level being a wisdom theme.

25. Kidner, *Wisdom*, 118.

or a shameful servant (14:35), while strife can be stirred up by a man with a hot temper (15:18). The poor can be people of integrity (19:1, 22). It is easy to appeal to a selection of proverbs to show support for a simplistic doctrine of retribution, but not if the book as a whole is considered.

The book of Job is best understood as a protest, not against Proverbs, but against a misunderstanding of Proverbs. This false view had misrepresented the mainstream wisdom tradition.[26]

Retribution in the Prologue

The opening scene of the book of Job assumes the truth of the retribution idea. In 1:1-5 there is a clear correlation between Job's ideal character (described in four ways in 1:1) and his flourishing family (1:2, 4), for whom he interceded (1:5), and wealth so abundant that he was the "greatest" among all the people of the east (1:3). Job is pictured as utterly righteous and suitably rewarded.

However, this nexus between righteousness and reward is also broken in the prologue, as Job loses these outward symbols of his righteousness (1:13-19) without his character having changed (1:22; 2:10). The accuser suggests that he only appears to be righteous, and that his motive is to enjoy the material blessings that come from acting in this way (1:9-11). The reason why Job suffered these losses (and the further afflictions in ch. 2) was not that Job *deserved* to do so, or that they were in proportion to his "wickedness" (the idea of retribution), for God himself comments that this was done "without reason" (2:3), meaning that it could not be accounted for on the grounds of justice alone. Thus the beginning of the book clearly shows that Job's suffering, at least, was not a consequence of his sin. This is meant to guide our reading of the debate between Job and his friends, which focuses quite strongly on this idea of retribution.

Job's Friends and Retribution

Duck-Woo Nam asserts that "the doctrine of retribution underlies the thought worlds of Eliphaz, Bildad, and Zophar."[27] Yet, although they clearly operate within a framework of retribution thinking, the development of their ideas is interesting. They begin with a less rigid approach in 2:11-13, since they would not

26. Holmgren, "Barking Dogs Never Bite," 341-47.
27. Nam, *Talking about God,* 58. Examples of this way of thinking include 4:7-11; 5:13-15, 17-26; 8:1-7, 11-13; 11:1-6; 15:7-16, 20-35; 18:5-21; 20:4-11, 23-29; 22:1-11, 15-20.

have come at all if the reason for all suffering is sin. Their purpose in coming was to "show him sympathy and comfort him" (2:11), which implies that they must have viewed this as a temporary setback (Prov 24:16a) and not proportionate to his offenses. When they arrive, they identify with him in his grief (Job 2:12) and do not use words to correct him (2:13). This notion that Job is suffering for a short-lived period seems to be reflected in Eliphaz's first speech (5:19).

Clines argues that "the author of Job does not portray any development in the position, theology or argument of Job's friends: their minds are set in familiar patterns."[28] However, this is not entirely correct when it comes to the idea of retribution. There is, for example, a significant change from Eliphaz's optimism in 5:17-26 to his strong condemnation of Job in 22:5-11. John Walton rightly points out that in the first round of speeches the focus is on the positive aspect of the retribution idea — that God rewards the righteous — at least in the first two speeches (4:6-7; 5:18-27; 8:5-7). There is only a brief statement of the flip side — that God punishes the wicked — by Zophar (11:11), and Bildad applies this to Job's children rather than to Job himself (8:4). In the second round, the balance shifts almost totally to emphasize the outcome for the wicked (15:20-35; 18:5-21; 20:4-29), and this is also the focus of the third round (22:15-20).[29]

This progression implies that the friends represent those who increasingly ignore the flexible and partial flavor of the idea of retribution in the book of Proverbs. They appear to harden their views as the debate progresses. Initially, they view the concept of retribution as an incentive to act righteously. When Job's experience does not match the idea of retribution, they suggest that this is only a minor deviation (5:19). Bildad tries to draw comfort for Job from the observation that he must not be as much a wrongdoer as his children, as they are dead and he is still alive (8:4-6).[30]

As the dialogue progresses, there is an escalating trend to condemn Job as wicked. Zophar even suggests that he has been given a discount, and is suffering less than he deserves (11:6), even though this introduction of the idea of mercy serves to undercut the doctrine of retribution. Increasingly they deduce Job's spiritual state from his ongoing suffering, his words of protest and his refusal to admit his sin. Their theological system must be trusted even when it no longer works. Gustavo Gutiérrez claims that "the friends believe in their theology [i.e., retribution] rather than in the God of their theology."[31]

This is not to say that the friends' understanding of retribution is totally

---

28. Clines, "Arguments," 213.

29. Walton, "Retribution," 652-53.

30. Clines, *Job 1-20*, xlii.

31. Gutiérrez, *On Job*, 29. See also Terrien, *Job*, 41; Holmgren, "Barking Dogs Never Bite," 347-48.

untrue. God does, in part, operate on the basis of this principle (see 5:13a, quoted by Paul in 1 Cor 3:19). But they are wrong in claiming that it is the basis for what is happening to Job, since it does not match the information given in the prologue. M. Pierce Matheney comments, "Job's friends know their text-book theology, quote it correctly *ad nauseam,* but consistently mis-apply it to the exceptional experiences of their 'friend.'"[32]

In passing, it seems that none of the friends bases the retribution idea on the Israelite covenant traditions. Instead, they all — like Proverbs rather than Deuteronomy — appeal to creation to support their theory of retributive justice as the basis of God's relationship to humanity (Eliphaz in 4:9-11; 5:8-16; 22:12-14; Zophar in 20:27-29; and Bildad in 8:11-13). The problem is not, however, the source of the idea, but rather the way that they develop and apply it.

Job and Retribution

Job, despite his protests, is also operating within the doctrine of retribution throughout the book. Thus Job affirms the doctrine when he invites the friends to show him his sin and that he will then accept his suffering (6:24; 13:23).[33] His persistent cries for justice through litigation are based on the presupposition that God must reward righteousness and punish wickedness. Job's pursuit of litigation is based on an understanding of justice as merely forensic and retributive, and that such a concept binds God to act in certain predictable ways. Indeed, James Crenshaw notes, "Job has no case at all against God apart from an operative principle of reward and retribution, for in a world devoid of such a principle good people have no basis for complaining that the creator has abandoned the helm."[34]

The litigation motif climaxes in Job's oath of clearance in chapter 31, and this clearly appeals to ideas of retribution.[35] This is first seen in its negative form (the wicked will be punished) in v. 3, while in v. 6 Job indicates that it is a matter of God weighing the scales of justice. Job expects to be vindicated on the ground of his "integrity." Other examples of retribution thinking can be seen in vv. 9-10 and 21-22. What is being assumed is that there is a necessary or automatic correlation between action and consequence.

Job's problem stems from an inability to hold together a firm belief that God is justly running his world, a conviction of his own righteousness, and

32. Matheney, "Major Purposes," 23-24.
33. Viberg, "Job," 201.
34. Crenshaw, *Whirlpool of Torment,* 62. See also Scholnick, "Poetry in the Courtroom," 189.
35. Humphreys, *Tragic Vision,* 107.

his lack of experiencing God's care.[36] The friends have used this concoction to condemn Job, while Job uses it to complain of the miscarriage of justice. They conclude that Job must have sinned; Job contends that God should be treating him differently. They have the same ideas, but the friends choose to question Job's godliness, while Job complains about God's lack of justice.[37] What is missing from such an understanding is a recognition of the sovereign freedom of God — not a freedom to act inconsistently with his revealed character, but a freedom not bound by an imperfect theological understanding based on a narrow form of human retributive justice. So Karl Barth insists, "The relationship between Yahweh and Job has the character of freedom. . . . it is not, as the false and lying theology of the three friends presupposes and maintains, a moral or juridical law which is secretly above Him."[38]

A progression in the friends' view of retribution has already been noted, but Job's understanding also changes as the debate unfolds. Job starts off with unquestioning submissiveness (1:21; 2:10), but this soon leads into lament (ch. 3). In the dialogue he begins to formulate his ideas and explores a number of hypothetical scenarios in order to secure his vindication. At the same time, he both anticipates and yet despairs of litigation with God, until he finally calls for a verdict in the oath of clearance (ch. 31). His conviction that God will ultimately act justly is the reason for him saying that he would approach God like a prince (31:37). In the end, Job finds no solution to his dilemma in the concept of retribution.

Elihu and Retribution

Elihu has a more ambiguous role in relation to the idea of retribution. He concedes that the three friends, with their increasingly sharp doctrine of retributive justice, were not able to refute Job. This is pointed out by the narrator (32:3) and repeated by Elihu himself (32:12).

Moreover, Elihu argues that one purpose of suffering is to educate a person (33:19-22), which takes him outside a purely retributive view. He is saying that there is another reason why people can suffer, in addition to receiving what they deserve. A pure retribution view insists that all suffering is in proportion to one's actions, not in order to achieve some other goal.

A further difference between the friends and Elihu is that Elihu is not con-

---

36. Polzin, "Framework," 183, describes it as "a contradiction between what he has been taught to *believe* about divine justice and what he *experiences* almost daily in his life."

37. Fingarette, "Meaning of Law," 251, 256.

38. Barth, *Church Dogmatics*, IV, 3/1:386-87.

cerned with Job's prior actions, but focuses only on his words in the debate (e.g., 33:8-11; 34:5-6, 9, 35-37; 35:16). He has at least moved on from the friends' position that Job's actions before the dialogue can account for his suffering. If he holds to a view of retribution, he applies it in Job's case only to the way he has conducted himself during the interchange of ideas with his friends. This focus on his "wrong speaking" is also moving outside a retributive framework because the suffering was inflicted in the opening two chapters, before he had spoken "wrongly." His great suffering would therefore not be in proportion to any prior wrongdoing.

Despite this, Elihu is firmly committed to the doctrine of retribution. Clines is correct: "Even Elihu, while recognizing that there are more important theological truths than strict retribution, still affirms its validity."[39] He has a strong view that God is a God of justice and is committed to acting in accordance with what is right (34:10, 12, 17-19). A key criterion for assessing Job's words is whether or not they are "just" (35:2a). Indeed, Elihu gives a clear outline of retributive thinking when he explains how God deals with wrongdoing:

> For according to the work of a man he will repay him,
> and according to his ways he will make it befall him. (34:11 ESV)

Elihu may espouse ideas about God's sovereign activity in addition to retribution, but retribution is clearly still a key component.

The Yahweh Speeches and Retribution

When God breaks his silence in chapters 38–41, there is a clear implication that a narrow view of human retributive justice cannot restrict God's free and sovereign running of his world. These speeches testify to a God who is, as Creator and sustainer, beyond human challenge. No human dogma, even that God must act with justice, can bind or restrict God (41:11, cited in Rom 11:35).[40] While God is undoubtedly just, his ordering of the world extends far beyond justice, and especially beyond a reductionistic human concept of retribution that is limited to rewarding righteousness and punishing wickedness. Gutiérrez insists that "justice alone does not have the final say about how we are to speak of God."[41]

The key to unraveling God's activity is realizing that God's concerns are

39. Clines, *Job 1–20*, xlii.

40. Clines, "Not a Problem," 103, says, "the divine speeches may be said to put forward other competing values . . . even such a highly prized value as justice might be only one value among others."

41. Gutiérrez, *On Job*, 87.

wider than a narrow understanding of justice as merely retributive. In fact, Yahweh opens his first speech by referring to one such broader concept, namely his "design" or "plan" (38:2). The contrast between Job's concern for litigation and Yahweh's exploration of the order in creation points to the truth that Yahweh's concerns are wider than those that preoccupy Job.[42] A clear example of this is found in 38:25-27, where Yahweh explains how rain falls on land where there are no human beings, so that this life-giving rain cannot be in response to the amount of human righteousness or wickedness.

In 40:8 Yahweh addresses Job's need to prove him wrong in order to establish Job's own integrity. Yahweh replies that this is only so if he is bound to run the world on the basis of the principles of justice epitomized by the traditional doctrine of reward and retribution. Norman Habel rightly concludes, "If in his governance of the cosmos God is not bound by that principle but by an integrity of his own, then the ground for a court case, where the operation of this principle is assumed, has been removed."[43] This, of course, is not to say that God is unjust, nor is it to assert that justice has nothing to do with the way God runs his world. The divine speeches simply illustrate that our understanding of justice is not the sole criterion for how God acts.

The doctrine of retribution is thus not rejected, but rather marginalized or qualified. Clines explains it well:

> God's speeches (chaps. 38–41) are remarkable as much for what they omit as for what they contain. There is, in the first place, not a word of the retributive principle here. This must mean that it is not so fundamental to understanding the world as all the previous characters of the book have thought. But it must also mean that it is not entirely wrong, either. If God were passionately in favor of it or violently against it, would he not have had to mention it? . . .
>
> What does this viewpoint expressed by the character of God do to the doctrine of retribution? It neither affirms nor denies it; but it marginalizes it. In Job's case, at least, the doctrine of retribution is beside the point. . . . All that Job learns from God is that retribution is not the issue, but whether God can be trusted to run his world.[44]

---

42. Habel, *Book of Job,* 65, notes Yahweh first answers Job's challenge by depicting a world in which God is free: "these natural laws are not governed by a higher law of reward and retribution which is applied mechanically each dawn."

43. Ibid., 66. He adds that the principle of retributive justice as a mechanical law of the cosmos has thus been "repudiated in three contexts — by the message of the prologue, by the experience of Job, and by the answer of God."

44. Clines, *Job 1–20,* xlv-xlvi.

Thus in 41:11 Yahweh clearly asserts that as owner or ruler of the universe he can never be compelled by the principle of retribution.[45] If there is more to Yahweh's purposes than retributive justice, he cannot be *bound* simply by justice, as if it is an objective principle that can be used to restrict his freedom.[46]

Sylvia Scholnick has argued that the term מִשְׁפָּט/*mišpāṭ* itself has a wider meaning than simply "retributive justice." She notes that within the book the root שׁפט/*špṭ* is used in two distinct ways: "as jurisprudence and sovereignty. Contained within this single root are two ideas which in the English language are distinct: judging and ruling."[47] While Job and his friends understand the legal sense of judging, God uses it here with the alternative meaning of ruling.[48] Yahweh is not simply judge; he is also the king who is actively exercising his sovereign rule. The Yahweh speeches thus serve to redefine *mišpāṭ* as sovereignty, God's right ruling of the universe.[49]

This argument has some merit, since the issue at stake in the Yahweh speeches is how God sovereignly rules his world. Yet a simpler and more cogent explanation is that Yahweh's purposes are seen as wider than "justice." It is not the meaning of "justice" that needs to be broadened; it is rather the reality of how God rules. God's purposes are broader than justice alone. If the term "justice" is filled out to include God's sovereign sustaining and ruling of his creation, then it is in danger of becoming too broad and inclusive, thus rendering it useless as a category. It is better to preserve the distinction between ruling and acting justly, while seeing both as important parts of God's activity.

The Epilogue and Retribution

Some scholars regard vv. 10-17 as a later addition to, and a contradiction of, the message of the book, largely because of the idea of retribution.[50] This view is usually based on the assumption that the Yahweh speeches have rejected the

---

45. Parsons, "Structure and Purpose," 145.

46. Whybray, *Two Jewish Theologies*, 8; Greenberg, "Job," 299. Gutiérrez, *On Job*, 72, remarks that "God will bring him to see that nothing, not even the world of justice, can shackle God; this is the very heart of the answer."

47. Scholnick, "Meaning of *mišpaṭ*," 521-22.

48. Scholnick, "Poetry in the Courtroom," 194. Scholnick, "Meaning of *mišpaṭ*," 523, argues that God uses *mišpaṭ* in 40:8 as a term for the divine governance of the world. It is used in the sense of ruling in, e.g., 1 Sam 8:9.

49. Scholnick, "Poetry in the Courtroom," 192.

50. Whybray, *Two Jewish Theologies*, 5-6; Gibson, "On Evil," 412; Polzin, "Framework," 185-86.

concept of retribution as a description of how God runs the world. Such views misunderstand both the Yahweh speeches and the epilogue.

They misinterpret the Yahweh speeches, which have only qualified — not overturned — the role of retributive justice in God's running of creation. The Yahweh speeches simply claim that justice cannot exhaust or fully describe God's plan for the world. The examples given there are exceptions to reorient Job away from thinking that God acts on the basis of human retributive justice alone. God is not only "just" — he is also actively and freely ruling as owner of the creation. Retribution is not being denied, but neither can it give all the answers. For God to act partly on the basis of retribution in the epilogue is not a contradiction of the previous chapters.

They also misinterpret the epilogue. While Job is given twice as much as he previously enjoyed (1:3; 42:10, 12), this is not simply because he is righteous. Two other reasons are given. In 42:10 God links the restoration of Job with his act of intercession for the friends, rather than to his righteous character. In addition, Job is restored because the test is now over. The test was to reveal whether Job feared God for nothing (1:9-11; 2:4-5), and the taking away of his possessions, family, status, and health were the form that the test took. Now that God has pronounced in favor of Job (42:7-9), the test has been completed and Job is restored at least to his former state. That is what normally happens when a test is finished. H. H. Rowley even suggests that "Job is prosperous at the end, not because he is righteous, but because he was prosperous at the beginning."[51] Thus there are good reasons for Job to be restored by a gracious God apart from the doctrine of retribution.

Yet in a sense a more nuanced concept of retribution is behind the picture given in the epilogue. In the prologue, the possessions of Job were outward symbols of his righteous character, in accordance with the teaching of Proverbs. The book of Proverbs did not teach that such wealth was guaranteed, but did point out that such a connection can often be observed and was certainly appropriate. Retribution does not cover the field about how God relates to people, though it is part of his plan. Now that the reader has seen that Job is inwardly righteous — that he fears God for nothing — the outward evidence of his righteousness is appropriately restored. Possessions may still be a sign of a righteous man. Roland Murphy comments: "The author does accept the doctrine of the goodness of the Lord and he now expresses this concretely in the case of Job."[52]

John Hartley sees the epilogue as preserving an essential statement of

51. Rowley, "Job and Its Meaning," 267.
52. Murphy, *Wisdom Literature*, 45.

biblical faith — that fear of Yahweh leads to an abundant life. He suggests that the book of Job is seeking rather to correct wrong applications of the idea of retribution, such as that suffering is conclusive proof that a particular person sinned, or that the extent of their suffering is always in proportion to the extent of their sin, or that the wicked will always suffer immediately.[53] But retributive justice is still a crucial component of God's active rule of society.

What Is the Teaching of the Book as a Whole on Retribution?

Don Carson observes that "the book does not disown all forms of retribution; rather, it disowns simplistic, mathematically precise, and instant applications of the doctrine of retribution. It categorically rejects any formula that affirms that the righteous always prosper and the wicked are always destroyed."[54] Yet it no more denies the idea of retribution than it rejects the notion of God's justice. It is affirming the flexible and partial perspective of retribution that is found in Proverbs but that had been calcified over the years until it had become a weapon wielded against sufferers like Job. Job's friends eventually arrive at the view that they can read off Job's wickedness from the extent of his suffering, but the book as a whole rejects this view. Human retributive justice is not the only principle on which God runs his world. God's purposes are broader than humanity and extend far beyond justice. God is free and sovereign, and must be treated as such. God is God!

Tracing the idea through the book of Job has also revealed, however, that there is a key place for retributive justice in God's purposes. Indeed, the book of Job affirms what is evident in the book of Proverbs. Yet the teachings of Proverbs must be understood as being true to life, not as promises or guarantees. Retributive justice is a true but partial description of God's ordering of creation. When it is forced to become the only truth, it flips over into untruth.

The Litigation Motif

Overview

The pursuit of litigation is one of Job's two major forms of protest in the book (the other is lament). The litigation motif is often identifiable by reference to

53. Hartley, *Book of Job,* 544-45.
54. Carson, *How Long,* 155.

legal terminology or procedure, centering on the taking of a lawsuit against God in order to secure "justice." Habel has maintained that a "legal metaphor" (or "litigation motif") pervades much of the book of Job, especially in the dialogue.[55] This is not entirely surprising, since Job's plea is fundamentally a call for justice. It is often missed by readers who do not naturally think about a relationship with God in litigation categories. However, the use of legal parallels and terms is vital to a right understanding of the book.

Habel outlines the structure of the motif in a chiastic pattern, which serves as a useful starting point:

A   Ironic Anticipation (1:6-11; 2:1-6)
    B   Contemplating Litigation (chs. 9–10)
       C   Challenging the Accuser (ch. 13)
          D   Announcing an Arbiter (16:18-21; 19:21-29)
             E   Testimony of the Accused (chs. 29–30)
             E1   Oath and Challenge by the Accused (ch. 31)
          D1   Verdict of an Arbiter (chs. 32–37)
       C1   Challenging the Accused (38:1ff.; 40:6ff.)
    B1   Retracting Litigation (42:1-6)
A1   Ironic Exculpation (42:7-9)[56]

This outline highlights that the motif peaks in chapters 29–31, after which time it is systematically unraveled.

There are two distinguishable streams of the litigation motif in the book. The first is Job's use of forensic categories such as taking God to court as a way of resolving his present dilemma. The second is Job's calling on a legal figure, variously described as an arbiter, witness, redeemer, and hearer, to intervene and settle the dispute. A crucial issue is whether these actions are being presented as consistent with Job's piety in the prologue.

Litigation and the Prologue

Legal categories enter the book at an early stage. Habel entitles the heavenly court scenes of the prologue (1:6-11; 2:1-6) as "ironic anticipation," but this is probably giving too much to the role of the accuser in the heavenly court.

---

55. Habel, *Book of Job,* 54, views it as "integral to the structure and coherence of the book . . . a major literary device which integrates narrative progression and theological motif."

56. Habel, *Book of Job,* 54. Some of the "labels," however, require some revision.

However, the heavenly court setting is in part a legal one, and the litigation motif commences here.

Another fruitful concept is the suggestion that Job is God's champion in a trial by ordeal, a common legal category throughout history.[57] The book as a whole is then a description of Job's successful completion of the ordeal or test, and thus a vindication of God's claim that humans can fear God without ulterior motives (1:9).

In both the court setting and the trial of Job's faith, the prologue is relying on an underlying legal analogy.

The Pursuit of Justice in the Dialogue

Within the dialogues, Job sees that his righteousness is at stake (6:29), but at that stage he does not explore any legal action. Job first contemplates entering into a legal dispute with God in 9:3. In chapter 9 he explores the problems in bringing God to trial (9:3, 14-16) and the difficulty of getting a fair hearing (9:17, 19, 32-34). His underlying theology of justice is retributive, and his assumption is that God has sovereign power (see 9:22-24). Although Job still uses some legal language in 10:1-2, the rest of that chapter shows that he moves on from litigation to lament.

As chapter 13 begins, Job is addressing the friends (13:2, 4-5), and rehearses before them his intended course of action. He announces his plan to argue his case (13:3, 6). Having prepared his case (13:18), he calls for litigation (13:19, 22) and asks for details of the charges against him (13:23). From 13:24 until the end of the speech in chapter 14, the focus changes and he again lets the idea of litigation lapse in order to express the depth of his pain.[58] This pattern of floating the possibility of litigation, then letting it go, suggests that the pursuit of litigation is an imaginative exploration of any possibility, rather than a realistic proposal.

Job closes the cycle of speeches in chapter 27 with an insistence that he be vindicated. Here Job resumes his case (27:1) and complains that God has denied him his "right" (27:2, מִשְׁפָּט/*mišpāṭ*, lit. "justice" or "judgment").[59] He asserts with an oath that he has not perjured himself (27:2-4), that he will not concede that God is in the right (27:5), nor will he give up his claim

---

57. Kline, "Trial By Ordeal," 93.

58. Habel, *Book of Job*, 231; Clines, *Job 1–20*, 316.

59. Frye, "Use of *māšāl*," 63-64, has argued persuasively that מָשָׁל/*māšāl* is to be understood as a litigation term here and in 29:1, where it is a departure from the stereotyped formula that begins all Job's other speeches.

to be a person of integrity (27:5) and righteousness (27:6). Job has thus not withdrawn or renounced his intention to take God to court to have his innocence declared.

The Possibility of a Legal Figure in the Dialogue

Job calls for a legal figure on three different occasions in chapters 3–27 and uses three different terms.[60] Job first considers the possibility of a legal figure in 9:32-35, when he calls for an arbiter or mediator (9:33). In 16:19-22 he looks to a heavenly witness, and in 19:25-27 he envisages a redeemer.

In 9:32-35 Job views the idea of litigation as a daunting challenge, since there is a power imbalance between God and him (9:32, 34). Job searches for someone who will act as a go-between, ensuring that there would be a fair trial (9:33).[61] Very little detail is given of this figure, which suggests that his identity should not be our main concern. Commentators speculate whether some unidentified third party is in view, or whether it is ultimately an appeal to God as mediator between Job and himself. The latter is conceptually difficult, since having God as an arbiter could not force God to play fair. So many suggest that it must refer to a third party, perhaps a helper in a lawsuit to get justice done.

However, it is also useful to ask whether Job is looking for an actual or simply an imaginary figure. Three factors suggest the latter. First, this passage is set in a chapter of highly fluctuating emotions, and Job is still only exploring possibilities, not actualities. Second, the image of 9:32 is one of terror, not comfort, and therefore more likely to be a possibility than an actual request.[62] Third, what is asked for is a hypothetical figure, whom Job cannot find (9:35b). This would account well for the little detail given of his identity.

At this stage, then, the precise identity of this figure is not yet clear, but there is a hint that to look for such a figure may be clutching at nonexistent straws.

In the second passage (16:19-22), Job calls for his witness who is in heaven or "on high" (16:19). The most natural way of reading this is as a reference to God, but v. 21 describes the function of the witness as being to argue the legal case of a person with God.

Hartley considers the alternatives and concludes that "the best candidate for the defender that can be found is God himself." He concedes that there are

---

60. On this figure see L. Wilson, "Realistic Hope or Imaginative Exploration?"
61. Habel, "Only the Jackal Is My Friend," 232.
62. Roberts, "Job's Summons to Yahweh," 160.

difficulties with this view, but suggests that they are not insurmountable.[63] This view is buttressed by 17:3, which indicates that Job is pleading *to God* for relief. It is also supported by Job's consistent practice of appealing to God, the one who is regarded as "on high."[64] However, these arguments are not particularly strong, and the impression given is they are based on the view that Job's big view of God elsewhere would preclude him from calling on someone else to stand in judgment on God. Clines usefully remarks, "All agree that in the end that is who Job's effectual 'witness' will turn out to be (cf. 42:7-8), but is that what Job thinks now?"[65]

Yet the most obvious difficulty still remains as to how God could argue a person's case against himself (16:21). This leads many to conclude that it refers to a third party.[66] However, there is no agreement about the nature of this "witness" if it is not God. John Curtis proposes that Job envisaged a "personal, private" God to take on the high God, but there seems to be no evidence for this in the text.[67] Alternatively, Habel sees that a major argument against seeing the figure as God is the role of the accuser in the prologue, where he is a third party in the heavenly court. He concludes, "A third party is clearly being described. Job is not contemplating the good side of a schizophrenic deity."[68] While Job is not aware of this figure from the heavenly court scene, he explores the possibility of a third party who is a counterpart of the accuser.

However, both Habel and Curtis make some revealing comments that suggest a third option. So Curtis writes, "As long as one holds that Job finally returned to the god who had abandoned him, the idea of a heavenly witness is little more than a strident outburst of total frustration."[69] Habel makes this concession: "This hope of a celestial mediator, however, remains but a flight of faith."[70] They appear to assume that the heavenly witness is an identifiable rather than an imaginary figure. Since, on their view, God seems precluded by the text, they conclude that it must be a third party. Yet why can it not be an "outburst of total frustration" or a "flight of faith"? Clines, who also precludes identifying this figure with God, makes an interesting observation:

---

63. Hartley, *Book of Job*, 264, claims that "he is affirming genuine confidence in God regardless of the way it appears God is treating him." See also Dhorme, *Job*, 239; Gordis, *Book of Job*, 178.

64. Andersen, *Job*, 183.

65. Clines, *Job 1–20*, 389.

66. So Smick, "Job," 933; O'Connor, "Reverence and Irreverence in Job," 98; D. Williams, "Speeches of Job," 476; Pope, *Job*, 118.

67. Curtis, "On Job's Witness in Heaven," 549.

68. Habel, *Book of Job*, 275.

69. Curtis, "On Job's Witness in Heaven," 550.

70. Habel, *Book of Job*, 276.

"And yet, it is hard to believe that, if the witness is not God, it can be some other heavenly being."[71]

Another proposal is that this witness is not a person or heavenly being but some object. Clines proposes that it is Job's protestation or affidavit of innocence, while Gerald Wilson hints that it could be Job's cry (16:18).[72] It is difficult to see how such objects would argue Job's case with God (16:21) any better than Job could, and such a view would not account for some other occurrences of the legal figure (e.g., 9:33).

This leads to the third option, which sees the first two views as partially right. No figure other than God is in view, and thus there is no third party. Yet the difficulties of identifying this figure with God (especially 16:21) suggest that Job is not making a straightforward avowal of trust in God. The third possibility is to see Job reaching out to an imaginary figure, grasping at even the most remote possibilities. No option, however unlikely, is left unexplored by Job. Along this line, J. Gerald Janzen contends that to try to identify the witness is to miss the point. Rather, "Job imaginatively reaches out into the dark and desperately affirms the reality of a witness whose identity is completely unknown to him."[73]

Several factors suggest that this third option is the most likely. First, Dale Patrick notes that in the second and third cycles, "expressions of hope and wishes to appear before God replace Job's requests for an explanation and a fair hearing."[74] That is reflected in 16:18-21, where Job does not mention the issues of justice, righteousness, or integrity that have earlier been prominent. This makes it appear that Job does not have a precise, identifiable legal figure in mind. This section is not a closely reasoned legal argument, but rather a despairing cry of hope. Second, the first two views have difficulty in explaining parts of the text. It does seem that no one other than God is in view (17:3), but there are problems in identifying him as God (16:21). The third option can best account for all the texts. Third, the similar pattern makes it likely that the figure here is the same as that in 9:33 and later in 19:25. Thus each exploration of this legal figure follows a burst of angry complaint and protest, and after each of these passages a cry of despair follows the floating of unfulfilled hope (9:35b; 16:22; 19:27c).[75] That a different title is used in each case implies that no identifiable figure is in view. Rather, Job is grasping after any possible solution. Fourth, the possibility of a heavenly advocate is a wish that would be reasonable for Job to explore. It did

---

71. Clines, *Job 1–20*, 389-90.

72. Ibid., 460; G. Wilson, *Job*, 182-83.

73. J. G. Janzen, *Job*, 125.

74. Patrick, "Job's Address of God," 275.

75. Gutiérrez, *On Job*, 66; Habel, "Only the Jackal," 232.

not seem to be a novel thought in that society, for such a figure is mentioned by others in 5:1 and 33:23.

The third call for a legal figure, and for many the high point of Job's faith and hope, is seen in the statement about a redeemer in 19:25-27. The identity of "my redeemer" in 19:25 is a moot issue. Gutiérrez sees a progression through the three figures in 9:33, 16:19, and 19:25 from "a nebulous request for the presence of an arbiter . . . to the need of a witness and thence finally to an expression of confidence in a liberator."[76] Looking back to the witness of 16:19 and the arbiter of 9:33, Habel sees the figure in chapter 19 as a member of the heavenly council, a counterpart to the accuser, who acts on behalf of God to vindicate Job.[77] Ronald J. Williams suggests that the redeemer is the Canaanite Baal, as an impartial judge who would call even Yahweh to task.[78] However, this rests on a doubtful parallel with the Ugaritic Baal and Anat epic. Clines develops a different view, that it is Job's protestation of innocence that is his "redeemer."[79] This is perhaps the most promising of the options in that he proposes that the "witness" is not God, but nor is it someone other than God.

However, there is no need to precisely identify the nature of the intermediary if we properly understand the function of these pictures in Job. I have already argued that the figure described differently in 9:33, 16:19, and 19:25 are not three separate identities — they are the one "hope" who is variously described. In other words, this "redeemer" is none other than the "witness" of 16:19 and the "umpire" of 9:33. The study of these earlier passages has suggested that this figure is, however, neither God nor an actual third party, but rather an imaginary figure as Job clutches at any possibility. As suggested in the commentary on this passage, Job's immediate sinking back into despair (19:27c) suggests that he is simply exploring possibilities at this stage. This longing for a "redeemer," then, is much less of a confident hope than it appears to be at first sight.[80]

One significant feature of the litigation motif here is that Job is not just making a demand for justice or vindication but looks forward to seeing God. It is true that a nuance of "my redeemer" is redemption or vindication, but that concept is not elaborated in this passage. Verses 26 and 27 focus rather on seeing God, as if that will meet both his existential dilemma and his desire to be vindicated. So underlying the picture of taking God to court is Job's deeper

76. Gutiérrez, *On Job*, 66.

77. Habel, *Book of Job*, 306.

78. R. Williams, "Theodicy," cited in Crenshaw, "Popular Questioning," 381.

79. Clines, *Job 1–20*, 459-65.

80. Whedbee, "Comedy of Job," 17: "What to many interpreters is the high point in Job's odyssey of faith is finally submerged in the sea of incongruities that surge through the book." See the commentary on 19:23-27.

desire for a restored relationship. Thus it seems that Job's pursuit of a legal figure is presented as part of genuine piety, for he makes an unconditional affirmation about God's commitment to him despite all the evidence to the contrary.

Thus the two strands of the litigation motif emerge very clearly in the dialogue. The first, most prominent in chapter 13, focuses on taking God to court since he must be bound to deliver justice. The other centers on a figure described in different legal terms in 9:33, 16:19, and 19:25. In these cases, Job seems to push beyond a litigation framework in seeking a restored relationship with God.

Job's Summing Up (Chapters 29–31)

The climax of the developing legal process is Job's address to the assembled crowd in chapters 29–31, in what is best viewed as Job's summing up his legal case. In this final and comprehensive review, Job rehearses his former righteousness (29:14), set against his present sufferings in the following chapter. This leads to an extended oath of innocence in chapter 31, culminating in a call for a "hearer," another legal figure, and for the Almighty to set out the charges in writing (31:35-37). If neither a "hearer" nor his adversary appears, Job's oath of innocence stands and he is cleared of all charges and vindicated. It is important that this summing up begins with a longing for a restored relationship with God (29:2), so that it is clear that Job's aim in pursuing litigation is not to belittle or defeat God.

In 29:7-16 Job is pictured as someone taking a prominent role in the legal affairs of the city, a righteous and just man (29:14) championing the cause of the powerless and actively working to overcome injustice (29:11-17).[81]

Chapter 30 contrasts starkly with the previous chapter, emphasized by the threefold use of "But/And now" (30:1, 9, 16). Formerly he was honored by all (29:21-25), and now he is despised by all (30:9-15). At 30:20-23 Job confronts God with a number of specific accusations, all suggesting that God has treated him in a way he did not deserve. Yet, even here, what hurts Job most is that when he cries out to God, God does not answer (30:20). Michael Dick makes the telling observation that "the author of Job . . . does not complete the lament with the customary final appeal for divine intervention, rather he substitutes in Chapter 31 a legal fiction."[82] That is, in his final speech Job transforms his personal lament into the call for a legal remedy.

---

81. For more detail on this and the following passages, see the commentary.
82. Dick, "Job 31," 31.

The implied legal procedure behind chapter 31 has already been explained.[83] This is essentially a way of ensuring that a resolution be found by putting one's life on the line. It is not an example of hubris, but rather stems from a deep conviction that justice can ultimately be found, and that God cares for justice.

Dick sees "Job 31:35 as the key to the legal metaphor in Job," being an appeal that would compel the plaintiff to present his evidence, after other less drastic attempts have failed.[84] Job's call for a שֹׁמֵעַ/*šōmēaʿ*, ("one to hear me," 31:35) is another call for a legal figure. Elsewhere this term is used for a person deputed by the ruler to hear and pass judgment on his behalf. For example, in 2 Sam 15:1-6, where people have a case to bring before the king, Absalom notes that there is no "hearer" (2 Sam 15:3) appointed by the king to hear their case. That is, the "hearer" is one chosen to hear and pass judgment on behalf of the king.[85] This means that Job has not given up his earlier wish for an arbiter, witness, or redeemer. That strand of the litigation motif is still active, as Job strives for God's intervention. This is another way of describing the figure mentioned in chapters 9, 16, and 19.

Job is still looking to God for a resolution, not only by lament but also by litigation. That Job has put his life on the line by his oath of clearance before God is further indication that his motives are right.[86] By the end of chapter 31 all the loose ends seem tied together. The notion of seeking litigation against God and the hope for some "legal figure" to intervene have both been elements of the litigation motif, which has fluctuated between them. Now they are brought together and merged with his cries to God. We now await the resolution in the unraveling that is to come in the Elihu and Yahweh speeches.

The other major function of this chapter is to cause the reader to reflect radically on the nature of a relationship with God. Is God bound by retributive justice? Is there a difference between God's justice and human justice? Is Job's understanding endorsed or denied? These questions peak here, but they are not yet answered.

Elihu and the Litigation Motif

Elihu has a very significant function in both strands of the litigation motif. Elihu regards himself as the answer to Job's call for a "legal" figure to deliver

83. See the commentary on ch. 31.
84. Dick, "Legal Metaphor," 38.
85. O'Connor, "Reverence and Irreverence in Job," 92.
86. Ibid., 94; also Gros Louis, "Book of Job," 256.

him, although he understands this in terms of being God's messenger who will instruct Job (32:12). Job has called for a mediator, and "Elihu steps forward as an ostensible umpire."[87] Chapter 32 is essentially Elihu's apology for assuming this role, as he acts as an authority figure calling Job before him for a civil trial (33:5). Elihu then summons Job to a hearing, answers the charges raised by him, appeals to the assembly of local "judges," and pronounces a verdict, defending the justice of God. The speeches of Elihu are thus a logical conclusion to the legal metaphor that has climaxed in Job's oath (ch. 31).[88]

Yet, since Elihu's self-perception is often awry, perhaps the case should not be regarded as closed. Indeed, some see Elihu's proposal of an angelic mediator (33:23-24) as an answer to the search for a legal figure, one who can intercede with God on behalf of humans. Norman Snaith, for example, thinks of such a figure as an angel who carries away the dead, and envisages the scenario that if such an angel saw a just man undeservedly near death and took on himself to declare to God this man's uprightness, then God might turn the man back to life again.[89] James Ross sees Elihu's main contribution to be "his description of the heavenly transaction between God and the interpreting angel, and in the results thereof for the salvation of the individual."[90] He sees this as the answer to Job's assertion that "God will answer none of my words" (33:13). However, Ross concedes that the figure Job had in mind was a legal official, whereas Elihu speaks of a cultic functionary in heaven.

Elihu also speaks forth on the other major strand of the litigation motif. Job has raised the possibility of bringing litigation against God in order to secure justice. Elihu delivers a verdict in God's favor, declaring that humans cannot summon God in litigation. The substantive argument of 33:15-28 is a calculated response to the specific claim by Job that no human can win a lawsuit against God (33:13), because God would not answer human beings. In chapter 34 Elihu argues that Job cannot expect a civil suit with God (34:23), so Elihu as a surrogate will judge in God's absence. Thus his reply to Job's call for litigation is that he must settle for a human arbiter.

In chapter 35 Elihu attempts to prove to the "court" that Job's demand for a trial is empty and meaningless in the context of his community (35:13-14). The transcendence of God (35:5-8) implies that his will is to be discerned through life and nature (35:10-11), not through direct contact. All this implies that Job's pursuit of litigation has been a result of rebellion, not faith.

87. Barth, *Church Dogmatics,* IV, 3/1:398.
88. Habel, "Role of Elihu," 83-85, 95.
89. Snaith, *Book of Job,* 89-90.
90. Ross, "Job 33:14-30," 39.

In the final two chapters, Elihu turns to a public defense of God (36:2-3). In 36:3 he sets out his purpose: to ascribe "righteousness" to his Maker. At 36:22, when he turns to the nature analogies, he mentions God's power and paints a rich picture of his transcendence. These themes are tied together in 37:23, when Elihu concludes that God is great in power, justice, and abundant righteousness.

Thus the Elihu speeches give a variety of responses to the litigation motif. First, Elihu appears to believe that he is to act in place of the "legal" figure(s) sought by Job. Second, his words appear to argue cogently that God will not respond to his call for litigation. Ultimately, however, Elihu's human verdict, including his insistence that God will not appear to humans, is overturned by the appearance of Yahweh in the theophany that begins in chapter 38.

The Yahweh Speeches and Job's Response

Scholnick has maintained that in chapters 38–41 Yahweh accepts Job's legal challenge and presents his arguments from the natural, animal, and mythological worlds as evidence in the courtroom. On her view, the creation poetry of these chapters serves as legal testimony so that the lawsuit continues.[91] In calling on Job as a litigant to answer (40:2), Yahweh is enforcing a courtroom procedure, while the barrage of questions function as cross-examining interrogatories.[92]

However, it is better to understand the Yahweh speeches as an invitation to cease the process of litigation, rather than as the continuation of a "lawsuit drama." Robert Alter thus sees a discontinuity between the issues of human justice raised in the courtroom and the response of God in the arena of creation.[93] In the light of a broader understanding of God's purposes in creation, the pursuit of litigation seems futile. Thus God is not giving evidence but questioning the point of furthering the process.

This is buttressed by Henry Rowold's observation that the inclusion of the purpose clauses shows that the goal is not to win the argument but rather to restore a proper relationship.[94] It also serves to prepare for what is best understood as Job moving away from the path of litigation in 42:6. Yahweh uses the examples not to crush Job into submission, but rather to invite him to withdraw the litigation. In modern legal terms, Job must file a nonsuit.

Some scholars see in 42:6 a formal retraction by Job of his legal case. For

91. Scholnick, "Poetry in the Courtroom," 187, 196, 200.

92. Ibid., 189. Habel, *Book of Job,* 33, and Kline, "Trial By Ordeal," 90, also point out the legal procedures here, though they differ on the details.

93. Alter, "Voice from the Whirlwind," 39. Also Parsons, "Literary Features," 222.

94. Rowold, "Theology of Creation," 64-65.

example, Habel views מָאַס/*mā'as,* the first verb (often translated as "despise"), as better translated as "retract," and notes that the previous time Job used this verb was with a "legal case" as an object (31:13). He concludes that this provides the resolution of the litigation motif as Job withdraws his legal challenge of God.[95] While this is not the most likely interpretation, there is a sense in which Job's choice to move in a new direction involves an informal, but just as real, renunciation of his legal case. Now that his other longings have been satisfied, he does not need a litigation process to force God to become present. Thus the book ends on Job renouncing the path of litigation as the appearance and words of God have now rendered it inappropriate.

Litigation and Retributive Justice

The previous section has pointed out that Job's desire to pursue litigation against God is apparently based on an understanding of justice as merely forensic and retributive. Once the Yahweh speeches explode the reductionism of such a view, the very foundation of litigation has dissipated. Even Job had pushed the doctrine of retributive justice further than it was intended to go. It was never meant to bind God to act only on the basis of justice and in proportion to a person's righteousness or wickedness.

Job was one step ahead of the friends. They had insisted that Job must have been desperately wicked since he was suffering severely. Job, however, was in the midst of a struggle. He held on to God's justice with as much fervor as the friends, but he believed just as firmly that he was not as wicked as his circumstances seemed to imply. As Robert Polzin notes, "there is a contradiction between what he has been taught to *believe* about divine justice and what he *experiences* almost daily in his life."[96] Unlike the friends, Job keeps on believing in the apparently irreconcilable truths of God's justice and his own innocence.

Job cannot see a resolution to this until the Yahweh speeches imply that God's justice is not the only principle on which he runs the world. Not every good or bad thing that happens to a person occurs as a reward or a punishment. God's purposes are wider than justice. Since Job's pursuit of litigation was impliedly based on the presupposition that God must always and only act justly, his desire for a legal remedy was no longer appropriate once God had torpedoed his presupposition. What was missing from such an understanding was a recognition of the sovereign freedom of God — not a freedom to act

95. Habel, *Book of Job,* 582-83.
96. Polzin, "Framework," 183.

inconsistently with his revealed character, but a freedom not bound by human constructs and imperfect theological systems.

The Legal Figure: "Imaginative Exploration" or Realistic Hope?

The study of the litigation motif has caused us to question the popular understanding of passages like 19:25-27. Job's calling on a figure variously described in chapters 9, 16, 19, and 31 cannot readily be identified as high points of faith. There does not appear to be any confident assertion here that Job expects his dilemma will be solved by resurrection.

Yet that is not to conclude that his outbursts show a lack of faith. Job's faith is not shown by the content of his assertions, but by the fact that he is paradoxically crying out to God against God himself. It is more the person *to whom* he cries rather than *what* he cries that makes his cry one of faith. Thus Job seems to vacillate between a call for a hearing date (9:32-35; 13:22; 31:35) and his call for deliverance and restoration (13:16; 19:26-27).[97] His goal appears to be deliverance from his present situation and a restoration of a wholesome relationship with God. His tactics — based on a forensic model — are to pursue a lawsuit against God claiming "justice." Such a bold and largely unparalleled course of action leads Job to investigate any possibilities that may facilitate his task.

Litigation and Lament

The litigation motif is distinct from, yet related to, the complaints to God (see the following section). One clear distinguishing feature is that the litigation motif appears predominantly when Job is addressing the friends. Unlike the complaint to God, when Job contemplates litigation he generally talks *about* God rather than to him. This use of the third person contrasts with the first person address to God that is characteristic of the complaint to God and will be shown to be a significant factor in viewing the complaint as a legitimate expression of faith.

As with the complaints, the litigation motif is largely developed in the first two cycles, and is largely absent (except for 27:1-6) from the third cycle. Both expressions of protest surface in the climactic unit of chapters 29–31, which suggests a linking or at least close relationship between the two.

In the early stages, the litigation motif petered out and was subsumed by the complaint to God. Thus the prospect of litigation, or an arbiter in chapters

97. Gros Louis, "Book of Job," 241.

9 and 13, is replaced by complaints in chapters 10 and 14. In chapters 16 and 19, where complaint is not prominent, Job largely explores the other strand of some legal figure to aid him in his quest.

In chapters 29–31 Job seems to use both expressions of protest in a two-pronged search for a resolution. Though they may explore different channels, they are not independent of each other, and both appear to have an underlying goal of a restored relationship with God.

Litigation and Faith

The question must arise as to whether the pursuit of litigation is inconsistent with Job's piety as shown in the prologue. Daniel O'Connor concludes that the "conviction of Job that God is the final source of justice is ultimately the factor which stamps Job's pleas as reverent."[98] The goal behind Job's desire for litigation appears to be to secure justice. This is a praiseworthy goal, but Job fails to see that his adopted course of action was flawed because of a wrong presupposition. This accounts for Job's acknowledgment in 42:3 that he spoke about what he did not understand fully and what was beyond his knowledge. His knowledge of how God runs his world was limited, since he assumed that one single principle explained it all. That Job took this principle of justice seriously, and yet was honest about his own experience as well, speaks of a genuine and humble submission to God that led to open verbal disputes. In refusing to reject God, or to reduce his view of God, Job is left in his confusion, but perseveres in faith.

This suggests that Job's faith is being stretched and tested rather than broken. While it appears at times to be a misguided or incomplete faith, the very fact that Job knows he has to deal with God implies that "righteous" Job has not yet abandoned his God. It seems that Job has retained his faith while still seeking further understanding.

Lament and Complaint to God

What Is Lament and Where Is It Found in Job?

When people think of prayer in the OT, most will think of the great prayers of faith. Perhaps it will be the intercessory prayers of Moses, Abraham, or Elijah; perhaps the majestic prayers of David and Solomon; it may be the trusting

98. O'Connor, "Reverence and Irreverence in Job," 101.

prayers of Daniel. While there are many different kinds of prayer in the OT, one that we often neglect or do not know how to use — individually as Christians, or corporately in the church — is the lament.

The lament is the most common type of psalm, is prominent in books like Job and Lamentations, and is sprinkled through Jeremiah and some other prophets. Claus Westermann comments that "any survey will show that laments pervade the entire Old Testament and that they are an essential part of what the Old Testament says happened between God and man."[99]

What, then, makes up the lament? While there is no rigid form for the laments, there are a number of commonly recurring parts. The basic skeletal structure of the individual lament typically includes an invocation (or calling on God), the lament or complaint itself, an expression of confidence, a petition, and a vow to praise (or actual praise).[100] In the lament or complaint, there are characteristically three parts, focusing on I, you (God), and they (enemies). William Morrow identifies these in Job as follows:

I-complaint	6:2-4, 11-13; 7:3-6; 9:25-28; 10:1; 16:16-17; 17:6-7; 19:13-20
God-complaint	7:11-21; 9:17-18, 22-24; 10:2-7, 13-17; 16:7-14; 19:6-12
Enemy-complaint	6:14-27; 12:2-6; 16:2-5; 17:12; 19:2-5; 21:34.[101]

The focus of the lament is not primarily about venting feelings, for it is fundamentally a plea or petition for help.[102] It is designed to bring about change, for those lamenting are seeking a resolution of their distress. Thus Job laments in order to change or restore his relationship with God. Westermann rightly observes that "petition, or at any rate something like petition, intrinsically belongs to the lament."[103] In biblical laments, the writers do not stop with the voicing of the complaint, but come before God with a request.

In the book of Job, laments are found in Job's speeches right through the dialogue section. Richard Hughes identifies seven laments here: 3:11-26; 6:2–7:21; chapters 9–10; 13:3–14:22; 16:1–17:16; chapter 19; and chapters 23–24.[104] We should probably also include his reflection on the prospering of the wicked in chapter 21 and his summary lament of his present life in chapter 30.[105]

---

99. Westermann, "Role of the Lament," 24.

100. Westermann, *Structure,* 33. He sees the movement from plea to praise as crucial to the lament.

101. Morrow, *Protest against God,* 132.

102. Westermann, *Elements of Old Testament Theology,* 169.

103. Westermann, *Structure,* 67.

104. Hughes, *Lament, Death, and Destiny,* 37-39.

105. Westermann, *Structure,* 31, suggests, in addition to the opening and closing laments

Hartley has argued that Job has deliberately adapted the lament form, altering some of these elements and omitting others.[106] The greatest overlap is in the lament proper and petition. The three elements of the lament proper (self, God, and enemy; or I, you, and they) are all present, but sometimes it is not only the friends who are the enemies (6:13-20; 12:2-5) but also God (16:9-14; 19:7-12). Hartley notes that his petitions center on the friends' listening to him and treating him better (6:28-29; 19:21; 21:5) and that God might ease his suffering and enable him to understand it (7:7, 16; 10:20-22).

Hartley suggests that Job departs from the usual form by initially not addressing God, and it is certainly a feature of Job's speeches that he often moves from addressing the friends to speaking to God. He also suggests that there is no review of God's past faithfulness, a feature common to the psalms of lament. However, that Job appeals to God's activity as his creator and preserver (e.g., 10:9-12; ch. 29 as a prelude to the lament in ch. 30) suggests that Hartley is overstating his case here.

However, he is on stronger ground in noting that Job has omitted the affirmation of trust or expression of confidence, replacing it with protestations of innocence (6:29; 16:17; 23:10-12). Furthermore, there is no vow to praise on Job's lips, for he instead reverts to the use of oaths. Hartley helpfully points out this movement within the dialogue from "despairing laments to determined oaths" in 27:2-6 and chapter 31.[107] He also suggests that there are no assurances of being heard, which often in the lament psalms account for the movement from lament to praise. The absence of assurances suggests that, while Job thought that God should hear, he had no confidence that it would actually happen.

Complaint to God as a Subset of Lament

While the lament genre is undisputedly prominent in the book of Job, it has a variety of forms.[108] In 3:11-26 Job utters a self-lament *(Ichklage)*; in chapter 19

(chs. 3 and 29–31), 6:4-20; 7:1-21; 9:17-31; 10:1-22; (12:13-25); 13:20–14:22; 16:6–17:16; 19:7-20, 23, 27.

106. Hartley, "From Lament to Oath," 89-91.

107. Ibid., 89.

108. Westermann, *Structure*, 8-13, et passim, argues that the book as a whole has the structure of a lament. However, in order to maintain his thesis, he has to excise the Elihu speeches as well as trim the material down to fit his argument. It seems much better to propose that individual complaints are prominent right through the dialogue, and are crucial to the understanding of Job's speeches.

he simply bemoans his present lot, seemingly addressing the friends (19:2-6, 21); yet at other times (7:7-21) he addresses God directly.

Craig Broyles has argued strongly that the various forms that fit under the umbrella category of lament need to be seen as distinct forms of appeal. In particular, he observes the need to distinguish between a general "lament" category (including I/we and foe laments and some "God-laments") and those "God-laments" that connote complaint. He summarizes the differences:

> Lament can be addressed to anyone; complaint must be addressed to the one responsible. A lament focuses on a situation; a complaint focuses on the one responsible. A lament simply bemoans the state of things; a complaint contains a note of blame and rebuke.[109]

Others have suggested that lament is the "bemoaning the troubles that one has undergone," while complaint is "arguing with and complaining to God about one's situation and protesting its continuation."[110] Walter Brueggemann defines a "lament" as

> a complaint which makes the shrill insistence:
> 1. Things are not right in the present arrangement.
> 2. They need not stay this way but can be changed.
> 3. The speaker will not accept them in this way, for it is intolerable.
> 4. It is God's obligation to change things.[111]

This distinction between laments and complaints to God is very helpful when it comes to the book of Job. All of Job's "laments" are not protests directed at God, but his complaints addressed to God clearly are. Of all Job's "laments," the "complaint to God" is the one most likely to be pictured as an illegitimate expression for a person of faith. Of those passages often identified as lament, chapters 7, 10, and 14 most clearly contain complaints directed to God.

Christian Difficulties with Laments

Yet most modern Western Christians entirely ignore the laments. Walter Baumgartner has described the laments as "Old Testament unevangelical prayers."[112]

---

109. Broyles, *Conflict of Faith and Experience*, 40.
110. S. Brown and Miller, "Introduction," xv.
111. Brueggemann, "Costly Loss of Lament," 62.
112. Quoted in Davidson, *Courage to Doubt*, 9.

Some features of the lament are, indeed, awkward for interpretation:

1. They contain strong outbursts of anger and vengeance directed at one's enemies.
2. They include bold, seemingly irreverent, accusations pointed at God.
3. There is rarely any explicit explanation for the general movement within a lament from complaint to praise.
4. There is uncertainty over whether the laments constitute a failure of faith, or whether the courage to doubt and question should be viewed instead as a legitimate part of faith.
5. It is not clear how, if at all, these laments are to be models for us today, or incorporated into our liturgies and our personal prayers. This is essentially the question of how they function as Scripture today.
6. There is also a lack of clarity about whether laments still have a place after Christ's victory in his death and resurrection, or whether they are no longer appropriate.

The net result is that the laments have "all but disappeared from Christian prayer."[113] However, several studies have urged us to rediscover the lament and its contribution to individual and corporate prayer. Brueggemann comments that "the lament psalms offer important resources for Christian faith and ministry even though they have been largely purged from the life of the church and its liturgical use."[114]

It appears that the lament has been both deliberately ignored and subtly replaced. The negativity of lament seems to be on a different wavelength from our world, which is so strongly committed to the need to be positive and affirming. Hence Page Kelley notes that the lament "has been repudiated by purveyors of positive thinking."[115] Many Christian leaders urge their followers to "claim the victory" rather than complain or lament.

On another front, the lament has been overshadowed by repentance for sin. Indeed, Westermann has proposed that "the confession of sin has become the Christianized form of the lament."[116] The setting of suffering presupposed in a lament is seen to pale in comparison to the drastic consequences of sin and guilt. Yet this does not need to be an either/or situation, for a high view of sin does not necessarily lead to minimizing the reality of suffering and despair.

113. Kelley, "Prayers of Troubled Saints," 381.
114. Brueggemann, "Formfulness of Grief," 263.
115. Kelley, "Prayers of Troubled Saints," 381.
116. Westermann, "Role of the Lament," 33.

There is room for both. To lament one's circumstances is not necessarily to deny one's sinfulness, but simply to assert that the present difficulties are not the outworking of judgment on sin. In the book of Job, the friends decree that his suffering is due to sin, and the only way to restoration is confession, but their analysis does not square with the prologue. Job does not confess any sin, but rather laments his situation, a stance endorsed by God himself at the conclusion of the book (42:7-8).[117]

Many Christians have been too quick to censor and discard the laments, based on an implicit understanding of them as embarrassing, perhaps even sub-Christian. But the laments add a useful, maybe necessary, dimension to a well-rounded faith. A striking feature of the laments is that, even in the darkest times of feeling forsaken by God, the sufferers still lament and complain to God. They are expressions of a faith that is not shaken by God's seeming silence. Thus the movement within the lament is of crucial significance — the move from questioning to a restored relationship. Yet it does not skip too quickly to hope and praise. It lingers on the present distress and allows it to be expressed and faced. Finally, however, the lament does not stop at complaining, but moves through the crisis of faith to a newer understanding of God's goodness and steadfast love (e.g., Lam 3:22-23). Though Job's complaints include blame and rebuke, the underlying dynamic is Job's desire to have his relationship with God restored.

It is therefore not surprising to find the word of a lament psalm on the lips of Jesus as he is hanging on the cross. In his genuine humanness, with the awfulness of the sin of the world separating him from the Father, he turns to Psalm 22 — and utters those now-familiar words: "My God, my God, why have you forsaken me?"

The words of God must control our reading of Job's laments, and it is God's verdict that not only was Job blameless and upright at the beginning (Job 1:8; 2:3), but also that what Job said about God during the debate was right (42:7-8). In the dialogue, Job speaks to his friends about God in laments. God must therefore be endorsing at least the general thrust of Job's laments and complaints.

Christians have not generally known how to incorporate lament in either corporate worship or private devotions.[118] Yet a fundamental insight from both Job and the lament psalms is that praise and lament need to be held together in tension. If we neglect lament, we will not fully understand praise. Followers

---

117. Westermann, *Elements of Old Testament Theology*, 173, notes that "Job defends himself against the friends who want to press him into a confession of guilt."

118. See the helpful suggestions of B. Webster and Beach, "Place of Lament."

of God need a language that will express their deepest feelings to God both in times of joy and in times of great suffering and anguish. The Bible provides both in songs of praise and thanks and in laments. Praise of God, or a restored relationship with him, is the goal of the lament, but this will sometimes only be reached through the use of honest laments and complaints poured out to God. Real life is not always easy, and Job provides resources to help us live out our lives authentically before God.

The Strong, Honest Language of Protest

It is of course Job's strong words of protest addressed to God in the dialogue that seem to sit most awkwardly with his earlier piety. He pictures God shooting poisoned arrows (of suffering) at him and complains that God is terrifying him (6:4). He accuses God of making him his target (7:20) and multiplying his wounds without cause (9:17). He complains that God is oppressing and despising him (10:3), hiding his face from Job and counting him as an enemy (13:24). Indeed, he pictures God as having mounted a full-scale attack on him (16:7-16).

Can true faith include such statements, accusations, and protests, or has Job overstepped the boundaries of genuine godliness? Are Job's laments and complaints pictured as legitimate expressions of faith or not? The study of Job's complaints in this commentary has revealed nothing that disqualifies Job from being a person of faith. There are bold questions and even accusations leveled against God, but God is still the one he turns to. He still firmly believes that God is the one in charge, and therefore the person to come before. The complaints are addressed to God, and this marks them off from the speeches of his friends. Thus F. I. Andersen comments that "at least he keeps on talking to the heedless God. His friends talk about God. Job talks to God."[119]

The ancient Hebrews, more familiar with the lament psalms, would recognize in Job the anxious "why" and "how long" of the laments, and would see in Job a representative of the tradition of doubt and protest seen in the OT. J. C. L. Gibson comments, "They would not be expecting him to be totally rebuffed. On the contrary, they would be looking for God to come to his aid; for the genre of the lament was above all a strategy designed to move God to action."[120] The parallels between the laments in Job and the lament psalms suggest that both seek to motivate God to respond.

---

119. Andersen, *Job,* 98. Simundson, *Message of Job,* 107, also observes that "Job had wanted to lament, but his friends wanted to argue theology."

120. Gibson, "On Evil," 410.

Job's words do contain strong and even accusatory language, just like the complaints and laments in the book of Psalms. They need to be interpreted as part of this broader genre. There are a number of reasons for understanding this strong language as acceptable to God in the midst of such trying circumstances. Most obviously, there is God's endorsement of Job's words "about him" (42:7-8). Furthermore, the laments are directed to God, assume God is in control, expect that no one else except God can right the situation, and are ultimately a call for the presence of a seemingly absent God. Despite the strength of the expressions used, they are still a call for a restored relationship with God.

Within the book, Elihu reaches a human verdict on the appropriateness of Job's laments and complaints. Elihu sees the issue to be whether Job has spoken rightly of God. In focusing only on the words of Job, Elihu has missed the point of the complaint to God as a call for God's presence. He thus regards Job's problems as intellectual rather than existential. There is no willingness to understand why Job is saying such things, but only a compulsion to correct impiety or bad theology. From this point of view, the Elihu speeches do not resolve the issues raised by Job's complaint to God, and the reader — whose sympathies are with Job — awaits a further resolution.

A key feature of the book of Job is that the main character persists in talking honestly to God, not breaking off the relationship. As Murphy expresses it, "One of the significant gifts of the book is honest language in conversing with God."[121] The book affirms that the honest pouring out to God of our deepest hurts, our raw emotions, even our strongest accusations, is an appropriate way to channel our pain. It is always appropriate to be honest before the God of the theophany, who knows and sustains all things. God will never be blown away by the strength of our language. Simundson suggests, "The lament gives the sufferer words to use, a way of bringing into the open what is difficult to express, so that it may be acknowledged and worked through in some meaningful process."[122]

We need to recover that sense of bold, honest faith that moves from a questioning of God's ways through to a settled and deep conviction that he is a God who is "for us." Rather than an embarrassment to faith, the laments of the OT are a challenge to genuine faith in the midst of trouble, a faith that knows that, even when God seems silent, help can come from no one else except God. This is not a failure of faith, but part of a genuine faith that has the courage to doubt, to complain, to protest — knowing that God and God alone can meet him in his utter darkness. So "even words of doubt expressed to God become

121. Murphy, "Last Truth about God," 586.
122. Simundson, *Faith under Fire*, 58-59.

statements of faith because they are addressed to the right person."[123] This is not a laid-back, easygoing faith we find here, but a desperate struggle of faith, for faith — trying to make sense of the world around him in the light of what he knows about God.

The Goal of Lament or Complaint

A vital feature of Job's laments is that his goal is to have his relationship with God restored. The lament is not static, but is heading toward a goal of moving through one's present trouble in order to praise God. When the present circumstances of the lamenter are found to be overwhelming, as they are expressed, the person is able to clarify their settled convictions and turn expectantly to God. Thus the complaint is expressed in order to move on in a relationship with God.

As already noted, petition is at the very heart of lament; hence Job calls out or appeals to God in order to change his situation. Westermann points out, "What the lament is concerned with is not a description of one's own sufferings or with self-pity, but with the removal of suffering itself. The lament appeals to the one who can remove suffering. . . . it is the means by which suffering comes before the one who can take it away."[124] Or as Brueggemann observes, "The laments are addressed to someone! And precisely in the presence of God himself is where the hurtful issues must be dealt with."[125] Job is not looking for an intellectual solution for his suffering. He wants a way out of the conflict between his faith and his experience. His understanding of God has given him an expectation about how he should be treated in life. Yet his current experience points him in a completely different direction. He refuses to form his ideas solely from his present experience, without reference to his past dealings with, and knowledge of, God. The goal of the lament is thus "to lay out one's own inner sufferings before the one who alleviates suffering, heals wounds and dries tears."[126]

As in the lament psalms, Job's goal is not to belittle God but to befriend him. It is not primarily to defy God, for defiance is only a means to an end. Thus it is right to see him showing "continuing fidelity even when his quest for God assumes the paradoxical form of defiance."[127] Job does not even insist on winning the litigation, since the goal of his court case was to secure the presence

123. Ibid., 59-60.
124. Westermann "Role of the Lament," 26.
125. Brueggemann, "From Hurt to Joy," 4.
126. Westermann, "Role of the Lament," 32.
127. Lévêque, "Job's Suffering and Transformation," 137.

of God. Such is Job's trust in God that he believes that, if only he could come before God, then the just God he knows would clear and restore him. This end is always in sight, so that Job's complaints can never be understood as merely mouthing off at God. Their underlying dynamic is well expressed in 14:15a: "You would call, and I would answer you." At times, lamenting is for Job the only way of clinging on to a God who seems silent or absent.

Persevering Faith

The only time Job is used as an example in the NT is in Jas 5:11, when James encourages his readers to persevere in faith in the midst of suffering. He reminds them, "you have heard of the steadfastness of Job" (ESV). The word translated "steadfastness," ὑπομονή/*hypomonē,* was rendered "patience" in the KJV, and so the phrase "the patience of Job" came into the English language. But *hypomonē* has the sense of steadfast, persevering faith, a commitment not put off by difficulties or obstacles.

Options Not Taken by Job

One way of seeing Job's perseverance more clearly is to look at the options that were open to him but that he did not take. In adopting his twin protests of pursuing litigation and complaining or lamenting, Job has effectively excluded a number of quite foreseeable options that would have been a failure of faith.

First, he has resisted the temptation to go through the motions of repenting so that God would have to ease his suffering and restore his blessings. This was the response suggested by his friends. Since they believe that he must have sinned, they urge Job to repent in order to have his former life restored. If he were to follow their advice, Job, knowing that he had not committed such severe sins, would be simply using God for personal gain. He would be undertaking a godly action (a prayer of repentance) not because he believed it, but simply because it was the pathway to blessings. This is the very thing that the accuser asserted in 1:9 — that Job did not fear God for nothing, but for what he could get out of it. This path would not be the way of faith for a righteous person, because it would be using God as a means to an end, not an end in himself.[128] In refusing to go down this path, Job shows his faith in God.

Second, he nowhere contemplates the path of suicide. On one reading of

---

128. McKeating, "Central Issue," 246.

the words of Job's wife, she may be suggesting that Job should "curse" God and so bring down on himself God's wrath, which would kill him (and put him out of his misery). This is not quite suicide, but it at least shows that suicide was a thinkable option for Job. Job rejects her proposal in saying that she is speaking like one of the foolish women (2:9). Especially in chapters 7 and 14, Job outlines the strong limitations and fragility of human life. While he loathes his life and asks God to leave him alone (7:16; 10:1) — even wishing he were never born (3:3-10) — he does not take steps to end his life but rather explores imaginary scenarios like being hidden in Sheol (14:13-17). As Hartley notes, "in his desire for death, Job never entertains the option of suicide. Suicide was not acceptable for the person of faith, because it signified that one had lost all hope in God."[129] While the suicide of a believer is always an anguished pastoral situation, it takes greater faith not to give up on life and God, and to persevere in what seems to be a living hell.

Third, he does not curse God. The prologue makes clear that the way to test the genuineness of Job's faith is whether he curses God. The accuser twice makes this the litmus test of Job's faith as he responds to the loss of his possessions, family, and health (1:11; 2:5). Job's words in the prologue are not words of cursing God, and the dialogue opens with Job cursing not God but the day of his birth (3:1). While the laments and complaints in the dialogue contain many strong and accusing words, none of that amounts to cursing God. This is made clear in God's words in 42:7-8, where he says Job spoke of him what is right. This could not be said if Job's outbursts in the dialogue should be viewed as "cursing God." There is a place for an open and honest pouring out of our deepest hurts to God, without constantly fearing that we may have stepped over the line. God seems more robust than some of his defenders, both ancient and modern.

Fourth, Job does not take time out from his relationship with God. Job does call on God to leave him alone (7:16; 10:20; 14:6), but this is only part of the picture. He still asks God to "remember" him and what he is like (7:7; 10:9; 14:13), and it is Job who keeps on initiating conversation with God as he characteristically turns in his speeches from talking to the friends (6:1-30; 12:1–13:19) to addressing God (7:1-21; 13:20–14:22). His deepest longing is not for God's absence but for a restored presence (14:15). The alternative for Job would have been to stop calling out to God in lament and to avoid God and his ways entirely. This is a common pastoral issue today as many churchgoers or believers respond to deep pain and horrific trauma by cutting themselves off from God and his people — no longer praying and reading God's Word, and avoiding their Christian friends. The apparently easy way out is to waste days,

---

129. Hartley, *Book of Job*, 92.

weeks, months, living as if God does not matter any more. Tragically some give up their faith entirely, and sentence themselves to a godless life. If this is the alternative chosen by many, we can see how Job's desperate clinging to a God who appeared absent or uncaring was in fact a choice of great faith.

Lament and Faith

Complaint to God was indeed a response of faith. It is perhaps even better than the path of silent submission, for that would not allow for expression of the loss or for petition for a restored relationship. Lament provides "for both the articulation of the experience and a means of coping with the experience."[130] The strength of Job's response is that he seeks to do justice to both his experience and his past knowledge of God. He refuses to opt for one or the other, because he wants an understanding of God that explains both. This will stretch faith to its very extremes, but it is still faith. In a sense, the friends were prepared to rewrite Job's life rather than rethink their doctrine. Job is not content with the arid theology of the friends since life does not always match the script that they take for granted.[131] They have replaced faith by an overly rigid doctrine of retribution. Robert Davidson comments, "There was more faith in such deeply questioning protests and scepticism than in the pious affirmation of untroubled, but blind, certainty."[132] Job's struggle is to break through the straitjacketed thinking of his friends to an encounter and restored relationship with God himself. Job takes risks as he pushes the boundaries of faith with bold and untested words, but his speech stems from genuine faith rather than rebellion.

The laments and complaints uttered by Job model a faith that refuses to surrender despite difficult circumstances. This is a faith that knows that its only solution is with God, even when God himself seems to neither hear nor care. Those who utter these laments pour out to God their honest reaction to whatever has befallen them. They do not cease speaking to God, nor do they pretend and play games with him. They pour out their hearts, hoping against hope that God will intervene and answer their longings. While it is sometimes inappropriate to share our deepest feelings with one another, it is always appropriate to bring them to God. Of course, that is not all that there is to faith, nor is it an end in itself, but it is so often a helpful and legitimate stage in working toward the goal of trusting God in the midst of troubles. We can be too quick

130. Balentine, *Hidden God,* 165.
131. Davidson, *Courage to Doubt,* 174, 178-79.
132. Ibid., 183.

in moving to an easy, half-baked trust. We do need to move on from lamenting to see God's faithfulness afresh, but we will not do so if we bottle up our hurts and our anger, or pretend they do not exist. We need to lay out our inner sufferings before the one who can change both us and our circumstances, helping us through to a deeper, growing trust in our God.

In OT studies, Brueggemann has been particularly attuned to the value of lament in a life of faith. For example, "The faith expressed in the lament is nervy, that honest facing of distress can only be done effectively in dialogue with God who acts in transforming ways."[133] It is easier in the midst of trials to give up rather than to hang on. Referring to the wider concept of lament, he notes,

> The use of these "psalms of darkness" may be judged by the world to be acts of unfaith and failure, but for the trusting community, their use is an act of bold faith, albeit a transformed faith. It is an act of bold faith on the one hand, because it insists that the world must be experienced as it really is and not in some pretended way. On the other hand, it is bold because it insists that all such experiences of disorder are a proper subject for discourse with God. There is nothing out of bounds, nothing precluded or inappropriate. Everything properly belongs in this conversation of the heart.[134]

The laments are a legitimate part of a robust adult faith that knows that God will not be shattered or provoked by strong words of protest. God does not, unlike many of us, avoid conflict, for he knows that the honest expression of where we are at is essential for our transformation. To ask "Where is God?" in the midst of one's sufferings is based on faith that God could do something about the circumstances if he chose. Desmond Tutu, as he reflected on the struggle in South Africa, pointed out that the perplexity behind laments comes from a belief that God is good, loving, and powerful. This big view of God becomes a problem when God does not seem to act in response to those calling out to him.[135]

Not many would suggest that the complaint is at the *core* of Israelite faith. Yet the book of Job presents it as a legitimate part of faith when a righteous person, not being punished for his sin, undergoes unspeakable loss and suffering and experiences God as silent or absent. Complaint can then be a proper expression of anguish and a desire to have his relationship with God restored. In such situations, Job's laments reflect a fundamental trust in God despite his

---

133. Brueggemann, "From Hurt to Joy," 5.
134. Brueggemann, *Message of the Psalms*, 52.
135. Desmond Tutu, quoted in Gutiérrez, *On Job*, xv.

circumstances. Just as belief and doubt can mark the life of a believer, so too can praise and lament. Faith includes responding not only to life's delights but also to its difficulties, and the silent submission of Job in the prologue is not the only possible response. Since God has made us as humans with raw emotions, there must be some opportunity to process them in a way that will enable us to keep on believing in a good and powerful God.

Of course, if the complaints arose out of a lack of faith, that would not make sense of the final form of the book, with so much of the central section devoted to Job's laments. If the Yahweh speeches could have followed immediately after Job's first lament in chapter 3, then we could make Job a much shorter book. Graeme Goldsworthy rightly argues: "We cannot suppose that the entire middle section of the book containing Job's search for understanding is put there so that it can be ruled out of order."[136] There was a need for the cut and thrust of the debate, and we cannot bypass this process without changing the message of the book. It is placed there because it has something to teach us, and it is most likely to concern the struggle to persevere in faith. Brevard Childs concludes that "the movement of the dialogue thus assigns a positive note to Job's struggle to meet God."[137] Job uses lamenting to come to terms with his anguish, and to cling to God when his situation is pushing him in the opposite direction. We may find here resources that help us cope with those "extremities of life which shatter, alienate, and destroy."[138]

In the dialogue, it is clear that the friends misunderstand Job's laments and complaints as words of rebellion. The friends act as if Job needed advice and correction rather than support. When Job is asking "why" and "how long," he stands in the tradition of the lament psalms, which use such questions as a way of voicing the depth of the hurt or loss. Job was hoping that someone would respond to the depth of his pain. The friends, however, see his questions as "armchair questions" when they are really "wheelchair questions."[139] Their category mistake renders them unable to hear and respond to the real issues in Job's words, and provoke Job into further despair. Andersen appropriately notes that even "true words may be thin medicine for a man in the depths."[140]

This reading of the complaints of Job suggests that Job is presented here as having a struggling faith trying to come to terms with his bewildering experi-

---

136. Goldsworthy, *Gospel and Wisdom*, 92.

137. Childs, *Introduction to the Old Testament as Scripture*, 536.

138. Brueggemann, "From Hurt to Joy," 6.

139. Ash, *Out of the Storm*, 12-13. Andersen, *Job*, 190, sees the difference between Job and the friends as follows: "the friends are detached, Job is involved; they are on the balcony, he is in the street."

140. Andersen, *Job*, 123-24.

ence. What we see in Job is that "God knows the difference between struggling faith and contemptuous unbelief," a phrase used by Derek Kidner in relation to Psalm 78.[141] As Tennyson has said,

> There lives more faith in honest doubt,
> Believe me, than in half the creeds.[142]

Job's levels of hope and despair are certainly fluctuating with the dialogue, but such is the nature of faith in times of struggle. His way of complaint, confrontation, and confusion is then a paradoxical way of expressing faith. Job is at the very least being genuine and honest before God. Nancy Duff has expressed it well:

> Psalms of lament allow us to speak from the darkest regions of the heart, where our despair threatens to overwhelm us. In so speaking we do not exhibit a lack of faith, but stand in a biblical tradition that recognizes that no part of life, including the most hideous and painful parts, is to be withheld from God.[143]

This is ultimately a stance of faith — genuine, honest, persevering faith.

The Fear of God

The "Fear of the LORD" in Proverbs

The "fear of the LORD/Yahweh" is an idea prominent in both wisdom and non-wisdom texts of the OT.[144] In the covenant strand, the "fear of the LORD" is most evident in Deuteronomy (e.g., Deut 4:10; 5:29; 6:2, 13, 24; 10:12, 20), but it is also common in the historical books (e.g., 1 Sam 12:14, 24; 1 Kgs 8:40, 43; 2 Chr 19:7, 9) and the prophets (e.g., Isa 11:2-3; Jer 5:22-24; Mal 3:5). Moreover, this fear of Yahweh is also woven into the fabric of the wisdom books, from which Israel's salvation history is strangely absent.

The idea of fearing God in the book of Proverbs is important background for understanding its function in the book of Job. The phrase "the fear of the

---

141. Kidner, *Psalms 73–150*, 282-83.
142. Tennyson, *In Memoriam*, stanza xcvi.
143. Duff, "Recovering Lamentation," 13.
144. See L. Wilson, "Fear of God," on which this section was based.

LORD" occurs frequently in Proverbs (1:7, 29; 2:4-5; 8:13; 9:10; 10:27; 14:26-27; 15:16, 33; 16:6; 19:23; 22:4; 23:17; 31:30), while the verbal form ("fear the LORD") occurs twice (3:7; 24:21). However, more important than the number of occurrences is its important structural location in the book of Proverbs. The present form of the book invites us to pass through chapters 1–9 first, so that the teaching of this section shapes the way that the rest of the book is to be read. The sentence literature of chapters 10–29 is not meant to be understood in isolation from the book as a whole.

The twin themes of chapters 1–9 are the importance of the fear of the LORD and the formation of a godly character. Therefore, it is significant that the fear of the LORD sayings are prominent toward the beginning and end of Proverbs 1–9 as a unit. Proverbs 1:7 is the climax to the prologue (1:2-7) and is the foundational, perhaps even programmatic, "fear of the LORD" saying. A similar saying is also found in 9:10 by way of *inclusio*. This strong emphasis on the fear of the LORD is also evident in the coda that ends the book in 31:10-31 (especially v. 30). The positioning of the motif in the book testifies to the centrality of the idea in the book as a whole, and that the concept is assumed in the rest of the proverbial sayings. Thus the fear of the LORD is foundational to wisdom, but not every piece of wise advice is explicitly related back to the fear of the LORD.

The "Fear of the LORD" and the "Fear of God"

The expression "the fear of Yahweh/the LORD" itself appears nowhere in the book of Job. There are several occurrences of "fearing God" in Job (1:1, 8, 9; 2:3; 4:6; 6:14; 15:4; 22:4; 28:28; 37:24), though the title for God does vary. The word for "God" is "Elohim" in 1:1, 8, 9; 2:3; it is "Shaddai" in 6:14 and 37:24 (implied from v. 23); in 4:6, 15:4, and 22:4 the verb "to fear" occurs without an expressed object to refer simply to piety. In 28:28 the phrase used is the "fear of Adonai." In other places, "fear" is used, but not with reference to "fearing God" (5:21, 22; 6:21; 9:34, 35; 11:15; 39:22). At times different roots occur (3:25; 4:14; 21:9; 22:10; 25:2; 31:34; 39:16, 22; 41:33) that are sometimes translated "fear" in English, but speak rather of "terror" and are unrelated to the wisdom notion of the "fear of the LORD."

The question of whether the "fear of God" is the same as the "fear of the LORD" is important for the book of Job since it does not use the phrase "fear of the LORD." The term "fear of God" at times seems to refer to little more than a basic morality, a sense of right and wrong. Thus Abraham in Gerar is fearful and lies because he distrusts the moral atmosphere of Abimelech's court, saying, "there is no fear of God in this place" (Gen 20:11). Similarly, the midwives, who show a basic respect for life in Exod 1:17, 21, are described as having "feared God." R. N. Whybray therefore defines the "fear of God" as "a standard of moral conduct known and accepted by men in general," a concept included in, but much more restricted than, the "fear of Yahweh."[145]

Whether "fear of God" has this narrower sense or is coextensive with the "fear of the LORD" cannot be decided a priori, but rather must be determined from the context in each case. However, it seems fairly clear from Eccl 8:12-13 that a writer can refer to the wisdom "fear of the LORD" motif, yet do so by speaking of "fearing God." It is further likely that the reference to fearing God in the epilogue of Ecclesiastes (12:13) is an allusion to the foundational wisdom principle of Proverbs. Terminology, in particular the use or nonuse of "Yahweh" does not appear to be decisive. This is not surprising since the wisdom writers were Israelites for whom Yahweh alone was God. As Goldsworthy comments, "These were Israelites and, although salvation history is not a theme of their writing, they were not unbelieving philosophers professing a humanistic alternative to the covenant faith."[146] Since the book of Job is written in response to a misunderstanding of the book of Proverbs, the Joban term "fear of God" needs to be equivalent to the mainstream wisdom idea of the "fear of the LORD."[147]

A clearer understanding of the "fear of God" in Job is vital for discerning how to read this very important OT book. Since the book of Job deals with the nature of authentic faith, it will indicate what kinds of address to God are portrayed as permissible. Has Job strayed from the fear of God in his bold words and actions — in which case he is held up before the reader as a warning? Or does he hold on to the fear of God, which means that Job's words are permissible? Does Job need to return to the "fear of the LORD," or does the idea of the "fear of the LORD" need to be broadened or qualified in order to include or legitimate Job's responses? Such are the questions raised by the book.

The "Fear of God" in the Prologue

At the outset, the narrator establishes Job as one who "feared God" (1:1). Such a statement in the prologue could on its own refer to a common morality, since the setting is in Uz (1:1), not in Israel. This is unlikely, however, for several reasons. First, the book was written for Israel, and Yahweh's endorsement of Job in 42:7-8 implies that he is to some extent a model for Israelites. Second, there are

---

145. Whybray, *Wisdom in Proverbs*, 96.
146. Goldsworthy, *Gospel and Wisdom*, 70.
147. For similar conclusions see Iwanski, *Dynamics of Job's Intercession*, 98-101.

good reasons to use "Yahweh" sparingly in the book of Job. Not only is the story deliberately set outside Israel, it also seeks, as wisdom books characteristically do, to deal with universal problems and not simply those of Israel's national history. In such a context the name Yahweh is used only in the prologue, Yahweh speeches, and epilogue (with one exception — 12:9). Third, it is clear that, in the context of Job 1, the God who is feared is Yahweh, for there is no other God in the prologue. The narrator's description of Job as one who "fears God" (1:1) is repeated by Yahweh himself (in 1:8 and 2:3), who describes Job as "my servant Job" who "fears God." Fourth, there appears to be an *inclusio* between Job fearing God in 1:1 and the programmatic statement of 28:28. In chapter 28 the expression is even more clearly referring to the mainstream wisdom idea (see below), and this confirms that "fearing God" in the prologue is the same. Finally, the coupling of "fears God" and "turns away from evil" (1:1) likely echoes the pairing of the book of Proverbs, which pairs the "fear of the LORD" and "turning away from evil" (Prov 3:7; 16:6; also 14:16).[148]

The prologue's repeated insistence that Job fears God serves to shape our understanding as we read the book. The fear of God is not something that Job learns in the process of the debate, for he already has this fear in the prologue. The disasters that befall Job in chapters 1 and 2 occur in spite of the fact that Job has feared God.

Thus the case of Job puts in doubt the maxim that those who fear God will prosper. On a quick reading of Proverbs, Job may well appear to have become one who did not fear the LORD. He does not seem to have found a refuge for his children (Prov 14:26), "a fountain of life" (14:27), absence of trouble (15:16), a satisfied life (19:23), or "riches and honor and life" (22:4). If these characterize those who fear the LORD, what does this mean for Job?

The "Fear of God" in the Dialogue

Of the three friends, Eliphaz is the only one to use the word יִרְאָה/*yir'â*, "fear (of God)," to Job. He employs it three times (4:6; 15:4; 22:4), once in each cycle. In all instances the object is implied, and *yir'â* is perhaps best translated "piety." In 4:6 Eliphaz urges Job to trust in his "fear/piety"; in 15:4 he accuses him of undermining "piety"; in 22:4 he appears to use it ironically to ridicule Job. Despite the fact that Eliphaz is not an Israelite (indeed, this could be the reason why "Yahweh" is not explicitly mentioned), he appears to have in mind

---

148. Derousseaux, *Crainte de Dieu,* 330-32, concedes this parallel but draws different conclusions.

the traditional wisdom concept of the "fear of the Lord."[149] Eliphaz is espousing a typical wisdom stance, linking piety with prosperity, based on the doctrine of retribution.

Job's sole use of it during the dialogues is in 6:14, where he alleges that Eliphaz's treatment of Job was not "fearing the Almighty" (שַׁדָּי/*šadday*). In the cut and thrust of debate, Job is surely referring to the mainstream wisdom concept (raised by Eliphaz in 4:6).[150] Job may be arguing that the doctrine should be understood more broadly, or that it has been unhelpfully applied in his case.

As readers of the book, we have an advantage over the participants, for the friends are not privy to the heavenly scenes in the prologue. The three friends conclude from Job's adversity that he no longer fears God. Even when they do not use "fear of God" terminology, they nonetheless urge Job to fear God more as the solution to his problems (5:8-9; 8:20; 11:7-20). The reader must view the advice of the friends ironically, since the prologue has demonstrated that this is not the reason for Job's sufferings. The reader sees the friends' analysis of Job's problem as mistaken, and it is later corrected by God himself (42:7-8). While the solution is not revealed in the dialogue, the call to fear God gives Job little comfort when God appears to be silent or absent. The friends, in proposing the fear of God as the remedy, serve as a foil when the issues are finally resolved.

The "Fear of God" in Chapter 28

The occurrence of the saying in 28:28 is clearly the peak of the "fear of God" idea in the whole book. However, the term "the fear of Adonai/the Lord" occurs only here in the OT.[151] Several factors indicate that this phrase is used here to denote the "fear of Yahweh."

First, chapter 28 is a poem extolling the virtues of human wisdom and reads like a mainstream wisdom discourse. Alter rightly notes, "The Hymn to Wisdom, Chapter 28, is in certain obvious ways cut from different cloth from the rest of the Book of Job. Lexically and stylistically, it sounds more like Proverbs than Job."[152] Second, it has already been argued that Job's fearing God in 1:1 is a reference to the traditional wisdom idea. If so, the apparent *inclusio* between Job 1:1 and 28:28 strongly suggests that the "fear of Adonai" is also intended to

---

149. Fuhs, "יָרֵא *yārē*'," 312, describes the absolute form as shorthand for the "fear of the Lord."

150. Fuhs, ibid., views the "fear of Shaddai" in 6:14 as equivalent semantically to the "fear of the Lord."

151. Zerafa, *Wisdom of God,* 155.

152. Alter, *Art of Biblical Poetry,* 92. Also Habel, *Book of Job,* 392.

refer to the wisdom precept of Proverbs. Third, the form of the saying in 28:28 appears to echo the "fear of Yahweh" mottoes found in Prov 1:7, 9:10, and Ps 111:10, and it seems to be placed here to allude to this foundational wisdom principle.[153] Fourth, this chapter is given a literary setting in the dialogue between Job and his friends. As has already been shown, "fear of God" in the dialogue clearly refers to the traditional wisdom idea and, since this chapter functions as an interlude that reflects back on the dialogue, it is likely that it retains the same meaning here. Thus most commentators find in 28:28 a reference equivalent to the traditional wisdom concept of the "fear of Yahweh."[154]

Is the fear of God, then, being proposed in chapter 28 as the answer to Job's dilemma? Much will depend on how chapter 28 is understood. At first glance this chapter suggests that Job is searching out something that is unobtainable and that belongs only to God. On this view, Job should give up his quest and return to a proper fear of God. Some therefore use the conventional wisdom ethos of this chapter to tie Job into the more orthodox mainstream of the wisdom movement. Thus in v. 28 they see the book's answer: "The fear of the Lord, that is wisdom." Moshe Greenberg has contended that this verse anticipates the book's conclusion — that "for mankind wisdom consists of fearing God and shunning evil; more than that he cannot know."[155] Such a view implies that true wisdom involves Job renouncing his earlier outbursts, complaints, and protests, and turning back to fearing God. However, the present context of Job 28 suggests a different reading of the chapter. Within the framework of the whole book, such a view is being aired here in order to be corrected by the remainder of the book.

I have previously argued that the location of this chapter before the summing up in chapters 29–31 (where protest and complaint reappear) preclude it being intended as the solution to Job's quest.[156] If fearing God was intended to be the answer of the book, it would have been given *after* Job's summing up, not before it. While the contents of chapter 28 may be true, they are not sufficient to resolve Job's dilemma. It is revealing that, in chapter 29, Job goes back to the days when he was respected in the community for his wisdom, presumably because he feared God and turned away from evil. That did not prevent his present distress or give him an awareness of God's presence. The orthodox and traditional conclusion of v. 28 is thus undercut by chapters 29–31, for there Job speaks of the way in which he lived fearing God, yet is left with his dilemma.

153. So Becker, *Gottesfurcht*, 246-47.

154. Whybray, *Wisdom in Proverbs*, 98; Fuhs, "יָרֵא *yārē'*," 312.

155. Greenberg, "Job," 299. Similarly, Eaton, *Job*, 19.

156. See the commentary. Also Westermann, *Structure*, 136; Habel, *Book of Job*, 393; Geller, "Where Is Wisdom?" 173-74.

His fear of God did not fully resolve the issues raised in his struggle of faith. Job 28:28 instead recalls 1:1, serving to remind the reader that Job already feared God. However, that has given him no answers in the face of God's continuing silence. The maxim found in v. 28 is not the key to evaluating Job's anguished words.

The form of the expression, "the fear of the Lord, that is wisdom," is important. This verse is asserting that the fear of God is no longer just the foundation of wisdom (Prov 1:7); but rather that the concept of wisdom is exhausted by, or equated with, the idea of the fear of God.[157] If so, this is an excessive claim, based on a fossilized misunderstanding of the book of Proverbs, and one that is qualified by the final form of the story of Job.[158] Clines, however, has suggested that while its prima facie meaning is that it equates fear of God and wisdom, it may not mean this but simply "that to fear God is a very wise thing to do, an act that is full of wisdom, or that the fear of God arises from wisdom."[159] This is unlikely, but even on this reading it is not presented as the final teaching of the book in Job's case.

It is evident that Job 28:28 creates rather than removes the difficulty for Job. The friends have applied the doctrine to Job and urged him to turn from his evil, which must have caused his suffering. Job has already replied, "I do fear God and turn from evil, yet my suffering continues." That tension is not faced in this chapter, and therefore this wisdom interlude must be serving another purpose.

As in Proverbs and Ecclesiastes, the location of the "fear of God" concept in a book is important for its overall significance. The structure of Job precludes this being read as the anticipated conclusion, and the speeches that follow make that manifest. When rightly understood, this chapter does not preclude the legitimacy of Job's earlier complaints as he has been striving in faith for the presence of God. Job is not telling himself, nor being told, to revert to his earlier quiet submission. The perspective of chapter 28 is qualified in the book as a whole.

The "Fear of God" in the Elihu Speeches

In chapters 32–37 the idea of fearing God occurs only once, at the conclusion of Elihu's final speech (37:24). It is, as in 28:28, in a very significant structural

157. Michaeli, "Sagesse," 43.
158. Goldsworthy, *Gospel and Wisdom*, 96.
159. Clines, "Fear of the Lord," 75.

position. If the answer of the book is that Job needed to learn a true fear of God, then this strong closing note in Elihu's final speech would have been a suitable conclusion. Instead, the contribution of Elihu is ultimately inadequate. Elihu's role within the book is to give the human verdict, summing up the words of Job and the friends, and delivering judgment. In such a context, it is likely that he means by the "fear [of the Almighty]" the wisdom concept as used by the previous speakers — Eliphaz, Job, and perhaps also its occurrence in chapter 28.

Elihu's implied remedy ("fear him [God]") does not lead to a resolution of the issues in the book. While Elihu says much that is true, his human verdict — that Job is in the wrong, and God does not appear to humans — solves nothing. It is essentially overridden by the Yahweh speeches, which follow immediately, and the epilogue, where Yahweh declares Job to have spoken about him what is right (42:7-8).

The "Fear of God" in the Yahweh Speeches and in the Epilogue

Even more significantly, the idea of fearing God is not brought up in the Yahweh speeches or in the epilogue. The Yahweh speeches and the epilogue are crucial for interpreting the book as a whole, yet they make no reference to the fear of God. In those very parts of the book where the central issues are resolved (as far as they are resolved!), the "fear of God" idea speaks with a deafening silence! This strongly suggests that the issue of the fear of God is not part of the solution of the book.

Of course, it is possible that the Yahweh speeches propose the fear of God as the solution, even if they do not use the term. If the essential meaning of fearing God is respecting God as God, it could be that the Yahweh speeches are saying, "Let me be God and run the world according to my sovereign purposes — this is the true fear of God." Although this is appealing, it does not work for several reasons. First, the focus in these speeches is not on how humans should respond to God (as if that were the theme), but on God's active ruling as king over all of creation. Second, when Job does respond (42:2-6), he concedes a limitation in knowing God's purposes, not an error in his fundamental attitude to God. The Yahweh speeches simply inform Job of the breadth of God's purposes. Third, when God reflects on what Job has said about him in the dialogue, he endorses his basic stance rather than corrects it (42:7-8). This would be anomalous if Job's problem was that he had ceased to fear God.

If 28:28 contained the anticipated conclusion, then it would need to resurface either when God finally speaks or when the narrator concludes. Yahweh has twice said that Job "fears God" (1:8; 2:3); the narrator agrees (1:1); even the accuser concedes that Job "fears God," though he questions his motive (1:9). Nowhere in chapters 38–41 does Yahweh claim that Job has given up his fear of God. Whether Job fears God for nothing is the question that hangs over the book, and Yahweh's verdict is that his servant Job spoke of him what was right (42:7-8). Surely this suggests that the overall message of the book is not that Job, through his sufferings, came to a truer understanding of what it means to fear God. It appears that, all along, Job's strong protests and complaints have been consistent with the fear of the LORD, and so are legitimate expressions of the faith of a righteous person.

The relationship between God and Job, seemingly broken by God's silence, is restored without any need to refer to the "fear of God" idea. Thus the Yahweh speeches and the epilogue perform an important literary function. The failure to mention the "fear of God" concept as the book concludes shifts this motif to the sidelines as the issues of the book are resolved in other ways.

The "Fear of God" in the Book as a Whole

What does the book as a whole conclude about the idea of the fear of God? Despite the variety of terminology throughout, the "fear of the LORD" concept is on view in the prologue, the dialogue by Eliphaz and Job, in chapter 28, and at the conclusion of Elihu's speeches. The friends, as well as Elihu, use the concept with its usual meaning as the solution to Job's problems, yet this is rejected in Job's case (and presumably in some others) by both Job and Yahweh. It is still important to fear the LORD, but this stance is not all that is important. The need to fear God is still important and undoubtedly true, yet it is not the whole truth.

Chapter 28 raises as a possibility that returning to the fear of God will resolve Job's struggle, but Job knows that he has feared God and yet is still left without answers. Fearing God is a good place to start, and important as an ongoing attitude — but Job is one who has feared and does fear God. That is not his issue. The solution to every pastoral situation cannot be reduced to, "You need to fear God more." The nonmention of the fear of God in the crucial final sections of the book implies that it is beside the point in Job's case.

The book of Job does not deny that the fear of the LORD is the beginning of wisdom, but it does show that fearing God is not all that there is to wisdom. It warns against reducing wisdom to the fear of God as if the extent of our fear of God will always determine our circumstances. God is bigger than that. Just as the doctrine of retribution is qualified, so too the "fear of the LORD" idea is clarified by showing its boundaries.

In Job's case, it is neither the reason for his suffering nor the solution to his struggle of faith. The function of the "fear of God" motif in the book of Job is to insist that the totality of wise living cannot be subsumed under the "fear of the LORD" concept. Wisdom is a wider category than the "fear of the LORD." An appeal to fear God more may often be appropriate, but it can also stifle authentic, honest faith in times of great hardship. There is sometimes a need to fear God boldly!

The "fear of God" thus functions in the book of Job to broaden our understanding of both wisdom and faith. Neither is exhausted by the fear of God, but in both the fear of God will continue to have an important role to play.

Humanity

The book of Job begins with a hint that the nature of humanity will be a key issue. The very first word in the book is אִישׁ/*'îš*, "a man," which is unusually (for Hebrew) placed before the verb. This change of word order is often a way of signaling emphasis in Hebrew. Wisdom literature also tends to focus on people as human beings rather than as Israelites. What, then, does the book say about human beings?

Humanity in Perspective

The prologue indicates that humanity is only one part of the picture, and that the events and difficulties of human life can be a result of what is happening in the larger heavenly realm. Job's losses and afflictions are thus determined by heavenly events that Job and his friends can neither control nor even know about. Of course, this is not confined to the prologue, for Job assumes that he can be affected by the heavenly realm when he accuses God (e.g., 6:4) or when he turns to God in prayer. As in the rest of the OT, the human world is not a closed or self-sufficient one.

It is also clear in the book that God's purposes for his creation are wider than simply for human beings. One of the features of the friends' understanding of retribution is that all actions can be accounted for on the basis of either rewarding human righteousness or punishing human wickedness. While their views have a number of flaws (e.g., not all justice is retributive, and justice is not the only criterion for God's actions), it is also based on the defective assumption that God's concern is always to reward and punish human conduct, rather than humanity being just one aspect of the whole creation. This is made clear in Yahweh's first speech, when he points out that his purposes for creation include rain falling on a land where there are no human beings (38:26-27). Verse 26 twice mentions that there is no man, no human, on this land. God's purposes are wider than simply to bless humans, and his actions do not require the presence of humanity. The full details of God's plan and purposes for his creation are never explained, but it is obvious that God has a bigger brief than simply considering humanity.

The Difficulties of Human Life

In his anguished reflections, Job casts his mind over the human condition on several occasions. While his initial stance is that human life is a gift from God, who is in charge (1:21), he notes that it can include disaster as well as pleasure (2:10). Indeed, he quickly comes to the view that a bitter and miserable life, hedged in by God (3:20, 23), makes people long for death (3:21-22).

Job's first response to Eliphaz unpacks this further by his discussion of various axioms about humanity (7:1-2, 9-10, 17-18). He compares human life to the miserable, hard service of a hired worker (7:1-2), implying that humans are not being treated in accordance with their true value. Bergant has argued that the focus in chapter 7 is on the misery of human life, while chapter 14 will develop the idea of its brevity.[160] However, there is some mention of the brevity of human life in chapter 7 as well (7:6-7), even if the greater problem is the lack of hope (7:6b).

The second axiom in chapter 7 highlights that human life is a one-way trip to death (7:9-10). Job's objection here is that he (and perhaps all humanity) is being treated as if humans were a major threat to God's plans, like the mythological allusions to the sea or sea monster. Job is lamenting the powerlessness of humans before a mighty God.

The final axiom appears to be a reference to Ps 8:4-5; this psalm is a key text in the OT understanding of humanity. In Psalm 8 human value is shown by God making so much of human beings and setting his heart on them. However, the imagery is turned on its head here, as it is used to refer to God's testing and punishing of people (7:17-18). Job now accuses God of targeting him (7:20) and begs for relief (7:19).

The juxtaposition of the short-lived nature of human life and the topic of hope, already joined in 7:6, is filled out in chapter 14. The predominant focus of vv. 1-6 is on the brevity of life (like a flower and shadow, v. 2), but there is some

---

160. Bergant, "Anthropological Traditions and Motifs," 150. The idea of brevity is also seen in 9:25-26; 10:20.

mention of its misery ("full of trouble," v. 1) and that he is not being treated as he deserves ("a hired hand," v. 6). The next part of the chapter (vv. 7-12) contrasts the hope of a pruned tree to sprout forth new life (vv. 7-9) with the human inability to do so (vv. 10-12). Despite their special place in God's economy, humans do not have the resilience of trees. After a short passage exploring an imaginative hiding in Sheol (vv. 13-17), Job focuses again on the hopelessness of the human plight as this chapter ends (vv. 18-22).

Humans' Responsibility before Their Creator

It is very clear in the book that humans have a responsibility before God. This is, in part, based on the creation theology of wisdom (e.g., Prov 8:22-31; Eccl 3:11), since creatures are accountable to their Creator (e.g., Eccl 12:1; Prov 14:31). The first Yahweh speech (chs. 38–39) outlines how God is creator of the physical and animal spheres, a truth already known to Job. In chapter 10 Job outlines how God has carefully and intricately made him in a physical sense (10:3, 8-11), and has also extended to him life, steadfast love, and care (10:12).

Job sees that he has moral obligations to God as a result of his creation, most clearly in chapter 31. Here he identifies his maker as "God above" and "the Almighty on high" (31:2) who numbers all his steps (31:4). He calls on God to test him by weighing his actions in a pair of scales (31:6), and seeks to avoid being "false to God above" (31:28). He expects to have to give an account to God of his treatment of his servants (31:14). This is particularly significant because it is based on the fact that God has made both Job and his servants (31:15). Being a creature of God brings obligations toward him and others.

Allied to the notion that God is the Creator is the idea that the God who has all things in his hand (12:10) actively watches over creation. This point is made several times by Job. God is seen as the one who has his eye on humans (7:8), and is called "the watcher of humanity" (7:20). Indeed, it is a recurring motif, since he later depicts God as watching him (10:14) and seeing all his ways (31:4). This last reference is significant in that God seeing his ways is linked with numbering his steps, and leads on to evaluating his conduct (31:6). Life is lived, according to Job, in the sight of a watching God who will call humans to account.

A Robust and Positive View of Humanity

A significant landmark in our understanding of the OT view of humanity was Brueggemann's *In Man We Trust*. He contended that the wisdom strand asserted a positive place for humanity in God's purposes: "Creation is viewed as a good place to live, a healthy environment, intended by God to be enjoyed. It is a place of orderliness and security, a friendly place, a healthy environment, one which opens to man its fruits and its secrets if he will have it so."[161] Of course, this is based largely on the book of Proverbs, but such is the background to the intrawisdom discussion evident in the book of Job. Brueggemann suggests that we have largely neglected those traditions that affirm the world, celebrate culture, and affirm human responsibility and capability. In particular, the criterion for one's actions is whether an intended act helps to order and make sense of the world. This gives striking importance to human activity in God's creation.

However, a more careful look at the protest wisdom of Job and Ecclesiastes might put some qualifications on this perspective. Job, for example, strongly emphasizes that humans are not God, and that our human choices are rendered more difficult by our imperfect knowledge. However, even Job's complaints to God are based on a high view of where humans fit in God's purposes. At least we can say that a noble view of humanity is a significant strand in the book of Job.

Indeed, Job contributes many insights for a better understanding of human potential. Job's successful passing of the accuser's test (1:9, 11) establishes that he does fear God for nothing, and thus it is humanly possible to have faith in God without ulterior motives. Sincere and wholehearted human faith is celebrated by the God who boasts about Job (2:3).

This robust view of human value and potential contrasts with the opinions of Job's friends. They are concerned to defend God's honor, but think that this requires a denigration of humanity. In his first speech, Eliphaz asks (with the implied answer no) whether any person can be pure or in the right before God their maker (4:17), for not even the angels are reliable (4:18). People are fragile like clay and dust and so will be crushed like the moth (4:19). Bergant comments that "the entire unit is a poetic statement of the inability of man, precisely because he is man, to be righteous/clean before God."[162] Eliphaz comes back to a similar idea in 15:14-16 — humans cannot be pure or righteous (15:14), nor are the angels (15:15), and the parallelism suggests that he thinks that all humans are abominable, corrupt, and unjust (15:16). In his final speech, he concludes that humans cannot benefit God in any way (22:2a). While Bildad and Zophar tend to focus on wicked humans (e.g., chs. 18 and 20), their failure to talk about righteous people implies that they do not think there are many of them. Bildad's position is made clearer in his final short speech, when he

161. Brueggemann, *In Man We Trust*, 25
162. Bergant, "Anthropological Traditions and Motifs," 164.

picks up Eliphaz's idea that humans cannot be pure or in the right (25:4; see 4:17; 15:14). His conclusion — indeed, the last words spoken by the friends — is that humans are maggots and worms (25:6).[163] It is the friends in the book who have a low view of humanity. While God rebukes them for what they say about him in the dialogue, the book as a whole also rejects this negative assessment of human beings.

Elihu, focusing on Job's words in the debate, delivers his verdict that humans cannot summon God to appear (34:23; 35:13-14). This is based on a view of God as transcendent and just (35:5-7; 36:5; 34:10-15; 36:22–37:23), while humans are from the dust (34:15b) and simply pieces of common clay (33:6) who are in need of a mediator (33:23-26). He concludes that the appropriate human response to God is simply to fear him (37:24a).

Job, by contrast, expresses his deepest human longing as the restoration of his relationship with God (e.g., 14:15). It is an image of relationship, of calling and responding, and of finding his true humanity through his connection with God. It is a robust and positive view of what it means to be a person.

God's speeches say very little about humans, although he does mention that his purposes are wider than humanity (38:26). However, his point is picked up by Job, who concedes that, as a human being, he spoke with limited knowledge (42:3). God's rebuke of the friends and his siding with Job (42:7-8) suggest that Job's robust view of humanity is closer to the mark than the negative view of the friends.

Humans and Sin

The wisdom literature of the OT does not deny the sinfulness of humanity, nor does it draw particular attention to it. This is particularly the case in the book of Job. Job is pictured not as sinless but as utterly righteous (1:1, 8; 2:3), so that his suffering could not be accounted for on the basis of any supposed wickedness. Job's insistence throughout his speeches is that the extent of his afflictions does not reflect his sin. He concedes that he may sin (e.g., 10:14), but objects to the suggestion of the friends that this is only a temporary and minor setback (as in 5:17-19) or even that he has been let off lightly (11:6c). Job insists that his integrity extends even to his internal thoughts and attitudes (31:1, 9, 24-25, 29), not simply to his outward actions.

---

163. Nam, *Talking about God,* 57, sees a change in focus from humanity in 4:17-21 to sinful man in 15:14-16, and sees this developed by Bildad into the "infernal being of mortals" in 25:4-6, so that through the dialogue there is a degrading of humanity.

Although some have used the book of Job as a source for the doctrine of original sin, this needs to be reconsidered. Origen, for example, argued that Job 14:4-5, together with Psalm 51, established the doctrine of original sin, in that this "taint of sin" affects every human being.[164] Similar passages in 4:17 and 25:4 are best understood as referring to the actual sinfulness of people rather than the original, inherited sinfulness. Along similar lines, Eliphaz's comment that "man is born to trouble as the sparks fly upward" (5:7) is not a statement about the human inclination to sin, but simply that living in the real world is often difficult. It should also be remembered that these references largely come from Job's friends. Since they are rebuked in the book as a whole (42:7-8), it is foolhardy to build a case based on their words.

Humans as Social Creatures

While the focus in the wisdom books generally is on individuals, the book of Job also understands that all individuals are part of a community. This book does not confine itself simply to Job's personal struggle for faith. This is clear at the very beginning of the book, when Job offers sacrifices for his whole family (1:4-5). His relationships are such that three friends come from a distance to comfort and console him (2:11). Chapter 29 outlines what Job's life was like before it was shattered by disaster, and it is a picture of life in vibrant community. His prime time was when he was surrounded by his children (29:5) and had earned the respect of others in the city (29:7-11). He fulfilled his obligations to the marginalized by caring for the poor, the widows, the orphans, the blind, the lame, and the needy (29:12-17).

This social dimension to Job's understanding of human life is even more clearly reflected in the oath of clearance in chapter 31. The picture of righteousness that can be distilled from this oath is one that affects sexuality, marriage, justice for the powerless, active care of the needy, proper use of wealth, inner attitudes toward others, and even opening up your house to those in need of a bed. This is a series of cameos that make clear that no person is an island insulated from the needs of our fellow human beings. It is therefore most fitting that, at the end of the book, Job is restored to an active part in society (42:11).

Job's struggles throughout the book are intensely personal, but Job always understands that he is part of a community of other human beings.

---

164. Origen, *Commentary on Romans,* cited in McDonald, *Christian View of Man,* 54.

God

The strong emphasis on Job's human struggle might suggest that the nature of God is not a major concern of the book. Such a view would not take sufficient account of the fact that Job's anguish is largely a consequence of trying to fathom God's character and purposes in the light of Job's changed circumstances. *God* is Job's issue. What is he like? What is he doing? Does he care? Can I keep on trusting him? This has led a number of scholars to claim that the book is as much about God as it is about Job.[165] While this may be taking it a bit far, the emphasis in the book on the relationship between God and humans requires any study of the theological themes of Job to give due weight to what it says about both humanity and God.

Names of God

Five names are used for God in Job: El, Eloah, Elohim, Shaddai, and Yahweh. El and Eloah are general names for God, with Elohim the plural form of Eloah. The majority of references to God in Job use El (118 times), while in the Elihu section Elohim is used exclusively.[166] Shaddai is the name used by God to make himself known to the patriarchs according to Exod 6:3, and is translated as "Almighty" in most English versions, following the lead of the Greek (LXX) and Latin (Vulgate) translations.[167] Shaddai occurs alone in 11 verses in Job, and in combinations with El or Eloah in 17 other verses. Of the 48 OT references to Shaddai, 31 of them are in Job, 16 in the mouths of the friends and Elihu and 14 from Job. The other one (40:2) comes from God himself.[168] The three principal names of God in the dialogue are El, Eloah, and Shaddai, and they are paralleled in 27:2-3, 8-11 (vv. 2-3, all three; in v. 8 Eloah and El; in vv. 10-11, El and Shaddai twice in parallel). The most common sequence is El followed by Shaddai (8:3, 5; 15:25; 22:17; 23:16; 27:2, 11, 13; 33:4; 34:10, 12; 35:13).[169] The names sometimes emphasize different aspects of God. Thus, in the dialogue, Shaddai is never used in the doxological passages (5:8-16; 9:2-10; 12:13-25) but only in passages that deal with the human individual (5:17; 6:4; 8:5; 29:5; 31:35).[170]

---

165. Habel, "In Defense of God the Sage," 21; Clifford, "God Who Makes People Wise," 65.

166. Oswalt, "God," 252.

167. This factual information is well set out in Reyburn, *Book of Job*, 21-24, on which this section is based. See also Reymond, *New Systematic Theology*, 153-60.

168. Oswalt, "God," 252.

169. Reyburn, *Book of Job*, 22.

170. Nam, *Talking about God*, 60.

The name "Yahweh," often translated "the LORD" to avoid pronouncing the sacred divine name, is used in the rest of the OT to describe the covenant God of Israel. Since the story of Job is set in patriarchal times (before the establishment of Israel as a nation), and outside the promised land, it is not surprising to see that the three friends, as well as Elihu, do not refer to God as Yahweh, and Job does so only twice — once in the prologue in a formulaic saying (1:21) and once in the dialogue (12:9). "Yahweh" is used 38 times, mostly in the prologue and epilogue, but also in the Yahweh speeches (38:1; 40:1, 3, 6; 42:1).[171] In the prologue, while the narrator uses "Yahweh," God himself uses "Elohim" (1:8; 2:3), as does Job (1:5; 2:10), the messenger (1:16), Job's wife (2:9), and the accuser (1:9). In the dialogues the name Elohim is used only twice (both parallel to El, 5:8; 20:29).[172]

There seems to be a lot of interchangeability of names, referring to the same deity but in fairly generic terms. The few references to Yahweh makes sense in the setting, but the occasional slip (1:21; 12:9) probably reflects a theological conviction that the God who is generally described generically by a number of titles is the same as the God of the rest of the OT. Much of the terminology (especially the infrequent use of "Yahweh") can be accounted for on the basis that the issues being dealt with are not confined to those relevant for the covenant believer. What is clear in the book is that the variety of names for God does not imply a plurality of gods, but are simply different terms for the one God.

God in the Prologue

The prologue is a potentially fruitful source of information as the narrator describes God and his setting, while God both speaks and acts. However, some scholars react against the view of God they discern in these opening chapters. Campbell, for example, complains, "It may be storytelling, but any sense of human decency is outraged by it.... What is shocking is that God should be presented as responsible for such fate, apparently motivated by pride, and inflicting such disaster on a faithful follower."[173] In a similar vein, Richard Clifford observes, "Perhaps no scene in Job is more disturbing than Yahweh betting with the Satan, handing over Job's family and finally Job himself to the malevolent Satan in a wager on whether Job reveres God for love."[174] Habel notes that the

---

171. Oswalt, "God," 252.
172. Reyburn, *Book of Job*, 22.
173. Campbell, "Book of Job," 16.
174. Clifford, "God Who Makes People Wise," 63.

way God is depicted as acting in the conversations with the accuser seems to be arbitrary, out of character, and not typical of the wisdom tradition.[175] A closer look is in order.

If the book is understood as a wisdom tale rather than an historical tale, then at least part of this difficulty dissipates. The transaction between Yahweh and the accuser is then simply literary artistry designed to draw attention to the issue of whether rightly motivated human faith is possible. It is not meant as a source for the characterization of the deity. In the introduction, I have suggested that this is the most likely literary genre for the book. On this view, the tests are not meant to disclose God's character, but simply to precipitate the raising of the opinions and issues that are the subject of the book.

Even if the book is understood more historically, certain observations can still be made. First, even in this heavenly court setting, there is neither dualism nor any suggestion of deities who can rival Yahweh. The accuser is not pictured as a god, and can only act if Yahweh permits it (1:12; 2:3, 6). God is pictured as the one who is actively ruling his world as the sovereign Lord, who can determine from the heavenly court what will happen on earth.

Second, while many view God's permission to let the accuser act on earth as arbitrary, no explanation is given about why God does so. To interpret God's actions as accepting a wager, or gambling with Job's life, is based on an unfounded assumption that God is being manipulated by the accuser. Much more likely is the view that God permits this suffering for his own (unexplained, but good) purposes, though it is not clear whether these purposes are simply good for Job or for humanity as a whole. While the extent of Job's suffering does not appear to be in his interests, the refining and confirming of his faith is certainly a long-term benefit. At the very least, the representation of God in the Yahweh speeches and epilogue should lead us to view generously God's motives and purposes in the prologue, rather than to impute shady motives to God, or to picture him as powerless or outmaneuvered.

Third, the portrayal of God as the one who has absolute freedom is one that many find offensive, but may nonetheless be true. Modern men and women — a bit like the friends — often want God to act in predictable and self-evidently good ways, but the book as a whole resists our putting constraints on God. The prologue unsettles us as readers because it presupposes that God is free to do as he likes and does not have to run his plans past an ethics committee for approval.

Thus, while the opening story raises questions for us about the nature of God, the best way to deal with these questions is to read on and see what the book as a whole tells us about God's character and purposes. We are simply not

175. Habel, "In Defense of God the Sage," 26.

told why God permits these disasters to happen, but we are left in no doubt that God is running the show. The prologue is not so much harmful to our image of God, but rather a challenge to our preconceived ideas. It seems to unsettle and provoke readers, but the literary effect is to cause us to want to read on in search of a resolution.

God according to the Friends

The friends have articulated an understanding or doctrine of God, although they are rebuked for what they have spoken about God (42:7-8). Yet the dialogue only works because so much of what the friends say sounds like truth rather than gross error. This is clear from the study of each of the friends.

Eliphaz begins by asserting that God's ways and actions cannot be fully explored or fathomed (5:9). He insists that God is the giver of water, which sustains life (5:10), and that he is active in and over his creation to both care for the needy and disavantaged, and to punish the wicked (5:11-16). Nam describes 5:8-16 as "a hymnic description of divine acts."[176] God's activity is sometimes seen in using suffering to discipline humans (5:17), and in such situations he is a God who will deliver and restore (5:18-27). The key motif here is that God is able to bring about reversal due to his graciousness evident in his promises of protection and prosperity.[177]

Bildad also wishes to speak in defense of the Almighty. God never perverts justice or rejects a blameless or righteous person (8:3, 20-22), for justice is at the very heart of God's character. Thus Bildad insists that God punishes the wicked (18:5-21), though possibly through the agency of others. In his final brief speech, he depicts God as a powerful ruler over both the cosmos and human armies (25:2-3).

Zophar is less forthcoming in his description of the nature and activity of God. However, he proclaims that God's wisdom and understanding are far beyond human comprehension (11:6-9), and his power is irresistible (11:10). He is a God who blesses the righteous and brings the wicked to judgment (11:13-20). Zophar appears to place greater emphasis on God's judgment of the ungodly (rather than his prospering of the righteous), as this theme entirely fills his final speech in chapter 20. Nam concludes that Zophar views God as "mysterious, omniscient and retributive."[178]

176. Nam, *Talking about God*, 38-39.
177. Ibid., 40.
178. Ibid., 56.

In the light of what they have said, how is it that they have not spoken of God what is right (42:7-8)? God's verdict in 42:7-8 is not a condemnation of their orthodox beliefs about God and his nature, but rather a rebuke of their pronouncements about God's activity in general and specifically as it touches Job. They have not correctly described how God acts in his world, for they each assume that God can only act on the basis of rewarding human righteousness and punishing human wickedness. God is not the initiator or the one who sets the world running, but is simply "a God who reacts,"[179] or "the engineer of the mechanisms of retribution."[180]

As a result of this, they all have another common feature. The friends insist that, in Job's case, the way forward is for Job to repent in order to restore God's favor. This is seen in the speeches of Eliphaz (5:8, 18-20; 22:21-24), Bildad (8:5), and Zophar (11:13-14).[181] Their assumption about God's activity is that God must be correcting or punishing Job, so Job must repent. They are thus wrong in their belief about what God is doing to Job.

Thus the friends are rebuked for strident views about what God is doing in his world, not for what God is like. Gregory Parsons expresses it well: "Though the three friends basically have an orthodox view of God, they often misapply the doctrine to Job's situation."[182] For this reason, God says that they have not spoken of him what is right.

Job's Understanding of God

On the other hand, God has announced that Job has spoken about him what is right, and this makes Job's words an important place to look for the book's doctrine of God. Some scholars view this verdict with suspicion. T. N. D. Mettinger, for example, claims that "the Job speeches depict a God who is not merely amoral but actively immoral, the omnipotent tyrant, the cosmic thug."[183] Such an assertion needs to be tested by a closer look at Job's words.

The prologue begins with Job seeing God as one worthy of respect ("fear," 1:1) and worship (1:5). After his losses, he acknowledges that God has the power of life and death ("the LORD gave, and the LORD has taken away," 1:21), and the one who can send both prosperity and disaster (2:10).

In the self-lament that opens the dialogue, Job still sees that God has

179. Habel, "In Defense of God the Sage," 27.
180. Mettinger, "God of Job," 41.
181. Parsons, "Job, Theology of," 416.
182. Ibid., 415. See also Oswalt, "God," 254.
183. Mettinger, "God of Job," 44.

power over birth and death (3:3-4) and is actively working through disasters ("God has hedged in," 3:23). Nam understands Job cursing the day of his birth as a challenge to God as creator, but this is best seen as an expression of his anguish.[184] His next speech begins with Job addressing the friends, and he again reveals his view that God has power over life and death (6:8-9) and the power to send disaster (6:4). Thus, from the very beginning, Job understands God's active control over the world and his intervention in it. Parsons describes this as "an ambivalent view of his Maker."[185]

As the dialogue continues, Job reveals his fuller understanding of God. Chapter 9 has a long description of God as "wise in heart and mighty in strength" (9:4). He outlines God's unstoppable power in the heavens and earth over mountains, the sun, stars, and the sea (9:4-9) before concluding that God does more great and marvelous things in creation than can be counted (9:10). His power is irresistible (9:12). Behind all this is a strong view of God as creator and sustainer of creation.

This picture of God active in his creation is filled out further in chapter 26. He catalogues God's hands-on involvement in the cosmos — the earth, the clouds, the moon, the seas, the skies (26:7-13). This is filled out further by his control over Rahab (26:12b) and "the fleeing serpent" (26:13b), both of which are images of anti-God forces in the created world, but which are under God's control.[186] Similarly, Sheol and Abaddon, death and destruction, are powerless before God (26:6). Thus Job understands that God is not only the creator and sustainer, but also the one who controls evil, death, and destruction.

Consistent throughout the book is Job's unshakable belief in God's unrivaled power. God is able to bring about his goals and cannot be blocked (23:13-14). After the Yahweh speeches, Job voices the view that he has held at all times in the book — that God can do all things and that no purpose of his can be thwarted (42:2). This is not a new understanding for Job but simply a restatement of the view he has held throughout. There is never a question in Job's mind about whether God is able to intervene or achieve his purpose.

This high view of God is also evident in chapter 12. God is again portrayed as the source and sustainer of all forms of life (12:7-10). The life and breath of every living thing is in his hands (12:10). Job depicts God as both mighty and wise (having counsel and understanding, 12:13, 16), and fills this out with an extensive description of his activity in creation and in daily life (12:14-25). Many of these examples could be described from a human viewpoint as disasters, with

---

184. Nam, *Talking about God,* 77-78.
185. Parsons, "Job, Theology of," 416.
186. Ibid.

counselors and priests stripped bare (12:17, 19), and kings, princes, nations and the mighty brought low (12:18-25). He is a God who intervenes in the real world to bring about his purposes.

Job also regards God as the one who should judge the wicked. This is assumed in chapter 21, as he complains about when the godless and unrighteous seem to prosper (21:7-18), and he calls on God to judge them (21:19-20).[187] The goal is that they should be repaid according to what they have done (21:31). Similarly in chapter 27, he outlines that God is responsible for punishing the wicked (27:7-23).

Job's summing up also reveals further aspects of his understanding of God. In 29:2-5 he explores his understanding of God prior to the disasters that came upon him. Here he speaks of God watching over and protecting him (29:2-3), of experiencing God's friendship (29:4), and God being with him (29:5a) and giving him light to walk by (29:3). The combined picture is one of God blessing him as a righteous person (29:14). However, he also speaks of God being active in reversing his circumstances (30:11, 19). In his oath of clearance Job discloses his belief that God is the one to whom will give account (31:2, 6, 14, 23, 28), the creator of all human beings (31:15), and the God who expects active justice from his people. The entire chapter outlines what God values in society.

It is clear from this survey that Job has a big view of God as the creator and sustainer of the cosmos. Even in the midst of his suffering, he does not come to believe that God is just one among many deities, or that God is only partly in control. He refuses to shrink God down to explain his circumstances. He has known what God was like (29:2-5), and he clings to that view of God even when his present situation makes no sense.

While he shares with the friends the retribution framework that God punishes the wicked and rewards the righteous, he diverges from them when his circumstances can no longer be explained on that basis. The friends insist that Job must be a sinner who needs to repent, for God must act only on the principle of human retributive justice. Since he is suffering, it must mean that he is a sinner.

Job, however, holds in tension a firm belief that God is a God of justice and that God is not dealing with him justly. He speaks of God treating him as a target (6:4) and having taken his right to justice (27:2). He complains that God, in treating him (wrongly) as an enemy (6:4; 13:24-28; 16:9-14; 19:6-12), is oppressing (7:12-21; 10:14-17; 14:3-4) and unfairly condemning him (7:21; 9:19-20,

---

187. Clifford, "God Who Makes People Wise," 64, suggests that at this point Job views God as an enemy.

25-35; 10:14-15).[188] Yet this represents Job's sense of loss and confusion, not his settled convictions about the character of God. He is seeking to hold together a belief in God's goodness and justice, and a conviction of his own basic righteousness before God. Job's speeches evidence this struggle to hold on to both.

In the end, Job does speak rightly about God because he refuses to reduce his view of God and yet proclaims that his current circumstances cannot be explained by God acting in accordance with the principles of human retributive justice. Job's friends insisted that God's treatment of Job was based on retributive justice — and they were wrong. Job insisted that God's treatment of him could not be based simply on retributive justice — and Job was right. Job shares the same theological presupposition as the friends but draws a different conclusion about God's actions.[189] What Job needed to see, however, was that God's active ruling of his world is much bigger than this principle of retribution, and this broadening of Job's understanding of God's activity is achieved in the Yahweh speeches.

The God Who Appears

In chapters 32–37 Elihu presents the human verdict on the friends and Job, but incidentally makes comments about the nature of God. Like the friends, he makes a number of true statements about God's nature. In chapter 34 he observes that God will not act wickedly (34:12), is in charge of the earth (34:13), has the power of life and death (34:14-15), is just, righteous, and powerful (34:17), and sees the ways of all people (34:21-22). Elsewhere he speaks of God's power, wisdom, and justice (36:5-6), and of his great and majestic work in nature (37:1-2, 14-18, 22-24). He dispenses lightning (36:32-33) and thunder (37:2-5), but his ways are beyond human understanding (36:29).

Against Job's view that God's ways are hidden, Elihu argues that God does make himself known in various ways (dreams, pain, illness, and angels — 33:13-23).[190] While this may be true, it is not the way God is speaking in Job's case. Indeed, Elihu's conclusion that God will not appear to humans (34:23) is certainly overridden by the coming of Yahweh in the theophany. Thus a key part of Elihu's role is to be a theological foil to Yahweh, and so we should not try to build too much on his view of God.

A much more fruitful and accurate source of information is what God

---

188. Nam, *Talking about God*, 73; Parsons, "Job, Theology of," 416.

189. Nam, *Talking about God*, 105.

190. Parsons, "Job, Theology of," 416.

discloses about himself when he appears and speaks. Habel rightly notes, "The reply of God from the whirlwind . . . offers a profound alternative to the various characterizations of God offered in the rest of the book."[191] In the first Yahweh speech, we see that he is lord over the physical earth (38:4-21), over the weather or "forces of nature" (38:22-38), and over the animal world (38:39–39:30). The implied answer to most of God's rhetorical questions ("no one but the Lord") highlights God's sovereignty as the ruler of the universe. His sovereignty is not restrained by his having to act according to an inflexible doctrine of retribution.

He is the one who has a plan or design for creation (38:2) and who possesses knowledge; hence he can rebuke Job for not speaking with knowledge (38:2). The picture that emerges from 38:4-7 is that God is "a God of stability and precision, not anarchy and disorder."[192] He is the creator, architect, and planner of the physical world, the one who knows it exhaustively. He is the one who imposes boundaries (e.g., on the sea, 38:10-11). He is the one who exercises his power to control the natural world. According to Nam, the cosmological section (38:4-21) establishes three truths about God: "First, God is the wise designer of creation who upholds the world order within it. . . . Second, Yahweh is the sovereign lord who can control such a hostile force as the sea. . . . Third, Yahweh is the recreator of the cosmic and moral world as the sustainer of creation."[193] Thus there is a clear picture of God as the one who is purposefully working out his plans in creation and sustaining the physical world. This includes some moral shaping of the world, in that the wicked are shaken out of creation (38:13, 15), an image that implies God's moral ordering of the world.

God's control of the weather forces means that he can use them to reward and punish (38:22-23) and to sustain life through water in its various forms (38:22-30). God is also in control of the heavenly bodies (38:31-33), which means there are no rival forces to God in the heavenlies. The mention of wisdom and understanding in 38:36-37 shows that God alone is able to attain his divine purposes for his creation.

The point of the animal section (38:39–39:30) is that God is sovereign over even the most remote and apparently useless members of the animal world. In particular, "the fabulously stupid ostrich is stupid by design (39:13-18). The speech shows that the world includes the useful, the bizarre, and even the playful, all by God's design."[194] He is the creator, sustainer, and preserver of those animals beyond human reach and control. As Nam observes, "Yahweh is the

---

191. Habel, "In Defense of God the Sage," 21. On 33 he notes that this speech is "God talking about God."

192. Ibid., 34.

193. Nam, *Talking about God*, 134-35.

194. Clifford, "God Who Makes People Wise," 64.

patron of life itself in his created world. He facilitates freedom, hilarity, agility, and hostility in the wild animals."[195] All this is done in a manner far beyond Job's understanding.

The manner of God's ordering his creation makes clear that his concerns are wider than humans alone. He is sovereign over all of creation, not just humanity, and so causes rain to fall where there are no humans (38:26-27). The series of impossible questions indicates that God's ordering of his cosmos is beyond human comprehension.

It is also worth noting that God's dominion allows for chaotic forces. There is room for the destructive lightning flashes (38:35), and for animals to feed on their prey (38:39, 41; 39:29-30). The ostrich eggs can be crushed (39:15) and the young mistreated (39:16). The spirited warhorse is involved in battle (39:21-25), which will lead to death and destruction. This is not a sanitized playground, but the real, fallen world over which God is actively ruling.

In terms of a doctrine of God, this first speech is a celebration of God's freedom and active sovereignty. There is no mention of any rules that bind God to act in certain ways. God is the main actor, not simply a reactor to others, whether human or not. God is certainly active in his creation, but neither threatened by it nor dependent on it. The God of the friends seems to be a hollow and shrunken version of the one who appears and speaks in chapters 38–41. No human dogma, even that God must act with justice, can bind or restrict God (41:11, cited in Rom 11:35). While God is undoubtedly just, his ordering of the world is broader than a reductionistic human concept of retributive justice in which he can do no more than reward righteousness and punish wickedness. He can and does run the universe as its creator and sustainer.

In Job 40:8 God raises the issue of justice, which he develops in his second speech. Whether the figures of Behemoth and Leviathan are mythological symbols of cosmic chaos (or even Death and Satan) or natural creatures described hyperbolically, the point of chapters 40–41 is that even the most powerful rival forces are under God's complete control, yet beyond human mastery. Since Behemoth was the "first of the works of God" (40:19), God's control over this primal creature implies his power over all others. The example of Behemoth shows that Job's belief that he knew how the world runs was overly optimistic. Behemoth also represents all those who are proud and wicked (40:12), with the implication that God is sovereign over all of them as well.

In terms of Leviathan, there is the motif of the control or hunt (41:1-11) and the physical description of him (41:12-34). In 41:12 Leviathan is pictured as the high point of God's creation, which is unpacked in the description that

---

195. Nam, *Talking about God*, 145.

follows. Nam rightly points out that "Yahweh uses Leviathan to demonstrate divine control of even the most awesome forces in the created world."[196] This is a picture of a God who has subdued and organized chaos to enable living creatures to keep on dwelling in the created world. This second speech proclaims that "God *can* control ultimate cosmic evil (symbolized by the land beast Behemoth and the sea beast Leviathan) but does not necessarily exercise control for the benefit of human beings."[197] It is at least clear in the case of Behemoth and Leviathan that no powers in the world are beyond the control of God.[198] God is able to contain evil, chaos, and destruction in whatever form.

Overall, the Yahweh speeches depict a God who is far beyond the formulas of the friends, and even the most imaginative hopes of Job. Yahweh is a God without rivals and without peers. He is not bound by human rules, but free and sovereign to implement his goals and design. His activity in his creation cannot be reduced down, even to the important principle of justice. As he deals with evil and chaos, he establishes his purposes and cannot be called to account. He is to be treated as the Lord of the universe, which he actively rules and sustains.

God in the Book as a Whole

The God of the book of Job is portrayed in ways that differ from (yet are consistent with) much of the rest of the OT. In this book, there is no focus on God active in history in rescuing his chosen people, but rather an elaboration of the God who is sovereign over all humanity and the entire creation. God owns and controls all of the cosmos. This picture peaks in the Yahweh speeches, and is thoroughly consistent with that of the other wisdom books.

Clifford has observed, "The book skillfully plays off the portraits of God drawn by Job and by the friends against the portrait of the prologue, divine speeches, and epilogue."[199] While the friends speak with great authority, the god they describe is only a shadow of the one who reveals himself in the theophany. Their reductionistic views satisfy neither Job nor God himself. In the final chapter, Job concedes that he spoke with limited knowledge of the God who was far beyond his comprehension (42:3), and it is this realization that enables him to move in a new direction.

196. Ibid., 158.
197. Clifford, "God Who Makes People Wise," 65.
198. Nam, *Talking about God,* 163.
199. Clifford, "God Who Makes People Wise," 65.

Yet the book does not just describe God as a majestic creator. Yahweh's endorsement of Job as one who has spoken of him what is right (42:7-8) implies that he also cares for human beings who struggle to cling to him in faith. Indeed, "Yahweh proves to be the God of cosmic justice and wisdom and, astonishingly, also of compassionate commitment to Job."[200] God is big enough to take genuine human hurt and bewilderment, and is not shattered by Job's protests, questions, and even accusations. Yahweh is thoroughly committed to the rawness of relationships with humans who trust him. He is not simply a cosmic God, but is also one who draws near to those who draw near to him.

Thus the book of Job makes a distinctive and rich contribution to the depiction of Yahweh in the OT. The one who is elsewhere depicted as the covenant God who intervenes in history is here seen as the creator and sustainer of the universe, and the one who relates to trusting — if protesting — human beings.

Creation

Wisdom and Creation

One of the distinctive features of the OT wisdom books is an emphasis on God as creator and sustainer of the whole world rather than simply the redeemer of Israel. God's redemptive work in history is not being denied, but neither is it the particular focus of wisdom literature. Instead, the concept of creation provides the theological undergirding for Israelite wisdom literature. Walther Zimmerli's maxim, "Wisdom thinks resolutely with the framework of a theology of creation," is often quoted in this regard.[201] However, Zimmerli's basis for arguing this is largely a negative one, the absence of mention of the God of Israel in the older wisdom texts, rather than the positive argument based on the frequency and importance of creation references. Zimmerli sought to anchor wisdom theology in Gen 1:28, where the Lord authorizes human dominion over and harmony with the rest of creation. He saw wisdom as growing out of this human dominion.

In early Israel the focus seems to be on the doctrine of redemption, but the doctrine of creation was always presupposed. It was the sages who moved Israel to appreciate the dimensions of a creation faith, since the wisdom mastery

---

200. Ibid., 57.

201. Zimmerli, "Place and Limit," 316. Schifferdecker, "Creation Theology," 63, notes, "Biblical Wisdom literature speaks of God primarily in terms of God's role as creator rather than in terms of God's covenant relationship with Israel or God's involvement in Israel's history."

of life depended on the regularity of observable phenomena. Leo Perdue thus also notes, "Each of the wisdom texts finds its theological center in creation."[202]

In three respects wisdom can be regarded as reflecting a "creation theology." First, in its emphasis on God as creator. Second, in its emphasis on human beings as human beings (not Israelites — Yahweh is the God of the world and its inhabitants, not simply a national deity). Third, in its emphasis on the natural world as divinely ordered. All three of these emphases are prominent.

The overall picture in the wisdom texts is that of a world well ordered, at least partially comprehensible with the forces of chaos kept under control. Wisdom thus sought to provide some explanation for the experience of this wholesome order in the world, an order that could be recognized, described, and catalogued. Wisdom can thus be seen as a search for at least a certain regularity in the diverse phenomena of this world. In this sense the search for wisdom is a search for the order in creation. There are interrelationships in this world, and all things are related to their Creator, who oversees his cosmos.[203] The idea of the active sovereignty of God is also noted by Perdue: "for the sages, God is the universal deity who created and providentially guides the world and its inhabitants."[204] It is important to remember that his sovereign rule is seen not only in the fact of creation, but even more so in his providential rule of what has been brought into being.

Of course, there are some differences among the wisdom books. While they all focus on God as the creator, they differ on their particular emphases.[205] While Proverbs focuses on order in creation (and Song of Songs delights in one specific dimension of the human creation), Ecclesiastes sees that this creational order is sometimes confused and confusing. A key emphasis in the book of Job is on the hiddenness of God's purposes in creation, as Job and his friends never discover what has occurred in the heavenly court scenes of the prologue (1:6-12; 2:1-6).

At the very least, then, it is clear that sages glean their truths from their experience of the world, of creation, rather than God's saving actions, and in this sense wisdom theology is strongly dependent on creation theology as one of its key strands. The issues that emerge in the book of Job include whether God is still active and in charge of his creation and, if so, in what ways. Job will also explore whether God's purposes in creation and for human beings are good.

202. Perdue, *Wisdom and Creation*, 340.
203. Murphy, *Tree of Life*, 124.
204. Perdue, *Wisdom and Creation*, 327.
205. Schifferdecker, "Creation Theology," 63. As an example, she mentions humanity's role in creation.

Creation in the Prologue and Dialogue

At the outset of his struggle of faith, Job understands God to be the creator and sustainer. Job's first reaction to his loss is that God is free as the creator to give and take away as he chooses (1:21). He thus starts from the stance that God is in charge of his creation, and that he has been made by God and must acknowledge his creator.[206]

In the heavenly court scenes, the accuser is not just questioning Job but also, by implication, God's management of the universe. He is implying that God is rewarding Job for a virtue he does not possess, as Job has simply disguised his self-interest (1:9-11). Thus, while Job is certainly being tested, the issue at stake is whether God has ordered his creation in accordance with what is right.

Terence Fretheim suggests that creation theology is seen most clearly in the dialogue in 3:3-9; 7:16-19; 9:4-24; 10:8-13; 12:13-25; 25:1-6; and 26:5-14.[207] It is not surprising to find creation theology in the dialogue, given that the protagonists are among "the wise." Several of these speeches contain hymn-like passages (9:5-10; 26:5-14), but not all of them. Job also urges his friends to learn from the natural world (12:7-10; 14:7-12, 18-19; 24:5, 19). The image of God as creator overcoming the forces of chaos is reflected in the dialogue (3:8; 7:12; 9:8, 13; 26:12-13), though Kathryn Schifferdecker suggests that the sea and Leviathan are more "wild and beautiful forces in which God takes delight" rather than images of chaos.[208]

Some understand Job's cursing the day of his birth in chapter 3 as Job asking for the undoing of creation, and thus a rebellion against the God who orders creation.[209] But his despairing and anguished longings that things could have worked out differently is exactly like many modern pastoral situations (e.g., death in a car or plane crash, divorce, rape) where people wish that they could turn back time or wind the clock back. These are expressions of deep pain, and issue from a desperate desire that matters could have turned out differently, not an attempt to usurp the role of the God who orders time. Job's self-curse is not rebellion against the one who has ordered creation — it is a cry of deep pain from one who is overwhelmed by his loss. Hartley, who classifies Job's words

---

206. Prideaux, "Creator and the Creature," 10-11. On 136 he adds that "his fundamental understanding of his relationship to God is defined in terms of him being a creature of the Creator God."

207. Fretheim, *God and the World*, 220.

208. Schifferdecker, "Creation Theology," 63-64. This theme will be later picked up in the Yahweh speeches (38:8-11; 41:1-34).

209. See the debate outlined in the commentary.

as a "counter-cosmic incantation," suggests that it is best to see these words as revealing the acuteness of Job's misery.[210]

Chapters 7 and 14 have been dealt with in the section on humanity, which could be seen as a subset of creation theology. One significant feature of these passages is that they echo the creation rather than redemption threads of the OT. Thus 7:16-19 appears to be an allusion to Psalm 8, though it establishes a different point. Furthermore, the imagery in Job 14 is creational, as humans are compared to other aspects of the created world. They are like a withering flower (14:2); they are worse off than a tree (14:7-10); they dry up like receding water (14:11-12); and their fading hopes are like mountains, rocks, stones, and soil that is worn down and washed away (14:18-19). Thus not only the theology but also the imagery is creation-based.

Job's poetic description of God as a powerful creator in 9:5-10 shows that his basic assumption is of the greatness and unrivaled power of the God of creation. He is also the one who determines what happens in the creation he sustains, and so he concludes in v. 24, "If it is not he, who then is it?" Later in this speech Job describes himself as God's creature ("the work of your hands," 10:3), and elaborates on his self-understanding in 10:8-12. Here he sees God actively involved in making him, and uses this truth as the foundation for asking God why he has allowed his current situation to come into being (10:18).

In chapter 12 Job uses examples drawn from creation such as the beasts, birds, plants, and fish (12:7-8), and then concludes that God is actively at work since the life of every living creature, and the breath of every human being, is under his control (12:9-10). This image of God active in his world is filled out in 12:13-25 as Job explores God's activity in creation (e.g., 12:15, 22) and in everyday life.

The third cycle of speeches shows that this emphasis on God as creator is not left behind as the debate proceeds. Eliphaz describes God as high in the heavens, and draws conclusions from the height of the stars and the thickness of the clouds (22:12-14). Job responds using creational imagery of donkeys and wasteland (24:5), water and vineyards (24:19), and harvested grain (24:24). Bildad sees the deity as God "in his high heaven" (25:2), and compares humans to maggots or worms (25:6). Job gives an extended description of God's majesty and power in the creation in 26:5-14, beginning with his control of destructive waters, and death and destruction (26:5-6). Job outlines God's control of the earth, seas, clouds, winds, and heavens (26:7-13) but suggests that this is simply scratching the surface (26:14a). His powerful work in creation can never be fully understood (26:14b).

---

210. Hartley, *Book of Job*, 102. This identification is based on the many parallels between Job 3:1-13 and Gen 1:1–2:4, so that this is seen as a systematic reversal of the acts of creation.

The interlude on wisdom in chapter 28 is also based on a marveling at the complexity of creation and the resourcefulness of the human creature. On the surface 28:1-11 is a description of mining, but it also speaks about how humans have observed and shaped the creation. In v. 5 corn is pictured as growing in the fields, while miners are working deep below. On the surface there is no conception of this activity under the ground. Humans show great wisdom, however, in preventing seepage in the shafts (v. 11) and in hanging by ropes to reach inaccessible areas (v. 4). The listing of precious stones and the proliferation of different words for gold in vv. 15-19 reflect a concern to comprehend and categorize the variety found in creation. This shows the concerns of the wisdom movement to classify the natural world. Finally, in vv. 23-27 God used and implanted wisdom in the creation as he made it, even though this wisdom is not fully accessible to humans.

While most of Job's summing up is a review of his past life and an outline of his current circumstances (though with occasional creational references, as in 30:29), the oath of clearance in chapter 31 provides some evidence of Job's fundamental values. It is clear from 31:13-15 that Job believes that he has a moral obligation to treat his servants well on the basis that the creator God has made all humans, both rich and poor. Since a poor person has been equally created by God, they must be treated fairly. For Job, then, the doctrine of God as creator has real moral implications for living.

Creation in the Elihu and Yahweh Speeches

One way in which Elihu acts as a theological foil for Yahweh is his introduction of creation theology in the second half of his last speech (36:22–37:24). God's greatness (36:26) and power (36:22) are filled out in his control of the weather forces, including rain, clouds, thunder, lightning, snow, whirlwinds, and ice (36:27–37:11). His management of creation is beyond human comprehension (37:5) and cannot be resisted by humans or animals (37:7-8).[211] These mighty forces in creation are controlled by God and accomplish his plans (37:12-13). Up to this point of the speech, Elihu has largely spoken truly.

However, Elihu is on shakier ground as he seeks to draw conclusions from his creational observations. In 37:14-24 he turns to apply this to Job. While rightly speaking of God's wondrous works (37:14, 16), he concludes that humans should not enter into a dispute with God (37:19-20), the very thing that Job

---

211. Perdue, *Sword and Stylus*, 151, suggests that "Elihu also asks Job impossible questions that pertain to the 'wonderful works of God.'"

has done. Instead, he urges all people (including Job) to fear God (37:24). Yet God will appear and substantially endorse Job's stance before him (42:7-8), and does not mention fearing God as something that Job needs to learn.[212] Elihu's earlier conclusion that the Almighty will not appear to humans (35:12-14) is also overridden by Yahweh speaking out of one of these weather forces, the whirlwind (38:1).

In chapters 38–39 Yahweh gives a poetic description of the physical universe, referring to the sea, dawn, snow, rain, and stars, then considering animals like the lion, ass, ox, ostrich, horse, and hawk. This indicates that he knows all about his creation and that he understands its origins and life stories or development. He also preserves the creation as he provides food for the lion, raven, and eagle (38:39-41; 39:29-30), and keeps the does and mountain goats safe when they calve (39:1).

Job 38–39 has been described as "a God's-eye view of creation in all its complexity and beauty,"[213] and is best pictured as a leisurely guided tour through the creation. As God describes each item, the little and unnecessary details that are added speak of a pride or delight in the world he has made and sustained. God also shows his delight with parts of the physical world by personifying them or describing them using analogies from human life. In 38:4-7, for example, creation is compared with the building of a house. There is also a playfulness about some of the descriptions such as the singing stars (38:7). In 38:39–39:30 there is evident pleasure in animals, such as the powerful warhorse (39:19-25). Effectively, God allows creation to speak for him. The colorful world pictured in the Yahweh speeches is bubbling with "wild and beautiful creatures that are allowed the freedom to be and become what they were created to be."[214]

The purpose of this guided tour through creation and references to Behemoth and Leviathan are not to inform Job about the beginnings of creation, but to broaden Job's horizons about the way God currently orders his world. In the Yahweh speeches, Job is confronted with God's kingly rule as sustainer in everyday life, and this broadens his understanding of God's purposes. Until God spoke, Job had understood too narrowly how God rules his creation, but now he sees that it is wider than the dispensing of justice according to the human principle of retribution. These speeches testify to a God who is sovereign over all creation. The God of the friends seems to be a hollow and shrunken version of the one who appears and speaks in chapters 38–41.

Two aspects of creation are particularly significant. First, the flavor of the

---

212. See the section above on "The Fear of God."
213. Schifferdecker, "Creation Theology," 65.
214. Ibid., 67.

speeches does not make humanity the sole focus of creation. Schifferdecker observes that "the divine speeches answer the question 'What is humanity?' with a deafening silence."[215] The creatures of chapter 39 have a common thread of not being under human control, nor being tamed by humans.[216] While the horse (39:19-25) is a possible exception, the picture that emerges is one of an animal whose spirit is not broken by its human masters. The peripheral nature of humans can also be seen from the dawn shaking out the wicked (38:13), God sending rain where there are no humans (38:26-27), the wild ass scorning the noisy tumult of the city (39:7), the ostrich who laughs at the horse and its human rider (39:18), and the eagles feeding on the blood of slain people (39:30).[217] Even the series of impossible questions indicates that God's ordering of his cosmos is beyond human comprehension.

In the second speech, Behemoth is described as the first of the works of God (40:19), which is the status claimed by humans. Of Leviathan, it is said that there is no creature like him (41:33), a description reminiscent of the way other OT texts describe humans (Gen 1; Ps 8).[218] Furthermore, neither Behemoth nor Leviathan can be captured by humans (Job 40:24; 41:8-9), and all human weapons are powerless against Leviathan (41:26-29). These descriptions prevent a purely anthropocentric view of creation. Of course, humans do have a place in this creation, and it is worth noting that a human (Job) is the sole recipient of this guided tour of creation.[219]

Second, creation includes some elements of disorder, yet it is the context in which God will carry out his purposes. The nature analogies include several examples where the ordering of creation is incongruous or ambiguous, or at least not rigidly governed by "justice." There is the destructive lightning flash (38:35), and rain falls where it cannot be used by humans (38:25-27). Creation includes the clumsy and "wisdomless" ostrich who carelessly leaves her eggs where they can be crushed, as well as neglecting her young (39:13-18). There are animals like the lion, the raven, and the eagle that feed on other animals (38:39-40; 39:29-30). The sea (a symbol of chaos), Behemoth, and Leviathan have a place in God's creation, but they also have boundaries (38:11; 41:10-11, 33).[220] Both order and apparent disorder are manifest in the way God orders his creation.

---

215. Ibid., 69.

216. Gordis, *Poets, Prophets, and Sages*, 293. Schifferdecker, *Out of the Whirlwind*, 2, comments that the picture of the creation here is "radically nonanthropocentric." On 83 she notes that the otherwise common words for "man" or "humans" are quite infrequent in chs. 38–41.

217. Schifferdecker, "Creation Theology," 69-70.

218. Greenberg, "Job," 299.

219. Schifferdecker, "Creation Theology," 70.

220. Habel, *Book of Job*, 66; Schifferdecker, "Creation Theology," 64.

The Role of Creation

Creation often functions in the OT as a way of leading people to praise God's power and majesty. Most clearly in Psalms and Isaiah, it is the task of creation to praise the Creator.[221] The closest we get to this in Job is the morning stars singing with joy (38:7). While this is not praise of the Creator, it does at least picture a joyful creation at the establishment of the earth.

Yet the book of Job uses creation with a different purpose. The creation theology of the Yahweh speeches is designed to broaden Job's horizon by teaching him that God's plan is much more panoramic than he thought. While a classic retribution understanding saw God as limited to rewarding human righteousness and punishing human wickedness, Yahweh is insisting that he is free to run the world as its sovereign ruler. God's purposes include justice, but cannot be confined to justice. God's plan is broader and more subtle than the protagonists imagined. God actively runs his world as he pleases, rather than simply in accordance with a humanly written instruction manual.

Habel also comments that "God's cosmic design is to be explored not obscured. After all, being hit by a theophany is only the beginning of wisdom."[222] The description of creation given in the Yahweh speeches acts as an invitation to study it more carefully and to learn from it. There is a clear hint that such study will yield greater understanding of God, his purposes, and his world.

One might object that a theophany is a very unwisdom-like aspect of the book, since wisdom theology is usually based on observation rather than revelation, and revelation of God and his purposes is given in Job 38–41. However, a closer look at the speeches indicates that there is no new content revealed to Job through the theophany. Unlike the appearances of God to, say, Abraham or Moses, there are no commands or promises given, and no detailed requirements are set out. Indeed, God speaks like a wisdom teacher as he points to aspects of the creation that Job could have noticed but had not, and his plethora of examples hints at the implication of all this. God reveals nothing new or additional, but calls Job back to learn from the creation. Thus, while theophanies are rare in wisdom literature, the nature and content of the Yahweh speeches makes this a very appropriate inclusion in the book of Job.

In the end, the book of Job adds greatly to the riches of an OT creation theology. While other significant themes of the OT include a leading role for humanity and a focus on order in creation, the Yahweh speeches reveal that the one who is the Ceator must be free to rule over it as he pleases. God must be allowed to be God!

221. Fretheim, *God and the World*, 267-68.
222. Habel, "In Defense of God the Sage," 38.

Job and Theology

Job and Biblical Theology

In order for us to understand the book of Job more fully, we need to place it in the context of the Bible as a whole. To use an analogy, if we want to assess how useful a particular boat will be as a means of river transport, it needs to be put it in the river, seeing how it floats and steers, identifying its strengths and weaknesses in the various sections in situ. We will later take the boat out of the water (see the next section, "Job and Systematic Theology"), but there is merit in viewing the book of Job as part of the river of biblical thought, and observing how its ideas form part of the flow of the whole.

Job as Part of Wisdom

We first need to examine how the book of Job can be understood as wisdom literature, and to identify what it contributes to the wisdom corpus.

Most of the OT books belong to groups or clusters (books of law, historical narrative, prophecies, etc.). While the book of Job could legitimately be viewed as part of the Writings, or one of the poetic books, the primary cluster that it belongs to is the wisdom literature. Proverbs, Job, Ecclesiastes, and Song of Songs are generally understood to be wisdom books in their entirety, and a number of other books contain wisdom-like elements.[1] The wisdom material is one strand that is woven into the rest of the OT and makes a rich contribution to the theology of the OT as a whole.

---

1. See D. Morgan, *Wisdom in the Old Testament Traditions*.

Connections between Job and Other Wisdom Books

In the introduction to this commentary I set out some ways in which the book of Job connects with the other canonical wisdom books. As a group, the wisdom books and the wider wisdom-like elements of other books seek to explore how to live successfully in the created world. While many of the other OT books deal with the history of the covenant, the covenant people Israel, and God's entry into history to redeem his people, the wisdom books have a broader, more universal concern with all of creation. Thus there is often a greater focus on everyday life issues than on what God has done in order to save us. This intellectual setting of the book of Job is much more important than its historical setting.

To read Job as part of the wisdom strand of the OT, we must interpret it against the backdrop of the mainstream wisdom book of Proverbs. Proverbs is based on a doctrine of creation, concerned with issues of everyday life and faith, and presumes an orderly world in which the righteous prosper and the wicked are punished. Job is seemingly written in response to those who have misunderstood these partial perspectives of Proverbs and turned them into rigid, calcified rules and promises. Job sits alongside Ecclesiastes as protest wisdom, asking hard questions about whether life can be mapped out so simply. So there is in biblical wisdom both an affirming or orientation wisdom — the wisdom of order — and also a protest or questioning wisdom, which raises hard questions about this order, or at least about our perception of it.

Proverbs is probably the foundational wisdom book, setting out the undergirding wisdom precept ("The fear of the Lord is the beginning of wisdom," 1:7; 9:10). It perceives the order that exists in the universe, and this means that the righteous will be rewarded and the wicked punished (3:9-10; 10:27-32). However, even in Proverbs this retribution principle is not without exceptions (e.g., 24:15-16).

The other wisdom books further qualify or reframe the mainstream view of Proverbs. Ecclesiastes notes that this order is sometimes confused and confusing, while Job points out that this order is also hidden from people. The book of Job is, in part, seeking to correct the notion that good people always prosper and sinners suffer, so that one's righteousness can be read off from one's circumstances — a fossilized misunderstanding of the book of Proverbs. While some scholars see a contradiction between these three books, Derek Kidner has offered an alternative image. They are rather, he suggests, three voices in counterpoint. Each of them will be misunderstood if they are heard alone; they need to be listened to alongside the others and nuanced by them.[2]

---

2. Kidner, *Wisdom*, esp. 116-24.

Fred Holmgren has persuasively argued that "Job's Friends are persons who have cast flexible proverbial sayings into rigid laws."[3] Their fundamental flaw is that they have grasped one truth (the idea that God rewards the righteous and punishes the wicked) and pushed it further than it was ever intended to go. Indeed, they also have turned it back-to-front. The idea in Proverbs shows the outcome of certain character traits and actions as a way of urging people to embrace or avoid them. Job's friends read from the outcome back to the underlying virtue or vice, using it as a diagnostic tool to discern a person's godliness or integrity. Since they see suffering in the life of Job, they detect a failing in his character. This works solely if the principle of retribution is the only one that affects human existence and God's governing of his world. In this they are wrong, and the Yahweh speeches are designed to make this very point. If they were to read Proverbs more closely, or examine the world around them, it is clear that the righteous sometimes do suffer and the wicked sometimes prosper. It is right to see a connection between righteousness and reward, but it is wrong to work the other way and conclude that every example of suffering has been caused by a specific sin.[4] So Holmgren concludes that "barking dogs never bite, except now and then." This is what Proverbs teaches, and it is also evident in everyday life.

Job is responding to this misunderstanding of the idea of retribution in Proverbs. He knows that God punishes the wicked (Job 27:13-23), but he also has observed occasions when the wicked have prospered (21:7-26). Both conclusions are true, but the friends can only see the first (e.g., 4:17; 8:3-4). While Proverbs puts most weight on the first, there are examples of both the righteous suffering setbacks (Prov 24:16) and the ungodly receiving unjust gain (10:2; 16:8, 19; 22:16). Sometimes this is just a matter of timing (e.g., 24:15-16), but on occasions no explanation is given. I have set out this shadow side of the book of Proverbs in the discussion of retributive justice in the previous chapter.

This has significant implications for how the book of Job is intended to be read. In order to understand the role of the friends, we must recognize that they have derived their ideas from Proverbs, but lost the flexibility and partial application of the original source. The debate between Job and his friends — and Job's final endorsement by God (Job 42:7-8) — needs to be interpreted against the backdrop of the book of Proverbs as a whole. Job is not trying to correct what Proverbs says elsewhere, but rather teasing out a minor and balancing strand within the book of Proverbs itself. It is not overriding Scripture, but

---

3. Holmgren, "Barking Dogs," 347.

4. It is interesting that Jesus addresses the same issue when speaking to his disciples about the man born blind (John 9:2-3). Not every example of suffering is caused by a particular sin.

reminding us of all that the earlier book teaches, which has been conveniently forgotten by Job's friends. Proverbs puts more weight on the prospering of the righteous and the punishment of the wicked, but Job is exploring those other times when life is not structured that simply. In order to understand either book, they need to be read together as voices in counterpoint.

Wisdom Themes in Job

The outline of the theological themes of Job also has revealed much overlap between Job and the other wisdom books. As in Proverbs (Prov 3:19-20; 8:22-31) and Ecclesiastes (Eccl 3:11; 12:1), the book of Job portrays God as creator rather than redeemer or savior.[5] This is not a different God, for he is called "Yahweh" (the LORD) in the prologue of Job (e.g., Job 1:7-12) and in Proverbs (e.g., Prov 1:7). However, there is a focus on who he is as creator/sustainer of the whole world rather than his more specific role as the rescuer or deliverer of Israel.

This is a key wisdom distinctive. The narrative of Job is set before the creation of Israel as a nation, and perhaps even before the time of Abraham. This enables the book to address the question of faith more generically than is possible in the Pentateuch, historical, or prophetic books. While it is still written for the people of God (hence the use of the name "Yahweh"), it seeks to address the issues it considers without any special help from the traditions linked with God's chosen people. By setting the story before the giving of the law and outside Israel, it has more freedom to explore questions that will affect all human beings rather than just Israelites.

While there is occasionally an explicit reference to God as the maker or creator (e.g., Job 31:15), the more common use of the creation idea is that God sustains the creation. This is the picture of the prologue, where God's decisions in the heavenly realm will determine what will take place on earth (1:6-12; 2:1-7a). Job's understanding is that God has given and taken away (1:21), exercising active responsibility for the events that take place. So Job addresses God as the one who can do something about what happens in his creation. Job nowhere suggests that God has any rivals in his active rule over creation, and the Yahweh speeches enable Job to see how this can be. God's purposes in superintending creation are much broader than Job imagined them to be.

This is a shared understanding with Proverbs and Ecclesiastes. In Proverbs the many examples of everyday life in the sentence sayings (chs. 10–29) describe

---

5. For a recent and comprehensive study of creation in Job, see Schifferdecker, *Out of the Whirlwind*.

a God who has ordered this whole area of human existence. While the book is given an historical anchor (Prov 1:1, as also Eccl 1:1), the events and central ideas of Israel's history (Sinai, covenant, Davidic kingship, promised land, law, exile, etc.) are conspicuously absent. Similarly, the later book of Ecclesiastes focuses on what happens in the created world (e.g., 1:3-11; 3:1-8; 12:1-7), and the distinctive ideas of much of the rest of the OT are simply bracketed out. In the covenant stream, God speaks directly to his servants; in the wisdom books, God makes his values known in creation. Job shares this wisdom focus with Proverbs and Ecclesiastes.

This affinity of Job with the other wisdom books is also seen in the book's understanding of humanity. The focus in Job is on people as human beings, not as Israelites. This is clearest in Job 7:1-6, 17-21, and 14:1-12, when Job describes humanity and their troubles generically. Ecclesiastes also opens with a focus on whether there is any gain for humans from their effort (Eccl 1:14), before reflecting in general terms on the human condition (1:13; 3:9-14). Rather than outline what God has revealed in his word, the Teacher (the main speaking voice in Ecclesiastes) concludes that no human can find out what God is doing (8:16-17). His advice to young men (11:9–12:1a) and his reflections on death (12:2-7) are again expressed in categories that apply to all humanity. Distinctively Israelite advice could also have been given, but Ecclesiastes, like Job, chooses not to do this.

Job shares with Ecclesiastes a focus on the setbacks and frustrations that can happen to people, such as sickness, loss, anguish, confusion, and death. While they concentrate on these difficulties and enigmas, Proverbs lays the foundation by outlining the usual and more predictable patterns of daily life. Yet what draws them together to give a coherent view on humanity is that Proverbs too is concerned with observations that are true of all human beings and not simply of those operating within Israelite traditions. For example, its advice on how to gain wisdom (Prov 2:1-11) or how to prosper (3:1-10) does not rely on any reference to specific laws or incidents in the life of Israel. Even when the book deals at length with adultery (5:1-23; 6:20-35; 7:1-27) there is no mention of the obvious commandment prohibiting adultery (Exod 20:14; Deut 5:18). The reasons given would apply to the situation of any young man — the way of the adulteress is the way of death; one should instead rejoice in one's own wife; God will judge our ways; responding to the enticements of an adulteress is playing with fire; and there is the prospect of a jealous husband.

While none of these three wisdom books places a great emphasis on sin, they do refer to sin. In Job the friends try to account for Job's sufferings on the basis of various theories of his sin (4:6-8; 5:17; 8:4-6; 11:4-6), but that is not the solution of the book, and sin is not mentioned in God's words addressed to Job in chapters 38–41. No substantial theology of sin emerges from the book. Both Ecclesiastes and Proverbs mention the reality of oppressors (e.g., Prov 1:10-19;

Eccl 4:1-3), folly (e.g., Prov 9:13-18; Eccl 4:5; 10:12-15), crookedness (e.g., Prov 2:15; 11:20; Eccl 1:15; 7:13), sorrow/sadness (e.g., Prov 15:13; 23:29; Eccl 7:3), and death (e.g., Prov 13:14; 14:27; Eccl 12:5-6), all of which have a connection with the presence of sin in the world. Yet the solution in these books (as in Job) is not to deal with the sins and their causes, but rather to commit oneself to God and his way of wisdom (e.g., Prov 3:5-6, 21-23; Eccl 12:1, 13).

In other words, the book of Job finds its ideological home with the other wisdom books of (at least) Proverbs and Ecclesiastes. The three books are not saying the same thing, but they are operating within a similar conceptual framework. There is little historical analysis, but much weight given to truths that can be gleaned by observation of the world. There is little focus on the distinctive concepts of Israel, but there is much consideration given to our common humanity and what it teaches us.

Job as Protest Wisdom

Like the book of Ecclesiastes, Job's emphasis on questioning and protesting also fits well within the counterpoint structure of the wisdom corpus. It builds upon some of the regularities outlined in the book of Proverbs, but it also wants to see how far these ideas stretch. While Proverbs outlines a well-ordered creation infused with wisdom, a broader picture is given in the book of Job. The friends, Elihu, the narrator, God, and Job himself all describe some order in creation (9:5-10; 10:8-13; 11:7-9; 12:13-25; 22:12-14; 25:1-6; 26:5-14; 28:1-11; 31:13-14; 36:24-33; 38:4–39:30), but Job also uses creation as the setting for his probing questions. He asks for an undoing of the day of his birth (3:3-10) and questions how God treats humanity (7:16-19; 14:1-12). All of this is expressed firmly within the wisdom tradition of creation theology, but the tradition is stretched and pushed to its extremities.

Similarly, Job prays to God, the God before whom all must give an account of their lives (31:6, 14). His assumption is a wisdom viewpoint that God is running the world and daily life. Yet this also grounds his serious questioning of God's actions, accusing him of firing arrows at him (6:4) and launching attacks against him (16:11-14). Instead of just outlining God's control of creation, he uses that truth to ask why God acts the way he does. It is not just wisdom or simply protest — it is protest wisdom. William Morrow describes this as "the arguing with God tradition."[6]

6. Morrow, *Protest against God*, 1. He is borrowing the terminology here from Laytner, *Arguing with God*.

Such protests are not seeking to dishonor or denigrate God, but to bring Job's legitimate concerns and questions before his creator. He is struggling to make sense of God's ordering of the world, so he brings his circumstances before the one whom he believes is in total control of creation. In this sense, Job belongs with the Teacher as a boundary rider, not huddling around the central religious community, but listening to the challenges and questions posed by the world. Rather than sticking to the safe, core truths of wisdom theology, they explore the edges in order to discover how far faith can stretch.

Job's Contribution to Wisdom

What does the book of Job add to the wisdom corpus? Clearly it is not in the assertion of order in the created and human world, for that is precisely what Proverbs outlines (e.g., Prov 3:19-20; 8:22-31). This is the starting assumption of the book of Job (1:1-3), and the finishing point as well (42:12-17), but it is not its distinctive contribution. It is rather the mainstream wisdom teaching that the author wishes to examine, discuss, and qualify.

Job's friends, as well as Elihu and the poem of chapter 28, set out a standard but often calcified connection between actions, words, and consequences. However, not everything they say is false — far from it. The friends rightly understand the greatness of God (e.g., 11:7-9) and his commitment to justice (e.g., 8:3), but they wrongly apply these truths to Job's situation. They sometimes push a truth (e.g., God judges sinners) further than it was intended to go, with the result that it no longer rings true to our experience of life. For example, Eliphaz's suggestion that no innocent or upright person ever perished (4:7) strikes most readers as contrary to what they observe in daily life. Thus the contribution of the book can only come from reading each part in the context of the book as a whole.

What, then, does it add to the foundational wisdom book of Proverbs? First, it draws attention to the way in which Proverbs can be misused. The possibility of wrong use of proverbs is already set out in the book of Proverbs itself. Proverbs 26, for example, indicates that a proverb in the mouth of a fool can be either useless ("like a lame man's legs," 26:7) or even dangerous (like a thorny bush in the hand of a drunk, 26:9). The book of Proverbs is intended for use by those whose character has been shaped by embracing Lady Wisdom, and whose stance in life is built upon the fear of the Lord.

Another limitation on the use of a proverb is that they are sometimes applicable and sometimes not. This is clearly seen in Prov 26:4-5, where we are exhorted to "answer a fool according to his folly" (26:5) and to "answer not a fool according to his folly" (26:4). We need to know when to apply one proverb and when to apply the other. This is of great significance for the book of Job, for the friends' shortcomings are often not in expressing theologically unsound ideas, but rather in applying truths wrongly to Job's circumstances. Clearly, the friends are right in their contention that God punishes wickedness (e.g., Job 20:23-29), but they are wrong in suggesting that this is the explanation for the extent of Job's suffering. Indeed, often they need to show care to Job rather than to offer him correction and advice.

While the limitations of proverbial wisdom are hinted at in the book of Proverbs itself, one of the key contributions of the book of Job is to make this very clear. There are times in pastoral ministry when wisdom should lead us not to give advice, and certainly not to offer advice unsuitable to a person's real circumstances. The book of Job reminds us that wisdom is not just about speaking truth, but first requires attentive listening and discernment to ascertain what is the actual need.

The book of Job also expands the understanding of faith found in the book of Proverbs. From Prov 3:5-6 faith might appear to consist solely of utter trust in God, and acknowledging him rather than leaning on one's own understanding. However, while Job starts in this way (1:20-22; 2:8-10), chapter 3 begins his litany of protest that characterizes most of the dialogue. Since God himself twice endorses what Job has spoken about him (42:7-8), it is clear that these robust complaints are also expressions of genuine faith. While Proverbs draws our attention to a need to trust God utterly, the addition of the book of Job to the canon implies that the language of protest is not alien to faith, but rather a different expression of faith or trust. Proverbs largely applies to our times of normal equilibrium, but Job shows how faith can be expressed in times of great struggle and uncertainty.

The book of Job also explains that the life of a follower of God is not always smooth or easy sailing. While Proverbs does mention temporary setbacks for the righteous (e.g., Prov 24:16), its dominant flavor is that life is orderly, and that in our world righteousness is rewarded (e.g., Prov 3:13-18). The book of Job places the emphasis on a complementary truth. While Job himself does not deny that a wicked person will be punished (e.g., 27:13-23), much more weight in his speeches is placed on the assertion that he is suffering even though he is righteous. The book as a whole seems to be a counterbalance to Proverbs in its insistence that righteous people do suffer, both extensively and sometimes inexplicably.

The flavor of the book of Proverbs is that God's sovereign sustaining of his creation results in an orderly, well-planned society in which righteousness blossoms. The book of Job does not undermine this truth, but qualifies it by insisting that God's active rule is not simple or straightforward, for God is free to pursue his complex goals for humanity and creation. A crucial contribution of the Yahweh speeches is that Job's Proverbs-like view of how God runs the world has zoomed in on a partial perspective but needs to be expanded to the whole panorama of God's purposes.

Furthermore, it is not possible to take a snapshot at any specific time and guarantee that this will provide a reliable indicator of who is righteous and who is wicked. Thus an analysis taken in the time of the prologue or epilogue would lead to a conclusion about Job different from one taken in the midst of the dialogue. However, Job's character of integrity remained the same during all these periods. The doctrine of retribution thus applies (but not as an absolute rule) to a person's life as a whole, not at any and every instant.

One key contribution of the book of Job is that it allows its readers to look at what a person of integrity is like on the inside, especially in times of setback and hardship. Our look inside the mind and emotions of Job is gained from the prologue, epilogue, and the dialogue. The prologue depicts Job as one who is proactive about his faith and persevering in the midst of difficulties. His customary practice was to be concerned about the possible failures of his children, taking initiative to make sacrifices on their behalf (1:5). In his own walk with God, he acknowledges that he is the gracious recipient of all that God gives, and so cannot complain if any of it is taken away (1:21-22). He continues in worship and praise even when it might seem to others that he has been abandoned by God (1:20, 21b). This is the groundwork of his faith and piety.

His response to his initial suffering is submissive (1:21) but also involves the appropriate expression of loss. He tore his robe, shaved his head (1:20), and sat among ashes; and later he sought to relieve his physical symptoms (2:8). He even rejected the false encouragement of his wife, who urged him to renounce his trust in God (2:9-10). The words of Job in all these scenarios show that these overt actions are the outworking of an active inner faith.

The epilogue is significant both for what Job does and what he does not do. Job's lack of a vengeful spirit is seen in him not getting even with those who mocked, abused, and spat at him (e.g., 30:10-14). Nor does he bear a grudge against his "miserable comforters" (16:2) who have withheld kindness from their friend (6:14). Instead, he intercedes for them, that God will not deal with them according to their folly (42:8-9). Indeed, Job welcomes those from his family and friends who had shunned him in his time of trial (42:11). He also shows great delight in his new family and extends generosity toward them (42:14-15).

However, it is probably in the dialogue that Job contributes most to the understanding of what faith on the inside looks like. Throughout this section, there is clear expression of deep pain. In chapter 3 he describes himself "in misery" and "bitter in soul," so that he "longs for death" (3:20-21). Even at this early stage, he is free to describe his suffering as the work of God ("whom God has hedged in," 3:23 ESV). He does not resort to the curious (but understandable) modern custom of saying that suffering is not caused by God but only allowed by him, often perceived as a way to ease the pain. Genuine, persevering faith can stretch this far.

Crucial to Job's inner life is his freedom to speak honestly to God, even if that involves accusing God. In 6:4 he speaks of God shooting metaphorical but painful arrows at him as terrors from God are lined up against him (see also 16:13). The extent of his "vexation" and "calamity" (6:2) is what drives the raw emotions of his accusations. This is not cool, unemotive language, and he often moves on to consider fanciful and imaginative possibilities. He thinks of undoing the day of his birth (3:3-4); that he might have died at birth (3:11, 16; 10:18); that God might crush him and cut him off (6:9); that he might argue a legal case with God (9:3, 14-20); that he might be hidden in Sheol (14:13). He longs for a figure variously described as an arbiter (9:33), a witness (16:19), a redeemer (19:25), and a "hearer" (31:35), though no such person actually exists. He is not really calling out for such a legal figure, but is driven by his pain to look in every corner for a solution.

At their heart, the speeches of Job are an outpouring of his deep pain to a God he refuses to abandon. He describes himself as giving free utterance to his complaint and speaking in the bitterness of his soul (10:1). Even his accusations, such as when he charges God with oppressing and despising his creatures (10:3), are simply the unrestrained hurt of deep pain. It is the friends who rebuke Job for this strength of language (e.g., 15:2-6), and they are themselves corrected by God at the end (42:7-8). Thus, when Job laments that God has put him in the wrong (19:6), this is not a theological statement to be weighed up or analyzed by scholars in armchairs; it is a projectile of pain. One feature of Job's speech that marks him out as a person of genuine faith is that he keeps on talking to God, even when God seems to him to be either absent or uncaring.

It is this whole roller coaster of emotions that the book of Job includes in the list of speaking about God what is right (42:7-8). Such strong, honest, emotive words are not a denial of faith but rather its outworking in Job's extreme circumstances. This is a picture of a vibrant if somewhat colorful faith too often missing in our modern, nice churches, and the book of Job adds this balance to the more even-tempered book of Proverbs. This is another part of Job's contribution to a wisdom understanding of spirituality.

One final aspect of Job's significance is what the book adds to wisdom ethics. The book of Proverbs is a rich source of moral teaching, touching on both individual and social ethics. Even here, however, Job has much to contribute. The comprehensive picture of chapter 31 outlines an ethic that is communal but also personal; an ethic that involves both inner thoughts and outward actions; a way of treating others with dignity and respect because they have been equally made by God (31:15); and a pattern of living that acknowledges that they need to give account of their lives to God (e.g., 31:14).

Yet there is an even richer depiction of living righteously in Job. An assessment of the nature of humanity is an essential component of any ethical theory, and the book of Job contains a robust view of the human condition. Though all humans are creatures made by God (e.g., 31:15), Job pleads for God's more obvious care because human life is frail and ephemeral (e.g., 7:1-10). He outlines the difficulties of human life (e.g., 14:1-6) as the grounds for God to care for them (14:13-17), with God having a moral obligation because of his commitment in making them in the first place. Humans are, says Job to God, "the work of your hands" (14:15).

Character or virtue ethics is also an important part of wisdom thinking. Here Job adds to Proverbs a picture of what virtue looks like in a setting of suffering and hardship. Proverbs most commonly depicts an ordered world where the righteous prosper and the wicked face disaster. The book of Job does not deny that aspect of how God rules his world, but it does assert that this is not the whole picture. However, for many who live in the majority world, and for those undergoing trials and setbacks even in the Western world, Job is a rich source of material for clarifying a godly character in a more challenging setting. Perseverance, for example, is a virtue one can develop only against a background of hardship. Refusal to take revenge implies that we have suffered wrong at the hands of another in the first place. Generosity of spirit is called for most clearly when the people we are counseling start to speak honest but forthright truths. Thus the book of Job draws out some virtues that are not as evident in the book of Proverbs.

Job as Part of the Old Testament

Links with the Rest of the Old Testament

The book of Job, then, is clearly indebted to the wisdom traditions established in the book of Proverbs. The latter's creation theology, doctrine of retribution, view of humanity, and understanding of God working behind the scenes in daily life are all assumed and explored in the various sections of Job. This section covers links between the book of Job and the nonwisdom parts of the

OT. As part of the wisdom corpus its avoidance of focusing on Israel, Sinai, covenant, law, exile, and so on mean that it will have significant differences from much of the rest of the OT, where these are often crucial themes. Yet discovering the connections that do exist will clarify the extent of theological overlap between Job and the other OT books.

Job's story is not considered at any length in the rest of the Bible, though Job is listed as a righteous person together with Noah and Dan(i)el in Ezek 14:14, 20. Here a major OT prophet sees no incompatibility between the integrity of a wisdom figure like Job and a prophetic understanding of righteousness. Indeed, Ezekiel argues from the assumed righteousness of Job to say that it would deliver only Job since one individual's righteous standing cannot deliver another person. It is not clear that the book of Job would have been written at this stage, so it may simply have been a reference to the story of the same righteous figure that the book of Job is based on. However, if the book was written by the exilic period, it would presumably be an endorsement of Job's stance in the book, and especially the outline of his righteousness in Job 31.

In any event, the ethical teaching of Job has significant overlap with the rest of the OT. The understanding of justice and righteousness seen in the law or prophets is assumed rather than denied. Job too is committed to justice in the legal system (31:13) and to care for the poor, widows, and needy (31:16-21). While Job gives no covenantal undergirdings, the ethical values are not only consistent with but often exactly the same as those in the covenant. The book of Job may add the importance of internal attitudes (e.g., 31:1, 7, 9, 24, 27, 29), but this is arguably the drawing out of what is previously implied. The language of Deut 6:5-9 includes loving with all one's heart, so that the external actions of Deut 6:7-9 also presuppose a prior internal response. While it is true that prophetic and pentateuchal ethics are certainly social more than individual, whereas wisdom ethics are primarily personal, my explanation of Job's ethics in this commentary draws attention to the social aspects of his thinking about right and wrong (see below, "Job and Moral Theology").

In broader terms, other issues grappled with in the book also find strong echoes in the rest of the OT. The endorsement of Job's lamenting is understandable in the light of the significant OT theme that regards protest addressed to God as legitimate. Much of the central dialogue of the book of Job (chs. 3–31) consists of lament and its subgenre "complaint to God."[7] J. C. L. Gibson suggests that many ancient Israelite readers of Job would regard him as a kindred spirit

---

7. See Broyles, *Conflict of Faith,* for a detailed discussion of the "complaint to God" subgenre and its relationship to the broader category of lament.

to the writers of the lament psalms. Indeed, the individual lament is the most common psalm type in the book of Psalms. However, this view of lament also is building on that tradition of doubting and protest before God that is evident in Moses (Exod 5:22-23) and Abraham (Gen 18:25).[8] This endorsement of lament can be further seen in the complaints of the book of Lamentations, as well as the lament of Jeremiah. These do not picture doubt and protest as illegitimate, but rather needing to be directed to God, since he has the power to rectify any crisis.[9] While the acrostic forms of Lamentations are not found in Job, there are particularly close parallels between the self-imprecation in Job 3 and that in Jer 20:14-20.[10]

The strong theology of creation in Job also integrates well with the rest of the OT. Genesis 1–11 proclaims that God is king over the whole world that he has created, not just over Israel. We must not lose sight of this focus on the whole of creation as the place where God rules, even though it is backgrounded for much of the covenant strand of the OT. This whole-creation focus is echoed in the setting of Job's story outside Israel and before the giving of the law (Job 1:1), apparently to render a universal twist, typical of wisdom literature, to the issues that the book explores. In the Yahweh speeches Job is confronted with God's kingly rule as sustainer in the realm of the cosmos, and this broadens his understanding of God's purposes. Until God spoke, Job had understood too narrowly how God rules, but now he sees that it is wider than the dispensing of justice simply for humans. While the invitation for Job to focus on creation is primarily meant to elicit change and not simply praise, the multiplicity of examples in chapters 38–39 (as well as earlier descriptions such as 9:5-10; 26:7-14; 36:22–37:18) result in a picture of God's majestic work in creation not dissimilar to that of Psalm 104.

Henry Rowold has also argued persuasively for the existence of close links between the Yahweh speeches in Job and what he calls the challenge-to-rival addresses found in the first half of Isaiah 40–55. In the book of Job, Yahweh challenges Job's claim or right to be an adversary. In Isaiah, Yahweh enters into forensic disputes with the idols/gods of the nations.[11] These so-called trial speeches (Isa 41:1-5, 21-29; 43:8-15; 44:6-8; 45:20-25) are characterized by the use of similarly structured challenge questions and a call on the antagonists to display their knowledge. Rowold maintains that the similar patterns suggest that a distinct genre, which he labels a "challenge to rival," occurs in these two

---

8. Gibson, "On Evil," 410.

9. See, e.g., Davidson, *Courage to Doubt*.

10. This is pointed out by many commentators. Fishbane, "Jeremiah IV 23-26," also notes similar references to the undoing of the creation of Gen 1 in both Job 3:3-13 and Jer 4:23-26.

11. Rowold, "Theology of Creation," 61-64. See also his "Yahweh's Challenge to Rival."

books (and not elsewhere) that differs from the covenant lawsuit commonly found in other places in the OT.[12]

This parallel between Job 38–41 and Isaiah 40–48 is remarkable given the wisdom provenance of Job and the prophetic origin of Isaiah, but it highlights that wisdom thought is compatible with many prophetic ideas and is not a foreign body in OT theology.[13] This section of the book of Job is clearly part of the OT as a whole, rather than being separated off in a hermetically sealed container. There are interconnections and a cross-fertilization of traditions, consistent with both Job and Isaiah being part of one testament. Of course, both books are compatible with the Sinai/legal traditions, which include the first commandment and its call for unrivaled commitment to Yahweh.

This is not to minimize the distinctive features of each, and Rowold points out that the significant additional element in Job is the purpose or result clause. While Yahweh's aim in Isaiah was to expose the emptiness of the idols and their claims, his purpose in the book of Job is to enable Job to move on from being an adversary and have his relationship with God restored.[14]

A final way in which the book of Job connects with some other parts of the OT is in its description of God working behind the scenes. In Job this is portrayed dramatically with the earthly and heavenly court scenes of the prologue. Yahweh does not appear on earth in the prologue; he does not speak to Job; nor does he act to inflict any suffering on Job without the agency of others such as the accuser, the Sabeans/Chaldeans, or forces of nature. God's fingerprints are on everything, but he would never be caught by a security camera. He is present and active but not visibly so. Instead, he acts behind the scenes and without direct contact with Job or his partners in argument. In much of the rest of the OT, God is not pictured as acting according to this pattern. He is often the God of mighty acts such as the plagues, the crossing of the sea, and the victor in battle. However, significant parts of the OT echo the pattern of the book of Job. For example, Job fits well with the cameos of God's providential involvement in everyday life in books like Ruth and Esther. God is not recorded as speaking to either Ruth or Esther, but is clearly the one who effects a good outcome in both books. Similarly, the Joseph story of Genesis 37–50 is one where God never appears to Joseph or gives him commands, but he is similarly in control of the outcome.[15] Joseph, Ruth, Esther, and Job are called on to act with initiative and wisdom against the backdrop of God's behind-the-scenes, providential outworking of events.

---

12. Rowold, "Theology of Creation," 63.

13. See L. Wilson, "Wisdom in the Book of Isaiah," 154-56, 159, 163-66.

14. Rowold, "Theology of Creation," 64-65.

15. I have developed some of these parallels further in *Joseph, Wise and Otherwise*, 258-72.

Though Job at many times feels isolated, the book that bears his name has many connections with the rest of the OT. While it makes a distinctive contribution to OT theology, it also shares much in common with a wide variety of texts taken from a number of different genres and traditions. It clearly belongs in its wisdom home, but there is no need for DNA testing to reveal that it is part of a wider family of books as well.

Job's Use of Other Old Testament Traditions

Another way of discerning the connections between the book of Job and the rest of the OT is also to examine its use of ideas derived from this source. Since it is part of the wider OT, it is worth seeing if some OT traditions other than wisdom ones have also found their way into the book of Job. Not everyone is persuaded that the book of Job relies significantly on earlier OT books and movements. Åke Viberg, for example, has suggested that "there are few theologically significant references in the book of Job to other parts of the OT."[16] However, this needs to be nuanced by a closer look at a number of possible influences on the book.

In the 1970s J. B. Frye explored how the pentateuchal traditions were picked up in the book of Job, using this to argue that the writer's dependence on earlier traditions is evidence that the author was an Israelite. While the book of Job is a book with many foreign elements (such as setting, names, language), it is not a foreign book with an Israelite veneer, but rather a fundamentally Israelite book.[17] The use of the name "Yahweh" in the prologue, theophany, and epilogue shows that the God of Job is to be identified as the God of Moses and the prophets. The parallels Frye sees with the Pentateuch come from the patriarchal period (e.g., Jacob and Esau), as well as the descriptions of God and the heavenly court in the early creation accounts and Deuteronomy 32.

Ronald Clements later explored how the wisdom books pick up and use earlier parts of the OT, focusing mainly on creation, the concept of *torah,* and Solomon. The first of these is important for Job (especially the Yahweh speeches), while the last is confined to Proverbs and Ecclesiastes. In connection with the second (the concept of *torah*), Clements notes a number of connections between Deuteronomy and wisdom, such as the fear of Yahweh and the doctrine of retribution. He suggests that the connection between wisdom and *torah* in Deut 4:6 may explain the assimilation of the notion of the revealed

16. Viberg, "Job," 203.
17. Frye, "Use of Pentateuchal Traditions," 13.

torah to the concept of wisdom, and thus a move from the earlier legal flavor to a set of more timeless and universal principles.[18]

William Green has also explored how the covenant categories might relate to the book of Job. He addresses the charge that the book of Job is unrelated to Judaism, and notes that what distinguishes Judaism from other religions of antiquity are its monotheism, covenant, and cult.[19] While he concedes that Job is essentially monotheistic, it is more problematic in relation to covenant and cult. He contends that Job cannot avail himself of what would in Israel be the means of keeping covenant. In other words, he cannot use cultic means to restore his relationship with God because "Job cannot atone for a transgression he did not commit."[20] However, he does argue that Job, especially in chapter 31, insists that "the covenant categories must apply"; and he concludes: "By bringing a complex and challenging picture of God into the covenantal framework, the Book of Job makes the structure of levitical religion better adaptive to the actual vagaries of life and supplies a realistic ground for Israel's persistent loyalty to God."[21]

However, what Green has not established is that the categories are exclusively covenant ones. My analysis of chapter 31 in this commentary has suggested that Job believes that he is indeed accountable to God, but that there is no specific, let alone exclusive, link to the requirements of the covenant law. Whereas the covenant focused primarily on religious obedience, only 31:26 would fall into this category. It is more likely that the book of Job is grounded in the assumption that God is in charge of every area of life, and a broader theological principle (God's active kingly rule) better accounts for the specific teaching of the book.

Most recently, Yohan Pyeon has studied the intertextual connections between the book of Job and earlier traditions. He relies for his methodology on the work of Richard Hays, who set out seven criteria for identifying scriptural echoes.[22] Of these, Pyeon suggests that four are especially relevant to the book of Job:

1. Availablity — was the source of the echo available to the author and/or original readers?
2. Volume — the degree of explicit repetition of words or syntactical patterns, but also how distinctive or prominent is the precursor text and does it receive any rhetorical stress?

18. Clements, "Wisdom," 75-76.
19. Green, "Stretching the Covenant," 571.
20. Ibid., 574.
21. Ibid., 574, 577.
22. Pyeon, *You Have Not Spoken*; Hays, *Echoes of Scripture*, 1-33.

3. Recurrence — how often does it cite or allude?
4. Thematic coherence — how well does the alleged echo fit in with the line of argument the book is developing?[23]

Pyeon concludes that "Job and his friends argue with one another by citing, quoting, echoing words, phrases, or ideas taken from the previous speeches, and also earlier biblical texts in order to present a debate concerning divine righteousness."[24] While none of the examples cited refers to earlier legal traditions, Pyeon notes the significant overlap between Job 3:3-13 and Gen 1:1–2:4a; between Psalm 8 and Job 7:17-18; and between Jeremiah and Job. This again suggests that Job is building upon the traditions of an earlier creation stream or tradition.

Thinking a bit more laterally, James Bruckner has proposed one possible way forward by arguing for a category of "implied law" in the pre-Sinai period. He has made an interesting study of implied law in the Abraham narrative, especially in Genesis 18–20. Of interest to our concerns is the quest to find implied law in the patriarchal period, in which the story of Job is ostensibly set. Bruckner maintains that in the Abraham narrative the implied law is grounded not in covenant but in creation.[25] In other words, law can have a creational as well as a covenantal context in the OT. What Bruckner means by "implied law" is an "ought" or "ought not," not in the forms of prohibition or command but "when behaviors or habitual conditions are implied, beyond a reasonable doubt, to be right or wrong."[26] Elsewhere he uses the term "implied ought,"[27] which may be a better term since some of the implied behaviors are moral and ethical categories rather than legal ones. His conclusion that we can find "implied oughts" in pre-Sinai narratives does show that some of the implied obligations in the OT are best traced to a theology of creation rather than a theology of covenant.

A Case Study: Job and the Decalogue

An interesting case study for the use of earlier traditions in the book of Job is the foundational legal text of Exodus 20. At first sight, it is unlikely that the

---

23. In relation to this criterion, Pyeon, *You Have Not Spoken*, 64, notes that this is complicated in Job by the fact that the present text's aim might be to negate or realign its previous meaning (e.g., Ps 8 and Job 7).

24. Pyeon, *You Have Not Spoken*, 4; see also 40: "Job and his friends . . . also quote, cite and echo earlier biblical texts in order to critique and argue with each other."

25. Bruckner, *Implied Law*, 12, 208.

26. Ibid., 12, slightly varied on 53.

27. Ibid., e.g., 53.

Decalogue has somehow influenced the book of Job. After all, the story of Job, whatever its date of writing, seems to be set purposefully in patriarchal times, in other words, before Moses and Sinai. Job is not specifically portrayed as an Israelite, but as one who lived outside Israel. Should we expect any reference to the Decalogue? The Decalogue is also based on God's prior act of grace in redeeming his people ("I am the LORD your God, who brought you out of the land of Egypt," Exod 20:2), and thus were never intended to stand alone simply as moral teachings. They were given in response to God's action is rescuing his covenant people, an idea not found in the book of Job.

Furthermore, the book of Job is part of the wisdom corpus, and one of the features of biblical wisdom literature is its paucity of references to salvation history, covenant, Israel, law, and so on. It is not that such motifs and ideas are actively opposed or even undermined; rather, it is simply that they are not where the canonical wisdom books focus. In the words of Roland Murphy, these covenant concerns are "bracketed but not erased."[28] Thus it would not at all be surprising to see little, if any, reference to the Decalogue in the book of Job.

In addition, the name Yahweh appears only in the prologue (1:6, 7-8, 9, 12, 21; 2:1, 2, 3, 4, 6, 7), one speech of Job (12:9), the frame narrative of the Yahweh speeches (38:1; 40:1, 3, 6; 42:1), and the epilogue (42:7, 9, 10, 11). Since the name Yahweh is crucial to the covenant formulations of the law, its absence in much of the book would reduce the likelihood of allusions to or echoes of the Decalogue. However, Dale Patrick has argued strongly that the first commandment ("you shall have no other gods before me") is not a concern in Genesis 1–Exodus 18. It is simply assumed that Yahweh is the only god on stage.[29] If the patriarchal era is the time in which the story of Job is set, then this explains the focus of Job.

Yet it is still worth looking for these echoes and allusions, since the book of Job is an Israelite book written after the time of the giving of the law and addressed to the people of God. Like all OT books, it is best read canonically. It seems likely that the author and/or editor(s) of the book of Job would be Israelites. The wisdom writings are intended for God's covenant people, and so must be read at some stage as a complement to, or perhaps a filling out of, the requirements of the covenant law, of which the Decalogue is the foundation. The book of Job has been incorporated into the Hebrew canon, presumably on the basis that what it teaches is compatible with (even if not identical to) the teaching of the rest of the OT, a prominent part of which is the covenant

---

28. Murphy, *Tree of Life*, 124.
29. Patrick, *First Commandment*, 105-18.

obligations, which are grounded in the Ten Words. Thus when reading Job, we need to be alert to the possibility that the (sometimes veiled) ideas sourced from the Decalogue may be behind the teaching of the book.

Furthermore, it is worth pointing out that the Pentateuch indicates that the Decalogue underwent changes even in the time of Moses. The reason for keeping the Sabbath varies from the account in Exodus 20 and that in Deuteronomy 5. It does not seem to matter that this command is grounded in redemption rather than creation. This alerts us to the possibility that there is more fluidity here than we might have imagined about these foundational commands written in stone.

Lastly, it is a characteristic of people to pick up ideas from previous generations. So Ralph Waldo Emerson in his essay "Quotation and Originality" says (and I quote!), "All minds quote. Old and new make the warp and woof of every moment. There is no thread that is not a twist of these two strands. By necessity, by proclivity and by delight, we all quote."[30] If there is a human inclination to refer back to older ideas and traditions (a key emphasis in wisdom literature),[31] then there is every likelihood that the foundational Ten Words of Israel will somewhere in Job find a place to lodge.

Two passages are especially significant. First, chapter 24, where Job addresses the issue of wrongdoing, and especially why this wrongdoing is not punished by God. In 24:13-17 he builds to a peak with a consideration of murder (v. 14), adultery (v. 15), and stealing (v. 16). Interestingly, this is in the same order as these three appear in the Ten Commandments, which may suggest literary dependence. However, there is a need to be cautious here, for the key image in this section is of darkness (v. 17) and light (vv. 13, 16), which does not appear to have derived from the Decalogue. There is consonance, to be sure. Job sees murder, adultery, and stealing to be wrong, but so would many other people who would not hold to the authority of the Ten Commandments. It may be that there is some literary influence here, but the evidence is hardly conclusive.

Second, in chapter 31 we find the most developed teaching in the book of Job about righteousness. F. I. Andersen provides some encouragement: "Connections with ancient lists, such as the Decalogue, can be traced, but direct dependence on any one of them has not been demonstrated."[32] John Hartley, however, is less hopeful of a link with the Decalogue: "Because Job is focusing

---

30. Emerson, *Letters and Social Aims*, vol. 8 of *The Complete Works of Ralph Waldo Emerson* (1875; repr. New York: Wise, 1920), 178. Cited in Schultz, *Search for Quotation*, 9.

31. Clements, "Wisdom," 67-68, notes that wisdom's broader perspective "required of it a skill in sifting, harmonising and re-interpreting a variety of inherited teachings."

32. Andersen, *Job*, 240.

on his attitudes toward others he mentions only two sins that are found in the Decalogue, adultery (vv. 9-12) and covetousness (vv. 7-8)."[33]

I have already made a closer study of this chapter in the body of this commentary, and nothing in Job seems inconsistent with the Decalogue. Yet, while there is overlap in content with the Decalogue, there are no absolutely clear examples of literary dependence on it. Indeed, there is a much greater concern for motives and underlying attitudes than is found in the Decalogue.[34] This does not mean that there is no influence, but it is clearly not simply an attempt to repeat the teaching of the Decalogue. At the very least, the book of Job is looking behind the specifics of the Decalogue to the broader principles on which they are based.

Job and God's Active Kingly Rule

The Concept of God's Active Kingly Rule

The Bible, including the OT, is about God revealing and establishing his active kingly rule, teaching and enabling God's people to live under this kingly rule. It outlines God's kingly rule past, present, and future; exercised through special people and through his word, in the world and among his people; and climaxes in the coming of Jesus. The Gospels highlight the "kingdom of God," a term not often found in the OT (and never in Job), even though the idea is there. This concept is rebadged in the Gospels, and in the Epistles it tends to become "proclaiming Jesus as Lord and Savior."

For all its diversity, and in both its Testaments, the Bible is concerned with God's active kingly rule. This active kingly rule *centers* or *climaxes* in the life, death, resurrection, and return of the Lord Jesus, but the totality is wider than this center, even though it is always finally understood in the light of this center. Peter Enns has proposed the term "Christotelic" (seeing Christ as the climax of Israel's story, based on the Greek word τέλος/*telos*, "goal," "end") as a way of describing the connection between the OT and Christ.[35] Christ is not the subject of every OT passage, but every passage is part of the larger story that leads to Christ as its proper climax.

Graeme Goldsworthy has observed that the Bible is essentially about God's

---

33. Hartley, *Book of Job*, 407.

34. Birch, *Let Justice Roll Down!* 332: "Some of the virtues here reflected are also embodied in the traditions of covenant and law, but the concern of Job does not primarily reflect the fulfillment of the law. Much of his recitation goes beyond the law's requirements."

35. Enns, *Inspiration and Incarnation*, 152-63. He applies this to the wisdom book of Ecclesiastes in Enns, *Ecclesiastes*, 27-29.

people in God's place, living under God's rule.[36] Pushing beyond Goldsworthy, I suggest that it is about revealing the nature and establishment of God's kingly rule (the kingship or kingdom of God) in a wider sense. It concerns God's active involvement in history, in creation, in everyday life, in the world, in God's people, in the future — and outlining the implications of God's kingly rule — for God's people and for others, in terms of how we are to respond to him as king, how we are to live, what we are to look forward to, and back to. The Bible is not just about God, but about his ordering, ruling, controlling his creation and his people, regulating life in his creation and calling for response from people.

The notion of God's kingly rule is a cluster concept, an idea with many components. It is my view that it is a central concept in biblical theology. It embraces God's right to rule as the creator, his ongoing upholding of the world, and his intervention in history to implement his plans. Sometimes as king God intervenes to do an action or bring something to pass (e.g., Jesus' death, healing a skin disease, answering prayer); sometimes he uses his kingly rule to keep things going (sustaining order in creation, sending rain); but when God acts, implements, manages, he does so as the one who is in absolute charge of his world.

Yet there is an inescapable connection between what the OT says about God's kingly rule and the person and work of Christ. For example, Acts 1:3 describes Jesus' spoken ministry between the resurrection and ascension as "speaking about the kingdom of God." Yet when Luke outlines the content of this message (Luke 24:25-27, 44-47), it concerns how the OT as a whole find its fulfillment in the death and resurrection of Jesus, which leads to the worldwide proclamation of a message of repentance and forgiveness of sins. Despite the views of some scholars, there does not appear to be a disconnection between the kingdom of God and the work of Christ. Luke and Acts are two volumes of one work (Acts 1:1), and so if we want to understand what Luke meant by the "kingdom of God," the words of Jesus in Luke 24 show that the kingly rule of God is unpacked by speaking from the OT about Jesus, how the various parts of the OT point to and climax in him. It is obvious, then, that rightly understanding the kingly rule of God presupposes reading the OT in the light of Christ (though not necessarily seeing that Christ exhausts the meaning of the OT), and reading Christ in the light of the OT.

Similarly in Acts 20:25 Paul's ministry is described as preaching the kingdom, but the content of his speeches in the book of Acts is about Jesus' death and resurrection. Thus Luke fittingly summarizes Paul's ministry at the end of Acts as "proclaiming the kingdom of God and teaching about the Lord Jesus Christ" (Acts 28:31).

36. Goldsworthy, *Gospel and Kingdom.*

Thus the kingly rule of God cannot be properly understood unless the OT is read in the light of Christ, and God's kingly rule in Christ cannot be understood without building on that wealth of material about his active rule right through the OT. As Goldsworthy points out, "Jesus drives us back to the Old Testament to examine it through Christian eyes and to see that it leads us back to him."[37]

Of course, some OT books do not neatly fit into a covenant framework. For example, the wisdom books of Proverbs, Job, Ecclesiastes, and Song of Songs focus on common human concerns, and not the distinctives of Israel as the people of God. In apocalyptic works like parts of Daniel, Isaiah, and Zechariah, the writers often leapfrog over the historical people of God, and only expect wrongs to be righted at the winding up of history. Some psalms speak of God's activity in creation or of humans struggling with issues in their daily lives.

There is a need to go right back to the beginning, to the doctrine of creation, to God as creator as well as redeemer. God is the creator who both brings order into being, but who also sustains the regularity of the created world. God's purpose in choosing a particular people is ultimately to minister through them to all of humanity (Gen 12:1-3). In the wisdom books, there is a widening of the focus to a panoramic view of what is true for all people as human beings — the people created by God, wherever they might be, seeking to make sense of this world. This includes key wisdom pursuits such as God's people attempting to find order in the wider human world.

This broader category, one that embraces both covenant and creation, is that of God's active kingly rule. God rules over all of humanity, but in a more focused way over his covenant people. God rules everywhere, not only where his covenant people are, but over the entire planet, and even the cosmos. Living under God's rule — as set out not just in his covenant stipulations but also by discovering the order in the creation and what sensible living is all about — involves learning not only from God's words but also from God's world. This fusion of covenant/redemption and creation accounts for what we find at the end of the book of Isaiah, when God's rescue work to redeem his covenant people is described as a new creation (Isa 65:17-25).

God's Active Kingly Rule in the Book of Job

While the book of Job does not deal with all of these areas, the idea of God's sustaining and governing rule in the arena of creation is fundamental to the

---

37. Goldsworthy, *According to Plan*, 69.

book. Job's starting assumption is that God sustains moral order in the world by rewarding human righteousness and punishing human wickedness. He rigorously pursues righteousness (1:1, 5) and is rewarded with being wealthy beyond compare (1:3). The retribution calculus seems to be working well and appears to explain how God rules the world. This is Job's initial assumption, but he progressively abandons it, even as his three friends cling to it doggedly.

For Job, this narrow understanding of God's rule no longer makes sense of his life circumstances. His character has not changed, but he experiences loss of possessions, family, social standing, and finally health (1:13-19; 2:7-8). Previously he had thought that this principle alone was the basis on which God exercised his power and initiative. Now he asks the typical lament questions of "why" and "how long."

The dialogue is largely a time of exploration and asking questions. Although Job has discarded his former solution (at least so far as its claim to cover the field), during the dialogue he does not replace it with anything else. He is left with questions rather than answers, and seeks to explore some imaginative possibilities in his quest for a solution.[38] Part of Job's unsettled emotional state in the dialogue is due to his assumption about the way the world is run, which is taken away well before he has any replacement for it. His anguish and distress at having no answers show the importance of asking the question about how God rules his world, in times of adversity as well as those of prosperity. Job's initial response of fearing God (respecting God for who he is, the one who rules the world) lays the foundation for when life is running smoothly, but does not give Job the additional answers he is looking for. The friends refuse to budge, but Job insists that there must be something more. Gary Smith suggests, "Fearing God is the starting point, but it does not adequately encompass the variety of responses that God desires of people after that initial step."[39] That is what Job progressively sees.

In the book as a whole, Job does not discover the answer, but has hints revealed to him. The Yahweh speeches address Job's anguished search with an answer based on the physical and animal realms of creation (chs. 38–39). While much of the rest of the OT views God ruling as king through intervening in history, usually on behalf of Israel, this is not the focus of Yahweh's speeches here. God describes his knowledge and control of the earth, sea, stars, and weather, then turns to his care of a range of animal creatures outside human control, yet nonetheless cared for by God. A key purpose in describing the features of the physical world is to emphasize that they are not simply random

38. On this see L. Wilson, "Realistic Hope."
39. G. Smith, "Is There a Place," 10.

in their operation. The God who speaks knows their workings intimately, and is able to use them to bring about his desired ends. While they seem to us to be outside anyone's control, they are portrayed as part of the picture of God's active ruling of creation. Similarly, the animals seem to have little to contribute to the world, especially from a human-centered perspective. The animals mentioned in chapters 38–39 are largely outside human control, and would rarely even have contact with people. However, since God's rule is wider than ruling over humanity (for he brings rain where there are no humans, 38:26), the description of this menagerie of creatures shows his active concern and care for all living creatures. His rule is over the entire creation, not just those areas deemed important by human beings.

The concept of God's rule or ruling is implied by a number of features of the book. The assumption of both Job and his friends is that human beings are accountable to God. This is made clear by Job in his oath of clearance (31:6, 14-15, 28), but also grounds the friends' call for Job to confess (5:17; 8:5-6; 11:13-14; 22:21-23) and their condemnation of him (11:4-6; 15:4, 12-13; 18:21; 20:28-29; 22:12-13). Their common belief is that God is running the world, determining among other things the identity of those who will be punished or rewarded. The friends differ from Job as to what God is doing, but they all agree that God will determine, and is determining, whether people will be blamed or vindicated. This makes the nature of God's rule a vital question, because our obligation to God is dependent on the principles God uses to run his world. Job comes to realize that the friends' insistence that God acts on the basis of human retributive justice alone simply does not account for his experience of daily life.

The prologue makes an important contribution to our understanding of God's kingly rule, for it establishes that God can be active in bringing about his purposes, but for that not to be evident on earth. Since he can work behind the scenes and through intermediaries (the accuser, Sabeans, Chaldeans), his activity might not be attributed to him. However, the prologue insists that through the actions of others, God is actively at work furthering his purposes.

The significance of God's kingly rule has been well-explored in an astute article by Gary Smith. He argues that both wisdom and covenant texts in the OT are grounded on the same belief that "God sovereignly rules over Israel, the nations, and nature," and that this is "a broad theme that is distinctively developed in wisdom and non-wisdom texts but constructively tied to the central theological teachings of both."[40] God's rule may be expressed in different ways in the various parts of the OT, but in every case it is God's sovereign rule that is in view. In the book of Job none of the characters doubts the reality of God's rule.

---

40. Ibid., 11, 16.

Smith suggests that the concept of God's rule is developed in two main ways in the wisdom book of Job. The first concerns God's just treatment of people. While the friends defend the justice of God against Job's perceived attack (e.g., 8:3), Job's pursuit of a legal resolution reveals that his underlying assumption is that God is just and must act justly. In their dialogue about Job's life and culpability, they are applying a common theology that God rules justly, but coming up with different applications. As a result, "Job probes the deeper issue of the relationship between God's sovereignty and his justice," believing that the slick formulas of his friends simply cannot account for reality.[41]

The second way in which the book develops the concept of God's rule is in its outline of "God's mysterious freedom and wisdom." Smith sets it out like this:

> In his wisdom he is free to allow sin, suffering, and the Accuser to exist; yet still fulfill his purposes. In the midst of negative circumstances justice exists, but it is mysteriously tempered with divine wisdom and freedom. This perspective is a unique contribution that wisdom theology makes to OT theology, and it is an essential part of a wholistic understanding of God's rule.[42]

God's kingly rule cannot be straitjacketed by the narrow formulations of Job's friends. He cannot be viewed as a puppet whose entire movements are controlled by the tugging of strings like the principle of human retributive justice. He is not bound to act only in ways that make sense to our limited, telescopic human perceptions of what he must do. Smith comments, "Life with God cannot be neatly systematized, but it is not a blind alley with no light. There is a way that seems right, but it is filled with divine surprises."[43] The idea of God's rule in the Yahweh speeches is that God must be treated as the God he is. Elsewhere in the OT, God rules over history in raising up nations and delivering in battle, based not simply on the principle of justice but on his wider covenant goals. So too in Job God rules over the creation he sustains, not simply to bring justice but also to further his broader creational ends. Yet the common theme is that "God rules over everyone and everything,"[44] and it is this common thread that establishes a unified biblical theology among the diversity of the OT.

John Goldingay had earlier sought to unify OT theology around the two conceptual poles of redemption (common in the covenant stream) and creation

41. Ibid., 17.
42. Ibid.
43. Ibid., 18.
44. Ibid.

(more prominent in wisdom literature).[45] Smith rightly insists that the concept of God's active rule (over nations, individuals, and nature) is a more fruitful integrating idea, and for four reasons.

> 1) It does not focus just on the two powerful events of creation and redemption, but on all God's powerful deeds and words. 2) It encompasses not only God's great positive deeds (creation and redemption) but his just judgment of nature and nations and his daily providential control of history and nature as well. 3) It is not focused on a few historical points, but on the many ways his wisdom instructions, laws, and prophetic warning bring about his rule over individuals, nations, and parts of nature. 4) It does not depend on the chronological relationship of creation and redemption, which makes one more prominent at one time and the other at another time, but applies to all times and in many ways.[46]

The distinctive contributions of the book of Job to this important motif of God's active kingly rule are that it must be understood more broadly than simply human retributive justice, and that it must be grounded in God's freedom to be God.

Job and Christ

One of the difficulties for Christian readers of the book of Job is to understand the connection between the book and Christ. Does the book speak about or even predict the coming or work of Christ? Does the book point forward to the NT? Does the NT look back to or even fulfill the book of Job? Or, since it was written B.C., is it about Christ at all? Is it a case of "the New is in the Old concealed, the Old is in the New revealed" (so Augustine), or is it rather "the Old is by the New restricted, and the New is on the Old inflicted"?[47]

Various approaches have been made to this topic. A typological connection between Job and Christ looms as a very attractive option at first but is ultimately not persuasive. There are, of course, parallels between the life of Jesus and Job. Both Job and Jesus are righteous and suffer undeservedly; both are rejected by those close to them; and both intercede for those who have wronged

---

45. Goldingay, *Theological Diversity,* 200-239. See my discussion in *Joseph, Wise and Otherwise,* 292-97.

46. G. Smith, "Is There a Place," 19.

47. W. VanGemeren, "Israel as Hermeneutical Crux," 268.

them.[48] But these parallels are only superficial, for many have been wronged by their friends and yet have prayed for them. There is also a difference in kind between Jesus' suffering and death, as a substitute for others, and Job's suffering, which was neither vicarious nor salvific. Furthermore, it is good practice not to make typological connections where the NT chooses not to do so, and Job is not referred to by any NT writers in a typological way. The only way in which the character Job is used in the NT (indeed, the only explicit reference to Job in the NT) is in Jas 5:11, where he is used as an example of steadfast perseverance.

Another popular connection made between Job and Christ is to see Jesus as the answer to Job,[49] in the sense of fulfilling Job's longing for a mediator. On this view, Job is an OT person of faith who foresees, perhaps even predicts, that the only solution to his problem is through bodily resurrection and the intercession of a mediator who stands between God and humanity. This is also an attractive option, as it connects this puzzling book to the key salvific act of the whole Bible. It would make Job a model of one who finally trusts in God despite his extreme circumstances, but only after he abandons his angry outbursts and hard questions.

Objections to this common Christian way of reading Job are several. First, it is not properly grounded in the exegesis of the text, but rather finds what some want to find. Job's angry, bold, and sometimes accusatory words in the debate are not words of rebellion but rather "speaking of God what is right" (42:7-8). They may not be the words we often use in church, but in the study of Job's speeches I have argued that they are expressions of a hurting, struggling, but persevering faith. They are the outworking of a faith that will not let go of God in the face of pain, but still clings to him even when he seems absent or silent. While many Western Christians are uncomfortable with such words, this is perhaps a sign that we do not understand lament. In many other cultures such raw honesty in the face of suffering would be read quite naturally as genuine faith, and the book of Job presents these outbursts in this way. When these bold words are regarded as revealing a lack of faith, it is natural to find that those passages where Job longs for a mediator (chs. 14, 16, 19) are where his faith finally breaks through. They become the purple passages that are the high point of the book — *I know that my redeemer lives* (19:25) or *though he slay me, yet will I trust in him* (13:15). The assumption seems to be that if these are not expressions of Job's real faith, then God cannot be correct in saying that Job has spoken of him what is right. I have maintained in this commentary

---

48. A recent example of this is Guthrie, *Wisdom of God.* The subtitle makes the intention clear: *Seeing Jesus in the Psalms and Wisdom Books.*

49. A concept based on G. Morgan, *Answers of Jesus to Job.*

that Job's uncomfortable words are themselves expressions of faith, and even if these purple passages were not in the book, Job would still be a person of persevering faith.

I also indicated that a closer analysis of the "mediator" passages renders it unlikely that they are the high point of the book. I am not convinced that they are great passages of confident hope, and they are certainly not what drives and legitimates the book. I have proposed that there is no assertion in chapters 9, 16, 19, and 31 that a mediator, witness, redeemer, or hearer actually exists, but rather they are expressions of a deep longing for some kind of resolution of Job's situation. In any event, what is envisaged in Job's cries is not a mediator like Jesus, who stands in the place of sinners, but instead someone who will plead Job's actual (not imputed) righteousness to a seemingly hostile God. It is true that Christ is the mediator between God and humanity (1 Tim 2:5; Heb 9:15; 12:24), but that role is not what is envisaged in the book of Job.

I have also argued that there is no definite hope of resurrection in connection with this hoped-for redeemer. A closer study of 19:25-27 suggests that this is not a fruitful source of a preincarnation prediction of the resurrection of Jesus, even though it draws attention to the usefulness of resurrection life as a way of easing Job's ongoing struggle. The doctrine of this world's wrongs being righted in the next could have been a reasonable solution to the issues raised in the book, but that is not how the author of Job chose to address those concerns. Thus identifying Christ with the mediator figure of the book does not do justice to the book of Job in its canonical form. Instead, such an identification proposes too easy a solution that actually domesticates or sanitizes what is meant to be an unsettling book. There is a need for a more robust doctrine of Scripture that can include this book with its refusal to opt for a facile solution.

But does this mean that the book of Job is not about Christ? Far from it. In the end the book is about Christ in the same sense that all of Scripture is about Christ. It is not that Christ is speaking or being spoken about at every point of the book, but that it, like the rest of the OT, speaks of God's active kingly rule, which climaxes in Christ and which cannot be fully understood without a Christotelic perspective. All Scripture needs to be understood in the light of the coming of Christ, but that is not to say that Christ is the exclusive and exhaustive subject of all Scripture. Since Christ is Lord of sustaining and ruling the creation, the perspectives of the book of Job need to be read with those truths in mind. For example, God's answer in chapters 38–41, that God's purposes in creation were wider than Job had realized, can be filled out in the light of Christ and his role in creation and sustaining the world, highlighting the even more intricate way in which God orders his world. The book of Job is, in this sense, about Christ, for it explores the complex way in which God orders creation, a theme that reaches its biblical climax and final clarification in Christ (Col 1:15-17).

Some evangelical scholars suggest, however, that any OT book is "about Christ" in a more specific way. For example, Goldsworthy asserts, "The OT is the word of God about Christ."[50] In favor of this view, he cites three NT references (Luke 24:25-27, 44-45; John 5:39), which deserve a closer look. In Luke 24:25-27, on the road to Emmaus, two disciples speak of Jesus' life, death, and disappearance. Jesus rebukes them as slow to believe, then v. 27 says, "beginning with Moses and all the prophets, he interpreted to them the things about himself in all the scriptures."[51] A similar passage occurs in Luke 24:44-45, when Jesus appears to the eleven disciples, and says, "everything written about me in the law of Moses, the prophets, and the psalms must be fulfilled. Then he opened their minds to understand the scriptures."

Two observations can be made about these passages. First, they do not say that *all of the OT* is about Christ, or that the OT is *all about* Christ. It is clear in v. 44 that the Pentateuch, prophets, and psalms (presumably as the first of the Writings) do speak at least in part about Christ, and where they do so that must be fulfilled. In v. 27 the Pentateuch and the prophets do speak about Jesus. In neither verse is there any claim that they speak of nothing but Jesus. In other words, they speak in part about Christ, and perhaps in part about other things. The text does not claim that the OT speaks of nothing but Christ. If we see only Christ in the OT, we will be seeing something that is there, but not all that is there.

A similar point could be made about John 5:39-40, where Jesus rebukes the Jewish leaders for their failure to see that the Scriptures testify about him. A key purpose is to testify about Jesus, so that people may come to him and find life, but the verses do not say that the OT is all about Jesus.

In what sense, then, is the OT about Jesus? Consider the following parallel. We could say that "being a tennis professional is all about playing well and winning tournaments," but my response is yes and no. It is also about such matters as preventing overuse injuries, earning and managing your money (income, cash flow, tax, investments), keeping your relationships healthy, improving your rankings, networking and making contacts, promoting the game, mentoring

---

50. Goldsworthy, *According to Plan*, 67. In *Christ-Centered Biblical Theology*, 186, Goldsworthy puts this claim in an even more extreme way: "*There is no aspect of reality that is not involved in the person and work of Christ.* . . . Our world view and our Christology make it necessary to enlarge the idea of typology to encompass everything found in the Old Testament." However, he does add that this does not mean that we should read every detail of the OT as a type of Christ.

51. The ESV translation is "he interpreted to them in all the Scriptures the things concerning himself." This understands the connection in a slightly different way.

others, planning for your postplaying days. Ultimately, it is about playing well and winning tournaments, but it is not just about these things.

However, we also need to observe the close link in the NT between Jesus and God's active kingly rule, whose prominence in Job has been set out earlier. What the OT says about God's kingly rule needs to focus on Christ and be understood in the light of Christ. This is made clear in Acts 1:3, which notes that before Jesus' ascension he appeared to the apostles during forty days and spoke to them about the kingdom, or kingly rule, of God. If we want to understand what Luke meant by the "kingdom of God," we need to see what words of Jesus he recorded in the first volume of his two-volume work, and he does this in Luke 24. In Luke 24:24-25, 44-47, speaking about the kingly rule of God is revealed to be the same as speaking from the OT about Jesus, and how the various parts point to and climax in him. It is obvious, then, that rightly understanding the kingly rule of God presupposes reading the OT in the light of Christ, though not necessarily seeing that Christ exhausts the meaning of the OT.

Tom Wright has said, "The great story of the Hebrew scriptures was . . . inevitably read in the second-temple period as *a story in search of a conclusion*."[52] There are a number of ways in which the threads or stands of the OT find their climax in Christ, but not all of these apply to the book of Job. The NT adopts OT concepts when it describes Jesus as the second Adam (Rom 5:12-21), the word (John 1:1-3, 14), the final prophet (Heb 1:1-2), the great high priest (Heb 7:22–8:1), the messianic king (Luke 1:31-33; Rev 1:12-20), the apocalyptic son of man (Mark 14:61-64; Rev 1:7, 13), and the suffering servant (Mark 10:45; Phil 2:5-11; John 13:12-16). However, it is clear that at least two OT streams lead from the book of Job to Jesus. The NT depiction of Jesus as the firstborn over all creation (Col 1:15-17) crystallizes what the book of Job has been grappling with and provides a suitable capstone. In addition, the concept of the wisdom of God finds its fulfillment in Jesus' wisdom speech forms, and in Matthew's portrayal of Jesus as the repository and embodiment of wisdom (Matt 11:25-27, 28-30).[53] This leads Paul to describe Jesus as the wisdom of God (1 Cor 1:18-24).

The book of Job, then, is not about Christ in the sense that Job is a type of Christ, or that it predicts the resurrection of Jesus. Neither is it about Christ in the sense that it is "*all* about Christ," nor in the sense that it is "about *nothing other than* Christ." Yet the book of Job is about Christ in a more fundamental way. The central theme of the book of Job is God's active kingly rule, an idea that finds its biblical climax in Jesus as the embodiment and implementer of God's rule over his world.

---

52. N. T. Wright, *People of God*, 217, emphasis added.
53. Witherington, *Jesus the Sage*, 201-8.

Job and the New Testament

The New Testament Use of the Character Job

The NT is an important and often neglected source of information about how we are to interpret parts of the OT. Significantly, the only time that the NT names Job is in Jas 5:11, where it singles out his steadfastness or perseverance (ὑπομονή/*hypomonē*). This verse is the origin of the phrase "the patience of Job," as it was translated this way in the KJV. Such a translation has caused many commentators to question the appropriateness of "patience" and "Job" being in the same sentence. As Douglas Moo says, "Few of us would single out Job as a model of faithful endurance in the midst of suffering."[54] In the eyes of many, it might at best be a reference to the Job of the prologue, or more likely to his portrayal in the *Testament of Job*.[55] However, my analysis of Job in this commentary suggests that a robust, persevering faith is exactly what the book depicts when read in its ancient Near Eastern setting. Indeed, Moo concedes as much, commenting that although Job did complain, he never gave up his faith but continued to cling to God and hope in him.[56]

James 5:11 also invites us to understand Job's faith in light of his vindication in the end or the outcome (τέλος/*telos*, "goal, end"; ESV "purpose") of his restored situation. Don Carson notes that the word "end" could refer to the Lord's intended end or purpose.[57] If it meant "purpose" (ESV, i.e., the end that God intended), then it refers to Job's refining through the testing process, which would make sense of many readings of Job 42:5-6. If, however, it meant "end" (cf. NIV "what the Lord finally brought about"), then it refers to Job's restoration as set out in 42:10-17. Scholars are evenly divided between these two possibilities.[58] It seems to me that the second is most likely in the context, for it draws attention to the gracious restoration, the outworking of the Lord's character, which provides a better motivation to be steadfast than the fact that God refines his servants.[59] On this reading, Peter picks up the thrust well when he urges his

---

54. Moo, *James*, 228.

55. See, e.g., Davids, *Epistle of James*, 187. Richardson, "Job as Exemplar," 214-19, 223-26, 229, argues at length that the canonical book of Job is the source of James's teaching. On 224 he suggests that Jas 5:2 is a citation of Job 13:28, giving evidence "that James had real familiarity with the book of Job."

56. Moo, *James*, 229.

57. Carson, "James," 1011.

58. This has been pointed out by Moo, *James*, 230; and Carson, "James," 1011.

59. Davids, *Epistle of James*, 188, cites a number of analogous examples in Greek literature that make it likely to refer to the result (i.e., restoration) rather than purpose.

readers to humble themselves under God's hand, casting their cares on him, for he cares for them. With the devil prowling for prey, we need to resist him, standing firm in the faith until the God of all grace restores us (1 Pet 5:6-10).

However, on either reading, it is clear "that James is using Job as a moral example under the providence of God."[60] This exemplary use of Job and the highlighting of his virtues or character confirm the legitimacy of such an application of the story of Job for Christians today. Job is not being displayed as a type of Christ, nor as a model of repentance, but as an exemplar of persevering faith. This is the exact picture of Job that has emerged from the book of Job in this commentary.

The New Testament Use of the Book of Job

The book of Job is also the source of a number of quotations, allusions, and references made in the NT. Explicit quotations are limited to the use of Job 5:13 in 1 Cor 3:19,[61] though some also include the partial quotation of Job 41:11 in Rom 11:35.

The most challenging feature of Paul's use of Job 5:13 is that it is a quotation not from Job or Yahweh but from Eliphaz. God has said of Eliphaz and his two friends, "You have not spoken of me what is right," and yet Paul cites his words in support of his argument in 1 Cor 3:19. In Job 5 Eliphaz is arguing that God will expose those using crafty schemes to project that they are wise. This is certainly a true observation, but he is seeking to apply it to Job. In 5:8 he urges Job to "seek God" and commit his cause to him; in 5:17 he tells Job not to "despise . . . the discipline of the Almighty." In its context, the implication is that Eliphaz thinks that Job is now suffering for some of his crafty schemes. However, this application to Job is overruled by Yahweh's verdict (42:7-8).

It is unlikely that Paul is endorsing Eliphaz's assessment of Job, for that would be irrelevant to his argument in 1 Corinthians 3. Instead, he is citing a true observation made by Eliphaz (but misapplied to Job) and exploring its implications for the Corinthians' misplaced trust in their own wisdom. Hays writes, "Paul cites Job 5:13 here as an authoritative disclosure of the truth about God's debunking of human wisdom."[62] Job's friends, although rebuked at the end, do utter some truths that might be helpful in other contexts. Paul has one such other context in mind, and applies this truth to it. He appears to be

---

60. Carson, "James," 1011.
61. So Newsom, "Job," 380.
62. Hays, *1 Corinthians,* 59, cited in Ciampa and Rosner, "1 Corinthians," 704.

citing it as a truth rather than citing it as Scripture. This is perhaps similar to his quotation elsewhere of the Cretan poet who says, "Cretans are always liars" (Titus 1:12), for in both cases the hearers will find that the words cited have a ring of truth about them. Paul's use of Job 5:13 may have added weight in that the truth (misapplied in its context) comes from Scripture, but it is used primarily because Paul's readers would be able to agree with its compelling truth.

Paul's looser rendering of Job 41:11 in Rom 11:35 is less problematic as it is a citation of God's words, which are clearly part of the final teaching of the book as a whole. The truth here is that God is not indebted to humans, but far beyond their scrutiny and judgment. This has the ring of truth about it but is also exactly how it is used rhetorically by Yahweh in his second speech. However, even here Paul could have taken the same truth from Elihu's words in 35:7: "if you are righteous what do you give to him? Or what does he receive from your hand?" This implies that it is a true observation even if it were not found in God's speech in chapter 41. Mark Seifrid suggests that Rom 11:33-36 is Paul's hymnic composition, weaving allusions to Scripture into a doxology that climaxes this section of his argument in Romans.[63]

It is also possible to hear a number of echoes in the NT that have a lesser degree of overlap with the text of Job. These are probably more important for showing consistency between different parts of the Bible than they are for revealing how the NT authors understood and used the book of Job. Thus the mention of Satan as the accuser of humans in Rev 12:9-10 recalls the picture of the Joban prologue. Paul's reminder in 1 Tim 6:7 that "we brought nothing into the world, and we cannot take anything out of the world," seems to be a rewording of the same truth in Job 1:21. The lesson that truths about God can be discerned from the created world can be learned from both Job 12:7-9 and Rom 1:20. The metaphor of God shutting a door so that it cannot be opened is used in Job 12:14 and applied to a church setting in Rev 3:7.

Certain virtues are commended in the book of Job and picked up similarly in the NT. That God will exalt those who humble themselves before him is clear in Job 5:11 and 22:29, but crystallized in Jas 4:10 and 1 Pet 5:6. The folly of showing partiality is clear in Job (34:19) but developed by James (Jas 2:1-9, especially v. 1).

Other parallels between the book of Job and the NT could no doubt also be drawn. However, two significant features of the NT use of Job are already evident. First, the way in which the NT adopts both the example and text of Job

---

63. Seifrid, "Romans," 678. He suggests that Paul's words correspond closely to the Targum of Job, and that there might have been a septuagintal version similar to that of the Targum. This is more speculative.

is not explicitly christological or typological. When the NT refers to Job or his words, it is to illustrate truths about matters other than Christ. Second, there is a willingness to refer not only to parts of the book that are uttered by Job, Yahweh, or the narrator, but also to those of his friends (e.g., Eliphaz) and of Elihu. Often, the truths in the book are repeated simply because of their ring of truth, rather than because they are part of the final teaching of the book of Job.

New Testament Developments of Job's Ideas

The NT affirms many of these distinctive contributions found in the book of Job.[64] The legitimacy of lament, for example, is reinforced by Christ uttering the opening words of a lament psalm while hanging on the cross (Matt 27:46, citing Ps 22:1; see also Heb 5:7-8). This can be a legitimate part of the faith of a righteous person who is undergoing hardship and loss. That Christ has won a decisive victory in the cross and resurrection does not render lament illegitimate, but rather a matter of honesty in the midst of difficulties. This can be seen even in the (post-cross) book of Revelation, in which the righteous saints continue to call out with the typical lament cry, "*how long* before you will judge and avenge our blood?" (Rev 6:10 ESV).

Furthermore, God's purposes in Christ are clearly wider than human justice, for the NT teaches that in his love and mercy Christ died for undeserving sinners, not for those who merited it on the grounds of retributive justice (e.g., Eph 2:8-9). The book of Job helps us to see that the principle of retribution can be pushed further than it was intended to go, and that there are limits to its power to explain what happens in the world. Those of us who are located in a comfortable Western world, or in some rich settings in the majority world, must be careful not to interpret our material wealth (or health, etc.) as a sign that we are more righteous than those who have less. The Lukan motif of the judgment as a time of reversal of expectations is apt here (e.g., Luke 13:22-30; 14:12-24; 16:19-31; 18:9-14). Justice is still important to God, and so are human beings. However, justice is not the only principle to be taken into account, and humans are not the only ones whose interests are considered. The teaching of the book of Job in this regard is still true "in Christ."

In addition, while the NT focuses less on the mighty creator and rescuer of the OT, and more on God assuming humanity in Christ, some full-orbed descriptions of Jesus as lord of creation do occur. He was in the beginning and all things came into being through him (John 1:1-4). Colossians 1:15-23 describes

---

64. This material fills out my earlier, briefer outline in L. Wilson, "Job, Book of," 387-88.

Christ not only as redeemer but also as the firstborn over all creation, in whom all things were created and hold together. Thus, while there is a focus in the NT on the redeeming work of Christ, there is certainly no denial of Christ's sovereign lordship over creation. The challenge that Yahweh gives in Job 38–41 can equally be said by Christ, who is lord of creation. This lordship over the natural world is evident particularly in his nature miracles, which show his authority over life and health (Mark 1:23-27; 2:1-12; 5:21-43), over the forces of nature (Mark 4:35-41; cf. Job 38:8-11), over the multiplication of food (Mark 6:35-44; 8:1-10), and even over walking on water (Mark 6:45-52). The closest parallel here is between Jesus' stilling of the storm in Mark 4:35-41 and God's claims in Job 38:8-11 that he alone can say to the sea, "here shall your proud waves be stayed" (Job 38:11 ESV). Jesus displays the ability to meet this divine challenge, since he, like Yahweh, is the lord over creation. Indeed, in the world to come there will be a new creation (Rev 21–22), in which the Lamb's majesty will be fully seen (Rev 5:11-14; 21:22-23).

The connection between Christ as lord of creation and the need for persevering faith is also manifest in the NT. At the climax of Col 1:15-23, Paul's hearers are reminded to "continue in the faith, stable and steadfast" (Col 1:23 ESV). The supremacy of Christ as creator and sustainer is meant to lead to persevering faith. Furthermore, in the miracle of stilling the storm Jesus asks the disciples, "have you still no faith?" (Mark 4:40), expecting them to keep on trusting him in the light of his demonstrated power over nature. Christ's lordship over nature is not simply a truth to be believed, but also the basis for an ongoing response of trust or persevering faith.

Reading Job as a Christian

Of course, seeing how the NT uses the book of Job does not exhaust how it can be legitimately and fruitfully read by Christians today. Indeed, there does not seem to be a single, prescriptive NT template anyway, based on different parts of the books and the various needs of contemporary believers. However, what is clear is that, if one wishes to read Job as a Christian, the book needs to be approached as Christian Scripture.

The notion of reading Job as Scripture needs some exploration. Our understanding of Scripture and how it works must be as broad as the texts that God has seen fit to include in the Bible. We must be careful that we do not read our own a priori assumptions into the book, and so find only what we expect to be there. People who approach the book of Job for the first time are often surprised with what is actually in the book and what is not included. There are substantial sections of complaint, protest, and accusation against God, typically on the lips of Job, but endorsed by God in the book as a whole (42:7-8). As modern readers, we can easily be like the friends, wanting to defend God's honor (implying that God needs our help?) and to find fault with Job's words. It is tempting to sanitize the stark conclusions of the book by making them milder, nicer, and more polite, but this comes at a cost of ignoring the robust faith shown by the character of Job. Just as the Yahweh speeches insist that we need to "let God be God," so we need to "let the book of Job be the book of Job," and not Deuteronomy or Romans.

Certainly the book of Job challenges some of our preconceived views of the nature of Scripture. Life is not always simply a matter of submissive obedience. There is room even in Scripture for imaginative exploration and honest grappling with life's troubles. This is the pastoral setting for many of today's readers in the majority world and for many in a Western context as well. We need Scriptures that help us to deal with the difficulties and despair we face. We need to hear those texts that face up to the disorientation in which some of us find it hard to know what God is doing or how he is running his world. Rather than try to make such texts more "Christian" by sanitizing them, we would do better to be challenged, confronted, and changed by them.

One further issue in reading Job as Christian Scripture is the need to read any section or text as part of the book as a whole. The advice of the friends, for example, is often true but misapplied to Job's circumstances and therefore not the final teaching of this book, even if it is taught elsewhere in Scripture. Thus when Zophar tells Job that God is exacting from him less than his guilt deserves (11:6), he is basing that on the true belief (well attested in the rest of Scripture) that God will punish human sins and wrongdoing. Zophar was wrong to apply this to Job (42:7-8), and we would be wrong to apply it to our congregations — this is not the solution to the book.

Therefore a key part of the process of reading Job as Christian Scripture is reading any section as part of the whole book, and as part of the Bible as a whole. I want to demonstrate how this can be done with three different texts we find in the book: the Yahweh speeches, the narrative in the prologue, and the complaints of the dialogue.

The first step in reading is to study the text itself, noting any literary features, thematic and theological ideas, and exegetical issues. This is letting the text speak in its own right first, and is an essential step to prevent the sharp edges of a text being planed away by our theological frameworks. The main temptation experienced by evangelical readers is to bring Christ in too early, without fully listening to the text first.

This is one area where we need to be cautious about the approach of Goldsworthy's otherwise helpful input on biblical theology. Goldsworthy contends that instead of starting with the OT and working through to Christ, we should rather start with Christ and read the OT in the light of the gospel:

> In doing biblical theology as Christians we do not start at Genesis 1 and work our way forward until we discover where it is all leading. Rather we come first to Christ and he directs us to study the Old Testament in the light of the gospel. The gospel will interpret the Old Testament by showing us its goal and meaning. The Old Testament will increase our understanding of the gospel by showing us what Christ fulfils.[65]

Much of this is right, but I think it is slightly wrongheaded. Biblical theology not only traces ideas through the Bible but is also a valuable tool for dealing with individual passages of Scripture. However, starting with Christ may sometimes obscure the questions raised by an OT passage in the first place, by jumping too quickly to christological questions. We need to listen to a passage first before we place a grid on it — even a helpful grid like Christ. It is better to let the ideas of a passage unfold in the way they are built on in Scripture, while ultimately seeing them in the light of Christ. I usually find it most productive to understand an OT text first as a text in its own right, then in the ever-widening context of section of book, book, section of the OT, the entire OT, and the Bible as a whole. What is helpful here (and does not appear in Goldsworthy's diagrams) is a feedback loop from Christ back to the OT passage under consideration. In other words, having traced the idea through the OT into the NT, we need to ask whether the coming of Christ has affected what we have read in the OT as we reread any particular passage.

This use of biblical theology is the focus of the rest of this section. What I propose is essentially to read any particular portion of Job as part of the biblical theological flow of the whole. It is based on beginning with a detailed reading of a text in its own right, working hard to understand its basic thrust, as well as the meaning of its details. Then there is a need to put it in the context of that part of the book in which it is found. Next it must be read as part of the book of Job as a whole, then as part of the wisdom collection of books, especially as a counterpoint to some understandings of Proverbs. The text would then be considered in terms of its place in the flow of the OT as a whole, and the penultimate step would be to read it as part of the Bible as a whole. The final stage is an important and often overlooked one: to *reread the passage* in the light of

---

65. Goldsworthy, *According to Plan*, 69. He unhelpfully labels the first as a "non-Christian approach to the Old Testament" (70).

the coming of Christ, asking whether that will affect the way we understand it.[66] In other words, we do not read any part of the OT through Christ, but we always need to reread it in the light of Christ. After we read part of the book of Job in its own right, then and only then we reread it in the light of how the OT is part of the whole Bible, which climaxes in Christ.

Chris Wright has argued that, if we come to Christ through the OT rather than coming to the OT through Christ, we can often gain three additional insights, the latter two of which are of most value in relation to Job. First, we may understand the "significance a particular event had, in terms of Israel's own experience of God." Second, "we may legitimately see in the event, or in the record of it, additional levels of significance in the light of the end of the story — i.e. in the light of Christ." Third, "the Old Testament event may provide levels of significance to our full understanding of all that Christ was and said and did."[67]

A biblical theological approach to reading the book of Job can be demonstrated in the following examples. (For reasons of space, I will assume rather than outline the meaning of the text itself, based on the exegetical sections of this commentary.)

Reading Job 38–39

Our study of the Yahweh speeches or theophany has highlighted issues such as creation being God-centered (not human-centered), and that God's active ruling as king over creation is based on much more than simply human retributive justice.[68] After the exegetical work on chapters 38–39, the first context to be considered is that of the Yahweh speeches and Job's responses as a whole (38:1–42:6). This would highlight a parallel between the form and structure of the two speeches and draw attention to the different challenge questions (38:2; 40:8), which focus on God's design and his justice. This context clarifies a concern with the broader question of how God orders his creation. The need for Job to change his stance is then reflected in 42:2-6, in which Job moves on from his complaint now that God has expanded his horizons.

The function of chapters 38–39 within the book as a whole would be the next context. In this commentary I have outlined the false trails of Job's friends, the wisdom poem of chapter 28, and the speeches of Elihu. Instead, Job is vin-

---

66. This is adapted from the outline of this approach in L. Wilson, "Job 38–39," 122.

67. C. Wright, *Knowing Jesus*, 28.

68. For more detail on this, as well as the role of biblical theology as a reading strategy, see my "Job 38–39."

dicated, and his words are endorsed by God (42:7-17). Clearly, then, the Yahweh speeches should not be seen as belittling Job, but simply seek to move him in a new direction now that a bigger picture of God's active rule has been explained.

Since Job is part of the wisdom group of books, we recognize the principle of retribution espoused by Proverbs, but it loses its flexibility with the friends and is balanced by the freedom of God to rule his creation in accordance with his wider purposes. The two ideas need to be held in counterpoint. Indeed, as we move to the rest of the OT, we see that God's broader aims in his creation, begun in Genesis 1–11, show that God's active ruling of his world is broader than simply rescuing his covenant people. The purpose of referring to creation in Job 38–39 is not so that the readers will marvel at the creation, but rather that they will begin to understand God's creationwide perspective, and so trust him with persevering faith through life's struggles. Of course, the Bible as a whole depicts God taking on human flesh (John 1:1-4) and Christ as the Lord who sustains creation as well as the Lord of redemption (Col 1:15-23). His active rule over creation was seen in his nature miracles, with some strong parallels between his stilling of the storm (Mark 4:35-41) and the theophany (especially Job 38:11). Here too God's active lordship over creation is meant to lead to persevering faith.

When we reread Job 38–39 in the light of these ever-expanding contexts (climaxing in Christ), then it is clear that the thrust of these chapters is much more than "look at the majesty of God as creator." For those of us who know Christ's sustaining work in creation and his ongoing rule in all of everyday life, we are meant to respond to our triune Creator by trusting in his kingly rule and persevering in faith. Our reading strategy of exploring the biblical theological contexts of this passage has helped to clarify how to apply its truths in preaching and in daily living.

Reading Job 7

Job 7 is an example of the common complaint-to-God genre, echoing the characteristic lament questions of "why" and "how long" (7:17-21). Job struggles with the presence of suffering coupled with the apparent absence of God, and expresses his loss and confusion in graphic ways. He accuses God ("Why have you made me your mark?" 7:20; also 7:12, 14); he complains without restraint (7:11); he loathes his life and tells God to leave him alone (7:16, 19). He prefers death (7:15) and does not want to live forever (7:16). At first sight, this is not a promising passage either for a preaching text or for one's personal devotions. However, if we look closer, it is clear that Job is grappling with the question of what it means to be a human in God's world ("What is man," 7:17). Furthermore, his underlying assumption is that God is the only one who can resolve his circumstances (7:21), and so he calls on him to "remember" him (7:7).

Again, this passage needs to be placed progressively in its wider contexts. It comes as the second half of Job's response to Eliphaz (chs. 6–7), in which Job, unlike the friends, turns from debate to address God directly. This turning to speak to God is Job's characteristic move, especially in the first round of speeches, and itself shows a lively faith. As part of the first cycle of the debate, Job is under attack by his friends, who accuse him of sin, brand him as wicked, and urge him to repent. The still wider context of the prologue informs us that they are not justified in their views. These are not the words of a scoffer, but of one who is under attack for his faith.

This context provides a clue for what Job is doing here. He is assuming the positive view of God's care for humanity found in Ps 8:4 (ESV):

> what is man that you are mindful of him,
> and the son of man that you care for him?

However, he is trying to make sense of his circumstances against the backdrop of this psalm, as he says (Job 7:17-18 ESV):

> What is man, that you make so much of him,
> and that you set your heart on him,
> visit him every morning
> and test him every moment?

He is not denying the truth of the psalm but is exploring how it applies to his life. Just as he does with the doctrine of retribution, he is seeking to qualify or nuance the simplistic views of his friends, who assume that a psalm like this will always govern how God treats his people. This is an example of what Katharine Dell describes as taking a familiar form and filling it with unexpected content.[69]

In this broader context, Job is pouring out the seemingly contradictory aspects of God's treatment of him, but shows ongoing faith as he still calls on God to remember him. This language of "remembering" is present in the second half of each of his speeches in the first cycle (7:7; 10:9; 14:13), and clarifies

---

69. Dell, *Shaking a Fist at God,* 58-59. She uses the parallel of starting a story "once upon a split second" (instead of "once upon a time") and ending it not with "they lived happily ever after" but rather "they were miserable unto eternity." Dell, however, thinks that Job is rejecting the idea rather than qualifying it.

that his deeper goal is not to be abandoned by God. The first cycle of speeches thus clarifies that his call for God to "leave him alone" is not to be taken at face value. Even in chapter 7, Job is expressing a deep and genuine faith in God but exploring what it means to be human in times of adversity.

This picture of Job's robust faith is reinforced in the wider context of Job. Yahweh's words in chapters 38–41 are not intended to accuse or condemn Job. Job's partial horizons had been expanded, and he is called on to take a new direction, which he duly acknowledges (42:2-6). While both humans and justice are important to God, his concerns are not limited to these aspects of reality. God is concerned for all of creation (e.g., 38:26) and is sovereignly free to exercise his more abundant purposes. Crucial to Job's dilemma is that he is assuming a tight nexus between actions or character and consequences (the intrawisdom debate), but the solution to how God treats humanity takes him to a bigger view of God and his active rule. The lives of humanity before God are governed by much more than one principle of human retributive justice.

Job's discovery is filled out in the wider OT as well. The God over creation in Genesis 1–2 is the same God who will stand no rival (Isa 40–55), and before whom even whole nations are like a drop of water or speck of dust (Isa 40:12, 22-23). Yet that same God over creation will raise up nations in history to attack his people. Though these nations are unrighteous and evil, God will use them for his purposes, which will again cause a believer like Habakkuk to cry out "why" and "how long" (Hab 1:2-3). In a world in which the new creation of Isa 65:17-25 is not yet a reality, God's people will still live with unanswered questions but cling to God in faith in the meantime.

This robust, lamenting faith is also seen in the NT. Lament itself is legitimated for Christians when Christ adopts the opening words of a lament psalm as he is hanging on the cross (Matt 27:46, citing Ps 22:1). The book of 1 Peter addresses God's people who are suffering because of their faith but are tested and refined by it (1 Pet 1:6-7). Peter calls his readers to stand firm in the midst of their unjust troubles (1 Pet 5:6-9). Job is even used by James as an example of persevering faith (Jas 5:11). The writer of Hebrews appeals to Jesus as one who was also tested and so can help others undergoing trials (Heb 2:14-18; 4:14-16). Finally, the NT closes with pictures of God's people undergoing great hardship (e.g., Rev 12:17), pouring out their laments (the "how long" of Rev 6:10), and holding fast to their God (Rev 14:12). Only then will God's ultimate purposes prevail.

When Job 7 is read in this ever-widening context of the rest of Scripture, it can be reread not as a story of failure of faith ("don't ask God to leave you alone, like Job did") but rather as one who clings on to God with a robust faith and asks God to remember him. The wider biblical context enables us to discern how

331

Job's questions and challenges still permit him to be described as one who has spoken about God what is right (42:7-8). Job is tested, even taunted, but longs for the God he knows to come near with comfort. In refusing to abandon God in such a setting of anguish and loss, Job shows a persevering faith.

Job and Systematic Theology

In a number of areas of systematic theology we would expect the book of Job to have little impact. It does not speak of ecclesiology, sacraments, the person and work of Jesus, election, pneumatology, or eschatology. However, this simply reflects that not every book of the Bible will speak to every issue in theology. The possible areas of contribution need to be examined more closely. Some topics in systematic theology, such as resurrection, Satan, sin, and the Scriptures, need some careful exploration as Job may contribute to some of the current debates. Even more clearly, Job makes a vital impact on such areas as our thinking about the nature of God, how God runs his world, and our understanding of creation and of humanity.

Job and the Doctrine of God

We have already partially explored the book's teaching about God in an earlier section.[70] Here I aim to supplement that with a brief discussion of systematic theologies of God in the light of the book of Job.

However, we need to be cautious in drawing out truths about God from the various parts of the book of Job. This is particularly the case of verses from the dialogue: we need to consider whether this is asserted or endorsed by the book as a whole. Thus some systematicians view Job 37:16 as establishing that God is perfect in knowledge.[71] There are two difficulties with this. First, these are the words of Elihu, and there needs to be some rationale for why his view should be regarded as that of the book as a whole. He also says that Job is an evil scoffer (34:7-9) and that God will not appear to humans (34:23), yet neither of these assertions is endorsed by the book as a whole. Second, while it seems right to describe God as "perfect in knowledge," Elihu earlier had described himself in exactly the same terms (36:4). Why should one be read as true and the other not? The extent of God's knowledge might better be conveyed by the lengthy

70. See the earlier section "Theological Themes: God."
71. For example, Reymond, *New Systematic Theology,* 184; Horton, *Christian Faith,* 240.

description in the first Yahweh speech (chs. 38–39), which clearly establishes the parameters of what God knows, but couples it with an explanation of his care for all his creatures.

Other systematic theologians, perhaps daunted by the complexity of the book, do not allow it to make a contribution to the doctrine of God. For example, the only reference to Job in Wayne Grudem's large volume is to use 19:25-26 as proof of OT belief about the resurrection.[72] The book's rich description of God seems to make no other contribution to his book.

A clear contribution of the book is its outline of God's providential workings. The principles on which God bases his activity are not set out, but the assertion of the book is that God is bringing about his purposes, but doing so behind the scenes. God appears in the heavenly court in the prologue, not at all in the dialogue, and only in a whirlwind in the theophany. God's providence is most clearly seen in the prologue, where the events that occur on earth are not directly performed by God himself, but by the agency of the accuser, who also uses both natural forces (lightning, east wind; 1:16, 19) and human actions (Sabeans, Chaldeans; 1:15, 17). Notwithstanding the intermediaries used, what happens on earth is what God has done.

When God does appear in chapter 38, he performs no action other than to address Job with verbal challenges. In the epilogue God gives a further address, this time to Eliphaz, Bildad, and Zophar, and forgives them after Job's intercession (42:7-9). We read of God "restoring" Job's fortunes (42:10), giving Job double (42:10), and blessing Job with much livestock (42:12). However, the means of doing so is not made explicit. The mention of human agency in this restoration (42:11) and the parallels to the prologue suggest that these actions of restoration and blessing were theological interpretations of God acting in the background.

The book of Job may also impact our understanding of God's omnipresence. The traditional understanding of God being present everywhere can be seen most clearly in Psalm 139. Yet, even within the book of Psalms, the lament genre struggles with the issue of the apparent absence of God in daily life (e.g., Pss 13, 22). The lament cries of "why" and "how long" are really ways of asking, "Where are you, God?" Of course, the laments and complaints of the book of Job function in a similar way, nuancing what is meant by the words of God's presence, "you are there" (Ps 139:8). Both Job and the book of Psalms are calling not for God's mere presence but for God to be present with blessing. The systematic theologian's issue of God being present or accessible or able to see is not the issue of the book of Job. Rather, Job is calling out to the God who does

72. Grudem, *Systematic Theology*, 830.

not seem to be present and asking him to act in accordance with his implied creational commitments (10:8-12). The question is never whether it is possible for God to be everywhere at the same time, but of God acting consistently with his nature in sustaining human beings. Thus the book seeks to reorient the systematician's question about the extent of God's presence by raising the dichotomy of presence and absence that is found elsewhere in the OT.

The book of Job may also be seen to nuance the doctrine of the immutability of God — that God does not and cannot change. Is Yahweh's varying treatment of the righteous human, Job, consistent with him remaining true to his nature and purposes? The idea of God as immutable is often misunderstood. While God does not change in his nature or essence, the notion of unchangeableness does not mean that he is frozen or unresponsive to humans and their needs. God answers prayer; he intervenes to deliver his people and is constantly at work in his world. As Robert Reymond expresses it, "He is not static in his immutability; he is dynamic."[73] God certainly responds to the intercession of righteous Job (1:4-5; 42:7-9), but he does not swerve from his ongoing goals.

The book of Job clarifies the unchangeableness of God by coupling it with the idea that God is sovereignly free to rule his world. Although God is unchanged, he is not in chains. Humans cannot say to God, "you cannot do that" or "you must act in this way," if that cuts across God's purposes for the whole of creation. Job's friends insist that God can only act to reward human righteousness and punish human wickedness, for that is his character as one committed to retributive justice. However, God can change in his treatment of Job because justice is only one part of God's character, and God must be free to act in accordance with his wider and longer purposes.

An openness-of-God theologian, John Sanders, has argued that God can change to the extent that he can even be manipulated by human beings: "One of the most remarkable features of the Old Testament is that people can argue with God and win."[74] Yet the book of Job insists that the relationship between God and humans is not one of a contest of competing wills, but rather one of God actively ruling, even if at times behind the scenes. In the end, Job sees the wisdom of abandoning his litigation against God due to the shortcomings of an adversarial approach.

The book does have a contribution to make to God's role in creation. Alister McGrath observes, "Job 38:1–42:6 sets out what is unquestionably the

---

73. Reymond, *New Systematic Theology*, 178. Berkhof, *Systematic Theology*, 59, reminds us, "There is change round about Him, change in the relations of men to Him, but there is no change in His Being, His attributes, His purpose, His motives of actions, or His promises."

74. Sanders, *God Who Risks*, 64.

most comprehensive understanding of God as creator to be found in the Old Testament."[75] While I have already dealt with the book's theology of creation,[76] it is worth recalling its distinctive contributions. Against a Deist view of God, in which God winds up the clock of creation and lets it go without further attention, the book of Job insists that God is actively ruling through his sustaining work. This is especially seen among the animal creation, where God draws a contrast between Job's lack of both knowledge and care and God's "hunting" (38:39), "providing" food (38:41), setting free (39:5), covering and making horses leap (39:19, 20), and "commanding" (39:27). God does not merely provide a home for the animals, but deliberately sustains them even in difficult places. The focus of the theology of God as creator in the book is more on this subsequent sustaining rather than the initial acts of creation.

The book also insists that God's active ordering of creation is not always transparent to human beings. Chapters 38–39 assume that God does the detail work and not just the big picture planning, but the point of the book as a whole depends on humans being unable to fully understand God's plans or purposes. Until the theophany, the three friends presume (wrongly) that God's management of creation is determined solely by the principle of retribution. This would make God's sustaining work transparent to wise human beings, but it is a view built on a false premise. This is not the only basis on which God acts in the human sphere, and certainly not in all of creation. His rule of creation is more complex than we imagine and is, at least partially, hidden from humanity.

In the prologue the accuser challenges not only Job's righteousness but also God's right ordering of creation. If God has wrongly rewarded Job (since his faith is based on self-interest, 1:9), then the Creator is basing his active rule on the false premise that Job deserves to be rewarded. However, the book as a whole concludes that Job is indeed a righteous person (42:7-8), so that no injustice has been done, even though the basis for God's sovereignly free activity is not bound by this principle. God's ordering of the creation is righteous, but is certainly not constrained by a narrow, human-centered view of retributive justice. Reymond concludes that the book is a rich source of illustrative material about God's active rule of his world.[77] In 36:32 Elihu claims that God commands lightning to strike its mark, and this is broadened out to the rest of the creation in the Yahweh speeches. Furthermore, Job, who has spoken about God what is right, outlines in 12:10-23 that God's activity is comprehensive. To him belongs

---

75. McGrath, *Christian Theology*, 216.
76. See the earlier section "Theological Themes: Creation."
77. Reymond, *New Systematic Theology*, 358.

the life of every creature, and all wisdom and power. He raises up some nations and their leaders, and pulls down others.

At first glance, the book of Job might also be viewed as a fruitful source of images of God that might fit well with a process theology or openness-of-God viewpoint. Does God allow Job to be tested because he does not know the outcome of the test? Are the events of the world a cooperation between a God who risks and human endeavors, as if God alone cannot determine what will happen?

Process theology claims that God cannot cause people to act in a certain way but only influence or seek to persuade them. In terms of the story of Job, God could thus be absolved of blame for inflicting suffering on Job or failing to stop it. Even natural disasters like those in the prologue would not bring moral culpability to God, since he can work only by attempting to influence the natural processes, but cannot override or control them.[78] This would provide an easy solution to the problem of suffering in Job, but the book does not take this path. However, the prologue shows Yahweh initiating the processes, and God's speeches portray him as actively in control of the natural forces in the world (38:4-38). In particular, the theophany does not depict God simply as interacting with the world, seeking to influence it. Instead, God is transcendent over the creation, even though the means he uses to control it are not explained.[79] Process theology could have been used in the book of Job but was not. In any event, its diminished view of God makes it an unattractive option.

Open theism (or openness-of-God theology), to some extent building on the process theology debate but arising as an intraevangelical discussion, argues that God cannot have knowledge of future events. Thus God could not have known for sure whether Job would pass the testing of his faith. Sanders, for example, proposed that God could only know what can be known and that "the future actions of free creatures are not yet reality, and so there is nothing to be known."[80] Along these lines, it could be claimed that the testing of Job took place in order for God to know Job's character, and whether his devotion to God was genuine or simply based on self-interest.[81] However, there is no hint of God's uncertainty in the text, and he virtually boasts about the genuineness

78. McGrath, *Christian Theology*, 214-15.

79. Burnett, *Where Is God?* 111, notes that "the divine speeches affirm the divine transcendence without explaining it."

80. Sanders, *God Who Risks*, 198-99. For a useful summary of this issue, see Allison, *Historical Theology*, 227-30; and Erickson, *Christian Theology*, 305-8.

81. However, Boyd, *God of the Possible*, 63-66, explores a number of possible places where God tests people to know their character, but does not include Job.

of Job's faith (1:8; 2:3). If God has wrongly described Job as a person of utter integrity, then it is not simply a matter of God not knowing the future but of God making a mistake about something in the present. Open theism, then, does not account for the story of Job, which insists that God's purposes will and do triumph.

Job and Theodicy

Theodicy is a term used to describe attempts to justify the ways of God in the face of the existence and effects of evil in the world. The story of Job invites reflection on the issue of theodicy. Here is a righteous man who apparently suffers out of all proportion to any wrongdoing; here is seen the activity of the "accuser," whom God allows to inflict suffering on Job; here both Job and the friends explore why Job is suffering; here God speaks about the way he runs his world; finally, here Job has all his possessions restored and even increased.

Theodicy emerges because readers of the Bible notice three crucial ideas, and find difficulty in working out the relationship among them:

1. God is all-powerful, all-knowing, and is active in his world.
2. God is perfectly good.
3. Disasters and suffering exist in the world.

Some find these three statements mutually incompatible, while others use the Bible's claims as grounds for doubting the existence of the biblical God.

In practice, an excessive amount of suffering (e.g., the Holocaust, the Lisbon earthquake of 1755, or the Boxing Day tsunami of 2004) makes this issue more acute, but the mere existence of even a small amount of suffering logically raises the issue of God's character and his abilities. Our interest, however, is not in the (complicated) nuances of the philosophical theories, but in what this means for the book of Job. Does the book of Job shed light on this theoretical discussion, and does the philosophical debate elucidate the story of Job? It is an important topic, since it "deals with the core of theology: what is God like, and how does he relate to the world?"[82]

Some scholars emphasize that the source of the suffering is morally significant, and that moral evil (that caused by humans) and natural evil (those acts not apparently or immediately caused by humans) need to be justified separately. However, the suffering inflicted on Job in the prologue is a mixture

---

82. Davies, "Theodicy," 808.

of moral evil (e.g., the Sabeans and Chaldeans in 1:15, 17) and natural evil (e.g., the "fire from God" and the mighty wind of 1:16, 19, and the sores of 2:7). There is the added complication of the accuser being the instrumental cause of both categories (e.g., 1:12; 2:6). In the debate and its resolution, neither Job nor God makes anything of the different sources of the suffering. Furthermore, even at the end of book Job is content but has never found out about the heavenly court scenes or the agency of the accuser. The source of the suffering, and even the instrumental use of the accuser, do not appear important in the book as we have it.

Others see the activity of the accuser as the key to theodicy in the book. This feeds into a more popular view that Satan ("the accuser") causes suffering while God takes the credit for blessing. Even though this may seem an attractive way out, it leads to a dualistic understanding of two competing wills in the heavens, which is a less-than-biblical understanding of God. It also does not account for the text of Job, which pictures the accuser as powerless to act without God's permission (1:9-12; 2:4-7), and God as responsible for both blessing and trouble (2:10). There still remains the difficulty of explaining why God allows Job to suffer.

Justifications for the existence of suffering and/or evil are often based on the positive value of the suffering.[83] At many places the friends try to justify Job's suffering as retributive (e.g., 4:7-9; 8:3-4; 11:14-20), but Job realizes that, while retribution is important to God, it does not account for all that Job notices in the world (e.g., 21:7-13; 24:1-17). Both Eliphaz and Elihu propose that suffering can have an educative role (5:17-19; 33:19-20; 36:15), but this possible solution is not the reason for Job's suffering in the prologue and is not picked up by God when he appears. Zophar proposes that God's ways are mysterious (e.g., 11:7-9), and this is also reflected in the interlude in chapter 28 (e.g., 28:13-27), which I have argued is not endorsed as the answer of the book as a whole. God's verdict on the friends (42:7-8) would further preclude any of these reasons being the justification of Job's suffering.

James Crenshaw suggests that the book of Job reveals the probative value of suffering, with God subjecting Job to a "monstrous test" so that he can know Job's true motives.[84] Yet if the motive is probative, it is not God who finds out information but rather Job or the reader. Crenshaw divides responses to evil

---

83. See, e.g., Crenshaw, "Theodicy," 552-54. He outlines the retributive, educative, probative, eschatological, revelational, mysterious, determinist, substitutionary, trans-generational, and denial views. Of these, the eschatological, determinist, substitutionary, trans-generational, and denial views play no part in the book of Job. See also the discussion and categories in Laato and de Moor, *Theodicy in the World of the Bible*, xxix-liv.

84. Crenshaw, "Theodicy," 553.

into ten categories, the fifth of which is the revelational, by which he means that a close encounter with God — even though it involves suffering — is of benefit to the person because it reveals more of God's nature. In Job's case it might arguably bring Job closer to God, or give him a more intense relationship, perhaps hinted at in 42:3, 5. However, while this is often a possible result of suffering, there is no suggestion of this being God's motive in the prologue, nor is it raised by him in the Yahweh speeches.

Systematic and philosophical theologians have looked to theoretical more than text-based responses to justify the ways of God in a setting of suffering. Kenneth Surin outlines four key types of theodicy:

1. The freewill defense, most clearly espoused by Alvin Plantinga, who maintains that God is all-powerful, all-knowing, and perfectly good, but "evil exists because of the actions of free, rational and fallible creatures." For Plantinga, it is logically impossible for God to make creatures in such a way that it is necessarily the case that these creatures can only do actions that are good and beneficial. The freewill defense works best when the suffering is caused by human actions. However, in the book of Job, the issue of suffering arises indiscriminately from both human and natural causes (1:13-19).

2. The "natural law" theodicy, as seen in the writings of Richard Swinburne, who contends that there is a good reason for permitting both natural and human evil to exist. The essence of this argument is that one needs to see harmful consequences of previous actions in order to learn that certain actions have bad consequences, and there must be natural evils for human agents to know how to create or prevent bad consequences. This makes it harder to justify the extent of Job's suffering, since only some evil is required for this theodicy. It certainly would not require Job to be afflicted a second time (2:7).

3. Process theodicy, as reflected in the views of Charles Hartshorne, who argues that God depends on his creatures to overcome evil. David Griffin, also an exponent of the process view, asserts, "To have the good is necessarily to risk the chance of the bad." One cannot have the capacity to enjoy if one does not also have the capacity to suffer.[85] J. Gerald Janzen incorporates many process ideas in his commentary, but the resulting picture seems far away from the picture of a sovereignly free God in the theophany.

4. The "soul-making" theodicy, as seen in the views of John Hick, who, based

85. Griffin, "Creation out of Chaos," 107.

339

on Irenaeus, regards evil as an integral element of the environment in which all people can grow into a perfected relationship with God. God creates us as free beings for a purpose to enable us to fulfill our nature in relation to God by exercising our freedom. In this life we are involved in the soul-making process, still needing completion. We are created as imperfect and developing creatures. The book of Job, however, insists that Job begins the story as one who is blameless and upright, fearing God and turning away from evil (1:1, 8; 2:3).[86]

Karl-Johan Illman has undertaken a thorough study of theodicy in Job, proposing that "the entire Book of Job is a theodicy in itself."[87] He argues, however, that a proper understanding of its theodicy is dependent on a diachronic study of the different and often conflicting parts, especially the prologue/epilogue and the dialogue. He refers, for example, to "two incompatible attitudes to God in the figure of Job, one in Chapters 1–2 plus 42:7-17, and another in Chapters 3–42:6."[88] So he separately considers these "two Jobs," suggesting that the "Job of the prologue/epilogue . . . expresses the view that God has the right to do what he likes with his creation, the other directs severe criticism against God precisely because God does what he pleases with his creation."[89] He suggests that the kind of classical theodicy that best represents the view of the friends is the educative theodicy (that suffering has an instructional role), but that this does not and cannot do justice to the way the book begins and ends.[90] In this commentary, however, I have argued for a unified reading of the book of Job, though one that contains differing emphases in its various parts. An understanding of the book's theodicy, then, would require an analysis that allows for all sections of the book.

In the end, the book of Job seems content to leave the question of theodicy unresolved. It precludes certain common answers in the case of Job, but insists that the God who is sovereign and free to act for his own reasons does not have to account to humans for his running of the universe. The intellectual need to explain or justify the works of God is not Job's deepest problem. As readers of this significant book, we might have hoped for more light to be shed on the vexed issue of theodicy, but we need to rest content with what we have been given.

86. Surin, *Theology and the Problem of Evil*, 70-111.
87. Illman, "Theodicy in Job," 305.
88. Ibid., 308-9.
89. Ibid., 314.
90. Ibid., 318.

Job and Satan

Satan is explicitly mentioned in the OT only in 1 Chr 21:1, Zech 3:1-2, and possibly Job 1–2. The serpent in Genesis 3 is not initially identified as Satan, although this connection is made in the NT (Rev 12:9; 20:2). In view of the sparse number of explicit references to Satan in the OT, it is not surprising that scholars want to make much of the figure in the prologue of Job. A number of questions need to be addressed.

Is the Accuser Satan?

The Hebrew noun שָׂטָן/*śāṭān* has the core meaning of an accuser or adversary, either an earthly one (as in 1 Sam 29:4) or a heavenly one (as in Num 22:22). Thus in 1 Kgs 11:25 Rezon was Israel's adversary or "satan" in the time of Solomon. In a legal setting it can have a more specific meaning of a human prosecutor or legal accuser (e.g., Ps 109:6).[91] Its use with the definite article in Job and in Zechariah 3 implies that it refers to someone who in the role of an accuser or adversary, rather than a person's name. Most English versions obscure this feature by translating *haśśāṭān* ("*the* accuser") as "Satan." This may be reading later ideas of Satan or the devil back into Job 1–2. The use of *śāṭān* without a definite article in 1 Chronicles 21 suggests that it functions there as a personal name or title, just as one would expect if the devil was being described.

The presence of the article in the prologue of Job is also often ignored by systematic theologians. For example, Grudem notes that "satan" is the personal name of the head of the demons, and gives Job 1:6 as one place where his "name" is mentioned.[92] Similarly, Hendrikus Berkhof asserts, "In Job 1 and 2 he is called *śāṭān*, that is, accuser, where apparently he is already a figure with a definite name and function."[93] However, the use of the article in the Hebrew text of Job 1:6 implies that it is not a personal name. Clarity on this matter is important before considering the extent to which "the accuser" of the prologue can be identified with Satan.

One view is to identify this figure with the investigators in the service of the king during the Persian period. His task is to serve the king by spying out and reporting on people who had been regarded as loyal servants to the empire. In making these accusations that the king is wrong to trust and reward a given

---

91. Page, *Powers of Evil*, 23-24.
92. Grudem, *Systematic Theology*, 414.
93. Berkhof, *Christian Faith*, 200.

person, the investigator is not being insolent, but simply doing his job. Such a spy is an adversary or accuser as a loyal servant and is ultimately working for the benefit of the king.[94] Thus the accuser in the prologue is not God's adversary but rather his agent. This view requires a certain view of dating the book and presupposes that a Hebrew reader would discern this role.

An increasingly popular theory is to regard the accuser as a projection of part of God himself. Meir Weiss argued that this figure was "the embodiment of God's apprehension," expressing God's own doubt or even the shady side to his character.[95] Gibson viewed it as "little more than an extension of Yahweh, representing that side of divinity which for whatever reason visits affliction on men," while Carol Newsom called the accuser "the externalizing of divine doubt about the human heart."[96] This seeks to solve the issue of theodicy by redefining the character of God, but has no grounding in the book.

A closer look at the text reveals a number of indicators about the identity of this accuser. His insidious nature is implied by the tone of his comments. His language is abrupt and peremptory, using imperatives to address God, and he fails to use the deferential language associated with court etiquette (addressing a superior as "my Lord," not "you"; himself as "your servant," not "I"). These seem to be indicators of insulting speech, hinting that he does not belong to the circle of God's respectful servants. David Clines, however, suggests that this simply reflects the naivete of the prologue and its economical use of words (e.g., there is no description of the heavenly court).[97] This is more difficult to determine, for at times the description is wordy, not brief (e.g., the repetition of "the accuser said to the LORD," or "the LORD said to the accuser," rather than "he said" or "the accuser said"). The careful selection and use of words in the prologue suggest that the accuser's tone and language are significant details.

In addition, the content of the accuser's attack on Job is really an attack on God's management of creation, so that he is not only the accuser of Job but also the accuser of God himself. Peggy Day notes, "The *śāṭān* is implicitly challenging Yahweh's blueprint for world order."[98] The accuser is arguing that God is showing favoritism to an unworthy person and thus not ruling the world with justice.

---

94. For example, White, "Purpose and Portrayal," 64-65. At 64 she notes, "Just like the Persian spies, the vocation of the *śāṭān* in the Book of Job was to search out the faithful and report the unfaithful to Yahweh."

95. Weiss, *Story of Job's Beginning*, 41.

96. Gibson, "On Evil," 418; Newsom, "Book of Job," 348. See also Kluger, *Satan in the Old Testament*, 119; Clines, *Job 1–20*, 22. Even Habel, *Book of Job*, 89, thinks he may be "verbalizing Yahweh's own latent misapprehensions."

97. Clines, *Job 1–20*, 23, 30.

98. Day, *Adversary in Heaven*, 80.

Sydney Page suggests that, since the author never seeks to explain the term "the accuser," this implies that the readers of the book were expected to be familiar with his identity. This, he says, should incline us to think it is Satan or the devil.[99] However, other figures in the book such as the umpire, witness, mediator, and hearer are never explained, yet no identifiable character seems in view there. Another reason for his identity not being explained is that the literary focus is not on the character described as "the accuser," but on Job. Thus it would make good literary sense not to explain a character who could be a potential distraction. Page is on stronger ground when he contends that the accuser exercises a different role than that of a prosecutor. This includes scouring the world looking for human shortcomings, not initiating the report on Job (Job is raised by God), and calling God's judgment into question by suggesting that he is hoodwinked by Job's outward actions.[100] In addition, his role of scouring the earth looking for human failings makes him much more than simply a prosecutor.

In terms of the whole Bible, three characteristics of the accuser are picked up in the NT to describe the activity of Satan:

1. He roams the earth, bringing affliction (the roaring lion of 1 Pet 5:8).
2. He accuses believers before God (Rev 12:10).
3. He sifts out loyalty to God (like Satan with Peter in Luke 22:31).[101]

Thus, although the accuser is not given a personal name in Job, the Christian reader of the book is likely to interpret this figure as the one later named as Satan or the devil. In a similar way, the serpent of Genesis 3 is not explicitly named in that chapter as Satan or the devil, although this identification is explicitly made in Rev 12:9 and 20:2. The accuser's work in Job 1–2 provides a strong hint that this figure is to be identified as the one later revealed more explicitly as Satan.

Where Is the Accuser Found in the Book?

A number of scholars have been puzzled by the absence of the accuser (or Satan) in the rest of the book, especially in the resolution offered. If suffering is sometimes a result of the activity of "prince of this world," then that would

99. Page, *Powers of Evil*, 24.
100. Ibid., 26-27.
101. Ibid., 30.

provide at least a partial answer to the problem of why there is so much pain on earth. It is worth commenting that some scholars have found the presence of the accuser subsequent to the prologue. For example, Day maintains that the umpire of 9:33 is the accuser of the prologue, who can argue with God about his ordering of the world, as is the witness of 16:19-21. His new titles indicate a changing function. Furthermore, both the mediator of 19:25-27 and Elihu's proposal of a mediator (33:23-25) ironically conjure up the figure of the *śāṭān* from the prologue.[102] This view, however, lacks textual support.

More plausibly, several scholars have sought to counter the perceived absence of the accuser in the book's resolution by identifying him with the mythological figures of the second Yahweh speech (chs. 40–41). Thus Gibson has proposed that both Behemoth and Leviathan have a metaphorical link with Satan (all are "figures of evil"), especially against the background of Canaanite mythology.[103] His student Robert Fyall has modified this by suggesting that Leviathan is a picture of Satan, while Behemoth is the personification of Death.[104] While I have argued that this reading should not be adopted, it would have the merit of bringing "Satan" into the question of theodicy in the book.

What does the book tell the reader about Satan?

Even if we assume that the accuser can be identified as the one we later know as Satan, there is not much detailed information about him in the book. His role is not to inform readers about himself but rather to implement the forms of testing of Job's faith. There is nothing in the book about his origin or his "fall," and his nature can only be inferred by his words and actions. The pre-history of the accuser is simply not a focus of the text. There is also not enough information to decide whether he belongs to the heavenly court or whether he is there as an intruder. He is simply a tool in a narrative that is focused on the issue of whether genuine human faith in God is possible. He instigates a test and reports back on it.

The most important insight of the prologue is that the accuser is not portrayed as an "equal but opposite" force opposed to God. He is at all times subordinate to Yahweh and can do nothing to Job without God's permission (1:12; 2:6). Calvin clearly describes the limits on the accuser's power: "he can do nothing unless God wills and assents to it . . . with the bridle of his power God holds him bound and restrained, he carries out only those things which have been divinely permitted to him."[105] He has the power to carry out activities on

---

102. Day, *Adversary in Heaven,* 88-103.
103. Gibson, "On Evil," 417-19.
104. Fyall, *Now My Eyes,* 128-29, 137, 157, 173-74.
105. Calvin, *Institutes,* 1.14.17.

earth that can cause human suffering, but his power is derived and limited. The agency of the accuser is not part of the solution of the book. Since Job never discovers the accuser's involvement, his existence makes no contribution to Job's moving in a new direction or in his understanding why all these struggles have been his lot.

Job and Sin

The book of Job has a clear focus on the nature of humanity and the possibility of genuine human faith in God. It begins with, "A man there was . . ." (1:1), placed emphatically at the start of the prologue; it focuses on Job as a righteous human being (1:1-5); and the challenge is whether even the one who is apparently very godly is serving God only from ulterior motives. The way the book is set up leads us to expect that the idea of sin will be prominent in the book.

The entries on sin in standard systematic theologies usually focus on the nature of sin, the extent of sin, the consequences or penalty of sin, temptation and sin, the forgiveness of sin, the origin of sin, and so on. However, the book of Job's teaching on sin is confined to certain specific topics or areas, and most of the traditional foci are backgrounded.[106] Furthermore, much of what is said emerges from the cut-and-thrust of debate, not a reflective fireside chat on the topic, so we need to be wary of extracting timeless teaching from emotive outbursts.

One important issue in the book is the correlation between sin and suffering. The prologue sets this in train by juxtaposing the utter righteousness of Job (1:1, 4-5, 8; 2:3) and his abundant prosperity (1:2-3). This positive nexus of righteousness and prosperity was one-half of the doctrine of retribution. The flip side of this idea is that there would also be a correlation between a person's unrighteousness or sin and that person's suffering or hardship. This connection is broken in the prologue, when Job suffers for reasons other than his sin (1:10-12). He suffers the loss of wealth and possessions (1:14-16), which were outward symbols of his godliness, but also his family members (1:18-19) and his health (2:7-8). However, God insists that Job is still righteous (2:3), and this is twice stated by the (reliable) narrator (1:22; 2:10). Clearly, the reader is meant to understand that the mere fact of Job's suffering cannot justify the view that Job must have sinned greatly.

The friends, however, assume that suffering is an infallible indicator of a person's sin, and this understanding guides their contributions to the dialogue.

---

106. On the terminology of sin in the book, see Boda, *Severe Mercy*, 380-81.

Eliphaz is reminded in a vision that no one can be sinless (4:17), so he initially views Job's suffering as a (temporary) discipline (5:17). Bildad suggests that his very survival when his children have died is evidence that he is a sinner, but less sinful than his children (8:4-6). Zophar even concludes that Job has been suffering less than his sins deserved (11:6). God's verdict is that the three friends have not spoken about Job what is right (42:7-8).

If the three friends focused on suffering as a consequence of Job's sinful actions, the human arbiter Elihu focuses on Job's words uttered during the debate as indicators of his wrongdoing. In his opening speeches, he cites Job's words to God, and then rebukes him for his sinful speech (see p. 156 above). The essence of his conclusion is that God does not appear to humans, and that Job is in the wrong. Unfortunately for Elihu, God then does appear, and in the Yahweh speeches does not seek to correct Job's supposed errors, but rather wishes simply to expand his horizon. God even says to the friends that Job has spoken of him what is right (42:7-8), which makes clear that neither Job's prior actions nor his subsequent speech are the reasons for his extensive suffering. The book as a whole, then, denies that a person's sin is always the explanation for any suffering that comes one's way.

The book is also curiously silent about the distinction between suffering caused by nature and that caused by other humans. It is common in theodicies to differentiate between disasters that have come from living in the (fallen) world and those that are the result of violent or selfish human actions. When Job loses all his possessions and children, some happen as a result of natural forces (lightning and storms, 1:16, 19) and some from human agents (Sabean and Chaldean raiders, 1:15, 17). Job makes no attempt to divide them into two groups, and he ascribes all of his losses to God — "the LORD has taken away" (1:21). While it is true that human sin has affected creation (Gen 3:17-19), this is not explored by Job as an explanation ("we live in a fallen world") or a potential source of comfort.

Nor is the agency of the accuser, *haśśāṭān*, part of the answer of the book. While he is the agent who causes the losses (1:12; 2:6), he is absent after the prologue and so does not fit in the solution. Indeed, Job never finds out about the agency of the accuser, so it is not crucial to the resolution of his dilemma. Job's stance throughout is that God is the ultimate cause of what happens. God gives and God takes away (1:21); we receive both blessing and disaster from God (2:10). While many Christians and some scholars use the book of Job to explain that Satan is the cause of sin, our protagonist cannot and does not take this path, and neither does the book as a whole. The accuser is not at center stage when the book seeks to explore the origin of sin; he is simply one who wrongly accuses Job of false motives.

What, then, does the book teach about sin? Not as much as we might like! The book of Job could have been a riveting account of the implications of sin, but it has not gone down this path. It focuses instead on the opposite template, that of the righteous life. Yet the way in which this is handled gives some insight into the wisdom writer's view of sin. The oath of clearance in chapter 31 is a legal device in which an accused can get vindication if proof of particular named sins cannot be provided. While I have used this chapter elsewhere to outline the nature of righteousness, the examples cited also paint a fairly comprehensive view of sin.

Like its counterpoint, righteousness, sin involves not only outward actions but also inner thoughts (31:1, 7, 9, 25, 29, 33). It includes, but is not confined to, religious unfaithfulness (31:26-27). Both personal (e.g., 31:9) and social breaches (e.g., 31:16-21) of obligation can constitute sin. Finally, the essence of sin is a failure to honor and be true to God (31:28). Job 31 provides a very comprehensive picture of sin, which mirrors the equally expansive portrait of righteousness in the chapter.

In the dialogue, an interesting insight is given into what kind of speech is regarded as sinful. Many Christians would believe that it is sinful to speak to God in terms that are complaining, accusing, or angry, but this may have more to do with our cultural values than with God's own mind. Job accuses God of shooting poisonous arrows at him and terrifying him (6:4), of hiding his ways and hedging Job in (3:23), and of acting vexatiously against him with wave after wave of troops (10:17). He asks why he did not die at birth (3:11; 10:18), why God does not crush him and cut him off (6:9). He speaks in his anguish and complaint (7:11; 10:1), accuses God of oppressing and despising him (10:3), and even summons God to court (13:3; 31:35). He loathes the life God has given him (10:1) and complains that God has hidden his face and counted Job as an enemy (13:24). Yet when God speaks he does not accuse Job of any sin, and twice says that Job has spoken *of him* what is right (42:7-8).

Job does not deny he has sinned (e.g., 10:14; 13:26) and knows that a person cannot be in the right before God (9:1).[107] However, he insists that his suffering is out of all proportion to any sin he has done. God's endorsement of what Job has said *of him* surely establishes that bold, assertive, even accusatory speech to God by one who is righteous is part of faith, not sin. Such words addressed to other human beings may well be sinful; but, when poured out to God in times of great stress, they can be part of a robust and persevering faith. Lament and God-directed complaint may not be socially acceptable, but they are theologically sanctioned in this book.

107. Ibid., 380.

Since accusations of sin come from the lips of the friends — those who have not spoken of God what is right (42:7-8) — the book draws attention to the pastoral and theological danger of using sin to explain more than it was meant to (e.g., all suffering). Job's pattern of addressing the friends before turning to God helps us to isolate his response to this approach by the friends. In 6:14-30 he rebukes the friends for their treatment of him; he describes their words as withholding kindness or loyalty (חֶסֶד/*hesed*) and abandoning a proper respect for God ("the fear of the Almighty," 6:14). The implication is that to wrongly accuse someone of sin in God's name is to cease treating God as God. Job perceives that their false accusations have come from their shame and disappointment (6:20), their fear (6:21), and perhaps their anxiety about their own wealth or obligations (6:22-23). Instead of abandoning their relational and community commitments (6:27), Job urges them either to instruct him (6:24) or to turn from their accusations (6:29). As readers of the prologue, we know that Job is in the right and that the friends have got it wrong in attributing Job's suffering to his prior sins.

Related to this is Job's temptation to confess sin in order to improve his circumstances, thus using confession as a means to an end. Eliphaz urges him to repent (5:8) in order to regain his prosperity (5:24-26), a call made more explicit by Bildad (8:5-7) and Zophar (11:13-19). Job responds by saying that pretending to agree that his sin has caused this suffering (and so forgetting his complaint, 9:27; also cleaning up his life in v. 30) will still lead to his condemnation because that is not the reason for his suffering (9:28-29, 31). Job is a person of integrity and so refuses to (falsely) repent just to make his living conditions more comfortable. Such repentance might have the outward appearance of piety, but would only serve to prove the accuser right when he claimed that Job's godliness was only a means to an end — his real goal of comfort or prosperity.

There does not appear to be any focus on original sin in the book. While some systematic theologians might quote 5:7 ("man is born to trouble as the sparks fly upward"), these are words found in the mouth of Eliphaz, and so cannot be assumed to be the teaching of the whole book. Even if they were, they are better understood as a description of the hardships that are the constant lot of humans right through life (as Job also claims in 7:1), rather than as an assertion that this has come about because of the original sin of Adam and Eve. The doctrine of original sin is neither being affirmed nor denied; the focus is rather on the constant hardship of human existence.

Job 15:14 may be thought to render support for the concept of original sin: "What is man, that he can be pure? Or he who is born of a woman, that he can be righteous?" (ESV). Some systematic theologians imply that being born of a woman is the means of transmission of this original sin. However, this is

348

again a polemical assertion by Eliphaz, used by him to condemn Job for the words he has spoken; and it would be hard to insist, in the light of 42:7-8, that Eliphaz's words would be the authoritative teaching of the book on the subject. Furthermore, the context in chapter 15 of words (15:3b) and actions (e.g., 15:16) indicates a focus on actual rather than inherited sin. Eliphaz is twisting Job's observations (14:1, 4) about human hardship that need to be seen as an emotive pathway into exploring his own struggle of faith. Again, the passages cited are consistent with original sin, but do not demand it or build anything on it. The focus in the book of Job is much more on allegations and denials of the extent of actual sin.

Job, Justice, and Retribution

The concept of justice, especially in its retributive aspect, is clearly crucial in the book as a whole. For Bildad justice is so foundational to God that he cannot even conceive of the possibility that God would act unjustly (8:3). Eliphaz is also committed to the notion of retributive justice, first in its two-sided form (4:7-8), but later with a more pronounced emphasis on the just judgment of the wicked (15:17-30), and still later as the basis for condemning Job (22:5-11). Zophar knows the positive aspects of the idea of retributive justice (11:13-19), but believes that Job has been punished less than his guilt deserved (11:6c), and focuses only on the consequences for the wicked in his final speech (ch. 20).

Job too grounds his stance on the doctrine of retribution. His recourse to the unlikely concept of litigation is based in the view that God is bound by justice. This is why Job cannot make sense of disaster coming upon the innocent (9:23b), and why the outcomes for the righteous and the wicked are not drawn more clearly (9:22). His exploration of a legal figure (arbiter, 9:33; witness, 16:19; redeemer, 19:25; and hearer, 31:35) is an imaginative way of calling God back to what Job knows he is committed to — justice. Taking God to court is not an act of arrogance but builds on his firm conviction that God will finally act justly. Job believes in the justice of God, but cannot explain how his current treatment is still consistent with God's justice. However, the promise of good consequences for just actions is not the basis for his godly living. The prologue has already established that Job respected God for who he is, not for what he got out of it — he "feared God for nothing."

If, then, the friends and Job are all firm believers in God's justice, what is the teaching of book on the subject of justice and retribution? Clines has argued that the book deconstructs itself on this very message of retribution, noting that the idea is assumed in the prologue, rejected in the dialogue, and reaffirmed in the epilogue.[108] However, this is to misunderstand the way that wisdom books deal with retribution. Even the mainstream book of Proverbs, which asserts that God will honor the righteous (e.g., Prov 3:1-10), observes that a righteous person can stumble seven times (24:16). The second observation is simply a qualification of the first, not a contradiction. Similarly, Job never denies that God rewards righteous people, but he does claim that the retributive principle is not working at that time in his case. Indeed, the retributive principle is affirmed in the prologue and epilogue, and is qualified in the dialogue. Job's questioning of his circumstances is based on him holding so tightly to a theology of retribution but making no sense of his life. His response is not to jettison the doctrine, but rather to seek to come before God so that the principle can be acted upon.

However, in the Yahweh speeches Job is shown that a narrow view of human retributive justice does not exhaust the way in which God runs his world. Mark Boda comments that the real problem is the "tendency to limit human experience and divine action to this theological model."[109] Job had previously sought to qualify the doctrine by arguing that it was not being applied in his case. Yahweh responds by giving examples that show that this is not the only basis on which he is running his world, thus qualifying the doctrine in a different way. Indeed, Yahweh opens his first speech by referring to a wider concept than justice, namely his עֵצָה/'ēṣâ, "plan" (or "counsel," 38:2). The contrast between Job's concern for litigation and Yahweh's exploration of the order in creation points to the truth that Yahweh's concerns are wider than those that preoccupy Job and his friends. Retributive justice is only part, not all, of how God is sovereignly active in his world.

Sylvia Scholnick maintains that the Yahweh speeches do not qualify the application of justice but rather redefine the Hebrew term. She has proposed the broadening of the meaning of מִשְׁפָּט/mišpāṭ to include Yahweh's sovereign ruling of creation.[110] She notes that within the book the root שׁפט/špṭ is used in two distinct ways: "as jurisprudence and sovereignty. Contained within this single root are two ideas which in English are distinct: judging and ruling."[111] She asserts that Job and his friends have understood it in the legal sense of judging, but that God uses it here with the other meaning of ruling. On this view, God is responding in court to Job's legal challenge, with a barrage of questions by way of cross-examination.

However, it is better to see that Yahweh is inviting Job to discontinue the

---

108. Clines, "Deconstructing," 108-16.
109. Boda, *Severe Mercy,* 384.
110. Scholnick, "Poetry in the Courtroom," 201.
111. Scholnick, "Meaning of *mišpāṭ*," 521-22.

process of litigation, which was based on the view that God must run the world on the basis of justice and justice alone. Instead, Yahweh is saying, and Job has come to see, that the way God sovereignly rules his creation is much broader than simply meting out human retributive justice. God is also the king who is actively exercising his sovereign rule of the universe. The strong emphasis on retributive justice in the dialogue and the restoration in chapter 42 also suggests that it should be given its more common meaning. Yahweh's concerns in running his world are much wider than a narrow legal understanding of human retributive justice. God is concerned with more than humanity and with more than justice.

Gustavo Gutiérrez expresses it well:

> Now that the Lord has overthrown that doctrine by revealing the key to the divine plan, Job realizes that he has been speaking of God in a way that implied that God was a prisoner of a particular way of understanding justice. . . . What is it that Job has understood? . . . The truth that he has grasped . . . is that justice alone does not have the final say about how we are to speak of God. . . . God's love, like all true love, operates in a world not of cause and effect but of freedom and gratuitousness.[112]

Job and Resurrection

The OT does not deal at length with the resurrection of individuals. The clearest teaching is found in early apocalyptic contexts (e.g., Dan 12:2 and perhaps also Isa 26:19). Understandably, the centrality of this truth in the NT (e.g., 1 Cor 15, or the sermons in Acts) has encouraged both scholars and earnest Bible readers to see if they have missed some of the earlier hints of this doctrine.

Some scholars have argued that several texts in the book of Job indicate belief in resurrection, especially 19:25-27 and perhaps also 14:13-15. In the body of the commentary I have maintained that neither passage establishes a firm belief in resurrection. However, the imaginative longing in both cases does highlight the value that the doctrine of individual resurrection would have in Job's case. While the text does not confirm that Job believed that he could be raised from the dead, it does testify to the value that resurrection would have in righting wrongs beyond this life. If evil could be punished after death and godliness rewarded as well, this changes the choices confronting humans in their daily lives. That Job so quickly slides back into despair (19:27c) again suggests

---

112. Gutiérrez, *On Job*, 87.

no identifiable figure is in view. Indeed, the dialogue contains many other hypothetical scenarios — in 3:3-10 he curses the day of his birth; in 13:15 "although he may slay me"; in 14:13-17, being hid in Sheol; in 9:14-20, considering taking God to court. None of these are *realistic* possibilities, but Job explores them all. Perhaps anyone would if they were in Job's sandals. Job is exploring resurrection only as an imagined possibility to which he is driven by his anguish, rather than a confident affirmation that he will be raised. He no more affirms his resurrection than he affirms the possibility of hiding in Sheol or undoing the day of his birth. Thus what may initially strike the reader as a great expression of trust is rendered ambiguous as it is more closely examined.[113] N. T. Wright, for example, contends that, in the light of Job's denial of life beyond death in chapters 7 and 14, and in view of the translation difficulties, the passage in 19:25-27 cannot be understood as presenting "a hope for bodily life beyond the grave."[114]

Can, then, an incipient doctrine of resurrection can be found here? Does the phrase "in [or apart from] my flesh I shall see God" (19:26) imply that Job will be in an embodied or disembodied existence after his death? The concept of bodily resurrection is neither endorsed nor rejected here. Just as Job's "redeemer" is a hypothetical rather than identifiable figure, so too is the thought of bodily resurrection. It is, in the words of Daniel Simundson, "more like an expression of longing and yearning (even 'wishful thinking') than a confident assertion that there is more to life than we can see from this side of the grave."[115]

From a Jewish perspective, Jon Levenson states that "a central belief in rabbinic Judaism" is that "God will resurrect the dead and restore them to full bodily existence."[116] His wider thesis is that readers should be more open to seeing the concept of resurrection throughout the OT. However, he notes that in Job a major focus is not on personal resurrection but on continuing one's lineage through one's descendants, and he does not even consider chapter 19 as a source of teaching on resurrection. Thus, in seeing four generations of his family (42:16), Job dies content. Levenson does, however, propose a distinction between those who go down to Sheol and those who die blessed like Job. He concludes that the way the book ends (42:17) does not connect the dying of the blessed with Sheol, but "offers instead the possibility of a happy ending to individual existence."[117] This seems to conclude too much from the tantalizing hints at the end of the book.

113. See L. Wilson, "Realistic Hope."
114. N. Wright, *Resurrection*, 96-98. For a more optimistic view see Alexander, "Old Testament View."
115. Simundson, *Job*, 105.
116. Levenson, *Restoration of Israel*, ix.
117. Ibid., 73-80.

It would be surprising to find a clear doctrine of resurrection in a wisdom book like Job, for one of the distinctives of wisdom theology is a this-worldly orientation in which wrongs must be punished and rights rewarded in this life. There is little room for eschatology in wisdom. Interestingly, though, some have also argued for the concept of resurrection in two wisdom-like psalms (Pss 49:15; 73:24).

However, there is no contradiction between the OT and NT in this matter. It is not that the NT affirms life after death for believers while the OT denies it; nor do both affirm it equally. Rather it is that the OT is, on this point, very un-developed, in that it neither affirms nor denies the existence of life after death. Yet the questions raised in the OT actually cry out for some clearer teaching about the nature of life after death, and this is what is provided in the NT.

Job and the Nature of Faith

I have maintained that the central issue in the book of Job is not suffering but rather faith. It is the matter raised by the accuser in 1:9 — does Job fear God for nothing? Or to put it in other words, is it possible for a person to have faith in God simply because of who God is, rather than because of what God will do for them? This is the essence of faith in the book of Job.

It is not the only possible expression of faith in the book. Some readers are so disturbed by Job's strong outbursts and forceful words that they look else-where for expression of genuine faith. Job's responses in the prologue provide the readiest examples of a "safer" faith in God. When Job loses all his posses-sions and family, he rightly mourns his great loss (1:20a), but he also turns to God in worship (1:20b). His attitude in worship is disclosed in his words. He realizes that he is the recipient of grace ("naked I came . . . and naked shall I return," 1:21a) and that God can both give and take away (1:21b). He has a high view of God actively ruling in his world. Against this backdrop, he pronounces that God (his "name" or character) is blessed (1:21c). This is genuine faith, and is endorsed as such by the narrator (1:22).

In a similar vein, after he is afflicted with terrible sores and urged by his wife to curse God, he insists that the life of faith involves a readiness to receive either prosperity or disaster from God (2:10b). The narrator also approves of Job's response here (2:10c).

The kind of faith that Job shows in the prologue is unproblematic, but it is clearly the foundation of his faith as expressed in the rest of the book. The friends, however, appear to insist that sentiments such as those uttered by Job in the prologue virtually exhaust the nature of faith. Job will be moved by

God's ongoing silence to explore whether faith can stretch much bigger than his initial stance, and this will be a crucial point of contention between Job and his friends. Job will not abandon his starting faith ("fearing God for nothing"), but will come to see that there is room in God's economy for a more robust expression of faith as well — at least in extreme circumstances.

Another common proposal for reconciling God's later endorsement of Job (42:7-8) and Job's strong complaints and accusations is to focus on the purple passages — arguably clear expressions of hope and trust in the midst of his despair. Some even find here the prospect of resurrection or a heavenly redeemer (usually seen as a glimpse of Christ).

The most commonly cited example is Job's call for a redeemer in 19:25-27. With the music of Handel's *Messiah* echoing in the background, a number of readers see that here finally Job is breaking through his dark clouds of despair into the light of christological and resurrection hope. Once this is established, they often see this hope supported by his call for a "renewal" after "being hidden in Sheol" (14:13-17), or a "mediator" (9:33) or "heavenly witness" (16:19), or "one to hear him" (31:35). In each image, they assert, Job's true faith emerges from the surrounding debate, and this is what is endorsed by God at the end of the book (42:7-8).[118]

This *may* be the case, but *need* not be. I have dealt with each of these passages in the commentary, and I suggested there that this is not the best way of viewing these images. Without repeating the arguments made there, the more substantial point is that one does not have to read these passages as high points of faith in order to view Job as a person of faith. Even if one concludes that these are great and clear expressions of firm trust, that is not the only basis for finding Job to have "spoken about God what is right." Job's questioning faith is genuine and legitimate faith as well.

Of course, there are expressions of hope, as well as protest, in Job's words. Job 13:15, despite the textual debates (see the commentary on this verse), is best translated as "though he slay me, I will hope in him" (ESV). Through his anguish and questioning, Job still is committed to trust the God whose purposes he does not fully understand. This is genuine faith, but it must also be seen in its context. The rest of the verse adds, "yet I will argue my ways to his face." True hope is not in conflict with ongoing protest and questioning, and so Job continues to explore the possibility of litigation (e.g., 13:18-19). In this robust faith, there is even room for despair (13:28).

What are some of the identifying characteristics of Job's protesting faith?

---

118. In the previous section I dealt with the issue of whether there is a doctrine of resurrection in the book.

Job continues to insist that the solution must be found with God and keeps on talking to him. In the face of unimaginable difficulty, he continues to direct his gaze and his words to God. He does not turn away when it becomes too hard. To pursue God into uncharted territory takes greater faith than the approach of the friends, who attempt to tidy up our messy world with a series of glib propositions about what must be true. C. L. Seow rightly observes, "To Job . . . people who are afraid of confronting the tough, faith-shattering questions are not fearers of God. Rather, they are simply fearers, theological cowards, for they fear the truth."[119] It is Job, not the friends, who demonstrate a robust faith.

Faith encompasses trusting God in the midst of distress, not simply positive thinking once the adverse circumstances have passed. It is possible to show faith even when God appears not to answer our cries for help or apparently fails to act on our behalf. It is not dependent on change (in us or our circumstances) already having taken place. Faith looks to God as the one who is able to help, and who is strong enough not to be shaken by an outpouring of our pain. It is not expressed in glib words, but emerges from a deep commitment to cling to the God we have known, no matter what. Sadly, faith like this is today more likely to be among the persecuted church in the majority world than in the lives of comfortable Christians in the West.

Job and Moral Theology

Some scholars have genuine moral difficulty with the book of Job and have reservations about it as a source of ethical teaching. Clines, for example, calls for a "fifth friend" who will call into question the ethical integrity not of the person Job, but of the book that bears his name.[120] He raises four areas of moral difficulty within the book:

1. The rationale for the imposition of Job's suffering.
2. Job's being kept in ignorance of the reason for his suffering.
3. The nature and tone of the divine speeches.
4. The apparent reaffirmation of the principle of retribution at the end of the book.

These are, however, primarily theological rather than ethical difficulties, and I have dealt with them in other parts of this commentary. But the teachings and

119. Seow, "Job," 421.
120. Clines, "Job's Fifth Friend."

implications of the book make a positive contribution to theological ethics in a number of areas.

The Source of Job's Ethics

The Ten Commandments (or Decalogue) are often viewed as the foundation for OT ethics. It is not surprising, therefore, to find some scholars making connections between the Decalogue and the ethical teaching of Job, especially in the most ethically oriented passage in Job 31. Waldemar Janzen even calls Job 31 "a wisdom decalogue" and argues that "there is nothing in the Decalogue or in Job 31 that is incompatible with the other."[121] He observes that the considerable overlap is reflected in the concern of both passages with idolatry, family and servants, adultery, hatred, honesty, and covetousness. While there is no focus on the Sabbath in Job 31, there is a genuine concern for the poor and the marginalized.

However, the book of Job has been deliberately set in the times of the patriarchs — before Moses and Sinai — and outside Israel. It seems that the Sinai covenant (and therefore the Decalogue) has been deliberately bracketed to deal with more timeless and universal issues. There is none of the particularity of the Decalogue, which is based on God's prior act of grace in redeeming his people (Exod 20:2). The Ten Commandments were never conceived as a stand-alone set of rules, but were given in response to God's action in rescuing his covenant people, an idea not found in the book of Job.

More likely is the view that "wisdom teaching was the place of origin for the ethics found in Job 31."[122] Wisdom literature goes back to the theology of creation and draws out the behavioral and character implications of what it means to be human before God. While the OT wisdom books ground their teaching on God, it is largely on God's activity as creator rather than redeemer or covenant maker. It is a common wisdom practice to ground instruction in observation of the world, so that the lazy person is urged to learn a lesson from the industrious ant (Prov 6:6-11).

Job's consideration of the human condition in chapters 7, 10, and 14 is grounded in God's activity as creator (7:16-18; 10:3-12; 14:1-12). In his arguments Job uses examples from nature, as he likens the brevity of human life to that of

---

121. W. Janzen, *Old Testament Ethics,* 128.

122. Fohrer, "Righteous Man," 9. Birch, *Let Justice Roll Down!* 332, also notes that while some of the virtues echo the covenant law, they are not essentially about fulfilling the law but going far beyond it. Hartley, *Book of Job,* 407, suggests that Job's focus is more on attitudes, and there is overlap with the Decalogue only in relation to adultery and coveting.

a flower (14:2), compares human vulnerability to a leaf or dry chaff being blown around in the wind (13:25), and views human decay as similar to a moth eating away at a garment (13:28).[123]

What Job derives from creation is consistent with what is found in the other OT traditions, but the core source of his ethics is clearly an understanding of God as the one who creates and sustains.

The Content of Job's Ethics

The book of Job fills out both the nature of right action and the nature of a righteous character. At the very beginning of the book of Job, God says (1:8; 2:3; see also the narrator in 1:1) that Job is blameless and upright, fearing God and turning from evil. This fourfold description of Job's character and actions draws attention to what it means to live righteously before God. Indeed, we see from 1:9 ("does Job fear God for nothing?") that it is precisely Job's righteousness (and what motivates it) that is at stake in the book.

Much of the dialogue deals with Job's subsequent struggles in his relationship with God, but it does contain some clues about Job's ethical values. He mentions in passing, and condemns, a few specific social wrongs, including bribes and bribery (6:22), deceit and deceitfulness (27:4; 13:7, 9), and partiality (13:8, 10).[124] In chapter 24 Job explores why God does not punish wrongdoing, and in so doing outlines the nature of unrighteous behavior. This includes unlawful seizure of property (v. 2a), theft (vv. 2b, 11), mistreatment of and lack of care for the marginalized (vv. 3-8, 21), ruthless financial transactions (vv. 3b, 9b), killing the vulnerable (v. 14), and adultery (v. 15).

However, in both chapters 29 and 31 Job reflects on his way of life before he suffered the tests of chapters 1 and 2. In the survey of his former life in chapter 29, Job gives us further glimpses of what is valued by a righteous person. While it includes positive relationships with God and family (vv. 4-5), prosperity (v. 6), and social respect (vv. 7-11), it does not stop there. Job outlines how he proactively cared for those often shunned by society — the poor and needy, orphans, widows, disabled, strangers (vv. 12-16) — by standing up to their unrighteous oppressors (v. 17). He did not live just for himself but served his community.[125] His life was characterized by righteousness and justice (v. 14).

123. In this last example, W. Brown, *Ethos of the Cosmos,* 332, suggests that "Job recognizes that he is eminently biodegradable"!

124. Maston, "Ethical Content," 44.

125. W. Brown, *Character in Crisis,* 78, suggests that this chapter "describes the apotheosis of Job's character *that once was.*"

His care for his neighbors stemmed from his relationship with God; hence in vv. 4b-5a he describes this time as "when the friendship of God was upon my tent; when the Almighty was still with me" (NRSV).

The oath of clearance in chapter 31 is a legal form in which Job asserts that if he has done any of these unrighteous things he may justly be punished. Like chapter 29, chapter 31 outlines Job's actions and character at the time when God says he is "blameless and upright, fearing God and turning away from evil," and is therefore a very useful insight into the book's understanding of righteous living. The well-known OT scholar T. H. Robinson even calls this chapter "the highest ethical standard which the Old Testament contains."[126]

Chris Wright sees in chapter 31 an "identikit" picture of the personal ethics of a righteous person. He suggests that the negatives (what Job claims he has not been guilty of) can be processed into positive prints to build up a picture of a person fulfilling their obligations, or doing what is "good."[127] As Wright points out, this chapter includes integrity in the following areas:

- refraining from lust (v. 1) and adultery (vv. 9-12)
- honest dealing in business (vv. 5-7)
- treating his servants justly (vv. 13-15)
- being generous and compassionate, not hard-hearted, to the poor, the needy, and the fatherless (vv. 16-23)
- not trusting in money to give security and purpose in life (vv. 24-25)
- renouncing idolatry in the form of astrology (vv. 26-28)
- controlling his thoughts and speech toward his enemies (vv. 29-30)
- showing hospitality (vv. 31-32)
- not avoiding open confession of sins (vv. 33-34)
- treating properly both land and its laborers (vv. 38-40)[128]

Three aspects are especially important here.[129] First, a wide range of moral accountabilities is in view. It is not simply a matter of having a right heart before

126. Robinson, *Job and His Friends,* 64.

127. Most recently in C. Wright, *Old Testament Ethics,* 372. See also W. Janzen, *Old Testament Ethics,* 127, who suggests that it is useful to "transpose the negative protestations of purity into their positive opposites."

128. C. Wright, *Old Testament Ethics,* 372. Fohrer, "Righteous Man," 7, finds twelve specific transgressions that are denied — lasciviousness, falsehood, covetousness, adultery, disregard for the rights of servants, hard-heartedness against the poor, trust in riches, superstition, hatred of enemies, inhospitality, hypocrisy, exploitation of land. For a fuller description of these verses, see the earlier comments on ch. 31. See also Ryken, *Literature of the Bible,* 116; Seow, "Job," 421-22.

129. C. Wright, *Old Testament Ethics,* 371-72; idem, *Eye for an Eye,* 203-4.

God, or staying unblemished by the world. Rather it includes both his inner thoughts and his outer actions, his words and deeds; what he does in private and in public, on his own, in his family, in his community. Thus it includes legal, social, sexual, and economic areas. The impression given by these samples is that no area of life can be immune from a need for righteousness.

Second, there is particularly a stress on a person's inner thoughts. Job's morality takes in not only righteous external acts, but inner attitudes or character as well. His right living extends even to those areas that you could never pass a law about. Thus Job's integrity extends to such thoughts and attitudes as not looking lustfully at a girl (v. 1). This emphasis on what goes on inside Job is evident in a number of other verses as well (where his heart is — vv. 7, 9; what he rejoices over — vv. 25, 29; hiding guilt in his heart — v. 33). As T. B. Maston put it, "Job understood that out of the heart are the issues of life."[130] There is an understanding that a righteous person's actions must build upon what drives one internally.

Third, his ethical reasoning highlights the importance of being accountable to God.[131] Job reveals the motivation for his righteous behavior most clearly in vv. 14 and 15 — accountability to God and God as creator. Righteousness is not just a matter of acting in accordance with accepted social norms, but is based on being accountable to the God who will judge. God is all-seeing (v. 4) and evaluates every act (vv. 6, 14). He has made all people, and therefore insists on them being treated fairly (v. 15). To commit adultery would have been, in the words of v. 11, "wicked, a sin to be judged" (NIV). In v. 23 Job sees that God has the sanction of judgment on wrongdoing, while v. 28 (echoing v. 11) shows that his motivation is to be faithful to God. In short, God is the one he seeks to please, and the whole of life is lived in the sure knowledge that he is accountable to God for the way he has used his freedom and opportunities.[132]

Job and Character Ethics

The very beginning of the book of Job focuses on Job's character. That Job is "blameless and upright, fearing God and turning from evil" (1:1, 8; 2:3), describes not simply his actions but also his underlying character. Samuel Balentine suggests that the terms "blameless" and "upright" describe Job's character,

---

130. Maston, "Ethical Content," 53; see also Raurell, "Job's Ethic," 135; Dick, "Job 31," 48-49; Fohrer, "Righteous Man," 13-14.

131. Seow, "Job," 422, notes that 31:14 "makes it clear that his is a theological ethic."

132. This section is strongly indebted to the insights of Chris Wright.

while the expressions "fearing God" and "turning away from evil" describe his actions.[133] While this may be an overly precise distinction, it is clear that Job's character is at least in view in this cluster description.

Then we see from 1:9 ("does Job fear God for nothing?") that the accuser is delving into the question of whether Job's apparently righteous actions are authentic or simply pragmatic. The underlying issue concerns Job's motive and therefore his character. If he is only motivated by the rewards offered, then he is not righteous but only a shrewd operator. As William Brown points out, "if he fears God *for something*, then his integrity is simply a facade."[134]

When it comes to the issue of character, the friends appear to be blinded by holding on to a very inflexible doctrine of retribution. Eliphaz initially appears convinced of Job's godly character (his "integrity" and "fear of God," 4:6) but only because righteousness is always rewarded (4:7) and Job has been prosperous. In other words, he is reading back from Job's wealth to his righteous actions, which must have come from a righteous character. Bildad too simply assumes that God would not reject a blameless person (8:20). Zophar takes this to its logical conclusion. He argues that Job's current outward suffering must establish that his actions are impure and that his underlying character is unclean (11:4-6). For the friends, Job's outward circumstances, both good and bad, are reliable indicators of the moral status of both his actions and his character.

The descriptions of Job's character in chapters 29 and 31 are instructive for character ethics, since God both initially (1:1, 8; 2:3) and finally (42:7-8) endorses Job's stance and values.[135] It is clear that Job's character is founded on a right relationship with God (his fear or respect of God, 1:8; 2:3), for this is mentioned at the beginning in chapter 29 (29:2-5) and throughout chapter 31 (31:2, 4, 6, 14-15, 23, 28). Thus Job's character is God-centered and God-dependent, aiming for the goal of honoring God.

Some, however, see an unevenness of Job's character in the book. William Brown, for example, has maintained that the book of Proverbs is about the formation of character, Job 1–31 concerns the deformation of Job's char-

---

133. Balentine, "Sanctuary of Silence," 66.

134. W. Brown, *Character in Crisis*, 53.

135. Newsom, "Narrative Ethics," 125, notes that, in the prologue, God and Job are characterized as positive and trustworthy, while the *satan* and Job's wife are pictured as negative and untrustworthy. Timmer, "Character Formed," 5, argues that "fear of God" is the crucial element of character in 1:1, 8, and 2:3 "because it is used alone as a summary for Job's relationship with God in 1:9." W. Brown, *Character in Crisis*, 28, suggests that the concept of the fear of the Lord "deals fundamentally with the heart and center of character, namely the position of the person *in relation* to God."

acter, and Job 32–42 focuses on its reformation.[136] Brown suggests that the epilogue in particular indicates Job's transformed character in that he shows compassion for others (praying for the friends, 42:8-10), does not criticize those who shunned him, and is generous to his daughters (42:15).[137] However, he has already prayed for others (1:5), and there is no suggestion that he did not care lovingly for his family previously (1:1-5; 29:5). Daniel Timmer, building on Brown, thinks that this deformation of his character begins in chapter 3 and that a gradual reformation of his character occurs only in chapters 38–42.[138] Yet it is the friends who make these allegations in the course of the dialogue. Although Eliphaz initially assumes Job's basically upright character (4:6), he later launches a scathing attack on Job's integrity. In chapter 22 Eliphaz accuses Job of a variety of social injustices (22:6-9) that come from his character of evil (22:5). Seow points out that this stance of the friends is a breach of the virtue of loyal friendship. It is the friends, not Job, who have failed to act with integrity.[139]

Toward the end of the dialogue, Job insists that he has maintained his integrity (27:6), and in chapters 29 and 31 he outlines the nature of his righteous character at length. In these chapters we see that he honors God, is a person of wise speech (29:7-11, 21-22), proactively cares for the marginalized (29:12-17; 31:16-23), and is innocent of a wide range of possible offenses (ch. 31). This is the conclusion of the book as a whole. Even Elihu concedes that the friends have not succeeded in proving Job to be unrighteous (33:3, 5, 12), a human verdict endorsed by God (42:7-8). Thus Job's extended description of his former life in chapters 29–31 provides important insights into wisdom understandings of character ethics. The ethical traits and values displayed here provide a useful supplement and complement to those sourced from the covenant law or the prophetic books.[140]

Job and Social Ethics

While the book of Job is about an individual, it is wrong to think that community concerns have no place in its ethical teaching. Maston has pointed out that quite a few social sins are condemned by Job in the dialogue, such as

136. W. Brown, *Character in Crisis,* passim.
137. Ibid., 112.
138. Timmer, "Character Formed," 6-9.
139. Seow, "Job," 421, citing 6:21. He speaks of "friendship that does not depend on one's theology."
140. W. Janzen, *Old Testament Ethics,* 129.

bribery (6:22), deceit (13:7, 9; 27:4), as well as partiality (13:8, 10).[141] As the dialogue comes to a close, Job outlines his former stage of life in chapter 29. Here he describes not only his physical circumstances but also his social standing (e.g., people deferring to his views — 29:7-11). This chapter is building on an important theme through the dialogue, where Job commonly refers to his loss of social status. Joel Burnett argues that, for Job, "being in right standing in life is reflected in being held in high esteem within the community."[142] Frequently in his speeches Job bemoans his poor treatment by his former friends and associates (12:4; 16:20; 17:6; 19:21-22) and elaborates on this in his litany of woes (30:1-15). Bildad latches on to this as proof of Job's wickedness (18:17-21). Job's position in society is crucial to the book.

Indeed, he outlines the community values by which he lived. He has acted positively on behalf of the poor and orphaned (29:12), the wretched and the widow (29:13), the blind and lame (29:15), the needy and stranger (29:16); and he has opposed the unrighteous (v. 17a). His life has been characterized by righteousness and justice (29:14). This active social care for his neighbors stems from his relationship with God, which he describes by referring to the time "when the friendship of God was upon my tent, when the Almighty was yet with me" (29:4b-5a ESV).

The picture given in chapter 31 is also one of a righteousness that is not just individual but social as well. For Job, integrity is not simply a matter of keeping oneself pure but actively caring for others. Thus Job has cared for the poor (31:16); provided for the orphans (31:17-18); been generous to the needy (31:19-20); treated his servants (31:13), his business partners (31:5), and even his enemies (31:29) fairly. In short, he has acted to build up his surrounding community. In some cases we are given insight into his motivation. His way of life was not only based on accountability to God (31:2, 4, 6, 14, 23, 28) but also on an assumption of the common humanity of people of different status (31:13-15), which is an echo of the social teaching of Proverbs (Prov 14:31; 17:5; 22:2; 29:13).[143] It is telling that when Job is finally vindicated, he resumes an active involvement in the community (42:11). The modern division of ethics into personal and social seems overridden in the book of Job. A model life needs to straddle both areas.

141. Maston, "Ethical Content," 44.

142. Burnett, *Where Is God?* 95.

143. Seow, "Job," 422, also argues that Elihu assumes that ethics has a social dimension, in that a person's wicked or righteous actions affect others. Elihu, he says, promotes acting ethically for the common good.

Job and the Environment

The book of Job has implications for thinking about the physical and living environment in a number of ways. A foundational presupposition is that the creator God has authority over the environment. At a simplistic level, he is able to send down lightning (1:16) and destroy seven thousand sheep. As the creator and therefore owner of the world and what it contains, he is sovereignly free to act in his creation. Murphy sees this assumption in the whole wisdom corpus, noting that "the Lord's dominion over the created world is at the core of wisdom's effort to help one to live in the world."[144] On this view, creation can have great significance, but its value can only be secondary — derived from the value that God assigns to it and his attitude toward it.

The selection of examples in the first Yahweh speech draws attention to the comprehensive nature of God's authority over the created world. They are grouped into the physical world — the sea, the dawning of each new day, the hidden places, the weather forces, the stars, and the clouds (38:4-38) — and a selection of animals and birds (38:39–39:30). The impossible questions asked by God imply that he alone can understand such a complex creation, and yet these examples are paraded before Job to remind him that God alone can run the world. God's pride in the physical and animal world, evident as he takes Job on this scenic tour, indicates that God both delights in and values the creation.

The created world is also a rich source of knowledge. It was a common practice among the sages to learn truths from the natural world (e.g., Prov 6:6-11), and it is not surprising that both the friends (Job 4:10-11; 5:8-10; 8:11-14; 11:12; 15:31-33; 18:15-16; 25:4-5) and Job (12:7-10; 14:7-12, 18-19; 24:5, 19) urge each other to learn in this way. Creation is a place of learning and a location of true knowledge of God and his ways.[145]

Humanity is given both a special and qualified status in the book of Job, and this has significant consequences for the book's teaching on the environment. The very fact that God is boasting in the heavenly court about the possibility of a righteous human (1:8) hints that humanity is of central interest to God. Within the book this is ultimately reinforced by God speaking to Job and giving him an honorific title ("my servant," 1:8; 2:3; 42:7-8). Job's self-understanding that he is accountable to God for his moral choices (e.g., 31:6, 14, 23, 28) also sets him apart from the rest of creation. While the focus here is on his accountability to

---

144. Murphy, *Tree of Life*, 124.

145. Habel, "Wisdom in Earth," 294-96, pushes this farther (and probably too far) in suggesting that not only is the earth valued because it is the place Yahweh searched to discover wisdom, but also because it still incorporates a web of wisdom that Yahweh searches as sage.

God, this can only arise because humans are in a unique relationship with God that is not shared by other creatures or the physical world.

However, it is also true — and a distinctive contribution of the book of Job — that God values creation apart from its utility for human beings. This is shown in relation to the physical earth in that it still rains where there are no human beings (38:26). In terms of the animal world, the creatures catalogued in 38:39–39:30 share a common element that they are not tamed by human beings or even exist to be useful for humanity. Even the spirited warhorse of 39:19-25 does not have his spirit broken by its (implied but not mentioned) human rider, though it is useful to people in battle. The value of creation derives not only from the fact that God values humanity. Instead, the value given to all parts of creation (the physical earth, animals, and humans) is not inherent but derives from God's kingly decision.

Some in today's environmental movements (including Christians) conclude that humanity has no mandate to exercise dominion over creation or use its resources. Even William Brown argues that, in chapter 12, "Job implies that the human pursuit of wisdom has fallen into the fallacy of arrogant 'species-ism.'"[146] While the book of Job does not address this question of the human mandate head-on, it does seem to endorse human use and management of the earth's resources. This is indicated in relation to the animal world by the restoring to Job of his flocks and herds (42:12), and in relation to the physical world by the positive descriptions of human mining (28:1-6) and water management (28:9-11) activities. It is also worth suggesting that the positive view of community in the book (seen in his description of his integrity in ch. 31) would imply that the shared use of the environment would take priority over individual use.

The teaching of the book seems therefore to be as follows: (1) the environment should be valued since it belongs to God and he delights in it; (2) the environment should be valued as a source of knowledge about how to live in God's world, and about God himself; (3) humanity has a special place in God's created world, but the environment is of value to God even in the absence of human beings; (4) this high view of the environment does not preclude humanity shaping the created world and using its resources.

Job and Suicide

Job's circumstances would provoke many to wonder if taking one's own life (by suicide, or even euthanasia/assisted suicide) would not become an option to

---

146. W. Brown, *Ethos of the Cosmos*, 331.

explore. The prologue shows that Job suffers the loss of all his children, the support of his wife, his place in society, and his physical health. This is poignantly set out in the contrast between his former prosperity in chapter 29 and his current circumstances in chapter 30, which include feeling abandoned by God (30:20-22).[147] While Job explores some examples of imaginative hope (e.g., the legal figure of 9:32-35a; 16:18-21; 19:23-27a), each time he reverts to his earlier despair (9:35b; 16:22; 19:27c).[148]

Job's wife appears to articulate the possibility of suicide, urging him to "curse God and die" (2:9). While this could mean to curse God in order to ensure that he does not die without cursing God for his suffering, it is most likely proposing either a defiant or compassionate attempt at suicide. Whether her motive is to defy God (by cursing him) or to have compassion on her husband (his death will put an end to his suffering), Job's wife raises the issue of suicide for the readers of the book. Job's rejection of this option is part of his not sinning with his lips (2:10).

Hartley is one commentator who draws attention to the importance of the prologue for the issue of suicide.[149] Suicide comes from a total loss of hope in God. While it is never our role to speculate on the spiritual state of believers who have suicided, the book of Job implies that this choice is never right, even in the most difficult of circumstances.

Job, by contrast, continues to reach out for any kind of hope despite the severity of his physical and emotional pain, and the apparent absence of a God who cares. He hopes against hope right through the dialogue. It is striking that, in the plethora of words that make up Job's speeches in chapters 3–31, there is no exploration of suicide as an option. Job does call for the (hypothetical) undoing of the day of his birth (3:1-10), but does not take any action to end his life. Kenneth Gros Louis lucidly sums up Job's stance in chapter 3:

> While Job clearly longs for death, here and elsewhere in the dialogue, he never thinks of suicide. It may be that Job does have a sense of his dignity and the dignity of all life. It may also be that he has an underlying faith in his God, not faith that he will get everything back again, but simply faith that there is a reason for his present suffering, that God has something in mind for him.[150]

---

147. For greater detail see the section above, "Theological Themes: Suffering."

148. Habel, "Only the Jackal," 232.

149. Hartley, *Book of Job*, 92. See the discussion above in "Theological Themes: Persevering Faith."

150. Gros Louis, "Book of Job," 232.

In the rest of the dialogue, Job does not even explore with his friends whether taking his own life is permissible in his situation.

Job and Wealth

Job is an interesting case study for the biblical understanding of wealth, for here we find a person who is wealthy because God has caused him to prosper. The book builds on the positive understandings about wealth seen in other wisdom literature like Proverbs (e.g., Prov 3:9-10; 14:24). The introduction to the prologue (Job 1:1-5) portrays Job as very wealthy. His wealth was measured in livestock (1:3), as was common in patriarchal times (e.g., the animals and servants listed in Gen 12:16). The narrator's ambiguous verdict in Job 1:3 was that Job was the greatest (in wisdom and/or wealth) of all the people of the east. His possessions were suitable indicators and appropriate accompaniments of his blameless life (1:1, 8; 2:3). It is not possible, however, to conclude from this that all wealth is a reward for righteousness, but it is seen as fitting that godly character could lead to material prosperity.

The possibility of Job honoring God simply to retain his wealth is explored in the dialogue between God and the accuser. In 1:9-10 the accuser argues that Job could have base motives for serving God, since God is the one who has caused Job to prosper by putting a protective barrier (a "hedge") around his possessions. God does not dispute this, but allows Job to be tested (1:12). The result of the first round of testing is that all of Job's possessions are taken or destroyed (1:14-17), but Job retains his faith (1:20-22). At this stage he does not even lament the loss of his property, nor does he ask God to restore it. The second round of testing concerns his health (2:7), not his wealth, for his possessions have all been taken away in the first test.

Job's words during the dialogue show that he sits loose to his former possessions. In his opening salvo in chapter 3, Job never asks for a restoration of his possessions. This pattern continues in the dialogue and can be seen most clearly in the first round. Job's threefold call is for God to remember him (7:7; 10:9; 14:13). What does he long for during the dialogue? Restoration of fellowship with God, not his possessions. As R. N. Whybray notes, "For Job the good life consisted not in his wealth but in his friendship with God."[151]

Eliphaz accuses Job of having gained his wealth in the first place through wickedness and oppression (22:5-9), and implies that Job trusted in his wealth rather than in God (22:23-26). This does not accord with the description of the

151. Whybray, *Good Life*, 141.

prologue. Job agrees that many who are poor are victims of oppression (24:2-12). They are cheated out of land and livestock (24:2-3), physically intimidated (24:4), forced to forage for food (24:5-6), left without proper clothing and shelter (24:7-8, 10), and oppressed by unjust loans (24:9).[152] However, he denies that he is a perpetrator of any such injustice (23:7, 10-12).

In chapter 29 Job describes his former period of prosperity, outlining how he used his wealth to assist the needy. He responded to cries of help from the poor, orphaned, and widowed (29:12-13); he aided the blind and lame (29:15); and he was even proactive in seeking out and acting to defend those who had been unfairly treated (29:16-17). His underlying attitude (not just outward actions) toward the victimized and needy is set out in 30:25 — he wept and grieved for them. He understood that responsibility toward the needy properly accompanies great wealth. Thus the book explains both how the poor are often oppressed by the rich and how they should be treated.[153]

In chapter 31 Job again outlines his active care for the poor and marginalized (31:16-23), but adds a further note about his attitude to wealth itself. He sees that placing trust in wealth, or relying on it, or being enticed by it (31:24-25), would be an iniquity deserving of punishment since it amounted to being false to God (31:28). He thus concedes the danger of having wealth, but denies that he has transgressed in this regard.

Elihu, giving the human verdict, concludes that the friends have not shown that Job sinned prior to the debate. Elihu confines his verdict on Job to the words offered during the dialogue, the time when Job had no possessions to trust in. His possessions are appropriately restored to Job once the test has been completed, since Job has shown that he trusts in God and has not used God as a means to the end of material prosperity. Some are concerned, however, that the doubling of Job's possessions in the epilogue (42:12) might provide support for versions of prosperity theology. Of course, the book does reflect the mainstream wisdom view that wealth is a common consequence of a righteous character. As Craig Blomberg put it, "The ending of Job provides important support for those who stress riches and wealth as good gifts from God to those he loves."[154] Blomberg even suggests that God knew that Job would be as generous with this doubled wealth as he was the first time around, since he has acknowledged that God is the giver of all things (1:21). However, the book as a whole negates the possibility of any automatic nexus between righteousness and wealth (crucial

152. Hoppe, *There Shall Be No Poor*, 109, who speaks of this passage as "a powerful indictment of the way people of means treated the peasants."

153. Hoppe, *There Shall Be No Poor*, 110, concludes, "The book also assumes that the wealthy are to take actions that benefit the poor rather than harm them."

154. Blomberg, *Neither Poverty nor Riches*, 59.

to prosperity theology), since Job remains righteous throughout the book yet is deprived of his wealth for most of the time. Since the trial is now over, and the loss of wealth was one aspect of the test, then it is appropriate that his possessions are restored at the close. The doubling of his property is simply a reminder of God's grace.

Job and Practical Theology

A neglected area of theology is practical theology, which asks how a particular section of Scripture should affect and shape our pastoral or ministry practice. Four areas are important for the book of Job: pastoral care, prayer, preaching, and mission.

Job as a Resource for Pastoral Care

The book of Job is an underutilized tool in pastoral ministry. Those who are hurting deeply, crying out to God without any apparent answer, and those tempted to give up on life will find here echoes of their own pain. Just as many derive pastoral comfort from others reading to them from the lament psalms, those struggling with life often find it quite liberating to find Job talk as he does and still receiving the commendation from God that Job has spoken of him what is right (42:7-8).

The pulpit is often overlooked when thinking about pastoral care, but it presents a great opportunity to set out proactively issues of faith, of coping with difficulties, of living with God's apparent silence, and so on. Before such items become urgent and immediate, the preacher can outline a framework and some useful principles. This is one reason why it is so useful to teach and preach from the book of Job. While these issues will need to be revisited in times of testing or suffering, having a healthier and more biblical framework in place beforehand will make easier the task of responding in a genuine but godly way.

Three different perspectives are given in the book, as the friends, Job, and God all have a say.

The Approach of the Friends

Job's friends come with the best of intentions, "to show him sympathy and comfort him" (2:11 ESV). As was the custom, they lament loudly and identify with Job by sprinkling ashes on themselves (2:12). They even observe a seven-day period of silence with Job, seemingly as they understand the limits of words at such times of great loss. They start so well!

However, they soon depart from their considered approach (2:11-13), and react to Job's angry words in chapter 3. Job's vocal disquiet triggers a knee-jerk response in the friends as they rally to defend God. Eliphaz hears Job questioning God's ruling of his world (4:7-11) and the presence of sin (4:17-19) and discipline (5:17). Bildad is provoked to respond when he understands Job to question God's justice (8:3) and the traditional teachings of the elders (8:8-10). Zophar is exasperated by Job's bold, self-justifying words and the implication of sinlessness (11:2-4).

In responding to Job's apparently wrong understandings, they show that they have moved on from caring for Job as a person to correcting his defective theology. They seek to straighten out Job's warped thinking, and in so doing they have reduced his despair to an intellectual problem. Of course, wrong thinking can often cause pastoral issues (e.g., I am not a complete person unless I express my sexuality; I should always be happy and healthy and prosperous). However, the friends respond so quickly to Job's outbursts that they do not take the time to work out the real nature of Job's dilemma. Thus they may say many true words (God is just, God runs the world, God will judge sin), but these were not the words that Job needed to hear, for they did not address his deepest problem. He longs for the presence of a seemingly absent God, but the friends never hear that and never address this issue. Their concern to correct Job's "wrong thinking" prevents them from listening for the deeper questions. They fall into the trap of an expert giving advice, but they have failed to actively listen for how Job sees his circumstances.

This failure is compounded by an increasing defensiveness as the debate continues and they come to question more and more of their own theological ideas. Even in the first cycle there is a progression from the respectful correction of Eliphaz (5:8) to the sterner rebuke of Bildad, who suggests that he is less of a sinner than his children (8:4-6). Zophar even more aggressively claims that Job has been punished less than he deserves (11:6c). Within the dialogue, the friends become stronger in their accusations against Job, so that in the third cycle Eliphaz, the most moderate of the friends, brings out a long list of Job's offenses (22:5-9). God's verdict on the friends is that they have not spoken about him (and presumably his ways in Job's case) what is right (42:7-8).

Job's Expression of His Needs

Job's bold, forthright words are the fruit of a deep but anguished relationship with God. Carson describes them well as a "rhetoric of outrage," words that come from raw pain that are not meant to be analyzed outside that context.[155] His opening self-curse (ch. 3) is not a rational request for the undoing of his day of birth, but is a means of expressing how deep the hurt goes. Even behind the common question "why" (e.g., 3:11, 12, 20) is not ultimately a plea for explanation but rather a call for God's presence and care.

He does make some strong accusations and complaints against God. He laments that God is treating him as an enemy, firing poisonous arrows at him (6:4; 16:12-14). He robustly urges God to end his life (e.g., 6:9) or to depart from him (e.g., 10:19). These might be misunderstood as Job wanting to be abandoned by God, but it is Job who in each of his first three speeches asks God to remember him (7:7; 10:9; 14:13). Throughout the dialogue, he keeps on addressing God. The friends characteristically speak to Job, but Job begins by responding to the friends but then turns to address God directly. He does not give up on God.

That God finally endorses Job's words (42:7-8) has implications for pastoral care. Rather than rebuke people for strong, accusatory words addressed to God, we should encourage them to pour out before God all their hurt and pain. There is great value in sharing about Job's struggles during pastoral visits. As Nancy Duff notes, "Reading and understanding psalms of lament can inform individuals that they are not the first to feel abandoned by God."[156] Rather than censor our words to God, we need to be honest before him about what we are thinking and feeling, even if it does not reflect reality. The God of the book of Job is big enough to field our accusations and complaints.

God's Reorientation of Job

God's responses to Job's words — and the corrections of the friends — are telling. He does not respond to each accusation that Job had made, apparently understanding that Job's deepest need was not to have an intellectual answer to his many questions. Yet God's very appearance to Job and what he chooses to say do help Job from a pastoral point of view.

Job's deepest longing is for the presence of God, for God to remember him and act toward him in care. Whybray notes, "it is the loss of his former personal relationship with God that is Job's chief lament."[157] The appearance of God to Job meets this need in a transforming way. However, God's words

155. Carson, *How Long,* 87-88.
156. Duff, "Recovering Lamentation," 10.
157. Whybray, *Good Life,* 139.

in the speeches also help Job to be reoriented away from his narrow formula of human justice and toward God's more panoramic perspective. He does not need to understand how God runs the world; he needs instead to see that God can be trusted to run the world. Job had confined God to rewarding human righteousness and punishing human wickedness, but God's sovereign ruling of the world involves the wider picture of the entire creation. Job has his thinking corrected, not by it being addressed, but by God expanding Job's parameters and removing his blinkers. Seeing something of God's wider plan, he can trust God in a new way and resume his former role in society (42:11). God discerned the deeper, underlying issue, addressed this in his words to Job, and this set Job free.

There is a danger in pastoral ministry to respond with advice (even an answer backed up by a Bible verse) to each question asked by someone in pain or confusion. Often there is a need to look beyond the presenting question to the more fundamental issue that needs to be addressed in order to bring lasting healing or change. While the book of Job is not intended as a manual for pastoral care, the way that God treats Job is very instructive.

Job and Prayer

The book of Job does not provide examples of all kinds of prayer, but it does provide several insights into prayer itself, especially lament.[158]

Prayer and God

Job is distinguished from his friends by his practice of talking *to* God rather than simply *about* God. For the friends, God is in the third person, the object of debate, the one they seek to defend. Job does talk about God, but in each of his first three speeches he moves on from this to address God directly. Indeed, in the whole book, only Job and the accuser talk to God, and only Job prays. Even in the final chapter, it is not the friends who pray to God, but Job who prays on their behalf (42:8-10). It seems to be easier to talk *about* God than to talk *to* him.

Job's words to God (or prayers) are based on his understanding of what God is like, that is, based on his past relationship with God. The quality of this relationship is clearly pictured in the prologue. He fears God (1:1); he is diligent in the offering of sacrifices (1:5); he trusts God even in adversity (1:20; 2:10);

---

158. Many of these have been outlined above in "Theological Themes: Lament and Complaint to God."

and he acknowledges that God has the sovereign right to give and take away all things (1:21). This same time period is also described in chapter 29 as "the days when God watched over me" (29:2), "when the friendship of God was upon my tent" (29:4), or "when the Almighty was yet with me" (29:5). Job prayed to God, because he was in relationship with God. He keeps on talking to God in prayer in the dialogue as he desperately seeks to maintain that relationship despite God's silence and seeming absence.

Throughout these chapters, Job's prayers are based on God's character. While this is clearly seen in the prologue (1:21; 2:10), it is also true in the dialogue. In 10:8-12 Job rehearses God's past care of him as a careful, caring creator and the giver of life and steadfast love. It is this past understanding of God that leads him to question what God is doing. This is why he describes his former way of life in such detail in chapter 29. He cannot reconcile the God he knew with the God he feels he is experiencing. Yet even in the lament genre the basis for this answer to prayer is the character of God.

The final aspect of God and prayer in the book is that God responds to prayer. While Job's constant complaint is that God is making no response (e.g., 19:7), the reality is that God does respond in his own time and way. This, however, means that there are times when God has not yet given a clear answer, even if he finally responds. Against this setting, the last chapter of the book is telling. Rather than the book as a whole leaving the reader with the impression that God does not answer prayer, Job acknowledges that God's presence is the very answer he needed (42:5). Then God informs the friends that he will answer Job's intercessory prayer, and he does so (42:8-9). While there will be occasions when responses will be delayed, the normal pattern is that God does indeed answer prayer. Sally Brown and Patrick Miller remind us that "what ultimately shapes even the biblical lament is . . . the faithfulness of the God who hears and acts."[159]

The Goal of Prayer

Laments are sometimes misunderstood as simply cathartic releases of pain. Such a view omits two vital elements of Job's cries. First, his complaints are essentially petitions; second, his goal is to draw closer to God. Job's prayers are motivated by a desire to secure change, in particular for the seemingly absent God to become present and to reveal his genuine care of Job. This longing for God's presence has been evident in the first cycle of Job's speeches, all of which call on God to remember (7:7; 10:9; 14:13). Though in his pain he calls on God

---

159. S. Brown and Miller, "Introduction," xix.

to leave him alone (7:19; 10:20; 14:6), his deeper longing breaks through as he envisages a restored relationship: "you would call, and I would answer you; you would long for the work of your hands" (14:15). John Sanders misconceives this as an example of his view "that people can argue with God and win."[160] Yet Job's final goal is not to win, or even to be vindicated; it is rather to have his relationship with God brought back to life.

With this broader context in mind, however, it is still clear that Job is petitioning for change. He does not want things to stay the same, and he pursues the thought of litigation against God in the fanciful hope that this will bring change. He summons God to appear and to answer (31:35); he calls out for justice (23:2-7); he even imagines being hidden in Sheol (14:13) or some kind of impossible, post-death vindication (19:26). Even when God does not appear to answer, he refuses to reduce the power of God. Thus, toward the end of the dialogue, he outlines God's kingly rule over creation (26:7-14), just as he earlier described God ruling over both creation and history (12:7-25).

The nature of his petitions is very telling. Noticeably absent is any call for his health to be renewed, his family to be replaced, his social standing to be restored, or his wealth to be reestablished. They would be obvious things to ask for, since in material terms they were his greatest losses. Yet he asks for none of these, and is satisfied even before they are made right (42:1-9). Instead, his petitions are for justice, for the presence of God, and for the care of God. He refers to his physical and social misery (e.g., 7:5, 19:17-20), but his most significant losses were that his way was hidden from God (3:23), that he might die before God seeks him out (7:8, 21), and that he is cut off from God's light (10:21-22). He pleads to be given a chance to argue for justice (e.g., 13:3, 15), for that will mean that God will finally be present (13:22) and then show his care (14:15). He persists in his bold petitions for vindication, help, and justice (19:7), but what is driving him is that he might find the God who would answer him with care and a sense of right (23:3-7). Job's approach is therefore thoroughly petitionary, but the objects he asks for further reveal the godliness of his character and his prayers. This is a portrayal of petitionary prayer that is robust, bold, and demanding, but that is driven by a deep longing for God's true character and purposes to be shown to all.

The Nature of Authentic Prayer

What does the book reveal about the reality of genuine prayer? The prayer pictured in the book is largely that of an individual talking persistently with

---

160. Sanders, *God Who Risks*, 64.

God. While he does talk to the friends, he often moves on the next stage of addressing his words to God. In his first response to Eliphaz, he begins by speaking to the friends in chapter 6 (e.g., 6:22-27), but moves on in chapter 7 to speak directly to God (e.g., 7:12-21). While these words are overheard by the friends and those gathered around,[161] they are from Job's perspective addressed to God. Even in the midst of great angst, Job's natural response is to come before God in prayer. He longs to be hurt no more by this seemingly silent or absent God, and tells God to leave him alone (e.g., 7:19; 10:20; 14:6). Yet Job keeps on initiating conversation with God and insists on arguing his ways in God's presence (e.g., 13:15b). God's apparent refusal to answer him never stops Job from talking to God. Such is the nature of persistent prayer that issues from a persevering faith (Jas 5:11).

Patrick Miller rightly points out, "If lament is the voice of *pain,* it is also the voice of *prayer.*"[162] Once we classify Job's words addressed to God as prayer, we gain further insights into the kinds of prayer that are acceptable to God. The desperate prayers of Job exhibit a raw honesty before God in which nothing is off-limits. Andersen notes that calmness is not the only godly path in prayer (citing Hannah in 1 Sam 1:13 and the example of Jesus in Heb 5:7): "Job makes his way to God with prayers that are sobs. Narrow and inhuman is the religion that bans weeping from the vocabulary of prayer."[163] Duff also insists that any definition of prayer must include these bold complaints, such as we find on the lips of Job. She observes that laments "allow us to speak from the darkest regions of the heart, where our despair threatens to overwhelm us. In so speaking we do not exhibit a lack of faith, but stand in a biblical tradition that recognizes that no part of life, including the most hideous and painful parts, is to be withheld from God."[164]

Honest words are more acceptable to God than empty but fine-sounding phrases. Job's friends seek to restrain his audacious words (e.g., 4:2-5; 8:2; 11:2-3; 15:2-6; 18:2; 20:3; 22:3-5), as does the human arbiter Elihu (e.g., 34:7-8). God's appearance trumps Elihu's words (33:12-18), and his rebuke of the friends overrides their rebukes of Job (42:7-8). However, Job keeps on talking to God (in prayer) because he knows that God alone can change him or his circumstances (12:7-10). He boldly demands an answer from God (31:35) so that justice is done. He does not pretend that his suffering is minor, or that his sense of God-forsakenness is something that can be overcome by the power of positive thinking.[165] His life

---

161. Bildad, for example, responds in 8:2-3 to Job's words to God in ch. 7. Later, Elihu will respond in 33:8-11 to Job's direct address of God in 13:23-24, 27.

162. Miller, "Heaven's Prisoners," 16.

163. Andersen, *Job,* 136.

164. Duff, "Recovering Lamentation," 13.

165. Sheriffs, *Friendship of the Lord,* 215-24.

is one of misery, bitterness, longing for death, and feeling hedged in by God (3:20-23); but the question "why" (3:20) governs his whole response. Since he is desperate, his prayers are desperate. Job's internal struggles are exactly what surface in his prayers. He models the value of honesty rather than pious pretense in prayer, and he responds to his enormous challenges and trials with a raw passion that is an indicator of the importance of his relationship with God.

Even today, we need to relearn how to lament as we look at our world — when we see that selfishness and pride have become a national way of life; when we see the wicked prosper; when Christians are persecuted; when, in our churches, spiritual coldness and division are rampant; when people around us harden their hearts, as they ridicule the gospel and mock the name of Christ — we too need to cry out and lament. There is much in this world that seems so wrong, and should drive us to God with honest questions. We need to pour out our hearts, hoping against hope that God will hear and answer. As Duff puts it, "just as we confess our sin, profess our faith, and bring forth praise, we also bring our sorrows, anger, frustration, and anguish before God."[166]

Job and Preaching

The variety and importance of the issues raised in the book of Job clearly make it a very contemporary book to preach on. Yet many pastors and students find it too daunting a book for a sermon series. It is long and seemingly repetitive, and some pastors tell me that they are afraid that their congregations might be as depressed as Job by the end of the series. In this section I will therefore reflect on some principles that might help in preaching on Job and make some practical suggestions on how to develop a series of expository sermons on the book.

Guiding Principles for Preaching and Teaching from the Book of Job

Three presuppositions should guide any preparation.[167] First, Job must be read as part of the wisdom strand in the OT. This means that it must be read against the backdrop of the mainstream wisdom book of Proverbs, based on a doctrine of creation, concerned with issues of everyday life and faith, and presuming an

---

166. Duff, "Recovering Lamentation," 9.

167. While this section reflects many years of preaching and teaching from Job, I have previously written on this in "Preaching and Teaching from Job," *Essentials* (September 2003): 11-13, and much of this section is based on this earlier writing.

orderly world in which the righteous prosper and the wicked are punished. Job is seemingly written in response to those who have misunderstood the partial perspectives of Proverbs and turned them into rigid, calcified rules and promises. Job sits alongside Ecclesiastes as protest wisdom, asking hard questions about whether life can be mapped out so simply.

Second, Job must be read as part of the OT as a whole. While the wisdom stream is generally not concerned with OT staples like covenant, law, Israel, temple, sacrifices, exile, and land, the God of Job is the same as the God of the rest of the OT, and the book is primarily addressed to Israelites. It must not be interpreted in a way that contradicts the rest of the OT, but neither must its distinctives be trimmed down simply to make the preacher's life easier.

Third, Job must be interpreted and preached in the light of the coming of Christ. This does not mean that Job must be seen as a type of Christ, or that the final message of the book is found in Job's search for a redeemer or in his glimpses of resurrection. Rather, it is that the issues the book raises and the answers it gives must be reframed by the clearer understanding of God's purposes in the coming, example, and teaching of Christ. In addition, what Christ has accomplished in his life, death, resurrection, and promised return transforms some of the issues that plague Job in his struggle of faith.

Practical Issues

A common problem in preaching on Job is that so much of the speeches sound the same. It is hard to say, "This is my seventeenth sermon on the speeches of the friends," and expect a high level of congregational interest. There is a need for variety in preaching, and for the essential point (the "sermonic sentence") to change from sermon to sermon.

A useful way forward in developing a series on Job is to identify distinct and discrete themes around which to fashion a string of sermons. I will give some examples below, but it is possible to develop a series from three to ten weeks on Job, without repeating the same things. It is obviously vital to know your group, and choose your themes and arrange your application accordingly.

You will almost certainly be using larger sections of text in preaching on Job. Rarely in Job do we find a key truth neatly packaged in five verses. As a preaching unit, you might look at the prologue, the epilogue, the Elihu speeches, the Yahweh speeches, and so on. This means that you are effectively preaching on a few chapters at a time. Of course, it does not follow that all of the text has to be read out in the context of a church service. Sometimes it is enough to read the first part of the story, or the end of the section, or a string of passages through the sermon. The preacher will need to guide the congregation through a section and fill in the gaps.[168]

It is also vital to read any section of Job as part of the book as a whole. Indeed, Donald Gowan has written that "it may be questioned whether one can legitimately preach from any part of [the book of Job] without taking the entire book as one's text."[169] There is a need to be clear about how the book hangs together, so that the preacher can communicate the flow and movement of the book to those listening.

Finally, in a sermon series as a whole, it is best to focus away from the details of the dialogues, to the various answers and perspectives of the book. Many issues are explored in the dialogue, but they are often picked up in the chapters that follow. In particular, some ways forward (with various degrees of merit) are proposed in chapters 28, 29–31, 32–37, 38–41, and 42. Furthermore, it is often better to deal with the friends' speeches before you preach on Job's speeches.[170] This makes it clearer that Job's friends do not satisfactorily answer Job, and also highlights that Job, unlike his friends, speaks not only to the friends but also moves on to address God. It also reflects the situation that Job gets the final word in the dialogue, not the friends.

Sermon Series

A series of consecutive sermons is an ideal way of picking up the different thrusts of each part of the book.[171] The following are some of the themes I draw out of the book, with the actual composition of the series depending on its length. The minimum series size would be three sermons, and in such a series I would preach on the prologue, Job's complaints to God in the dialogue, and how the book finishes (the Yahweh speeches and epilogue).

However, there is scope for a much longer series. These are some crucial ideas that are worth preaching from the book:

---

168. There is much value in integrating small group Bible study material for the church with a sermon series. If midweek Bible study groups are covering some of the details of the passages, the larger chunks on Sunday can be covered more quickly, knowing that the rest can be picked up in this other setting.

169. Gowan, *Reclaiming the Old Testament*, 100.

170. This insight, which came from Atkinson, *Message of Job*, has been very useful as I have preached on Job.

171. This is not to deny that it is possible to give a single sermon on Job. I heard a fine example of this when Frank Andersen preached in Ridley College chapel on the book as a whole, with Jas 5:11 as his text.

- Faith with no strings attached (chs. 1–2).
- Truth misapplied — the advice of Job's friends. I often call this, "Lord, deliver me from my friends," and base it on passages such as 4:12-17, 8:2-10, and 11:2-6.
- What does it mean to be human? (ch. 7 or 14).
- Job's laments can be dealt with under such headings as "Complaining to God," "Living with Unanswered Prayer," or "Feeling Cut Off from God." Others may wish to reflect on topics such as "Being God's Enemy," "Lessons Learned in Suffering," or "Is Life Worth Living?" I often use chapters 10 or 14, where Job addresses God directly.
- What lies beyond death? Is death the end? (ch. 19).[172]
- What is wisdom? Is the fear of the Lord enough? (ch. 28).
- The righteous life (ch. 31).
- The human verdict (chs. 32–37).
- How does God run his world? Is there justice in the world? God and creation (chs. 38–41). I often call this "Let God Be God."
- Is Job a person of faith? (ch. 42).

One of my students gave me the transcript of a creative series of five Lenten sermons by Norman Habel, the author of a major commentary on Job. Habel weaves into the book of Job a developing story of a lady who has been sexually abused as a child, and whose son is burned alive, and who is dropped by her friends. He sets it out, with parallel NT passages, as follows:

- Senseless suffering — Why, God, why? (Job 1 and Matt 27:45-50)
- Suffering of the soul — What did I do? (Job 3 and Luke 22:39-46)
- Suffering — the second wound (Job 4–6 and Luke 22:54-62)
- Suffering injustice — a no-win case? (Job 9 and Luke 23:1-16)
- The pain of healing (Job 31 and 42 and Luke 22:14-22)

Fyall covers the book in this way:

- Is God the author of evil? (Job 1–2)
- Where is God when it hurts? (Job 3)
- When counseling does not help (Job 4–11)
- If it is not he, then who is it? (Job 9)
- Where can wisdom be found? (Job 28)

172. This sermon will depend on the precise nature of the hope found in this chapter. See the commentary above.

- Trying to tie him down (Job 32–37)
- The grandeur of God (Job 38–39)
- The enemy unmasked (Job 40–41)[173]
- The vision glorious (Job 42)[174]

My former minister (and teacher of preaching) Peter Adam developed this series:

- Job on Trial (Job 1–2)
- Job's Endurance (Job 2–3)
- Job's Friends (Job 4; 8:1-19; 11; 32–33)
- Job's Autumn Years (Job 1:1-5; 29)
- The Lord Speaks (Job 40–41)
- My Servant Job (Job 42)
- Jesus Answers Job (Job 1:1-5; 19:23-29; 42:7-17)

What emerges from all these series is that it is possible to put together a varied and interesting series of many weeks on the book of Job.[175] There is room for creativity, but in each case there is a desire to draw out the distinct threads of the book, while giving the shape of the book as a whole.

Job and Mission

The book of Job is not the first book to come to mind in thinking about mission. Danie van Zyl even suggests that it "is on face value probably one of the least likely candidates among all the books of the Bible to contribute to a biblical understanding of mission."[176] However, a recent and helpful group of scholars (including Chris Wright and Michael Goheen) have advocated for the need of a missiological hermeneutic of the Bible and its constituent books. Not much work has been done yet on applying this to OT wisdom, but several attempts have raised the possibility of considering the book of Job in this light.

---

173. This is based on his identification of Behemoth and Leviathan as Death and Satan.

174. Fyall, *How Does God Treat His Friends?* This is based on a series of talks at the Christian Union at Durham.

175. The longest series of sermons I know of is that of the Puritan preacher Joseph Caryl (1602-1673). Barker, *Puritan Profiles*, 130, notes that Caryl preached on the book of Job for nearly three decades. I owe this reference to Peter Adam.

176. Van Zyl, "Missiological Dimensions," 24.

Rethinking Mission in Job

Van Zyl notes that mission has been commonly understood as either winning people from the world to faith or bringing the kingdom into the world. However, it can also refer to questioning and challenging aspects of one's own culture in order to become a "missional" church. Job has little to say on the first two, van Zyl suggests, but its critique of a narrow theology of retribution is of missiological significance. In the way they relate to others, God's people need to learn not to impose or build upon this self-confident ideology, seen for example in prosperity theology. Just as Job is stripped of almost everything in order to see more clearly, so the church needs to be set free from its Western agendas and to learn how to do mission in "bold humility."[177] In other words, the book of Job does not clarify the *content* of our mission, but rather the *way* in which God's people need to do mission.

At the same time that van Zyl was writing from a South African perspective, Wayne Allen was writing from a Caribbean setting, with an eye to mission in Gambia. Allen suggests that the message of Job to those who are not currently suffering is its "missionary message." By this he means that, like the rest of the Bible, it proclaims that "God wants to heal the nations of the disease of sin."[178] He maintains that even someone as righteous as Job did not know enough about God to satisfy his deepest longings. In the midst of a "diseased and suffering world," the church needs to outline what God requires of humanity. In the story's patriarchal setting, where sacrifice was the style of worship and God seemed distant yet powerful, the book suggests the need for a new way of understanding what pleases God and what he is like. In this sense, the book might be thought of as "pre-missional," showing why mission was needed then and is needed now. People will not find their way to God unless someone makes the path known to them.

The importance of voices such as these from the majority world is that they expand the question. Reading a book from the Bible missiologically is much wider than asking, "What does the book say explicitly about mission?" It might also include how those going on mission might need to change in their thinking or values in order to be part of God's mission in his world. Chris Wright, in his magnum opus on mission, has echoed such a call for self-examination. He notes that the biblical wisdom books call out loudly that any mission endeavor must be carried out with a critical openness to the world, a respect for God's image in humanity, and a humility and modesty in our approach and answers.[179]

177. Ibid., 24-28.
178. Allen, "Missionary Message," 18.
179. C. Wright, *Mission of God,* 453.

Since that time, Larry Waters has indeed argued that the book has a "missionary" purpose in a broader sense. By this he means that "a believer's suffering should be viewed, as seen in Job's experience, as a witness not only to God's sovereignty but also as a witness to His goodness, justice, grace, and love to the nonbelieving world."[180] As believers undergo undeserved suffering (like Job), their response will proclaim to the watching, skeptical world that God is still someone worth trusting. Waters sees this happening in the book as Job struggles with a false theology devoid of grace and in God's remarkable speeches communicating his love for humanity.[181]

Waters suggested that the setting of the book outside Israel meant that God was "on mission" through the impact that the life of Job would have on those around him, as well as later readers. In an ancient Near Eastern setting, the assumption would have been that God would relate to an individual only on the basis of the principle of retribution. Against this backdrop, the book of Job proclaims that God is free to act graciously, giving a message of hope to those undergoing undeserved suffering.[182] The missiological significance of the book is its conclusion that God can use suffering for his purposes, correcting the view that God is capricious, and impacting the world with the reminder of his grace. God's desire is still to bring the world to faith, and to bring faith to the world, by means of the testimony of suffering believers.[183]

Further Reflections

This exploration of Job and mission is still in its infancy, and so it is appropriate to add some further reflections. First, we need to learn from majority-world scholars that some of the ways in which mission has been, and is being, done may be far from helpful and less than scriptural. Job's friends refused to assess the validity of their ideology and traditions, and so prevented the pursuit of truth. Their approach hindered Job in his pursuit of faith in a setting of undeserved suffering. Mission can sometimes be done without proper self-examination, and the coupling of the Christian message with Western cultural values may hinder the task of mission. Furthermore, the method of mission may need to be critiqued. God's kingly rule over the world and his call for responsive faith is seldom furthered by a triumphalism that can blind those of

180. Waters, "*Missio Dei*," 19.

181. Ibid., 20. He also argues for a more positive role for Elihu, correcting and guiding Job into God's presence. I am not persuaded by this aspect of his argument, for reasons outlined earlier.

182. Ibid., 24-29.

183. Ibid., 32-35.

us who know we have a living word of hope. There is a need for humility, for patient listening, and for rethinking our customs, preferences, and assumptions. We see in the book of Job, for example, a need to regard all people with dignity (e.g., 31:15) and a high value placed on the natural environment (e.g., chs. 38–41, but most clearly in 38:26) that is wider than a focus only on humanity. There is also a concern for justice and the building up of community, particularly in chapter 31, and not simply making a verbal response of faith. These might give rise to a more holistic understanding of mission. The Yahweh speeches also remind us of the danger of trying to fully describe how God must act, and thus seek to limit his freedom. Sometimes our neat formulas and slick gospel presentations can fail to encompass the freedom and surprising grace of God. The book of Job does not exhaust our understanding of mission, but it may lead us to examine ourselves, our message, and our methods to make sure that they are honoring to God and further his kingly purposes.

Second, while mission in the OT often concerns the proclamation of the mighty acts of God, the wisdom books may add an important balancing contribution. The book of Job, for example, proclaims that God is worth trusting even in adverse circumstances. Suffering is still for many a big obstacle to belief in God's goodness or trustworthiness. In the majority world, suffering is not uncommonly associated with Christian commitment, in a way not fully realized by believers in the "developed" world. God's actions in history provide powerful evidence of God's care, but so does a focus on God's character of grace and his active ruling of the world that is beyond human comprehension. Yahweh's insistence that everything under heaven belongs to him (41:11) shows why all people need to respond to God. The invitation of the book is for people to trust God with no strings attached, like Job (1:8; 2:3), and to speak about him what is right (42:7-8). Thus the book of Job is really about living as humans in the light of God's sustaining the created world, acknowledging his rule over all, even those outside Israel, and responding with living faith. Faith like this is able to accept that God's purposes may never be fully known by humans, but that God can be trusted.

Bibliography

Adam, P. *Hearing God's Words: Exploring Biblical Spirituality.* NSBT. Leicester: Apollos, 2004.

Aitken, J. K. "Lexical Semantics and the Cultural Context of Knowledge in Job 28, Illustrated by the Meaning of *ḥāqar.*" In *Job 28: Cognition in Context.* Ed. E. van Wolde, 119-37. BIS 64. Leiden: Brill, 2003.

Alden, R. L. *Job.* NAC. Nashville: Broadman and Holman, 1993.

Alexander, D. "The Old Testament View of Life after Death." *Themelios* 11 (1986): 41-46.

Allen, W. A. "The Missionary Message of Job: God's Universal Concern for Healing." *Caribbean Journal of Evangelical Theology* 6 (2002): 18-31.

Allison, G. R. *Historical Theology: An Introduction to Christian Doctrine.* Grand Rapids: Zondervan, 2011.

Alter, R. "The Voice from the Whirlwind." *Commentary* 77 (1984): 33-41.

———. *The Art of Biblical Poetry.* New York: Basic Books, 1985.

Andersen, F. I. *Job.* TOTC. Downers Grove, IL: InterVarsity Press, 1976.

———. "Yahweh, the Kind and Sensitive God." In *God Who Is Rich in Mercy: Essays Presented to Dr. D. B. Knox.* Ed. P. T. O'Brien and D. G. Peterson, 41-88. Sydney: Lancer, 1986.

Ash, C. *Out of the Storm: Grappling with God in the Book of Job.* Leicester: InterVarsity Press, 2004.

Atkinson, D. J. *The Message of Job: Suffering and Grace.* BST. Downers Grove, IL: InterVarsity Press, 1991.

Baker, J. A. "The Book of Job: Unity and Meaning." In *Papers on Old Testament and Related Themes.* Vol. 1 of *Studia Biblica 1978.* Ed. E. A. Livingstone, 17-26. JSOTSup 11. Sheffield: JSOT Press, 1979.

Balentine, S. E. *The Hidden God: The Hiding of the Face of God in the Old Testament.* Oxford: Oxford University Press, 1983.

———. "Inside the 'Sanctuary of Silence': The Moral-Ethical Demands of Suffering." In *Character Ethics and the Old Testament: Moral Dimensions of Scripture.* Ed. M. D. Carroll R. and J. E. Lapsley, 63-79. Louisville: Westminster John Knox, 2007.

Barker, W. S. *Puritan Profiles.* Fearn: Mentor, 1996.

Barth, K. *The Doctrine of Reconciliation.* Vol. 4, part 3/1 of *Church Dogmatics.* Trans. G. W. Bromiley. Ed. G. W. Bromiley and T. F. Torrance. Edinburgh: T&T Clark, 1961.

Bartholomew, C. "Wisdom Books." In *New Dictionary of Biblical Theology*. Ed. T. D. Alexander and B. S. Rosner, 120-22. Downers Grove, IL: InterVarsity Press, 2000.

————. *Ecclesiastes*. BCOTWP. Grand Rapids: Baker Academic, 2009.

Becker, J. *Gottesfurcht im Alten Testament*. AnBib 25. Rome: Pontifical Biblical Institute, 1965.

Beeby, H. D. "Elihu — Job's Mediator?" *South East Asia Journal of Theology* 7 (1965): 33-54.

Bergant, D. "An Historico-Critical Study of the Anthropological Traditions and Motifs in Job." Ph.D. diss., Saint Louis University, 1975.

Berkhof, H. *Christian Faith*. Trans. S. Woudstra. Grand Rapids: Eerdmans, 1979.

Berkhof, L. *Systematic Theology*. London: Banner of Truth, 1941.

Bias, M. P., and L. J. Waters. *Job*. Asia Bible Commentary. Manila: Asia Theological Association, 2011.

Birch, B. C. *Let Justice Roll Down: The Old Testament, Ethics, and Christian Life*. Louisville: Westminster John Knox, 1991.

Blomberg, C. L. *Neither Poverty nor Riches: A Biblical Theology of Possessions*. NSBT. Grand Rapids: Eerdmans, 1999.

Boda, M. J. *A Severe Mercy: Sin and Its Remedy in the Old Testament*. Winona Lake, IN: Eisenbrauns, 2009.

Boström, L. *The God of the Sages: The Portrayal of God in the Book of Proverbs*. ConBOT 29. Stockholm: Almqvist & Wiksell, 1990.

Boyd, G. A. *God of the Possible: A Biblical Introduction to the Open View of God*. Grand Rapids: Baker, 2000.

Brown, S. A. "When Lament Shapes the Sermon." In *Lament: Reclaiming Practices in Pulpit, Pew, and Public Square*. Ed. S. A. Brown and P. D. Miller, 27-37. Louisville: Westminster John Knox, 2005.

Brown, S. A., and P. D. Miller. "Introduction." In *Lament: Reclaiming Practices in Pulpit, Pew, and Public Square*. Ed. S. A. Brown and P. D. Miller, xii-xix. Louisville: Westminster John Knox, 2005.

Brown, W. P. *Character in Crisis: A Fresh Approach to the Wisdom Literature of the Old Testament*. Grand Rapids: Eerdmans, 1996.

————. *The Ethos of the Cosmos: The Genesis of Moral Imagination*. Grand Rapids: Eerdmans, 1999.

Broyles, C. C. *The Conflict of Faith and Experience in the Psalms*. JSOTSup 52. Sheffield: Sheffield Academic Press, 1989.

Bruckner, J. K. *Implied Law in the Abraham Narrative: A Literary and Theological Analysis*. JSOTSup 335. London: Sheffield Academic Press, 2001.

Brueggemann, W. A. *In Man We Trust: The Neglected Side of Biblical Faith*. Atlanta: John Knox, 1972.

————. "From Hurt to Joy, from Death to Life." *Int* 28 (1974): 3-19.

————. *The Message of the Psalms*. Minneapolis: Augsburg, 1984.

————. "The Costly Loss of Lament." *JSOT* 36 (1986): 57-81.

————. "The Formfulness of Grief." In *The Psalms and the Life of Faith*. Ed. P. D. Miller, 84-97. Minneapolis: Fortress, 1995.

Burnett, J. S. *Where Is God? Divine Absence in the Hebrew Bible*. Minneapolis: Fortress, 2010.

Byrne, P. H. "Give Sorrow Words: Lament — Contemporary Need for Job's Old Time Religion." *Journal of Pastoral Care and Counseling* 56 (2002): 255-64.

Calvin, J. *Institutes of the Christian Religion.* Trans. F. L. Battles. Ed. J. T. McNeill. 2 vols. Philadelphia: Westminster, 1960.

Campbell, A. F. "The Book of Job: Two Questions, One Answer." *Australian Biblical Review* 51 (2003): 15-25.

Capps, D. *Reframing: A New Method in Pastoral Care.* Minneapolis: Fortress, 1990.

Carson, D. A. *How Long, O Lord? Reflections on Suffering and Evil.* 2nd ed. Grand Rapids: Baker Academic, 2006.

————. "James." In *CNTUOT* 997-1013.

Ceresko, A. *Job 29–31 in the Light of Northwest Semitic.* Biblica et orientalia 36. Rome: Pontifical Biblical Institute, 1980.

Childs, B. S. *Introduction to the Old Testament as Scripture.* London: SCM, 1979.

Ciampa, R. E., and B. S. Rosner. "1 Corinthians." In *CNTUOT* 695-752.

David J. Clark, "In Search of Wisdom: Notes on Job 28," *The Bible Translator* 33 (1982): 401-5.

Clements, R. E. "Wisdom." In *It Is Written: Scripture Citing Scripture. Essays in Honour of Barnabas Lindars, SSF.* Ed. D. A. Carson and H. G. M. Williamson, 67-83. Cambridge: Cambridge University Press, 1988.

Clifford, R. J. "The God Who Makes People Wise: The Wisdom Literature." In *The Forgotten God: Perspectives in Biblical Theology.* Ed. A. A. Das and F. J. Matera, 57-74. Louisville: Westminster John Knox, 2002.

Clines, D. J. A. "The Arguments of Job's Three Friends." In *Art and Meaning: Rhetoric in Biblical Literature.* Ed. D. J. A. Clines et al., 199-214. JSOTSup 19. Sheffield: JSOT Press, 1982.

————. *Job 1–20.* WBC 17. Dallas: Word, 1989.

————. "Deconstructing the Book of Job." In *What Does Eve Do to Help? and Other Readerly Questions to the Old Testament,* 106-23. JSOTSup 94. Sheffield: Sheffield Academic Press, 1990.

————. "Does the Book of Job Suggest That Suffering Is Not a Problem?" In *Weisheit in Israel: Beiträge des Symposiums "Das Alte Testament und die Kultur der Moderne" anlässlich des 100. Geburtstag Gerhard von Rads (1901-1971): Heidelberg, 18-21. Oktober 2001.* Ed. D. J. A. Clines et al., 93-110. Altes Testament und Moderne 12. Münster: Lit, 2003.

————. "'The Fear of the Lord Is Wisdom' (Job 28:28): A Semantic and Contextual Study." In *Job 28: Cognition in Context.* Ed. E. van Wolde, 57-92. BIS 64. Leiden: Brill, 2003.

————. "Job's Fifth Friend: An Ethical Critique of the Book of Job." *Biblical Interpretation* 12 (2004): 233-50.

————. "Putting Elihu in His Place: A Proposal for the Relocation of Job 32–37." *JSOT* 29 (2004): 115-25.

————. *Job 21–37.* WBC 18A. Nashville: Nelson, 2006.

————. *Job 38–42.* WBC 18B. Nashville: Nelson, 2011.

Course, J. E. *Speech and Response: A Rhetorical Analysis of the Introductions to the Speeches of the Book of Job (Chaps. 4–24).* CBQMS 25. Washington: Catholic Biblical Association of America, 1994.

Cox, D. "The Desire for Oblivion in Job 3." *Studii biblici franciscani liber annuus* 23 (1973): 37-49.

————. *The Triumph of Impotence: Job and the Tradition of the Absurd.* Rome: Università Gregoriana Editrice, 1978.

————. *Man's Anger and God's Silence: The Book of Job.* Slough: St Paul Publications, 1990.

Crenshaw, J. L. "Popular Questioning of the Justice of God in Ancient Israel." *ZAW* 82 (1970): 380-93.

————. *A Whirlpool of Torment: Israelite Traditions of God as an Oppressive Presence.* OBT. Philadelphia: Fortress, 1984.

————. "Theodicy." In *The New Interpreter's Dictionary of the Bible.* Ed. K. D. Sakenfeld, 5:551-55. Nashville: Abingdon, 2009.

Curtis, J. B. "On Job's Witness in Heaven." *JBL* 102 (1983): 549-62.

Dahood, M. "Some Northwest Semitic Words in Job." *Bib* 38 (1957): 306-20.

Davids, P. H. *The Epistle of James.* NIGTC. Grand Rapids: Eerdmans, 1982.

Davidson, R. *The Courage to Doubt.* London: SCM, 1983.

Davies, J. "Theodicy." In *DOTWPW* 808-17.

Day, P. L. *An Adversary in Heaven: śāṭān in the Hebrew Bible.* Harvard Semitic Monographs 43. Atlanta: Scholars Press, 1988.

Dell, K. J. *The Book of Job as Sceptical Literature.* BZAW 197. Berlin: de Gruyter, 1991.

————. *Shaking a Fist at God: Struggling with the Mystery of Undeserved Suffering.* Liguori: Triumph, 1995.

Derousseaux, J. *La crainte de Dieu dans l'Ancien Testament.* Paris: Cerf, 1970.

Dhorme, E. *A Commentary on the Book of Job.* Trans. H. Knight. Nashville: Nelson, 1967.

Dick, M. B. "The Legal Metaphor in Job 31." *CBQ* 41 (1979): 37-50.

————. "Job 31, the Oath of Innocence, and the Sage." *ZAW* 95 (1983): 31-53.

Diewert, D. A. "Job 7:12: *Yam, Tannin* and the Surveillance of Job." *JBL* 106 (1987): 203-15.

Driver, S. R., and G. B. Gray. *The Book of Job.* ICC. Edinburgh: T&T Clark, 1921.

Duff, N. J. "Recovering Lamentation as a Practice in the Church." In *Lament: Reclaiming Practices in Pulpit, Pew, and Public Square.* Ed. S. A. Brown and P. D. Miller, 3-14. Louisville: Westminster John Knox, 2005.

Dumbrell, W. J. *The Faith of Israel: A Theological Survey of the Old Testament.* 2nd ed. Grand Rapids: Baker Academic, 2002.

Eaton, J. H. *Job.* Old Testament Guides. Sheffield: JSOT Press, 1985.

Enns, P. *Inspiration and Incarnation: Evangelicals and the Problem of the Old Testament.* Grand Rapids: Baker Academic, 2005.

————. *Ecclesiastes.* THOTC. Grand Rapids: Eerdmans, 2011.

Erickson, M. J. *Christian Theology.* 2nd ed. Grand Rapids: Baker, 1998.

Estes, D. J. *Handbook on the Wisdom Books and Psalms.* Grand Rapids: Baker Academic, 2005.

————. *Job.* Teach the Text. Grand Rapids: Baker, 2013.

Fingarette, H. "The Meaning of Law in the Book of Job." In *Revisions: Changing Perspectives in Moral Philosophy.* Ed. S. Hauerwas and A. Macintyre, 249-86. Notre Dame: University of Notre Dame Press, 1983.

Fishbane, M. "Jeremiah IV 23-26 and Job III 3-13: A Recovered Use of the Creation Pattern." *VT* 21 (1971): 151-67.

Fohrer, G. *Das Buch Hiob.* KAT. Gütersloh: Gerd Mohn, 1963.

————. *Introduction to the Old Testament.* Nashville: Abingdon, 1968.

————. "The Righteous Man in Job 31." In *Essays in Old Testament Ethics.* Ed. J. L. Crenshaw and J. T. Willis, 3-22. New York: Ktav, 1974.

Fontaine, C. R. "'Arrows of the Almighty' (Job 6:4): Perspectives on Pain." *AThR* 66 (1984): 243-48.

Freedman, D. N. "The Structure of Job 3." *Bib* 49 (1968): 503-8.

Fretheim, T. E. *God and World in the Old Testament: A Relational Theology of Creation.* Nashville: Abingdon, 2005.

Frye, J. B. "The Use of Pentateuchal Traditions in the Book of Job." *OTWSA* 17-18 (1977): 13-20.

————. "The Use of *māšāl* in the Book of Job." *Semitics* 5 (1977): 59-66.

Fuhs, H. F. "יָרֵא *yārē*." *TDOT* 6:290-315.

Fyall, R. S. *How Does God Treat His Friends?* Fearn: Christian Focus, 1995.

————. *Now My Eyes Have Seen You: Images of Creation and Evil in the Book of Job.* NSBT 12. Downers Grove, IL: InterVarsity Press, 2002.

Gammie, J. G. "Behemoth and Leviathan: On the Didactic and Theological Significance of Job 40:15–41:26." In *Israelite Wisdom: Theological and Literary Essays in Honor of Samuel Terrien.* Ed. J. G. Gammie et al., 217-31. Missoula, MT: Scholars Press, 1978.

Geller, S. A. "'Where Is Wisdom?': A Literary Study of Job 28 in Its Settings." In *Judaic Perspectives on Ancient Israel.* Ed. J. Neusner, B. A. Levine, and E. S. Frerichs, 155-88. Philadelphia: Fortress, 1987.

Gibson, J. C. L. "On Evil in the Book of Job." In *Ascribe to the Lord: Biblical and Other Essays in Memory of Peter C. Craigie.* Ed. L. Eslinger and G. Taylor, 399-419. JSOTSup 67. Sheffield: JSOT Press, 1988.

————. "The Book of Job and the Cure of Souls." *SJT* 42 (1989): 303-17.

————. "A New Look at Job 41.1-4 (English 41.9-12)." In *Text as Pretext: Essays in Honour of Robert Davidson.* Ed. R. P. Carroll, 129-39. JSOTSup 138. Sheffield: JSOT Press, 1992.

Glatzer, N. N. *The Dimensions of Job: A Study and Selected Readings.* New York: Schocken, 1969.

Goldingay, J. E. *Theological Diversity and the Authority of the Old Testament.* 2nd ed. Carlisle: Paternoster, 1995.

Goldsworthy, G. L. *Gospel and Kingdom: A Christian Interpretation of the Old Testament.* Exeter: Paternoster, 1981.

————. *Gospel and Wisdom.* Exeter: Paternoster, 1987.

————. *According to Plan: The Unfolding Revelation of God in the Bible.* Downers Grove, IL: InterVarsity Press, 1991.

————. *Christ-Centered Biblical Theology: Hermeneutical Foundations and Principles.* Downers Grove, IL: InterVarsity Press, 2012.

Good, E. M. *In Turns of Tempest: A Reading of Job with a Translation.* Stanford: Stanford University Press, 1990.

Gordis, R. *The Book of God and Man: A Study of Job.* Chicago: University of Chicago Press, 1965.

————. *Poets, Prophets, and Sages: Essays in Biblical Interpretation.* Bloomington: Indiana University Press, 1971.

————. *The Book of Job.* New York: Jewish Theological Seminary, 1978.

Gorringe, T. J. "Job and the Pharisees." *Int* 40 (1986): 17-28.

Gowan, D. E. *Reclaiming the Old Testament for the Christian Pulpit.* Atlanta: John Knox, 1980.

————. "God's Answer to Job: How Is It an Answer?" *HBT* 8 (1986): 85-102.

Green, W. S. "Stretching the Covenant: Job and Judaism." *RevExp* 99 (2002): 569-77.

Greenberg, M. "Reflections on Job's Theology." In *The Book of Job: A New Translation Accord-ing to the Traditional Hebrew Text*. Ed. M. Greenberg et al., xvii-xxiii. Philadelphia: Jewish Publication Society of America, 1980.

———. "Job." In *The Literary Guide to the Bible*. Ed. R. Alter and F. Kermode, 283-304. Cambridge, MA: Belknap Press of Harvard University Press, 1987.

Greenfield, J. C. "The Language of the Book." In *The Book of Job: A New Translation According to the Traditional Hebrew Text*. Ed. M. Greenberg et al., xiv-xvi. Philadelphia: Jewish Publication Society of America, 1980.

Greenspahn, F. E. "The Number and Distribution of *Hapax Legomena* in Biblical Hebrew." *VT* 30 (1980): 8-19.

Greenstein, E. L. "The Poem on Wisdom in Job 28 in Its Conceptual and Literary Contexts." In *Job 28: Cognition in Context*. Ed. E. van Wolde, 253-80. BIS 64. Leiden: Brill, 2003.

Griffin, D. R. "Creation out of Chaos and the Problem of Evil." In *Encountering Evil: Live Options in Theodicy*. Ed. S. T. Davis, 101-19. Atlanta: John Knox, 1981.

Gros Louis, K. R. R. "The Book of Job." In *Literary Interpretations of Biblical Narratives*. Ed. K. R. R. Gros Louis et al., 226-66. Nashville: Abingdon, 1974.

Grudem, W. A. *Systematic Theology: An Introduction to Biblical Doctrine*. Leicester: Inter-Varsity Press, 1994.

Guthrie, N. *The Wisdom of God: Seeing Jesus in the Psalms and Wisdom Books*. Wheaton, IL: Crossway, 2012.

Gutiérrez, G. *On Job: God-Talk and the Suffering of the Innocent*. Trans. M. J. O'Connell. Maryknoll, NY: Orbis, 1987.

Habel, N. C. "'Only the Jackal Is My Friend': On Friends and Redeemers in Job." *Int* 31 (1977): 227-36.

———. "'Naked I Came . . .': Humanness in the Book of Job." In *Die Botschaft und die Boten: Festschrift für Hans Walter Wolff*. Ed. J. Jeremias and L. Perlitt, 373-92. Neukirchen-Vluyn: Neukirchener Verlag, 1981.

———. "Of Things beyond Me: Wisdom in the Book of Job." *CurTM* 10 (1983): 142-54.

———. "The Role of Elihu in the Design of the Book of Job." In *In The Shelter of Elyon: Es-says on Ancient Palestinian Life and Literature in Honor of G. W. Ahlström*. Ed. W. B. Barrick and J. R. Spencer, 81-98. JSOTSup 31. Sheffield: JSOT Press, 1984.

———. *The Book of Job*. OTL. London: SCM, 1985.

———. "In Defense of God the Sage." In *The Voice from the Whirlwind: Interpreting the Book of Job*. Ed. L. G. Perdue and W. C. Gilpin, 21-38. Nashville: Abingdon, 1992.

———. "The Implications of God Discovering Wisdom in Earth." In *Job 28: Cognition in Context*. Ed. E. van Wolde, 281-97. BIS 64. Leiden: Brill, 2003.

Harris, R. L. "The Book of Job and Its Doctrine of God." *Presbyterion* 7 (1981): 5-33.

Hartley, J. E. *The Book of Job*. NICOT. Grand Rapids: Eerdmans, 1988.

———. "From Lament to Oath: A Study of Progression in the Speeches of Job." In *The Book of Job*. Ed. W. A. M. Beuken, 79-100. BETL 114. Leuven: Leuven University Press, 1994.

Hays, R. B. *Echoes of Scripture in the Letters of Paul*. New Haven: Yale University Press, 1989.

Hemraj, S. "Elihu's 'Missionary' Role in Job 32-37." *Bible Bhashyam* 6 (1980): 49-80.

Hess, R. S. "חפץ." In *NIDOTTE* 2:234-35.

Hoffman, Y. "The Use of Equivocal Words in the First Speech of Eliphaz (Job IV–V)." *VT* 30 (1980): 114-19.

————. "The Relation between the Prologue and the Speech-Cycles in Job: A Reconsideration." *VT* 31 (1981): 160-70.

————. "Irony in the Book of Job." *Immanuel* 17 (1983/1984): 7-21.

Holbert, J. C. "The Function and Significance of the *Klage* in the Book of *Job* with Special Reference to the Incidence of Formal and Verbal Irony." Ph.D. diss., Southern Methodist University, 1975.

————. "'The Skies Will Uncover His Iniquity': Satire in the Second Speech of Zophar (Job xx)." *VT* 31 (1981): 171-79.

————. "The Rehabilitation of the Sinner: The Function of Job 29–31." *ZAW* 95 (1983): 229-37.

Holmgren, F. "Barking Dogs Never Bite, Except Now and Then: Proverbs and Job." *AThR* 61 (1979): 341-53.

Hoppe, L. J. *There Shall Be No Poor among You: Poverty in the Bible.* Nashville: Abingdon, 2004.

Horton, M. S. *The Christian Faith: A Systematic Theology for Pilgrims on the Way.* Grand Rapids: Zondervan, 2011.

Hughes, R. A. *Lament, Death, and Destiny.* StBL 68. New York: Peter Lang, 2004.

Hulme, W. E. *Dialogue in Despair: Pastoral Commentary on the Book of Job.* Nashville: Abingdon, 1968.

————. "Pastoral Counseling in the Book of Job." *Concordia Journal* 15 (1989): 121-38.

————. *Christian Caregiving: Insights from the Book of Job.* St. Louis: Concordia, 1992.

Humphreys, W. L. *The Tragic Vision and the Hebrew Tradition.* OBT. Philadelphia: Fortress, 1985.

Illman, K.-J. "Theodicy in Job." In *Theodicy in the World of the Bible.* Ed. A. Laato and J. C. de Moor, 304-33. Leiden: Brill, 2003.

Iwanski, D. *The Dynamics of Job's Intercession.* AnBib 161. Rome: Pontifical Biblical Institute, 2006.

Jackson, D. R. *Crying out for Vindication: The Gospel according to Job.* Phillipsburg, NJ: P&R, 2007.

Jamieson-Drake, D. W. "Literary Structure, Genre and Interpretation in Job 38." In *The Listening Heart: Essays in Wisdom and the Psalms in Honor of Roland Murphy.* Ed. K. G. Hoglund et al., 217-36. JSOTSup 58. Sheffield: JSOT Press, 1987.

Janzen, J. G. *Job.* Interpretation. Atlanta: John Knox, 1985.

Janzen, W. *Old Testament Ethics: A Paradigmatic Approach.* Louisville: Westminster John Knox, 1994.

Johns, D. A. "The Literary and Theological Function of the Elihu Speeches in the Book of Job." Ph.D. diss., Saint Louis University, 1983.

Keel, O. *Dieu répond à Job.* Paris: Cerf, 1993.

Kelley, P. H. "Prayers of Troubled Saints." *RevExp* 81 (1984): 377-83.

Kidner, D. *Psalms 73–150.* TOTC. Downers Grove, IL: InterVarsity Press, 1975.

————. *The Wisdom of Proverbs, Job, and Ecclesiastes: An Introduction to Wisdom Literature.* Downers Grove, IL: InterVarsity Press, 1985.

Kissane, E. J. *The Book of Job.* Dublin: Browne and Nolan, 1939.

Kline, M. G. "Trial by Ordeal." In *Through Christ's Word: A Festschrift for Dr. Philip E. Hughes.* Ed. W. R. Godfrey and J. L. Boyd III, 81-93. Phillipsburg: P&R, 1985.

Kluger, R. S. *Satan in the Old Testament.* Trans. H. Nagel. Evanston: Northwestern University Press, 1967.

Knight, H. "Job (Considered as a Contribution to Hebrew Theology)." *SJT* 9 (1956): 63-76.

Köhler, L. *Hebrew Man*. Trans. P. R. Ackroyd. London: SCM, 1956.

Laato, A., and J. C. de Moor, eds. *Theodicy in the World of the Bible*. Leiden: Brill, 2003.

Laurin, R. "The Theological Structure of Job." *ZAW* 84 (1972): 86-89.

Laytner, A. *Arguing with God: A Jewish Tradition*. Northvale: Aronson, 1990.

Levenson, J. D. *Resurrection and the Restoration of Israel*. New Haven: Yale University Press, 2006.

Lévêque, J. *Job et son Dieu*. 2 vols. Paris: Gabalda, 1970.

———. "Job's Suffering and Transformation." *TD* 26 (1978): 134-38.

Lewis, C. S. *The Problem of Pain*. New York: Harper, 1940.

Lo, A. *Job 28 as Rhetoric: An Analysis of Job 28 in the Context of Job 22–31*. VTSup 97. Leiden: Brill, 2003.

Loader, J. A. "Job — Answer or Enigma?" In *Old Testament Essays*. Vol. 2. Ed. J. A. Loader and J. H. Le Roux, 1-38. Pretoria: UNISA, 1984.

Long, V. P. "On the Coherence of the Third Dialogic Cycle in the Book of Job." In *Studies on the Text and Versions of the Hebrew Bible in Honour of Robert Gordon*. Ed. G. Khan and D. Lipton, 113-25. VTSup 149. Leiden: Brill, 2012.

Longman, T., III. "Reading Wisdom Canonically." In *Canon and Biblical Interpretation*. Ed. C. G. Bartholomew et al., 352-73. Grand Rapids: Zondervan, 2006.

———. *Job*. BCOTWP. Grand Rapids: Baker Academic, 2012.

McCabe, R. V. "The Significance of the Elihu Speeches in the Context of the Book of Job." Th.D. diss., Grace Theological Seminary and College, 1985.

———. "Elihu's Contribution to the Thought of the Book of Job." *Denver Baptist Seminary Journal* 2 (1997): 47-80.

McDonald, H. D. *The Christian View of Man*. Westchester, IL: Crossway, 1981.

McGrath, A. E. *Christian Theology: An Introduction*. 5th ed. Chichester: Wiley-Blackwell, 2011.

McKay, J. W. "Elihu — A Proto-Charismatic?" *ExpTim* 90 (1979): 167-71.

McKeating, H. "The Central Issue of the Book of Job." *ExpTim* 82 (1972): 244-47.

MacKenzie, R. A. F. "The Transformation of Job." *BTB* 9 (1979): 51-57.

Maston, T. B. "Ethical Content of Job." *SwJT* 14 (1971): 43-56.

Matheney, M. P., Jr. "Major Purposes of the Book of Job." *SwJT* 14 (1971): 17-42.

Mettinger, T. N. D. "The God of Job: Avenger, Tyrant, or Victor?" In *The Voice from the Whirlwind: Interpreting the Book of Job*. Ed. L. G. Perdue and W. C. Gilpin, 39-49. Nashville: Abingdon, 1992.

Michaeli, F. "La sagesse et la crainte de Dieu." *Hokma* 2 (1976): 35-44.

Michel, W. L. "Confidence and Despair: Job 19,25-27 in the Light of Northwest Semitic Studies." In *The Book of Job*. Ed. W. A. M. Beuken, 157-81. BETL 114. Leuven: Leuven University Press, 1994.

Miller, P. D. "Heaven's Prisoners: The Lament as Christian Prayer." In *Lament: Reclaiming Practices in Pulpit, Pew, and Public Square*. Ed. S. A. Brown and P. D. Miller, 15-26. Louisville: Westminster John Knox, 2005.

———. *The Ten Commandments*. Interpretation. Louisville: Westminster John Knox, 2009.

Moo, D. J. *The Letter of James*. Pillar New Testament Commentary. Grand Rapids: Eerdmans, 2000.

Morgan, D. F. *Wisdom in the Old Testament Traditions*. Atlanta: John Knox, 1981.

Morgan, G. Campbell. *The Answers of Jesus to Job.* London: Marshall, Morgan & Scott, 1934.

Morrow, W. S. "Consolation, Rejection, and Repentance in Job 42:6." *JBL* 105 (1986): 211-25.

————. *Protest against God: The Eclipse of a Biblical Tradition.* Hebrew Bible Monographs 4. Sheffield: Sheffield Phoenix, 2006.

Muntingh, L. M. "Life, Death and Resurrection in the Book of Job." *OTWSA* 17-18 (1974-75): 32-44.

Murphy, R. E. *Wisdom Literature: Job, Proverbs, Ruth, Canticles, Ecclesiastes, and Esther.* FOTL 13. Grand Rapids: Eerdmans, 1981.

————. "The Last Truth about God." *RevExp* 99 (2002): 581-87.

————. *The Tree of Life.* 3rd ed. Grand Rapids: Eerdmans, 2002.

Nam, D.-W. *Talking about God: Job 42:7-9 and the Nature of God in the Book of Job.* StBL 49. New York: Peter Lang, 2003.

Neville, R. W. "Job's Ethic in Job XXXI 13-15." *VT* 53 (2003): 181-200.

Newell, B. L. "Job: Repentant or Rebellious?" *WTJ* 46 (1984): 298-316.

Newsom, C. A. "The Book of Job: Introduction, Commentary, and Reflections." In *The New Interpreter's Bible.* Ed. L. E. Keck, 4:317-637. Nashville: Abingdon, 1996.

————. "Narrative Ethics, Character, and the Prose Tale of Job." In *Character and Scripture: Moral Formation, Community, and Biblical Interpretation.* Ed. W. P. Brown, 121-34. Grand Rapids: Eerdmans, 2002.

————. "Dialogue and Allegorical Hermeneutics in Job 28:28." In *Job 28: Cognition in Context.* Ed. E. van Wolde, 299-305. BIS 64. Leiden: Brill, 2003.

O'Connor, D. J. "Job's Final Word — 'I am Consoled . . .' (42:6b)." *ITQ* 50 (1983/1984): 181-97.

————. "Reverence and Irreverence in *Job.*" *ITQ* 51 (l985): 85-104.

Oswalt, J. N. "God." In *DOTWPW* 246-59.

Page, S. H. T. *Powers of Evil: A Biblical Study of Satan and Demons.* Grand Rapids: Baker, 1995.

Parsons, G. W. "The Structure and Purpose of the Book of Job." *BSac* 138 (1981): 139-57.

————. "Literary Features of the Book of Job." *BSac* 138 (1981): 213-29.

————. "Job, Theology of." In *Evangelical Dictionary of Biblical Theology.* Ed. W. A. Elwell, 415-19. Grand Rapids: Baker, 1996.

Patrick, D. "The Translation of Job XLII 6." *VT* 26 (1976): 369-71.

————. "Job's Address of God." *ZAW* 91 (1979): 268-82.

————. *The First Commandment in the Structure of the Pentateuch.* VTSup 45. Leiden: Brill, 1995.

Peake, A. S. "Job: The Problem of the Book." In *Theodicy in the Old Testament.* Ed. J. L. Crenshaw, 100-108. Philadelphia: Fortress, 1983.

Perdue, L. G. *Wisdom in Revolt: Metaphorical Theology in the Book of Job.* JSOTSup 112. Sheffield: Almond, 1991.

————. *Wisdom and Creation: The Theology of Wisdom Literature.* Nashville: Abingdon, 1994.

————. "Creation in the Dialogues between Job and His Opponents." In *Das Buch Hiob und seine Interpretationen.* Ed. T. Krüger et al., 197-216. Zurich: Theologischer Verlag, 2007.

————. *The Sword and the Stylus: An Introduction to Wisdom in the Age of Empires.* Grand Rapids: Eerdmans, 2008.

Polzin, R. "The Framework of the Book of Job." *Int* 28 (1974): 182-200.

Pope, M. H. *Job.* 3rd ed. AB 15. New York: Doubleday, 1973.

Prideaux, A. R. "The Relationship between the Creator and the Creature in the Book of Job:

An Exploration of the Theme of the Book of Job." M.Th. thesis, Australian College of Theology, 2006.

Pyeon, Y. *You Have Not Spoken What Is Right about Me: Intertextuality and the Book of Job.* StBL 45. New York: Peter Lang, 2003.

Raurell, F. "Job's Ethic and God's Freedom." *TD* 29 (1981): 133-37.

Reiske, J. J. *Coniecturae in Iobum et Proverbia Salomonis.* Leipzig, 1779.

Reyburn, W. D. *A Handbook on the Book of Job.* UBS Handbook Series. New York: United Bible Societies, 1992.

Reymond, R. L. *A New Systematic Theology of the Christian Faith.* 2nd ed. Nashville: Nelson, 1998.

Richardson, K. A. "Job as Exemplar in the Epistle of James." In *Hearing the Old Testament in the New Testament.* Ed. S. E. Porter, 213-29. Grand Rapids: Eerdmans, 2006.

Roberts, J. J. M. "Job's Summons to Yahweh: The Exploitation of a Legal Metaphor." *Restoration Quarterly* 16 (1973): 159-65.

Robertson, D. "The Book of Job: A Literary Study." *Soundings* 56 (1973): 446-69.

————. "The Comedy of Job: A Response." *Semeia* 7 (1977): 41-44.

Robinson, T. H. *Job and His Friends.* London: SCM, 1954.

Ross, J. F. "Job 33:14-30: The Phenomenology of Lament." *JBL* 94 (1975): 38-46.

Rowley, H. H. "The Book of Job and Its Meaning." *BJRL* 41 (1958): 167-207.

————. *Job.* Rev. ed. NCBC. Repr., Grand Rapids: Eerdmans, 1980.

Rowold, H. L. "The Theology of Creation in the Yahweh Speeches of the Book of Job as a Solution to the Problem Posed by the Book of Job." Th.D. diss., Concordia Seminary in Exile, St. Louis, 1977.

————. "Yahweh's Challenge to Rival: The Form and Function of the Yahweh-Speech in Job 38–39." *CBQ* 47 (1985): 199-211.

Ryken, L. *The Literature of the Bible.* Grand Rapids: Zondervan, 1974.

Sanders, J. *God Who Risks: A Theology of Providence.* Downers Grove, IL: InterVarsity Press, 1998.

Sarna, N. M. "The Mythological Background of Job 18." *JBL* 82 (1963): 315-18.

————. "The Book of Job: General Introduction." In M. Greenberg, J. C. Greenfield, and N. M. Sarna, *The Book of Job: A New Translation according to the Traditional Hebrew Text,* ix-xii. Philadelphia: Jewish Publication Society of America, 1980.

Schifferdecker, K. M. "Creation Theology." In *DOTWPW* 63-71.

————. *Out of the Whirlwind: Creation Theology in the Book of Job.* Cambridge: Harvard University Press, 2008.

Scholnick, S. H. "The Meaning of *mišpaṭ* in the Book of Job." *JBL* 101 (1982): 521-29.

————. "Poetry in the Courtroom: Job 38–41." In *Directions in Biblical Hebrew Poetry.* Ed. E. R. Follis, 185-204. JSOTSup 40. Sheffield: Sheffield Academic Press, 1987.

Schreiner, S. E. *Where Shall Wisdom Be Found? Calvin's Exegesis of Job from Medieval and Modern Perspectives.* Chicago: University of Chicago Press, 1994.

Schultz, R. L. *The Search for Quotation: Verbal Parallels in the Prophets.* JSOTSup 180. Sheffield: Sheffield Academic Press, 1999.

Schwab, G. M. "The Book of Job and Counsel in the Whirlwind." *Journal of Biblical Counseling* 17 (1998): 31-43.

Seifrid, M. A. "Romans." In *CNTUOT* 607-94.

Seow, C.-L. "Job." In *Dictionary of Scripture and Ethics*. Ed. J. B. Green, 421-22. Grand Rapids: Baker Academic, 2011.

———. *Job 1–21: Interpretation and Commentary*. Illuminations. Grand Rapids: Eerdmans, 2013.

Sheriffs, D. *The Friendship of the Lord*. Carlisle: Paternoster, 1996.

Simundson, D. J. *Faith under Fire: Biblical Interpretations of Suffering*. Minneapolis: Augsburg, 1980.

———. *The Message of Job*. Augsburg Old Testament Studies. Minneapolis: Augsburg, 1986.

Skehan, P. W. "Strophic Patterns in the Book of Job." *CBQ* 23 (1961): 125-42.

———. "Job's Final Plea (Job 29–31) and the Lord's Reply (Job 38–41)." *Bib* 45 (1964): 51-62.

Smick, E. B. "Mythology and the Book of Job." *JETS* 13 (1970): 101-8.

———. "Another Look at the Mythological Elements in the Book of Job." *WTJ* 40 (1978): 213-18.

———. "Semeiological Interpretation of the Book of Job." *WTJ* 48 (1986): 135-49.

———. "Job." In *The Expositor's Bible Commentary*. Ed. F. E. Gaebelein, 4:843-1060. Grand Rapids: Zondervan, 1988.

Smith, G. V. "Is There a Place for Job's Wisdom in Old Testament Theology?" *Trinity Journal* 13 (1992): 3-20.

Smith, R. L. "Introduction to Job." *SwJT* 14 (1971): 5-16.

Snaith, N. H. *The Book of Job: Its Origin and Purpose*. SBT 2/11. London: SCM, 1968.

Stump, E. *Wandering in Darkness: Narrative and the Problem of Suffering*. Oxford: Clarendon, 2010.

Surin, K. *Theology and the Problem of Evil*. Oxford: Blackwell, 1986.

Tate, M. E. "The Speeches of Elihu." *RevExp* 68 (l971): 487-95.

Tennyson, A. "In Memoriam." In *Poetical Works of Alfred Lord Tennyson*. London: Macmillan, 1935.

Terrien, S. "Job." In *The Interpreter's Bible*. Ed. G. A. Buttrick, 3:877-1198. New York: Abingdon, 1954.

———. *Job*. Commentaire de l'Ancien Testament 13. Neuchâtel: Delachaux et Niestlé, 1963.

———. "The Yahweh Speeches and Job's Response." *RevExp* 68 (1971): 497-509.

———. *The Elusive Presence: Toward a New Biblical Theology*. San Francisco: Harper & Row, 1978.

Thomas, D. *Calvin's Teaching on Job: Proclaiming the Incomprehensible God*. Geanies House: Mentor, 2004.

Timmer, D. C. "Character Formed in the Crucible: Job's Relationship with God and Joban Character Ethics." *Journal of Theological Interpretation* 3 (2009): 1-16.

Tsevat, M. "The Meaning of the Book of Job." In *The Meaning of the Book of Job and Other Essays*, 1-37. New York: Ktav, 1980.

Tur-Sinai, N. H. *The Book of Job*. Jerusalem: Kiryat-Sefer, 1967.

Urbock, W. J. "Job As Drama: Tragedy or Comedy?" *CurTM* 8 (1981): 35-40.

VanGemeren, Willem. "Israel as the Hermeneutical Crux in the Interpretation of Prophecy (II)." *WTJ* 46 (1984): 254-97.

van der Lugt, P. "Stanza-Structure and Word Repetition in Job 3–14." *JSOT* 40 (1988): 3-38.

van Hecke, P. J. P. "Searching for and Exploring Wisdom: A Cognitive-Semantic Approach to the Hebrew Verb *ḥāqar* in Job 28." In *Job 28: Cognition in Context*. Ed. E. van Wolde, 139-62. BIS 64. Leiden: Brill, 2003.

van Leeuwen, R. "A Technical Metallurgical Usage of צֵיר." *ZAW* 98 (1986): 112-13.

van Wolde, E. J. "Job 42,1-6: The Reversal of Job." In *The Book of Job*. Ed. W. A. M. Beuken, 223-50. BETL 114. Leuven: Leuven University Press, 1994.

―――. *Mr and Mrs Job*. Trans. J. Bowden. London: SCM, 1997.

―――. "Wisdom, Who Can Find It? A Non-Cognitive and Cognitive Study of Job 28:1-11." In *Job 28: Cognition in Context*. Ed. E. van Wolde, 1-35. BIS 64. Leiden: Brill, 2003.

van Zyl, D. C. "Missiological Dimensions in the Book of Job." *International Review of Mission* 91 (2002): 24-30.

Vawter, B. *Job and Jonah: Questioning the Hidden God*. New York: Paulist Press, 1983.

Vermeylen, J. *Job, ses amis et son Dieu*. Studia biblica 2. Leiden: Brill, 1981.

Viberg, Å. "Job." In *New Dictionary of Biblical Theology*. Ed. T. D. Alexander and B. S. Rosner, 200-203. Downers Grove, IL: InterVarsity Press, 2000.

Walton, J. H. "Job 1: Book of." In *DOTWPW* 333-46.

―――. "Retribution." In *DOTWPW* 647-55.

―――. *Job*. NIVAC. Grand Rapids: Zondervan, 2012.

Waters, L. J. "Reflections on Suffering from the Book of Job." *BSac* 154 (1997): 436-51.

―――. "*Mission Dei* in the Book of Job." *BSac* 166 (2009): 19-35.

―――. "Suffering in the Book of Job." In *Why, O God? Suffering and Disability in the Bible and in the Church*. Ed. L. J. Waters and R. B. Zuck, 111-25. Wheaton, IL: Crossway, 2011.

Webster, E. C. "Strophic Patterns in Job 29–42." *JSOT* 30 (1984): 95-109.

Webster, B. L., and D. R. Beach. "The Place of Lament in the Christian Life." *BSac* 164 (2007): 387-402.

Weiss, M. *The Story of Job's Beginning*. Jerusalem: Magnes, 1983.

Westermann, C. "The Role of the Lament in the Theology of the Old Testament" (trans. R. N. Soulen). *Int* 28 (1974): 20-38.

―――. *The Structure of the Book of Job: A Form-Critical Analysis*. Trans. C. A. Muenchow. Philadelphia: Fortress, 1977.

―――. *Elements of Old Testament Theology*. Trans. D. W. Stott. Atlanta: John Knox, 1982.

Wharton, J. A. *Job*. Westminster Bible Companion. Louisville: Westminster John Knox, 1999.

Whedbee, J. W. "The Comedy of Job." *Semeia* 7 (1977): 1-39.

White, M. E. "The Purpose and Portrayal of the *śāṭān* in the Old Testament." M.Th. thesis, Tyndale Seminary, 2004.

Whybray, R. N. *Wisdom in Proverbs: The Concept of Wisdom in Proverbs 1–9*. SBT 1/45. London: SCM, 1965.

―――. *Two Jewish Theologies: Job and Ecclesiastes*. Hull: University of Hull, 1980.

―――. "Wisdom, Suffering and the Freedom of God in the Book of Job." In *In Search of True Wisdom: Essays in Old Testament Interpretation in Honour of Ronald E. Clements*. Ed. E. Ball, 231-45. JSOTSup 300. Sheffield: Sheffield Academic Press, 1999.

―――. *The Good Life in the Old Testament*. London: T&T Clark, 2002.

Williams, D. L. "The Speeches of Job." *RevExp* 68 (1971): 469-78.

Williams, R. J. "Theodicy in the Ancient Near East." *Canadian Journal of Theology* 2 (1956): 14-26.

Wilson, G. H. *Job*. NIBC. Peabody, MA: Hendrickson, 2007.

Wilson, L. "The Book of Job and the Fear of God." *Tyndale Bulletin* 46 (1995): 59-79.

―――. "The Role of the Elihu Speeches in the Book of Job." *RTR* 55 (1996): 81-94.

———. "Realistic Hope or Imaginative Exploration? The Identity of Job's 'Arbiter.'" *Pacifica* 9 (1996): 243-52.

———. "Job 38–39 and Biblical Theology." *RTR* 62 (2003): 121-38.

———. "Preaching and Teaching from Job." *Essentials* (September 2003): 11-13.

———. *Joseph, Wise and Otherwise: The Intersection of Wisdom and Covenant in Genesis 37–50*. Paternoster Biblical Monographs. Carlisle: Paternoster, 2004.

———. "Job, Book of." In *Dictionary for the Theological Interpretation of the Bible*. Ed. K. J. Vanhoozer, 384-89. Grand Rapids: Baker Academic, 2005.

———. "Wisdom in the Book of Isaiah." In *Interpreting Isaiah: Issues and Approaches*. Ed. D. G. Firth and H. G. M. Williamson, 145-67. Downers Grove, IL: InterVarsity Press, 2009.

Witherington, B. *Jesus the Sage: The Pilgrimage of Wisdom*. Minneapolis: Fortress, 1994.

Wolfers, D. "Elihu: The Provenance and Content of His Speeches." *Dor le Dor* 16 (1987/1988): 90-98.

———. "Job: The Third Cycle: Dissipating a Mirage — Part I." *Dor le Dor* 16 (1988): 217-26.

———. *Deep Things out of Darkness: The Book of Job. Essays and a New English Translation*. Grand Rapids: Eerdmans, 1995.

Wright, C. J. H. *An Eye for an Eye: The Place of Old Testament Ethics Today*. Downers Grove, IL: InterVarsity Press, 1983.

———. *Knowing Jesus through the Old Testament*. London: Marshall Pickering, 1992.

———. *Old Testament Ethics for the People of God*. Downers Grove, IL: InterVarsity Press, 2004.

———. *The Mission of God: Unlocking the Bible's Grand Narrative*. Downers Grove, IL: InterVarsity Press, 2006.

Wright, N. T. *The New Testament and the People of God*. Minneapolis: Fortress, 1992.

———. *The Resurrection of the Son of God*. Minneapolis: Fortress, 2003.

Zerafa, P. P. *The Wisdom of God in the Book of Job*. Rome: Herder, 1978.

Zimmerli, W. *Man and His Hope in the Old Testament*. Trans. G. W. Bowen. SBT 2/20. London: SCM, 1971.

———. "The Place and Limit of Wisdom in the Framework of Old Testament Theology." *SJT* 17 (1964): 146-58.

Zink, J. K. "Uncleanness and Sin: A Study of Job XIV 4 and Psalm LI 7." *VT* 17 (1967): 354-61.

Zuck, R. B. "A Theology of the Wisdom Books and Song of Songs." In *A Biblical Theology of the Old Testament*. Ed. R. B. Zuck, 207-55. Chicago: Moody Press, 1991.

Index of Authors

Index of Scripture References

405